MW01286430

A
FLOWER
TRAVELED
IN MY BLOOD

THE INCREDIBLE TRUE STORY *of the*
GRANDMOTHERS WHO FOUGHT *to* **FIND** *a* **STOLEN**
GENERATION *of* **CHILDREN**

Haley Cohen Gilliland

AVID READER PRESS
New York Amsterdam/Antwerp London
Toronto Sydney/Melbourne New Delhi

AVID READER PRESS
An Imprint of Simon & Schuster, LLC
1230 Avenue of the Americas
New York, NY 10020

First Avid Reader Press hardcover edition July 2025

AVID READER PRESS and colophon are trademarks of Simon & Schuster, LLC

Simon & Schuster strongly believes in freedom of expression and stands against censorship
in all its forms. For more information, visit BooksBelong.com.

For information about special discounts for bulk purchases, please contact Simon & Schuster
Special Sales at 1-866-506-1949 or business@simonandschuster.com.

The Simon & Schuster Speakers Bureau can bring authors to your live event.
For more information or to book an event contact the Simon & Schuster Speakers Bureau
at 1-866-248-3049 or visit our website at www.simonspeakers.com.

Interior design by Silverglass
Map by Paul J. Pugliese

Manufactured in the United States of America

1 3 5 7 9 10 8 6 4 2

Library of Congress Control Number: 2025005407

ISBN 978-1-6680-1714-2
ISBN 978-1-6680-1716-6 (ebook)

FOR MY PARENTS,
WHO WOULD DO ANYTHING FOR THEIR
CHILDREN AND GRANDCHILDREN

EPITAFIO

Un pájaro vivía en mí.
Una flor viajaba en mi sangre.
Mi corazón era un violín.

Quise o no quise. Pero a veces
me quisieron. También a mí
me alegraban: la primavera,
las manos juntas, lo feliz.

¡Digo que el hombre debe serlo!

(Aquí yace un pájaro.
                    Una flor.
                              Un violín.)

EPITAPH

A bird lived in me.
A flower traveled in my blood.
My heart was a violin.

I loved and I didn't. But sometimes
was loved. I also
was happy: about the spring,
the hands together, what is happy.

I say a man has to be!

(Herein lies a bird.
                    A flower.
                              A violin.)

—Juan Gelman, translated from Spanish by Ilan Stavans.

Contents

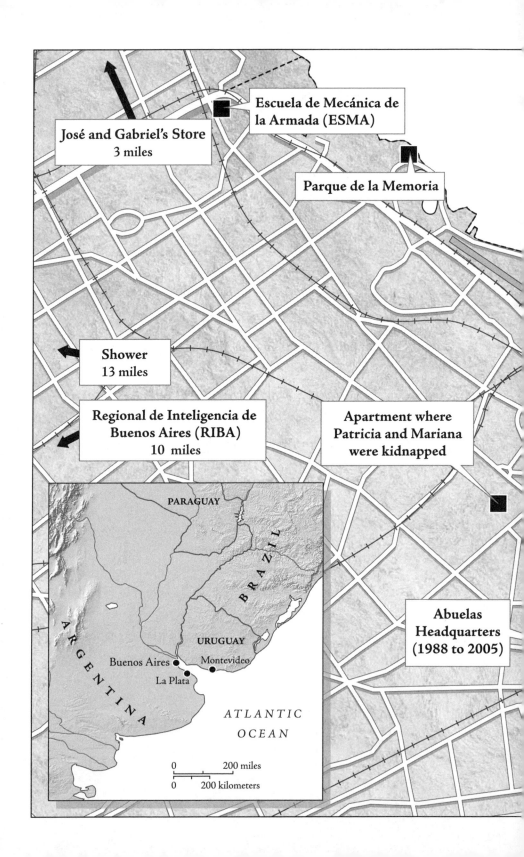

Escuela de Mecánica de la Armada (ESMA)

José and Gabriel's Store
3 miles

Parque de la Memoria

Shower
13 miles

Regional de Inteligencia de
Buenos Aires (RIBA)
10 miles

Apartment where
Patricia and Mariana
were kidnapped

Abuelas
Headquarters
(1988 to 2005)

PARAGUAY

BRAZIL

URUGUAY

ARGENTINA

Buenos Aires

Montevideo

La Plata

ATLANTIC
OCEAN

0   200 miles

0   200 kilometers

Buenos Aires

0   1 mile

0   1 kilometer

Río de la Plata

Aeroparque Jorge Newbery

Catedral Castrense
Stella Maris

Plaza San Martín

Abuelas
Headquarters
(1982 to 1988)

Plaza de Mayo

Abuelas
Headquarters
(2005 to Present)

Casa Rosada

Iglesia de la Santa Cruz

Timeline of Historical Events

1810

+ May 18–25: Argentina launches the May Revolution, marking the beginning of its independence fight.

1816

+ July 9: Argentina declares independence from Spain.

1930

+ September 6: General José Félix Uriburu unseats democratically elected president Hipólito Yrigoyen, marking the first of six coups that would occur between 1930 and 1976 and ushering in a period of instability known as the Infamous Decade.

1943

+ June 4: A shadowy faction within the Argentine military seizes power, ousting civilian leader Ramón Castillo.

1946

+ June 4: Juan Domingo Perón assumes the presidency after his election victory.

1952

+ July 26: Perón's wife Eva Perón, known to all as Evita, dies at the age of thirty-three.

1955

+ June 16: The Plaza de Mayo is bombed by Argentine navy and air force aircraft in an attempt to overthrow Perón. Over three hundred civilians are killed. Perón manages to escape and continues in office.
+ September 19: Perón is overthrown in a coup.
+ November 13: General Pedro Eugenio Aramburu becomes president of Argentina's military government.
+ December 22: Evita's corpse disappears from its resting place.

1956

+ June 9: General Juan José Valle attempts to depose President Aramburu and restore Perón to power. Soon thereafter, Valle and twenty-six of his collaborators are executed.

1962

+ March 29: The military overthrows democratically elected president Arturo Frondizi. He is replaced by another civilian leader, José María Guido.

1966

+ June 28: General Juan Carlos Onganía seizes power from democratically elected president Arturo Umberto Illia.

1969

+ May 29: The Cordobazo, a protest against the Onganía regime in the city of Córdoba, turns violent, killing around thirty people.

1970

+ May 29: The Montoneros kidnap former president Pedro Eugenio Aramburu.
+ June 1: The Montoneros kill Aramburu in retaliation for his overthrow of Perón and for his role in the execution of Juan José Valle and others involved in an attempted Peronist coup.

1973

+ June 20: At least thirteen people are killed when left-wing and right-wing supporters of Perón clash during a celebratory event marking his return from exile, an event later known as the Ezeiza Massacre.
+ June 27: The military takes power in Uruguay.
+ September 11: General Augusto Pinochet topples democratically elected president Salvador Allende in Chile.
+ October 12: Juan Perón assumes the presidency for his third term and his third wife, María Estela Martínez de Perón—known as Isabel—is sworn in as his vice president.

1974

+ July 1: Juan Perón dies at seventy-eight, leaving Isabel in power.
+ September 19: The Montoneros kidnap Juan and Jorge Born, the heirs to one of Argentina's largest conglomerates. They set the ransom at $60 million.
+ November 1: The Montoneros kill Argentina's federal police chief, Alberto Villar, and his wife by placing a bomb on their yacht.
+ November 6: Isabel Perón declares a state of siege, giving the military and security forces the power to search and detain people without a warrant or legal charges.

1975

+ November 28: The military regimes of Argentina, Bolivia, Chile, Paraguay, and Uruguay gather and launch Operation Condor, a transnational campaign to suppress "subversion." (Later on, Brazil, Peru, and Ecuador will also join.)

1976

+ March 24: The military deposes Isabel Perón in a coup and army chief Jorge Rafael Videla is named president.

1977

+ April 30: The mothers who will become the Madres de Plaza de Mayo convene in the plaza for the first time.

+ October 22: During one of their regular Thursday marches, a Madre who is also missing a grandchild asks other Madres whose daughters or daughters-in-law were pregnant at the time of their abductions to step aside and confer separately.
+ November 21: US Secretary of State Cyrus Vance visits Buenos Aires and twelve women who are missing their grandchildren in addition to their children gather after his visit. Later, they will become known as the Abuelas de Plaza de Mayo.
+ December 8: Seven people, including two Madres, are abducted from the Iglesia de la Santa Cruz.
+ December 10: Madres founder Azucena Villaflor is disappeared.

1978

+ June 25: Argentina hosts—and wins—the World Cup final.

1979

+ July 31: The Committee for the Defense of Human Rights in the Countries of the Southern Cone (CLAMOR) announces that Anatole and Victoria Eva Julien Grisonas had been located living in Valparaíso, Chile.

1980

+ March 19: Half-sisters Tatiana and Laura Britos reunite with their biological family in a Buenos Aires court, becoming the first grandchildren directly found by the Abuelas.

1981

+ March 29: Jorge Rafael Videla steps down as president of Argentina's military government. He is replaced by his close friend Roberto Eduardo Viola.
+ December 22: Leopoldo Galtieri is declared president of Argentina's military government after Viola's ouster.

1982

+ March 19: Argentine scrap metal workers land on South Georgia Island, igniting what will become the Falklands War.

+ April 2: Argentine soldiers invade the Falklands, officially marking the beginning of the Falklands War.
+ June 14: The British declare victory in the Falklands War, during which 649 Argentine soldiers and 255 British soldiers were killed.
+ July 1: Reynaldo Bignone replaces Galtieri as president of Argentina's military government and allows political activities to resume.

1983

+ December 10: Raúl Ricardo Alfonsín assumes the presidency and democracy is restored to Argentina after nearly eight years of military rule.

1984

+ June 8–17: A committee of American scientists, including Mary-Claire King, visits Argentina to present on how their areas of expertise might be used in service of identifying the disappeared and, in King's case, their surviving children.
+ November 30: La Comisión Nacional sobre la Desaparición de Personas, or the National Commission on the Disappearance of Persons (CONADEP), publishes its findings about the dictatorship in the form of a bombshell book titled *Nunca Más*, Never Again.
+ December 13: Paula Logares becomes the first grandchild who is returned to her biological family by the courts thanks to the creation of the Index of Grandpaternity.

1985

+ December 9: Argentina's Supreme Court rules in the Trial of the Juntas, sentencing Jorge Rafael Videla and former naval chief Emilio Eduardo Massera to life imprisonment, Roberto Eduardo Viola to seventeen years, another former naval leader, Armando Lambruschini, to eight years, and former air force chief Orlando Ramón Agosti to four years in prison.

1986

+ December 24: Alfonsín enacts the Full Stop Law, which sets a sixty-day deadline for prosecutions of most dictatorship-era crimes.

1987

+ April 15–19: A radical sector of the Argentine army known as the *carapintadas*, or painted faces, attempts to mutiny.
+ June 1: Alfonsín enacts a law creating the Banco Nacional de Datos Genéticos, or National Bank of Genetic Data (BNDG), to collect genetic information from relatives of the children stolen during the dictatorship.
+ June 8: Alfonsín promulgates the Due Obedience Law, which shields most military personnel from prosecution for dictatorship-era crimes. Kidnapping and rape are explicitly excluded from the amnesty.

1989

+ July 8: As Argentina wrestles with hyperinflation, Alfonsín is forced to renounce the presidency early. Carlos Saúl Menem takes his place, marking the first time in sixty-three years that one constitutionally elected Argentine president has handed power to another.
+ October 7: President Menem signs a decree pardoning most military officers who had not benefited from the Full Stop or Due Obedience Laws. This pardon did not include several top commanders, such as Jorge Videla and Roberto Viola.

1990

+ December 29: Menem pardons Jorge Videla and other top military leaders who remained in prison despite his earlier amnesty. He also pardons Mario Firmenich, a leader of the Montoneros.

1996

+ December 30: The Abuelas lodge what will become known as the Plan Sistemático de Robo de Bebés case, or the Systematic Plan of Baby Kidnapping case, alleging there was a coordinated plan to steal their grandchildren.

1998

+ June 9: Videla is detained after having been implicated in the Plan Sistemático de Robo de Bebés case.

1999

+ December 10: Menem hands off the presidency to Fernando de la Rúa, who promised to clean up corruption, campaigning on the slogan "They say I'm boring."

2001

+ December 1: De la Rúa limits bank withdrawals to $250 a week to avert a banking crisis. The measure becomes known as the *corralito*, or little corral.
+ December 20–January 1, 2002: Amid widespread looting and rioting, De la Rúa steps down after just two years in office, fleeing the Casa Rosada by helicopter. Three interim presidents try and fail to contain the economic chaos over the course of twelve days before Eduardo Duhalde takes office.

2003

+ May 25: Political newcomer Néstor Kirchner assumes the presidency.

2004

+ March 24: Kirchner removes portraits of dictatorship-era army chiefs Jorge Videla and Reynaldo Bignone from the Colegio Militar. He officially declares the former grounds of the Escuela de Mecánica de la Armada (ESMA) a public museum.

2005

+ June 14: Argentina's Supreme Court strikes down the Full Stop and Due Obedience Laws, enabling renewed prosecutions of dictatorship-era crimes.

2006

+ September 18: Torture survivor Jorge Julio López disappears after testifying against Miguel Etchecolatz, the former commissioner general of police for Buenos Aires Province.
+ September 19: Etchecolatz is sentenced to life imprisonment.

2007

+ December 10: Cristina Fernández de Kirchner replaces her husband as president. That same day, coast guard officer Héctor Febres, remembered by witnesses as overseeing pregnant women at the ESMA, dies of cyanide poisoning in his jail cell while awaiting sentencing for torture.

2010

+ October 27: Néstor Kirchner dies of a heart attack at the age of sixty.

2011

+ October 23: Cristina Fernández de Kirchner is reelected in a landslide.

2012

+ July 5: The Abuelas prevail in the Plan Sistemático de Robo de Bebés case. In addition to eight other convictions, Jorge Videla is sentenced to fifty years in prison.

2013

+ March 13: Jorge Mario Bergoglio, the former archbishop of Buenos Aires, is elected pope and assumes the title Pope Francis.
+ May 17: Jorge Videla dies in prison at the age of eighty-seven.

2016

+ March 24: On the fortieth anniversary of the coup, US President Barack Obama announces that the United States will declassify more records from the dictatorship period, including those from military and intelligence sources.

2023

+ November 19: Javier Milei is elected president.

Glossary of Terms

AAA or Triple A
Alianza Anticomunista Argentina (Argentine Anticommunist Alliance)
A covert right-wing death squad composed largely of off-duty police and
military officers that operated in Argentina before the 1976 coup.

AAAS
American Association for the Advancement of Science
An American nonprofit organization committed to promoting science
around the world.

appropriator
A term used by the Abuelas de Plaza de Mayo to refer to the people who
stole their grandchildren.

asado
Argentine term for barbecue, derived from the word "asar," which means
to cook over an open flame.

BNDG
Banco Nacional de Datos Genéticos (National Bank of Genetic Data)
A genetic bank, established in 1987, to collect and preserve the genetic
profiles of relatives of the Abuelas' stolen grandchildren.

CLAMOR
The Committee for the Defense of Human Rights in the Countries of the
Southern Cone
A small ecumenical group founded in 1977 to research and publicize
human rights atrocities in the Southern Cone.

colectivo
Argentine term for public bus.

CONADEP
Comisión Nacional sobre la Desaparición de Personas (National
Commission on the Disappearance of Persons)
A fact-finding commission established by President Raúl Alfonsín in
December 1983 to investigate the disappearances of the dictatorship.

CoNaDI
Comisión Nacional por el Derecho a la Identidad (National Commission
for the Right to Identity)
A government body established by President Carlos Menem in 1992 to
help locate the stolen children of *desaparecidos*.

desaparecido
A person forcibly disappeared by Argentina's security forces.

EAAF
Equipo Argentino de Antropología Forense (Argentine Forensic
Anthropology Team)
A team of Argentine forensic experts, founded in 1984, responsible for
exhuming and identifying the remains of *desaparecidos*.

ERP
Ejército Revolucionario del Pueblo (People's Revolutionary Army)
The combat branch of the Partido Revolucionario de los Trabajadores
(PRT).

ESMA
Escuela de Mecánica de la Armada (Navy School of Mechanics)
A naval academy in Buenos Aires which operated as one of the largest and
most feared clandestine detention centers during the dictatorship.

habeas corpus
A legal writ requiring a person in government custody to be brought before
a judge or released unless their detention is proven to be lawful.

H.I.J.O.S.
Hijos e Hijas por la Identidad y la Justicia contra el Olvido y el Silencio (Sons
and Daughters for Identity and Justice Against Oblivion and Silence)
An advocacy group founded by the children of *desaparecidos* in 1995.

Montoneros
A leftist Peronist group active in the 1960s and 1970s.

Nunca Más
The title of the report released by CONADEP in November 1984, which
documented dictatorship-era human rights abuses.

Operation Condor
A transnational network of South American dictatorships that shared
intelligence and planned joint operations between 1975 and the early 1980s.

pampas
Argentina's fertile grasslands, which stretch from the Atlantic to the
Andean foothills.

parrilla
Argentine grills heated with wood or coals.

picana
Electric prod used by Argentina's torture squads during the dictatorship.

Proceso de Recuperación
A program run at the ESMA during the dictatorship, through which the navy sought to "rehabilitate" prisoners through forced labor.

PRT
Partido Revolucionario de los Trabajadores (Workers' Revolutionary Party)
A Marxist group active in Argentina during the 1960s and 1970s.

RIBA
Regional de Inteligencia de Buenos Aires
An intelligence center in the western suburbs of Buenos Aires operated by Argentina's air force during the dictatorship.

verde
Nickname for guards at the ESMA.

villa miseria
An impoverished settlement, often lacking basic services like electricity and sewage, with homes typically built from scrap materials.

The Toy Store

October 6, 1978

The men crept in so quietly she didn't notice them at first. They moved fast, too fast for her to remember if there were two or three, or to see their faces. The workday was almost over, and Teresa Izaguirre was distracted. But as soon as she spotted them, it was obvious that something was wrong.

It was a rainy Friday afternoon in October 1978, and the toy and party supply store where Teresa worked in Martínez, a dense suburb north of Buenos Aires, had started preparing for the pre-Christmas throngs. On the wood-paneled walls hung wreaths of shimmering green tinsel and cartoonish ornaments depicting Papá Noel—Santa—smiling over his white beard.

The intruders passed the shelves stacked with Nativity scenes and slunk into the office, where José Manuel Pérez Rojo and Gabriel Pontnau were working. José had recently opened the shop to support his growing family. He and his partner, Patricia Roisinblit, already had one infant daughter and were expecting their second baby soon. José had always been fond of toys— he was an only child and, when he was young, his extensive collection of Superman and Elongated Man comic books had kept him entertained while his parents worked. He had recruited his old friend Gabriel, and they had gathered toys and decorations to sell from the small storefront tucked in a shopping arcade called Galería Saint George.

Teresa sat, paralyzed, as the men punched José into submission and clamped handcuffs over his wrists. Less sure of what to do with Gabriel, the assailants left him for the moment and stormed into the driving school located in the office next door, demanding to use the phone. They announced themselves as members of Defraudaciónes y Estafas, the federal police's fraud department. "Qué hacemos con el rubio? Que se la coma?" the owner of the driving school heard one of the men ask into the receiver, referring to Gabriel. What should we do with the blond guy? Should we take him, too?

The answer must have been yes. Through the glass walls of the shop, other storekeepers could see the men cover José and Gabriel with long beige raincoats, drag them out of the building, and shove them into the bed of a military truck. The truck screeched off, accompanied by several other cars.

No one—and particularly not Teresa—made any attempt to seek help. Even had she wanted to, whom would she call? If Argentines had learned anything in the two and a half years since the military had seized power, it was that little good came from paying attention, and even less came from attracting it. The armed men who now roved the city as agents of the dictatorship were at once secretive—driving cars without license plates and obscuring their faces with women's stockings—and brazen, abducting people off the street in broad daylight. It was almost as if they were daring bystanders: acknowledge you've noticed us, see what happens.

No. Better to forget what she'd witnessed. Teresa waited for her husband to pick her up, locked up the store, and left. Her employers had always treated her well, but a thought lingered—one that many others in Argentina had come to believe over the years: "Si se los llevan así, es por algo." If they were taken, there must be a reason.

The convoy made a brief stop at a garage two blocks from the shop, where José and Gabriel stored their excess merchandise. What their captors could have wanted with a warehouse worth of toys and holiday decorations was a mystery; perhaps they planned to resell it or dole it out to fulfill their own children's Christmas wishes. (Men like this didn't tend to be discriminating. In other raids, they had dragged away refrigerators full of food, vinyl records, and even boxer puppies.)

From there, the caravan headed south toward Buenos Aires, passing through the commercial district of Martínez and into Olivos, the leafy suburb where the leader of the ruling military junta, Jorge Rafael Videla, lived in a manicured presidential compound with his wife—with whom he shared six children—and their beloved German shepherds. Eventually the cars reached the neighborhood of Palermo. They bumped up the cobblestones of Gurruchaga and stopped in front of the eight-story apartment building where José lived with Patricia and their fifteen-month-old daughter, Mariana.

The men walked past the tall ash and plane trees near the building's entrance, through the front door, and into the dim lobby. For months now, José and Patricia had passed through that lobby each day as they went about their lives. They were just starting to settle into a mundane rhythm after more than a year of darting from safe house to safe house, trying to outrun the security forces. Now their days were blissfully boring. Each weekday, José left the apartment to manage his store, while Patricia cared for Mariana. In the evening, she gave Mariana dinner, but waited for José to return from work before giving her dessert so he, too, could enjoy her delighted expressions.

The crew reached the third floor and crossed the threshold of apartment 20, where they found little Mariana, who had just started toddling around, and Patricia, who had reached the stage of pregnancy where even walking was strenuous. Her belly bulged and her normally thin legs had swollen. They shuffled mother and daughter to a car waiting downstairs, and once both had been loaded inside, one of the men demanded Patricia give them the address of a relative where they could leave Mariana. "We don't kidnap children," he explained.

Patricia spat out the address of José's parents, José Manuel Pérez and Argentina Rojo, in Belgrano, a verdant residential neighborhood about three miles away. The cars took off again, heading north. José's parents lived on the ground floor of a three-story building, with their bedroom window facing the street. If the couple had been home, they would have heard the wheels of the convoy swishing to a halt on the wet pavement outside, but the small apartment was empty. Unbeknownst to Patricia and José, his parents were at the hospital, attending to a nephew who had fallen ill.

And so the captors were given another address: Francisco Beiró 2998, the home of Argentina's sister Francisca in Olivos, back in the direction from which the cars had originally come. By then it was late, around ten, and when they finally reached the quiet neighborhood, the streets were dark. Eucalyptus trees and Paraná pines shuddered in the breeze as the caravan sped by. Beiró was a one-way street with neat sidewalks and well-tended one- and two-story homes set behind iron gates. It was the type of place where people moved to escape the chaos of the big city, in search of some little slice of peace.

The convoy stopped in front of a small white home across the street from the high walls of the Olivos cemetery, whose marble mausoleums housed the remains of tango singers, actresses, and politicians. Each year, José's family gathered at the cottage to celebrate Christmas—though lately they had avoided inviting José to their reunions out of caution. Now their fears had been realized: he had brought the security forces to their doorstep. The men—at least twenty of them—poured out of their cars and fanned around the house, blocking the doors and windows. Most of them wore starched brown fatigues and carried rifles. Some climbed the walls of the cemetery to surveil the cottage from above, while a few others, dressed in civilian clothing, approached the front door.

"Open up or we'll knock it down!" they demanded.

After a pause, the door creaked open to reveal José's elderly aunt Francisca and her eighteen-year-old grandson, Marcelo—José's second cousin. Despite his efforts to contain her, Francisca slipped under Marcelo's arm, begging the men to leave him alone. Marcelo asked the men for a few minutes to calm Francisca down and shooed her back into the house, where his eleven-year-old cousin waited along with two of his friends, who had been getting ready to go out dancing. Marcelo shut one of his friends and his cousin with his grandmother inside her room and left his other friend cowering under the kitchen table.

When Marcelo returned to the front door, he found five men shuffling anxiously around the porch, where they had balanced a basket on the entrance gate. One man, a redhead, seemed the most nervous of all. Nestled inside the basket was Mariana; on the ground was a bag of her tiny clothing. Out on the street, tied up inside the bed of a Chevy Brava, José tried to stand, yelling to Marcelo to take care of his daughter. Fifty meters away, from the back seat of a car that looked suspiciously like the green Fiat 125 Patricia and José shared, Patricia strained out the window to scream to Marcelo: "I'm pregnant! They're taking me to—"

Before she could finish, one of the men clapped a hand over her mouth and pushed her back into the car.

Marcelo hurried Mariana inside the home, where she began tracing frantic circles around Francisca's rough orange sofa, howling: "Papá, Papá, Papá, Papá, Papá." When he stepped outside again to fetch the bag of her things, the men were already back in their cars, speeding away into the night.

PART I

The Disappeared

1

The Castaways

Patricia Julia Roisinblit, the cosseted only child of Rosa Tarlovsky de Roisinblit and her husband, Benjamín Roisinblit, was blessed with a sheltered upbringing. Her birth, on December 8, 1952, had been the fulfillment of long unrealized dreams: Rosa, an obstetrician who had delivered hundreds of other women's babies, had a difficult time with pregnancy. Soon after marrying Benjamín, she suffered a traumatic miscarriage at five months, when her belly had already started to expand. Upon becoming pregnant with Patricia, her uterus rippled with premature contractions, and she was ordered to remain on bed rest for eight months.

When Patricia finally emerged into the warm Buenos Aires air, she was perfectly smooth and round, like a porcelain doll. Immediately, she became the center of her parents' universe. Though both had demanding jobs—Rosa in an obstetrics clinic, and Benjamín as an accountant— they fixed their schedules so that one of them was nearly always with her. When they couldn't arrange that, Rosa brought Patricia to work, where nurses let her admire the sleepy newborns and sang her "Mantantirulirulá," a popular children's song of the era.

Rosa dressed Patricia like "a princess," in embroidered dresses and purses that she made herself. She and Benjamín encouraged Patricia's passions:

the Roisinblits joined an athletic club with a pool so Patricia could learn to swim; when her doodles showed promise, they got her a private teacher and began taking her to Saturday classes at the Instituto Bernasconi, a Florentine-style grade school with a weekend art program. Such support nourished the young girl's talents—and her confidence. At one point, the artworks Patricia brought from home were so precise and lifelike that one of her teachers snapped: "Tell your mother not to do your drawings for you." The young Patricia responded: "Fine, I'll draw something here in class so you can see I know how to draw." Eager for her to excel in school, her parents did lend a hand in other areas from time to time. Rosa pitched in with Patricia's geometry homework and Benjamín, who wrote poetry, helped her with compositions. Education was a family value, and Patricia relished the opportunity to learn. When Benjamín returned from work around eight in the evening, the family would sit down and chat over plates of Rosa's specialties: succulent roast chicken and kamish broit—crunchy Jewish cookies with cinnamon and nuts. During one of these study sessions, conversation turned to ancient Egypt. Benjamín explained that the pyramids had been built before Egyptians had access to the wheel to help with construction. The next day, Patricia shared this information with her class, leading her teacher to ask where she had read about such things. "I didn't read about it," she said proudly. "My papá taught me."

The Roisinblits were Jewish—Rosa and Benjamín's parents had both emigrated from the Russian Empire to Argentina around the turn of the twentieth century—and to ensure Patricia felt connected to that heritage, they enrolled her in a weekend class at the Peretz, a Jewish center just outside Buenos Aires. On the white classroom walls hung banners that read: "The new Argentina provides us with happy schools and happy children."

Indeed, Argentina had once seemed like a haven, a place where families like the Roisinblits could lead prosperous lives. In the years preceding World War I, crop and cattle exports had made it among the richest nations in the world—better off than France and Germany in terms of GDP per capita. Flocks of mostly Italian and Spanish immigrants sailed across the Atlantic to seek their fortunes in the country's vast and fertile pampas and burgeoning cities, bringing their refined tastes along with them. A Roman or Madrileño stepping off the boat at the bustling Buenos Aires port in the early twentieth century would have felt at home among the wide, tree-lined avenues and newly constructed Beaux-Arts buildings. The grand opera house, Teatro Colón, whose red velvet seats and stained glass skylights were unveiled to the public in 1908, had helped turn the city into a cultural hub to rival Milan or Barcelona. (The acoustics of the concert hall were rumored to be so crystalline that audience members seated in the fifth balcony could hear a soprano's teardrop splash on the stage during an emotional performance.) For a time, the French described exorbitantly wealthy people as "riche comme un Argentin."

Then, in 1929, the Great Depression hit, crushing demand for Argentina's farm exports in the United States and Europe. Customs revenues plummeted and the government struggled to pay its employees, fueling discontent. Influenced by Italy's brand of fascism, the Argentine military took advantage of the tumult to seize power in 1930, and over the decades that followed, the country ping-ponged between military and civilian rule, with its economy following a similarly jagged trajectory of booms and busts. The chaos gave rise to a series of strongmen and spawned a snide joke among outside observers: When God was creating Argentina, it begins, he endowed it with the never-ending pampas, towering Andean peaks full of minerals, sprawling oil fields, and countless other natural resources. Saint Peter asked God if he was being overly generous, pouring so many advantages into just one nation. "Don't worry," he replied. "I'm also giving it the Argentines."

By the time Patricia grew more interested in politics, as she entered her teenage years, Argentina was under the draconian control of General Juan Carlos Onganía, who had swept to power in a 1966 coup and proceeded to outlaw political activity—and just about everything else. Women were arrested for wearing their skirts too short, and men for wearing their hair too long. Police officers would sometimes take the liberty of cutting it before releasing them; longer than eight centimeters above their shoulders and boys were barred from secondary schools. Nabokov's *Lolita* and Henry

Miller's *Nexus* were forbidden for being "obscene"; Miloš Forman's *Loves of a Blonde* and Michelangelo Antonioni's *Blow-Up* were banned from theaters. Kissing was prohibited in public parks. Couples seeking privacy at one of Buenos Aires' many *boliches*, or nightclubs, were out of luck, too: Onganía's regime ordered the clubs to keep their lights bright at all times. Even ballet was too risqué for the general. Once, halfway through a performance of Stravinsky's *The Rite of Spring* at the Teatro Colón, Onganía stomped out of the presidential box and rushed his wife and twenty-eight-year-old daughter outside. "My wife and daughter had to look at indecencies performed by seminude dancers," he griped to the mayor of Buenos Aires the following day. "Today, we had to go to confession."

Patricia, meanwhile, navigated the cultural austerity with aplomb. At Escuela Normal Número 8, the prestigious public school she attended, there was a strict uniform. Girls had to wear long smocks; nail polish and makeup were banned. Each morning, one of the head teachers met students at the door of the Greek Revival building to examine their hands, faces, and outfits as they walked in. One day, the teacher clucked at Patricia for wearing her skirt too short—it covered only half her knees. Patricia provoked hysterical laughter from her friends when, the following morning, she showed up with a smock down to her ankles. "You want long?" the look suggested. "Here you go!"

Within Número 8's wrought-iron gates, students were taught mostly patriotic music. "Coronados de gloria vivamos, O juremos con gloria morir!" went the Argentine national anthem. Crowned in glory, let's live, or let's swear with glory to die! But outside, Patricia and her friends sang songs from the thrilling new world of Argentine rock, or *rock nacional*. Influenced by the Beatles and the Rolling Stones, and fueled by Onganía's repression, a wave of homegrown rock-and-roll bands had become a sensation among Argentina's youth. Vinyls by bands like La Joven Guardia, Sui Generis, and Pedro y Pablo were in frequent rotation on the girls' turntables. But it was Los Gatos who sparked revolutionary fervor among Patricia's generation. Like many bands in the *rock nacional* scene, Los Gatos often camped out in La Perla del Once, a twenty-four-hour café across the street from the Once train station that was frequented by university students and haggard workers waiting to travel home. The bandmates would sit at their table laughing boisterously, swapping ideas, and trying to write songs. They couldn't afford many *cafés con leche* or *medialunas*, Argentina's buttery-sweet interpretation of the croissant, and sometimes exasperated waiters chucked them out, annoyed by the racket and their frugality. One night in 1967, to avoid such scrutiny, the young musicians retreated to the men's bathroom with their instruments, where they composed their most famous song, "La Balsa," which describes building an imaginary raft and purposely shipwrecking it to escape the repressive world of 1960s Argentina:

> *I'm very sad and lonely here,*
> *In this deserted world . . .*
> *I'll build a raft*
> *and I'll go and get shipwrecked*

The single sold 250,000 copies in six months—fifty times more than most other rock records at the time—and inspired a movement of *náufragos* (literally "castaways," a reference to the song's lyrics), young hippies who spent their days puffing on shared cigarettes, debating philosophy, and reading poetry under the trees in the city's plazas. In protest of Onganía's vow to boost productivity and "modernize" Argentina, *náufragos* came to embrace performative idleness, spending much of their time on one city block—the Manzana Loca, or Crazy Block—in Retiro, one of the wealthiest neighborhoods of Buenos Aires. As they lingered outside French-style mansions wearing tight pants and denim vests embroidered with the words PAZ Y AMOR, the castaways delighted in the looks of horror they provoked from stiff businessmen and their prim housewives. Many *náufragos* visited the Instituto Torcuato Di Tella, a center for avant-garde art, to partake in "happenings," interactive artistic experiences that sometimes spiraled into barefoot dance parties. Other days, they took naps under the tipa, palo borracho, and jacaranda trees of Plaza San Martín, a lush park half a block from the Di Tella.

A rocker known as Tanguito—José Alberto Iglesias—had helped Los Gatos write "La Balsa." Once, to mark the arrival of spring, Tanguito picked up a guitar and led hundreds of free-spirited young people wearing jeans and flowered shirts in a musical procession through the streets. An organizer of the event passed out copies of a manifesto he had penned titled "I'm Tired." "I'm fed up with a civilization that has made humans hate other humans, has forbidden men from sleeping anywhere on His Planet, has forced everyone to live a sad, mundane life, locked up in themselves and their homes as if in trenches," it read.

This kind of whimsical protest never posed any real threat to the Onganía regime—Argentina's hippie movement was much smaller than the one surging in the United States—but the police hounded the *náufragos*. The Argentine newspaper *La Razón* announced the start of an "anti-hippie war" in Buenos Aires beginning in January 1968, when security forces arrested fifty-five young people in "multicolored shirts, tight pants, and long manes of hair, carrying records from the Beatles and other new wave musicians." In another incident, a waiter at a café in the upscale Barrio Norte neighborhood called the police on four patrons sipping lemonade, claiming that they were disrespecting the military government with their fitted pants, boots, and "crypto-military" jackets; they were promptly arrested. A lead singer of Los Gatos was detained twenty times in one month. "Once, I was released, I walked one block, and I was picked up by another police car," he later recalled. A fellow musician started traveling around the city with his address scribbled on a sign tied around his neck—he was sick of the police demanding to know where he lived each time he was jailed.

While she and her friends were attracted to the culture and fashion of *rock nacional*, Patricia herself was in many ways the antithesis of an Argentine drifter. Ever since elementary school, Patricia's grades had been superlative, landing her on the honor roll every quarter. On top of her normal schoolwork, she attended English classes at a British-language school, where she earned a teaching certificate. Yet as the hippie movement swelled around her, she began to chafe against the conservativism of her school and family. She fell in with a clique of girls known as *las avivadas*—the smart alecks—

who delighted in pushing boundaries. Once, Patricia led her friends to escape school before the end of the day, an infraction for which they received their first official group reprimand. Another time, shielded by her peers, she disrobed in the corner of a classroom to change out of an outfit she had stained. She was unabashedly confident in her good looks, once responding to a boyfriend who teased her about her small breasts: "With the legs and ass I have, can you imagine if I also had tits?"

This brassiness, combined with her chestnut hair and perfectly even smile, made Patricia irresistible to men. She showed off her legs in red high heels and newly fashionable miniskirts and applied bright red lipstick to her full lips. "She made herself up like a doll," Rosa would later say. Friends likened her voice to a songbird's and her laugh to the tinkling of bells. "Watching her seduce someone was a party," one said.

It was the late 1960s, and the whole world seemed on the brink of implosion. The unmitigated bloodshed of the Vietnam War and the assassination of Martin Luther King Jr. had plunged the United States into chaos, while in France, student protests over education reform had devolved into a general strike over workers' rights that involved roughly two-thirds of the country's workforce. Fiery demonstrations roiled Czechoslovakia after Soviet-led forces invaded, and the armed forces in Mexico massacred an estimated three hundred students who had gathered in the capital to oppose their country's hosting of the Olympic Games.

While Patricia was finishing high school and the *náufragos* milled about Plaza San Martín, a more serious strain of resistance began to emerge in Argentina. Onganía had not only banned racy ballets and arrested hippies, but also cracked down on unions, prohibited strikes, raised the retirement age, froze wages, and devalued the peso by 50 percent. Thousands of workers were pushed out of their rail, port, and other public sector jobs, and large state-run sugar mills were shuttered. *Villas miseria*—literally "misery slums," poor communities composed of makeshift structures fashioned from corrugated iron, cardboard, and whatever other materials residents could scrape together—ballooned in and around big cities.

The spark that ultimately led to the inferno was seemingly trivial: a cafeteria at a university in Corrientes, a city in Argentina's northeast, was privatized, pushing prices up. On May 15, 1969, angry students gathered outside the school to protest and were met with police gunfire that killed a medical student. Young people around the country took to the streets, allying themselves with workers, who were similarly fed up with Onganía's austerity and repression. Two weeks later, on May 29, union workers in Córdoba, one of Argentina's largest cities, made plans to walk off their jobs and march to union headquarters, in clear defiance of Onganía's ban on strikes. They collected steel bars and bolts from the plants where they worked—just in case things got hairy. Meanwhile, students gathered across the city in support.

As the coalition of laborers and young people set off from various neighborhoods, older women shuffled out of their homes to supply them with matches, bottles, and brooms for protection. At first, it didn't seem they would need such objects. The day started peacefully, with some participants describing the mood as "joyous." But around noon, as the jumble of workers in dusty uniforms and middle-class students in khakis and loafers closed in on Córdoba's central plaza, the police grew jumpy. They replaced their rubber bullets with lead ones. Then they opened fire, killing an autoworker named Máximo Mena. As Mena lay bleeding on Boulevard San Juan, one of Córdoba's main thoroughfares, the marchers grabbed whatever rocks and chunks of pavement they could find and began hurling them at police.

News of Mena's shooting spread rapidly. Soon, residents who had seen the mayhem from their windows or heard about it on their radios charged out of their apartments, dragging furniture and mattresses behind them to build barricades and bonfires. Overwhelmed, the police retreated, leaving the crowds to rampage through the city. Protesters set fire to the Citroën and Xerox stores, the Development Bank, the upscale Jockey Club, and other symbols of elitist snobbery and foreign imperialism. Around the country, ten million Argentines—nearly half the population—sat glued to their televisions, watching reports of what would become known as the Cordobazo. By the time the tumult subsided the following day, Córdoba was littered with husks of burned-out cars and shattered glass. Approximately thirty people had been killed, and hundreds of others had been wounded or arrested.

Pinning the event on "an excess of freedom," Onganía responded with a mix of vengeful repression and panicked change, shutting down several news outlets, ripping up his economic plan, and sacking several important ministers. These measures did little to boost his popularity, which was waning among his military colleagues and civilian subjects alike. Some of his generals had taken to calling him El Cano, or The Pipe. "He is very straight, but also very hollow," one explained.

There was not a peep about the Cordobazo in Patricia's Democratic Education class, where teachers stuck to a sanitized curriculum the Onganía regime would have approved of. She was occupied with other pursuits anyway, having decided that she, like her mother, would go into the medical field. While most students took a year to exclusively study for the entrance exam to the rigorous Facultad de Medicina at the University of Buenos Aires, Patricia prepared while still in her final year of secondary school, gaining admission without trouble. When the students began dissecting cadavers, many reconsidered their career paths, but not Patricia. Rosa had never shielded her from the realities of the human body; in fact, she had drawn diagrams to teach her daughter about fertilization and genitalia. "This is the uterus," she would say as she scribbled. "This is the vagina." Now she sometimes helped her daughter prepare for exams. Patricia performed well in embryology and, to Rosa's delight, received a perfect score in obstetrics.

2

Perón or Death

Around nine o'clock on the morning of May 29, 1970, precisely a year after the Cordobazo, in the wealthy Buenos Aires neighborhood of Recoleta, two young men in military uniforms arrived at the front door of General Pedro Eugenio Aramburu. From 1955 to 1958, Aramburu had presided over Argentina as dictator after helping to overthrow democratically elected president Juan Domingo Perón. But that business was behind him now, and at sixty-seven, the general was enjoying his retirement. Aramburu was still in his pajamas when the doorbell rang—neither he nor his wife, Sara, had been expecting visitors. When the young men told Sara that they had come to guard her husband, though, she thought little of it. The family had suffered scares before. Once, a gardener had stumbled on a bomb while tending to the grounds of the Aramburus' country home; on another occasion, Sara discovered someone had left a bouquet of black flowers in the lobby of their apartment building. Tensions had been particularly high since the Cordobazo, and just the other day her husband had said that military personnel were at risk of being killed. She invited the young officers inside and asked her housekeeper to serve them coffee as they waited for the general to get dressed. Then she excused herself to go buy meat at the market.

Aramburu emerged, greeting the young men warmly. If he had looked more closely at their uniforms, he might have noticed that one of them was far too big and had been tailored by an amateur. Nevertheless, the general did not resist as they shuffled him outside into a white Peugeot sedan and sped away. A few hours later, at one thirty, radio stations across the country interrupted their programming with breaking news: General Pedro Aramburu had been kidnapped.

Journalists, photographers, and concerned Argentines descended upon the entrance to the general's apartment, eager for updates. In the meantime, the kidnappers had switched cars twice, eventually shoving Aramburu in the back of a Jeep Gladiator pickup and covering him with hay bales. Then they drove eight hours out of Buenos Aires, where they hid him on a remote farm.

Later that same day, the kidnappers released a communiqué to the public, accusing the retired general of betraying the nation and of the murder of twenty-seven Argentines. At the bottom of the message, capital letters spelled out an ominous vow: "PERÓN OR DEATH."

Six feet tall, with broad shoulders and a Cheshire cat grin, Juan Domingo Perón was the most important Argentine politician of the twentieth century. He had clawed himself from a lower-middle class upbringing to become a decorated army colonel and, when the military took over the government in 1943, a powerful political fixture, serving as secretary of labor and social welfare, minister of war, and, finally, vice president.

In 1946, when the military held democratic elections, Perón ran, becoming the first Argentine politician to direct his campaign at the working classes, who represented a huge and increasingly disgruntled swath of the country. In the late 1930s, one-fifth of Argentina—an area larger than the entirety of France—had belonged to just two thousand ranching families, cattle czars who could "gallop for days without finding the end of [their] land." They modeled their homes after Spanish castillos and French châteaus, with hand-planted eucalyptus trees lining their miles-long driveways. Much of the actual ranching was done by hired help while the landowners gallivanted around Europe, sometimes bringing home French prostitutes and a year's stash of champagne and foie gras. Meanwhile, millions of other Argentines—*los descamisados*, or the shirtless ones—struggled for survival. Perón's booming voice, chummy demeanor, and promises to improve the economic lot of the disenfranchised soon won him their ardent devotion.

But Perón's greatest asset was his second wife: María Eva Duarte de Perón, known to all as Evita. Willowy, with a pert nose and perfectly coiffed blond hair, Evita was born in 1919—the same year as Rosa Roisinblit—in a small agricultural town, where she was raised by a poor single mother. At a time when most Argentine women didn't leave home until they married, she moved to Buenos Aires on her own at age fifteen and became a screen and radio actress, a rags-to-riches fairy tale that was vanishingly rare in 1940s Argentina.

Perón and Evita inspired hope among their working-class followers, convincing them that their dreams for a better life were not futile. Crisscrossing the country on a train car named El Descamisado, the couple gifted candy, kilos of meat, shoes, and toys to adoring crowds. During these trips, Perón eschewed suits for button-down shirts, to seem closer to the people. But rather than dressing down for the occasion, Evita wore sparkling jewels and couture clothing.

"You, too, can have these things someday," she told those who came to greet her. "I once had nothing."

Perón won the 1946 election handily and, true to his word, worked to uplift the *descamisados* by rolling out universal social security and popular new labor laws, including a minimum wage, the right to sick leave, and paid holidays for the entire workforce. While he occupied the Casa Rosada (the Pink House, Argentina's presidential palace), wages rose—jumping 62 percent between 1945 and 1949—the number of young people enrolled in secondary education nearly tripled, the number of beds in public hospitals doubled, and homeownership shot up. In one of the world's most famously carnivorous countries, he put a price cap on meat, promising "steak on every plate." Some of his followers began calling him El Líder—not *a* leader but *the* leader.

Perhaps emboldened by such a title, Perón was soon acting more like an autocrat than a servant of the people, even rewriting the constitution to include language taken verbatim from a speech that he had delivered. His critics, meanwhile, struggled to write much at all. During his first years in office, a commission set up by his administration shut down forty-five newspapers over their "anti-Argentine coverage." The international press was not spared either. After running a cover of Evita that the Peróns apparently found distasteful, *Time* magazine was banned in Argentina for over a year.

All the while, Evita continued courting *el pueblo*, the people, and lambasting the wealthy. "Shall we burn down the Barrio Norte?" she once cried from the Casa Rosada's balcony, referring to one of the ritziest neighborhoods of Buenos Aires as the crowd below whistled and cheered. She held frequent open houses in her office, where Argentines were invited to ask her for favors. One person might plead for medical treatment for a sick child; another would ask for housing for a group of mothers living in a swampy shantytown. Evita listened attentively and, within a few days, the requests would be granted. During such office hours, she would often kiss female visitors in greeting. Once, a woman showed up with a syphilitic sore on her mouth, prompting one of Evita's staffers to jump in between her and the first lady. Evita shooed him away with a flick of her delicate wrist and kissed the woman on the lips. "Never do that again," she later admonished her employee. "It's the price I have to pay."

Not long into Perón's first term, Evita's health began to falter. A newspaper article from mid-1948 reported: "An acute bronchitis makes her cough often. She asks for aspirin and tea. The rings under her eyes are even more pronounced because of the paleness of her face." Already petite, she lost twenty-two pounds in a single year, transforming from a glossy femme fatale to someone who looked as though she might float away with the breeze. One sweltering January day in 1950, Evita was inaugurating a building for the taxi union near the Buenos Aires port when she fainted in front of her adoring fans. Her frailty only served to fuel her popularity—and by extension that of her husband. When she released her autobiography in 1951, it sold 150,000 copies in a single day. Following galas at Teatro Colón, one newspaper printed 400,000 copies of special "Colón night" issues, dedicated almost entirely to photos and descriptions of her fur stoles, elegant gowns, and glittering gems. Later that year, millions of people showed up to see an increasingly feeble Evita join Perón during a speech from the balcony of the Casa Rosada, chanting "La vida por Perón!" Life for Perón.

On July 26, 1952, as Rosa Roisinblit lay in bed pregnant with Patricia, Evita died of cervical cancer at the age of thirty-three. Braving frigid winter rain, two million people streamed into the streets of Buenos Aires to mourn, some waiting fifteen hours to glimpse Evita's ashen face through her glass casket. Outside her resting place in the Ministry of Labor, 8,340 funeral wreaths and twenty-foot-high piles of flowers accumulated in the days following her death, giving the building the look of an enchanted castle. Argentina's florists—the only businesses that remained open in all of Buenos Aires—ran out of blooms and had to import roses, tulips, and carnations from Chile. The minister of public health commissioned a 220-pound, 5-foot-5-inch candle (the same height as Evita) to be lit for an hour on the twenty-sixth of each month to mark the day she died. A food workers' union wrote to Pope Pius XII to ask that she be canonized.

No one, however, was more shattered by Evita's loss than Perón himself. Since taking office, the general's domineering style—shaped in part by his brief tenure as a military attaché in Mussolini's Italy from 1939 to 1940—had unsettled many Argentines, including Rosa Roisinblit. His grief seemed to fuel his tyrannical tendencies. He had already nationalized Argentina's railways and other utilities, stuffing their boards with corrupt cronies; cracked down on imports and exports; and imprisoned political critics. Right before Evita died, he pushed through a law ordering that her autobiography, La Razón de Mi Vida, or The Reason for My Life, become required reading in schools. "Mommy loves me" was replaced by "Eva loves me" in first-grade reading textbooks. Now, as the mourning Perón turned fifty-eight in 1953, his actions grew even more extreme. He took up with a fourteen-year-old schoolgirl, lavishing her with gems from Evita's collection, and riled the powerful Catholic Church by pushing to legalize divorce and prostitution. When the church predictably resisted such measures, he jailed one curate for "disrespect." The church and the heavily Catholic Argentine military were apoplectic. Both institutions decided Perón needed to go.

On June 15, 1955, rumors swirled that the Vatican had excommunicated

Perón; the following day, a cold and cloudy Thursday, planes flown by the Argentine navy and air force dropped more than one hundred bombs on the Casa Rosada in hopes of assassinating him. They also strafed the Plaza de Mayo, the palm-studded square in front of the presidential palace, where masses of Perón's defenders had gathered to show their support amid his standoff with the Church. The attack killed over three hundred people and maimed more than twelve hundred. Perón escaped unscathed but was toppled and ejected from the country a few months later, effectively dividing all of Argentina into two hostile groups: Peronists and anti-Peronists.

Shortly after the coup, General Pedro Eugenio Aramburu, a top commander in the Argentine army, took power as de facto president of Argentina and began working to purge the country of his predecessor's considerable influence. He stuck several Peronist generals in jail and felled statues of Perón and Evita, hacking up the Carrara marble to donate to art students. Argentines were banned from mentioning Perón by name—newspapers tended to call him the *tirano prófugo*, or fugitive tyrant, while Aramburu himself preferred "the monster." Merely possessing a picture of the former president could land an Argentine in prison for up to six years. Worried that Evita's embalmed corpse had taken on too much symbolic power, Aramburu's regime stole her casket from its resting place in the dead of night and hid it.

Incensed by these measures, a Peronist general named Juan José Valle staged a failed coup in June 1956 to oust Aramburu and restore Perón. Aramburu had known General Valle from the Colegio Militar de la Nación, or National Military College, where they'd both trained, but any personal rapport paled in comparison to the responsibility Aramburu felt to keep Perón from rising again. With Aramburu's approval, Valle and twenty-six other military personnel and civilians suspected of involvement in the attempted coup were put to death without a trial. The general supposedly wept as he signed the order for Valle's execution.

The following year, Aramburu did something else that would enrage Peronists for decades to come. Despite his regime's efforts to sequester Evita's body in secure military buildings, supporters manged to find her, laying flowers and candles nearby. By April 1957, Aramburu could take no more. He enlisted the help of a priest to spirit her casket out of the country, forbidding the cleric from divulging her final resting place—even to him. A devout Catholic, he wanted to truthfully say that he did not know where she was, but that she was in "Christian hands." With secret assistance from the Vatican, she was buried in a cemetery in Milan under a false name. In 1958, Aramburu stepped down and allowed democratic elections. But in a final insult, he decreed that Peronists were not allowed to run.

Aramburu's kidnappers were part of a small group of Peronist militants who called themselves the Juan José Valle Command of the Montoneros, an allusion both to the Peronist general Aramburu's troops had executed in 1956 and to the ragtag mounted soldiers who had helped free Argentina from Spanish control in 1816. When two of their members showed up at the general's door in May 1970, the Montoneros in their entirety numbered just twelve young men and women, all Catholic, none older than thirty. Several of the young people had begun their political lives in conservative Catholic organizations, but, inspired by Che Guevara and the Cuban Revolution, ultimately gravitated toward socialism. They viewed Argentina as a country divided in two antagonistic factions: "the liberal oligarchy, clearly anti-nationalist and *vendepatria*," or willing to sell out the homeland, and "the people," committed to its defense. The Montoneros believed that defense would necessarily require taking up arms. Two of the group's founding members had received military instruction in Cuba; the others had no combat training whatsoever. Even so, they were, according to one scholar, "intent upon responding to the military violence with violence in the name of the people."

They defined their ideology simply, stating: "We are peronists [*sic*]." Only one founding member of the Montoneros, however, had any direct connection with the Peróns: years prior, Evita had saved his mother's life by sending a plane to pick her up in Corrientes so that she could have a vital operation at a modern Buenos Aires hospital. The Montoneros had all been too young to vote for Perón when he twice ran for president, and they had never met or corresponded with their patron saint, who was now living in exile in Spain.

But they were convinced he shared their commitment to building a "free, just, and sovereign fatherland," and were hell-bent on returning him to lead Argentina.

Two days after abducting Aramburu, on May 31, the Montoneros announced they had formed a "revolutionary tribunal" and interrogated the former general about what they deemed to be his crimes, including the "killing of 27 Argentines without a prior trial or justified cause." The following morning, they shot him twice in the head and once in the chest. They vowed to reveal the location of Aramburu's corpse only when the military government disclosed the whereabouts of Evita Perón's.

Ever since the uprisings in Córdoba the year before, General Onganía had been clinging to power by his fingernails. Aramburu's kidnapping was his final undoing. Mounting economic frustration and social unrest was one thing. But now, a former president of the nation had been abducted from his own home on Onganía's watch. He had clearly lost control; his military colleagues felt compelled to act. A week after Aramburu vanished, mutinous troops surrounded the Casa Rosada and forced Onganía to resign, replacing him with another general.

On July 16, after a frenzied search involving twenty-two thousand men, officials found Aramburu's corpse in the basement of a farmhouse owned by one of the Montoneros' families in the tiny farming village of Timote. The general had been gagged and his hands were tied behind his back. His body had been covered in lime to dissolve his flesh and bones.

With their very first operation, the Montoneros had assassinated one dictator and toppled another. Almost overnight, they became household names.

3

Perón *and* Death

1971–1974

In 1971, Patricia Roisinblit's father, Benjamín, became gravely ill. Benjamín had long suffered from health issues, but this time was different: an exploratory operation found that he had advanced stomach cancer. The doctors predicted he had four months to live.

To the Roisinblit women, the news was earth-shattering. While Rosa's job as an obstetrician meant that the Roisinblits had defied certain gender stereotypes, Benjamín had always played a traditional patriarchal role. He was strikingly handsome, with olive skin, thick, dark eyebrows, and a crackling sense of humor that electrified every room he entered. His relatives described him as "a sun," and indeed his family seemed to revolve around him. He saw himself as Patricia's protector, and he doted on Rosa. Before marrying, they had both lived with their families, meeting mostly at parks and cafés. On one early date, the couple sat on a bench in Plaza San Martín, the same picturesque square Argentina's hippies would later inhabit. Finding the lighting unromantic, Benjamín chucked a stone at one of the streetlights, knocking it out to better set the mood. On the twenty-first of each month, they celebrated the anniversary of their first date, which had taken place in October 1949; without fail, Benjamín would meet Rosa at the movie theater carrying chocolates, a bouquet of flowers, or a book he'd picked out for her.

As time went on, he saved a napkin from every café and restaurant he and Rosa visited—eventually presenting them to her in a brown leather album with gilt edging as a surprise. He wrote her scores of effusive letters and intimate poems that she tucked away like treasures, and he found every opportunity to compliment her. Once, upon watching Rosa walk in from the kitchen, a friend of Benjamín's exclaimed: "Rosita, what nice legs you have!" Instead of telling his friend off, Benjamín smiled slyly, satisfied that someone else appreciated what he already knew.

Benjamín's final months were torturous for Patricia and Rosa, but even as he faded away, he tried to lighten everyone's mood. When a friend came to check on him, he quipped: "I can't complain. They dote on me like a prince, and I sleep in the bed of a king." (The couple had an ornate Louis XV–style headboard.) Aware of the little time he had left, Benjamín threw himself into his writing. Apart from his family, it had always been his purest passion. In December 1971, he completed his third book: *Pampas de Sión*, a compilation of twenty-one poems inspired by Rosa's parents and other Jewish immigrants who had settled in Argentina's grasslands. Rosa's favorite, "La Fronda Ennoblecida," told the story of a woman who gave birth on the side of a road in Moisés Ville, the ranching town where she had grown up.

After that, it became difficult for Benjamín to do much at all. He had always celebrated Rosa's cooking—she joked that she could put a rock on a plate, and he would praise the rock—but as he grew sicker, strong scents disgusted him. He stopped reading the newspaper because he couldn't tolerate the smell of the ink, instead listening as Rosa read articles to him. ("He wanted to know everything," Rosa would later recall.) Since Aramburu's assassination, militant groups like the Montoneros had proliferated, and the military government that had replaced Onganía fought to crush them. "SHOOTOUT," blared one headline. "Giant Military Operation in Search of Subversive Elements," read another. Over time, Rosa had to move her chair farther away from the bed—the ink smell was still too strong for her husband's increasingly sensitive nose. In February of 1972, Benjamín—just fifty-six—was gone.

Patricia was nineteen when her father died, and the loss unmoored her. Benjamín had been strict, and without him, she began to look for meaning outside the comfortable confines of the apartment in middle-class Boedo where she had been raised. Her early steps into rebellion took a personal tack. From the age of thirteen, she had dated a clean-cut student she had met at the Hebraica, a Jewish social club in downtown Buenos Aires where Rosa and Benjamín had also connected. Patricia and her boyfriend had begun to prepare for a life together, gathering towels, sheets, and other items for the home they would one day share. Before he died, Benjamín had talked about buying them an apartment so they could get married. The whole Roisinblit family adored him.

But when she arrived at the University of Buenos Aires for medical school, Patricia discovered an intoxicating sense of freedom. All around her, young people were starting to push back against Argentina's conservative Catholic mores. Sex, many of them believed, was a natural part of being in love, not a rite reserved for marriage. In this new environment, Patricia was overwhelmed with romantic choices. "Boys chased after her like flies to honey," Rosa would later recall. "She did not lack candidates!" She soon broke things off with her boyfriend and began dating a fellow medical student named Miguel Benasayag, a philosopher type who played drums in a rock band and described himself as an "anarchist-hippy." She became more interested in history and, through Miguel, began dabbling in leftist activism. "Until that moment, she had lived a comfortable middle-class life," a school friend would later recall. "This swerve from the good student, bourgeois momma's girl concerned about being pretty and attracting boys to the deeply committed militant was a very important chapter for her."

Many of her peers were undergoing the same transformation. Galvanized by the Cordobazo, France's protests of May 1968, and other demonstrations worldwide, Argentine youth threw themselves into political action throughout the early years of the 1970s, convinced the status quo was not only unsustainable but immoral. Universities and high schools became hotbeds of political organization. As one student in La Plata, a tranquil city an hour from Buenos Aires, put it: "There was a contagious effervescence in the streets." To their parents' concern and confusion, young leftists began organizing in *villas miseria*. The settlements were not connected to official electric, water, or sewer systems, and in the rain, their dirt roads tended to transform into filthy rivers. An Argentine newspaper described how, in one *villa*, children swarmed around a garbage dump scrounging for food instead of attending school. *Villas* had once been transitional places, where immigrants and countryfolk who had come to find work in the city could land temporarily. But over time, the slums became permanent—and much larger. Between 1955, when Perón was unseated, and 1970, the number of people living in them swelled from eighty thousand to eight hundred thousand. The military government responded by vowing to eradicate the neighborhoods. In protest, young people worked to improve conditions, painting houses and schools, hosting literacy classes, organizing trade unions, and recruiting fire brigades.

Patricia began visiting a *villa* in Bajo Flores, in southern Buenos Aires. The warren of haphazard residences was less than three miles from her family's apartment, which Rosa and Benjamín had filled with fine furniture and art, but it felt worlds away. "When it is cold, it's even colder here. And when it's hot, it's hotter here than in other places in Buenos Aires," another young leftist who worked in Bajo Flores wrote at the time. "Only seldom do we see a car on the villa streets. The children, barefooted, play in the mud or throw things in the ditch that give the neighborhood a fetid smell." Miguel would later remember Patricia weeping as she took in the poverty.

As Patricia confronted Argentina's social realities, the Montoneros continued to gain traction, and over a dozen other leftist groups intent on revolution—and admiring of acronyms—gained a foothold as well. Among them were the Fuerzas Armadas Revolucionarias, or Armed Revolutionary Forces (FAR); and the Partido Revolucionario de los Trabajadores, or Workers' Revolutionary Party (PRT), along with its armed branch, the Ejército Revolucionario del Pueblo, or People's Revolutionary Army (ERP). Convinced, like the Montoneros, that violent resistance to autocracy was righteous, several of the groups combined political advocacy with combat operations, staging attacks against government forces, detonating bombs, and kidnapping business executives. Some of the early actions of the Montoneros seemed designed to serve as "armed propaganda" rather than to cause physical harm. Before setting off bombs at the golf courses and country clubs of the wealthy, for instance, the Montoneros first blocked the roads with signs that read "Danger! Dynamited Zone." They did not want to alienate the public with indiscriminate violence; instead their goal in undertaking such actions was to reveal the incompetence of the military government and restore Perón to power.

The leftist organizations also hijacked food and milk trucks and stole toys, distributing the loot among the needy. Some groups provided construction and medical services in *villas* like the one where Patricia worked, and nearly all of them handed out impassioned propaganda. One US government memo from the time reported that the Montoneros had "devoted as much of their energies to proselytizing and legitimate reform as to guerrilla tactics."

During this time, existing right-wing ultranationalist groups began to intensify their actions in resistance to these leftist organizations, and new ones began to form. Curiously, some of these groups also embraced Perón, considering him the only leader capable of taming the left-wing movements and halting the spread of communism. Sensing an opportunity, the former president, still in exile in Spain, sought to keep both sides happy as he plotted his eventual return to Argentina. His greatest strength had always been his ideological expediency, figuring out what people wanted to hear and saying precisely that. "A Maoist would speak to Perón and leave convinced he was a Maoist," a journalist said of Perón at the time. "And a Fascist would talk to him and also leave convinced he was a Fascist." From his fieldstone villa in Madrid, Perón somehow rallied his disparate followers around a single goal: bringing him home to run for president once more.

By early 1973, the military dictatorship ruling the country realized that it was losing its grip on power and agreed to hold free elections. But even as they decided that Peronists would be allowed to run for the first time since 1955, they instituted a series of restrictions to prevent Perón himself from seeking the presidency. Undeterred, Perón handpicked a puppet candidate he could control from Madrid and eventually replace: Héctor José Cámpora, a dentist turned lackluster politician. The duo did little to hide their end goal, with Cámpora campaigning under the slogan

"Cámpora to government, Perón to power." Cámpora won the election, and Perón began plotting his grand return.

According to a carefully devised plan, Perón would land at Ezeiza, Argentina's main international airport, on a chartered Aerolíneas Argentinas jet at three in the afternoon on June 20. The airport itself, on the grassy outskirts of Buenos Aires, was too small to support the multitude that would surely come to greet him, so instead a helicopter would whiz him to a nearby landing area next to a highway, where a massive stage had been erected. The National Symphony Orchestra would perform Argentina's solemn anthem as well as the zippy "Peronist March," whose chorus rang: "Perón, Perón, how great you are! My general, how worthy you are! Perón, Perón, our great leader, you are the first worker!" Perón would then command the crowd to silence in honor of Evita before releasing eighteen thousand doves into the crisp winter sky to signify the end of his eighteen-year exile.

As Perón prepared to leave his Madrid villa on June 19, his followers began gathering by the stage in Ezeiza, eager to secure the best views even if it meant camping out overnight in the cold. A massive photo of Perón—as tall as a ten-story building—smiled down at them from behind the platform as they passed around gourds of mate, strong Argentine tea, and snacked on chorizo sausages cooked on hot *parrillas*, open-flame grills as core to the Argentine identity as the flag itself. They warmed their hands over bonfires made from wood donated by trade unions and the government, and entertained themselves with broadcasts of faraway boxing matches.

When the day of Perón's arrival dawned, it was chilly and wet. But the general's followers didn't seem to care; the crowd that amassed to welcome him had swelled to become the largest recorded in Argentina's history. Vendors offered up banners and buttons, old men peddled cups of lemonade, and folk music piped from speakers. In the early afternoon, the clouds gave way to bright sun, inspiring the excited masses to peel off their overcoats and sweaters. It was turning into a true *día peronista*, which was how many Peronists referred to pleasant days.

Thousands of left-wing militants showed up for the event, beating drums and bearing banners that stretched 160 feet. As one Montoneros leader would say later, they were eager to impress Perón with their sheer numbers: "Look, General, the future runs through us. It's not with the old bureaucratic unions."

But sprinkled among the crowd were members of such bureaucratic unions and other right-wing groups, who were not pleased by the presence of the left-ists. At first, the scuffles between the two sides were merely verbal. Young men and women on the left chanted, "Perón, Evita, the Socialist Fatherland," and those on the right spat back: "Perón, Evita, the Peronist Fatherland." Then, around two thirty in the afternoon, a group of right-wing Peronists pulled themselves onto the stage in front of Perón's massive photo. Later they would claim knowledge of a leftist plot to assassinate Perón—a plan the leftists denied. Armed with a formidable arsenal of machine guns, shotguns, and rifles, the men on the stage took aim at those who looked like *zurdos*—or lefties—with their flowing hair and tight pants. As Perón's plane flew over southern Brazil toward Buenos Aires, shots rang out from the podium.

The orchestra abandoned their violas and cellos and flattened themselves to avoid flying bullets. Thousands of terrified doves fluttered through the air as leftist youths holding banners reading "Perón or Death" sought refuge in nearby homes and churches. (An anti-Peronist writer would later reflect that "Perón *and* Death" would have been a more appropriate slogan.) The gunmen continued raining down bullets on the throng even as ambulances arrived to ferry away the wounded. By the end of the day, at least thirteen people had been killed and hundreds had been wounded. The plane carrying Perón was diverted to an air force base west of Buenos Aires.

Perón was livid: the chaos had ruined what was meant to be his glorious comeback. On top of that, for as much as he adored power, he viewed himself as a committed pacifist, or, as he put it, a "vegetarian lion." "Blood saves time," he'd once said. "But it costs a lot." In a speech the next day, he seemed to blame his left-wing followers for the bloodshed, not the conservatives who had fired the guns.

In the end, the events of June 20, later to be known as the Ezeiza Massacre, had little impact on Perón's reascent. Within weeks, Cámpora resigned, paving the way for the former president to reclaim his position. He breezed to election victory in September, with his third wife, María Estela Martínez de Perón—known as Isabel—serving as his vice presidential running mate, and returned to the Casa Rosada a few weeks later. Any illusion, however, that Argentina might come together under its leader shattered on May 1, 1974, when Perón was due to deliver a speech from the Casa Rosada in celebration of May Day. The theme was national unity. As Perón praised organized labor and his more conservative followers, some of the fifty thousand leftists gathered in the Plaza de Mayo began booing and shouting. The mood soured further when Isabel appeared on the balcony where Perón stood behind a panel of bulletproof glass, and the leftists began chanting: "There's only one Evita!"

Perón erupted, calling the young people "stupid" and "beardless youths." Fed up, the leftists wheeled around and walked out of the plaza, dodging right-wing groups who attacked them with poles and stones as they went. A few weeks later, Perón maligned the "revolutionary infantilism" that had interrupted his appearance, and, in a thinly veiled nod to his right-wing followers, announced that, just as the immune system forms antibodies by fighting a virus, the Peronist movement would grow stronger by crushing its internal enemies.

All the stress took a grave toll on the old general, who at seventy-eight was already ailing. In July 1974, after contracting a severe flu that provoked a heart attack, El Líder passed away. He'd served just nine months back in office. Offices, stores, and banks closed, and buses and trains stood still as hundreds of thousands of mourners flooded the streets to pay their respects. As they cried over his coffin, some wailed affectionately: "Chau, viejo"—Goodbye, old man.

Isabel immediately took her husband's place in the Casa Rosada, becoming the first female head of state in Latin America. Her credentials offered scant assurance that she would rise to the historic occasion. She had little formal education and an unsettling obsession with the occult. She had connected with Perón while working as a dancer at a Panamanian cabaret called Happyland. To make all important decisions, Isabelita, as she was known, turned to her shadowy minister of social welfare, José López Rega, a retired police corporal with sharp cheekbones, vacant blue eyes, and ultraconservative beliefs who had served as the Peróns' luggage carrier during the couple's time in exile. He and Isabel bonded over their shared interest in astrology, a topic on which he had written several books, and he eventually wheedled his way into the Peróns' inner circle. (In the preface to one of his astrology volumes, he suggested that he was an intermediary for God; in another, published years later, he ascribed coauthorship to the archangel Gabriel and rhapsodized about glories of the cow.) As his influence within the administration grew, people began calling him El Brujo—The Sorcerer—and Rasputin of the Pampas. When Isabel gave speeches, he adopted the discomfiting practice of lurking behind her and mouthing her words like a wicked ventriloquist.

"Isabel does not exist," he insisted once. "She is a creation of mine."

Another creation of López Rega's was the Argentine Anticommunist Alliance, or Triple A, a secret right-wing death squad. Dressed in civilian clothes with dark sunglasses and machine guns strapped over their shoulders, Triple A thugs, many of whom officially worked as police officers, roved the streets of Buenos Aires in unmarked cars. Few of their targets— mostly left-leaning Peronists—survived.

"The AAA makes the leftists look good by comparison," read one confidential US government cable at the time, referring to the group by its acronym. The memo argued that while the leftists restricted their violence to their proclaimed enemies—"policemen, army officers, business leaders, and foreign diplomats"—the Triple A targeted not just leftist militants but also popular singers, actors, writers, university professors, and congressmen thought to have leftist beliefs. After being forced into the cars, it was reported, the Triple A's captives were driven to quieter locations and shot execution-style, their corpses left to rot as a warning. While Isabel looked the other way, the Triple A began to publish lists of citizens it planned to assassinate, sometimes delivering typed threats directly to its intended victims. "You are hereby informed that you have been sentenced to death," one such message read. Estimates suggest the Triple A ultimately carried out two thousand murders in the three years it terrorized Buenos Aires.

In response, Argentina's leftist groups ratcheted up their own operations, continuing to ambush military barracks and police stations, and abducting businessmen and robbing banks to fund their movements. They seemed to be getting bolder. During one particularly volatile week in 1974, leftist militants detonated 110 bombs around Buenos Aires—mostly at car showrooms, banks, and other financial institutions—killing at least two men. In September of that year, the Montoneros went so far as to abduct Jorge and Juan Born, the heirs to Argentina's largest conglomerate. The kidnapping was spectacular. Montoneros dressed up as Buenos Aires city employees and used fake street signs and stolen public vehicles to ambush the brothers' chauffeured car, killing the driver and another employee in the ensuing melee. The ransom was even more astonishing: the Montoneros eventually extracted $60 million for Jorge and Juan's safe return. It was—and remains—the most lucrative kidnapping in world history.

While Patricia herself was not officially involved, her boyfriend, Miguel, was part of the ERP, the combat wing of the Marxist Workers' Revolutionary Party. At first he contributed to the movement in menial ways, transporting things and spray-painting buildings, but over time he began participating in the group's armed resistance.

"First you disarm a cop, then you're involved in robbing a bank or a police station," he recalled later. "It was all very gradual." Patricia was terrified. She threatened to break up with him if he didn't step back from the movement's tactical unit. Unwilling to lose her, he tried, but was arrested soon thereafter anyway.

Less than two months after the Born abduction, Argentina's federal police chief, Alberto Villar, and his wife, Elsa, boarded their yacht for a day of cruising on the Río de la Plata, the wide and powerful river that runs past Buenos Aires. In addition to his official post, Villar was rumored to be an important pillar of the Triple A and was generally known for his harsh tactics—sometimes torturing or even killing those he arrested. Around eleven in the morning, as the Villars pulled away from the jetty where their ten bodyguards stood, an eruption blew their boat thirty feet in the sky. The Montoneros had struck once again.

Within days, an overwhelmed Isabel declared a state of siege, giving the military and police free rein to search or detain anyone they liked without a warrant. From one day to the next, the decree deprived Argentina's twenty-five million inhabitants of all their constitutional rights.

4

Now, Now, Now

1975

By Patricia's early twenties, the crackle of gunfire and the thunder of bombs had become familiar soundtracks around Argentina. In Córdoba, the Montoneros kidnapped an honorary US consul, shooting him between the eyes when the Argentine government refused to negotiate for his safety. Corpses burned and bullet-ridden beyond identification—suspected victims of the Triple A—showed up in parking lots and along lonely dirt roads outside Buenos Aires. Twenty-nine murders were linked to the Triple A in May 1975 alone. Gunfights between police and revolutionary groups were constant. A bomb exploded in Argentina every three hours, and a political killing took place every five. "There seemed," one leftist militant remarked at the time, "to be a smell of death on the streets."

The country was hurtling toward collapse, and for many young people, the pressure was mounting to choose: in or out. Some retreated from the escalating violence. On a bus ride through the flat, green plains to Villa Gesell, a beach city four hours south of Buenos Aires that had become a vacation hot spot for leftist youth, one of Patricia's friends admitted that she was too terrified to join the struggle: "When you see a bomb explode here, and another there, and, at any moment, a bomb could explode in front of you—one thing is to read about it, another thing is to live through it," she would reflect later.

But Patricia saw matters differently. "When it comes to these things, one has to commit and push ahead," she declared. After that, the two grew apart.

Around mid-1975, twenty-two-year-old Patricia joined the Montoneros movement. As a doctor in training, she was recruited to Sanidad, the health division within the group. When members were wounded in clashes with security forces or paramilitary groups, they could not go to the hospital for fear of being abducted, and instead sought care at *dispensarios*, improvised clinics set up in the homes of Montoneros or their sympathizers and manned by members with medical experience. To keep the equipment well camouflaged, Montoneros would sometimes dig holes under the houses, bury their wound spreaders, clamps, and drills inside, and then tug a carpet over the hole. Even when they did not have anyone to treat, they gathered furtively to discuss best practices in first aid, such as how to identify hypovolemic shock from a gunshot or explosion.

Patricia worked at a clinic in Quirno, in the western part of Buenos Aires, that was headed by one of her classmates from medical school and his partner, who served as a nurse. Their names were Luis Fernando Kuhn and Amalia Larralde, but Patricia and the rest of the medical team referred to them by their *nombres de guerra*: Marra and Andrea. It was believed that the fewer identifying details they shared with one another, the safer they would be if someone was abducted and tortured for information. (For her own alias, Patricia adopted the name Mariana.) While they couldn't divulge much practical information, *compañeros*—comrades—poured out their emotional lives to one another, sharing hopes for what their "project" would accomplish in Argentina and fears about what would happen if they failed. As one Montonera put it: "Everything was now, now, now, because we didn't know if there was going to be a tomorrow."

To boost their chances of seeing another day, the Montoneros met only in pairs, as larger gatherings were viewed with suspicion. They arranged meetings over the phone using cryptic codes, then linked up in bars or to quietly sip coffee together. "Tell Doctor Rodríguez I expect the package with twenty shirts to arrive tomorrow," for example, meant to meet at eight in the evening (20:00 in military time) at Bar Rodríguez. Timeliness was critical; waiting made you vulnerable. One day, Patricia showed up to meet a fellow Montonero doctor at an arranged time and place, only to find him lying dead in the street. Though he was a close friend, she knew better than to stop—someone was surely watching. She walked past his body with her chin held high as though he didn't exist. He was only twenty-four.

Before long, she had dedicated her life to the movement. Schoolwork went by the wayside. So did the makeup and red high heels. Now, allergic to any bourgeois indulgences, Patricia went barefaced, used oversized glasses, and wore shoes so tattered Rosa was unsure how she could still walk. Once, when washing the white coat Patricia used at medical school, Rosa found scraps of bread and deli meat in the pockets. It seemed that Patricia would not allow herself to buy a full sandwich—just the separate components. When, four years after Benjamín's death, Rosa decided to downsize and offered her daughter half of the proceeds from the sale of the large Boedo apartment where she'd grown up, Patricia announced that she would pass the entire sum on to the Montoneros. Though Rosa did not approve, she knew Patricia could not be convinced otherwise— her daughter had inherited her own iron will. She did, however, persuade Patricia to let her come along for the handoff. They boarded the train at Estación Once, a short walk from Rosa's new apartment in the Congreso neighborhood, and rode about an hour west through the dense streets of Buenos Aires to the bustling suburb of Morón. At a café Patricia had agreed upon with a Montoneros superior, Rosa sat down several tables away, careful to avert her gaze, as she had been instructed. While waiters shuffled around serving patrons coffee and pastries, Patricia handed over her inheritance.

One morning, when Patricia was just four credits short of receiving her medical degree, Rosa found her asleep past the time when she usually left for university. "Patricia," her mother said, leaning over her bed. "What are you doing? You're supposed to be in school."

Patricia ignored her, refusing to leave the apartment for days. Finally, she told Rosa what was going on. "Mamá, stop insisting. I'm not going to go back to school. . . . My classmates told me that they came looking for me there."

Meanwhile, Isabel Perón's failure to steer the country back from the brink of anarchy led many Argentines to expect another military coup, and some to root for one. As political violence raged and inflation galloped toward 1,000 percent, graffiti reading "Chile," in reference to the neighboring country's 1973 brutal right-wing overthrow of President Salvador Allende, began appearing on walls around Buenos Aires and other major cities; a mysterious organization that called itself the Group for Action and Liberty painted signs that asked "Soldiers, how long must we wait?"

In a desperate bid to hold on to power, Isabel tried reshuffling her cabinet. In twenty months, she chewed through six economy ministers, six interior ministers, and four foreign ministers. But it was too late. Her ouster was seen as a matter of time. Newspaper vendors in the capital began shouting daily alerts as they hawked their broadsheets: "The coup has been delayed for another day."

It was during this time, shortly after she joined the Montoneros, that Patricia met a militant named José Manuel Pérez Rojo, alias Matías. Tall and thin, with dark, bushy eyebrows and full lips, José had much in common with Patricia. Like her, he was an only child. Though money had not always been plentiful, his parents had stretched to encourage his interests. They paid for him to take English lessons and piano classes, which fueled his obsession with music. As a teenager, he'd played the organ in a rock band called the Géminis that was good enough to perform in one of Argentina's massive soccer stadiums. An ardent fan of the Beatles, he listened to *Revolver* over and over on his Winco turntable, trying to translate the lyrics to Spanish. He named his dog Paulina, after Paul McCartney.

His parents were busy—they ran a restaurant, among other ventures—and José spent a lot of time alone. Once, when he was around nine, he took advantage of the lack of supervision to get drunk on alcohol his parents had stashed at home. One of his cousins, Graciela Tobar, interpreted it as a call for attention. José's father, José Pérez, had a mean streak that was often directed at his son, and as a child, José had found refuge and community in the Scouts, the Argentine equivalent of the Boy Scouts. Some Scouts groups were affiliated with the church; José's, Grupo Scout San Francisco de Asís, was led by Mario Bertone, a priest associated with the Movimiento de Sacerdotes para el Tercer Mundo, or the Movement of Priests for the Third World. In contrast to Argentina's Catholic establishment, which leaned conservative and tacitly supported the security apparatus, Third World Priests rejected capitalism and worked mostly in Argentina's *villas miseria*. In Caseros and, later, Villa Bosch, two working-class neighborhoods on the western outskirts of Buenos Aires, Bertone led Scouts to build a community chapel and help the neighbors improve their precarious living situations. The Scouts built septic tanks, attached roofs to improvised homes, and installed sidewalks. To unwind, they went camping together, playing guitar and singing around the fire. José's devotion to the group became so clear that his mother, Argentina, once sold her sewing machine to pay for him to attend a camping trip to Córdoba.

As leftist groups swelled in the early 1970s and tensions with the government intensified, many Scouts decided that these militant organizations were the way to make a real impact in the world; José got involved in the Juventud Peronista, Fuerzas Armadas Revolucionarias, and eventually the Montoneros. By the early 1970s, he was fully committed, slipping out of his family's house in the afternoon and staying out till the wee hours to convene with his *compañeros*. As the Triple A prowled Buenos Aires, picking off left-wing militants, José prepared to defend himself, practicing his shooting aim by firing at a photo of López Rega he had pasted on a sheet of metal. "It's not that we want to take over the country, it's that we want to improve things," he told his concerned mother. "We don't want people starving. . . . Does it seem good to you to have five-year-olds opening the doors of taxis? . . . Or a worker who can't earn a living wage? Or that people are living in shanty-towns where if one structure burns, all of them burn?"

Though almost a year younger than Patricia, José quickly climbed to prominence within the Montoneros. While Patricia worked in the clinic, he directed a unit on the west side of Buenos Aires, arranging surreptitious meetings and distributing pamphlets outside factories and other places where people might be ripe for recruitment to the cause. A letter he wrote to a fellow Montonero suggested that he was also involved in the group's armed operations; in it he encouraged "fighting like hell against the enemy," placing homemade bombs, and killing police officers. Graciela, José's cousin, once stumbled on a cache of arms José had hidden in a closet at her house.

As Argentina tore itself apart, Patricia and José fell in love. For them, as for many of their comrades, the times were tense but tinged with hope. The Montoneros believed that the state's brutality would, in the end, only help convince more Argentines to join their righteous struggle. They braced for gunfights in the street, home raids, and detentions. However bad things got, they believed, they had to keep fighting.

5

The Pink Panther

1976

Before dawn on March 24, 1976, military trucks rumbled past the monuments of the Plaza de Mayo to the Casa Rosada, where soldiers stormed through the palace's grand pink archways, slashed telex cables, and shuffled Isabel Perón onto a waiting helicopter.

"Señora," one of the coup collaborators told her at the airport. "You are under detention. The government you have led is a calamity. The armed forces are taking over."

Unlike some of Argentina's previous political transitions, not a drop of blood was shed during the takeover. But around three in the morning on the day of the coup, the new regime released an ominous statement that was printed in newspapers and read on radio stations across the country: "It is recommended that all inhabitants strictly adhere to the directives issued by the military authority . . . and avoid individual or group actions that could demand drastic intervention from military personnel." Argentina was now under the control of a military junta comprised of the heads of the country's army, navy, and air force, with army chief Jorge Rafael Videla at the helm.

Videla was known to his colleagues as El Hueso—The Bone—or the Pink Panther, for his gaunt frame and rangy gait. Fifty, with slick black hair and a severe mustache, his ramrod posture gave him the appearance of someone who bathed in starch each morning. "Faced with an audience," one newspaper put it, he looked like "a man enduring a pair of boots two sizes too small," bouncing awkwardly on his toes during speaking engagements as if hoping to eject himself from the situation. A US diplomatic cable stated that he did not like "to hear off-color stories" or "to discuss his job, the infantry, or his children." (That such preferences left little to talk about was just fine by him.) He was rarely spotted out of his military jacket, with its gold epaulets and lapels adorned with gilded leaves; he called conventional suits "uniformes de civil," civilian uniforms, and avoided them at all costs. Only his teeth defied his aura of strict control—on the rare occasion he smiled, his thin lips revealed one canine that jutted out of line from the others.

If ever someone was destined to commit their life to the Argentine military, it was Videla. Born on August 2, 1925, his parents had christened him in morbid honor of his twin older brothers, Jorge Mario and Rafael José, who had died from measles when they were just a year old. Videla's father, Rafael Eugenio Videla, was an army captain in Mercedes, a small, conservative town an hour and a half outside Buenos Aires. The family cottage was so close to Rafael's infantry regiment that the young Videla could have thrown a stone from his modest front door to the army property. Of course, he never would have thrown stones; his father wouldn't have allowed it. Rafael was exacting and proper, refusing to remove his military jacket even when relaxing at home. Years later, when Videla eventually joined the army, his father forbade him from doing so either.

Videla's childhood acquaintances—he didn't really have friends—described him as dull, pious, and unyielding. When they played hooky or engaged in other boyish mischief, he never partook. He had impeccable handwriting, wore gleaming white sneakers, and styled his black hair straight back. At the Colegio Militar de la Nación, the National Military College, he once ratted out a friend for dancing with the love interest of a superior. Thanks to his lack of curiosity about any other pursuits, Videla graduated when he was just nineteen and joined the army immediately thereafter. Around that time, he began his first-ever romantic relationship, with a woman named Alicia Raquel Hartridge, the daughter of a diplomat of Irish descent. Each Sunday promptly at three in the afternoon, Videla would arrive at the Hartridge family home to see her. The young girl tended to take her time while she made herself presentable, and after waiting patiently, often for two hours or more, Videla would ask Hartridge's stern father permission to take her out, vowing to return her before dinnertime. The budding couple would walk around a nearby plaza holding hands, perhaps exchanging kisses on the cheek to seal their farewells. A few years later, they married.

Videla's singular dedication and discipline helped catapult him quickly up the army ranks, from second lieutenant to captain to colonel. Eventually, he was appointed to lead the Colegio Militar, where, as an instructor, he had earned a reputation as an "excellent teacher and a stern, self-denying taskmaster." In 1975, as Argentina spiraled into bedlam, Isabel Perón named Videla head of the army in an attempt to placate the increasingly restive armed forces; an advisor had assured her that he was "apolitical," completely professional, and incapable of launching a coup.

They had underestimated him. As Isabel vacationed with Videla's wife and the wives of the heads of the air force and navy in September 1975, Videla and his colleagues began seriously plotting their putsch. They had already pressured Isabel into cutting ties with López Rega, her astrology-obsessed minister of social welfare; she had grudgingly booted El Brujo from the country a few months before. Now it was clear Isabel herself had to go, but Videla and the others did not want to appear to be strong-arming the country's first female president. The longer the military could wait, they figured—and the more Isabel flailed—the more likely the Argentine public would be to perceive the leaders of a coup as national heroes rather than power-crazed usurpers. Six months later, once public readiness had ripened to the point of impatience, the junta made its move.

At first, the Montoneros and other leftist revolutionaries viewed the situation as an inevitable step on the path to revolution. They had survived military dictatorships before. There was no reason to think that this time would be different.

Once installed in the presidential palace, however, Videla wasted little time in unleashing the junta's Proceso de Reorganización Nacional, or National Reorganization Process, a bland name for a brutal plan to quash political violence and restore what he saw as the essential values of the state. He did away with Congress, restricted all political activities, and banned trade unions. While Isabel Perón had condoned extralegal violence against groups like the Montoneros only tacitly, Videla now employed the formidable machinery of the government to purge them. Often dressed in civilian clothes and sometimes wigs, military men and police officers cruised the streets. They tended to drive one type of vehicle: drab green Ford Falcons without license plates. When they spotted a target, they would leap from the car, stuff the person inside, and drive away, tires screaming against the pavement. Some of their victims were involved in revolutionary groups, others were not. This didn't matter. To Videla, a terrorist was "not only someone who plants bombs but a person whose ideas are contrary to Western, Christian civilization."

It seemed no one was safe, particularly not those who happened to look like the leftists the military reviled. To avoid arousing suspicion, young people wrapped certain books in newspapers and men kept their hair trimmed short. Some took to walking against traffic through Buenos Aires' labyrinth of one-way streets so they could see potential assailants coming. The Montoneros shrouded their communications in new layers of secrecy, sometimes scribbling messages behind toilets and mirrors in the city's public restrooms. They avoided leaving the smoldering butts of their Parisiennes and Particulares—known to be the militants' favorite brands of cigarettes—on their coffee saucers in cafés for fear of being traced, and they buried or burned their copies of Crisis, a political magazine popular among revolutionary youth.

Since loitering on the street was dangerous, they sometimes sheltered in movie theaters if they needed to kill a few hours between activities. Miriam Lewin, a Montonera in José's column, recalled going to see Scorsese's Taxi Driver with José and other compañeros during one such interlude; the brutal violence depicted in the film felt hauntingly similar to her reality. Once, she arrived at a meeting twenty minutes late to find the area swarming with Ford Falcons, long rifles jutting out their windows. On the ground in a puddle of blood was a comb belonging to one of her comrades. She feared it was only a matter of time before she was taken too. In her pocket, Miriam carried a homemade cyanide pill, hidden inside a lipstick tube. Many Montoneros carried such pills. If they were caught, they wanted to be in control of how they died, before they could be forced to give up their friends. The meetings José led in the western suburbs of Buenos Aires became smaller and smaller; it seemed every day another *compañero* was taken. They no longer planned resistance operations or strategized about how to recruit more members. Instead, the Montoneros' ideological mission was displaced by a practical one: survival. They spent their days rushing around the city, emptying the safe houses that their captured comrades were privy to, in case electrical shocks or beatings induced them to give up the addresses.

But being careful could only get you so far in those days. Late one stormy night, military men invaded José's parents' apartment. They wrapped José's father up from head to toe like a mummy, leaving only his nose free so he could breathe, and savagely beat him. "Against the wall," they ordered José's mother, Argentina, covering her head with a robe as a makeshift hood. They aimed a gun at her and pulled the trigger. Only after a few seconds did she realize she was still alive. The gun was empty. The whole thing was a ruse to terrify and humiliate her.

The men demanded she tell them where José was. Argentina often didn't have a clue, but this time she happened to know that he was sleeping above their restaurant, a few blocks away. Still, she thought she would rather die than be the reason her son was picked up by the security forces. The men interrogated her for two hours, but she refused to say a word about José's whereabouts. When they finally left and the apartment was quiet, Argentina untied her husband, who was shaken but alive, and ran outside. It was raining hard. She glanced around to see if anyone was watching and, finding the street empty, pulled her umbrella low over her face. She raced the two blocks to the restaurant and climbed upstairs without turning on a single light. José was asleep.

"José, the cops came." No sooner had the words left her mouth than José sprang to his feet and escaped into the night.

Eventually, he and Patricia went into hiding together, moving frequently as locations were compromised. Many of their *compañeros* did the same, often living in precarious shacks or tenements. Still, they clung to their dreams of revolution. "It didn't matter," Miriam would say later. "I wasn't going to be able to be happy if this *'proyecto'* that we wanted didn't come to fruition. I believed I could never live calmly seeing that next to me there were people who couldn't eat, who didn't have jobs, who didn't have homes."

Patricia didn't visit Rosa's apartment anymore, but occasionally she and José would pick Rosa up at a prearranged location in a car provided by the Montoneros and drive around to talk with less fear of being ambushed. Conversation inevitably turned to politics. "Chicos, let's talk about something else. I'm not interested, I don't want to know," Rosa would implore them. "Let's talk about whatever you want, the weather—whatever—but I don't want to talk politics with you, period."

Patricia and José tried to persuade Rosa, who rarely attended temple but still considered herself Jewish, that the military leaders were as evil as the Nazis, and that they had to be stopped. Unconvinced, Rosa responded: "If you want to act that way, do it. But don't try to convince me."

During the junta's first year in power, Patricia showed up at the law office where her mother worked. After retiring from her career as a doctor years before, Rosa had gotten the office job to distract herself from her anxiety about Patricia's safety. But that day, Patricia brought happy news: she was pregnant.

Even as the country plunged into chaos, Rosa had not relinquished her attachment to middle-class norms, and she urged Patricia and José to wed. They reminded her that scribbling their real names on any official documents would be like signing their own death warrants. Instead, Montoneros married in unofficial ceremonies. Because he was the committed leader of a unit and a powerful orator, José was sometimes asked to officiate at such events, and even to serve as something of a revolutionary marriage counselor. Once, Miriam came to him with a quandary: her boyfriend, Juan Eduardo Estévez, another Montonero, was thinking about leaving her for a woman who was not part of the leftist movement. His parents' house had recently been raided and security forces had pressed a pistol against the head of his fifteen-year-old sister. Juan felt immense guilt and had asked Miriam if she'd wait for him while he figured out what he really wanted.

"It was a period where you didn't know if they were going to kill you the next day, so asking someone to wait for two months was like asking them to wait twenty years," she would later reflect.

After Miriam explained the situation to him, José sat down with her and Juan at a bar to talk things over. José reminded Juan that they all had a responsibility to keep fighting in honor of their *compañeros* who had already died. "You're wanting to leave the movement," José hissed. "Let's see if you have the balls to just say that to my face. Don't tell me that you want to date other girls." The chat convinced Juan to recommit not only to the Montoneros but to Miriam as well. Soon thereafter, the couple asked José to marry them. In a small room with blue curtains on the second floor of a gas station, the young man gave an impassioned speech. As the couple exchanged rings of nickel silver inscribed with the date, José expounded on what it meant to be a revolutionary couple, explaining that it required devotion not only to each other but to a more just society. If Miriam and Juan had children, he said, they too would be raised to fight for equality and stand up for those who were suffering. Miriam understood that, though José was talking about her relationship and her future children, he was also talking about his own.

As Patricia neared the end of her pregnancy and winter descended on Buenos Aires, she and José huddled in the tiny maid's quarters in the small Belgrano apartment where José's parents had moved after the traumatic raid on their previous home. Despite the risks of frequenting public places, the couple had decided to have their baby at the Sanatorio Güemes, a private hospital in the center of Buenos Aires. Rosa stayed with Patricia when she went into labor, just as she had sat with hundreds of patients as an obstetrician. On June 28, 1977, Patricia gave birth to a healthy baby girl, whom she named Mariana after her Montoneros alias. José ran into the visitors' area, where Argentina was eagerly waiting, and exclaimed: "It's a girl and she looks just like you!"

Shortly thereafter, the couple went into hiding again. Videla's troops seemed to be closing in; within days of Mariana's birth, nine people associated with José's former Scouts group disappeared, and a few weeks later, a doctor who had worked at the same Montoneros clinic as Patricia succumbed to the security forces in a frenzied chase. After realizing he was being followed, he had ducked out of a bar where he planned to meet someone and raced to a nearby hospital, where he had once worked. There, cornered in a bathroom, he swallowed a cyanide pill. When the military officers reached him, they fetched amyl nitrite to counteract the cyanide and drove him away in an ambulance as his petrified colleagues looked on. A month later, his family identified his lifeless body at a morgue in Buenos Aires.

Eventually, when he felt it was safe enough, José fetched Rosa in a borrowed car so that she could spend a few days with her new granddaughter. As he drove her to the place where he and Patricia were hiding, José demanded that his mother-in-law lower her eyes from the road. It wasn't that he didn't trust her. But it was better that she knew nothing about their whereabouts, just in case she was questioned.

In late 1977, when Mariana was five months old, José made a trip to Brazil on Montoneros business. Encouraged by the ease with which he exited the country, Rosa begged Patricia to do the same. She offered to sell her apartment to finance a move to another Spanish-speaking country and promised to take care of Mariana so Patricia could finish medical school.

Patricia's response was unwavering: "Those who leave the country are cowards."

6

El Proceso

The Casa Rosada did not suit Videla's austere personality. With its indulgent balconies, archways, and chiseled statues, the building was too decadent, too attention-seeking. And then there was the hue. In a futile bid to unite two warring political blocs, one of which was associated with the color red and the other white, a nineteenth-century presidential predecessor had painted the Italianate structure salmon pink. Videla had no such interest in conciliation.

Inside the presidential palace, the general had two offices: one formal, one personal. The primary office was regally commanding, with ornate lamps, graceful settees, and gilded chairs upholstered in sumptuous patterns. Videla's personal office was more reflective of its occupant—a visiting diplomat once described it as akin to a basilica, with religious art hanging from every wall.

Videla's was the most dangerous type of faith: the kind that convinces its possessor of their infallible moral rectitude. Driven by the belief that the very soul of the Republic was at stake, many in Videla's junta considered their purge a "Dirty War," invoking Saint Thomas Aquinas's concept of a "just war." By casting their enemies as "terrorists" and "subversives," they conveniently excused themselves from the normal rules of engagement. Indeed, Videla didn't seem to struggle with reports of his troops shoving electric prods up peoples' rectums or beating detainees to within an inch of their lives. "Dios nunca me soltó la mano," he would say later. God never let go of my hand.

And yet Videla made sure to obscure what, exactly, he believed God had guided him and his soldiers to do. The 1973 coup in Chile had taught him as much. Augusto Pinochet had been more brazen—openly vowing to "exterminate Marxism," and doing little to hide extrajudicial killings—and Chile's reputation had suffered for it. Concealing the true nature of El Proceso would enable the Argentine junta to avoid international moralizing. And covering its tracks—even lightly—would help the junta to remain in Argentines' good graces. The country had long conceived of itself as enlightened, European. (As one saying goes: "Argentines are Italians who speak Spanish who think they are British.") While many supported the dictatorship's ends, the junta suspected they might not be able to stomach the means. It was essential to maintain the illusion of Argentina as a civilized place full of civilized people—the type who wore suits to sit at cafés and kitten heels to do the shopping and went to church each Sunday. It would be better, then, for the junta to get rid of its perceived enemies quietly, without drawing too much attention. Put simply: it would be best to make them disappear.

There were no more bodies dumped conspicuously in the streets as there had been during the Triple A era; bodies were rarely recovered at all. There was no paper trail, either—no police logs or jail records of all the people vanishing. For the junta, these covert abductions were the perfect tool: brazen enough to incite fear, but subtle enough that Argentines could pretend they weren't happening. As one newspaper would later put it: "A nation traumatized by years of anarchy was willing to see law subordinated to order." While the armed forces claimed to be targeting "terrorists," they employed a conveniently loose definition of what that meant. In their crosshairs were not only militants but those on the further peripheries of the left. Students. Artists. Journalists. Musicians. Poets. Priests who ministered to the poor. Nuns who helped families looking for their missing relatives. In the eyes of the dictatorship, they were all "subversives." Even if they weren't involved in any armed movements, they could still be tortured for information—or forced into submission with outright barbarity. Not even the family members of prominent military officers were spared: two of Videla's own relatives were taken. A subversive was a subversive.

Those who tried to advocate for perceived enemies of the regime were targeted, too. Shortly after Videla's coup, two hundred petitions seeking information about missing people flooded into courthouses in just one week. The lines of anguished relatives looking for their loved ones snaked around the Ministry of the Interior building. The police allegedly kept a running list of lawyers who submitted requests about missing people; a news report at the time suggested that if a lawyer's name appeared "more than once or twice," it was forwarded to the military. Between March and December 1976, nearly one hundred lawyers were abducted by security forces. Some later turned up alive; others didn't.

So wide was the junta's dragnet that it gave rise to new vocabulary. The Montoneros and other leftists began using *chupar*, a verb meaning "to suck," to describe how the armed forces did not so much arrest people as hoover them up in the thousands, like a great hungry maw. When it became clear that these people were not registered in traditional prisons or police stations, another troubling word began to echo around the country: *desaparecidos*, the disappeared. "Many of the *desaparecidos* were innocent citizens abducted and murdered by soldiers and police in mufti," a *Time* correspondent wrote in 1977. Later, in a bid to doublespeak away the growing concern about this "ghostly army" of missing people, Videla used the word himself, explaining in a press conference: "The *desaparecido* is an unknown . . . they are an unknown entity, neither dead nor alive, they are disappeared."

The extent of what happened to those disappeared by the junta would not be fully revealed for years, but, slowly, hints began to filter out. About six months after the coup, a green Ford Falcon pulled up in front of house number 586 on calle 56 in La Plata. Inside, María Claudia Falcone was sleeping peacefully. It was after midnight on a Thursday, a school day. Claudia had turned sixteen only the month before and was still in high school, where she had recently attended a rally championing a discounted student bus fare.

Men in civilian clothes stepped out of the car and barged into the apartment, dragging the teenager and a friend who had been staying there outside. Over the course of the next day, eight more La Plata high school students who had attended the rally—the oldest of whom was just eighteen—vanished in similar raids.

The students were then taken to clandestine torture facilities like Pozo de Arana, a compound on the outskirts of La Plata surrounded by green fields, and Pozo de Quilmes, a tidy house in a residential neighborhood of Quilmes, a southern suburb of Buenos Aires. There they were blindfolded, beaten, and, in some cases, raped. Four of the children were released and eventually were able to share what they had experienced. "They tortured us with profound sadism," one, Emilce Moler, later said. "I remember being naked. I was just a fragile small girl of [less than five feet] and weighed about [one hundred and three pounds], and I was beaten senseless by what I judged was a huge man." The six other students were not seen again. The horrific affair eventually became known as La Noche de los Lápices—The Night of the Pencils.

Unbeknownst to most around the country, the junta had set up hundreds of secretive detention centers like the ones where the students were tortured. They varied in size and sophistication: some operated in small buildings owned by the military or the police force, holding one or two prisoners at a time; others, usually those at existing military and police compounds, held hundreds of people, such as the sprawling Campo de Mayo army base outside Buenos Aires or La Perla in Córdoba. Like Pozo de Arana, some detention centers were out in the countryside, while others, like Pozo de Quilmes, were located on busy city streets, disguised as auto repair workshops or residential homes. Inside these facilities, military and police officers plunged detainees' heads into tubs full of excrement, urine, blood—or a combination of the three—right to the edge of drowning. They raped women while other prisoners were forced to watch and electrocuted people until they lost control of their tongues.

Occasionally, the armed forces—most often the navy—freed people from these centers, perhaps in the hopes that they would sow further fear of the junta. Through the traumatized whispers of survivors, one detention center developed a particularly fearsome reputation: the Escuela de Mecánica de la Armada, or ESMA. Set on the northern edge of Buenos Aires on a verdant property spanning forty-two acres, the ESMA officially served as a naval training academy, and from Avenida Libertador, the wide avenue that ran past the compound's spiked iron gates, that's exactly what it looked like. During the day, swarms of naval officers and students marched about the imposing Greek Revival buildings and ran practice exercises on the property's fields.

Despite the ESMA's avowed purpose, there was gossip. *If your tire pops or goes flat, don't stop on Libertador by the ESMA,* one warning held. Sometimes men in green Ford Falcons exited the property and flew down the road against traffic, machine guns poking out of the windows. Then they would return, prisoners stuffed in the back seat or sometimes the trunk, stating a secret password to regain entry to the premises. Often, the codes related to chess moves. "Cerrar la partida con tres de alfil," for instance. Finish the game with three moves by the bishop.

The men then brought their captives to the compound's main building—the Casino de Oficiales—and dragged them into the dank basement, which was illuminated with harsh fluorescent lights at all hours of the day and night. Next to signs that read "Avenida de Felicidad"—Happiness Avenue—and "El silencio es salud"—Silence is health—were three rooms specifically dedicated to torture. "Where is the place that, based on what you know or what you've heard, you would least like to be?" the men asked one prisoner after they abducted her. "The ESMA," the woman responded. Rumors about the place had spread: In the ESMA they sawed off peoples' fingers. In the ESMA they put rats in women's vaginas.

"You're in the ESMA," the naval officers informed her.

Then the prisoners were stripped naked, tied to metal beds, beaten, and electrocuted with thick prods called *picanas*. Naval doctors stood by to tell the torturers whether they could increase the wattage without killing their victim or to revive them from heart attacks so the session could continue. In most cases, death was their destiny—but the men wanted to pump their targets for intelligence first.

Between torture sessions, most detainees were held in the third-floor attic in cramped makeshift cells separated from one another by wood beams. Their hands and feet were cuffed and their vision was blocked by hoods or eye masks. They were referred to by numbers, not names, and prohibited from talking to their fellow prisoners. The officers often played the radio at full blast, the dulcet voices of Mercedes Sosa and Joan Manuel Serrat not quite muffling the screams of people being electrocuted and beaten downstairs.

"Transfer days," however, were near silent. Prisoners held in the *capucha*, the main detention area on the third floor, strained to stay still in their cells. Eventually, the heavy iron door creaked open and naval officers called out the numbers of several detainees. Those prisoners stood and were led single file down the stairs, their leg chains scraping against the floor as they descended. In the basement they were injected with Pentothal, a strong sedative. Then they were loaded into trucks and driven away, often to Aeroparque Jorge Newbery, an airport a few blocks to the south.

A low, spindly terminal next to the Río de la Plata, the airport had opened in 1947 to ferry passengers to various Argentine cities and across the river to Uruguay. But now, each Wednesday, the armed forces loaded groups of prisoners—naked and drugged, but alive—into Skyvan and Electra warplanes and took off over the Río de la Plata's warm and muddy waters. Only a scattering of naval barracks and the crumbling, aluminum-roofed shacks of a shantytown once called Villa Unemployment lined the river's shores. It was as if Buenos Aires were built with its back to the river, encouraging residents to look away as violent currents pushed twenty-two thousand cubic meters of water per second into the Atlantic Ocean.

When the planes were far enough from land to avoid being spotted— sometimes the pilots flew 150 miles to the sea—the military men opened the plane doors and pushed their sedated captives out, watching as they plunged through the air and splashed into the water. "Fish food," the men called them.

7

Walls of Glass

In June 1978, Argentina was due to host the soccer World Cup. Soccer fandom in Argentina verges on evangelical, and the country's men spend much of the year squabbling about the preeminence of River Plate, Boca Juniors, San Lorenzo, or their other preferred teams; only the World Cup has the power to soothe these rivalries and rally the country behind the same flag. While Videla himself was more of a golfer, he hoped to capitalize on that fleeting unity. Reports of the junta's brutality had been trickling out, and a populace that was busy shouting about strikers and fullbacks would be less likely to whisper about *desaparecidos*.

Hosting the games though, he knew, was also a risk, inviting foreign attention and, by extension, foreign journalists. Ahead of the tournament, the junta retained the New York–based public relations firm Burson-Marsteller to polish Argentina's image. The firm's spin doctors had helped burnish the reputations of troubled corporations like General Motors and totalitarian countries like Romania. It hatched a plan that included wooing international journalists with tours of the Teatro Colón and dispatching Argentine reporters to newsrooms in Europe and America to promote a vision of Argentina's true "reality." Meanwhile, the junta poured $70 million into beefing up security and constructing gleaming new stadiums—and to prevent any embarrassing bombings or kidnappings during the games, Videla's security forces intensified their purge.

By the beginning of the year, the military had crushed the Montoneros and other revolutionary groups like a Parisienne under a combat boot. Abductions slowed considerably, in part because there were hardly any militants left to abduct. The Montoneros clinic that Patricia had once been a part of disbanded, as did most of the rest of the organization. Several Montoneros leaders who had not been killed fled the country. Feeling betrayed, some of their followers blew up their guns, ammo, and other weaponry. Amid the wreckage of twisted iron, they left behind leaflets stating that they too were abandoning the struggle.

Watching this steady decline, Patricia began to yearn for peace. She had already lost so many friends, and it was too dangerous to do anything of substance. She had a daughter now; fighting no longer seemed worth it. José's cousin Graciela sensed that José was similarly keen to focus on his growing family. But he had a harder time leaving the movement completely behind. Occasionally, he placed cryptic classified ads in the newspaper in hopes of connecting with *compañeros* who were still active. Yet most Montoneros had disappeared or moved on, looking for jobs and settling into civilian life.

As they too stepped back, Patricia and José began to let their defenses slip. Instead of dashing between safe houses, they rented an apartment on a leafy street in Palermo, a middle-class residential neighborhood of Buenos Aires. Rosa not only knew the address—Gurruchaga 2259, third floor, apartment 20—she was also the guarantor on the lease. The couple filled the apartment with books and vinyl records and set up Mariana's crib. In the heat of summer, they got pregnant again.

Having been only children themselves, Patricia and José were thrilled that Mariana would have a sibling. While they awaited that brother or sister, the couple delighted in caring for Mariana together. Though Patricia had been raised by parents who participated equally in her life, Argentines generally viewed parenting as women's work. That was starting to change—particularly among progressive youth—and José and Patricia shared not just the joyful moments of play but the mundane caregiving. José changed diapers, cheerfully toted around baby gear, and sang lullabies like "Arrorró mi niño" (Hush-a-bye my baby) while rocking Mariana to sleep on his shoulder. Patricia, meanwhile, seemed to take a deliberately laissez-faire approach to parenting their daughter. Perhaps in response to her parents' strictness, she liked to let Mariana explore and push boundaries without coddling her. If the child fell, Patricia encouraged her to get up on her own. Mariana once toddled to the bathroom and splashed toilet water on her face. José's mother, Argentina, was aghast.

"Ay, Patri! How are you going to let her do that?"

"Let her be," Patricia responded. "It'll help her build up immunity."

Meanwhile, José reconnected with a friend named Gabriel Pontnau, who had no known political involvement, and together they opened a business in the suburb of Martínez selling toys and party supplies. To help them, they hired Teresa Izaguirre, a middle-aged married woman who lived in a suburb a bit farther north. By early October, as Patricia neared the end of her pregnancy, they had begun to prepare the store for Christmas. Everything was visible through the store's glass walls. For the first time in a long while, it seemed they had stopped trying to hide.

8

Show Me the Body

October 7, 1978

Every Saturday, in what had become a weekly ritual, Rosa walked two blocks from her Buenos Aires apartment on Riobamba to a nearby salon, where her short hair was styled and her nails were slicked with polish. Blessed with the taut skin of someone much younger than her fifty-nine years, she didn't wear much makeup under her large wire-frame glasses, and she painted her toenails herself. Yet she had long granted herself the small indulgence of these salon visits. Even when she had worked twenty-four-hour shifts as an obstetrician, she still liked to look put together.

During the week, the one-way street outside her apartment building teemed with cars, motorcycles, and buses, all honking and sputtering and jockeying to overtake one another. Weekday Buenos Aires was a city in a rush, but Saturday mornings were different—languid and serene—especially in Rosa's neighborhood of Congreso, whose government buildings sat closed.

Rosa had moved to Congreso only a few years before, and her new apartment was smaller than the one in Boedo, where she had raised Patricia. Still, it was charming in its own way: a large floor-to-ceiling window faced west toward the apartment towers of Once and Abasto and the wood floors were laid in an inviting herringbone pattern. In the living area hulked a large wooden hutch with glass doors covered in gold lattice. On the walls, gilt frames held scenes of geishas that Rosa had cross-stitched while on call as a doctor as she waited to deliver a baby. She would sit beside her patients as they puffed and panted in labor, embroidering to pass the time.

The years since Benjamín's death had been difficult, but lately things seemed to be improving. Patricia and José had a beautiful child and another on the way. They seemed finally to be scaling back their political activities. Patricia had recently told Rosa she could stop worrying—the security forces were no longer hunting her.

October 7, 1978, should have been a Saturday like any other. But the phone rang early in Rosa's apartment. It was José's mother, Argentina.

"Venite rápido para acá," Argentina said breathlessly. Come quickly.

"Se llevaron a los chicos." They took the kids.

Rosa set down the phone and raced outside, where the morning air was earthy from the previous day's rain. She hurried to a nearby bus stop on Callao and looked up the wide avenue toward the copper dome of the Congressional Palace, searching anxiously for the rounded outlines of the 60, the bus she needed. *They took the kids.*

Finally, the mustard-yellow *colectivo* rumbled up and Rosa climbed aboard. The 60 ran the most famous route in the city, traversing Buenos Aires from its working-class south to its ritzy north, ferrying passengers to and from their jobs across the sprawling metropolis. On Saturday mornings, the city and its buses were often empty, as *porteños* slept in or started their days at local cafés. Traffic didn't ensnarl the city until later. Still, Rosa needed to make it all the way across town to Belgrano, where José's parents were waiting for her—a journey of six miles, about forty minutes at the best of times.

Each stop was maddening. The bus puttered past the Palacio de Aguas Corrientes, covered in 170,000 terra-cotta tiles, and through Recoleta, where men and women wearing imported clothing strolled in the cool shade of crape myrtle trees. It turned left on Las Heras, where a modern new library was being constructed on top of the ruins of the palace where Perón and Evita had once lived, and trundled by the elephants and giraffes of the Palermo Zoo. As the bus neared Belgrano, it passed the headquarters of the army's grenadiers, an elite mounted unit tasked with guarding the president. The blue-and-white flags hanging off the building's balconies fluttered in the breeze.

At last, Rosa leapt off the bus at Cabildo and Juramento. She headed toward Plaza Manuel Belgrano, where a large granite and bronze monument dedicated to the founding father stood surrounded by tipa trees and jacarandas. Rosa spotted her in-laws by the swings. José's father had prominent eyebrows and full lips that he had passed down to his son. Although he was not tall, he towered over his wife, Argentina, who wore large glasses that dipped over the tops of her round cheeks. The couple told Rosa what little they had been able to piece together: Armed men had wrenched José from his store in Martínez, then Patricia and Mariana from their apartment in Palermo. Later that night, a convoy of cars had left Mariana at Argentina's sister's house. Argentina and José had picked her up as soon as they'd heard. But by the time they reached the house, there was no trace of their children.

Rosa looked over at Mariana. José's parents had brought her with them to the plaza. Little Mariana, with her chubby face and stubby legs that had just started to carry her places. At fifteen months, she could muster a few words: Mami, Papi, cheese, water, and "aelo," for abuelo and abuela. If only she could tell her "aelos" what she had just witnessed.

Patricia was about to give birth to her second child, yet Rosa had no idea where her daughter was, what was happening to her, or how to find her. In her fifty-nine years, she had already lived through five coups d'état, but never one like this, one that threatened her so directly. She read the newspaper daily and voted in elections, when they were allowed, but she had always avoided politics, focusing her attention inward—on her career, her passions, her family. When it came to searching for her daughter, by her own admission, she "didn't know anything about anything."

Nor did she know where to turn for help. Benjamín was gone. Her father had passed away, her mother was in her eighties and frail, and her sisters were petrified of associating themselves with someone who might be marked by the junta. Most of her friends and extended family had begun to distance themselves when they had learned of Patricia's political involvement, afraid that Rosa might "contaminate" their children, too. The Sunday invites to her cousin's country club for *asados*, long, leisurely barbecues, had stopped coming long ago.

After some thought, she contacted a lawyer friend, who helped her draw up a habeas corpus—a petition demanding that the government bring Patricia before a judge and show lawful grounds for her imprisonment. Rosa submitted the document herself. There were rumors that making such demands—in Latin, habeas corpus roughly translates to "show me the body"—put you in grave danger. Rosa had a typewriter, a heavy Underwood upon which Benjamín had composed his poems and Patricia later drafted political screeds. On it, she typed out habeas corpus requests for José's parents as well, copying the language from the draft the lawyer had helped her with. If Rosa hesitated before preparing a document that clearly stated her name and home address—knowing her information would now be irreversibly in the government's talons—it did not stop her. She had to get Patricia home before she gave birth.

Five days after the abduction, on October 11, the habeas corpus petitions were ready. Rosa approached the Palacio de Justicia de la Nación, more commonly known as Tribunales, an imposing neoclassical building that spans an entire city block in front of Plaza Lavalle. Outside it was warm; soon it would be summer, when lime-green monk parakeets swoop and squawk among the city's trees. Diagonally across the plaza from the courthouse was the Teatro Colón, where, in what must have seemed like a different lifetime, Rosa had watched ballets and operas with Benjamín. She walked past the guards standing at attention and in through the courthouse's grand arched entrance. There was often a line of women like her—some crying, some stoic—all waiting to hand over their habeas corpus documents. Rosa left her papers with a clerk and walked back through the building's dark hallways, her footsteps echoing against the cold marble floors.

As she waited for a response to her petition, the few people who hadn't deserted Rosa tried to console her. "La van a soltar," they said soothingly of Patricia. They'll let her go. "What are they possibly going to do to a woman who's eight months pregnant?"

A week crawled by without any news of Patricia or José. Then, ten days after they had disappeared, around one in the morning, the phone broke the silence in Rosa's apartment.

She picked up groggily before snapping awake at the voice in her ear. It was Patricia.

"Mamá, I was mistaken. They're treating me well." She said the pregnancy was proceeding perfectly.

Then a man took the receiver.

"Señora Roisinblit, pay attention to what I have to say to you. Your daughter is doing very well. We don't want to hurt her."

He continued, barking instructions. Rosa should under no circumstances try to figure out where her daughter was, nor should she pay anyone for help in doing so. She should not file any complaints on Patricia's behalf. And she should stay far away from the apartment on Gurruchaga that Patricia had shared with José.

"Señora," he continued. "The charges against your daughter aren't serious—in contrast to those against your son-in-law. Your daughter will be released soon."

"Soon? How soon is soon?" Rosa asked.

Six months, maybe a year, the guard responded.

"But first, you need to prepare yourself to raise a grandchild. As soon as the baby is born, we will deliver it to you. I will call again. Goodbye."

Rosa set the phone receiver in its cradle, dazed.

The following day, October 17, Rosa received a single-page typed response from the criminal court about the habeas corpus she'd filed. The margins and spaces between the lines were wide—apparently the government did not have much to say. It was written in doughy legalese, but one word made the document's message clear: *Rechazar*. Reject. Without further explanation, it ended, "You have been notified."

Rosa was grappling with what to do next when, on October 23, at the same ungodly hour as before, the shrill ring of her phone pierced the pre-dawn quiet once again. She grabbed the receiver. It was the same man who had called the previous time; he said he was passing along a question from Patricia. *Was Mariana being kept up-to-date on her vaccines? Or was she due for a booster?*

Even in her dead-of-night fog, the question struck Rosa as curious. A doctor in training, Patricia would not have needed to ask her mother about Mariana's shots. She never let her daughter's vaccines lapse, and she kept assiduous track of what doses Mariana needed and when. Only later would Rosa wonder: Could Patricia have been looking for some way—some innocuous question that her guards wouldn't object to—to let Rosa know she was still alive?

"Behave yourself," the man warned. "Demonstrate that you've earned our trust, and you will see your daughter again very soon." The phone line clicked and silence once again settled over Rosa's apartment.

9

White Wool

October–November 1978

It had been more than two weeks since Patricia's disappearance, and her due date was imminent. As November approached, Rosa sat as though chained to her telephone, terrified of missing the promised call about her new grandchild. The editions of *La Nación* that she paged through each morning reflected a country that was similarly on edge. Things were heating up in Argentina's decades-long fight with Chile over several islands in the Beagle Channel, a treacherous strait at both countries' southernmost tips, and the Argentine army had moved troops and weaponry into the contested area. Every few nights, the military ordered "darkness operations" in preparation for a potential air assault from Chile. Residents were instructed to stay off the streets and cover their windows and doors to block all light. Meanwhile, Videla purged his cabinet, which had grown divided over his handling of the economy. The inflation rate had become the highest in the world, increasing the cost of living by 127 percent in less than a year. Prices for meat shot up 23 percent in a month. Argentines flooded exchange houses to swap out their devaluing pesos for dollars.

Three afternoons a week, Rosa went to see Mariana in Belgrano, where she was living with José's parents while they waited for news of Patricia and José. Rosa doted on the girl, lavishing her with fine dresses and children's books. To the rest of her family, she tried to project an illusion of normalcy, visiting her elderly mother, Alte, as usual.

"Where is Patricia?" Alte inquired when she realized she hadn't seen her granddaughter in a while. "What happened? Why hasn't she visited?" Rosa suspected Alte already knew, but she couldn't bring herself to tell the truth. "She's traveling," Rosa responded. "She had to go abroad."

As the days crept by, Rosa forced herself to continue waiting. Surely the call was coming.

November arrived, and the freshness of spring melted into the heaviness of summer, with jacaranda petals littering the streets like purple rain. Patricia's baby was due around mid-November, but the month ended just as it had begun: without news. At home, Rosa distracted herself by knitting tiny clothes. She didn't know whether Patricia was pregnant with a boy or a girl, so she chose white wool instead of blue or pink for her handmade hats and booties. The yarn ran through her fingers, the skein getting smaller and smaller.

In 1894, a steamship chugged up the Río de la Plata into the port of Buenos Aires carrying forty families, their Torah scrolls, and their hopes for a better life. Their passage from Russia had been encouraged by Baron Maurice de Hirsch, a German Jewish philanthropist with a curlicue mustache who aspired to rescue Jews from persecution in eastern Europe and help them resettle in agricultural colonies in North and South America. He dubbed this lofty mission the Jewish Colonization Association, and eventually he would help Jewish settlers in Argentina amass 600,000 hectares of land—an area ten times the size of Chicago. By 1920, Argentina's Jewish population had grown to around 150,000. At one point, Theodor Herzl, the founder of the modern political Zionist movement, supposedly considered Argentina as an alternative to Palestine.

Among the settlers on this particular ship in 1894 were Hirsch Tarlovsky, his wife, their daughter, and five sons—including nine-year-old Salomón, who would one day become Rosa's father. The family spoke no Spanish, but the unknowns of a life in Argentina could not be worse than the fear they had endured in Belarus; Hirsch had owned a grocery store near the city of Grodno, and when he would leave the shop in the care of his wife, Russian peasants would ransack the place. Once, they struck young Salomón across the face, leaving him with a fat scar that would remain for the rest of his life. In Argentina, the family settled in a hamlet near Moisés Ville, a small farming community in the province of Santa Fe, where they transformed themselves into successful ranchers.

Nearly everyone in the town was Jewish, and the few inhabitants who weren't had taught themselves Yiddish by necessity. Soon there were four synagogues to choose from, as well as two libraries full of Hebrew tomes and an elegant theater. Not all was utopian. By the dawn of the twentieth century, the town had suffered a series of mysterious murders at the hands of roving bandits. But Jewish ranchers cantering around the dusty streets were spared the generalized xenophobia of Argentina's larger cities: the town doctor was Jewish, the town lawyer was Jewish, and the mayor was Jewish.

In 1901, seven years after Salomón arrived, Rosa's mother, Alte Milstein, landed in Moisés Ville with her family, having traveled from Bessarabia. She was ten years younger than Salomón, but they connected easily. Sometimes, as he trotted a horse-drawn carriage full of clanking milk jugs past alfalfa fields to the rail station, he would spot Alte as she was walking to school and offer a ride. When he was eighteen, he promised that one day he would marry her; eight years later he fulfilled his vow.

Once wed, the couple bought a plot of land close to Moisés Ville where they could raise livestock and built a brick house, which they began to fill with children. Alte would ultimately give birth to five girls and two boys, but after a time, only the sisters remained. One of the boys passed away as an infant, and the other died at nine after falling off a horse he had mounted without permission.

Money flowed in readily at first. But after World War I, when demand for agricultural exports plunged, a brutal recession crushed the ranchers of the pampas. The Tarlovskys were forced to sell off cattle they had bought at three pesos a head for just forty cents and to mortgage the extensive farm they had amassed plot by plot. They couldn't afford books—borrowing from friends or the local library instead—but they were committed to educating their children however they could. They read and debated topics in the Jewish and Spanish newspapers and gathered around the table in the evenings to share stories about their ancestors. Rosa grew up speaking Yiddish at home, eating in a kitchen perfumed by the aromas of knishes and gefilte fish. When Kalman "Kalmele" Weitz, the famous "boy cantor" who had begun touring the world at age six, came to perform his liturgical music in Moisés Ville, Alte and Salomón scrimped so their children could attend the performance.

Rosa was plucky from the start. At ten years old, she was tasked with driving herself and one of her younger sisters the four miles to school in a horse-drawn cart. She attended Spanish school in the morning and Hebrew school in the afternoon, trotting home as the sun tucked behind the seemingly interminable grasslands. Her mother sewed fabric remnants together to create elegant dresses for her—embroidered confections and knits in vibrant colors—and sighed when her designs invariably returned home coated in mud from Rosa's puddle-hopping or covered in thorns from her scrambles up trees with her male cousins.

Even back then, Rosa dreamed of being something more than a *chica del pueblo*, or village girl. To escape the dusty roads, braying cows, and crushing flatness of Moisés Ville, she accepted a family friend's offer to train as an obstetrician when she was just fifteen, becoming part of a larger migration of first-generation Argentine Jews from the pampas to the medical universities of Argentina's big cities. So many children of Jewish immigrants left their families' farms to study medicine, in fact, that it inspired an Argentine Jewish saying: "We planted wheat and grew doctors."

Rosa's work took her all around the country, from the big city of Rosario to clinics in small farming villages like the one she had just left. Eventually a job opportunity led her to Buenos Aires, a city whose cultural richness thrilled her after years in sleepy hamlets. In what little free time she had, she avidly attended concerts and the ballet; Perón was president, and his administration often funded performances at the city's biggest law school. Rosa had also begun to earn more money, which she eagerly spent to see classical pianists or operas by Wagner. On Tuesday, Thursday, and Saturday mornings, she went to the local Hebraica, where she played half an hour of basketball and did an additional half hour of exercises at the gym that the association maintained. It was there that she fell for Benjamín Roisinblit, a charismatic accountant with a greater passion for words than numbers. The couple married in January of 1951, first in a civil ceremony and then in a Jewish service at the Gran Templo Paso, a Buenos Aires synagogue with soaring arches and twinkling chandeliers. Benjamín sported a slick black tuxedo with a bowler hat; Rosa wore a long-sleeved gown with a modest V-neck and a gauzy veil secured by a beaded head-band. The following year, Patricia arrived.

Both sides of Rosa's family had crossed the Atlantic on crowded steam-ships for one main reason: in search of safety. Now her pregnant daughter had been kidnapped—not by some street gang, but by the very state Rosa's family had hoped would protect them.

The man on the phone had explicitly told Rosa not to visit Patricia's apart-ment, and for a while she obeyed him. If she broke her end of the deal, he might renege on his, too. He could refuse to release Patricia and her baby. Or he might have Rosa apprehended. Who would look for Patricia and her child then?

Eventually, though, Rosa couldn't take any more waiting. She needed to visit the apartment, to search for clues—and to talk to the landlord. She could no longer afford to keep paying the rent, which inflation was pushing higher and higher each month, and she wanted to see if she could cancel the lease.

She'd tried to shield her family from what was happening as much as pos-sible, but she couldn't make this visit alone. She called her youngest sister, Sola. Blond, with small coffee-colored eyes, Sola was nine years younger and had long considered Rosa more of a second mother than a sibling; as children, it was Rosa who sang Sola to sleep. When Rosa moved to Buenos Aires to work as an ob-stetrician, Sola moved too. She had stepped in and taken Patricia on vacation when Rosa and Benjamín were too busy with work, chasing behind her niece on horseback in Córdoba and splashing around in hotel pools. In Buenos Aires, Patricia would sometimes help Sola get ready for outings, dusting eye shadow on her lids. Because Sola had a car, Patricia had often begged her aunt for rides when she was a bit older, asking to be dropped off at places like La Paz, a large café on the corner of Corrientes and Montevideo that was a popular gathering spot for left-leaning youths. Now it was Rosa who needed Sola.

"I am terrified," Rosa confided to Sola on the phone. "I have to visit the house and I'm afraid."

Sola picked Rosa up and drove her to the street in Palermo where Patricia and José had settled. She waited in the car as Rosa walked up the sidewalk to their building. Nestled midway up the block, shaded by towering London plane trees, the complex was blocky, with iron balconies that protruded from each floor. Rosa made her way to apartment 20. It was locked, so she called for a locksmith, posing as a forgetful homeowner who had left her key inside. Petite, elegant, and pushing sixty, Rosa did not arouse suspicion, and the locksmith gamely pried the door open without asking any questions.

Inside, Rosa found a disaster. The apartment was entirely hollowed out. The television and leather chairs that had graced the living room were gone. Cabinets had been yanked open. The shelves inside them were empty. Mariana's toys had been taken. Even the pantry had been ransacked. Rosa searched the rooms for the fur coat of rich nutria she had lent Patricia to keep her warm through the chilly Buenos Aires winter while her belly grew: gone. Missing, too, were the fine leather boots she had bought Patricia as a gift, and the folding door made from petiribí wood that had separated Patricia and José's bedroom from the living areas. The door to the shower had been wrenched off its jamb, and the gas stove had been disconnected and carted away. Either out of laziness or as a macabre taunt, the goons had left behind only one item: Mariana's baby crib.

The promises of the man who had called Rosa in the middle of the night—urging her not to take any action to find Patricia, suggesting that she would be released—suddenly seemed as empty as the deserted apartment. It was clear that whoever had taken Patricia and José had no intention of acting within the bounds of the law. Now, Rosa realized, she needed to make up for lost time. If she was ever going to find her daughter and grandchild, it seemed she would need to do so herself.

The headquarters of the federal police department, just a fifteen-minute walk from Rosa's own apartment, seemed as good a place to check as any. A white-and-yellow Italianate building that spanned an entire city block, it might have seemed beautiful in another context, with neat balustrades and an open-air courtyard adorned with palm trees. By visiting, Rosa would be flouting instructions even more brazenly than when she had gone to Patricia's apartment. But she was desperate. In addition to ordering Rosa not to look for Patricia, the man who had twice called in the middle of the night had referenced "charges" against her daughter. Maybe the police could tell her something about them.

Rosa was received by a man with a bushy black mustache. When she asked if he had any information about Patricia, the officer stepped away for a moment and returned with a document that he slid in front of her. "Look, señora," he said. "Your daughter's records are clean. There isn't a warrant for her." The neatly dressed grandmother before him must have aroused some pity in the man. After a pause, he added: "But there are some cases that don't go through us."

"What does that mean?" Rosa asked, perplexed.

"That even though she is not a person who is sought after—even though there is nothing in her records—she might still be detained." Then he moved on to the next person in line.

Rosa did not know what to make of the officer's comment. At a loss for what else to do, she continued visiting other places where Patricia might be held. One day, the husband of one of Rosa's other sisters shuttled her the twelve miles from her apartment to a walled prison compound, located at the same intersection where right-wing Peronists had opened fire on left-wing Peronists five years earlier during the Ezeiza Massacre. Rosa's brother-in-law parked his car on the side of the road as Rosa tramped up the path toward the security gate alone. As she wove through relatives hauling care packages for their imprisoned loved ones, her modest heels sank into the dirt.

When she reached the guard tower, a voice boomed from above asking her what she wanted. She craned her neck upward, responding that she was looking for her daughter: Patricia Julia Roisinblit. "No, señora," the guard answered immediately. Intimating that Rosa would have been notified if Patricia were imprisoned there, he added: "This is an open jail." Rosa trekked back to the car. Only later would she begin to wonder what it meant for a jail to be closed.

10

Nothing to Lose

Late 1978

R osa rarely attended temple, but she was of the mind that "Judío se nace, no se hace." (One is born Jewish, not made Jewish.) So when she heard that Jewish organizations were helping people find their missing relatives, she began to visit as many of them as she could. One of her first stops was the Delegación de Asociaciones Israelitas Argentinas, or DAIA, an umbrella group that united a large number of Jewish organizations and advocated against discrimination.

Over the past few decades, Argentina's Jewish community—which had grown to 300,000, representing one of the largest Jewish populations in the world—had dealt with plenty of antisemitism. Following World War II, word spread that Perón's government had sold fraudulent Argentine passports to Nazi war criminals, allowing them to assume new identities and quietly resettle around the country. In 1960, Mossad agents located Adolf Eichmann, one of the masterminds of the Holocaust, in a Buenos Aires suburb, where he had hidden for ten years, working at a Mercedes-Benz workshop under the name Ricardo Klement. Since the 1976 coup, a number of synagogues had suffered bombings and Jewish storefronts had been strafed by machine guns. In 1977, the son of DAIA president Nehemías Resnizky was abducted—though he was eventually released and allowed to seek refuge in Israel.

The DAIA headquarters was a short walk from Rosa's apartment through the barrio of Once, a buzzy area full of synagogues and discount fabric stores. If she strolled down Sarmiento, she would have passed the Hebraica, the social club where she had long ago connected with Benjamín, and where Patricia had later attended dances with friends. There was a chance that her mission would be fruitless. Other Jews looking for missing relatives complained that the DAIA staff had received them coldly, looking at their watches impatiently while they talked; some suggested that the organization had used all its political capital pushing for the release of Resnizky's son and couldn't help anyone else. But Rosa's experience was initially encouraging. As she walked through the brutalist black entrance, a man named Naum Barbarás, the organization's public relations head, received her with his arms raised in a warm welcome. "Ah, if a Jewish mother comes to the DAIA to ask for our help, we are going to provide it," he said emphatically.

Barbarás instructed his employees to take notes while Rosa told him about Patricia and José. As she recounted what information she'd been able to gather, a man burst through the doors with a wide grin on his face. He began to loudly thank Barbarás and the DAIA for having found his son, who, like Patricia, had been kidnapped. For the first time since she had begun her search, Rosa felt something resembling hope. "Now," she thought, "they'll bring me my daughter."

Rosa awoke the next morning itching for an update, but she forced herself to be patient. She didn't want to annoy the DAIA with a barrage of requests. She let a week pass before returning to see Barbarás, and to her surprise, he greeted her icily. "Go see our lawyer," he said. Deflated, she wandered through the DAIA's halls until she found the office she needed. Inside was a young man reading a book with his feet propped on his desk. With what seemed like disdain, he said: "Señora, did you *really* think we'd find your daughter so easily—overnight?"

Crushed, Rosa returned home, vowing to avoid the DAIA from then on. Nor did she have much luck with a group of rabbis who provided spiritual guidance to Jewish prisoners. She had asked them to look for Patricia in the Buenos Aires jail where they worked. They called her back shortly thereafter: there was no trace of her daughter. The Israeli embassy was no help either. The consul there nodded and sighed upon hearing Rosa's story. It was one that had become all too familiar to him. Haggard family members in similar situations had trekked to his office from across the country, hoping that being Jewish would be enough to compel his attention. While Jews made up a relatively small percentage of the Argentine population, they seemed to be disappearing at a disproportionate rate. People who had been arrested and subsequently released by the security forces described seeing swastikas emblazoned on police station walls and being forced to listen to cassettes of Hitler speeches while they were tortured.

The consul explained to Rosa that he met with the interior minister each Wednesday. But week after week, the government simply denied everything. "If he tells me there aren't any detained Jewish young people, what can I say? What can I do?"

Not everyone in the Argentine Jewish community was quite so defeatist: one rabbi, Marshall Meyer, took it upon himself to look for the disappeared. An American from Brooklyn, Meyer had moved to Buenos Aires in 1959 to champion the Conservative movement, a branch of Judaism that aims to preserve traditional Jewish practices while embracing modern culture. Influenced by his mentor, Abraham Joshua Heschel, a Jewish philosopher active in the civil rights movement, Meyer believed that social action was inextricable from Judaism. He had planned to stay in Argentina for only a few years, but soon became consumed by the goal of reinvigorating faith among Argentina's hundreds of thousands of largely assimilated Jews. As violence in Argentina had escalated in the mid-1970s, people began to approach him for something more than spiritual guidance: they wanted assistance finding their loved ones. Meyer came to see helping the families shattered by the dictatorship as his "supreme duty."

In his Shabbat services at Comunidad Bet El, the congregation he had established in Belgrano, the rabbi began to rail against the dictatorship, attracting Argentines of all faiths to the synagogue's sanctuary. "There they could hear what wasn't being said in their churches," he would later reflect. Even Christian mothers looking for their missing children showed up on Friday evenings, gamely trying to imitate Meyer's Hebrew prayers. Moved by the plight of these family members, he offered to scour jails on their behalf, at great risk to himself. Everywhere he traveled, he was trailed by plainclothes police officers; his home phone was tapped and constantly rang with death threats. Once, during a visit to a jail in the heart of Buenos Aires, Meyer was stripped naked in the courtyard and left to freeze in the winter air. He was released only after the prison director stomped by and muttered, loud enough for Meyer to hear: "This Jew is going to walk in one day through the front door, and he's going to go out in a coffin through the back door."

Still, he remained undeterred. "I think that the only thing that distinguishes the activist from the coward," he later explained, "is the fact that the coward permits the fear to paralyze him and the activist in spite of his fear knows what his duty is and he goes about it."

Rosa didn't have much confidence that the well-known rabbi would help her, but she went to Comunidad Bet El to visit him anyway. Meyer made no promises but listened compassionately, giving her a list of organizations to contact. One was the Permanent Assembly for Human Rights, an institution comprised of religious, legal, and intellectual leaders that had formed a few months before the 1976 coup in response to increasing reports of human rights atrocities. It was housed in a modest apartment that Rosa reached by trudging up a staircase. On the landing, she encountered a scattering of small tables at which affiliates of the organization sat listening to stories like hers. Rosa looked for an open table and took a seat facing a man with gentle eyes and a receding hairline. His name was Alfredo Galletti. He listened to Rosa's story attentively, penning careful notes.

"Señora, tomorrow a bunch of grandmothers are coming to my house because I'm going to help them file complaints," Galletti told her when she had finished. He explained that the documents would be sent to the Organization of American States, an international group dedicated to the promotion of democracy, human rights, and security in the Western Hemisphere.

The information surprised her. Rosa hadn't realized that there were other women in her position—women who were looking not just for their disappeared children but for grandchildren, too. Galletti gave Rosa the address, urging her to come. His apartment was in Almagro, a quick subway or bus ride from hers. Rosa considered his invitation. Though he looked kind enough, she knew nothing about the man. He could well be a mole for the dictatorship. Such infiltrators were rumored to be everywhere, trying to ensnare people. But her husband was already gone, and now they had stolen her daughter and grandchild—what more did Rosa have to lose?

PART II

The Grandmothers

11

Azucena

Nearly two years before Rosa began her search for Patricia, one December day in 1976, Azucena Villaflor de De Vincenti received a message from a woman who lived near her son Néstor, a twenty-four-year-old architecture student. What she had to tell Azucena was important, she said, but could not be shared over the phone. Instead, they arranged to meet at a produce shop half a block from Azucena's home in the Buenos Aires suburb of Sarandí. As oblivious shoppers browsed carrots and squeezed springtime tomatoes for ripeness, the woman wrapped Azucena in a tearful hug.

"I have to tell you something!" she said, choking back sobs. "A tu hijo lo han muerto, Azucena." They've killed your son.

Néstor's political involvement had become a source of constant worry for Azucena; while she was proud of his social conscience, her son's strong convictions seemed to be pulling him away from her and her family. The De Vincentis had worked themselves raw to build one of the nicest homes in their lower-middle-class neighborhood, and Néstor, the second of her four children, had seemed to reject such hard-earned comfort. "Was it really necessary to build such a showy house?" his sister, Cecilia, would later remember him complaining. He sparred incessantly with his father, Azucena's husband, Pedro De Vincenti, over his political activism and tendency to spend time in a nearby *villa miseria,* where residents inhabited dwellings improvised from scraps of metal that they illuminated with kerosene lamps. Noticing that the soles of Néstor's moccasins were riddled with holes, Pedro had Azucena buy him a new pair. The next time Néstor visited: the same old mangy shoes. "What the hell did you do with the shoes we bought you?" Pedro demanded. Néstor replied that he had passed them on to someone who needed them more.

Recently, Néstor had been living with his girlfriend, a seamstress named Raquel Mangin, in a small workshop where Raquel made and sold leather and suede clothing. They were both involved with the Montoneros, where Néstor, who was known as Paco, led a regiment. There had been scrapes with the authorities; a bullet scar on Néstor's leg proved it. But on the morning of November 30, 1976, things escalated. Armed men streamed out of seven military vehicles and stormed Raquel's workshop. Néstor wasn't around, so the troops lashed Raquel and the building's owner to chairs while they waited for him to return. When he walked through the door, the men pounced, punching and kicking him savagely.

At the produce stand, Azucena's friend had told her that Néstor was dead. But later, when Azucena talked to more of Néstor's neighbors, they insisted that they had seen the armed men yank Néstor and Raquel outside, bruised and bloodied but alive. If there was even a chance that they were right, she knew she needed to look for them. In early January 1977, Azucena and Pedro submitted a writ of habeas corpus at their local courthouse. Four days later, a judge responded: Néstor was not being held by the police.

Despite her anguish over Néstor's abduction, Azucena made sure her home was spotless and her family's meals were on the table promptly at nine in the evening. She still had three other children to care for. Now fifty-two, she had devoted herself to her family since marrying Pedro when she was twenty-five. She was of average height with a round frame, a wide smile, and toffee-colored hair that she styled into a helmet-like bouffant. Her body, a friend would later recall, "made you think of a great fortress," her arms strengthened by decades of cleaning and cooking. She relished making each of her children their favorite meals: milanesas for the boys, fish and fried sweet potatoes for Cecilia, the only girl. But after Néstor was taken, Azucena began to spend long hours out of the house, racing across the Matanza River to and from Buenos Aires, calling on any official who might know the whereabouts of her son. She visited hospitals, police stations, and morgues, but Néstor was nowhere.

One morning, her destination was the Ministry of the Interior, which managed Argentina's domestic affairs from the north wing of the Casa Rosada. Since the 1976 coup, the ministry had become a place where relatives with missing loved ones gathered to beg for information. The ministry granted only ten visits per day, so people—most of them women, despondent mothers like Azucena—often lined up overnight, sleeping on the sidewalk to ensure an audience in the morning. When it was her turn, Azucena approached the Casa Rosada's arched salmon entrance. In front of the building stretched the Plaza de Mayo, the symbolic heart of Buenos Aires. The summer heat shimmered off its tiled pathways and baked its palm trees. Inside, she handed over a lengthy complaint, detailing everything she knew about Néstor's abduction. Days later, when she hadn't heard back, she returned and shoved a shorter document across the desk. It pleaded, "I beg of you to help me with this sad situation."

It became a depressing routine: the trips to Buenos Aires, the crushing disappointment. Before long, Azucena and the other women outside the Ministry of the Interior began to recognize each other's weary faces. They started to talk, quietly and elliptically, sharing their stories and frustrations. None of them had managed to penetrate the junta's bureaucracy. Sometimes, officials stoked false hope—"I'll try to do everything possible; I promise you. Poor soul! Your case is so moving," an employee had said to one woman in a saccharine voice. Or they dropped ominous hints. "Señora, maybe he will never reappear," another mother was told. Police officers informed the women that the state had nothing to do with the abductions. Perhaps their children had been kidnapped by their own *compañeros*, officials sometimes suggested to mothers whose children were involved in leftist organizations. Burning for even a tiny crumb of information, some mothers turned to fortune tellers.

Eventually, an employee at the ministry told Azucena to visit Monseñor Emilio Teodoro Grasselli, a priest who served as the military vicar's private secretary. The address she was given led her to a strange flap of land in Retiro, hemmed in on one side by a busy avenue and on the other by the waters of the Río de la Plata. Nearby loomed the headquarters of Argentina's navy and air force, where, unbeknownst to Azucena, officials issued orders for abductions and death flights. Next to the charmless naval building stood Catedral Castrense Stella Maris, a military church with a sleek white facade and a gigantic stained glass window dedicated to Our Lady, the Star of the Sea, an ancient title for the Virgin Mary, who supposedly protected seafarers from the perils of the ocean.

Upstairs from the chapel, Azucena walked through a huge anteroom teeming with people waiting to see the monsignor, some of whom likely looked familiar from the snaking lines outside the Ministry of the Interior. Church employees demanded IDs and collected women's purses, advising those who smoked to take their cigarettes along with them, as the rest of their belongings would be held until they exited. Each person was given a number that functioned as a pass.

When she was finally waved through to Grasselli's office, Azucena encountered a middle-aged man wearing a black clerical collar. He swept his arm toward an empty seat across from his desk, atop which lay a metal coffer. Inside the box, out of view, were thousands of note cards containing information about missing people that Grasselli had gathered from conversations with people like Azucena. On the front of the cards were names of those missing and the estimated date of their abduction; on the backs were the names of those who had come looking for them and the dates of the interviews. One visitor noticed that several cards bore scarlet *M*s, seemingly a mark to denote Montoneros.

Though some would later come to suspect it, at first the men and women who came to see Grasselli did not realize that he regularly turned these cards over to the Ministry of the Interior, the federal police, and navy. Once, a distraught father visiting the priest dropped the crucifix he had been carrying for solace. When he bent to retrieve it from the floor, he saw a recorder whirring under Grasselli's desk. Like the officials at the Ministry of the Interior, Grasselli wavered between empty warmth and casual cruelty as he met with relatives of the missing. During one interaction, he told a mother in search of her abducted son and daughter-in-law: "Take a taxi home because your kids should be there waiting for you!" She flew out of his office to her house only to find it empty. He told another: "Look señora, perhaps he'll come back, because surely what happened is he got tired of his wife and left her for another woman. You know how men are." Other times he dismissed his visitors callously. "Go home," he said once after scanning his files. "They're all dead."

Indeed, apart from the Third World Priests who worked in the *villas*, much of the country's Catholic leadership supported—or silently tolerated—the junta, viewing its violence as an unfortunate consequence of Videla's mission to defend Argentina's "Western, Christian" values. Occasionally, after pushing prisoners from planes into the Río de la Plata, soldiers would seek guidance from the military's priests. The priests consoled them, insisting it was a "Christian form of death," because the victims did not suffer. Even the Bible mentioned separating the wheat from the chaff.

Azucena left her first meeting with Grasselli confused and frightened. He seemed more keen on extracting information from her than providing her with it. She was at a dead end. The hours she had spent on the sidewalk outside the Ministry of the Interior had been fruitless, her visits to jails and police stations futile. But in mid-April, she returned once again to Catedral Castrense Stella Maris. She didn't trust Grasselli, but she didn't know where else to go. Other officials avoided women like her—at least Grasselli agreed to see them. That day, church employees demanded visitors to remove their shoes for inspection, as if they might be concealing switchblades in their loafers. Then, lined up in the bustling waiting room, Azucena watched as a mother staggered out of the monsignor's office. Grasselli had just informed the woman that her child, who had been abducted a few weeks before, was dead.

Suddenly, Azucena couldn't take any more. The ministry workers feigning helpfulness. The church employees rifling through her purse, as though she were a common criminal. The desperation so profound you could smell it. The interminable lines. At the end of the long hallway that led to Grasselli's office, she stood as tall as she could muster and shouted into the waiting room: "All that we're doing, coming here, the habeas corpus, the interviews, the trips to the police and the military barracks, all of it is useless." Tapping her leg for emphasis, she declared, "What we have to do is go to the Plaza de Mayo."

A shocked silence fell over the crowd. The plaza had been instrumental in past revolutions and social movements, she reminded them. "Let's go to the Plaza de Mayo, and, when our numbers grow—because unfortunately we will soon be many, so many people are disappearing—we are going to walk through the plaza, we are going to cross the street, and we are going to enter the [Casa Rosada]—we won't let anyone chase us away—and we are going to reach Videla."

The waiting room erupted in chatter. Several women approached Azucena. "But what will we *do* in the plaza?" one ventured to ask. "Nothing," Azucena responded. "Nothing special, except sit, chat, and grow in numbers each day." A woman pulled a calendar out of her purse and tentatively proposed the thirtieth of April, a Saturday a few weeks from then, to give them time to spread the word. It was decided.

12

The Mothers

April–October 1977

The Plaza de Mayo is not particularly imposing. The length of two city blocks and the width of one, it is overshadowed by the grand buildings that surround it. On its northern edge sit the neoclassical headquarters of Argentina's main bank and the country's most important Catholic cathedral. On its narrower western side is the Cabildo, a white Spanish-style building with glazed red tiles that hosted the town council during the colonial era. To the south lies the boxy Palacio de Hacienda, the home of the Ministry of Economy. And to the east loom the pink columns and domed windows of the Casa Rosada.

The plaza features manicured patches of lawn punctuated by palms and jacarandas. Four tiled walkways cut through the grass, guiding visitors to its centerpiece: the Pirámide de Mayo, a sixty-foot white obelisk topped by a statue of a woman wielding a spear and shield. The "pyramid" and the plaza itself were both named for the May Revolution of 1810, which laid the foundation for Argentina's declaration of independence from Spain. Huddled within the Cabildo, whose windows overlooked the plaza, Argentines had created their first government. As their newly appointed officials hammered out the details, Argentines dressed in top hats and tall boots trudged through the plaza, the dirt paths turned to muck in the rain, to demand transparency. "El pueblo quiere saber de qué se trata!" they shouted.

The people want to know what's going on!

Ever since, the Plaza de Mayo had been both a garden for new ideas and a battlefield, hosting the births and deaths of political movements, massive celebrations, and angry protests. It had gained particular importance during the era of Perón, who would often speak to crowds gathered in the plaza from the Casa Rosada's central balcony. Later, in 1955, Peronists had run for their lives across the plaza's tiles when the military dropped bombs on it, killing hundreds of civilians while trying to unseat El Líder.

On April 30, 1977, Azucena and the other women filtered onto the plaza's pathways. They had purposely come alone, without their husbands or sons, and some brought only change purses, having left their pocket-books behind to avoid accusations that they carried anything suspicious. Since the coup, Videla's government had prohibited group meetings, and the mothers were in clear violation of that ban. But society often overlooks middle-aged women—and they hoped that, even as they tried to attract Videla's attention, the police would too.

They lit cigarettes, taking long drags to settle their nerves, and tapped the ash onto the tiles. The women were able to recognize one another by their tight, anxious faces and their shared aimlessness. "Are you here for the same reason as I am?" one mother timidly asked a few others who were walking together. Ultimately, fourteen women showed up. They loitered around the plaza's benches, sharing their names and snippets about how their children had disappeared, but avoiding deep engagement out of caution. "We were anonymous, distrustful people, united by the paperwork and the lives we were trying to recover," one mother would remember later.

If they had hoped Videla would notice them, however, that plan was soon dashed. It was an unusually warm autumn afternoon in Buenos Aires, yet despite the pleasant weather, there was nobody around to appreciate their plight. The only other souls in the Plaza de Mayo were the armed guards flanking the entrance to the Casa Rosada, a lonely peanut vendor, and pigeons pecking for scraps in the grass. They soon realized their mistake. They had picked Saturday, when the center of Buenos Aires—normally thrumming with office workers and government personnel—shuts down. President Videla wasn't even in the city: he was finishing up an official visit to Córdoba. The operation was, one woman would later express, "a disaster."

Eventually, Azucena stood up. "We have to do something!" she shouted to the others.

"A vos quién te manda?" one woman demanded, implying that perhaps Azucena was working for a political organization. Who sent you?

"What do you mean, who sent me?" Azucena shot back. "Together we can do something, alone, nothing." The group made plans to meet again the following week—but this time on a Friday, when the plaza would surely be busier. They did so once, still uncertain of quite what to do with themselves, until a mother requested yet another change. Fridays, she said, were "witches' days" and brought bad luck. "Worse luck than we've already had?" another quipped. Unwilling to test the limits of that question, they agreed to move the meetings to Thursday afternoon.

Even with the scheduling change, the mothers were not attracting the attention they wanted. They decided to write a letter to Videla, requesting an audience with him directly. He might not know that people were going missing, they thought; if they alerted him, perhaps he could help. One of the mothers scribbled a draft longhand before passing it off to another to type up at home. Upon finishing, the mothers sat in pairs on the hard benches of the Plaza de Mayo, reading the missive and writing each of their names at the bottom. Eventually they would call themselves the Madres de Plaza de Mayo, but that day, they signed the note with a wordier moniker: "the mothers who meet every Thursday at three thirty in the afternoon in the Plaza de Mayo." They walked across the plaza to the Casa Rosada to deliver it, vowing to return each Thursday until they received a response.

The letter went unanswered. But each week, word about the women spread, and their ranks grew. "Your daughter was at the Colegio Nacional de Buenos Aires? Mine too," one mother whispered to another while waiting at the Ministry of the Interior, referencing one of the finest public schools in Buenos Aires. Another woman murmured: "We have to go to the plaza. It's said many women are meeting there." By July, around sixty women gathered each Thursday at three thirty on the dot, in plain view of the Casa Rosada's arched windows, but there was still no word from the president. Their patience had run out. One afternoon, they strode through the Casa Rosada's grand pink entrance and made a demand: "We want a meeting with Videla. He has to answer us."

A colonel appeared, explaining that Videla himself would be unable to meet with them. He was too busy, some later remembered him saying. (Others recalled a harsher answer: Videla isn't interested.) But the colonel agreed to bring them to meet with Albano Harguindeguy, the stocky general who headed the Ministry of the Interior.

The sun had just dipped behind the Pirámide, and the streetlamps cast long shadows on the ground. Bundled up in warm coats to fight the winter chill, the mothers waited anxiously in the Plaza de Mayo as three from their ranks reported to the minister's office. They were Azucena, who had become the group's natural leader; Beatriz "Ketty" Aicardi de Neuhaus, who was married to a retired military officer and had the most military connections; and María del Rosario de Cerruti, a frail-looking woman with the temperament of a lioness who had drafted the original request to meet with Videla.

Guided by the colonel, the trio walked through the elegant hallways of the Casa Rosada to Harguindeguy's office. There, they encountered the general himself, dressed in full military regalia. Gilded epaulettes protruded from his blazer and a tie girded his beefy neck. His reputation was fearsome; in one government telegram, an American diplomat who had just divulged bad news to President Videla wrote: "I was happy I wasn't talking to MinInt. Harguindeguy, who weighs about 240 pounds and doesn't speak but instead roars."

Harguindeguy greeted the women, inviting them to sit in armchairs. He immediately recognized Ketty, whose husband was one of his acquaintances from the military. "But, señora, has your daughter still not appeared?" he said with surprise—real or feigned, they couldn't tell. "I thought your problem was already resolved."

"I still know nothing," Ketty responded evenly, "and there are many of us in this situation."

The general walked over to his desk, grabbed a logbook, and held it up for the women to see. "I have a list of friends, the children of friends, all of whom are disappeared, and I truthfully don't know what's happening."

Taken aback, Azucena snapped: "How can you not know what's happening?"

"I don't know what's happening," he said, doubling down.

"But you are a functionary of the Ministry of the Interior, you should know what is going on," Azucena pressed.

Turning once more to Ketty, he continued: "There was a girl who was disappeared, the daughter of a friend who came to see me, and later we learned that she was in Mexico. If I hear something about your daughter, I'll help you. You wouldn't believe the number of girls that fled the country. All subversives who left and now practice prostitution to make a living."

Ketty's eyes flashed with rage. "My daughter is not a prostitute," she sputtered. "My daughter is not in Mexico."

Azucena burst from her chair and began to shout. Alarmed by the ruckus, other ministry employees charged into the office to see what was happening. "We aren't going to leave the plaza until you tell us where our kids are. We will walk until our legs fall off," Azucena yelled.

Unable to contain herself, María del Rosario added: "Franco is a dictator, he killed thousands of people. But he owned up to it. You are lying! You are taking people away but not admitting it."

Harguindeguy rapped his burly fist on the table in front of him. "This meeting," he bellowed, "is over!"

A month later, news broke that Videla would be receiving a visit from Terence Todman, the US assistant secretary of state for inter-American affairs. Reports of the junta's brutality had reached the new American president, Jimmy Carter, and Todman planned to press Videla on his handling of human rights. Hoping to share their stories with the diplomat, the Madres decided to swarm the Casa Rosada to catch his attention.

On the day of Todman's arrival, the mothers stood near the pink presidential palace, waiting in near silence. When a fleet of cars pulled up and Todman stepped out, dressed in a dark blue suit and wide tie, they began to shout. The assistant secretary only craned his head curiously toward the women before disappearing inside the Casa Rosada, but the cries of the Madres attracted the attention of foreign journalists who had arrived to cover the visit. As plainclothes and uniformed police officers surveilled the scene, the reporters approached the women. Whether out of complicity or fear, Argentine news-papers had steered clear of the mothers—and most other stories that might ruffle the military government. Around thirty-five reporters had disappeared over the previous four years, and just a few months earlier, twenty men with machine guns slung over their shoulders had seized Jacobo Timerman, a prominent newspaper publisher, from his apartment. Foreign journalists, however, could afford to be bolder.

One showed particular interest: American Sally Chardy of NBC Radio. Short and slight, in her early twenties, Chardy dashed from mother to mother—capturing their testimony with a handheld cassette recorder and scribbling in her reporter's notebook—until a young man dressed in a pressed khaki suit sidled up behind her and demanded her passport. She handed over the navy booklet without resistance and the man dropped it into his pocket. Then he swiped her recorder and barked that he was tak-ing her to the police station.

Azucena and the other Madres were not about to let Chardy get hauled off. With her sturdy arms, Azucena grabbed the undercover cop by the la-pels and began shaking him. A mob of other mothers surrounded him and hoisted him above their heads like rowdy fans at a rock concert. As he flopped and flailed, one woman grabbed his testicles and squeezed. Hard. Another snatched back the recorder and passport and hailed a taxi for Chardy, in-structing the driver to rush her to the American embassy. Perhaps due to embarrassment—or a desire to avoid a scene while Todman sat inside with Videla—the other police in the plaza made no attempt to arrest the women, who had surprised even themselves with their audacity.

The next morning, the *Buenos Aires Herald*, an English-language news-paper in Argentina, gave the Madres their front-page debut: "Plaza Mayo Mothers Protect U.S. Newswoman," the headline read. "Members of the group of mothers say they do not wish to harm the image of the country," the article continued, "but are desperate for news about their children, who have all vanished without trace after being 'detained' by groups of armed men claiming some official connection." The fact that the paper's editor, Robert Cox, and many of its journalists had foreign passports, paired with the team's courage, meant that the *Herald* published pieces that other Argentine outlets wouldn't dare to. "It was an honor to scream when everybody else held silence," Cox would say later. Staring at the newsprint, one mother reflected that she did not exactly feel joy—joy was something consigned to her past life. But the Madres couldn't help but feel pride, and just a dash of hope.

The police were not so sanguine. At first, the mothers of the plaza had merely been an annoyance. "Las Locas," they called them. The crazy women. Now they were an embarrassment, perhaps even a threat. Three days after the mothers humiliated the plainclothes officer, cops again showed up at their regular Thursday march, which had swelled to several hundred. It was a brisk winter day and the women wore overcoats and scarves. Whereas usually the police had just watched menacingly from the sidelines, this time they forced their way into the flock of women, commanding them to disperse.

"Señoras, tienen que circular," they said. You have to move along.

The women stood their ground. They were gathered only to talk about their problems, without bothering anyone, Azucena insisted. The officers replied that groups of more than two were banned, and again demanded that they move.

"Fine," one mother recalled Azucena saying, to the surprise of the women shivering behind her. They had never known her to back down from a fight. Then she hooked her arm through the arm of the woman next to her. "We'll move two by two, in a line, without stopping, without meeting. But we are not leaving the plaza." The pairs of women began circling the bronze monument of founding father Manuel Belgrano, close enough to the front entrance of the Casa Rosada that Videla's guards could have spat at them.

The following week—on August 25—the police were ready. As the Madres reenacted their new tradition of marching around the Plaza de Mayo in pairs, a horde of cops encircled the women and ordered them to disband. They dragged about fifteen Madres into their patrol cars and took them to the police station. After another march, the police commandeered five *colectivos* and filled them with Madres. (They halted the buses, unloaded their terrified passengers, and shoved the Madres in.) When they arrived at the police station, the buses' floors were blanketed in tiny bits of white paper. The Madres had shredded anything in their pocket-books they thought might be compromising.

In both instances, the women were released, but the message was clear: mothers or not, the junta would not hesitate to punish them.

Around this time, Azucena Villaflor's husband, a fierce traditionalist who "wanted his wife to be at home at all times," reached a breaking point. He was frustrated by her absences and feared for her safety. One evening, Azucena had returned home to find Pedro waiting for her in an armchair in their dimly lit living room. "Basta, Azucena!" he said, exhausted. Enough! "If you keep searching for Néstor, I'm leaving."

Azucena stared at him evenly, then replied, "Want me to pack your suitcase?"

Azucena and the Madres were more determined than ever. As time went on, the Madres had figured that the more they could make their plight known, the safer they would be. While the junta was not shy about abducting people in broad daylight, wrestling them off the street and into Ford Falcons, they still tried to avoid drawing too much attention to their actions. The mothers believed their best hope for finding their children—and for surviving themselves—was to make themselves as visible as possible. The more people were paying attention to them, the more pressure the junta would feel to explain where their children were. The greater their ranks, the harder they would be to disappear.

To strategize, the most stalwart core of mothers got together at Las Violetas, an elegant café with stained glass windows, Italian marble floors, and Parisian furniture. As waiters in white jackets flitted about with trays of rich chocotorta and delicate petits fours, Azucena suggested that the mothers join the next pilgrimage to Luján, an annual Catholic procession to a basilica northwest of Buenos Aires. The ban on groups meant there were few large gatherings anymore, but as a religious event, the Luján pilgrimage was exempt. Hundreds of thousands of pious Argentines were expected to join, trekking thirty-seven miles from Buenos Aires to Luján to pay their respects to a seventeenth-century statue of the Virgin Mary inside the basilica.

"We have to wear something that can be spotted from far away so we can find each other," one normally shy woman piped up as the others sipped coffees from small ceramic cups. "A kerchief on our heads, for example."

"Better still, a cloth diaper," riffed another. "It looks like a kerchief, but it'll make us feel better, closer to our children." The group agreed—it was worth a try.

On the day of the march, in early October, the women tied white cloth diapers over their hair and set off for Luján from various starting points around Buenos Aires. As they padded along Ruta 7, leaving behind the bustling streets of Buenos Aires for flat green fields dotted with scrubby trees, people approached the women curiously. "Are you nuns?" they asked, eyeing the white diapers.

"No, we are the Mothers of the Plaza de Mayo," they responded. "We are looking for our stolen children."

The people stared, eyes wide with confusion and fear, then slipped back into the crowd. It was risky to be associated with anyone linked to the disappeared.

Finally, late in the afternoon, the women reached the plaza in front of the Luján basilica. Exhausted, several mothers held up a sign with black-and-white photos of their children, unwrinkled and smiling, frozen in time.

They approached the basilica's priest to receive communion of wine and bread. But when one mother shared that she would be accepting the offering on behalf of her disappeared son, the priest refused. There were soldiers watching.

After the journey to Luján, the Madres' circle continued growing larger and larger with each passing Thursday. Still marching in pairs, the group had begun tracing larger paths around the Pirámide de Mayo. The towering white monument rose from the plaza's very center; they would be impossible to miss. María Eugenia Ponce de Bianco, a dark-haired, fifty-three-year-old woman from the north of Argentina with a voracious curiosity about history, the economy, and poetry, became a fixture of the scene, as did Esther Ballestrino de Careaga, a fifty-nine-year-old with a warm smile. For a time, María (known as Mary) had belonged to the Communist Party, but she abandoned it when her daughter, Alicia, a philosophy student active in the Montoneros, was dragged from her house just outside Buenos Aires shortly after Videla's coup. Esther had moved to Argentina from Paraguay, where she had earned a doctorate in biochemistry and helped found the country's feminist movement.

Earlier in the year, the military had snatched her sixteen-year-old daughter, Ana María, who was three months pregnant, and brought her to a clandestine torture facility, where she was doused with freezing water, burnt with cigarettes, and electrocuted. After Esther spoke to the *Buenos Aires Herald* about her daughter's case, Ana María was released, eventually fleeing to Sweden. Esther, however, had refused to follow her daughter. "My obligation is to be here," she insisted. "I will go on until we find them all."

One chilly Thursday, a young man about the age of the mothers' missing children came to speak with them. He was muscular, with clear blue eyes and blond hair he swept to the side. Despite the crisp weather, he wore a white T-shirt that revealed tanned biceps. The Madres were stunned. Men never participated in the marches; they were clear targets for the police, and the young man would surely be nabbed if he stuck around long.

"You shouldn't be here," the mothers yelped, surrounding him like a brood of hens.

Little did they know, the man had been invited. The previous Sunday he had introduced himself to Azucena at a Mother's Day church service as Gustavo Niño, explaining that his twin brother, Horacio, had disappeared. He couldn't recall his brother's ID number for Azucena to record in her files, so she had instructed him to look it up and bring it to her in the plaza the following Thursday. He had showed up after all, handing Azucena a crumpled chit with his name, Horacio's name, and both of their ID numbers.

Perhaps because he was almost the same age as her son Néstor, Azucena took pity on the young man. She invited him to join the Madres' weekly marches, where he tended to stick close to her. Niño gradually won over many of the other mothers, too, giving them rides in his white Peugeot 504 and standing up to threatening police officers on their behalf. "He always looked a little scared, and we took care of him," one mother would later recall. When Niño complained that he had no place to sleep the night before an early morning protest, Azucena asked her husband if he could stay with their family in Sarandí. "But—you're crazy!" Pedro hissed. "You don't know this person. And you're going to bring him home? You have an adolescent daughter!" He didn't like Niño. It was unnerving how he attached himself to Azucena like a barnacle.

13

The Grandmothers

November–December 1977

Shortly after Terence Todman's visit to Buenos Aires, Videla met with President Jimmy Carter while visiting Washington, DC, to witness the signing of the Panama Canal treaties. Carter had campaigned to electoral victory on a platform of promoting justice and morality across the globe—"Because we are free," he proclaimed in his inaugural address from the United States Capitol, "we can never be indifferent to the fate of freedom elsewhere"—and he was adamant that human rights abuses perpetrated by American allies could not be ignored.

During their meeting, when Carter pressed Videla on reports of torture and disappearances in Argentina, the general ardently defended the junta's actions, citing a need to protect his nation against extremism: "Those who recognized that man was created in God's image must recognize his dignity as an individual," read a US government memo summarizing Videla's response. "Terrorists wanted to change that view of man, and Argentina had faced what amounted to a war over the issue." As a military man himself, Videla continued, Carter should know that all wars cause collateral damage. Suggesting that Argentina had nothing to hide, the general invited Carter to send his secretary of state, Cyrus Vance, to visit the country that November. Carter agreed.

When news of the invitation was made public, the Madres rushed to prepare. They had tried and failed to get Terence Todman's attention in August;

they would not let this new opportunity slip away. The women compiled folders with information about their individual cases to turn over to Vance. Inside, they enclosed photos of their sons and daughters, as well as testimony describing what had happened to them. Among the women hurrying to put together her dossier was a soft-spoken art history teacher with short hair and a predilection for pearl earrings. Inside, she placed not only photos of her son and daughter-in-law, but also their infant daughter—her granddaughter, who had gone missing the year before. On November 24, 1976, María Isabel Chorobik de Mariani, known as Chicha, had been home in La Plata, knitting, when, like much of the city, she heard the reverberations of bombs and the crack of the bullets in the distance. The next morning, she found out the sounds had come from the house her son, Daniel, shared with her daughter-in-law, Diana, and her three-month-old granddaughter, Clara Anahí.

Diana Teruggi and Daniel Mariani had operated a business making pickled rabbit. At least, that's what their neighbors thought. A false wall on their home's patio, however, hid the evidence of an entirely different endeavor: four brand-new printing presses for a Montoneros publication called *Evita Montonera*. Recently, the presses had run off an issue revealing the existence of death flights and clandestine torture centers; a month later, two hundred ground forces had surrounded the house as helicopters and airplanes droned overhead, strafing it with bullets and dropping bombs on its roof. Daniel happened to be out of the house that day, but Diana and several *compañeros* who had been inside were killed. Before they died, someone had thought to tuck Clara Anahí in the home's smooth white bathtub. After the gunfire faded into a heavy quiet, a witness described seeing an officer carry the infant out of the rubble alive, swaddled in a blanket. The officer asked his superior, General Ramón Camps, the merciless head of the Buenos Aires Provincial Police, what to do with the child. Camps nodded toward the back seat of one of the patrol cars, signaling for the man to put her there to be driven away.

After that day, even Chicha's dearest friends began steering clear of her, bolting to the other side of the street if they saw her coming. Daniel, she had found out, was still alive, but the security forces were on his heels. Once, they showed up at Chicha's house, holding her captive for a few hours while they searched it. Defiant, Chicha told them: "If you kill me, it doesn't matter, you already killed my whole family." Then, in August of 1977, she received the call she'd been fearing: Daniel, too, had been slain.

Chicha had been feverishly looking for her granddaughter, but no one in the military barracks, hospitals, and police stations she visited could, or would, tell her a thing. Now Clara Anahí was all Chicha had left. Finally, after months of hopeless searching, a woman working at a juvenile court felt sorry for Chicha, quietly sliding her the address for another grandmother in her situation. "You're very alone, señora," she said.

One morning soon thereafter, Chicha knocked on the door associated with the address. A tall, slender woman with clear blue eyes greeted her, dressed in a pink bathrobe and hair curlers. Her name was Alicia Zubasnabar de De la Cuadra, though, coincidentally, she went by Licha. She clearly hadn't been expecting company, but ushered Chicha inside all the same. The women talked for hours, sharing their ghastly stories. Licha had been especially battered by tragedy. In 1976, Licha's son was abducted; the following year, in February 1977, Licha's son-in-law and pregnant daughter had also been taken. Recently, she told Chicha, she had connected with other mothers whose children had been disappeared in the Plaza de Mayo. Some of the women were missing grandchildren, too. She invited Chicha to join them in Buenos Aires for Cyrus Vance's state visit, instructing her to bring a white handkerchief, which many of the mothers had started wearing on their heads instead of diapers, so as not to lose or sully one of the only mementos they had of their children, and a written record of her case. Chicha compiled a small stack of papers containing testimony about her granddaughter's disappearance. On her handkerchief, she sewed a photo of Clara Anahí, with her chubby cheeks, shock of dark hair, and dimply knuckles.

On Monday, November 21, 1977, Chicha and one hundred other mothers who had met for months in the Plaza de Mayo gathered instead in Plaza San Martín, the same Retiro park where hippies had loitered during the Onganía era. Before he met with President Videla, Vance was scheduled to appear there to lay a wreath on the red granite base of the plaza's namesake monument to José de San Martín, Argentina's liberator from Spain—a traditional diplomatic gesture to mark the start of a state visit. In the morning hours, men in fine Italian suits with copies of the day's *La Nación* tucked into their briefcases strolled beneath the tipa, jacaranda, and palo borracho trees toward the glimmering high rises of Microcentro, the business district of Buenos Aires. The Madres could easily have passed as their well-heeled housewives, with pressed blouses tucked into long skirts, prim purses, and umbrellas hooked over their arms—it had looked like rain that morning. Their hair was neatly styled and their heels were of a sensible height. (Months of confrontations with Argentine police had taught them the value of a speedy getaway.)

Before long, a limousine pulled up. Vance, lanky, with placid blue eyes, an affable face, and a pinstriped suit, emerged, still looking every bit the Connecticut prep school prefect he had once been. He strode down the red carpet that had been laid out for him and approached the monument with a waist-high corona of white flowers. Once he'd climbed to the top step, he leaned the wreath against the statue's base and turned to pose for the legion of photographers assembled in the plaza.

The square crawled with a sea of guards—a mix of American secret service, recognizable by their garishly wide ties, and Argentine military officers toting FAL rifles. It was terrifying for the Madres to stand so close to members of the very forces they suspected were responsible for their children's abductions, but they did not falter. As press cameras furiously clicked at the US secretary of state, the women fished white handkerchiefs out of their purses and tied them onto their heads or waved them like little flags.

"Vance! Vance! Ayúdenos, ayúdenos!" Help us, help us! They wailed. The cameras turned to capture their contorted, tear-streaked faces.

Vance smiled and waved as his security team shuffled him back toward the limousine. Unwilling to let the moment go to waste, various Madres plunged through the scrum of guards, dodging bayonets and snarling dogs. Suddenly, they were face to face with the American diplomat. He shot his security detail a look, urging them to practice restraint. The Madres thrust their papers at him, and to their relief, Vance accepted them.

Chicha, however, was too overwhelmed to pass her folder along. As Vance prepared to leave, she stood rooted in place like one of the plaza's tipa trees, her testimony clutched to her chest.

"What? You didn't hand yours over?" a woman next to her asked urgently. It was Azucena Villaflor. She snatched the papers from Chicha's hands and, swerving past helmeted soldiers, extended them to Vance, who had no choice but to receive them before ducking into his limousine. As the car pulled away, three women chased it down. Banging on the thick bulletproof window, they shouted: "Help us find our children!"

While Plaza San Martín emptied out, Chicha and Licha walked to the square's edge to meet with the other women who were missing not only children but grandchildren. Recently, during one of the Madres' Thursday marches in the Plaza de Mayo, a mother named Mirta Acuña de Baravalle had stopped walking and yelled to the others making their circular pilgrimage: "Those of you who have pregnant daughters-in-law or daughters, step aside!" They had arranged to meet after the Vance event. Standing under the violet blooms of a jacaranda tree, Chicha and Licha watched as those grandmothers now approached. Among them was Ketty Aicardi de Neuhaus, one of the three Madres who had met with Harguindeguy back in July. Her daughter, whom the interior minister had intimated might have fled the country to practice prostitution, had been pregnant at the time of her abduction. The other women were María Eugenia Casinelli de García Iruretagoyena, Eva Márquez de Castillo Barrios, Delia Giovanola, Clara Jurado, Leontina Puebla de Pérez, Raquel Radío de Marizcurrena, Vilma Sesarego de Gutiérrez, Haydée Vallino de Lemos, and Mirta Acuña de Baravalle herself.

The women determined that, in addition to attending the Thursday marches, they should continue to gather separately. Unlike the other Madres of the Plaza de Mayo, they were looking for two generations, not one. Through their fruitless visits to orphanages and juvenile courts, they had come to understand that the government was never going to help them. If they were going to find these children, banding together seemed a good place to start. They settled on the name Las Abuelas Argentinas con Nietitos Desaparecidos—the Argentine Grandmothers with Disappeared Little Grandchildren—though it didn't stick for long. Eventually, they would give in to the name that everyone called them anyway: the Abuelas de Plaza de Mayo.

As the holidays approached, there was still no word from either the American or Argentine governments regarding the folders pressed upon Secretary of State Vance. In their frustration and despair, an idea began to spread among the Madres and newly organized Abuelas. If Videla refused to engage with them at the Casa Rosada, perhaps they could force his response by publishing an open letter in the press.

The Madres had successfully published such a message a few months before in *La Prensa*. Now they decided to buy an advertisement in *La Nación*, an even larger newspaper, and write Videla a letter signed by the Madres, Abuelas, and their supporters. They would aim to publish it on December 10, Human Rights Day, in *La Nación*'s Saturday issue. Even if Videla didn't respond, the ad would surely reach tens of thousands of Argentines as they read their papers over *medialunas* and coffee.

Later, the Madres would remember that their initial inquiries to the paper went unanswered. They followed up several times, until, fed up, Azucena and another Madre marched to the newspaper's headquarters and convinced them to relent. Once things were settled, the Madres got to work polishing their message, meeting at apartments around Buenos Aires to collect money to pay for the ad and signatures to display the size of their movement. When they could find priests who were sympathetic to their cause, they gathered in churches, too. Even in such holy environments, they were careful. At the Parroquia Santa María de Betania in the Buenos Aires neighborhood of Abasto, two mothers stood out front, under the building's giant glass cross, gauging whether those who approached were familiar faces or potential infiltrators. They sent those they considered safe to the church's back entrance, where they signed the advertisement with their full names and identity numbers—a remarkable act of boldness—and contributed what money they could.

Another frequent meeting place was the Iglesia de la Santa Cruz, a Gothic-style church in the neighborhood of San Cristóbal. Late in the afternoon of December 8, the day before they planned to deliver the ad to *La Nación*, one group of Madres and Abuelas gathered there among the church's wooden pews: Ketty Neuhaus, Esther Careaga, María Ponce de Bianco, and about fifty others milled about, along with Sister Alice Domon, a French nun who had been supportive of the Madres, and Gustavo Niño, the young man who had been attending the Madres' marches in the Plaza de Mayo. Hundreds of churchgoers had come to celebrate a special mass in honor of the Virgin Mary, providing ample cover. There were so many people that the priests had to open a special room to accommodate everyone.

The Madres did not plan to meet for long that evening—there was little left to discuss. It was just a matter of collecting the last of the money and signatures. But even before they disbanded, Niño seemed anxious to get going. *Where is Azucena?* he repeatedly asked Ketty. His concern was not entirely surprising. The Madres had noticed that at marches and meetings, Niño always seemed to find their de facto leader, affectionately threading his arm through hers. Newcomers often mistook him for her son. But tonight, Ketty told him, Azucena was elsewhere. Niño seemed annoyed by the news, and announced he needed to leave. Before he departed, he kissed Esther Careaga, María Ponce de Bianco, and Sister Alice Domon, the nun, gingerly on the cheek, a customary Argentine farewell.

Money securely in hand, the Madres began to head out as well. But as they exited through the church's tall arched door, leaving behind the stained glass windows depicting Jesus and Mary, a large, mustachioed, blond man on the street suddenly grabbed Esther and shoved her into a waiting car. Other men seized María, Sister Alice, and several other activists who had come to the church to support the Madres, and dragged them toward five Renault 12s and a Ford Falcon double-parked on the street, all of them without license plates. A hefty man punched the women in the stomach so they couldn't scream. Others pinned Sister Alice's arms behind her back and pulled her toward the cars by her hair.

"Why?" shouted María del Rosario de Cerruti as she watched her friends hauled away. "Why?"

"This is a drug operation," the men grunted back.

After the Renaults and Falcon had peeled off, María del Rosario rushed straight to the house where Azucena and other Madres were ironing out the final details of the advertisement. She frantically rang the doorbell. When the other Madres opened up, her face was twisted in panic.

"Se las llevaron, se las llevaron!" she panted. They took them!

Once she had calmed down a little, the other mothers urged her to try to remember who had been taken so they could make a list. It had been so chaotic that it was hard to say. Eventually, they wrote down the names of Esther, María, Sister Alice, and several activists who had supported the Madres. But they were concerned: what about the blond boy, Gustavo Niño? Nobody had seen him after the abductions.

Only much later would the Madres would learn that Gustavo Niño was not, in fact, the grieving brother of a *desaparecido*, but Alfredo Astiz, a naval officer who worked in one of the junta's most brutal task forces: Grupo de Tareas 3.3.2 at the ESMA. His seemingly polite farewell gesture had in fact been a "kiss of death."

The next day, Azucena and the Madres reconvened at the apartment of Eva Castillo Barrios, a Madre and founding member of the Abuelas. Bleary-eyed and shaken, they discussed what to do next. Azucena was firm: despite the horrors of the previous evening, they needed to publish the advertisement, which more than eight hundred Madres, Abuelas, activists, and relatives of the disappeared had signed.

Other Madres protested. "I don't want to continue with this advertisement. Let's go look for our *compañeras*," one begged.

"Our *compañeras* were fighting for this advertisement to be released," Azucena responded. "We are not going to let them down." She understood the risks. As she and a handful of Madres headed back to *La Nación*'s headquarters that afternoon, she asked the women to make her a promise.

"If something happens to me, go on without me."

The rest of the day was full of petty annoyances. As the Madres later recalled, the staff at *La Nación* claimed they couldn't print the advertisement unless its content was typed up first. The Madres raced to one of their husbands' offices, and just before the newspaper's deadline, shoved a typed document at a *La Nación* staffer. Then someone tried to reject the clinking bags of coins and small bills the women intended to pay with, insisting they change them to larger bills before they made the transaction. But the Madres pushed back: money was money. Eventually, the staffer ceded.

"Writing this advertisement is a victory," Azucena told the group outside on the sidewalk afterward. As the Madres prepared to return to their homes, Azucena pressed sheets of paper into each of their hands. "Hagamos un Trato," it read at the top in bold black font. "Let's Make a Deal." It was a poem by Mario Benedetti, an Uruguayan poet whose searing writing and radical politics had made him popular among leftist revolutionaries—and forced him to flee neighboring Uruguay's dictatorship.

It ended: *You know you can always count on me.*

On December 10, Azucena woke early and prepared mate for her husband, Pedro, as she did every morning. Leaving her teenage daughter, Cecilia, sleeping at home, she walked down the street and under the train tracks to buy bread and pastries from her regular baker, Aníbal. On the way back, she stopped at a newspaper kiosk. There it was: the Saturday edition of *La Nación*. She slid eighty pesos across the counter and took the crinkly paper. The cover announced that the cost of living had jumped 9 percent the previous month and heralded Videla's trip to Patagonia in celebration of National Petroleum Day. She flipped to page 19. There, under an advertisement for a polo store hawking leather saddles and mallets, was the Madres' message.

"We only ask for the truth," it read. "We are the expression of the pain of hundreds of MOTHERS AND WIVES OF THE DISAPPEARED. . . . THE TRUTH that we ask for is to know if our *DESAPARECIDOS* ARE ALIVE OR DEAD." Among the 804 names typed under the message were María Ponce de Bianco and Gustavo Niño. (Esther Careaga and Alice Domon, it seemed, had not gotten a chance to sign before they were hauled off.)

The text was a bit smudged in places. Azucena decided she would head home, drop off the pastries for Cecilia, and then pick up another copy along with the ingredients for that day's lunch. Saturdays were for cooking, and after decades of living in Sarandí, she had regular vendors for each ingredient: meat from Chocho, vegetables from Don Sauro, pasta from La Bolognesa, and fish from a little stall beneath the overpass near her house. After lunch, she planned to wash the plates, clean the kitchen, and then take Cecilia to her aunt's house for a long, languid visit, just like she did every weekend.

At home, she poked her head into Cecilia's room and called: "What do you want to eat, honey, meat or fish?"

"Fish," came the groggy reply. It was Cecilia's favorite.

Azucena told Cecilia to go back to sleep and left the house once again. On her way to the fish market, she paused to greet Chocho, offering sheepish apologies for not buying meat from him that day. Then she started to cross Avenida Mitre, the busiest avenue in her neighborhood.

As she stepped onto the grass divider between the avenue's two directions of traffic, seven or eight men with rifles and handguns sprang out of several cars and tackled her. Her neighbors watched, frozen, as Azucena screamed and flailed, trying to fight the men off. But she was just one and they were many. They shoved her into a Ford Falcon and sped off.

A few weeks later, unusually strong winds buffeted Argentina's Atlantic coast and powerful waves pounded the beaches of Buenos Aires Province. Among the detritus washed ashore in Santa Teresita, a beach town four hours south of Buenos Aires, were several corpses. A police doctor called to examine the bodies determined that the cause of their deaths had not been drowning, but "crashing against hard objects after falling from a great height." No one tried to identify the deceased—they were quickly swept to a cemetery forty minutes inland and buried under the soil. On the register, the cemetery employees were instructed to write N.N.—*ningún nombre*, no name.

It would be decades before anyone identified the bodies of Azucena Villaflor, María Ponce de Bianco, and Esther Careaga.

14

A Visit to the Tailor

Late 1978–Early 1979

Rosa Roisinblit was a dedicated reader of *La Nación*, and she had likely paged past the Madres' advertisement when it was published in December 1977. But that was before Patricia was taken, and before Rosa had ever imagined that she might have something in common with the women in the Plaza de Mayo. "I didn't know anything about that," she would say later in reference to the disappearances. "I didn't want to know." Now after several months of searching for Patricia alone, Rosa walked up Avenida Rivadavia, scanning the buildings for the address that Alfredo Galletti had given her at the Permanent Assembly for Human Rights. She knew very little about the group of grandmothers she was going to meet—only that they were looking for their children and grandchildren too, and that Galletti claimed he was going to help them.

Rivadavia was a busy avenue, with people emerging from apartment towers and the mouth of the Línea A subway station. Las Violetas, the sumptuous café where Azucena and the other Madres had sometimes met, sat on the corner, its windows revealing a long case full of cakes and pastries. Rosa could very well be walking straight into a trap, but she thought only of Patricia and her grandchild. The baby would be a few months old already. By now their eyes would be taking in the world with increased sharpness. They might even have smiled their first gummy smile—that is, if Patricia had given birth at all, and if her baby was still alive. Rosa found the right building and rang the buzzer. The door clicked open.

Upstairs, Galletti waved her inside warmly. He and his wife, Elida, had moved into the apartment about a year earlier, but shortly after they unpacked their boxes, their daughter, Liliana, had been abducted while driving with her boyfriend in the countryside. The Gallettis had been home when they found out that she had been taken and they fell to the ground with shock, pressing their mouths against the floor so the neighbors wouldn't hear them scream. The couple hadn't gotten around to decorating much after that; the apartment was merely a place to sleep, until Alfredo got involved in the Permanent Assembly for Human Rights. Then, it became something else: a secret meeting place.

Galletti had gentle, mournful eyes and a penchant for ties with large, geometric patterns. His white hair had begun to recede, and he clasped his hands in front of him when he spoke, revealing long, twig-like wrists. Since Liliana had disappeared, he and Elida had struggled to eat—consuming food felt like a "gift to which [they] had no right." *What was Liliana eating?* they wondered. *What had become of her?* Even after her disappearance, Elida baked Liliana a cake on her birthday, just in case she returned in time. At night, she and Alfredo stared at photos of their daughter, thinking about her love of horoscopes and her terrible, off-key singing, which she proudly defended as her "style."

The other grandmothers had already arrived, and Galletti introduced Rosa around the room. There was Chicha, who was looking for Clara Anahí; Licha, who was searching for her grandchild; and Estela de Carlotto, a polished schoolteacher whose daughter, Laura, had been abducted by the military a year before Patricia. Unlike the rest of the women, Estela knew that Laura was dead. The police had claimed she died in a shootout, but when Estela had managed to recover her bullet-ridden body, she had seen that several of the shots—at Laura's face and stomach—had been fired from point-blank range.

Later, Rosa would not remember which other grandmothers she met that day, though Delia Giovanola was a regular at such gatherings. Delia had joined the Madres early, before Azucena Villaflor disappeared, and had worked with the grandmothers from the beginning. Before tragedy had darkened her life, she had been a spirited prankster. Thin and attractive, she smoked like a taxi driver; her friends called her "la tía loca," the crazy aunt. In October 1976, Delia's son, Jorge, had been abducted with his wife, Stella Maris Montesano, who was eight months pregnant, and in the years since, Delia had submitted more than forty writs of habeas corpus, to no avail. At first, she had feared that working with the Madres would be another "waste of time," but she quickly changed her mind when she met them. The Plaza de Mayo seemed to take individual grief and transform it into collective determination. Together, the women were bold enough to stomp into the offices of military officers or shove folders in the face of the world's most powerful diplomat. Even after the junta tried to crush them, disappearing three of their leaders, they had persisted. The Monday after Azucena was taken, the Madres and Abuelas had charged into the Ministry of the Interior to file a writ of habeas corpus on her behalf. That Thursday, they were back in the plaza, crying silently as they made their rounds arm in arm.

Rosa began to tell the women her story. As she spoke, Galletti scribbled down notes for the complaint that he planned to send to the Organization of American States. The other women in the room would later recall that she looked completely disoriented, "like a wet little chicken." But vibrating through the room was a feeling Rosa hadn't experienced in a long while: solidarity.

Rosa immediately threw herself into working with the Abuelas. Doing so did not magically ease her worry or pain, but it did provide her with a certain measure of peace. "I wanted to fight, I wanted to do something, I was in a rush to do something," Rosa would say later. The Abuelas' stories were like individual pieces of a puzzle. By comparing where they overlapped and where they diverged, they could reach a better understanding of what was happening. They knew that some of their children had been killed by the junta after giving birth, but perhaps others were still alive. Through the quiet testimony of survivors released by the junta, some women knew for certain that their grandchildren had been born.

Rallying behind the mission "to look for our grandchildren without forgetting our children," the Abuelas gathered in the Plaza de Mayo on Thursdays to march alongside the Madres, their pockets full of marbles to chuck at the stallions of the mounted soldiers if they got too close. Afterward, the group migrated to one of the area's many cafés, favoring those with two entrances so they could slip out the back if they saw the black combat boots of a military man or police officer clomp in the front.

The disappearance of Azucena Villaflor and the other Madres still cast a pall of terror over the women, and the Abuelas had developed a stringent system of precautions. When speaking on the phone, they couched their conversation in deceptively cheery code. *Cachorros* (puppies), *cuadernos* (notebooks), and *flores* (flowers) referred to their missing grandchildren; *las jóvenes* (the girls) were the Madres, whereas the Abuelas were *las viejas* (old ladies) or *las tías viejas* (old aunties). *Ir a la modista* (to visit the tailor) was used to schedule a gathering. At least at first, they avoided meeting in the same place each week, instead rotating between different cafés around Buenos Aires. They met at El Molino, just a few blocks from Rosa's apartment on Riobamba, and under the glimmering stained glass windows of Las Violetas. Sometimes they laid knitting needles on the table alongside their coffee cups. A group of little old ladies comparing cabling over chocotorta would hardly arouse suspicion, they reasoned—particularly not when the stitching was as expert as Rosa's or Chicha's. Other times they feigned birthday celebrations, carrying flowers and empty boxes tied up with ribbon to complete the picture. As they sang "que lo cumplas feliz!" in unison, they quietly passed around whatever document or letter they were working on for all the women to sign. When they were sure no one was listening, they plotted visits to orphanages and family courts and planned trips to registries where they might find relevant birth certificates. As their numbers swelled, however, such public meetings became challenging. A birthday party of twelve elderly women was reasonably likely to go unnoticed. A celebration with thirty women, less so.

They began gathering in their own apartments during the afternoon siesta, when the caretakers of Buenos Aires apartment buildings retreated from their lobbies to eat lunch or nap in their quarters. The Abuelas entered the residences individually or in pairs rather than all at once, avoiding clanking elevators in favor of the stairs; the smokers of the group abstained from their cigarettes, lest the smell alert the neighbors to their presence. Once tucked safely inside an apartment, they drew the curtains and spoke in whispers. The women hailed from a wide range of economic circumstances, and not all of them could afford to pay for lunch during their meetings. Chicha chipped in her husband's pension, and Julia Grandi, wife of the esteemed artist Mario Darío Grandi, sold some of her late husband's paintings, pooling the money to ensure everyone could eat. One of Grandi's relatives later recalled that, on the days the gaggle of grandmothers invaded their family art gallery, the tables swelled with an incongruous mix of habeas corpus petitions, tea sandwiches, photos of wide-eyed infants, and delicate cakes.

The Abuelas' meetings were long and intense, partially serving as group therapy sessions, where members could commiserate over rejected habeas corpus petitions or government officials who had lied to their faces. Mostly, though, the women strategized. Licha, whom many credited with having launched the Abuelas, was named president of the organization, while Chicha was appointed its executive secretary. One Abuela was put in charge of gathering photographs—those that existed—of their missing grandchildren, and another compiled a log of the Abuelas' visits to family courts. Chicha was one of the few Abuelas to own a typewriter—a green Royal so old and decrepit the military had ignored it when they raided her home—and so she was placed in charge of correspondence, which she typed out with just one index finger, to the giggles of the other grandmothers. Their first missive, to Pope Paul VI, had read: "We are some of the Argentine women who have suffered the disappearance or death of their children in these past two years, and to this piercing maternal pain, we have also been deprived of the children of our children, many of them newborns or several months old." They sent it by the regular Correo Argentino, just as one might casually send a postcard; they didn't know how else to reach him. Memos to ambassadors, journalists, the United Nations, the Red Cross, and other human rights organizations followed. Replies were rare.

Soon, the Abuelas were swimming in so much paperwork that gathering in the same place felt less risky than the danger of losing track of their files. Once a week, they borrowed a small room in an apartment where the Madres had started holding meetings, a twenty-five-minute walk from the Plaza de Mayo. Often, though, the Abuelas' work brought them out of the office, visiting orphanages, cemeteries, courthouses, and anywhere else they might be able to glean clues about their grandchildren. The judges were generally unhelpful, and sometimes outright hostile. The women would later remember one judge as being particularly cruel. An attractive blond in her forties, Marta Delia Pons oversaw the family court in Lomas de Zamora, a southern suburb of Buenos Aires. "Señoras," the Abuelas recall Pons saying in one of their first meetings, "I am personally convinced that your children were terrorists. For me, a terrorist is akin to a murderer. And I don't intend to return children to murderers."

Slowly, though, the Abuelas began to attract supporters. People nervously approached them during their Thursday marches, slipping them scraps of paper with names or addresses before hurrying away. One person might report that their neighbor had suddenly appeared with a chubby infant when her stomach had always been as flat as Argentina's grasslands. Another knew someone who had undergone a hysterectomy but was suddenly parading around a beautiful baby. Perhaps the couples had legally adopted these children. But perhaps they hadn't.

The Abuelas chased down every lead. Had their grandchildren been lost in the chaos of the abductions? Taken from their mothers and given away? Sent across the border? Killed? Were they being raised somewhere in secret? To seek the answers, the women got creative. When one case required the name of a recently deceased individual who might be connected to one of their grandchildren, three Abuelas traveled to Chacarita Cemetery, a famous graveyard in a working-class neighborhood of Buenos Aires. They figured the cemetery's guards might be suspicious of old women wandering around, dry-eyed, while scribbling notes on legal pads, so instead they posed as mourners. Clutching a bouquet of tastefully somber flowers, they walked under the Greek-style frieze at the entrance and wove among the mausoleums. One of them housed none other than General Juan Domingo Perón, whose embalmed corpse lay inside a coffin protected by seven centimeters of bulletproof glass and four locks, lest the military try to steal it as they had stolen Evita's. When the Abuelas managed to find the freshly sealed tomb of the person in question, they knelt as though praying until they determined the name, which they slyly recorded using a pen hidden among the blooms they carried.

Some cases required bolder performances. To confirm that a child lived in a certain home, the Abuelas pretended to be saleswomen promoting a new baby product. As the door swung open, they erupted into a lively chorus—"Is there a baby in this house?"—and proceeded to plug the benefits of the supposed appliance or cream. But their eyes were always trained past the homeowner and into the entryway beyond. *Were there tiny shoes stored by the door, or a stroller?* They got pedicures to extract information from salon owners who had also polished the toenails of suspected kidnappers and sought jobs as maids at homes that required more time to properly investigate, snooping around as they cleaned the windows until they sparkled. One grandmother even had herself committed to a psychiatric hospital in the interest of data gathering.

For months, their furious detective work yielded nothing. Then, in July 1979, incredible news reached the Abuelas from over the border. In the hardscrabble Chilean port city of Valparaíso, a small Brazilian nonprofit had helped locate two Uruguayan siblings who had been abducted with their mother outside Buenos Aires in 1976. Their names were Anatole Boris and Victoria Eva Julien Grisonas.

15

Operation Condor

1979

The Abuelas were overcome with joyous disbelief. They had previously been in contact with Anatole and Victoria's paternal grandmother, Angélica Cáceres de Julien, who had sought their help in looking for the children. When they had disappeared with her son and daughter-in-law, Angélica had rushed from her home in Montevideo to Buenos Aires, where she spent several months. "Sometimes I would travel by bus and think that I glimpsed my son on the street," she would later remember. "I would jump off and race through the streets, searching, always searching." She wrote letters to the queen of England, the king of Spain, and the president of France and scoured parks and orphanages for her grandchildren. Now, she had found them, giving new strength to the hope that had driven the Abuelas since their formation: perhaps their grandchildren were alive after all.

When the Abuelas' initial shock wore off, however, concerns and questions crept in. *Uruguayans abducted from Argentina found in Chile by a Brazilian group?* Their investigations within Argentina were difficult and risky enough as is. Could it really be that their grandchildren might be scattered across South America?

None of them could have known the full extent of the horror engulfing the region at that time. Though the Abuelas had the unfortunate distinction of being the only grandparents working together to find their missing grandchildren, they were not the only South Americans who suspected the state had taken their loved ones. Throughout the 1970s, the continent had echoed with whispers of torture, rape, and murder, from São Paulo to Asunción to La Paz. Around the time General Videla stalked the hallways of the Casa Rosada, dictators also occupied the presidential palaces in Bolivia, Uruguay, Brazil, Paraguay, Chile, Ecuador, and Peru. While Videla's junta took the scale of such terror to new levels, Argentina's armed forces were not alone in using electrified prods to shock people on their gums and genitals, or pushing them alive out of airplanes and helicopters.

That multiple Latin American dictatorships employed such gruesome methods at the same time was not a case of coincidence or mere mimicry; it was carefully coordinated. In November 1975, the dictatorships of Argentina, Chile, Bolivia, Paraguay, and Uruguay had quietly committed to a transnational crusade against "leftists, communists, and Marxists" that became known as Operation Condor, after the carrion-eating bird that soars high above the Andes. Brazil had joined the following year and Ecuador and Peru signed on in 1978. For decades, several of the regimes had received backing from the United States, which saw them as allies in the Cold War campaign against communism. In 1964, Lyndon Johnson's ambassador to Brazil urged the US government to send weapons to support a military coup that displaced a left-wing president, and that same year, Johnson's administration supported a similar uprising in Bolivia. But Henry Kissinger, who would eventually serve as secretary of state under Presidents Richard Nixon and Gerald Ford, was even more forceful in his support of Latin American regime change. In 1970, when he was Nixon's national security advisor, Kissinger backed the assassination of a prominent Chilean general in hopes of facilitating a military takeover of socialist president Salvador Allende; the plot failed, but later, when General Augusto Pinochet did finally topple Allende in 1973, Kissinger fervently defended him. Soon after the coup, America's ambassador to Chile complained that Pinochet was torturing his own citizens. In a handwritten note scribbled in the margins of a diplomatic

cable, Kissinger dismissed the ambassador's commentary with a swift ad-
monition: "cut out the political science lectures."

Condor masqueraded as an intelligence-sharing mission—and indeed,
the participating countries had compiled an extensive database of individuals involved in leftist movements, unions, and left-wing political parties.
But the collaboration between participating countries went much further
than investigations. The governments also identified shared targets and dispatched joint security teams to conduct abductions and extrajudicial killings. Most operations took place on Argentine soil, where political refugees
fleeing Chile and Uruguay, whose dictatorships had begun earlier, sought
safety. After the Argentine military launched its own coup in 1976, the
country became, in one description, "a hunting ground."

When rumors of the potential coup in Argentina had begun to rattle
around diplomatic circles, some in the American government "discreetly
and through third parties" suggested that the military dictatorship be formally recognized. Once the junta took over, the US Congress approved a
request from Kissinger to send it $49 million in military assistance. Even
as news of torture, rape, and kidnappings began to emerge, the secretary of
state was unflaggingly sanguine. "We want you to succeed," Kissinger told
an Argentine official a few months after the coup. "If there are things that
have to be done, you should do them quickly."

It would eventually become clear that Kissinger and other top officials
were fully aware of what the military was up to in Argentina and throughout the Condor countries. In fact, the United States had helped author the
playbook they followed. Several top Argentine generals were alumni of the
School of the Americas, an American military academy located in Panama
until 1984, which trained Latin American soldiers to fight communism.
(Among the graduates was Roberto Viola, one of Videla's closest confidants.)
Decades later, the Defense Department released documents showing the
school had used US Army manuals that encouraged counterintelligence officers to appeal to "fear, payment of bounties for enemy dead, beatings, false
imprisonment, executions and the use of truth serum." The Condor countries
exchanged intelligence with the FBI, CIA, and other foreign agencies; in one

case in 1975, the FBI actively investigated a leftist wanted by the Chilean secret police. Condor's members communicated most frequently through a protected telex system called "Condortel," which relied on encryption devices manufactured by a company that was secretly owned by the CIA. For a time, the Condor governments also utilized a US military radio network whose main transmitter was situated inside the Panama Canal Zone, a US concession until 1979.

Among those targeted by the Condor network were Mario Roger Julien and Victoria Grisonas, the parents of the children who had just been found in Chile. In the early 1970s, the couple had fled Montevideo, where they had been pursued by local forces for their involvement in the leftist political movement. To avoid capture, the two holed up with their young son, Anatole, in San Martín, a suburb outside of Buenos Aires, where their daughter, Victoria Eva, was born. With the help of Argentine intelligence provided in the context of Operation Condor, the couple was tracked, and on September 26, 1976, a mix of Argentine and Uruguayan security forces used two armored cars to cut off traffic on the street outside the house where the family was living. As bullets started to fly overhead, Mario stuck four-year-old Anatole and sixteen-month-old Victoria Eva in the bathtub to protect them, and then tried to slip out the back door, where he was ambushed by heavily armed authorities, who shot him dead. Four men dragged Victoria to the street by her arms and legs, where they savagely beat her in full view of her children, who had been carried outside, before shoving her into the trunk of a police car.

The toddlers were also taken, shuffled between clandestine prisons in Buenos Aires and Montevideo. Ultimately, the children were sent to Chile on a small aircraft. Having never flown before, four-year-old Anatole asked to enter the cockpit, and he would later recall staring down at the snowy tips of the Andes through the windshield. On December 22, a black car with tinted windows transported the siblings to a plaza in the Chilean port city of Valparaíso. Before they knew what was happening, they were pushed onto the pavement and the car sped off, leaving them alone.

In the center of the plaza, there was a children's park with rides. The park's owner spotted the neatly dressed children and assumed someone would return for them. He lifted them onto the carousel and let them ride its horses around for free. After a few hours, when no one had come to pick them up, the man grew concerned and called the Carabineros, Chile's military police force. The children were taken to an orphanage, where they lived for several months before they were adopted by a dentist, Jesús Larrabeiti, and his wife, Silvia Yáñez, who were oblivious to their awful odyssey. Eventually, news of Victoria Eva and Anatole's whereabouts wove its way through a serpentine network of contacts to the Committee for the Defense of Human Rights in the Countries of the Southern Cone, or CLAMOR, a small Brazilian ecumenical group dedicated to investigating and denouncing state terrorism in South America. CLAMOR, in turn, alerted Angélica Cáceres de Julien.

When Angélica heard the news, she raced to Chile with every intention of bringing Anatole and Victoria Eva home with her. "If my son and daughter-in-law don't appear, [the children] are all I have left of them," she said at the time. A large group accompanied her, including representatives of CLAMOR and UNICEF, who wanted to be present for the historic reunion, as well as lawyers Angélica had retained to help her fight the Larrabeitis, who didn't want to let Anatole and Victoria go. "We fell in love with them at first sight, and now they are our children and our reason for living," the couple said.

Seeing the children again after nearly three years was a shock. Victoria Eva—Vicky—looked exactly like her mother; Anatole had his father's almond-shaped eyes. Angélica yearned to hug them, but the psychologists who prepared her for the meeting had urged her to maintain her composure, and so she sat down on the couch to speak with the children from a distance. Soon, they were climbing over her, drawing her pictures.

As she spent more time with her grandchildren, Angélica's feelings began to change. Anatole was still haunted by the gory day he was snatched. He had seen his mother dragged across the pavement and his father shot. The Larrabeitis were dedicated parents who had not known Anatole and Victoria Eva were stolen. Now the children knew the truth, and maybe that was enough. Though it shattered her, Angélica ultimately agreed to leave her grandchildren with the couple who had adopted them, promising to visit often.

"I couldn't make them suffer again," she said.

Upon hearing that the Julien Grisonas siblings had been found, the Abuelas were desperate to learn more about CLAMOR and whether it had any other leads. But they couldn't call the group by phone; these matters were far too sensitive, and besides, they had no idea whom to call. They knew only that CLAMOR operated out of São Paulo. Using donations and money from Chicha's husband's pension, the Abuelas bought two tickets for Chicha and Licha to fly to Brazil and track down the organization's founders. They traveled with just one tip: an activist in Buenos Aires had given them the information for a Brazilian friar who was immersed in the country's human rights community. (After initially backing Brazil's coup, Brazil's Catholic Church—unlike Argentina's—had eventually opposed the dictatorships of South America and supported the groups that had sprouted in resistance to them.) Armed with the friar's contact, the two women packed their suitcases. Chicha made sure to save a little space in hers. She wanted to bring back a doll for Clara Anahí.

São Paulo is the largest city in South America, and as Chicha and Licha's plane hurtled toward Congonhas airport, it passed over a seemingly interminable parade of skyscrapers. The city lacked Buenos Aires' charm; it was known as a place to work rather than enjoy—"Earn in São Paulo so you can spend in Rio" went one popular adage. Neither Chicha nor Licha had visited the immense and intimidating city, nor did they know any Portuguese. When they landed and emerged from the terminal, heavy rain pelted the sidewalk. They found an open taxi, a Volkswagen, and dove inside, brushing water from their hair and clothes. They managed to communicate that they wished to be taken to a hotel.

Which one? the driver inquired in Portuguese. Whichever, they gestured.

They wove in and out of traffic as rain pounded the windshield. They stopped at a few hotels, but all of them were full. As it grew dark outside, the taxi driver started to get frustrated, and the women worried that they would not find a place to spend the night. Then, while the taxi was stopped at a red light, Chicha spotted a hotel through the rain-streaked window and asked the driver to drop them there. When he shook his head vigorously, she got insistent. Chicha had a voice like silk, but it could turn firm and stony when she wanted something. His patience frayed, the taxi driver swept his hand crabbily at the hotel, motioning for the grandmothers to get out. Inside, the man behind the reception desk gave them a worried once-over before informing them they could not stay, but with insistent Spanish and emotive hand gestures, the women wore him down also, and hotel staff led them to a room.

The door creaked open to reveal a strange sight. Most of the walls were covered in red and wine-colored tapestries, except for one that boasted a huge mirror. The bed was round. Next to it, on the nightstand, was a button. Chicha pressed it unthinkingly. Suddenly loud music blared from speakers and colored lights danced around the room. She scrambled to push the button again, and the music stopped. What *was* this place? Too tired to investigate, Licha lay down on the round bed and Chicha climbed into a small cot she found nearby. The women fell into a deep sleep.

The next morning, they met with Fray Alamino, the friar they were hoping could connect them to CLAMOR's founders. "What house are you staying in?" he asked, making conversation. "Oh, no, we're in a hotel," Chicha corrected him. When he asked which one, the women handed over a card they had taken from the reception desk. The friar's face turned bright red, and he immediately ordered his secretary to go pick up their things. The Abuelas had slept at a "love motel," usually rented by the hour and reserved for much less serious business than what had brought them to São Paulo, he explained with clear discomfort. Chicha and Licha laughed and laughed, harder than they had in years.

The friar ultimately connected the Abuelas to Jaime Wright, a tall, round-faced son of American missionaries who had followed his parents into Brazil's Presbyterian Church. His brother Paulo, a sociologist who had worked as a labor organizer and local politician in the Brazilian state of Santa Catarina, had been disappeared by the Brazilian army in 1973. As Catholic dioceses in neighboring countries like Argentina ignored— or justified—the military's abuses, the Brazilian religious community's staunch support of human rights had made São Paulo a popular place of asylum. Political refugees from Argentina flooded into the city, sharing harrowing stories of torture, rape, and death, and Wright, aghast at what he was hearing, decided he had to do something. In 1977, he joined Brazilian lawyer Luiz Eduardo Greenhalgh and British journalist Jan Rocha to establish CLAMOR.

Though CLAMOR's founders did not yet grasp the magnitude of the transnational collusion, they had begun to investigate, undertaking risky missions to visit political prisoners around the Southern Cone, organizing a massive list of the disappeared in Argentina, and researching claims about missing babies. Their location was an advantage. While disappearances occurred in Brazil, they were nowhere near as common as in Argentina, and the influx of refugees meant evidence was sometimes brought directly to them. The group aired its findings in a bootstrapped bulletin that it published in Portuguese, Spanish, and English. It was in one of those bulletins that CLAMOR had published grainy pictures of Anatole and Victoria Eva Julien Grisonas, allowing the children to be located.

CLAMOR's members had begun an archive, sorting documents into plastic boxes. Some boxes contained testimony from people who had been abducted by the armed forces in their countries and later released or, occasionally, from Uruguayan military defectors who shared sensitive information after fleeing to São Paulo. There were also boxes full of letters sent to CLAMOR from across the continent, supplying evidence or expressing suspicions. The majority of these had been postmarked from Argentina. Galvanized by the recovery of the Julien Grisonas siblings, many of the Abuelas had begun to send their own typed testimony to the organization so that it could run the information by its network of political refugees in search of answers. Rosa was among them, describing Patricia's story in two short pages. She explained how she had to remain on bed rest while she was pregnant with Patricia and how Patricia had been an excellent student, making the honor roll every quarter—a fact that she proudly underlined for emphasis. Finally, she described how, on October 6, 1978, Patricia had been disappeared. "I haven't heard any news of her or of my grandchild who was about to be born since," she wrote toward the end of her testimony.

The Abuelas soon returned for a second trip to São Paulo to consult CLAMOR's archive, with Estela de Carlotto, the graceful schoolteacher, replacing Licha as Chicha's travel partner. This time, Chicha and Estela avoided hotels, staying instead in a house offered to them by political asylees. It took them days to comb through the thousands of pages in the archive. Each morning, the women grabbed a box and settled into the house's garden, reading until their eyes could no longer stand it, taking in the names and details of disappeared person after disappeared person until everything ran together in a macabre blur. Occasionally, they were snapped to attention by testimonies mentioning births in clandestine detention centers. In one lengthy typed document, an Argentine man named Lisandro Raúl Cubas strained to remember everything he possibly could from his detention in the ESMA, the naval mechanics school, between late 1976 and early 1979. He wrote short descriptions of everyone he remembered seeing there, including a young woman named Susana Pegoraro, who had been abducted in June 1977 while five months pregnant. In November 1977, Cubas wrote, Pegoraro gave birth to a baby girl while detained. Susana's mother-in-law, Angélica Chimeno de Bauer, an active member of the Abuelas, had not known her grandchild was a girl. Suddenly, thanks to the CLAMOR archives, Estela would say later, grandchildren who had been "barely shadows began to have sexes and birth dates."

Bringing back copies of the CLAMOR documents was not an option. If Chicha and Estela were caught by the junta's forces, they would surely be detained—or worse. Instead, they bought several bright yellow packages of Garotos, a brand of Brazilian chocolate truffles enclosed in shiny wrappers. They carefully opened a few of the boxes, making sure not to rip anything, and ate the chocolates. Inside the empty wrappers, they placed pieces of crumpled silk paper, upon which they'd scrawled miniscule notes about what they had read in CLAMOR's files. They closed the boxes, smoothing out any creases to make it appear they'd never been touched, and placed them in their suitcases along with several packages that still contained all of their chocolates. On top they draped dirty socks and muddy shoes so that anyone examining their luggage would feel disgusted enough to move on quickly.

Despite its clear risks, Chicha delighted in the ploy. The Abuelas' work was usually so heavy that she never missed an opportunity to have a little fun, "like a child pulling a prank," another Abuela later remembered. The gambit worked perfectly. When Chicha and Estela arrived back in Argentina, they were stopped by police at the airport. Carefully removing one of the Garotos boxes that still held candies, they began eating the sweets and offered some to the officers. The men waved them through. Later, reflecting on the experience of her *compañeras*, Rosa would quip: "Who was going to suspect anything of the little old ladies carrying chocolates?"

16

The Britos Sisters

1980

In part through CLAMOR's bulletins, the Abuelas began to attract more international attention—and international mail. They received so many letters at such a rapid clip that it was hard to keep up. Such thick stacks of correspondence flooded into their homes that—unaware of who the women were or what they were up to—their mailmen sometimes winked at them when passing over the bundles, joking that they must be very important. Most were simple messages of support. Jagged drawings of children. Lots of broken Spanish. Poems. The missives arrived from Costa Rica, Brazil, the United States, and all over Europe. The Abuelas took heart in the messages of affection and kept their eyes peeled for potentially useful information.

One day, a letter arrived from Canada. He did not identify himself at the time, but later the Abuelas would learn its author was an Argentine Third World Priest who had fled north. In his missive, he described two Argentine sisters in great detail. The girls, he explained, had been adopted by kind people without connections to the dictatorship: Inés and Carlos Sfiligoy. Inés was a French teacher and the priest had been one of her students; sometimes they met at her home, which is where he had seen the girls. They were healthy and well-loved, but the priest suspected they might be the daughters of *desaparecidos*.

The descriptions seemed to square with Tatiana and Laura Malena Britos, half sisters who had disappeared in October 1977 when they were four years old and two months old, after their mother, Mirta Graciela Britos Acevedo, was abducted in a suburb of Buenos Aires. Recently, the Abuelas had connected with Laura Malena's paternal grandmother, María Laura Yribar de Jotar, who was relentlessly searching for both girls. (Tatiana was not her biological grandchild—she was the fruit of a previous relationship of Mirta's—but María Laura loved her as though she were.) After scouring endless registries, the Abuelas located a birth certificate for Laura Malena, the younger Britos sister. Clearly printed on it, to their surprise and delight, was the address Villarroel 562 in Villa Ballester, a suburb of Buenos Aires. Like many other leftist revolutionaries, María Laura's son, Alberto, had not told anyone where he was living. Now, equipped with this key information, María Laura set out to Villa Ballester, more than a fifty-mile haul from her home near La Plata, to beg the neighbors for more. A nearby butcher told the grandmother that, on the day Alberto disappeared, guitar music and singing had wafted from his windows, as though he had been having a party. Then the music had stopped, and the butcher had watched as uniformed men dragged Alberto out the door, his head covered by a hood.

María Laura and the Abuelas gathered all they could into a folder to bring to the family court closest to Villa Ballester, the Tribunal de Menores No. 2 in San Martín. They enclosed Laura Malena's birth certificate and documents summarizing the case inside. On one of the sheets, María Laura wrote down everything she knew, including the last time she had seen the girls (in October 1977, around Mother's Day) and the testimony of the butcher.

Not long after submitting the documents, María Laura heard a knock at her door. She opened it warily to find someone holding a judicial citation. The family court judge in charge of the Tribunal de Menores No. 2, Mario Basso, had studied her case; he wanted to see her.

On Wednesday, March 19, 1980, Estela de Carlotto accompanied María Laura to court. Expectations were relatively low—the women had often visited Judge Basso to ask for help with various cases, to no avail. Still, armed with more evidence than usual, they could not help but feel a whisper of hope.

When they arrived at court, Judge Basso motioned for María Laura to sit. He slid several photos in front of her. "Are these your granddaughters?" he asked.

The grandmother looked across the table at the pictures. Before her were two little girls—one around six, the other about three—with dark hair and brown eyes. The girls were very thin, with hair cut so short it looked almost shaved. María Laura's heart sank with uncertainty. The girls did not look like the images of Tatiana and Laura Malena that she had replayed over and over in her head for two and a half years. The last time she had seen Laura Malena, the child had been too young even to hold up her own head; it was hard to recognize the infant in the toddler who now stared back at her. She remembered Tatiana with the rounder face of a four-year-old and hair that brushed her shoulders.

Estela jumped in.

"Those are your granddaughters. Look at them, please," she urged María Laura, pointing at the photos. She had never met the girls, but just from the pictures she'd seen, the resemblance was clear to her. "This is Tatiana, the other is Laura Malena. There's no doubt about it."

"You think so, Estela?" María Laura said tentatively.

Judge Basso, to their surprise, was also encouraging. He told María Laura that the girls had appeared in his courthouse around the time she had reported her granddaughters missing. According to police, they had been abandoned in a plaza. Judge Basso had them placed in a youth home and they were eventually adopted.

What the judge did not mention was that the girls' adoptive mother, Inés Sfiligoy, had since come to visit him three times, asking whether the girls had any biological family. The idea that someone would abandon two healthy children, one of whom was an infant who could not so much as roll over, struck her as suspicious. When Tatiana began singing songs before bed, her concerns grew. The girls must have had a family—who else would have sung to them? Tatiana recoiled at the sight of police dogs and seemed scared to set foot outside their home. But each time Inés asked him, Judge Basso was firm: *The girls had no family. Don't ask again.*

Now, though, the evidence confronting the judge was overwhelming. From next to María Laura, Estela took a breath, pausing before she asked the judge a final question: "What are the girls' names?"

"One is Tatiana," he said. "The other is Laura."

The Abuelas fell silent. After a few moments, María Laura demanded: "Mr. Judge, I want to see my granddaughters."

"If you stay calm, I'll show you the girls," Judge Basso replied. "They're just in the next room."

María Laura padded cautiously next door and observed the scene. Inside, a pale man with a kindly face sat with an elegant woman and two girls with dark hair and dark eyes. One of the children looked around curiously, while the other fidgeted in Inés's lap. When María Laura saw the younger of the two girls, she felt a jolt run through her. Olive skin, arched eyebrows, wide smile. She was a "living portrait" of her son, Alberto. It was her granddaughter, Laura. She was sure of it.

But six-year-old Tatiana recoiled when she saw María Laura, lowering her gaze to the floor.

"Do you recognize me?" the grandmother asked gently.

Clearly perturbed, Tatiana silently shook her head no.

At another court meeting soon after, Tatiana was introduced to her other two suspected grandmothers. (Since Tatiana and Laura were half sisters, three grandmothers were involved in their identification.) Again, Tatiana insisted she didn't know them. One of the grandmothers broke down, becoming so distraught it seemed as though she might faint. Inés Sfiligoy, the girls' adoptive mother, walked over to console her, and proceeded to burst into tears herself. The documentation the Abuelas had collected had convinced Inés that Tatiana and Laura were indeed related to these women, and while she was glad to have solved the mystery of the girls' origins, she was terrified to lose them.

Once the scene had settled, Inés's husband, Carlos, stood and gave an impassioned speech to the Abuelas and the judge. He described how much they had bonded with the girls, and how they needed one another. It was clear to María Laura and the other grandmothers that Carlos and Inés Sfiligoy were loving and committed parents. Tatiana and Laura seemed fully at ease, clambering over them like kittens. The couple had never lied to the girls about the fact that they were adopted and, indeed, had tried to investigate their history. Tatiana's claims that she did not recognize her grandmothers, they suspected, were provoked by a fear of being separated from those she now considered her mother and father.

The Abuelas had always imagined that finding their grandchildren would be their greatest challenge. They had not anticipated that what happened after might prove just as complicated. Tatiana and Laura were the first of their grandchildren they had found as an organization, and no one quite knew what to do. Just as Angélica Cáceres de Julien had been when deciding whether to fight for her grandchildren, Tatiana and Laura's grandmothers were torn. The young girls had already endured incredible trauma. Tatiana was old enough to remember being wrenched from her family once before—she had watched from the sidewalk as men surrounded her mother and hauled her off. After all she and Laura Malena had been through, did the grandmothers really want to rip them from a family to whom they seemed so rooted? On the other hand, they were the girls' *true* family, bound by blood. Relinquishing them to anyone else felt like an affront to nature's laws—and to their disappeared children.

Eventually, the parties came to an agreement similar to the one Angélica had made with her grandchildren's adoptive parents in Chile. The girls would continue living with Carlos and Inés, but the grandmothers could visit whenever they wanted, even dropping in unannounced as if Carlos and Inés were their own children.

"Look, Inés, I want you to feel calm," one of the grandmothers said to the girls' adoptive mother. "The only thing that matters to me is playing the role of abuela, the role my daughter has given me."

17

The Survivors

1981–1982

Rosa and the other Abuelas celebrated finding Tatiana and Laura as if the girls had been their own. That their efforts had at last paid off gave their quest a new weight—something to grasp. Perhaps their sons and daughters were no longer alive; this seemed more and more likely as time passed. But the Abuelas felt a renewed resolve, certain their work was bringing them closer to their grandchildren.

Tatiana and Laura's case had aligned in remarkably lucky ways: the Abuelas had known the girls' names, their ages, and what they looked like. They had been able to track down their birth certificates. The judge in the case had decided to help them, and Tatiana and Laura's adoptive parents had been mercifully cooperative. Such conditions were not typical. In many cases, such as Rosa's, the Abuelas were looking for grandchildren who had disappeared while still in their mothers' wombs. Questions about such children far outnumbered answers. Were they tall for their age or petite? Round or rangy? Did Mariana have a little sister or a little brother? Rosa had no idea. While she remained deeply committed to the Abuelas' collective effort, she was no closer to personally finding her grandchild than she had been years before when she wandered into her first Abuelas meeting in Galletti's apartment.

Then, one day in 1981, Chicha and Estela returned from a trip radiating excitement. Thanks to a large donation from the World Council of Churches, they had spent several weeks traveling around Europe, meeting with international organizations that might be able to help the Abuelas. Their itinerary had brought them to Geneva for one of the first ever sessions of the United Nations Working Group on Enforced or Involuntary Disappearances. There, they had met several women who had been imprisoned in and later released from the ESMA. Chicha and Estela told Rosa the women had information she needed to hear—information so important she needed to travel to Geneva herself: these women had seen Patricia.

Airfare from Argentina to Europe was expensive, and sending Rosa to Geneva would not be possible right away. As the Abuelas saved up to buy her tickets, Videla took his final actions as president. The dictatorship had always strained to project the illusion that it operated as a legitimate government through sham legal processes and term limits, and the general's mandate was about to conclude. His exit was quiet—a stark contrast to how his presidency had begun—and not entirely victorious. While he had entered the Casa Rosada with bold promises to crush "subversion" and tame Argentina's economy, he had failed miserably on the latter goal. The previous year, one of Argentina's largest private banks—El Banco de Intercambio Regional—had collapsed. Within days, several other banks imploded as well. Combined, the institutions held deposits equivalent to 12 percent of the financial sector total, and their foundering sparked widespread panic as Argentines rushed to withdraw their savings.

On March 29, 1981, Videla handed over the reins—and the burden of the economic crisis—to Roberto Eduardo Viola, his longtime confidant and alumnus of the School of the Americas, in a strikingly lackluster inauguration ceremony. Surrounded by a handful of other generals in a rotunda of Argentina's Congressional Palace, Viola, a fifty-six-year-old lieutenant general with the build of a rugby player and a bristly gray mustache that kept vigil over his frowning lips, was handed a wooden scepter and draped with a blue-and-white sash. From there, he folded his stocky frame into a black limousine that crawled slowly down Avenida de Mayo to the Casa Rosada, flanked by a mounted military band. The crew moved at molasses pace so everyone could get a good look at their new president. Except no one had shown up. The route was mostly lined with police officers meant to control the nonexistent crowds and cavalrymen in feathered top hats.

With the collapse of Argentina's banks, and surges in inflation and unemployment, the military's grasp on power was slipping. Videla was gone. Disappearances had slowed to a trickle. Argentines were growing less afraid of the military and more frustrated with its incompetence. Amnesty International and the Inter-American Commission on Human Rights had released scathing reports on the junta's human rights abuses, making the brutality harder for Argentina—and the rest of the world—to ignore. Viola, a shrewd political operator, had made enemies within the army's more totalitarian ranks for promoting dialogue with political and labor organizations. But his conciliatory instincts, others thought, might make him just the person to restore popular confidence.

It was a grave miscalculation. Under Viola, inflation levels spiked from concerning to downright unlivable, soaring into the triple digits. For the first time since 1976, groups other than the Madres and Abuelas felt emboldened to openly criticize the junta. Flouting the ban on political gatherings, activists held dinners and publicly pronounced that military rule had "run out"; during one assembly, someone dared to call Interior Minister Harguindeguy—the formidable general who had met with the Madres in 1977—a "naughty fat little man." Workers staged massive protests decrying high levels of unemployment. Endless lines formed outside the consulate buildings for the United States, Canada, Spain, and France as two million Argentines plotted escapes.

Even Viola's military colleagues began openly upbraiding him—a development his ego could not abide. After former dictator Juan Carlos Onganía suggested Argentina needed to return to a "strong presidency," Viola's troops arrested him and imprisoned him in the Campo de Mayo, the army compound that had functioned as a clandestine torture center for the past several years. They also jailed former navy chief—and junta member—Emilio Massera, for disparaging the current junta in a newspaper he had started.

After nine painful months, Viola was forced to step down. He was replaced by hard-liner Leopoldo Galtieri, who, in an attempt to appease the increasingly restive public, promised to one day return the country to democratic rule (though he avoided specifying when). The international press published pieces about how the "unpopular Argentine Armed Forces" were "clinging" to power. The men who had once promised order and discipline, some observed, had grown used to the chauffeured sedans, the spending accounts, and the sumptuous dinners in the Beaux-Arts mansions of Argentina's elite. They were scrambling to retain control—not only for the love of power itself, but to avoid prosecution for the crimes committed during the junta's bloody reign.

Finally, in February 1982, it was time for Rosa to travel to Geneva along with Chicha. Saying goodbye to Mariana, who was now a precocious four-year-old, was brutal. In the departures area at the international airport in Ezeiza, where she had come to see Rosa off with her other grandparents, Argentina and José, the little girl wailed: "Baba, I want to go with you!" (Mariana could not pronounce bobe, the Yiddish word for grandmother, so Rosa was Baba.) "Baba bring me along, stay a little bit longer with me!" she shouted as Rosa rode the escalator toward the airport gates.

"Poor Angel, how she cried! Who knows what thoughts were passing through her head," Rosa wrote in her travel notebook that day. "I will think very carefully about leaving [her] again."

Upon reaching Geneva, Rosa and Chicha quietly arranged to meet the ESMA survivors. Despite the upheaval at home, Argentina was still in the clutches of the junta, and the military's tentacles certainly reached overseas; an intelligence center had been set up in the Argentine embassy in Paris. Discretion was paramount. The Abuelas were careful to avoid any written reference to the survivors' identities in their travel diaries, alluding to them only as "las chicas Argentinas." They met on February 21—a frigid Sunday when the streets in Geneva were quiet—in the hotel where Rosa and Chicha were staying. Rosa was in her room, pasting photos into the folders she and Chicha were compiling of the Abuelas' cases, when Chicha excitedly alerted her the women had arrived.

Chicha introduced the women to Rosa. Their names were Ana María Martí, who was thirty-six, with mournful eyes, and Sara Osatinsky, a forty-six-year-old with dark hair that she parted in the middle. While Martí had been able to reunite with her young children after her detention, both of Osatinsky's two teenage sons had been killed by the armed forces, as had her husband, a militant leftist leader.

During their imprisonment in the ESMA, both women had been tapped for Naval Chief Emilio Massera's twisted *proceso de recuperación*, or recuperation process, wherein prisoners Massera's troops judged to be "salvageable" were forced to work for the men who had abducted them. Martí and Osatinsky had been tasked with translating foreign newspapers, so the junta could follow what was being said of them abroad. Other prisoners with artistic flair were put to use falsifying passports and identity cards that the naval officers could use to obscure their identities. The prisoners hoped that by doing such work, they might live to experience freedom once again; Massera, in turn, hoped the "rehabilitated" prisoners would proselytize on his behalf and help him gain populist power so he might one day become a Perón-like figure.

Instead, Martí and Osatinsky had studiously written down every detail they could remember of their detention—including all the pregnant women they had seen. In November 1978, they recalled, one woman had arrived at the facility when she was practically to term. Two other ESMA prisoners, Amalia Larralde and Miriam Lewin, had known her from the Montoneros, but only by Mariana, her alias, or "la mujer de Matías," Matías's wife.

Now Rosa showed Martí and Osatinsky a picture of Patricia that was taken just before she was abducted. The women didn't hesitate. It was her, without a shred of doubt: la mujer de Matías. They had seen her in the ESMA. And Osatinsky had personally witnessed her give birth to a healthy baby boy.

18

A Drop of Life

October–November 1978

After the convoy of cars left José's aunt's home on October 6, 1978, Patricia and José were driven to a house west of Buenos Aires. Based on the quiet, it seemed as though they were the only prisoners there. The official overseeing them was tall and thin, with striking green eyes and deep grooves etched into his face like rivers. He went by the alias Gringo. Patricia was held upstairs while José was kept in a room downstairs. At eight months pregnant, Patricia wasn't much of a flight risk, but she was blindfolded and tied to the leg of a desk anyway. She was spared other physical harm, but José was tortured—shocked with an electric cow prod, strung up from the ceiling with cables, and beaten savagely. Occasionally the military men took him out of the building—Patricia suspected that he was brought to a nearby army base—returning in even worse shape than before.

When there were fewer officers around, sometimes a guard would lead José upstairs so the couple could talk—about Mariana, and the baby they were about to have. In another moment of relative compassion, Patricia was guided outside by a wiry officer with glasses and a smoker's growl into what seemed to be a garden, where the sun warmed her skin.

After a few weeks, as her belly expanded further, a man showed up to take Patricia away. Now José was left behind in the silent home as Patricia was transported into the unknown.

The car carrying Patricia traveled about forty minutes before pulling through large metal gates into a compound punctuated by white buildings with red tiled roofs: the ESMA. She was taken to a building on the property's northern edge that had arched windows and wooden shutters. Cars and buses rumbled up a busy avenue nearby. Planes roared overhead.

Once inside, she was led upstairs and shut into a stifling room above the barracks where the nation's admirals slept, next to the warehouse where they had stashed the refrigerators, radios, clothing, and fine china that they looted from their targets' homes after abducting them. The room's ceiling was slanted, making it difficult to stand, and it was only a few paces long—just big enough to fit a dingy cot for Patricia to rest on. The ESMA guards, young naval students of varying degrees of sadism whom the prisoners referred to as *verdes* for their green uniforms, often left the door to her cell slightly ajar, and other prisoners could see her panting uncomfortably in the heat as they were escorted by. To the passing prisoners, she was "a drop of life" in a place otherwise haunted by death.

Indeed, only three floors down, in the basement, men and women were stripped naked and tortured with electric prods. Prisoners who heard their screams over the cranked-up radio held hands until the blood-curdling sounds passed. Sometimes, the torture was psychological. The naval officers seesawed between depravity and disorienting chumminess—particularly with their female detainees—which many ESMA prisoners found even more disturbing than if they had been consistently brutish. The men who ran the ESMA's operations would periodically order their female captives to get gussied up, bringing them French perfume to spritz on their necks, and take them to meals at popular Buenos Aires haunts like Los Años Locos, El Globo, and Fechoría. As a small act of resistance, one of the women would invariably order the priciest thing on the menu—almost always fried calamari. At one such meal, Jorge Acosta, one of the ESMA's most feared leaders, an insomniac who was known to stalk the hallways at night like a tiger, reproached the women: "With you, one can talk about movies, theater, any topic . . . One can talk about politics . . .

you are the women we thought only existed in novels or movies, and this has destroyed our families! Because . . . what are we supposed to do now with the women we have at home?" Then Acosta and the other officers returned the women to the ESMA, where they slept on dirty foam mattresses or directly on the cement floor, dreading the moment when they might next be dragged to the basement and tortured.

The officers in the house where she'd been held with José had threatened Patricia that, once she gave birth, torture awaited her too. Until then, to supplement the ESMA's usual meals of putrid beef sandwiches, she was given pieces of fruit and extra portions of milk.

When her contractions started, on the morning of November 15, 1978, Patricia was led downstairs to the basement. As she descended, the dank odors of blood and filth gave way to the sharp sting of antiseptic. She was shuffled into a small room that was painted yellow and illuminated with fluorescent bulbs that were never turned off. In other moments, the room served as the ESMA's infirmary, where prisoners were injected with barbiturates before being loaded onto planes that would fly them to their deaths. That day, officers had improvised a "delivery table" from a desk and a mattress with a green sheet draped over it.

As Patricia lay on the table, she was attended by Jorge Luis Magnacco, a military doctor with frigid blue eyes who had been dispatched from the naval hospital. As he assessed her progress, he gave orders to two female detainees sent to assist with Patricia's labor. One of them was Sara Osatinsky. The other was Amalia Larralde, the nurse who had once worked alongside Patricia in the Montoneros clinic. On Magnacco's orders, Larralde injected drugs into Patricia's veins to intensify her contractions and speed her delivery, whispering encouragements as Patricia pushed and screamed.

Her labor proceeded as smoothly as birth in a dungeon could, lasting only a few hours. Around noon, Patricia's baby—a healthy seven-and-a-half-pound boy—slipped into Magnacco's hands. Patricia's smooth skin was pocked by a red rash from the effort, and Larralde recalled her sobbing uncontrollably. As she held her child for the first time, she murmured: "Hola, hijo." Hi, son. "Soy yo." It's me.

Rosa Tarlovsky (*fourth from the left*) and colleagues in their obstetrics uniforms.

Rosa Tarlovsky's
obstetrics license.

Juan and Eva Perón.

Juan and Eva
Perón wave to
supporters from the
presidential balcony.

Juan Domingo Perón.

Rosa Tarlovsky
and Benjamín
Roisinblit married on
January 20, 1951.

Argentines flood the streets for Eva Perón's funeral in 1952.

Flowers towered outside Evita's resting place following her death on July 26, 1952.

The Roisinblit family on the beach.

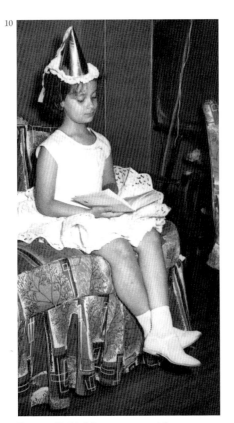

Jorge Rafael Videla photographed on March 25, 1976, the day after the coup.

Patricia Roisinblit as a young girl.

Soldiers stand guard outside the Casa Rosada shortly after the coup.

Videla and other military men observe a ceremony during the 1978 World Cup.

14

Patricia Julia Roisinblit.

José Manuel Pérez Rojo.

15

16

Several members of
the Madres de Plaza
de Mayo walk toward
the Casa Rosada.

17

Madres argue with police officers during a march in 1982.

18

Madres encounter mounted police while protesting.

19

María Isabel "Chicha" Chorobik de Mariani.

(left to right) Rosa
Roisinblit and Estela
de Carlotto.

(left to right) Jorgelina
Azzari de Pereyra,
Licha de la Cuadra,
Estela de Carlotto,
Chicha Mariani, Rosa
Roisinblit, and Emma
Spione de Baamonde
working together in the
Abuelas headquarters.

The Abuelas
marching.

Patricia begged the doctor not to cut the umbilical cord that connected him to her. "Don't take him away from me," she pleaded as her son lay on her chest. "Don't take him away!"

Magnacco snipped the cord.

Their bodies now separate, Patricia was left in the yellow infirmary to re-cover with her son, whom she had decided to name Rodolfo Fernando; Larralde was permitted to pull an extra mattress into the cramped room as well, so she could more easily attend to mother and baby. As Patricia nursed her newborn son over several days, she told Larralde about all that had happened since they had last seen each other in the Montoneros clinic. She recounted how the gang of men had taken her and Mariana from their apartment and how she had shouted desperately from the car as they turned her daughter over to José's relatives. She described the place where she had been held with José and how José had been electrocuted, strung up from the ceiling by cables, beaten, and drugged. She revealed that she had been able to call Rosa twice, and how, when she had asked for baby clothes in preparation for Rodolfo's birth, someone had delivered her a satchel full of little onesies and socks. She'd recognized them immediately as items she already owned; they must have been collected from her apartment.

Then, when the stump of Rodolfo's umbilical cord had hardened and fallen off—a few days after Patricia gave birth—Magnacco, the naval doctor, returned to the ESMA basement and prodded her to start moving around more. It was time for her to leave.

Several detainees begged the naval officers to let Patricia stay. Months of quiet observation had led them to suspect that transfers meant death. If Patricia could make herself useful at the ESMA as part of the recuperation plan, perhaps they would spare her. But the answer from the authorities was categorical: her fate was not theirs to decide; she was a prisoner of a different branch of the military.

Her womb empty, Patricia was torn between fear of the physical pain in store for her now that she was no longer pregnant and hope that she would ultimately be reunited with her son and partner. She had watched with her own eyes as Mariana was safely dropped off with family. Why should her destiny be any different?

The night before Patricia was set to leave, Larralde had been summoned to talk to Acosta, the ESMA chief who sometimes dragged prisoners out to dinner. *Forget what you've seen,* he told her in reference to Patricia. The next day, Larralde watched from the dim basement as guards led Patricia up the stairs and into the concrete parking area, Rodolfo Fernando cradled in his mother's arms.

PART III

Blood Ties

19

Las Malvinas

1982

Five days after Rosa returned to Argentina from her revelatory trip to Europe, on March 19, 1982, a group of forty Argentine scrap metal workers anchored their ship in Leith Harbor on South Georgia Island, an ice-crusted, uninhabited speck of land in the South Atlantic Ocean, 1,700 miles east of Argentina's southernmost tip. Between 1909 and 1965, the port had served as one of the largest whaling stations in the world, processing 175,250 whales into oil for margarine and fertilizer. It had been a busy place, with plants that hissed and burbled—and a smelly one, the chilly air ripe with, as one observer put it, the "pong of bad fish, manure, and a tanning works mixed together." Now, after seventeen years of abandonment, the plants were rusted and silent, with bone saws and harpoons strewn haphazardly across the hard ground.

The Argentine crew's job was to sort through the wreckage and salvage any hunks of metal their employer might be able to sell back in Buenos Aires. Times were tough, after all. But before they got to work dragging things onto their ship, they first hauled something off it: an Argentine flag, which they speared triumphantly into the icy soil. Across the bay, a group of British Antarctic researchers camping at Grytviken who, lacking other entertainment, had been curiously tracing the crew with their binoculars, spotted the flag, whose bright blue-and-white stripes contrasted with the gray sky as it whipped in the wind. They rushed to their ham radio and frantically called London. "By God," they cried. "The Argies have landed!"

The islands of the South Atlantic had long been a point of rabid dispute between Britain and Argentina. The countries had squabbled for decades over the sovereignty of South Georgia, and for even longer over a group of islands about eight hundred miles to the west: the Falklands.

A collection of two larger islands and around 220 tiny ones off Argentina's southern coast, the Falklands are remote, cold, gusty, and damp, with no arable land. Nearly all 4,524 square miles of the islands serve as rocky pasture for sheep and cattle. And yet, for centuries, Britain and Argentina had furiously jostled for ownership of them. Argentina based its claim on the fact that, after it declared independence from Spain in 1816, the Spanish crown had bequeathed the islands to it—and that Argentina's proximity to the territories should count for something. (The shores of Patagonia were three hundred miles away, whereas London was nearly eight thousand miles away.) The British countered that they had officially owned the islands since 1833, when they had expelled all Argentines, and that the "kelpers," as Falklanders called themselves in a nod to the profusion of seaweed off the islands' shores, identified as British. The countries even bickered over the true name of the islands. To the Brits they were the Falkland Islands. The Argentines called them Las Malvinas.

In 1982, the 1,800 inhabitants of the Falklands and their 600,000 sheep were overwhelmingly British, and the inhabitants of South Georgia were overwhelmingly penguins, but Argentines still insisted the islands were theirs. After the scrap metal crew planted their flag, *The Washington Post* called the act "either a prank or the kind of patriotic gesture a Boy Scout troop might undertake in the wilderness." The British, however, did not see humor in it. They viewed the deed as an unforgivable provocation, alleging that some of the ship's crew were not scrap metal workers but Argentine military personnel. Soon afterward, Brits swarmed the Argentine air force headquarters in Stanley, the Falklands' capital, replacing the Argentine flag with a Union Jack and smearing the message "tit for tat, you buggers" in toothpaste on a desk.

On March 24, the sixth anniversary of the Argentine coup, an Argentine naval ship commanded by none other than Alfredo Astiz, the rakish blond naval officer who had infiltrated the Madres de Plaza de Mayo as Gustavo Niño, showed up in South Georgia, creating further agitation.

Meanwhile, back on the mainland, the junta was facing an ever-worsening image crisis. At the end of February, a thirty-one-year-old metal worker named Ana María Martínez had disappeared from her home in a hardscrabble Buenos Aires suburb. Martínez, who was pregnant at the time, belonged to the Socialist Workers' Party, and her abduction had all the hallmarks of a state-sanctioned killing. As horrified neighbors looked on, she was forced at gunpoint into a drab green Ford Falcon, and a few days later, her bullet-riddled corpse was found in a neighboring area. She had been shot in the head and the stomach, and her hands had been sliced off. Had Martínez's murder occurred in 1976 or 1977, it likely would have gone unnoticed—lost among thousands of similar slayings, and ignored by the Argentine media. But in 1982, it made a big splash: it was the first such political killing recorded that year. The case was widely covered in the international media—during their stay in Geneva, Rosa and Chicha had cut out a clip about it from *Tribune de Genève*—and, more notably, highlighted on the front pages of Argentine newspapers.

The following month, the largest protests since the military had taken power erupted across the country over the state of the economy, in open defiance of the government ban on demonstrations. When police opened fire on protesters and arrested more than two thousand people, the news again made headlines.

President Galtieri and the junta needed to do something to whip up patriotic sentiment, and an easy war—far from the mainland, without any real threat to Argentine civilians—seemed like just the fix.

On April 2, several thousand Argentine troops flooded onto the Falkland Islands, quickly overwhelming the eighty-four British marines stationed there. In London, the surprised British sent a furious stream of telex messages to their compatriots in Stanley, trying to figure out what the devil was going on.

LONDON: What are all these rumors?

PORT STANLEY: We have lots of new friends.

LONDON: What about invasion rumors?

PORT STANLEY: Those are the friends I was meaning.

LONDON: They've landed?

PORT STANLEY: Absolutely.

LONDON: Are you open for traffic?

PORT STANLEY: No orders on that yet. One must obey orders.

LONDON: Whose orders?

PORT STANLEY: The new governor.

LONDON: Argentina?

PORT STANLEY: Yes.

LONDON: Are the Argentinians in control?

PORT STANLEY: Yes. You can't argue with thousands of troops
plus enormous navy support when you are only 1,800 strong.
Stand by please.

Then the Argentines slashed the lines.

The junta's gamble seemed to yield results. The Plaza de Mayo, which had recently seethed with angry protesters, now filled up with jubilant crowds chanting, "Argentina! Argentina!" and waving blue-and-white flags. When Galtieri gave a speech a few days after the invasion, there were so many people crunched together in the plaza's few square blocks that, from the balcony of the Casa Rosada, he could not see even a pin-prick of ground. Overcome by patriotism, around twenty-eight thousand civilians volunteered to help the war effort; the "Patriotic Fund" created to support the soldiers in Las Malvinas collected checks, cash, four hundred and fifty televisions, fifty video recorders, ten thousand liters of paint, a Mercedes-Benz, and other valuables estimated by one official to total $54 million. Argentine women did their part by staging "knit-ins," sitting on the street and knitting scarves, gloves, hats, and other items to keep the soldiers warm in the frosty conditions of the extreme south. It seemed that, after years of economic dysfunction and disdain from the rest of the world over human rights abuses, Argentines were ravenous to once again feel national pride. Even Mario Firmenich, a leader of the Montoneros, cheered the news from exile in Cuba. While the invasion had been accomplished "by the Armed Forces of the dictatorship," he said, "it still constituted an authentic national vindication."

After its fleeting moment of boldness in the weeks following Ana María Martínez's murder, the Argentine press quickly fell back in line, too. News coverage of the invasion resembled propaganda more than journalism: "Massive Euphoria for the Recovery of Las Malvinas!" celebrated the front page of *Clarín*, one of Argentina's largest newspapers, the day after troops landed in Stanley. "We are winning!" blared the cover of *Gente*, a glossy weekly magazine. (Later, *The New York Times* would accuse *Gente* of inventing an entire two-page interview with an Argentine commando and it would surface that *Clarín* had published a photo of Argentine soldiers proudly planting a flag in Falklands soil that had in fact been taken at the ESMA.)

In protest of Anglo influence, the country's main newspaper distribution society made the decision to stop circulating the *Buenos Aires Herald*. The move masqueraded as patriotism, but it had the benefit of quashing more realistic reporting. For years, the British-owned paper had been the lone news outlet to publish information about disappearances.

The Madres and Abuelas seemed to be the only Argentines unswayed by the tide of nationalistic fervor. On the Thursday after the invasion of the Falklands, the women gathered in the Plaza de Mayo for their usual three-thirty march. As they strolled arm in arm about the Pirámide, they were suddenly ambushed by hordes of men wearing headbands in the colors of Argentina's flag. In their hands, the men clutched pamphlets printed with a drawing of a typical Madre de Plaza de Mayo—white handkerchief on her head—stabbing Argentina in the back with a dagger. As they tossed the pamphlets in the air like confetti, the men pushed the Madres and Abuelas to the ground and punched them. The police were nowhere to be found. "They yelled all kinds of insults at us," one Madre would later remember. "There wasn't a thing they didn't yell at us."

One of the targeted Abuelas, Delia Giovanola, was filled with rage as she boarded the bus home. Every surface she could see—the windows, the back of the bus seats, the walls the bus passed by outside—were papered with leaflets that read: "Las Malvinas Are Argentine" and "Los Argentinos Somos Derechos y Humanos"—We Argentines Are Right and Human—a direct dig at human rights groups.

Then Delia had an idea. When she got home, she looked for something to make a sign of her own. She found a white cardboard tray that had recently held pastries and printed a short message on one side. The following Thursday, when she returned to the Plaza de Mayo, she brought the sign with her. The area teemed with foreign photographers who had come to Argentina to cover the war, and their shutters snapped incessantly as the Madres and Abuelas walked their usual rounds. As she approached one photographer, her handkerchief tied in a neat knot around her neck, Delia angled the sign in the direction of the camera. "Las Malvinas Are Argentine," she had written in neat black print. Right below it read: "The *desaparecidos* are too."

As Argentine newspapers fed their readers a steady diet of rosy news about the Falklands, Britain prepared to fight back. The junta had underestimated Prime Minister Margaret Thatcher. She too welcomed the opportunity to distract Britain from its domestic woes. Her austerity measures had incensed the country, and her approval rating had sunk to a measly 30 percent. If she didn't find a way to rally support, she was sure to lose the general election slated for the following year. She authorized an operation to take back the islands and code-named it Corporate, dispatching 127 warships, helicopters, and submarines.

It took the British fleet about two weeks to traverse the eight thousand miles of choppy Atlantic and arrive at South Georgia Island. After waiting out frigid temperatures and gales that reached 100 miles per hour, a troop of highly trained British special forces was lowered down to the island by helicopter. Caught entirely by surprise, the handful of Argentine soldiers stationed on South Georgia quickly surrendered without firing a single shot.

Argentines on the mainland were the last to find out. The junta had allowed only a few Argentine reporters into the islands, and then expelled them, so the newspapers found themselves relying on official press releases drawn up by the military itself. When rumors about the episode leaked out weeks later, readers were astounded—what was this about a bloodless capitulation? Alfredo Astiz, normally clean-shaven, had grown a scruffy beard during his weeks on the island, but, in photos released by international outlets, he could clearly be seen hunched over a table in the wardroom of the HMS *Plymouth*, a British frigate, signing the document that promised Argentina's surrender of South Georgia. It was through such photos that the Madres and Abuelas learned the real name of the man who had betrayed them.

More bruising losses followed. On May 2, even though it was outside the "Total Exclusion Zone," the radius within which Argentine ships and aircrafts were required to request permission to travel, the British launched a torrent of torpedoes at the ARA *General Belgrano*, a warship that the Argentines had acquired from the United States after World War II. The death toll was devastating—323 Argentines were killed as the ship sank to the bottom of the Atlantic—but Argentine newspapers focused instead on the number of seamen rescued and Argentina's retaliatory wrecking of the HMS *Sheffield*, a British destroyer.

After that, most Argentine warships were kept anchored in port, and the conflict moved to land and into the skies. The Argentines enjoyed superior air capabilities and pummeled British ships with Exocet missiles and bombs, but were soon confronted with an influx of British ground troops. While the Argentines still outnumbered the Brits, most of the Argentine crew were one-year conscripts, poorly trained and scantly equipped for the harsh conditions. Military officers received boxes containing The Breeder's Choice Whisky, hot cocoa mix, canned meat, and Chesterfield cigarettes, but newer recruits received much more modest rations that provided less than 1,500 calories a day, about a third of what they should have been eating. By mid-June, the better-prepared British soldiers had surrounded Stanley, raising the imminent threat of Argentine starvation. On the evening of June 14, the Argentine troops quietly surrendered and were taken prisoner, their mud-caked rifles emptied of bullets and heaped in a huge pile on the side of the road. A British general sent a telex message back to London sharing the news. "The

Falkland Islands are once more under the government desired by their inhabitants," he wrote triumphantly. "God save the Queen."

The Argentine press tried to frame the rout as a mutual truce, and Galtieri refused to publicly admit defeat, promising that the vanquishment of Stanley was "not the last link in the national undertaking" to reclaim the Falklands and South Georgia. But Argentines seemed to finally grasp the truth. After seventy-four days of war, the junta had ceded to the British. Not only had the military government disappeared thousands of its own citizens and bungled the economy, but it was not even good at the very thing it existed to do: fight wars. Hordes of fuming Argentines stormed back into the Plaza de Mayo. Only this time, instead of waving flags and chanting patriotic cheers, they lit Union Jacks and buses on fire until police in riot gear dispersed them with tear gas. Swaying arm in arm, they defiantly sang the national hymn. "Crowned in glory, let's live, or let's swear with glory to die."

Within days, Galtieri was pushed out as president.

The man chosen to replace him was a fifty-four-year-old general with drooping jowls named Reynaldo Bignone, whom colleagues described as placid or, in an odd characterization for a dictator, "nice." He officially lifted the six-year-old ban on political parties and vowed to work closely with their leaders to shape policy. He also promised to restore civilian rule by early 1984.

Quickly, it became evident he might have to accelerate that timeline. Almost a month after the war's conclusion, the rolling hills around Stanley remained strewn with Argentine corpses. Those who had survived shared horror stories of pestilence and hunger and complained of "corruption, cowardice, and incompetence among their commanders." These charges were strengthened when it came to light that Galtieri, Bignone, Harguindeguy, and other military higher-ups had borrowed $2.2 million from the government to build luxury apartments before defaulting on the loan. Meanwhile, regular wages had plunged 40 percent from the beginning of the year. The 1982 World Cup provided a distraction for a day or two, but even soccer could not rescue the country's morale—far from defending their 1978 win, Argentina's national team fumbled in just the second round.

That October, as disdain for the junta grew, the Madres and the Abuelas helped stage a larger-than-usual demonstration in the Plaza de Mayo. Calling it the Marcha por la Vida, or the March for Life, they partnered with other human rights groups to, once again, demand answers about the disappeared. The junta declared the march illegal, but tens of thousands showed up anyway. The crowd was a mix of old people and children, men in pressed suits and ties and others in tatty sweaters. It was as if the fear of the previous six years had fully transformed into anger. "Los desaparecidos . . . que digan dónde están," the crowd shouted. Tell us where the *desaparecidos* are!

Mounted police officers blocked the routes to the plaza that day, but the junta could not stifle the truths that kept surfacing. Later that month, the parents of a young union organizer who had been missing since 1976 stumbled on a mass grave in a cemetery not far from the Campo de Mayo army base. Further investigation turned up four hundred bodies stacked three to six deep in eighty-eight common graves; another probe found similar unmarked burial sites containing three hundred bodies in La Plata. The junta tried to shrug off the graves as the resting places of "beggars and indigents." But they could not explain why so many of the skeletons had bullet holes in their skulls.

The fragile economy, the humiliation of the botched war, and their waning control led some of the aggressive factions of the military to rail against Bignone for his rapprochement with political groups. The dictator struggled to balance the military's demands for a "constitutional presence" in the new government with those of the country's civilian political leaders, who found that idea inconceivable. As the specter of another internal coup began to loom, some warned against Argentina's return to anarchy. General Ramón Camps, the notorious former chief of police in Buenos Aires Province, praised the military for averting a communist revolution before warning ominously: "the struggle is not over, nor my role in it."

In the chaos, the junta's few remaining supporters channeled their frustrations at the country's most stalwart and visible opponents of the junta: the Madres and the Abuelas. The women had always endured threats, but now they were barraged by intimidating phone calls, accused of undermining national unity and pride. Sometimes the callers vowed to bomb the Abuelas. Other times, they played the portentous tune of Chopin's "Marche Funèbre." The least creative would just breathe menacingly into the receiver.

"We are going to blow all of you up, old ladies. Why don't you focus on sewing or cooking?" one anonymous caller warned Chicha Mariani. Normally mild-mannered and serene, Chicha exhibited no patience.

"Instead of messing around, why don't *you* look for a job, lazy devil!" she retorted. When other callers vowed to kill her, she would respond: "When? Tell me the date, because if not, why are you warning me?"

One morning in December, she discovered that someone had spray-painted all the buildings on her quiet street in La Plata. The graffiti, in red paint, continued down the block, covering her neighbors' walls in addition to her own, until the scrawled messages reached the home of Hebe de Bonafini, the head of the Madres, who lived up the street. Similar graffiti appeared outside the homes of Estela de Carlotto, Vilma Gutiérrez, Eva Castillo Barrios, Ketty Neuhaus, Clara Jurado, Nélida Moavro, and Emma Spione. "Madre de Terroristas" read the huge red letters on their doors and walls. Mother of Terrorists.

The day after the graffiti incident, the Abuelas returned to the Plaza de Mayo, this time for the March of Resistance, a twenty-four-hour march along with the Madres in honor of Human Rights Day. When they showed up, they were met by a phalanx of three hundred armed police, mounted officers, and armored cars blocking their path. Instead of returning home, the women adjusted their route to walk laps between the edge of the plaza and Buenos Aires' famed Obelisk, a white stone column that juts from the center of the city's widest avenue. They marched through the night, chanting: "La Plaza es de las Madres y no de los cobardes."

The Plaza belongs to the Mothers, not the cowards.

20

A Bird Lived in Me

1979–1983

The bond of a mother to her child was considered so powerful by the Greeks that it could change the seasons. It was the story of Demeter, the goddess of the harvest, that explained winter: the loss of her daughter, Persephone, to the underworld created a sadness so deep that the earth withered. In Hindu scriptures, Shakti, the force responsible for creating and sustaining all existence, was described as motherly, both nurturing and fiercely protective. The book of Isaiah in the Old Testament drew on the imagery of a mother to depict God's unfailing devotion to the Hebrew people—"Can a woman forget her nursing child?" Modern science has since affirmed what the ancients intuited. Even after a baby has left her womb—and even after that baby has grown and left her side—a mother remains permanently altered: Research has shown that she carries her child's genetic material in her veins, just as the child carries hers. To bear a child is an indelible act—it creates a memory in one's body that cannot be undone. "I *had* to look for my daughter," Rosa once said. "She was my daughter. Montonera or not, she was my daughter."

Before the coup, a well-known poet in Buenos Aires had been Juan Gelman, an ardently progressive son of Jewish immigrants who gained renown for writing that pulsed with social consciousness. In the 1970s, he and his son, Marcelo, were involved with the leftist movement and, as a result, became government targets. Gelman was living in exile in Europe when the military seized power, but his son and daughter-in-law remained in Argentina. Soon thereafter, in August 1976, Marcelo and his wife, María Claudia, who was seven months pregnant, were kidnapped from their home in Buenos Aires. In the aftermath of the disappearance, María Claudia's mother, María Eugenia Casinelli, a kindly psychoanalyst, became a founding member of the Abuelas, offering her apartment for surreptitious meetings. Gelman's ex-wife, Berta Schubaroff, joined as well and Gelman became a supporter, using his writing to challenge the junta from exile.

As the dictatorship faltered, Gelman strove to invoke the power of maternal attachment in a poetry collection he dedicated to the Madres, eventually published as *La Junta Luz*. It was a poem Gelman had written long before 1976, though, that seemed to best capture what the Madres and Abuelas knew both in their hearts and in their bodies. Titled "Epitaph," the poem celebrated the euphoria of young love and mourned its evanescence. But its eleven brief lines could just as easily have been penned about the fierce longing the Abuelas felt for their children, and now their children's children—a longing that had driven them to risk their own lives, however remote the odds of succeeding, and however malevolent the forces aligned against them.

"A bird lived in me," it began. "A flower traveled in my blood."

For almost all the Abuelas, that yearning remained painfully unfulfilled.

"Wherever he is, I want him to know that his grandmother has looked for him since the day he disappeared, when he was still in his mother's womb," Rosa said about her grandson. "Until the last day of my life, I will not stop looking for him."

Nor could other grandmothers, like Estela, turn off their impulse to search. On one of the Abuelas' trips to Brazil, Estela had learned from a woman who was imprisoned with her daughter that, before Laura was killed, she had given birth to a healthy baby boy, whom she had named Guido, after Estela's husband. But Guido could be anywhere, and sometimes Estela found herself following women with children on the street, pulled as if by a gravitational force to investigate whether the child looked like Laura. "My mother will never forgive the military for what they're doing to me," Estela was told Laura said while imprisoned. "And she will pursue them until her last breath." Estela had never been an activist, but Laura seemed to have known that her mother's grief would turn her into one. Now Estela spent her days combing through birth certificates, visiting jails, and marching defiantly in the Plaza de Mayo.

Thus far, most of the grandchildren the Abuelas had found were located through outside hints—people who sent them letters or furtively passed them notes during the Thursday marches. As the junta's influence weakened, the Abuelas began to pursue bolder strategies. Sensing that the danger of doing so had largely passed, they decided to solicit tips more publicly, traversing the dozens of barrios of Buenos Aires armed with large black-and-white posters. They pinned the posters on the walls of office buildings, next to snappy cartoon advertisements and concert announcements. They pasted them on Parisian-style apartment buildings. The signs featured photos of their grandchildren, their faces enlarged to show their pudgy cheeks and fuzzy hair—daring pedestrians to walk by without stopping. "If YOU know something . . . HELP US to find them," pleaded the bold black letters on one.

Anticipating that they would need more resources after the return to democracy, the Abuelas also intensified their call for donations. It was through such outside support that the group was able to rent a compact apartment on Montevideo, a bustling street in central Buenos Aires, to serve as their headquarters, furnishing the space with items gathered from their homes. Rosa contributed acrylic curtains and potted green plants to liven up the drab space. Argentina, José's mother, lugged over an armoire that had belonged to Rosa and Benjamín before Rosa had passed it down to José and Patricia. It had been one of the only pieces of furniture left by the military raiders in the apartment on Gurruchaga. Soon thereafter, the Abuelas bought a more permanent headquarters a few blocks up Montevideo, inviting their supporters to a party there to thank them for making the move possible.

Then, one day in 1983, the Abuelas were alerted that a check for

$10,000 had arrived for them at the Bank of Canada from a Canadian religious charity. The women were in shock. Ten thousand dollars was an unthinkable amount of money—particularly at a time of such great economic strife—and it could not have come at a more opportune moment. The Abuelas had recently decided to organize more formally, drawing up legal documents that officially established them as an association. By then, Licha had stepped down as Abuelas president to care for her ailing husband and Chicha had been unanimously elected to replace her. "She was very cultured, very serious, and an extremely hard worker," Rosa would say later. Chicha rarely took days off, often sleeping in the Abuelas' compact new headquarters instead of returning home to La Plata. "We can't rest," she would later reason. "Because each day we lose is a day in the life of a child." Estela was chosen as vice president. It hadn't been immediately clear what Rosa's role should be, but the day the check arrived, she raced with Chicha and Estela to retrieve the money, which the bank distributed to them in cash. The women were at a loss for what to do. Many Argentines hid their savings under their mattresses, but that didn't feel safe, especially while thugs with spray paint cans who viewed them as "mothers of terrorists" clearly knew their home addresses. They retreated to the bank's bathroom, divided the stack of bills into three piles, and stuffed the smaller piles in their underwear. As they discussed various possibilities, Rosa timidly volunteered that she had a safe-deposit box at a different bank. The women agreed that was their best option. With the bills concealed under their clothes, the Abuelas scrambled to the other bank. There, Rosa carefully unlocked her box and placed the cash in a fresh envelope.

"This envelope belongs to the Abuelas," she scribbled on the front.

And with that, Rosa Roisinblit became the Abuelas' treasurer.

A more pressing challenge faced the Abuelas as they eagerly awaited the junta's dissolution. It had become clear that the photos on their posters and in the case folders they distributed could only take them so far. Some of the images of their grandchildren were now seven years old. The cherubic babies pictured in them were now kids with gangly limbs and missing front teeth. And anyway, many Abuelas, like Rosa, had never met their grandchildren at all. They needed something else—a method that didn't rely on them knowing what their grandchildren looked like, or their gender, or their birth date. Something that transcended the subjective. Something undeniable. They had been working on finding that something for years, but now, as they braced for the return of democracy, the task became especially urgent.

Carefully tucked into Chicha Mariani's planner was a newspaper clipping from a 1979 issue of El Día, the main newspaper in La Plata, that she had optimistically toted around ever since. The article was about a paternity dispute—and a novel type of blood test that had been used to resolve it. On the surface, it was nothing radical. For decades, scientists had successfully compared blood groups to exclude suspected fathers during such disputes and, over time, the tests had grown more accurate by including other blood markers. (DNA testing would not be introduced until later.) But most tests were still only able to prove who a child's father wasn't. What caught Chicha's attention when reading El Día that day—compelling her to save the article—was that the new test described had revealed, with a high degree of probability, who the father was.

Chicha was a retired art history teacher, not a biologist, and she didn't understand the nuances of how the test worked. But the article sparked an exhilarating question: If a parent of a child could be positively identified through their blood, not just excluded, could the same be done for a grandparent?

She shuffled around from doctor's office to doctor's office, asking her friends who were medical professionals. The Abuelas also contacted Amnesty International and, on their travels abroad, met with any scientist or doctor who would agree to see them. In each audience, Chicha would fish the El Día clipping from her purse, hand it over, and ask whether the Abuelas' blood could be used to connect them to their grandchildren. The blood test described in the article had involved a direct parental relationship, but the Abuelas' children—and the blood in their veins—had been disappeared. Could a link still be proven without them?

No one seemed to have answers. The women were often met with drawn-out silences and raised eyebrows. One Swedish doctor became so overwhelmed as the Abuelas recounted their awful stories that he nervously scratched his face to a pulp. In Paris, a doctor considered the question for hours, consulting colleagues and textbooks, before shrugging and admitting that he couldn't figure out a solution. He gifted the Abuelas an ashtray to soften the blow.

Then, on a trip to Washington, DC, in November 1982, the Abuelas had made contact with a man by the name of Eric Stover, who worked for the American Association for the Advancement of Science (AAAS), a nonprofit dedicated to promoting science around the world. The Abuelas were in DC for a meeting at the Inter-American Commission of Human Rights, and had been given his name by Isabel Mignone, a human rights activist and the daughter of Emilio Mignone, an Argentine lawyer who had famously investigated disappearances and acts of torture committed by the junta. Stover ran the Science and Human Rights Program for the AAAS, she explained, and might be able to help them. With that, Chicha and Estela had tied white handkerchiefs over their hair and walked through downtown Washington to his office.

Stover was in his early thirties, with a neatly trimmed dirty-blond mustache and beard. After graduating from Colorado College in 1974, he had spent years hitchhiking from Alaska to his mother's home country of Chile, working odd jobs along the way. On March 24, 1976, he had found himself in the picturesque desert province of Jujuy, in northern Argentina, with his brother, Smokey. Stover would later recall that there was some sort of Carnival festival happening, and people had poured into the dry clay streets to celebrate, dancing in vividly colored costumes. The Stover brothers were standing in the crowd, enjoying the spectacle, when suddenly a taxi pulled up and unloaded a group of heavily armed military and police officers, who lunged into the mass of revelers. It was the day of the coup. They shoved the brothers against the wall, cuffed them, and brought them to jail, where they locked them in a cell with a bunch of other men. The long and sleepless night that followed was punctuated by the metallic clink of the cell door, which the police opened only to deposit even more detainees, many of them bloodied and beaten. One man was pushed in with a broken arm that dangled limply at his side. The following morning, a pair of police officers removed the brothers from the cell and drove them to the train station. They instructed them to get the hell out of Argentina—and stay out. Stover had heeded their warning at first. But his work for the AAAS now took him regularly to Buenos Aires, where he was investigating cases involving disappeared scientists.

Seated in Stover's spartan Washington office, Chicha and Estela passed him a one-page memo they had written by hand in Spanish. "To Identify Disappeared Children," they had underlined at the top. "To what point can it be demonstrated that a child is a member of a certain family without their parents, who have been 'disappeared'?" one part read. "How much can the new advances in genetics help?" Stover read the memo carefully. He had interacted with many scientists, and worked as a freelance science journalist during his travels, but he was not a scientist himself. He didn't know the answers to their questions, he told Chicha and Estela, but he would help them find someone who did.

It was better than a blank stare. Leaving DC, Chicha and Estela traveled to New York to attend a meeting at the United Nations and to meet with another contact Isabel Mignone had recommended: Víctor Penchaszadeh, an Argentine pediatrician and geneticist living in exile in Manhattan. A tall man with a corona of curly hair and a sturdy build, Penchaszadeh was around the age of their disappeared children—and had almost faced a similar fate. He was never involved in any militant groups, but he had been active in leftist student organizations, and had attended burials for people killed by the Triple A, the right-wing group that terrorized Argentina in the years before the 1976 coup. The week before Christmas in 1975, Penchaszadeh was abducted from his medical office by armed Triple A thugs. The men removed Penchaszadeh's glasses, blindfolded him, tied his hands behind his back, and beat him. Then they dragged him downstairs to the sidewalk toward an idling car outside his office building. He resisted so aggressively, kicking and flailing his long legs in plain view of *porteños* milling around the busy street, that the Triple A operatives got spooked and drove off. Two days later, Penchaszadeh boarded a plane and left the country.

Chicha and Estela invited Penchaszadeh to meet them at the bar of the Lexington Hotel, the art deco tower in Midtown where they were staying.

The doctor was a head taller than the women, and to greet them with an Argentine kiss on the cheek he had to lean down. As they settled in at a table, no time was wasted on small talk. The Abuelas peppered Penchaszadeh with dozens of questions before his coffee even arrived. "Their passion—this mixture of suffering and strength, the determination that no obstacle was going to stop them—that was my impression," he would later recall.

At one point in the conversation, the women, disheartened by the lack of answers they'd been given, expressed doubt that grandpaternity testing could be done at all.

"Who told you that?" asked Penchaszadeh.

They named the scientists, recounting their disappointing interactions across Europe.

Penchaszadeh paused for a moment. Those people were well reputed, to be sure, he told them, but they were not geneticists. If paternity testing could be done, he reasoned, grandpaternity testing should be possible as well. He did not immediately have the answer—"but there's every reason to be optimistic," he said.

The two Abuelas wanted more than optimism: they wanted a commitment. "You're Argentine and a geneticist," they replied. "Is there anything more important that you could dedicate yourself to than helping us to identify our grandchildren?"

After that, of course, Penchaszadeh agreed to help them.

21

Paula

Argentina held its first democratic elections in over a decade in late October 1983. After a vote count that stretched overnight, Raúl Alfonsín was declared president. Argentines flooded into the streets of Buenos Aires to sing and chant in the predawn darkness. Cars honked incessantly. Finally, they were free. A charismatic orator from the country's fertile grasslands, with thick black hair and a black mustache, Alfonsín was a member of the Unión Cívica Radical, or Radical Civic Union Party, which, paradoxically, was known for centrism. After nearly forty years of drastic swings between military rule and mostly Peronist democratic governments, Alfonsín's victory suggested a hunger for something fresh.

He inherited a country grappling with how best to move forward from the trauma it had just endured. In anticipation of the election, the military had announced plans to extend itself a blanket amnesty, declaring its crimes of the past decade "extinguished." The proposal provoked an uproar in the country and a forty-thousand-person march in Buenos Aires. The Madres and their supporters participated, painting thousands of faceless silhouettes to represent the disappeared and pasting them on trees and walls around the city. Ignoring the outcry, the military proceeded with their plans and signed the National Pacification Law, whose very title seemed a thinly-veiled threat. Immunity, it suggested, was the sole way to placate them.

Alfonsín had been involved in Radical Party politics since his twenties, but during the dictatorship he had also worked as a human rights lawyer, filing habeas corpus motions for the disappeared and advocating on behalf of the Permanent Assembly for Human Rights, the organization through which Rosa first connected with the Abuelas. On the campaign trail, he vowed to restore human rights, and promised to annul the military's amnesty. "With democracy, one does not only vote," he frequently repeated. "With democracy one eats, one heals, and one educates."

His inauguration took place on December 10—a date purposely chosen to coincide with International Human Rights Day. On that early summer Saturday, a day so hot that firemen occasionally misted water onto the crowd, the Abuelas donned their white handkerchiefs and joined the masses converging in the Plaza de Mayo to hear their new president's first address. In the very place where, for the past six years, they had demonstrated their resistance to the state, they now celebrated a new government. The air crackled with possibility. The crowd tossed confetti and waved flags and sang. It felt, observers said, like a giant party. "El pueblo, unido, jamás será vencido," the crowd bellowed. The people, united, will never be defeated.

As the Abuelas milled about, easily recognizable in their headscarves, members of the crowd cheered and hugged them. "With democracy, we thought that the heavens would open, that we were going to find all the kids and receive answers," one Abuela would later recall.

Still, others booed and insulted them. Alfonsín had promised healing, but for many Argentines, that would not happen by litigating deeds that could not be undone. The Abuelas were obsessed with old wounds, some felt. To heal, they believed, required leaving the past alone.

At seven in the morning three days after Alfonsín's inauguration, Elsa Pavón, a hearty, serious mother of four in her late forties, stood anxiously outside of Tribunales. The day promised to be scorching and, as she stood on the staircase that led to the building's entryway, the air was already thick with humidity. She was accompanied by Chicha, Mirta Acuña de Baravalle, and the Abuelas' lawyers.

Elsa had been waiting for this moment. It had been five years since her eldest daughter, Mónica Grinspon; son-in-law, Claudio Logares; and granddaughter, Paula Logares, had disappeared in Uruguay, where the family had fled after the coup. May 18, 1978, was a holiday, and Paula, who was just shy of two years old, had begged to go to Parque Rodó, a riverside park in Montevideo shaded by palm trees. To reach the park, the family had needed to take two buses. As they disembarked the first in front of Cine Miami, a large movie theater on a street lined by colorful buildings, a swarm of military officers that included some Argentine soldiers blocked them in with three cars. From the theater's ticket booth, an attendant saw the men throw hoods over Mónica's and Claudio's heads and stuff the family into separate vehicles—Claudio in one and Mónica and little Paula, who was also hooded, in another.

It was the last anyone had heard of them, but Elsa had refused to give up hope, joining the Abuelas after they recognized her as one of their own in a La Plata courtroom. ("Just as we could sniff out a policeman, even if he was disguised, we also were able to recognize one another," Elsa would say later.) In 1980, CLAMOR, the Brazilian group that found the Julien Grisonas siblings, offered Elsa and the Abuelas a first clue. That year, someone had hand-delivered several photos to them of a little girl with brown ringlets, dressed in a tracksuit. On the back of one of the images, in scraggly handwriting, was an address in Buenos Aires and a name. The writing was almost impossible to decipher, but it seemed to say "Paula." The person who had originally turned over the photos was someone close to the couple who was raising the girl, and had apparently overheard an argument one day in which the girl's supposed mother was shouting at her husband: "You killed this girl's parents and you found nothing better than to dump her on me to mess up my life!"

"Dios mío!" Chicha exclaimed when she saw the photos. "My God! It's Paula. It's Paulita. I'd bet my head on it." Elsa, though, was not so sure. Paula was not yet two when she disappeared. At the time, her hair had barely grazed her ears and her cheeks were pudgy and soft. The photos in her hand depicted a girl, not an infant. It was hard to trust that the child standing solidly on her own two feet was the same baby that Elsa had once rocked in her arms. The possibility that these children could be the same also gave rise to a terrifying question: If the girl was Paula, where was her mother?

Though she was skeptical, Elsa pursued the lead. First, she decided, she needed to see the child with her own eyes. The address printed on the back of the photo was in one of the greenest and poshest parts of Buenos Aires, near the city's manicured botanical gardens. It was also one of the hardest areas to investigate. The women of the neighborhood wore long strands of pearls around their perfumed necks; with her boxy dresses and sensible sandals, Elsa would stick out. There were no *colectivos* that ran down the narrow one-way street where Paula supposedly lived, nor were there any cafés or restaurants in which to wait for the girl to pass by. All of the apartment towers in the area had security guards who might grow suspicious if they continually saw the same unfamiliar woman wandering up and down the street. Elsa was careful to change her clothing and hairstyle each time she went.

Finally, one day, a school bus stopped in front of the apartment building and a small brunette girl dressed in a preschool smock stepped off. Elsa only glimpsed the girl's back, but a flash of recognition suddenly struck her. The girl's curls were soft and brown. Clad in white socks, her little legs twisted slightly inward at the ankles, just as Mónica's had. It was Paula.

As summer turned to autumn that year, torrential rains buffeted Buenos Aires for a month, making it impossible to take a casual stroll down Paula's street without arousing suspicion—who, after all, wandered around in a downpour? But when the rains finally stopped and Elsa returned to the apartment building, a sign reading For Rent hung on the balcony where Paula had lived. Elsa was crushed. She begged the building superintendent to tell her where the couple had moved, but he demurred. Elsa convinced herself she had been mistaken—she had only seen the girl from behind, after all.

Around that time, Elsa's husband grew ill and had to undergo heart surgery. While she cared for him, she asked Chicha and the Abuelas to continue searching for Paula on her behalf. Three years passed. With democracy on the horizon, the Abuelas had begun plastering the streets of Buenos Aires with posters of their missing grandchildren. Soon they received a tip from an anonymous male caller who recognized the wide-eyed little girl in one of the photos: Paula. She attended school with his daughter, he said, and lived in a ground-floor apartment at Fraga 488 in the residential neighborhood of Chacarita along with Raquel Teresa Leiro Mendiondo, who claimed to be the girl's mother, and her husband, Rubén Lavallen, who had worked as a police officer during the dictatorship.

Armed with the girl's address, Elsa and the Abuelas had been ready to fight for Paula's return. But the Abuelas' lawyers thought it would be prudent to wait to involve the courts until democracy was restored—which was how Elsa, Chicha, and Mirta now found themselves standing in front of Tribunales in the dull morning light.

Eventually the women were invited inside, where they presented their case before a judge. The evidence, they argued, was overwhelming. The girl looked identical to her mother and had the same first name she had been given at birth. They asked the judge to bar the girl's caregivers from leaving the country, to provide her with a social worker, and to dispatch a police officer to guard the door of the apartment building where she was living.

The judge asked the Abuelas to wait in his anteroom while he mulled over their request. They obliged, but the waiting soon became unbearable—every so often, Chicha would rise from her chair and rap on the judge's door to check if he had made a decision. Her dulcet voice and round pearl studs made her the picture of grandmotherly civility, but she was not about to let the judge off the hook. If something happened to Paula, she told him, the responsibility was his. Finally, around one in the afternoon, the women saw a pack of police officers leave the courthouse. Instead of heeding their demands, it seemed the judge had ordered a raid.

Elsa and Mirta raced to observe the proceedings firsthand. Elsa worried that Lavallen and Leiro Mendiondo might try to escape with Paula or that, despite the judge's orders, the police might not carry out their duty. It was hard to trust that the police force's loyalties had flipped over the course of a weekend, even if the system of government had. Elsa and Mirta traveled directly from the courthouse to the cobblestone street in Chacarita where Lavallen and Leiro Mendiondo lived and sat down at an outdoor table at the bar across the street.

Soon, they watched four police officers in civilian dress rumble up the street in a Ford Falcon and approach the café. From her table, Elsa could see the men walk toward two bricklayers who were drinking wine cooled with ice to combat the heat. One of the workmen was quite drunk and, as the cop approached his table, he all but flew out of his chair. Elsa couldn't blame him—it would take more than a few days of democracy to erase the terror associated with plainclothes men rolling around in Ford Falcons. But this man wasn't their target. At least, not in the way he may have thought.

"Alright, you two, come over here. I need to do a search, and I need two witnesses," Elsa heard the police officer say gruffly, before adding that a girl in the house had reportedly been kidnapped.

Jolted back to sobriety, the men walked across the street with the police and entered the apartment building. Minutes passed. Then half an hour. Then an hour. Then hours. Elsa had assumed that Paula would not have valid documents and so the police would seize her that day. But that evening, as dusk cast shadows over the cobblestones, Elsa and Mirta watched, surprised, as the police emerged without Paula.

Later that night, the Abuelas found out what had happened: Lavallen and Leiro Mendiondo had presented the police officers with a birth certificate suggesting that the girl was indeed their biological daughter and that she had been born in October 1977—not in June 1976, as Elsa's Paula had been. The document itself was dubious: it claimed Leiro Mendiondo had given birth in the home of one of her husband's police colleagues, an odd detail in a country with very few home births. From there, the couple's story only got more far-fetched. They could not point to anyone who had seen Leiro Mendiondo pregnant, nor did her medical records reveal any prenatal visits. After Paula was born, Lavallen and Leiro Mendiondo claimed they had moved temporarily to the small provincial city of Chivilcoy, but their supposed neighbors testified that they had never seen the couple. For the moment, though, the judge allowed Paula to continue living with Lavallen and Leiro Mendiondo.

Three days after the police visited the couple's apartment, Rosa received a frantic phone call from Chicha. The Abuelas had heard a rumor that Lavallen and Leiro Mendiondo planned to flee with Paula across the Río de la Plata to Uruguay that night, but Chicha and Elsa both lived too far from central Buenos Aires to do anything about it. Could Rosa help? She raced from her apartment to the home of Laura Conte, a Madre who often worked with the Abuelas, and together the women called Marshall Meyer, the American rabbi who had helped Rosa when she began her search for Patricia. They begged Meyer to rush to Buenos Aires' port to ensure Paula was not spirited away.

As Laura made their case, Rosa tugged insistently on her friend's skirt.

"Tell him that the girl is Jewish," she urged, thinking it would help persuade the rabbi to act. (Elsa's first husband, the father of her children, had been Jewish.) Laura ignored her at first, but Rosa kept wheedling until she relented, finally telling Meyer that Paula's mother was Jewish.

"She's a human being," he responded gently. He agreed to go. He was meant to attend the wedding of one of his children the following day, so he donned his tuxedo before heading to the port, just in case he ran out of time to change before the ceremony.

Meanwhile, Rosa and one of the Abuelas' lawyers squeezed into a small Citroën and drove to Chacarita, where Paula was living, parking on the corner to keep vigil over Lavallen and Leiro Mendiondo's building. Through the ground-floor window, they could see the couple setting plates and silverware on the table for dinner. Lavallen was wide and stocky, with biceps that bulged out of his shirt and a cross necklace that hung around his neck. Leiro Mendiondo looked like a waif in comparison, with a shaggy brown pixie cut and small features. Hours passed with no movement. Perhaps they would not leave after all. Finally, after the sun had risen the next morning and the city's parakeets and pigeons began to squawk and chirp, Rosa and the lawyer headed home.

Paula was safe for the moment. But now that the couple was aware the Abuelas were onto them, who knew how long they would stay put? The Abuelas needed a way—and soon—to persuade the judge of Paula's true identity.

Fortunately, they were closer than ever to having one. For months, Eric Stover and Víctor Penchaszadeh had called every contact they could think of in search of an answer to the Abuelas' question about blood testing. One name had seemed particularly promising: Stanford geneticist Luigi Luca Cavalli-Sforza. Originally from Genoa, Italy, Cavalli-Sforza had traveled the globe using genetics to trace human migration and evolution. He was an icon in the field and unabashedly committed to progressive causes.

Stover's close friend, a Chilean biochemist named Cristián Orrego, was ultimately the one to reach out. When Cavalli-Sforza had answered the phone, he insisted he could not take on the project. He did, however, know exactly the right person for the job.

22

Story Problems

1952–1983

Mary-Claire King had always loved puzzles. As a child, she often spent afternoons cross-legged on the floor in front of her family's black-and-white television, watching Ernie Banks, the Chicago Cubs' megawatt shortstop and first baseman, step up to the plate at Wrigley Field. Sitting beside her father and her younger brother, King would watch as Banks raised his bat, wriggled his fingers around its base to get a perfect grip, and slammed balls into the outfield—or, often enough, *out* of the outfield. Invariably, her father, Harvey, would turn to her with a question. "Ernie Banks is batting .277 and he'll probably have three at bats this game," he'd say. "What's he going to have to bat to bring his average above .280?"

"I don't know," King chirped. Most of her classmates in elementary school were still working on simple addition and subtraction.

"You're right," her father said. "I haven't told you enough. What else do you need to know?"

Harvey was born in 1890 in Saginaw County, Michigan, a farmer's son with a sharp mind who received what little formal education he got in a one-room schoolhouse. King's mother, Clarice, had enrolled in college at the University of Chicago, but was forced to drop out when her family went bankrupt during the Great Depression. After the couple married, they wanted their children to receive the best possible educations and so moved to the Chicago suburb of Wilmette in part for its unparalleled public schools. The community offered an idyllic 1950s childhood, with a quaint downtown lined with theaters, five-and-dimes, and a popular ice cream shop where King and her brother slurped down cones on hot summer days.

As King entered second grade, Harvey began to lose control of his muscles and develop other Parkinson's-like symptoms that the family would eventually suspect were late-onset effects of the 1918 influenza epidemic. He was forced to retire from his job as a labor relations manager for Standard Oil, instead spending his days at home on Forest Avenue, a mile and a half from the waters of Lake Michigan. With his body out of commission, he liked to entertain himself—and his equally inquisitive daughter—by devising math problems. Watching television, King and her father would solve his puzzles together; to figure out what it would take Ernie Banks to bring up his average, for instance, they first had to know how many times he had stepped up to bat that season.

For King, tussling with such problems felt like unlocking hidden layers of the universe. Harvey's puzzles took a theoretical practice and made it vital, teaching her to love the challenge of problem-solving almost as much as the solution itself. She would work intensely, scribbling notes with a pencil and paper, until she teased out the answer. Then her blue eyes would widen, and a grin would flash across her face, revealing deep dimples. As she grew into adolescence, this passion continued, but she also found others. She spent hours on music, playing flute in the symphony orchestra and piccolo in the marching band, and bumping bikes over the brick avenues of Wilmette with her best friend, Debbie Williams, an adventurous girl who lived down the street. Together, they played with each other's pets—King had a parakeet, Perky; Debbie owned a pug—and daydreamed about their futures. King adored children and hoped to one day become a teacher and a mother. Debbie wanted the same for herself.

But soon, Debbie got sick. Her family didn't talk about the illness, and it was only later that King would learn she suffered from a rare kidney cancer. All she knew was that Debbie was in constant pain and was forced to undergo an amputation of her leg. Then, not long after they began high school, Debbie passed away.

King reeled. That her vivacious best friend should die so young was unfair and inexplicable. She poured herself into her schoolwork, continuing to gravitate toward mathematics, with its precise rules and clear answers. She found inspiration in two female math teachers at her high school—a relative rarity in the 1960s. One of the teachers had a PhD, and she persuaded King that she too should aspire to graduate-level study. After graduation, King enrolled in Carleton College, a small liberal arts college in Minnesota, where she majored in math. She was consistently a B student, but despite her middling grades, a college advisor recognized her raw talent for applied math (as opposed to abstract theory) and suggested she apply for a graduate program in it.

By 1966, King was at the University of California, Berkeley, pursuing a PhD in statistics. It was a heady environment for a polite and studious transplant from the Midwest. Hippies dressed in bell-bottoms and jean jackets milled around at all hours. Marijuana perfumed the air. Huge protests over free speech had roiled the campus for the past two years, and just as the university ceded ground, changing its policies on political expression, ire over the Vietnam War and civil rights was escalating. Engaging in some measure of activism was unavoidable. King marched alongside fellow students as they paraded down Berkeley's streets holding signs with slogans like "Stop the Bombing" and "Get Out of Vietnam." When Martin Luther King Jr. delivered a speech on campus, in May 1967, she joined some five thousand others on the steps of Sproul Hall, straining for a good view.

It was during this time that King stumbled into the field of genetics. To break up her courses on probability and nonparametric statistics, she decided to sign up for a genetics class for fun, a lecture taught by legendary German geneticist Curt Stern. Stern's classes regularly attracted more than one hundred students, who packed into the Life Sciences building every weekday at one in the afternoon to watch the professor, soft-spoken and dressed in suit and tie, deliver presentations centered on a "puzzle of the day." To better hear, and ensure that she could read the chalkboard, where Stern scrawled equations in neat handwriting, King always sat in the first row.

Sometimes the puzzle dealt with a "cross," or the combination of two individuals' genes. Other days it was simply a question. The exercises filled

King with a sense of nostalgic excitement, reminding her of long afternoons working out baseball statistics with her father. The more of Stern's lectures she attended, the more enthralled she became. Stern would lay out data that seemed hopeless in its complexity, and then propose clear solutions. "I couldn't believe people were paid to do this," King would say later. Soon she had switched her PhD concentration from statistics to genetics.

Less than a year after his visit to Berkeley, Martin Luther King Jr. was assassinated on a hotel balcony in Memphis. Robert Kennedy, another advocate of peace, was killed two months later. The years that followed ushered in even more global unrest and violence. Protests calling for an end to authoritarianism and capitalism erupted around the world, including in France, Mexico, Senegal, and South Africa. In Argentina, the Cordobazo happened. Berkeley seethed with tension, and in May 1969, campus police in riot gear fired buck and bird shot at a large crowd of protesters who were occupying a vacant piece of land owned by the university. One young onlooker was killed. Other rioters were blinded or permanently maimed. Ronald Reagan, then the governor of California, called on the National Guard to quash the protests.

King was only a bystander in what became known as the People's Park protest, but when the Vietnam War lottery put her brother, Paul, and all her male friends at risk of conscription, the draft became her primary focus. "Everywhere around us were people who were vulnerable to being sent off to a war that we all opposed," she would later recall. King began not just participating in protests, but also helping to organize them. The day after the United States invaded Cambodia in 1970, she helped lead a letter-writing campaign denouncing the war that ultimately garnered thirty thousand signatures.

As she balanced schoolwork and social justice, she started to doubt if science was for her. She was studying bacterial evolution, and it was not going well. She understood the theory, but she could not get her experiments to work. She had recently spent a summer working for Ralph Nader, the political activist, researching the effects of pesticide exposure on farmworkers in California's Central Valley, and now she wondered if she should drop out of graduate school entirely. She did not want to stare at uninterpretable data; she wanted to make an impact now.

Nader had offered her a full-time job in Washington, DC, and as King considered the decision, she sought the advice of Allan Wilson, a renowned geneticist from New Zealand who ran the lab next door. An intense thirty-something with a lithe build and reserved manner, Wilson shared her social conscience (when two of his students were arrested during a Black Panther demonstration, he gamely bailed them out), and she figured he would understand her quandary.

To her surprise, Wilson was aghast. Usually a gentle communicator who saved his outbursts for racists and creationists, he passionately urged King not to quit science. "If you leave now, you can do good work," he acknowledged. "There's no question it's righteous work." Still, she would ultimately do more good for the world, he declared, by sticking it out in the lab.

"With only a bachelor's degree, you'll never set the agenda," he told her.

When King shot back that none of her experiments seemed to be working, and that her hands didn't seem to understand what her brain wanted them to do, Wilson was unmoved.

"If everybody whose experiments failed stopped doing science," he said, "there would be no one left." He invited her to work in his lab. He could help her devise a project, he insisted, that took advantage of her math prowess without being too challenging on an experimental level.

At the time, Wilson believed that humans and chimpanzees shared a common ancestor much more recently than other scientists supposed—a theory he had explored in his prior work. Because proteins and other molecules changed steadily over time, he posited, they could be used as "molecular clocks" to trace evolution. To further his understanding of the evolutionary distance between humans and chimpanzees, he tasked King with studying their molecular differences, with a focus on the genes that code for proteins. The study had massive potential—with possible implications for the history of humankind itself. King turned down the Nader job and got to work in Wilson's lab, dabbing drops of chimpanzee blood onto gel pads that separated charged molecules, like proteins, by size using a technique called electrophoresis. In a different slot on the same pad, she repeated the process with human blood, comparing the sizes and structures of the human and chimpanzee proteins based on the positions of their bands on the gel.

Curiously, though, they were identical. King began to despair. *Here we go again*, she thought. *More failed experiments*. She ran her tests again and again, scrutinizing the gels for any differences. Here and there, she would find one, but it was unusual. She was convinced her experiments were flawed—these were two entirely different species, one covered in fuzz and jungle-dwelling, the other a walking, talking, builder of empires. How could they possibly share such similar protein sequences? Sibling species of mice were more genetically distinct than the results she was seeing play out on her gels.

One day, King vented to Wilson: "They're the same again."

"You're doing fine," he said encouragingly. "The gels look beautiful. Have you ever considered the possibility that you've actually got it right?"

Scarred from years of failure in the lab, King had not. But Wilson was convinced that she had uncovered something groundbreaking: despite looking and acting very differently, humans and chimps shared 99 percent of the sequences of their protein-coding genes. Other scientists were dumbfounded. What set humans apart from other species if not their proteins? King's discovery suggested that differences between species might not always be due to differences in their protein-coding genes, but might instead be due to other factors like when and where these genes were expressed.

King was starting to set the agenda after all.

The death of her childhood friend Debbie still haunted King, and as she delved further into genetics, she decided she wanted to study cancer. Her PhD and pioneering work with Wilson complete, she landed a job researching the disease at the University of San Francisco. President Nixon had declared a "war on cancer," pouring ample government funding into research, and King was eager to explore if the illness might have a genetic component—a controversial idea at the time, since cancer was widely thought to be caused by viruses and other environmental factors. There was evidence that breast cancer, for example, was more common in certain families. If she could figure out what genes those families shared, maybe she could isolate what predisposed them to the disease and help spare the lives of women in the future. "I cannot separate doing science from doing good work," King would later say. "To do science is to try to improve the lives of people."

In 1973, she had married Robert Colwell, a Berkeley ecologist, on his family's Colorado ranch. Two years later, they welcomed a child, a daughter they named Emily. King delighted in being a mother, bringing Emily everywhere—including, very often, to work, where she breastfed during breaks in her office. In time, using family surveys compiled by the National Cancer Institute, King developed a statistical model proving that breast cancer did indeed cluster in families. The development was promising, but the existence of a gene remained hypothetical; she still had to locate it.

Meanwhile, King was quickly becoming something of a rising star in genetics. King and Wilson's findings about the similarities between humans and chimps had recently been splashed across the cover of *Science*, an honor in the scientific world akin to winning an Academy Award. Soon after, she was offered a tenure-track job at UC Berkeley. The university had just introduced affirmative action policies, and when King got the job, in the epidemiology department, not everyone was excited. "I just want you to know you are only here because of all these new regulations, and we are really scraping the bottom of the barrel in hiring you," the head of the department told her by way of a welcome. "We'll see how long you feel that way!" she retorted.

As King worked to earn the respect of her colleagues, her home life fell apart. One Sunday night in 1981, Colwell made an announcement: he wanted a divorce. "I was a young mother, a young scientist and a young wife," King would later reflect. "Something had to collapse, and it was the marriage." She was slated to teach the following morning; though she was shattered, she decided it was easier to show up to campus than explain why she couldn't. After class, she was summoned to the department head's office. She'd been awarded tenure in half the usual time, he told her jovially.

King broke down sobbing. "No one's ever reacted like that before," the professor said in surprise, reaching for a bottle of Jack Daniel's in his desk drawer after she explained the source of tears. The whiskey, and the congratulations from the very man who had told her he was "scraping the barrel" with her appointment, cheered her up marginally. (Later she would remind him of his comments, and he would scoff: "I never said that. I absolutely didn't say that. I totally wanted to hire you.")

King had once watched Julia Child on PBS each week, trying to replicate whatever she cooked. She loved mystery novels by P. D. James and chamber music. But if there had been precious little time for these things before, now as a single mother, there was even less. Every hour was devoted to caring for Emily or running her lab, and sometimes both at once. Her daughter grew accustomed to doing her homework surrounded by beakers and pipettes and postdoctoral fellows in lab coats. She had an area in King's office with picture books and toys where she liked to color posters to tape onto the door. "First Mommy to Walk on Land," read one. When King asked why she was making the posters, Emily responded: "They are to keep people happy while they have to wait for you."

Soon after she and Colwell separated, King was awarded a substantial grant from the National Institutes of Health to continue studying heriditary breast cancer. It was this work that, in the summer of 1983, led her to the lab of Luca Cavalli-Sforza, where she hoped to apply the Stanford geneticist's cutting-edge experimental techniques to her cancer research.

Cavalli-Sforza was Italian to the core, and fine coffee—brewed in a silver moka pot and served in ceramic demitasse cups—was a constant presence in his lab. He often wandered around to serve it himself. One morning, as he poured King a cup, Cavalli-Sforza announced: "I've just had a call from the AAAS." He was referring to the American Association for the Advancement of Science, where Eric Stover worked. The AAAS was helping a group of Argentine women called the Abuelas de Plaza de Mayo, Cavalli-Sforza continued. Their grandchildren had been stolen from them during the military dictatorship that had gripped Argentina for the past seven years. They were keen to develop a test that could prove their relationship to their stolen grandchildren without the blood of those children's parents, who were among the thousands of disappeared.

The Abuelas' challenge gripped King immediately. It was a story problem like those that had enchanted her since childhood—one whose solution would change lives. As she considered the Abuelas' plight, she thought, too, of her daughter, who was now eight, with a straight blond bob and glasses. Emily was the exact age of the children the grandmothers were searching for. It was not hard for King to imagine that, if she had been born in Buenos Aires and not suburban Chicago, she might have been disappeared for her activism, and *her* daughter might have been kidnapped.

This was just her type of project.

23

The Index of Grandpaternity

1983–1984

K ing quickly got to work. She was joined by Pierre Darlu, a young Frenchman who was doing a year's sabbatical in Cavalli-Sforza's lab. He agreed with King that there had to be a way to help the Abuelas—with a bit of statistical alchemy, they theorized, they should be able to extend the principles of traditional paternity testing to grandpaternity.

Mothers and fathers each contribute twenty-three chromosomes—threadlike structures that carry DNA—to their future children through their eggs and sperm. When those eggs and sperm are created, the parent's genes are shuffled and combined, meaning that every child, other than identical siblings, receives a unique set that determines everything from eye color to height to blood types. For decades, scientists had tested paternity by comparing a child's ABO blood type, of which there are three main variants, with those of potential fathers. While these tests could exclude possible fathers, no blood type was rare enough to definitively confirm a parental connection. Recently, though, scientists had begun using markers that provided much stronger clues to paternity. The new test Chicha had read about in *El Día* four years earlier—the one that had inspired the Abuelas to launch their quest for a grandpaternity test—involved markers called human leukocyte antigens, or HLA. Found on the surfaces of most cells in the human body, HLA are proteins that help the immune system detect potentially harmful threats, such as bacteria and viruses. In contrast to the ABO blood group system, HLA is highly variable—in the early 1980s, scientists knew of approximately eight thousand different types—and, while some were common, others were vanishingly rare. If you identified the same combination of rare HLA types in a child and a potential parent, the probability was extremely high that they were related.

Linking grandparents with grandchildren, however, would be a more vexing puzzle. Between grandparents and grandchildren, genetic building blocks have been mixed up and mingled together twice; children share only one-quarter of their genes with each grandparent. Determining the probability that grandparents and grandchildren were truly related—and that they didn't simply share certain traits by chance—would require more sophisticated calculations.

To make them, King and Darlu turned to a theory devised by the eighteenth-century English statistician, philosopher, and Presbyterian minister Thomas Bayes, which allows an experiment to begin with an initial hypothesis that is updated incrementally based on new information. Bayes' theorem is often used to make and adjust weather predictions. Say, for example, you know that on any given day, there is a 25 percent chance of rain in your town—one morning, you wake up, look out the window, and see that the sky is dotted with gray clouds. Bayes' theorem would enable you to calculate precisely how much the presence of those clouds boosts the likelihood of rain, generating a new, more accurate probability. If the clouds become towering thunderheads and the temperature plunges, the theory could incorporate these clues, too, updating its prediction of rain based on accumulating evidence.

In many cases, although the Abuelas could not prove the identity of a suspected grandchild, their detective work had reaped binders full of circumstantial evidence. By quietly hiding to catch a glimpse of a child as they entered school, perhaps they had seen that the boy had a birthmark on his left calf, just like their stolen grandson. Or maybe they knew their grandchild was born in May of 1977 and found a birth certificate from that period with all the features of a fake: a home birth, perhaps, signed by a military doctor rather than a civilian obstetrician. They couldn't be sure—and they certainly didn't have any evidence incontrovertible enough to convince a judge—but they often had strong initial hunches about the identities of suspected grandchildren.

With Bayes' theorem as a guide, King and Darlu worked to create an equation into which the Abuelas could layer biological data to probe those hunches. Some markers, like matching ABO blood types, might only increase the likelihood of a grandparental relationship slightly, but rarer markers, like certain HLA types, would dramatically boost the probability of a match.

After a few weeks of tinkering, King and Darlu had their formula, with "P" to indicate probability, "gp" to refer to grandparents, and "c" to mean children. They showed Cavalli-Sforza, a skilled statistician, who helped them mimic different scenarios, inputting information from hypothetical families to test whether the approach would provide accurate probabilities in every possible case. It worked seamlessly. For the first time ever, King and Darlu had invented a way to connect grandchildren to their grandparents, without any genetic information from their parents. They called the formula the Index of Grandpaternity—or Índice de Abuelidad.

Soon, six thousand miles to the south, another revolution was launched. Within days of moving into the Casa Rosada in December 1983, Alfonsín fulfilled his promise to annul the military's self-amnesty law and announced that he would prosecute nine of its leaders, including Jorge Rafael Videla. To avoid the perception that he was on an anti-military crusade, he also ordered the arrests of Mario Firmenich, the former Montoneros leader, and several other leftist bosses. A few days after that, he launched La Comisión Nacional sobre la Desaparición de Personas, or the National Commission on the Disappearance of Persons (CONADEP). Overseen by a group of the country's most prominent intellectuals—novelists, surgeons, journalists, and religious figures, from bishops to the American rabbi Marshall Meyer—CONADEP was tasked with uncovering everything possible about the disappearances of the dictatorship: how many people had been taken, who they were, where they were, and who had been responsible.

Military leaders showed little willingness to talk, so CONADEP turned to the only solid evidence they had to work with: bones. Almost as soon as it was formed, the commission began excavating unmarked graves across the country in a quest to identify the many bodies that lay within them. The team had given little thought to *how* the exhumations should be handled, however: all at once, excavators rumbled into cemeteries, digging deep into the earth and hurling the mixture of dirt and human remains into the air. The process was broadcast on televisions across Argentina—the secrets the junta had tried to bury suddenly, and quite literally, unearthed for the whole country to see.

It was a revelatory, agonizing time. Due to press censorship and self-censorship, many Argentines had not realized the full scale of what was happening during the dictatorship—or they had willfully ignored it. Even relatives of the disappeared had not grasped the magnitude of the carnage. Some of them had clung to hope that their loved ones were still alive, perhaps in some remote prison somewhere. But the mass graves clearly suggested otherwise.

Alfredo Galletti, the lawyer who had originally connected Rosa to the Abuelas, had never watched much TV, but suddenly he could not tear himself away from the screen, staring as the heavy construction vehicles and workers with spades churned up dark soil flecked with the stark white of bones. Perhaps they belonged to his daughter, Liliana. Perhaps they didn't. He would never know. Untrained cemetery workers mixed together the remains of various people, ruining the chance they would ever be identified.

On December 31, 1983, before he had to endure a new year without Liliana, Alfredo Galletti took his own life.

As they watched the excavation coverage, the Abuelas felt a similar despair. Bones, they knew, held clues not just about their children but also their grandchildren: the acts of carrying a child and pushing it through the birth canal can leave dents and grooves on a mother's pelvis. The skeletons in the mass graves might reveal whether or not their grandchildren had been born. Now that very evidence was being crushed. Distraught, they begged CONADEP to let Eric Stover, the human rights researcher at the AAAS, gather a scientific committee to teach the Argentines proper forensic protocols so that Argentina could form its own forensic anthropology team. Bringing American scientists to Argentina would be politically delicate—many Argentines resented America for tacitly supporting the dictatorship, and those sentiments had only deepened after the United States backed Britain in the humiliating scuffle over the Falklands. A more radical faction of the Madres, led by Hebe de Bonafini, opposed exhumations altogether, creating a fissure in the group that would ultimately lead to its division into two separate organizations—and the Abuelas' estrangement from the Madres. "We want to know who the murderers are; we already know who the victims are!" demanded one Madre in the anti-exhumations camp. But after repeated requests from the Abuelas, CONADEP agreed to contact Stover, who began assembling a small group of experts in February 1984. He recruited Lowell Levine, a forensic odontologist with a slight New York twang who used teeth to identify victims of plane crashes and homicides; Leslie Lukash, a medical examiner and self-proclaimed "diagnostician of death"; Luke Tedeschi, a pathologist from Massachusetts; and finally, Clyde Snow, a garrulous forensic anthropologist from a dusty farm town in West Texas.

If Stover was at all worried about parachuting into Argentina with a planeload of "yanqui" scientists, his selection of Snow would not have helped. The man was cartoonishly American. No matter where he traveled, he invariably wore leather cowboy boots and a jaunty felt fedora; a Camel cigarette often drooped out of his mouth as he spoke in his syrupy Plains drawl. He had worked for the Federal Aviation Administration as an accident investigator, flying to scenes of grisly crashes in a refurbished World War II P-51 Mustang that itself seemed fated to plunge to the earth. As his reputation as the "Sherlock Holmes of Bones" had grown, he had even been invited by Congress to testify on the authenticity of President John F. Kennedy's remains.

By June, a few weeks before the group was scheduled to travel to Argentina, the Abuelas were encouraged by how the AAAS committee was shaping up, but not entirely satisfied. Bones could only tell them whether or not their grandchildren had been born—it was blood that held the answers required to identify them. They had the formula, but they still needed someone to put the Index of Grandpaternity into practice, showing them how it might work in various cases—and who could possibly be better than one of its authors, Mary-Claire King? They implored CONADEP and the AAAS to invite her to join the committee.

King had never intended to implement the index herself, but the timing of the Abuelas' request was fortuitous. That summer, her ex-husband, Colwell, had arranged for Emily to come to his family's ranch for an extended stay, freeing King to join the AAAS crew in Argentina. Less than two weeks after the Abuelas asked her, she was on a plane to Buenos Aires.

The geneticist knew that nothing was guaranteed. The Index of Grandpaternity would provide decisive results only if the Abuelas could use genetic markers that were much more powerful than blood groups. HLA would be the best candidate, but HLA typing was complex, and King feared it would not be available in Argentina, particularly in the wake of a dictatorship during which droves of scientists had been unceremoniously dismissed from their jobs or disappeared altogether. Even if the Abuelas could conduct HLA analysis, there was the question of whether they could collect the blood samples required to reach a definitive conclusion. For most cases, King would need samples from at least five individuals—the suspected grandchild and all four grandparents. But most of the Abuelas and their husbands were in their fifties and sixties, and some had already passed away. Many of the grandchildren, the Abuelas had begun to suspect, were living with families who did not want them to be found.

King was not optimistic. She saw her trip as more symbolic than anything, a onetime event to express solidarity with the Abuelas' cause. Still, she was committed to helping in any way she could.

Years before, she had seen firsthand the destruction a dictatorship could bring. Back in 1972, as King was finishing up her PhD and about to get married, Colwell and several of his students had been awarded a US National Science Foundation grant to conduct research in Chile. Colwell was a field ecologist and the country was a wonderland for his work—a sort of California turned upside down, with the scorching Atacama Desert in the north, the jagged Andes mountains in the east, a long stretch of Pacific Ocean to the west, and the lakes and forests of Patagonia in the south. In love and always game for an adventure, King eagerly went along, joining for research visits to the Norte Chico, where pink, white, and purple wildflowers bloomed from the desert floor like a Technicolor carpet.

The following year, Colwell was invited to teach at the Universidad de Chile in Santiago through a Ford Foundation exchange program with the University of California and the couple jumped at the chance to return. As King and Colwell prepared to move down for the semester, simmering political tensions in Chile rose to a rolling boil. Salvador Allende, an upper-middle-class medical student turned Marxist politician, was president. His drive to redistribute the country's wealth had earned him the loyalty of Chile's farming and working classes, but it had also attracted the ire of the conservative Chilean military and the US government, which was then led by hard-line anticommunist Richard Nixon. Allende had particularly galled such critics when he seized large estates and nationalized telecom businesses and mining conglomerates, some of which were American-owned.

On June 29, 1973, the Chilean military attempted to mount a coup. It failed, but in its wake, friction continued to build. As one of Allende's top aides peeked out of the second-floor balcony of his home a month later, he was shot dead. Inflation surged, prompting widespread shortages and strikes by irate shopkeepers. On the days stores were open, lines for bread, meat, gasoline, and many other basic food and household items snaked down the block. There had been murmurings of another uprising for months, but as the South American winter passed, nothing materialized.

In early September, Colwell flew to Chile while King headed to a meeting of the National Cancer Institute in Washington, DC, with plans to travel to Santiago from there. After sessions had concluded one warm early fall evening, she was strolling by the White House when she passed a *Washington Post* vending machine. The front page displayed through the glass stopped her in her tracks. "Allende Dead in Chilean Coup," it read. The government had been seized by Chilean general Augusto Pinochet.

King raced to the nearest phone to call Colwell, but the lines were down. Panicked, she called her parents in Chicago, who begged her not to travel to Santiago. But her husband was there. She couldn't imagine *not* going. She rushed to the airport and flew to Miami. When she boarded her flight to Santiago in Florida, it was almost entirely occupied by journalists and conservative Chilean expats who had already begun knocking back drinks to celebrate the coup. Over Peru, the pilot took to the loudspeaker and announced that Pudahuel Airport in Santiago was shut down. They were being diverted to Buenos Aires.

Upon landing at the stout concrete terminal of Argentina's international airport in Ezeiza, King shared a taxi into the city with a few of the journalists who had been on her flight. It was spring, and emerald-green fields dotted with scrubby bushes lined either side of the highway. A few minutes into their drive, they passed the site where, just a few months earlier, Perón's homecoming event had devolved into a bloody massacre.

The journey became familiar to King as she shuttled frantically back and forth between Buenos Aires and Ezeiza each day to find out if Chile had reopened its airport. Finally, after ten days, she was granted a ticket into Pudahuel on the first commercial flight from Buenos Aires.

The roads from the airport to central Santiago, normally choked with traffic, were eerily quiet. As King made her way to the apartment where she and Colwell would be staying in Las Condes, an upper-middle-class neighborhood near the city center, military men in tanks and Chilean police in shiny patrol cars seemed to be the only people on the streets. Staring out the car window, she glimpsed a headless corpse that had been tossed on the side of the road like garbage.

Once reunited with Colwell, she learned that on the day of the coup, he and the rest of Santiago had been ordered to stay in their homes. Violators who ventured out were told they would be shot without question. Sometimes jittery soldiers would fire if a window opened too quickly, suspecting rival snipers. Colwell recalled that the TV screen went blank, flickering to life only periodically as members of the new junta appeared to remark how wonderful it was that the country had been saved from communism.

By the time King arrived, Colwell had already begun hearing disturbing rumors. It seemed Pinochet's forces were arresting activists, intellectuals, university students, and anyone else suspected of leftist tendencies. They'd supposedly sliced off the hands of Chilean folk singer Víctor Jara before killing him. Colwell had also learned that two Americans—a thirty-one-year-old journalist and a twenty-three-year-old economics student—had been killed during the brutal days after the coup. Their US passports had apparently not been enough to keep them safe.

In Santiago, the number of people arrested by the armed forces—around eight thousand according to the government's own estimates—soon exceeded the capacity of the city's jails. In response, Pinochet's men seized Santiago's main soccer stadium, which could seat more than forty-six thousand, and turned it into a massive makeshift torture camp. All the while, Chile continued to host international games there. In November, FIFA investigators came to follow up on accusations by the Soviet Union—not exactly a bastion of human rights itself—that the stadium was a "place of blood." To evade notice, the prisoners were forced at gunpoint into dressing rooms hidden below the playing field and told to shut up or die.

Amid the chaos, King and Colwell pushed forward with the work that had brought them to Chile. Once the university reopened, Colwell led his course and King taught classes on genetics, statistics, and evolution in what eventually became Spanish, but started as, in her description, "fractured, fractured French." She often joined Colwell and his students on ecological field trips. To reach their field sites, they drove roads punctuated with endless military checkpoints. Because she was a woman, King recalls she was often the one to speak with the soldiers, her blue eyes, halting Spanish, and the mist nets and vials in the trunk effectively convincing them that she was just a "clueless gringa scientist."

A few months after the coup, a student King and Colwell had grown close to discovered he was on a list of leftists being targeted by Chile's feared intelligence directorate. He fled to his ecology field research site just outside Santiago and, at his request, King and Colwell rushed to pick up his passport at his home, unsure if it was already being surveilled. Following careful instructions to interact only with a specific airline employee at the Braniff

International Airways ticket office, King and Colwell bought the student a plane ticket out of Santiago, stating: "We would like to invite a young Chilean friend to visit us, as soon as possible, in San Francisco, California."

Soon, King and Colwell felt it was time to leave as well. Most other academics participating in the Ford Foundation exchange had already packed up and headed home to California. "There were very few people like us there anymore," King would later say. The longer they stuck around, the more people might grow wary of them—and by extension their students. On Christmas Day, King and Colwell left Santiago. Once home in Berkeley, Colwell concealed cash in film canisters and sent it back to Chile to support the resistance to Pinochet. King worked to secure spots in American graduate schools for Chilean students she worried were still at risk. Still, she felt crushing guilt that she could escape and others couldn't.

"You are nothing more than a do-gooder if you can get on a plane and leave," she would say later. "Which means you owe more."

Now, eleven years later, King was headed back to the Southern Cone, to another country ravaged by a military dictatorship. This time, she wouldn't be able to pull anyone away from danger; the abductions and murders were in the past. But, if she could implement it, the index she had helped devise might still reveal the stolen children of those killed—the living disappeared.

24

Madame Defarge

June 1984

Outside an auditorium near La Plata's sweeping central plaza, a hand-written sign beckoned: "Seminar on the Forensic Sciences and the Disappeared . . . All welcome." It was the first time the AAAS delegation was introducing itself to the public, and King found herself before an audience of Abuelas, government officials, and relatives of the disappeared eager to hear her presentation. Carefully, she laid out how the Abuelas might use the Index of Grandpaternity to identify their grandchildren with "absolute precision." Just as children inherit their hair color and eye color, she said, they also inherit markers in their blood. Their looks might change over time. Their hair might darken, or their body shape might morph. But the markers they carried in their blood would endure.

Other members of the team explained their specialties and how they might be used to investigate the junta's crimes. As the scientists launched into their presentations, delving into the intricacies of bone excavation and dental forensics, it became clear that the translator hired for the event, a young Argentine woman, was in over her head. She began to bumble, struggling with various medical terms. When one of the experts expounded on the physical impact of torture, the translator burst into tears and said she could not continue. The event ground to an awkward halt as Estela and Chicha glanced around the room for a replacement. Without a translator, they would have to call the whole thing off. But there, seated in the back, they spotted Morris Tidball-Binz, a sprightly blond Chilean Argentine medical student who had participated in several marches with the Abuelas. Tidball-Binz had British ancestry and his knowledge of English medical terms was strong; he volunteered to take over, picking up the presentations where the other translator had abruptly left off.

As the event drew to a close, the scientists opened the floor to questions. A stooped and graying man named Juan Miranda rose laboriously from his seat.

"Tell me, Doctor," Miranda began in Spanish, directing his question to Clyde Snow, the foremost expert on skeletons in the group. "How long does it take for the bones of a six-month-old child to dissolve?"

Seated on the stage near Snow, King wondered if she had misunderstood the question. She hadn't spoken much Spanish since leaving Chile. But Tidball-Binz translated the question exactly as she'd thought. Unbeknownst to her and the other scientists, a few months earlier, in a sprawling cemetery to the north of Buenos Aires, the Abuelas had helped Miranda and his wife exhume the remains of their twenty-six-year-old daughter, her husband, and who they imagined would be the couple's three children. They found the adults and the two older children, who were five and three at the time of their abduction, had all been shot during a raid on their home in 1976, buried next to one another in unmarked graves, and categorized as N.N.: No Names. But when the team opened the wood coffin buried in the smallest grave, where they expected to see the bones of the Mirandas' infant granddaughter, Matilde, they had found only a pair of tiny socks, a spotless teddy bear, and a pacifier, all wrapped in a green blanket.

Snow explained to the man that bones do not dissolve.

"Then Matilde is still alive," Miranda murmured.

For the past several months, King had been thinking about the challenges faced by the Abuelas in terms of functions and formulas—gp's and c's in an equation. Suddenly, the horror—and the hope her index offered—was no longer so abstract.

It was Rosa Roisinblit who opened the door to King at the Abuelas' headquarters, ushering her inside. Now King's real work would begin: putting the Index of Grandpaternity into practice.

As Rosa showed her around, King felt an immediate affection for the older woman. Rosa was witty and sharp, but also maternal, tolerating King's broken Spanish and offering her mate and food. She focused exclusively on Abuelas business, never mentioning anything personal, but afterward, King would wonder if, with her age and scientific background, she reminded Rosa a bit of Patricia. Rosa's tour of the headquarters was quick, as there were just a few rooms to explore: a small kitchen, a bedroom that housed the Abuelas' new Bull desktop computer, and a living room whose shelves were lined with thick black binders, each one representing a case. King told Rosa that the Abuelas reminded her of Madame Defarge from *A Tale of Two Cities*, a seemingly unthreatening old woman who whiles away her days knitting as the French Revolution rages. Concealed in the long scarf she's making, however, is a list of targets to be beheaded. The Abuelas, likewise, might have been dismissed as "viejas locas," old loons, but King saw that they had been underestimated.

"My dear girl," replied Rosa, smiling wryly. "I don't have time to knit anymore; now I use a personal computer."

In the living room, a jumble of black-and-white photographs pinned to the wall caught King's eye. "Where are these children and their parents?" a note at the top read. Below, staring out at King, were the faces of dozens of smiling couples, dimply babies, and chubby toddlers.

"My God," she exclaimed, overwhelmed. "Where do we start?"

"Empezamos con Paula," Rosa responded, referring to Elsa Pavón's suspected granddaughter. We begin with Paula.

King and the Abuelas took seats around the wooden table where the Abuelas did most of their work. King sat in the middle. The table was often piled high with boxes and papers, but now they cleared a space for her demonstration. The case to get Paula back was stalled—she still lived with Lavallen and Leiro Mendiondo, and she would likely remain there until the Abuelas could produce firm evidence of her identity. As the Abuelas crowded around, King sketched out a genealogical tree to demonstrate how the Index of Grandpaternity would work in Paula's case, and in any other. At the top she drew four grandparents, using small circles to represent grandmothers and squares to denote grandfathers. Below one pair of grandparents, she drew another square: a son. Below the other, a daughter. Then she raised her pen and, with a quick stroke, crossed both shapes out. These were the Abuelas' disappeared children. Finally, at the bottom, King drew a square with a question mark next to it. "Niño o niña secuestrada," she labeled it. Kidnapped boy or girl.

Even without blood samples from the disappeared parents, King explained, if all four grandparents were living, scientists could compare the markers in their blood with those of the suspected grandchild. They could immediately rule out a relationship if the child's alleles, the variations of the gene in question, did not match any of the grandparents. But if one of the child's alleles matched a maternal grandparent, and another matched a paternal grandparent, they might be related. To calculate the likelihood that the match was due to biology and not coincidence, they would need to enter the genetic markers into the formula King and Darlu had devised. Reaching a truly decisive conclusion would require testing HLA, the most powerful genetic marker available.

Only three out of four of Paula's presumptive grandparents were alive. Elsa's first husband—Paula's putative maternal grandfather—had died before Paula was born. It was a challenge, but not an insurmountable one. King stared at the genealogical tree she had sketched out. She could use blood from Elsa's surviving children—Mónica's siblings—to re-create their father's genetics, she decided. If they could get samples from Paula, Elsa, Elsa's children, and Paula's paternal grandparents, they should be able to get a definitive result.

First, though, they would need a lab capable of conducting HLA testing. HLA had been identified in 1958, and since then, it had been used largely to determine whether donated organs would be compatible with their intended recipients. Such labs were fairly common in America, but King didn't know whether the method had arrived in Argentina. They would also need samples. Extracting blood from Elsa, her children, and the other grandparents should be simple enough, but King suspected reaching Paula, who was still living with Lavallen, the former police officer, and his wife, might be another matter.

The Abuelas waited politely while King listed her concerns. When she finished, they informed her they had already worked out a plan. They could request a court order compelling Lavallen and Leiro Mendiondo to submit Paula for testing. Then, to King's surprise, they announced they had identified an immunology laboratory in Buenos Aires that could conduct HLA analysis.

Located on Avenida Díaz Vélez, a bustling boulevard in the middle-class neighborhood of Caballito, the Hospital Durand was housed in a blocky gray building studded with small windows. Its metal entrance gate was rusted bright orange. Spartan stairs led inside to corridors that were patched precariously with wood. But when the Abuelas opened the door to the immunology department, King was flooded with relief. Inside she found a modern laboratory with well-maintained microscopes, clean beakers, and neatly stacked microtiter plates—like "an oasis in the middle of a desert," King would later recall.

The Abuelas introduced her to the lab's director, an angular wisp of a woman with a short brown bob named Ana María Di Lonardo. She was known to be exacting and intense, lurking over her team to ensure their work was completed her way. Using the lab's whiteboard to write out the Index of Grandpaternity, King explained to Di Lonardo and her team how she thought HLA might be applied in the Abuelas' case. The first part of the process was no different from the one the Durand team already used to test organ transplant compatibility. From each grandparent and suspected grandchild, they would need to extract twenty to thirty milliliters of blood—enough to fill two or three vials that had been pretreated with heparin or other anticoagulants to keep the blood from clotting. Then the blood would need to be rushed back to the lab and piped into a plate dotted with wells that had each been filled with antisera, or antibody-rich serum used to determine the particular types of HLA present. It was a complex process, and one that would need to take place quickly—within forty-eight hours, but preferably twenty-four. Once the analysis was complete, the team would plug the resulting data into the index. Since they didn't yet have a computer in the lab, they would need to conduct all their calculations by hand.

Undaunted, the Durand team got to work right away. They extracted blood from Elsa, her children, and her son-in-law's parents. They were also, to the Abuelas' great relief, able to extract blood from Paula. The Durand team carefully analyzed each person's HLA types and handed the results to King. From a cursory scan of the data, it was already clear that Paula could be related to the families. But King would have to enter the information into the Index of Grandpaternity to be sure.

King scribbled her calculations with a pencil on a sheet of paper. The results were so striking that the team checked them three times to be certain. The likelihood that Paula Lavallen was actually Paula Logares, the granddaughter of Elsa Pavón, was 99.82 percent.

25

Nunca Más

June–December 1984

A s King returned home to Berkeley, the Abuelas submitted the results of the index to a judge and waited, keeping her closely updated on the case. The Index of Grandpaternity was an entirely new tool, and it wasn't certain that judges would embrace it as evidence. Soon, however, the Abuelas shared good news. Despite the test's novelty, the judge presiding over Paula's case had accepted its results as valid. But the celebration was short-lived. Faced with the results of the Abuelas' test, Rubén Lavallen changed tactics. He stopped insisting Paula was his daughter, as he had claimed previously, but argued that wresting the girl from the only "parents" she remembered would be too traumatic. The court, for the moment, agreed.

The Abuelas were stunned. Democracy had been restored for eight months. Witnesses had seen Lavallen at the Brigada de San Justo, a clandestine torture center where Paula's parents had also been spotted. Paula had the same name her parents had given her and looked exactly like her mother had as a child. Most important, though, her blood had confirmed it. She was Paula Eva Logares. And still the court had sided against them.

The women took to the courthouse steps to protest, waving white signs with black lettering that read: "Paula Eva Logares: kidnapped by a repressor and prisoner of the justice system." They wrote fiery press releases, insisting that "Paula cannot continue as 'war booty,'" and appealed the ruling, arguing that it was akin to giving immunity to kidnappers around the world.

In November, as the Abuelas waited for an answer from the court, their appeal gained crucial recognition. Nearly a year after its formation, CONADEP, the commission tasked with investigating the junta's disappearances, published its final report: fifty thousand pages of raw testimony and evidence delivered to President Alfonsín a few months before had been distilled to 539 pages and bound with a bright red cover for the public. Its title, emblazoned in rough, white letters, was as much an exhortation as a description of the book's contents: *Nunca Más*. Never Again.

Not anticipating the Argentine public's hunger for the truth after years of censorship and lies, CONADEP had only planned for an initial print run of forty thousand copies. They sold out in two days. Those who did get their hands on a book were horrified by what they read.

"Many of the episodes recounted here will be hard to believe," the introduction warned. "This is because the men and women of our country have only known such horrors through accounts from other parts of the world." In searing detail, *Nunca Más* described how Argentines were dragged from their homes, offices, and off the street. One parent of a *desaparecido* described how her son had been recovering from a car accident in the hospital when armed men disguised as medical professionals stormed his room. They forced all the other patients in the ward to pull sheets over their heads and rolled the man away, never to be seen again. The book also revealed the existence of 340 clandestine torture facilities where prisoners were beaten, raped, shocked with electrical prods, hung from the ceiling by their arms, and waterboarded. A survivor of one of the torture centers recalled how a guard entered her cell while she was asleep, placed his boot on her face to keep her quiet, and raped her. The following morning, he brought her sugar for her mate, stating it was for "services rendered." In fact, the report clarified, almost every case investigated by the commission involved some sort of torture.

Nunca Más laid bare what the junta had tried to erase, assigning hard numbers and first-person testimony to previously blurry suspicions. It estimated that 8,960 people had been disappeared during the dictatorship, emphasizing that number was only approximate—before passing power to Alfonsín, the junta had ordered that all records related to disappearances be destroyed. (Other documents that surfaced later suggested a higher death toll. A classified Operation Condor intelligence memo reported twenty-two thousand people had been disappeared in Argentina by July 1978. Human rights groups argued the number was closer to thirty thousand.)

Most shocking for many Argentines, though, was the first official confirmation that the junta's forces had stolen babies. According to the report, "repressors" had dragged pregnant women to clandestine detention centers, where some were tortured as their pregnancies progressed. While in labor, they were attended by military doctors—who sometimes rushed along the process by performing C-sections—or other prisoners who were forced to help. A few hours after giving birth, the women were separated from their babies. One witness shared a rumor that, in the naval hospital, there was a list of officers without children of their own who wanted to "adopt" those of the disappeared.

Here, the report departed from its usual staid, academic language and ventured an explanation for why the military had done something as demonic as stealing babies: to indoctrinate them, severing them from the "subversive" philosophies espoused by their parents. "When a child is torn from their legitimate family to be placed in another family environment chosen according to an ideological notion of 'what is best for their salvation,' a vile usurpation of roles is being committed." It called the stolen children an "open wound" in Argentine society and highlighted the work of the Abuelas to heal it, calling them "indefatigable, constant, and discrete." About midway through the book, an entire page was dedicated to the case of Paula Logares.

A few weeks after *Nunca Más* was released, the phone rang in King's office. It was the middle of December 1984, and she was rushing to get as much done as she could before the Christmas holiday. (Not that she planned to vacation herself—she hadn't taken a true break in years.) When she picked up and heard the voice on the other end of the line, her heart began to race. Long-distance calls from Argentina to California were expensive. Estela would only be calling if it was important.

The court's verdict was finally in, Estela told her. Paula was home—the first of the Abuelas' stolen grandchildren to be returned to her family by the courts, all thanks to genetic evidence.

Staring out her lab's windows, toward Berkeley's iconic campanile and the gentle undulations of the Berkeley Hills, King listened to Estela describe Paula's reunion with her grandmother. When she was escorted back to Elsa's house—a home she had not seen since before her second birthday—the now eight-year-old girl strode in confidently and turned left into the bedroom where she used to sleep. Even though she had hardly been able to form words when she was last in the room, she seemed to remember it perfectly. "Where is my teddy bear?" she asked, observing the empty bedspread.

King had not indulged her emotions during the weeks she had spent in Argentina with the Abuelas. The Abuelas hadn't, and their attitudes had made clear that there was no time for anyone else to cry either. But now tears streamed down King's face as she took in the enormity of what the Index of Grandpaternity had accomplished. What had started as a formula sketched out in pencil had rectified a horrible crime, wresting back a child from her kidnapper. It had helped uncover Paula's true identity, ensuring she would grow up knowing who she really was, and restored the bond between her and her family. The test had salvaged a family history—and thus a small piece of Argentine history as well.

Estela interrupted King's brief moment of sentimentalism. There were many more grandchildren out there, and they needed King's help to find them. "Now," she said, "you need to come back."

26

A Mother's Mark

1984–1987

Around the time that Elsa Pavón learned the identity of her Paula, Rosa's granddaughter, Mariana, was grappling with a discovery of her own. One evening, while picking Mariana up from an English class, her grandmother Argentina delivered some delicate news: The next day, she told her granddaughter, she would need to get her blood drawn.

"But why? Why?" Mariana had whined. She was terrified of needles. The one time Rosa, the family's resident medical professional, had given her an injection, she remembered it had felt like being "pierced by a sword."

"Look, Mariana," Argentina said firmly. "I have to tell you something, but I don't want you to cry."

Rosa, Argentina, and Mariana's grandfather, José, often spoke to Mariana about her parents. Her grandfather had photos of Patricia and his son and namesake that he kept tucked under the glass top of their sideboard, and every morning, he would observe the images in silence before giving each one a kiss. The grandparents had been truthful with Mariana about her parents' fate since she was tiny. Once, during a tantrum when she was four or five, Mariana told Argentina that she wanted to leave—she wanted to go be with her mother—just to say something she knew would be hurtful.

"I wish you could go with your mother, too," Argentina had responded plaintively, "but the military took your parents and we don't know where they are." It was the first time Mariana would recall having an explanation for their absence. But her grandparents had never told Mariana that she might have a sibling. Now, as they walked together, Argentina continued: "When they took your mom, she was eight months pregnant. You have a brother that we're looking for."

Mariana didn't even think of crying—she was thrilled. She hated being an only child, playing alone all the time, bored to death. The next day, she sat stoically as technicians from the Hospital Durand told her she would barely feel a thing; it would just be like a "mosquito bite." Then, they inserted a needle in her vein and extracted several tubes of blood, which were quickly sent off for HLA typing. They did the same with Rosa's sample, and samples from Argentina and José. The truth they already knew was confirmed: Mariana was their granddaughter. Someday, they hoped the test would identify their missing grandson as well.

It had been a triumphant year for the Abuelas. In addition to Paula Logares's hard-fought restitution, they located eleven other grandchildren. Now that she finally understood what it was that Rosa did all day in the small apartment on Montevideo with the other grandmothers, Mariana became convinced that her brother would surely appear at any moment.

Soon, though, Mariana grew frustrated waiting for her missing family members. When Alfonsín had campaigned for president the year before, she had been a die-hard supporter, watching every one of his broadcast speeches—so long as the television worked, anyway. (The bulky television in the Belgrano apartment where she continued living with Argentina and José broke so often that her grandfather had established an unlikely friendship with the repair technician.) When the dark-mustached lawyer intoned about the return of democracy—"Argentinos! The dictatorship is over. Immorality and tyranny are through. Fear and repression are done"—the six-year-old had sat as rapt as if she were watching *Señorita Maestra* or *Burbujas*, two of her favorite children's shows. As time passed, however, her opinion of the president changed.

"I am disappointed with Alfonsín," she once complained to Rosa.

"Why?" Rosa asked, surprised.

"Because I thought that when he came into office, Alfonsín was going to open all the jails and the *desaparecidos* were going to return," Mariana replied. When that didn't happen, Mariana began to accept that her parents were dead. They *had* to be dead. Why else wouldn't they come look for her?

But now, with the knowledge of a brother, her yearning took a new shape. She imagined leading him to school by the hand and passing down her uniform to him. Eventually, she began writing him letters.

"Sometimes I think, when we find one another, 'What will I say to you?'" she wrote in one. "And I answer: Surely we will look at one another and I (the weak one, moved) will maybe start to cry; then, after looking at one another as though we can't believe it, maybe I'll give you a hug and say: 'My dream has come true.'"

In 1985, the case initiated by Alfonsín against Videla and other dictatorship-era leaders—known as the Trial of the Juntas—came to an end. Initially, Alfonsín had pushed for the proceedings to take place in a military tribunal, both to give the military an opportunity to clean up its own affairs without civilian meddling and to avoid further inflaming tensions with his administration. But the Supreme Council of the Armed Forces declared that the actions the military took against "terrorist subversion" during the dictatorship were "unimpeachable," and the case had landed in civilian court. There, it was publicly prosecuted by a civilian lawyer named Julio Strassera, who accused the defendants, including Videla and former navy chief Emilio Massera, of perpetrating "the greatest genocide" in Argentine history.

"The guerrillas kidnapped, tortured, and murdered," Strassera said during one hearing. "How did the state choose to respond? By kidnapping, torturing, and murdering on a vastly greater scale."

Over seven and a half months of emotional hearings, which were televised across the country, more than eight hundred witnesses condemned the cruelty of their former government. One particularly gut-turning session featured a young woman named Adriana Calvo, who recounted how she was forced to give birth to her baby in the back of a police car, blindfolded, hands tied behind her back, while being driven from one torture center to another. In the seat next to her was a female officer who had tortured her during her detention. Sensing the baby was coming, Calvo begged for help, but the men in the front had continued driving. In the grand courtroom, Calvo looked up to the ceiling as though summoning strength before continuing her testimony:

"My baby girl was born healthy, she was very little, and she hung from the umbilical cord, she fell off the seat, she was on the floor, I begged them to give her to me, but they didn't." No one knew how to cut the umbilical cord, so they left Calvo in the car for two or three hours, her baby girl still swinging from the umbilical cord, wailing, cold, before a doctor came.

Luis Moreno Ocampo, Strassera's assistant prosecutor, rubbed his temples as Calvo spoke, as though her testimony caused him physical pain. The judges listened intently.

"Señor Presidente," she said, directly addressing the head judge. "That day I made a promise that if my baby lived, if I lived, I was going to fight for the rest of my days for justice." It was seen as a turning point in the trial.

Assistant Prosecutor Moreno Ocampo's mother was the daughter of a military officer and a staunch defender of the junta. He relied on her as a bellwether for the prosecution's persuasiveness. After Calvo's testimony, mother and son spoke by phone. "I still love Videla," she said. "But you're right: He has to go to jail."

In Strassera's final argument before the judges, he channeled the anger and pain of an entire nation. "I want to use a phrase that doesn't belong to me, because it belongs to all Argentines," he bellowed. "Señores jueces: Nunca más."

The court ruled in December 1985. Videla, who had spent some of the hearings paging through a Bible, listened as the chief judge read the manifold counts against him: 66 aggravated homicides, 4 episodes of torture followed by death, 93 episodes of torture, 306 cases of illegal privation of liberty, and 26 robberies. He was sentenced to spend the rest of his life in prison. It was the first time in Latin American history that a civilian government had convicted a military regime for crimes against humanity, and Alfonsín was celebrated around the world as a human rights hero.

But the armed forces were predictably irate. While the military's power had been greatly diminished by the Falklands War, it was still strong enough to pose a credible threat to Argentine democracy, whose institutions were weak after decades of instability. Military leaders pressed Alfonsín to halt further legal actions. He and his administration were terrified of another coup—so much so that his aides rarely left him alone in the presidential residence, concerned that the military officers guarding him might mutiny. In December 1986, Alfonsín ceded to the pressure, announcing that he would enact the Full Stop Law, which prohibited new legal proceedings against the military for most crimes committed during the dictatorship after a sixty-day deadline.

The swift decision had unintended consequences. Before the deadline elapsed, the number of lawsuits lodged against military officers skyrocketed. Exasperated, a radical sect of the armed forces that called itself the *carapintadas*—or painted faces, after the camouflage patterns they smeared on their skin for combat—seized the Campo de Mayo army base around Easter 1987. They demanded a cessation of all trials, even those that had been pushed through before the Full Stop deadline. Rosa was among the massive crowd of Argentines who gathered in the Plaza de Mayo to express their support for Alfonsín—and their nascent democracy. As they cheered encouragingly, Alfonsín announced that he would personally fly to Campo de Mayo in a helicopter to negotiate with the insubordinate soldiers.

He returned hours later, declaring victory from the balcony of the Casa Rosada, only to succumb over the following weeks to the demands of the armed forces. That June, he passed the Due Obedience Law, which shielded lower-ranking military officials from punishment if they were following a superior's orders—legally enshrining the defense many Nazis had used during the Nuremberg trials. Alfonsín's "impunity laws," as they were often called by their critics, and the specter of yet another revolt, reminded the Abuelas of the precarity of their recent success. At home, Mariana channeled her own ire at the president into poetry. Splayed on the ground with a fat marker, she wrote: "I only hope that you think, President, about children like me, without my brother born in captivity, without my parents taken to heaven."

To make matters worse, the limitations of the HLA tests the Abuelas relied upon were starting to become clear. Earlier that year, the Abuelas had located a ten-year-old girl in the coastal city of Mar del Plata with a suspicious backstory: the girl's birth certificate indicated she was born was in September 1977, which would have made her supposed mother, a female police sergeant, in her fifties at the time she gave birth. After the Abuelas began legal proceedings to investigate, the sergeant quickly confessed the girl was not her biological child. (Later it would surface that she was employed at the Brigada de San Justo, the same facility where Paula Logares's appropriator had also worked. At birth, she had torn the newborn girl from her mother, stripped off her own shirt, and placed the baby on her naked chest, so the infant would smell her scent instead of her mother's.)

Though the Abuelas had hypotheses based on the girl's birthdate, at first, they didn't have a clear theory for whose family she might belong to, so they planned to compare her HLA types with several families. Then Chicha traveled to Mar del Plata to meet the child in person. Upon seeing her walk through the courthouse hallways, Chicha was stunned: the girl had the exact same gait as María Lavalle Lemos, the eleven-year-old granddaughter of Haydée Vallino de Lemos, an austere woman who had been one of the Abuelas' founding members. María had been kidnapped at fourteen months by the security forces along with her father and mother, who was eight months pregnant, but was later returned to Haydée. She often accompanied her grandmother to the Abuelas' headquarters. Chicha was confident. This girl had to be María's missing little sister, and Haydée's grandchild.

Unfortunately, the HLA data they would be able to obtain was limited. After Haydée's pregnant daughter and son-in-law were abducted from their home in the Buenos Aires suburbs, Haydée's husband, Alberto, died, his heart weakened by grief. Their other daughter had lived in exile since evading abduction by security forces and their son had also been disappeared.

Without blood samples from these crucial family members, it wasn't clear if the Index of Grandpaternity would be able to confirm Chicha's hunch.

Still, they pushed on. The Abuelas already had blood samples from Haydée and her in-laws; now they secured a court order to extract a sample from the young girl. Technicians at the Hospital Durand typed the samples and sent King each person's HLA data to review. To the uninitiated, the jumble of numbers and letters would have been as inscrutable as ancient runes, but as King stared at the paperwork, she all but gasped.

Haydée and the Abuelas had been extremely fortunate. Haydée, María, and the suspected grandchild all shared a very rare HLA type, making it unlikely that they shared it by chance. The index was conclusive: The likelihood that the ten-year-old girl with the familiar walk was Haydée's granddaughter exceeded 99 percent.

Haydée's family celebrated with a bottle of cider from the local bar, waking up María in the middle of the night to share the news. "Mirá, Mariquita," they had told her as, pajama-clad, she begged them to go back to sleep. "We found your hermanita," they said, snapping her wide awake.

Luck had been on their side this time. But the case underscored something King had long worried about: the HLA method was unsustainable. Confirming a grandparental relationship with HLA testing required drawing blood samples from many different family members of a suspected child—preferably all four grandparents. As time passed, so too would many of the Abuelas and their spouses, which meant there would eventually be genetic gaps that were impossible to fill. To devise another approach, King returned to the Abuelas' long wooden table in late 1987. A Spanish-English dictionary and a gourd of strong mate sat next to the papers that occupied her attention. The caffeine was welcome—the questions ricocheting around her mind were thorny.

For years, the Abuelas and their scientific allies had lobbied Argentina's Congress to create a national genetic data bank, where genetic information from families looking for their stolen grandchildren could be stored. Congress had recently granted their request, designating the Hospital Durand's immunology lab, which had managed the Abuelas' HLA testing for the past three years, as the headquarters of the newly formed Banco Nacional de Datos Genéticos (BNDG). It was welcome and historic news; the BNDG was the first "biobank" of its kind in the world, and would ensure that the Abuelas' genetic information—and their search—would endure even after they passed away. But the bank's establishment highlighted another lingering problem with the HLA method. Up until then, the Abuelas had been careful to pursue just the cases they knew they could solve, comparing the HLA types of a suspected child against those of a select few families, who were carefully chosen based on circumstantial evidence the Abuelas had gathered. More than three hundred families were still missing their grandchildren, and ideally the Abuelas would be able to compare the genetic profiles of each suspected grandchild against all of them to avoid missing a potential match. With HLA, that wasn't advisable. Since HLA types are rare but not unique, screening hundreds of families with HLA would increase the chance of a match occurring by coincidence, not because of biology—a risk the Abuelas could not afford to take.

Sensing her unease as she puzzled away in the Abuelas' office, one of the grandmothers gave King a fond hug. "Go back to Berkeley, dear, and give us a call in a couple of weeks when you've figured it out."

Until the 1960s, scientists believed DNA populated only the nucleus of our cells. Then, in 1963, a husband-and-wife team at Stockholm University noticed something curious while peering through an electron microscope at chick embryos: there were tiny white circles of DNA, more than a thousand times smaller than a grain of rice, floating within the embryo's mitochondria, the bean-shaped structures that generate a cell's energy. The finding was revolutionary, upending conventional beliefs about what shapes our genetic identities. Scientists rushed to analyze what exactly mitochondrial DNA, or mtDNA, could tell us about our families and ourselves.

One of those scientists was Allan Wilson, who since advising King's work on chimpanzees in the early 1970s, had largely been focused on using mitochondrial DNA to trace evolution. For the nuclear DNA that determines everything from the texture of our hair to the size of our feet, a child receives half his genes from his mother and half from his father. Mitochondrial DNA, by contrast, is passed down exclusively by mothers, without any shuffling or mixing. Almost without exception, each of us carries mtDNA that is an identical copy of our mother's, whose mtDNA is a carbon copy of her mother's, and so on. In fact, any two people who are related by an unbroken maternal lineage, including siblings, cousins, and even second cousins, should share an identical mitochondrial DNA sequence. The conservation of mtDNA across generations made it the perfect vehicle for mapping maternal lineages—and, by extension, evolution, Wilson's greatest academic passion.

Among unrelated families, in contrast, mitochondrial DNA sequences are clearly distinct. Though mtDNA remains constant from generation to generation, it does morph slightly over longer stretches of time due to natural mutations—random changes that can occur when genetic code is copied. Just as Wilson had used the concept of the "molecular clock" to analyze the evolutionary distance between chimpanzees and humans, similar principles were now being applied to compare human populations from all over the world. By tracing mtDNA mutations back in time and calculating the rate at which such shifts occurred, Wilson and his team were hoping to answer questions about the early origins of humanity. How old were the various geographic populations of modern humans? How closely related were they? Where did they originate?

As soon as she arrived back in California, King decided to pay Wilson a visit to discuss how mtDNA might be of use to the Abuelas. The idea had come from Cristián Orrego, the Chilean scientist who had originally helped connect the Abuelas to Luca Cavalli-Sforza and King, and who had recently begun working at UC Berkeley as well. Wilson's office was on the fourth floor of Berkeley's blocky biochemistry building, not far from his lab, where his graduate students liked to blast rock and roll. He was still as warm and humble as when King had first met him—but his patience had not deepened with age, and he did not bother with on/off switches. If he wanted to ask one of his students a question without the soundtrack of Bon Jovi or Aerosmith in the background, he would simply yank the stereo's plug out of the outlet and start talking. Now in his early fifties, his chin-length hair had turned silver, giving him the look of a sage wizard. The hair plus his daily uniform of pressed gray trousers had inspired some of his students to dub him "Grey Eminence." Over the years, his lab had hosted a collection of graduate students diverse even by Berkeley standards: punk rockers, gay rights activists, "belly-dancer enthusiasts," cave explorers, and Zen priests. He went out of his way to support scientists who were underestimated and overlooked; other male science professors sometimes quipped that his lab had all the women.

This was a more literal observation than most realized—Wilson's freezers were packed with hundreds of placentas, which had turned out to be especially rich sources of mtDNA. Many of them were donated by friends and colleagues, including King herself, who had personally carried her placenta, sealed in a sterile plastic bag and protected by a Styrofoam box, to Wilson's lab after giving birth to Emily. Sometimes Wilson's graduate students would attend Lamaze classes to source placentas, lobbying skeptical pregnant women to donate theirs after delivery. Along with the American samples, the lab had collected at least twenty placentas from women of African descent; thirty-four from women with ties to China, Vietnam, Laos, the Philippines, Indonesia, and Tonga; twenty-one from Indigenous Australians; and twenty-six from Indigenous New Guineans. The place was so flush with placentas that Wilson once ran out of freezer space and had to rent more from a commercial facility, where the organs were stored near roadkill and an entire frozen alligator. (Wilson was also a zoologist.)

To isolate the mtDNA from each placenta, Wilson and his team ground up slices of each tissue in a superpowered sterile Waring kitchen blender and poured the resulting puree into plastic tubes that were sent whirling in one of the lab's two high-speed centrifuges. After that, they used cesium chloride to release the mtDNA from the cells of the placenta, and spun everything in the centrifuge again for several days. The end product was a clear liquid containing miniscule rings of mitochondrial DNA. They repeated this process for all 147 samples and, based on the differences in their mtDNA sequences, estimated how long one would need to look back to find a common ancestor. They looked back further and further, and the giant genetic tree they were drawing got narrower and narrower. Eventually Wilson and his students realized that the mtDNA sequences of all 147 individuals, who came from all over the world, could be mapped back to a single mtDNA sequence that belonged to a woman in Africa 200,000 years ago—and by extension, so could everyone else, from Buenos Aires to Beijing. The implication was not that she was the *only* woman on earth—there would have been other men and women who lived at the same time—but at some point the descendants of those other women stopped having daughters and their mitochondrial DNA died off, just as a last name might in a traditional patriarchal family without sons.

The finding electrified the scientific world, and the media. After Wilson and two of his graduate students, Mark Stoneking and Rebecca Cann, published their work in *Nature* in January 1987, the common female ancestor in the study was dubbed "Mitochondrial Eve," and Wilson "The Father of Eve." (Wilson himself preferred the term "Lucky Mother" to "Mitochondrial Eve," to avoid the suggestion that the "Eve" he'd identified was the first known woman.) Whatever her name, Wilson's ancestral mother was as evocative of a feminist fantasy as she was scientifically revolutionary. She had gifted her daughters, and their daughters, and all the daughters of daughters to come after her, not only the power to carry and give life to children, but also an invisible, indestructible code imprinted within them. That code would endure, linking every mother to her children for the rest of time.

Now Wilson listened intently as Orrego and King laid out the Abuelas' problem. One of Wilson's most endearing qualities was his assumption that everyone understood everything that he did. He rarely bothered to explain his logic, skipping several steps ahead of everyone else. "Oh, of course," he murmured, as much to himself as to Orrego and King. "This will work."

Together, the three scientists talked through it. While mitochondrial sequences in unrelated families tend to differ by just a few chemical bases, the building blocks that make up DNA, those differences are clearly defined, Wilson said. Instead of needing the genetic material from all four grandparents, with mtDNA, the Abuelas would need just *one* maternal relative to connect a suspected grandchild with their biological family. The child's maternal grandmother would suffice, but so would a maternal aunt, cousin, or uncle. Since each family line was distinct, mtDNA would also allow the Abuelas to quickly cross-check suspected grandchildren against the hundreds of families looking for stolen children with far less risk of a coincidental match.

The junta had tried to make thousands of people disappear, and to erase the identities of their offspring. But mtDNA was like an indelible ID tag that every mother seals in her children's cells. What the Abuelas needed to find their stolen grandchildren was already within them: Their mitochondrial DNA contained the story of every mother that had come before them, and every child they had borne—no matter where in the world they had been taken. A flower that traveled in their blood.

This, King thought. *This will work.*

Like many scientists, Mary-Claire King is not a believer. But in that moment, and later as she shared the news with the Abuelas, she never had more faith that God was a woman.

Daughters of the State

1988–1989

In January 1988, a smartly dressed older couple strode into the immunology lab of the Hospital Durand, where the Banco Nacional de Datos Genéticos had been operating for a few months, holding the hand of a young girl. The woman had short gray hair and a predilection for large stud earrings; the man was bald, with thick black glasses. It was a busy time for the Abuelas—they were in the throes of moving to a larger space a thirty-minute walk up Corrientes, and their cramped office, which was often a flurry of legal papers, was even more chaotic than usual. But the couple's visit to the Banco was an important priority for the Abuelas.

Their names were Carmen Rivarola and José Treviño, and they were both journalists who lived in Barrio Norte, one of Buenos Aires' poshest enclaves. In 1978, after losing their three-and-a-half-year-old son to a genetic condition, they had adopted a ten-day-old infant girl they named Juliana.

Even when Juliana was tiny, the couple had never hidden the fact of her adoption from their daughter, and she often wondered aloud about her birth parents, lamenting that she didn't have any pictures of them. "Did my parents abandon me because they didn't love me?" she sometimes asked. After attending a press conference that discussed children stolen during the dictatorship and watching the film *La Historia Oficial*—The Official Story—a

1985 Academy Award–winning movie about an Argentine history teacher who comes to suspect her adopted daughter might have dark origins, Rivarola and Treviño began to nurse their own doubts. They had come to the Banco Nacional de Datos Genéticos to voluntarily submit Juliana to a blood test.

The Abuelas were stunned. Potential grandchildren were never dropped in their laps like this, and immediately they scrambled to figure out whose granddaughter Juliana might be. She was a thin, tan child with wavy brown hair. Based on her appearance and the timing of her birth—May 1978—the Abuelas determined she could be the daughter of Liliana Fontana and Pedro Sandoval, a couple who had been abducted by the military from their suburban Buenos Aires home in July 1977. The theory had some immediate holes: Liliana and Pedro's baby was supposed to have been a boy born in January 1978, not a girl born in May. But perhaps, the Abuelas thought, Liliana had miscarried while in detention and later gotten pregnant again while she and Pedro shared a cell. To test the hypothesis, technicians at the Hospital Durand drew Juliana's blood as she held her adoptive mother's hand.

One evening a few months later, in late June, Treviño and Rivarola were informed that the blood results were back. The Banco Nacional de Datos Genéticos did not yet have the capacity for mitochondrial DNA testing, but according to a comparison of Juliana's HLA types with those of her suspected grandparents, there was a 98.91 percent probability that they were related. The very next day, a judge ordered that Juliana be provisionally turned over to the Fontanas. There was little precedent to guide judges in these situations, and, in consultation with the court's psychologist, he decided the sudden move would be the best way to avoid further traumatization. "She needs separation from her adoptive family to be able to start the process of recovering what is her own, time to strengthen bonds with her relatives, and time to become a part of the family," the psychologist said at the time.

The Treviños were crushed. They had wanted to help Juliana find peace, but they didn't think that would mean losing her. As they reeled, Juliana settled into the Fontana household, which, unlike the Treviños' apartment in

Barrio Norte, was busy and boisterous, with thirty-two cousins who flitted in and out. There, she downed steaks with a surprising voracity and drew pictures of mountains and birds. She played with the family dog, a stocky, tawny thing named Coli, who seemed to recognize her. And of course she asked for photos of her mother and father—the photos she'd always dreamed of having. She was delighted to see that her dad had tan skin and soft curls, just like she did. Even the Treviños had been struck by Juliana's resemblance to the Fontanas and Sandovals when they'd seen the images. In legal proceedings, José Treviño declared that he and his wife were convinced Juliana had found her family, not only because of the blood test results, but undeniable inherited attributes, like Juliana's "toothpick" legs, which resembled Liliana's slender ones.

In Treviño's view, however, that did not mean that they should lose their daughter. The Treviños began publicly demanding that Juliana be returned to them, arguing that the identification of her biological family did not annul their adoption's validity. If theirs could be so suddenly overturned, the entire institution was at risk. They held press conferences to plead their case, wrote op-eds in La Nación, and allowed Gente to take photos of their posh apartment, which the magazine published next to photos of the humble Fontana abode in a Buenos Aires suburb. The message was clear: Juliana would be better off with the Treviños.

The conflict captivated the Argentine public and set off a media maelstrom. The conservative press, which tended to cast the Abuelas as vindictive shrews, lambasted them for illegally prying a young girl from her rightful adoptive parents simply because they could not move on. The country should not dwell on the past, went the thinking, and Juliana should be allowed to be who she was now: the daughter of the Treviños, whom she had loved as her parents for ten years. Supporters of the Abuelas, meanwhile, believed that only by reckoning with its trauma could Argentina recover. Juliana had been stolen from her biological family, and it was with her biological family that she belonged. The passage of a decade did not erase the crime that had been committed. As the case played out in the headlines, it was as if Argentines were really arguing over a bigger question. As one famous journalist wrote at the time, "The identity of Juliana is symbolic of the identity of this society."

Then, in August, the Treviños intensified their media campaign. Carmen Rivarola donned a crisp white button-down and appeared with her lawyer on *Tiempo Nuevo*, a popular political talk show. In a grave tone, she told one of the hosts: "Juliana should have been home with us. She should have been home. Not only because that's what is just under a legal adoption," she continued, "but for another much more serious reason. . . . I have to say clearly: Juliana is not the daughter of that couple who were disappeared."

The host's eyes widened behind his large spectacles.

Rivarola brought up the inconsistency in expected birthdates between Juliana and the grandchild sought by the Fontana and Sandoval families. While it was shocking news to the Argentine public, she and her husband had known about the discrepancy for months, but dismissed it after the blood results came back, with Treviño declaring in court: "It doesn't matter how that biological unknown is explained. Yes, we are convinced that at last Juliana has discovered her family."

A new judge had just taken over the case and ordered another HLA test. This time the results were even more conclusive: 99.91 percent that Juliana was biologically related to Fontana-Sandovals. At the end of August, the judge convened the Treviños, the Sandovals, and the Fontanas for a hearing. It was a temperate winter's day and a mixture of Abuelas, Madres, and other human rights activists gathered outside the courtroom in the golden sunlight, anticipating a decision. Rubén Fontana, Juliana's presumed grandfather, held a sign. One side was emblazoned with a photo of his daughter, Liliana. The other said: Mamá de Juliana. As the judge, a young man in a smart three-piece suit, passed by, a Madre yelled a reminder: "Ethics, judge!" She paused for a second before adding another exhortation. "Have heart, judge. Have heart."

The sunny day turned into a chilly night as deliberations began. Dressed in high-top sneakers and a skirt, Juliana slept on the carpet in the judge's office, curled up in the fetal position. Finally, after fourteen hours, the judge reached a decision. While he did not dispute the genetic evidence that Juliana was the granddaughter of the Sandoval and Fontana families, he temporarily returned custody to the Treviños, citing private conversations with Juliana. At 5:40 a.m., Juliana was led by fifty heavily armed police officers through the crowd of irate human rights activists and into an idling car. As she left, Juliana offered a tearful goodbye to her grandmother, Clelia. "Hasta mañana," she said. See you tomorrow.

As the car peeled away, Clelia stood crying on the sidewalk with her husband, Rubén. "They stole my daughter and now they've stolen my grand-daughter," Rubén wailed. The Abuelas were outraged—for the Sandoval and Fontana families, but also because they worried the case presaged something more sinister. "This," Chicha said at the time, "is part of a campaign to put an end to the search for disappeared children."

In December, the country marked five years of democracy. Colorful street art adorned the buildings of Buenos Aires. Young men and women freely walked around reading books that might have gotten them thrown in jail—or worse—during the dictatorship. A rock concert to mark the anniversary drew 150,000 people, a symphonic celebration of freedom that many of the Abuelas' children likely would have enjoyed if they were alive.

For the Abuelas, the month also marked a less felicitous five-year milestone: five years of waiting for answers regarding Ximena Vicario, a young girl they believed was one of their grandchildren. On February 5, 1977, Ximena's mother, Stella Maris Gallicchio, a gamine twenty-five-year-old with huge eyes she traced with dark liner, had brought eight-month-old Ximena to the federal police headquarters in Buenos Aires to pick up the infant's passport so they could leave the country. She was just exiting the building with the document in hand when she remembered she had a question and turned back. She and Ximena were seized on the spot; her husband, Juan Carlos Vicario, was abducted that same day from the family's home in Rosario, an agricultural city 185 miles northwest of Buenos Aires.

In 1983, the Abuelas had received an anonymous complaint revealing that, soon after she was kidnapped, Ximena had been left on the doorstep of Pedro de Elizalde, a children's hospital. The hospital was in a poor area of Buenos Aires, and Ximena did not fit the profile of the other children abandoned there; she was dressed neatly, with small stud earrings in her ears, and her stroller was of the highest quality. Some would later recall a more damning piece of evidence: a tiny sign dropped off with Ximena that read: "Daughter of guerrillas." But it was 1977—the height of the dictatorship's power—and the doctors and nurses at Pedro de Elizalde did not ask questions. Instead, one of the hospital's hematologists, Susana Siciliano, sought legal custody of Ximena in court. She was granted adoption and renamed the baby Romina Paola Siciliano.

Eventually, Ximena's maternal grandmother, Darwinia Gallicchio, was able to track her down at Siciliano's home. For a year or so, Darwinia enjoyed relatively harmonious visits with Ximena and Siciliano, frequently traveling from Rosario to Buenos Aires to see them. She tried to convince her young granddaughter to accompany her on visits to art museums and Ximena, in turn, tried to drag her grandmother on rides at Italpark, an amusement park in Recoleta. But then Darwinia decided to seek a full restitution of her granddaughter, according to which Siciliano's custody rights would be severed, and the relationship soured. The Abuelas took the information they had gathered about Ximena to the courts in the middle of 1984, thinking that soon she would be returned to Darwinia and her biological family. But the judge overseeing the case moved at a glacial speed. It wasn't until late 1985 that he finally ordered Siciliano to submit Ximena to blood analysis. Siciliano resisted, so the judge sent a technician to her house to force the issue. The likelihood that "Romina Siciliano" was related to Darwinia was deemed 99.82 percent, but the judge still didn't order her return. More years of delays and legal squabbles followed, during which time Ximena continued to live with Siciliano, with visits from her biological family. Once, according to a relative, Darwinia thanked Siciliano for taking care of her granddaughter for so many years. Siciliano allegedly spat back that she would sooner "cut off my hands" before giving up the girl.

Then, around New Year's Day in 1989, when Ximena was twelve, the judge summoned Siciliano to court for an important update. The reason for the hearing was meant to be a secret, and the ruling the judge intended to present was kept in a locked box, but a court employee leaked the information to Siciliano: the judge planned to grant guardianship to Darwinia. Anticipating that Siciliano might not obey the summons, the judge dispatched security forces early on the morning of January 3 to collect her and Ximena. Ximena would later recall awakening to the sight of multiple men with rifles in her room. The officers shuffled her and Siciliano into a patrol car and drove them to Tribunales, where journalists and photographers had amassed in a noisy scrum outside.

Siciliano and Ximena exited the car and stood in front of the press. Siciliano, like the Treviños, had become media savvy, and she sometimes welcomed reporters into her home to prove what a happy childhood Ximena was enjoying. She made sure they knew she was nurturing Ximena's passions for swimming and music, and introduced them to Ximena's fuzzy cocker spaniel, Pamela. Ximena was just a few months shy of becoming a teenager, and to court that morning she wore a tank top and white hoop earrings. Cameras captured a girl with straight brown hair tied back in a ponytail and cheeks streaked with tears. She had been adamant about her desire to stay with Siciliano. As reporters shoved microphones toward her, Ximena clutched Siciliano.

"I'm not going with that old lady!" she howled, referring to her grandmother. "Let me stay with my mommy please!" She wanted nothing to do with Darwinia, she told the journalists, vowing to commit suicide before going to live with her. To pry her and Siciliano away from the press, the police had to escort the pair to the judge's office. Ximena continued crying. Despite the emotional scene, the judge remained resolute. The court's decision, he told them, was inevitable and irreversible: Ximena would be returned to her biological family. Siciliano was sent away, and Ximena left the courthouse with her grandmother.

Later, though, one of the judges who helped decide the case would admit that he had not always felt certain about what to do. "Ximena's case kept me up for nights," he said. "I've had homicides and everything, but I've never had to resolve such a difficult question. My friends said, 'How can you do this, opting for the family of the womb over the family of the heart?' But we knew that we had to change the power relations, so that she could escape the lie and start living the truth."

28

Fallout

1989–1990

The day after the dramatic courthouse scene, *Página 12*, a new left-leaning newspaper, published a triumphant headline on its cover: "XIMENA VICARIO IS WITH HER GRANDMOTHER." The historically conservative *Clarín*, meanwhile, took a very different tone: "A daughter of *desaparecidos* resisted leaving her adoptive mother. Nevertheless, she was transferred to the home of her grandmother by blood." The accompanying photo showed Ximena and Siciliano intertwined in a tearful embrace, its caption referring to Ximena as Romina Paola Siciliano.

Public debate about the Abuelas escalated to a new level of ferocity. Radio hosts opined: "I wonder: why don't they respect what the girl wants?" or "How can they separate the girl from the people who raised her?" Such thoughts were echoed by Siciliano herself. "I understand how [the Abuelas] feel from a human point of view," she said. "But they are very bitter. Aside from their thirst for justice, I think they also have a thirst for vengeance. They don't think of the best interests of the child."

The Abuelas watched it all, stunned and disturbed. It was one thing to be vilified by the police and military officers who had stolen their grandchildren; it was another to suddenly find themselves in the crosshairs of a critical public—as if *they* were the perpetrators of evil, not the victims of it. The group had, by this time, found fifty grandchildren and, contrary to the perception that they prioritized their desires for reclamation over the well-being of the children, had left twelve of them to grow up with families who had adopted them in good faith, including the Julien Grisonas siblings and the Britos sisters. But they could not abide leaving their grandchildren with people they deemed "appropriators," who knew of the children's suspect origins and claimed them anyway, or had even stolen them directly from their real parents.

Gente, the same magazine that had displayed photos of the Treviños' swanky apartment next to the Fontanas' humble home, named Siciliano one of its people of the year, including her on its cover alongside Argentine actors, athletes, and musicians. Soon she was invited by Bernardo Neustadt to appear on *Tiempo Nuevo*. He was the same pundit who had railed against the restitution of Juliana Treviño. In one of his impassioned monologues, he accused the Abuelas of "kidnapping" Ximena. To him, the sinners were not the armed forces who had abducted her as an infant along with her parents. To Neustadt and his many viewers, the villains were the Abuelas de Plaza de Mayo.

"Well," Estela de Carlotto plaintively said to Darwinia after Ximena was settled at home in Rosario. "You won't be with us anymore."

"No," Darwinia corrected her. "Now is when I have to work hardest to repay what I received [from the Abuelas]."

The Abuelas de Plaza de Mayo had always derived their power from their unity. It was their togetherness that afforded them security, solidarity, and hope. They had given one another courage—to submit habeas corpus documents, to stand up to government officials, to risk their own lives to reclaim those of their grandchildren—and a forum for emotional release. One Abuela, Nélida Gómez de Navajas, would later recall that the only place she allowed herself was to cry was the Plaza de Mayo.

At a time when many of their own families pushed them away, afraid of getting mixed up in their dangerous business or being associated with "mothers of terrorists," the Abuelas had become like sisters to one another. Each woman threw herself into the search for the group's grandchildren with the same formidable intensity with which she looked for her own. Alone, their efforts could have only taken them so far, like the beam of a single flashlight in the dark. Together, their beams added up to a powerful floodlight, a stubborn rejoinder to the darkness.

Shortly after Ximena's case blew up in the headlines, however, that unity began to crack. Chicha and Estela, the organization's president and vice president, had always been very different people. They had figured out a way to work effectively together, but they had never been friends. Chicha was, by her own admission, detail-oriented and demanding. She would carefully comb through every court filing, pressing the legal team on minute details, and was seen as more staunchly committed to neutrality, whereas some Abuelas felt Estela was more inclined to wade into partisan politics. Estela was eloquent and stylish, dressing in fine tailored clothing and relishing media attention, while Chicha was more reserved. They had fiery disagreements about how the organization should be structured and how the legal team should be composed—Chicha was unhappy with its performance; Estela was supportive—and promoted different stories of how the Abuelas de Plaza de Mayo originally formed. Chicha considered the organization's birthday to be November 21, 1977—the day when she and eleven other Abuelas had gathered under a jacaranda tree after Cyrus Vance's visit. Though she had not yet joined the organization herself by then, Estela put the date at October 22 of that year, when Mirta Acuña de Baravalle had supposedly called for grandmothers marching in the Plaza de Mayo to identify themselves (and which also happened to coincide with her birthday).

Though Chicha had threatened to resign a few times ("I have tolerated insolence from Estela for a long time until I told myself: enough," she wrote to her husband during one fit of pique), the two had pushed through their differences in the interest of their shared mission. Now, in the wake of the Juliana Treviño and Ximena Vicario cases, the partnership fractured for good. On November 21, 1989—the day she viewed as the Abuelas' twelfth anniversary—Chicha Mariani left the Abuelas.

Estela took over as president and Rosa as vice president. The group never openly discussed Chicha's departure or the reasons for it; Abuela Vilma Gutiérrez later remembered that she showed up one day and Chicha was simply gone. In her resignation letter, Chicha wrote that the "cohesion" that had always sustained them "had been broken." Gutiérrez quit shortly thereafter, along with Mirta Acuña de Baravalle and Elsa Pavón, the grandmother of Paula Logares. Eva Castillo Barrios also stepped aside, irate that Chicha and Estela had let their personal animus affect their mission.

As Estela, Rosa, and the other remaining Abuelas fought to keep their organization together, external pressure continued to mount. Even after a judge had restored custody of Juliana to her adoptive parents, José Treviño and Carmen Rivarola had not stopped fighting for her; they wanted to ensure no one could ever take Juliana from them again. To accomplish that, they needed to prove the allegations that Rivarola had leveled in her appearance on *Tiempo Nuevo*: that, despite the results of two separate HLA analyses suggesting 98.91 percent and 99.91 percent probabilities of a biological link, Juliana was not related to the Fontana or Sandoval families.

The Banco Nacional de Datos Genéticos still only had the ability to conduct HLA analysis, so to perform a full retest at the Treviños' urging, the head of the BNDG, Ana María Di Lonardo, took blood from Juliana and the Sandoval and Fontana families with her to Paris, where she had been invited in 1990 to receive a prize. There, at a cutting-edge genetics center, she used two advanced technologies to assess the samples. First, she studied DNA polymorphisms, common variations in DNA sequences. Then she used DNA fingerprinting, a method developed by British geneticist Alec Jeffreys that built on the study of DNA polymorphisms, allowing scientists to look at specific sections of DNA called "minisatellites" and create visual barcodes for samples that could be easily compared.

Immediately, she noticed something concerning. Some of the minisatellites detected in Juliana's blood were not shared by any of her supposed grandparents. Given that every child inherits around one-quarter of their genes from each grandparent, the significance was clear. As the Treviños had argued for two years, Juliana was not related to the Sandoval family or the Fontana family, with whom she'd been sent to live for a few months.

The Abuelas scrambled to figure out what had gone wrong, though reaching a conclusive answer was challenging. Later, the Abuelas and their allies would blame Di Lonardo and the BNDG, insisting that the team had made errors in its HLA analysis and failed to include blood samples from other members of the Fontana family that would have influenced the results. When asked if the Abuelas had ever noticed inconsistencies in the tests, Estela reminded a journalist that the Abuelas were not scientists and "had no reason to doubt" those who were.

But Di Lonardo was staunch in her avowal that neither she nor anyone on her team had made a mistake. Even in the case of a 99.91 percent probability of a biological relationship, there was still a chance of nine in ten thousand that Juliana shared HLA types with two of her supposed grandparents by coincidence. It was not probable, but it was possible, and in Juliana's case, Di Lonardo argued, it was what had happened. ("How curious," a reporter would remark when interviewing Di Lonardo about the case later. "It's not curious," Di Lonardo responded. "It's how it is.") If there had been an error, she suggested, it was one of legal judgment. No other judicial decision in an appropriations case had relied so completely on genetic evidence, without the Abuelas' usual binders of circumstantial evidence to back it up.

The whole thing could have been avoided, she noted, if the government had invested in the equipment and personnel needed for more advanced forms of genetic testing. The immunology lab at Hospital Durand from which the BNDG operated did not have photocopiers or a reliable way to access international databases and scientific reports. The fax machine the team used was one Di Lonardo had borrowed from a friend. The government didn't even cover the personnel and goods needed for HLA analysis. Often, Di Lonardo had to drive her personal Citroën to the international airport in Ezeiza to pick up critical reagents, or chemical catalysts, that friends had sent her for free because they knew she couldn't get them in Argentina. Other times, she relied on the help of volunteers, like Eric Stover of the AAAS, who would shuttle down such chemicals in his carry-on and hand them over to Abuelas waiting impatiently for him in the arrivals area. On occasion, the Abuelas had traveled to Ezeiza to collect reagents for the BNDG themselves. ("And these chemicals, where do they come from?" a customs agent asked them sternly one day. "Che!" another agent called to his colleague. "These are the Abuelas de

Plaza de Mayo. When they put on their handkerchiefs, they have even toppled the president.")

Whatever had happened and whomever was at fault, politicians and commentators latched onto the Treviño fracas like attack dogs. One legislator campaigned to overhaul the BNDG so completely it would have essentially ceased functioning. *Tiempo Nuevo*'s Bernardo Neustadt questioned whether the "hysterical decision" to turn Juliana over to the Fontana and Sandoval families had been driven by ideology rather than certainty. An editorial in *La Nación* said the ordeal "allows one to question similar cases." The aura of infallibility around the Abuelas' scientific methods was pierced—perhaps mortally.

As the Abuelas navigated this extreme turbulence, the nation was doing the same. In July 1989, five months before the constitutionally mandated end of his term, Raul Alfonsín had been forced to resign the presidency. The monthly inflation rate had spiked to the triple digits, and Argentine currency lost three-quarters of its value in less than three months. After food prices tripled over the course of mere weeks, riots erupted around the country as hungry, angry Argentines looted supermarkets and exasperated housewives blocked roads in protest. At least fourteen people died in resulting clashes with police.

The successor who had accepted the gold-capped presidential scepter from Alfonsín seemed, at least on paper, poised to take a tougher stand with the military, which had continued threatening to mutiny even after the Full Stop and Due Obedience Laws were passed. The swashbuckling son of Syrian immigrants, with robust black sideburns and a taste for white suits, Carlos Saúl Menem had himself been imprisoned by the armed forces after the 1976 coup. Back then he had been serving as the Peronist governor of La Rioja, his hot and arid home province in Argentina's northwest, when the junta accused him of corruption and links to the leftist movement. He was eventually taken to Magdalena, a rural prison set among pastures two hours south of Buenos Aires, where he was held until 1978 along with a handful of other Peronist politicians. During that time, his mother died, and Menem had petitioned Videla to attend the funeral. Videla denied the request, leaving Menem to mourn in his cell alone.

After the dictatorship ended, Menem again won the governorship in La Rioja, and had recently used his platform to criticize, in a withering public letter, Alfonsín's Full Stop Law. "The final stop for murderers is jail," he wrote. "The only way to close the doors forever on this horrible past is not to interfere in the work of the Judicial Power. . . . No one has the right to forget."

But presidential authority, and a desire to hold on to it in the face of a combative military, soon seemed to soften Menem's views. (One Menem biographer, Olga Wornat, would later say that Menem loved "power more than anything, including his family.") Like those who argued the Abuelas should let their grandchildren go instead of fighting to reclaim them, Menem seemed to embrace the philosophy that to move forward required moving on. In October 1989, the new president freed more than two hundred officers who were awaiting trial despite Alfonsín's "impunity" laws. "I know there will be those who are unhappy," Menem announced from his home in La Rioja. But he insisted the action was necessary for "national reconciliation."

A year into his term, he went even further. On the evening of December 29, 1990, as much of the country was busy preparing for New Year's celebrations and the Abuelas were grappling with the fallout of the Treviño case, Menem sprang Montoneros leader Mario Firmenich from the jail where he was being held on the edge of Buenos Aires.

That same night, he also dispatched a government helicopter to Magdalena prison, where he had spent two years during the dictatorship. It was dark by then, but witnesses standing nearby could hear the staccato thrum of the blades. As they peered through the twilight, they were just able to make out the birdlike face and rangy gait of one of the men to clamber aboard the chopper before it sped away from the blocky white compound.

Fourteen years after the junta had locked up Menem in that very prison without charges, the Peronist president had freed Jorge Rafael Videla.

29

The Deli Fridge

1991–1993

The Abuelas' bleak period—burdened by internal tensions and the profound impact of the Ximena Vicario and Juliana Treviño cases—was alleviated by one merciful development: Mary-Claire King, back in Berkeley, had worked out how to use mitochondrial DNA to identify their grandchildren. She had also, after seventeen years of relentless searching, fulfilled her long-standing quest to uncover the genetic basis of breast cancer. Overcoming the skepticism of many, King traced hereditary breast cancer to chromosome seventeen, to a gene she would call BRCA1.

Both findings were groundbreaking, and King would eventually be considered a top candidate to replace James Watson, who famously helped discover the double helix structure of DNA, as head of the Human Genome Project, an exciting government effort to map all one hundred thousand human genes. She was also approached to lead the National Institutes of Health. But her first love was the lab: running experiments, brainstorming with students, and devising scientific solutions for human problems.

Indeed, she had no shortage of problems to occupy her—many of them assigned to her by the Abuelas. King had excitedly shared her thoughts about mitochondrial DNA with Di Lonardo and the Banco Nacional de Datos Genéticos team, but the laboratory had not yet been able to build the

capacity (or secure the funding) necessary to conduct such testing themselves. Then, on March 12, 1991, police officers dressed in plain clothes
burst into the immunology lab at the Hospital Durand and shut the doors
so no one could leave, separating the scientists for individual questioning.
The officers demanded to see the books, by which they meant the logs the
scientists had filled with family trees and HLA data scribbled in red ink.

The fallout from the Juliana Treviño case was still trailing the Abuelas,
and the police wanted something specific: the results of two HLA analyses
the BNDG had performed at the end of 1986 on a ten-year-old girl who, up
until then, had been named Nancy Viviana Madrid. The tests had found that
in fact she was Elena Gallinari Abinet, the daughter of *desaparecidos* Miguel
Ángel Gallinari and María Leonor Abinet, born while her mother was imprisoned. In 1987, the Abuelas had returned her to her biological family, making
her the first child born in a clandestine detention center whom they were able
to recover—a feat that would have been impossible without genetic testing.
But after the Treviño debacle, Elena's appropriators, a police officer and his
wife, had sensed an opening to try to get her back and ordered the court re-
examine her blood results. "You all studied the grandparents of the girl. Why
didn't you study the parents?" the police pressed. That indeed would have been
ideal, gamely replied the BNDG team, but her parents had been disappeared.
After pawing through the entire lab, creating a giant mess, the officers took
the logbooks and left. The materials were never returned, and the scientists
had to start new registries from scratch.

Between the Juliana Treviño scandal and the BNDG raid, it had become
clear: the Abuelas urgently needed a way to strengthen—and safeguard—
their scientific work. On August 27, 1991, the fax machine in King's office
shuddered to life. Its rollers whirred and chugged until they spat out a typed
letter. It was from Estela.

"Dear Mary," it began. "We have decided to make the mitochondrial DNA
bank in the U.S. our number one priority; even more so because of the results
that you and Víctor are familiar with." Estela was being purposefully elliptical,
but King recognized she was referring to the Treviño case. King had already
been conducting mitochondrial DNA testing for the Abuelas on a limited

basis, but now Estela had a larger request. To avoid "painful moments like the current one," she suggested that King reconfirm every HLA test with mitochondrial DNA in Berkeley, storing the samples to create a parallel genetic bank to the BNDG. The Abuelas' trust in Di Lonardo had been seriously shaken, the BNDG still wasn't able to undertake any sort of DNA testing, and, unlike the BNDG, a bank in California could not be raided by Argentine officials. Víctor Penchaszadeh, the Argentine geneticist, would be traveling to the United States in a month, added Estela. He could start bringing samples then.

King knew the project would require time she didn't really have: News of her breast-cancer discovery had unleashed a mad sprint among scientists in at least one dozen labs to be the first to clone and sequence the gene; her twenty-person team was working tirelessly to win what had become known simply as The Race. (One of her colleagues at a sister lab who ran marathons called the contest to clone BRCA1 just as intense.) She was also teaching multiple graduate and undergraduate courses—including a freshman genetics class for nonscience majors. She and her team essentially lived at the lab, working, in her words, "if not 24/7, at least 14/6."

But King did not waver. Sometimes, she told Estela, her team fought over who got to sequence the Abuelas' cases. She would happily reconfirm all HLA results with mitochondrial DNA in Berkeley, and she would do the work at no cost. She cleared space in a red, blue, and yellow vintage deli fridge for the incoming samples and outfitted the fridge with two locks, one combination and one padlock. Soon Penchaszadeh arrived with the first batch. When she traveled to Argentina, King carried samples back to Berkeley as well, tucking them in her pockets for safekeeping. Bored US customs agents running through their required list of questions would sometimes ask her if she was carrying any agricultural products. "I have some DNA," she would volunteer, jolting the official out of their stupor. Then, cheerily, she would add, "It's just from healthy people. It's not infectious."

In April 1992, the Abuelas celebrated their fifteenth anniversary. But, instead of a festive party with champagne and canapés, they marked the occasion with a three-day multidisciplinary seminar intended to rebuild confidence in their mission. King and Penchaszadeh were invited to Buenos Aires to present on the organization's scientific advances, and to a packed auditorium in the glassy Centro Cultural San Martín, King praised the power of mitochondrial DNA with the fervor—and language—of an evangelical preacher. "God put this method on earth specifically for the Abuelas," she declared, repeating what had become her favorite rallying cry. "It is exactly what they needed." By then, the test tubes in the deli fridge in King's lab that functioned as the Abuelas' mitochondrial DNA bank had mushroomed. No samples had yet presented a match, but King was certain that it was only a matter of time before mitochondrial DNA testing began to identify more of the missing grandchildren. Speaking in Spanish that newspapers would later call "rather correct," King declared that mtDNA analysis was "essentially infallible."

King's work with mitochondrial DNA was beginning to open up possibilities in human rights investigations beyond those of the Abuelas. Recently, King and her team had figured out they could extract mitochondrial DNA from dental pulp. Sometimes they got just 600 millionths of an ounce—but it was enough to analyze. Protected by hard enamel, the DNA in teeth was better preserved than in porous bones. By comparing the DNA contained in a single tooth with that from a single suspected maternal relative, King realized that she could identify even the most degraded remains. The Equipo Argentino de Antropología Forense, or Argentine Forensic Anthropology Team (EAAF), which formed after the 1984 visit from the AAAS committee, had continued its delicate mission of exhuming unmarked graves and immediately realized the power of the new technique. Together, by extracting DNA from the teeth of disinterred skulls, King and members of the forensic anthropology team quickly matched two bodies of *desaparecidos* with their families, providing long-awaited closure.

Soon, teeth began showing up at King's lab in droves, packed in brown bags and brown boxes with stamps from faraway places. Some arrived pristine, others riddled with chips and stains. There were molars, incisors, canines, and wisdom teeth. Adult teeth and baby teeth. They sat in freezers until King and her team could carefully break them open, crunching through the enamel to reveal the yellowish pulp inside. Bodies that had gone nameless for years, or even decades, could now be identified and properly grieved and honored. King's team identified fallen American soldiers who died fighting in World War II and worked with a US Army lab in Honolulu to identify an American television correspondent who had been taken prisoner by the Khmer Rouge in Cambodia during the Vietnam War she had protested so fervently while at Berkeley. She applied the technique to identify victims of El Salvador's El Mozote Massacre, in which at least 794 Salvadorans, many of them children, were killed by US-trained Salvadoran soldiers. She helped analyze the remains of the Romanovs, the family of the last Russian czar, all of whom had been shot by the Bolsheviks in 1918 and buried in a forest in Yekaterinburg until they were exhumed in 1991.

The advance was transformative for human rights investigations, and each tooth her team matched to a family gave King great satisfaction. But it did not bring her nearly the same joy as her collaborations with the Abuelas. By identifying children who had been stolen from their families by the junta, King felt it was almost as if she and the Abuelas could "bring the missing children back to life."

By mid-1993, King had analyzed the mitochondrial DNA of 189 people representing ninety families, still with no match. Since 1990, the Abuelas had only identified one living child. (Earlier in 1993, they found out one child they were searching for had died in the womb when his mother was killed.) But that December brought a flash of good news. After the BNDG had run HLA and other genetic tests on a seventeen-year-old boy the Abuelas deemed likely to be one of their grandsons, King compared his mitochondrial DNA to that of his supposed maternal family members to be sure. She found that he shared the exact same sequence as his suspected grandmother.

King relayed the results on December 23, 1993. "Very merry Christmas to all of the Abuelas and congratulations to the Falabella-Abdala families," she wrote in a fax. Anticipating the Abuelas' next request—because there was always a next request—she ended the note: "We will continue with other cases."

30

A Systematic Plan

1994–1998

In a dim and dingy Buenos Aires subway station in 1994, a short man with a full mustache approached Horacio Verbitsky, a former Montonero who had become a prominent investigative journalist for *Página 12*. "I was at the ESMA," the man said. "I want to talk to you."

At first Verbitsky thought he might be a survivor of the torture center, but then the man pulled a sheet of paper from the cheap briefcase he carried and thrust it at him. "Read it," he urged. "We did worse things than the Nazis."

The man's name was Adolfo Scilingo, and he had been a naval captain during the dictatorship. The document was his confession. While stationed at the ESMA, he explained, he had participated in what he called "aerial transports." First, he and his colleagues would separate a handful of prisoners from the rest of the pack and tell them they were being taken to a prison in the south and needed a vaccination. In reality, the military's syringes held sedatives that transformed the detainees into "zombies" who could hardly walk. The drugged prisoners were loaded into trucks and taken to Aeroparque, the airport next to the Río de la Plata, where they were packed onto planes owned by the armed forces. "Finally," Scilingo wrote in the document he handed Verbitsky, "they were stripped naked and thrown into the waters of the South Atlantic from the planes during the flight." Scilingo had personally participated in two flights, in which thirty people were killed. But he estimated that between 1,500 and 2,000 ESMA prisoners died in such a manner during the dictatorship. Verbitsky gathered the testimony into an explosive book, *El Vuelo*, or *The Flight*, which was published in March 1995, and penned front-page articles for *Página 12* released around the same time.

Argentines were aghast. In the previous months, two of Scilingo's colleagues at the ESMA had broken with the Argentine military's long tradition of silence and admitted that they too had tortured prisoners during the dictatorship. But their confessions were brief and vague. Scilingo's, in contrast, burst with grim detail, confirming the practice of death flights—long rumored to be true but never openly acknowledged by the military. President Menem was livid about such confessions. Though he had created la Comisión Nacional por el Derecho a la Identidad, or the National Commission for the Right to Identity (CoNaDI), a governmental body dedicated to identifying children stolen during the dictatorship, which would help the Abuelas carry out investigations with state resources and support, he still maintained that the best thing for the nation was to move on. He implored military men to save their confessions for their priests, to avoid "rubbing salt in old wounds."

Scilingo's admission unleashed a new level of fury among regular citizens, who, thanks to Alfonsín's "impunity laws" and Menem's pardons, had long been frustrated by the lack of justice for military men accused of crimes in the dictatorship. It was maddening that such men got to live free and normal lives—browsing at the grocery store, riding public transit—and some disgusted Argentines took it upon themselves to hold the officers accountable however they could. Astiz, the naval officer who infiltrated the Madres, could hardly walk outside without men throwing punches at him; once, while Videla was waiting in a bank line, another patron hocked a wad of spit at him. After spotting the man who had tortured his father in a Buenos Aires bar, one son of *desaparecidos* gathered his peers to form a new human rights organization called Hijos e Hijas por la Identidad y la Justicia contra el Olvido y Silencio, or the Sons and Daughters for Identity and Justice Against Oblivion and Silence (H.I.J.O.S.). "I could have smashed a glass over his head, but I felt that the release needed to be collective," he reasoned.

H.I.J.O.S. began staging *escraches*, public shamings in which members camped outside the homes and offices of suspected dictatorship-era criminals, shouting about the offenses they were accused of, singing songs comparing them to Nazis, throwing paint at the walls, and even reenacting rape scenes. The first ever *escrache* was directed at Jorge Luis Magnacco, the obstetrician who witnesses reported had delivered Rosa's grandson and several other babies in the ESMA. Through a television investigation, H.I.J.O.S. learned that he was working at a hospital in the heart of Buenos Aires—Sanatorio Mitre. ("I was following orders," Magnacco responded coldly when a journalist intercepted him to ask if the accusations against him were true.) Dozens of young people gathered out front of the hospital with signs that read: "Magnacco: Torturer and Thief of Lives." They shouted, painted swastikas on the doors in red spray paint, and generally made as much of a ruckus as they could. From there they marched about thirty minutes to do the same thing outside the doctor's apartment building. Before long, Magnacco was forced to resign from Sanatorio Mitre and his neighbors had asked him to move.

Among the crush of H.I.J.O.S. who had hurled insults at Magnacco was none other than Mariana Pérez, Rosa's granddaughter, who attended the *escrache* holding an enlarged photo of Patricia. Mariana was a university student by then, studying political science at the University of Buenos Aires, but she spent much of her time in the Abuelas' headquarters, working alongside her grandmothers. (A cook by trade, Argentina made sure the Abuelas stayed well-fed, whipping up tarts, pastas, and stews for them; Rosa continued to oversee the organization's various investigative, legal, and psychology divisions as vice president. Mariana admired them both, but she especially appreciated Rosa's clear-minded realism, a no-nonsense outlook on life that Mariana identified with.) In between classes, Mariana volunteered with the investigative branch, sometimes attending the phone. She found aspects of the job infuriating. Men and women would call in anonymously, speaking in oblique code "as if they fantasized about starring in a suspense movie." The calls took the same general shape: in 1976, the callers said, someone suddenly appeared with a baby even though they'd never been pregnant. Usually they couldn't supply facts—just flimsy suspicions. What irked Mariana the most, though, was how the callers seemed to expect gushing displays of gratitude for coming forward when they had remained silent for two decades.

While Alfonsín's impunity laws shielded military officers from punishment for most crimes, rape and the kidnapping of minors were still prosecutable offenses. Since democracy had been restored, the Abuelas had continuously brought those who had appropriated their grandchildren to court, and by the time of the *escraches*, they had prevailed in eight kidnapping cases, condemning their grandchildren's kidnappers to jail. Confident in their track record, they started to build a larger case, gathering evidence to argue that the kidnapping of children during the dictatorship was not the diabolical idea of a few wicked individuals, but rather a "systematic plan" endorsed by the dictatorship's top brass. Could it truly be just a coincidence that so many of their grandchildren had ended up in the homes of military and police officers? In 1996, the Abuelas initiated what would eventually be called the Plan Sistemático de Robo de Bebés case, or Systematic Plan of Baby Kidnapping case. In their complaint, the group accused several of the junta's top officials, including the former interior minister Albano Harguindeguy and Reynaldo Bignone, the junta's last leader, of facilitating a concerted plan to appropriate babies during the dictatorship. Soon, the list of defendants was broadened to include Emilio Massera, the former head of the navy. Listed as plaintiffs, among many other Abuelas, were Estela and Rosa.

For a few years, the proceedings limped along. Then, on June 9, 1998, a military gynecologist testified that, during the dictatorship, he had "received verbal and written orders to assist in the births of the prisoners and that later the babies were taken away based on orders from above." When pressed on what he meant by "above," the gynecologist implied that the orders would have been reviewed by none other than the junta's original chief: Jorge Rafael Videla.

That very evening, Videla was preparing to leave his compact, fifth-floor apartment in Belgrano, knotting his tie around his gangly neck, when his doorbell rang. It was curious; he was not expecting anyone on that chilly Tuesday night. He hardly ever had visitors anymore. To avoid events like the humiliating (and unhygienic) bank spitting incident, he largely kept to himself. He exited his apartment building rarely, only to walk the three blocks to mass at the nearby military church, or occasionally drive somewhere in the red Peugeot 405 he kept downstairs in the garage. His social life was limited to spending time with his wife, Alicia, his children, and his grandchildren. He was a man who thrived on rigid routine, content to do his daily push-ups, watch television, and read the Bible.

"We have an order to detain you," came a clipped voice from the other side of the door. Videla opened it to find three police officers dressed in black winter coats and black peaked caps. One of them held a piece of paper in his hand—a judicial order from a federal court judge.

Videla's head snapped toward the paper in a nervous, birdlike reflex. He finished tying his tie and asked to see the order. Through the large silver glasses that encircled his inscrutable eyes, he read that he stood accused of "facilitating and promoting" the kidnapping and identity suppression of five children during his reign as dictator.

He gave Alicia a peck on the the cheek and followed the officers downstairs. The police had cut off Avenida Cabildo, a bustling avenue that normally echoed with the horns and screeching brakes of buses, cars, and motorcycles. In front of Videla's apartment building, which was tall, thin, and uninviting— just like its most famous resident—a crowd had formed to see what was going on. Flanked by the police officers, who clutched him by the elbows, Videla was shuffled outside. The news had leaked; he strained to cover his face with his gray winter jacket as hordes of photographers followed him.

The officers helped Videla duck into the back of a white sedan, where he crouched to avoid the mobs. Led by a police car, the caravan pulled away and began driving toward a courthouse north of Buenos Aires. Upon arrival at the low-slung brick building on a quiet cobblestone street in San Isidro, Videla was led to a room next to the judge's office. The former general stood impassively, hardly even blinking. He did not think to sit down until someone told him it might a while before the judge would receive him. Word of his arrest had spread like blood in water and, outside the building, relatives of the disappeared had gathered in the hundreds, pacing restlessly and climbing the wrought-iron black bars, trying to get a look at the former dictator. They shouted: "Asesino! Hijo de puta!" Murderer! Son of a bitch!

Estela de Carlotto was across the Atlantic Ocean in Geneva on business for the Abuelas when the news reached her. She immediately found a bulky computer with an internet connection at her hotel and scoured the web for updates. As they loaded, a wide grin spread across her face.

Estela returned to Argentina to find that the Abuelas had become celebrities. Soon, she was invited to appear on one of the country's most-watched talk shows, *Lunching with Mirtha Legrand*, a program that featured a filmed conversation between the glitzy Mirtha Legrand and several guests as they enjoyed lunch served in an ornate mansion. Seated around a lacquered wood table set with fine stemware and sprays of flowers, Estela chatted with Mirtha. "What news do you have of your grandson?" Mirtha asked. Estela explained that he had still not been found.

"I am a grandmother, and my grandchildren are what I love most in the world," Mirtha said. "So I put myself in the place of this divine, wonderful grandmother, this woman who is admirable, by the way, who has been searching for her grandson for so many years, and I think she must walk down the street and see boys of twenty or twenty-one years old and think, 'That could be my grandson, right?' . . . He's going to appear." She repeated the encouragement again. "He's going to appear."

A few months later, Estela was declared one of the "People of the Year" by *Gente*, which felt particularly momentous given the magazine's past attention to Abuelas critics. Estela appeared on the magazine's cover in a tailored white skirt suit along with supermodel Valeria Mazza, TV host Susana Giménez, and President Carlos Menem, who was still stubbornly calling for reconciliation.

The Abuelas had other reasons for hope as they rang in 1999. They had some of the world's top scientists on their side and the BNDG had continued incorporating promising new genetic methods. They had put Videla back on the hook for his crimes. And the grandchildren they had been searching for were growing up. The children had mostly been born between 1976 and 1978, which meant they had now become legal adults, capable of investigating their own identities without direct interference from those who had raised them. "For decades we have been looking for our grandchildren," Mary-Claire King remembers Rosa telling her. "One day they will come looking for us."

PART IV

Rebirth

31

Guillermo

April 27, 2000

On Thursday, April 27, 2000, Guillermo Gómez awoke around nine thirty in the morning to the harsh trill of his telephone. It was supposed to be his day off from work, and he had hoped to spend it as any twenty-one-year-old guy might, sleeping late and playing *Metal Gear* on his friend's PlayStation. But the voice on the line belonged to his boss, Osvaldo. One of Guillermo's colleagues had called in sick. Could Guillermo fill in? Guillermo groggily agreed. If he worked a Thursday, he thought, maybe he could take a Sunday off to watch River Plate, his favorite soccer team, play at their massive stadium next to the Río de la Plata.

Guillermo showered and studied his round cheeks, thick dark hair and eyebrows, and pecan-brown eyes in the mirror. He slipped into a pair of jeans and pulled on his uniform, an egg-yolk-yellow polo shirt that smelled of grease from the combination fast-food-restaurant-and-music megastore where he worked. Argentines often reached for English words to give their businesses trendy appeal: a popular pizza chain was called Kentucky; an American-style barbecue joint modeled after Applebee's was Kansas Grill & Bar. Guillermo's workplace, in the Buenos Aires suburb of San Miguel, was Shower. He preferred working on Shower's music side—it gave him a chance to chat with customers, and he enjoyed trying to sell things. But that day Osvaldo needed him on the food side.

He normally took the 448, the bus line that stopped a block from the one-story brick home in José C. Paz that he shared with his mother, Teodora Jofré. But Osvaldo was counting on him, so Guillermo ordered a car service to take him the two miles to downtown San Miguel. Upon arrival, he got right to work. He was unloading bottles of Sprite and Coca-Cola into the restaurant refrigerator, listening to the melodies of the Backstreet Boys and Britney Spears waft in from next door, when, from across the restaurant, he noticed a coworker gesturing at him. His colleague was standing with two women, both about Guillermo's age. One was thin and brunette with large lips and a slightly upturned nose. The other had dark hair and pale skin. She was cradling a newborn in her arms.

Guillermo had never seen either of them before. He watched perplexed as the women wove around the tables toward him.

"Are you Guillermo Francisco Gómez?" asked the one without the baby.

"Yes, what's going on?" he answered reflexively. How did this stranger know his full name?

Guillermo went out dancing most weekends, drinking and improvising dance moves in local nightclubs. He never drank to the point of oblivion, but now he had a panicked thought. Maybe the women had come to claim the baby was his.

"Can we talk to you?" the same woman asked.

"No," he said curtly. "I'm working."

"Can I sit and write you a letter?" the woman persisted. Despite his unease, the request piqued his interest. What an odd thing to ask.

"To sit you have to order something," he snapped. "Once you've ordered you can do whatever you want."

Guillermo turned and went back to unloading the bottles, shoving them anxiously in the refrigerator. As another server took the woman's order, the colleagues who had caught the interaction teasingly congratulated him on his baby. "What's his name?" they chuckled. "He looks just like you."

When the woman motioned for him to come back over, Guillermo did little to mask his annoyance.

"Can I have a bag?" she asked.

Guillermo found a bag behind the counter and thrust it at her. She tucked the letter she'd been working on inside a book, slid the book inside the bag, then handed the bag back to him.

The women remained seated. Now itching with curiosity, he tore open the bag and scanned the note. In neat cursive, it said something to the effect of: *I am Mariana Pérez. My parents are* desaparecidos. *I'm looking for my brother who was born in captivity. Someone called the headquarters of the Abuelas de Plaza de Mayo suggesting you might be him.* It ended: *If you have doubts about your identity and want to come, I'll wait for you.*

Guillermo unclenched. The baby had nothing to do with him. Nor, as far as he was concerned, did the note.

He had heard of *desaparecidos.* He knew there had once been a dictatorship that imprisoned people, and that many had gone missing, but his knowledge stopped there. His teachers avoided mentioning it at the schools he attended—particularly at his high school, an air force academy—and even before his mother had divorced his father, Francisco Gómez, an air force employee, that ghastly chapter in Argentina's history had never come up around the dinner table. These things were horrifying, but they did not involve him.

This was clearly a mix-up. "If I had a lost sibling, I'd be doing the same," he told the women, still seated at the table. "But I can't be him." Guillermo fished his green identity booklet out of his pocket and pointed to the first page. It clearly stated he was Guillermo Francisco Gómez.

Mariana smiled wanly. She scribbled down the numbers for the Abuelas' headquarters and her personal phone. "Call me whenever," she said.

It was time for Guillermo's lunch break. Bewildered, he took the bag containing the book and sat down at a table on the mezzanine that overlooked the bustling food court, where waiters bobbed and weaved with trays of hamburgers, hot dogs, and pizza. Soon Osvaldo wandered over. "So, tell me, what happened with your future wife?" he asked.

"It's a little more serious than that," said Guillermo. He handed Osvaldo the letter to read while he took a closer look at the book Mariana had enclosed in the bag. The cover was divided into two sections. A banner on the top showed a black-and-white image of older women in white handkerchiefs carrying a large white sign reading: "Niños Desaparecidos." The bottom section displayed a mosaic of dozens of black-and-white photos featuring doe-eyed infants and smiling toddlers. The book was titled *Niños desaparecidos. Jóvenes localizados: En la Argentina desde 1976 a 1999*—Disappeared children. Located youths: In Argentina from 1976 to 1999. It was crisp and new except for one crease on the spine that caused the book to fall open to page 175.

Guillermo scanned the page. The text described how a young couple, Patricia Roisinblit and José Manuel Pérez Rojo, had been captured in 1978. "On the 6th of October in 1978 the couple was abducted by security forces, José at his business in Martínez (Buenos Aires Province) and Patricia at her home in Buenos Aires," he read. "Patricia was eight months pregnant." Guillermo's eyes floated to the two pictures above. The first was of a beautiful young woman, Patricia, with a perfectly straight smile, shiny brown hair swept across her forehead, and a slightly upturned nose. The second photo, of José, hit Guillermo like a punch in the gut: It was his face, in black-and-white. Round cheeks. Full lips. Thick, straight hair.

Osvaldo finished the letter. He stood up to peer from the mezzanine into the restaurant, where Mariana still sat with her friend. He looked back at Guillermo. "That," he announced with conviction, "is your sister." Guillermo sat quietly as zippy pop tunes blared over the speakers. "What are you going to do?" asked Osvaldo.

"I don't know," Guillermo responded. "You're older than me. What do *you* think I should do?"

Osvaldo paused. "Can you live your whole life not knowing whether or not you have a sister?"

Guillermo decided that he could not. A few hours later, he reached for the paper Mariana had left him and dialed the number she'd written down for the Abuelas' headquarters. The person who picked up insisted that there was too much to explain over the phone. He would have to come in person.

Guillermo walked to the closest train station and boarded the San Martín line to Buenos Aires. He sat silently as the squat, graffiti-covered buildings of the suburbs streamed by. Soon, the blue train chugged past Guillermo's former high school, on the edge of El Palomar Air Force Base. It was a familiar touchpoint on an unsettling day, though he was not paying much attention to the scenery. His mind reeled, frantically trying to make sense of Mariana's visit.

Guillermo's first memory, from when he was about three, was of ambling through the central plaza near his home in José C. Paz toward a swing set, as trees swished in the breeze. Holding his left hand was his father, Francisco Gómez, a short, wiry man who worked for the air force. On his right was his mother, Teodora Jofré, a heavyset woman with beehive hair and hands strengthened from cleaning homes for a living.

It was a nice image. But Guillermo's childhood was not a happy one. Though their single-story home had warm wood floors and a color television in the living room—a novelty for the time—the family lived in a poor neighborhood, marred by heroin use and rampant crime. And then there was his father's temper. Another one of Guillermo's earliest recollections was of passing Jofré pots and pans from under the sink so that she could defend herself against Gómez's blows. One night, Gómez had returned sloshed from a folklore festival and pummeled her bloody with the butt of a rifle. In other moments, he pointed a shotgun at her head and held a knife to her chest. He threw chairs and slashed tables and doors. His beatings were so savage they sometimes sent Jofré to the hospital. Their neighbor had once called the police on Gómez, but any record of the complaint eventually vanished, Guillermo later recalled, as though it hadn't happened.

Gómez never laid a finger on Guillermo, but he did sometimes call him names—"Jew" was one of his standards. Guillermo did not think to ask why, considering their family was Catholic. When Guillermo was small, he remembered Gómez as an affectionate and committed father. In the colder months, Gómez had warmed Guillermo's tiny socks on the stove so that his feet would not be chilly on the walk to kindergarten; once, he arrived to pick Guillermo up at school with candy for him and his friends. Sometimes on weekends, he brought the boy to the air force facility where he worked, a damp house surrounding a courtyard in Morón. There, other officers took Guillermo to eat ice cream cones and let him play with their unloaded .32 revolvers. One was a man his colleagues called El Colo or El Colorado—the Redhead—for his flame-colored mane. Guillermo felt comfortable around the men. Now and then they came to his house, and he played with their children.

One day, recognizing how brutal her brother was to Jofré, Gómez's own sister helped her and Guillermo escape. While Gómez was out of the house, Jofré swept a few belongings into satchels and took Guillermo with her on a train to San Luis, her mountainous home province. For a few blessed months, mother and son enjoyed peace. Six-year-old Guillermo learned to pedal a bike on rural dirt roads lined with cow pastures. He studied catechism and became an altar boy at their local church. But just as he had on the other occasions in which Jofré had tried to flee, Gómez tracked her and Guillermo down—this time using Guillermo's school records.

Eventually, when Jofré had collected enough money to afford a lawyer, she decided that enough was enough and returned to Buenos Aires to file for divorce, which had only just become legal in Argentina. After that, Gómez seemed to lose all interest in Guillermo, paying a paltry sum for child support each month and otherwise vanishing.

Ever since, Jofré had effectively been Guillermo's only parent. One day, when he was around eight, he had been lying next to his mother before his siesta when she asked him a peculiar question. *What would happen,* she said, their faces pressed close in her bed, *if a woman knocked on their door saying she was his mother?* Panic had coursed through Guillermo's small body. He wrapped his arms around her neck like a baby monkey and told her, "But *you're* my mamá!" Then he sobbed himself to sleep while clinging to her, terrified by the idea that someone might try to separate them.

Guillermo and Jofré settled into a rhythm as a team of two. While she cleaned other people's homes, Guillermo tended to theirs, doing laundry, fetching groceries, and cooking pasta and other simple meals. Jofré was Guillermo's place of refuge. "When I had a fever, it was her embrace that brought it down," he would say later. "When I got a scratch, it hurt less in her arms; when I felt like crying, her arms calmed me." As his face began to sprout hair, it was his mother who taught him to shave, not his father.

No matter what Guillermo tried, Gómez seemed to want nothing to do with him. As an adolescent, Guillermo had signed up for high school at an air force academy, hoping to ignite some spark of paternal pride; but when he graduated, Gómez didn't show up to the ceremony. This indifference, coupled with their disparate appearances, had sometimes led Guillermo to wonder about their connection. Guillermo was fair and tall, with large eyes and feet like serving platters; Gómez was tawny, short, and lithe, with small features and a thin mouth. Guillermo began to think that perhaps he was the product of an affair Jofré had. What else could explain his father's cold disinterest? Once, he asked Jofré as much. In response, she chucked a sandal at him.

It had never occurred to Guillermo that he might be the child of *desaparecidos*. He had only learned what a *desaparecido* was as a teenager, when he watched a movie on Channel 9 about the Night of the Pencils. Based on the events of September 1976, when ten high school students who had agitated for lower bus fares were abducted by state security forces, the film had been difficult to stomach. One particularly brutal scene depicted a student about Guillermo's age being stripped naked and electrocuted on a metal table that an officer had blithely sprinkled with water to conduct extra electricity. It was sickening to think the movie was based on recent events. At Guillermo's high school, history class had stopped somewhere before Perón's first term in 1946.

The tall towers of Buenos Aires came into view as Guillermo's train crossed into the city. Near the Chacarita Cemetery, he got off and walked to the subway station for the B line, which brought him to a stop directly in front of the Abuelas' headquarters on Avenida Corrientes. The city hummed all around him. *Colectivos* roared down the wide avenue as, across the way, shoppers entered the sweeping Abasto shopping center—one of the city's largest malls—to eat empanadas at one of its many restaurants or catch a movie in one of its twelve cinemas.

Guillermo hardly noticed all the activity. One thought consumed him: Could Mariana really be his sister?

One month earlier, in March 2000, the poet Juan Gelman had found his granddaughter, Macarena. Though both Gelman's son and daughter-in-law were Argentine, he had tracked Macarena down in Montevideo, where he learned she had grown up in the home of a Uruguayan policeman and his wife. Like Paula Logares and the Julien Grisonas siblings, it seemed Macarena had been a victim of Operation Condor, the transnational collaboration between the dictatorships of the Southern Cone. The happy news that, after twenty-three years, Macarena had been located was splashed across the covers of Argentina's largest newspapers.

"Finally, Gelman found his granddaughter," read the *Clarín* headline. Hoping to protect Macarena's privacy, the poet was purposely tight-lipped with reporters, but joy radiated from his pithy statements. "I have been looking for my granddaughter for a long time," Gelman said, his eyes visibly red.

Macarena was the sixty-seventh grandchild located by the Abuelas and their allies. Before her had come Hilda "Victoria" Montenegro, whose trail the Abuelas had pursued since 1984, when she was eight. That year, the group had learned that a military officer known by the nickname "El Gordo José"—Fat José—had likely stolen a child of *desaparecidos*. The details they could piece together seemed to square with Victoria's case. But by the time the Abuelas were finally able to confirm her identity, she was twenty-four years old and had given birth to three children of her own.

That the babies the Abuelas had once searched for were now adults made things easier in some ways: There were no more fierce custody battles, and the grandchildren could now come to them, as Rosa had predicted. In 1999, for instance, a young woman with wavy black hair and pale skin had visited the Abuelas along with her adoptive parents after recognizing herself in an array of baby photos published in a newspaper. A subsequent DNA test bore out her suspicions: she was the daughter of *desaparecidos* Silvia Beatriz María Dameri and Orlando Antonio Ruiz. The very next day, she reunited with her brother, whom the Abuelas had found years before. These were the dream cases. But of course, the Abuelas did not sit idly by, waiting for the hundreds of grandchildren who remained at large to flood into their headquarters. They searched, and when they found someone, they got to work persuading them to submit to DNA testing, which, in many cases, was proving to be fraught.

In 1999, they had located someone they believed to be the child of Susana Beatriz Pegoraro and Rubén Santiago Bauer. Since reading testimony that detailed her birth in the ESMA in the CLAMOR archives back in the early 1980s, the Abuelas had known they were looking for a daughter born in late 1977. Complaints led them to a girl—now a young woman—who had grown up in the home of Policarpo Vázquez, a retired naval officer. The Abuelas launched a legal case and, in March of 1999, Vázquez was arrested. He quickly admitted that the young woman, Evelin Vázquez, was not his biological child; she had been delivered to him by another Argentine naval officer who went by El Turco—the Turk. But Vázquez told the judge that he saw raising her as a "divine mandate."

"God put the baby in my hands and so I thought I should keep her and raise her," he explained.

With Vázquez's confession, the court already knew whose daughter Evelin wasn't. But they still didn't know whose child she *was*. Evelin met with the judge overseeing Vázquez's case soon after his arrest and was told she would need to submit to a DNA test. At first, she said she would be willing to give her blood. But a week later, she reneged, stating she would only do so if the results would not be used against Vázquez and his wife, the people who had raised her.

"I understand the suffering of the others, the twenty-two years that my supposed grandmothers have searched," she later told *La Nación*, before explaining her resistance to testing her DNA. "If for twenty-two years, he has been my father, don't expect me to abruptly cut him off. I don't want to hurt my father."

Evelin's case had been deadlocked ever since, but there were still hundreds of stolen grandchildren left to locate. To encourage people to come forward of their own volition, the Abuelas worked to make themselves even more publicly visible—and thus easier to find. They bought television ads that urged people born during the dictatorship to consider the question "Vos sabés quién sos?"—Do you know who you are?—and held massive rock concerts that filled the Plaza de Mayo with cheering youth. They worked with theater troupes to prepare theatrical performances as part of an initiative they called Theater for Identity, and participated in an array of film projects.

As Guillermo walked toward the Abuelas' headquarters, one of the theaters in the Abasto shopping center across the street was playing its five o'clock showing of *Botín de Guerra*, a documentary about the Abuelas that had been released just a week before. The director had spliced together historical images of the Abuelas marching in the Plaza de Mayo with current footage of Chicha Mariani, Elsa Pavón, Licha De la Cuadra, and other Abuelas describing how their children had been abducted and their grandchildren stolen from them. It also featured some of the grandchildren the Abuelas had found. One, a lean twenty-three-year-old who was still going by Claudio Novoa, the name with which he was raised, recounted how as a baby he was the only member of his family to survive a raid by the armed forces because his mother had thought to wrap him in blankets and enclose him in a closet. Another, a twenty-four-year-old who had grown up as María Carolina Guallane, detailed the moment in which she had first realized that she was related to her biological grandmother after recognizing herself in a baby photo.

In one scene, Rosa appeared, sitting on a patterned couch in her living room. She told the audience about the grandson she had sought for twenty-one years—the child to whom her daughter, Patricia, had given birth in the cold depths of the ESMA. She still had not found him. "I hope he knows that he has two Abuelas who are looking for him," she said, "and a sister who is looking for him desperately, who writes him letters, who writes him poems, and who desires more than anything else in her life to find him. Nothing more."

Had Guillermo been seated in the theater, he would have recognized one of the young women to also appear on-screen. "It must be terrible for these young people to have a memory of something they don't consciously understand," Mariana Pérez said solemnly into the camera, as the Río de la Plata lapped on the shore behind her. "Because I believe that, somewhere, that exists. I believe that being separated from your mother somehow imprints itself on a baby's psyche."

Amid the hubbub of Avenida Corrientes, Guillermo found building 3284—constructed in the Parisian style, with arched windows and wrought-iron railings—and rang the buzzer for 4H. The front door clicked open and he took the elevator up to the fourth floor. A tiny old woman with cherubic cheeks and the crackly voice of a smoker opened the door. As she ushered him inside, he noticed tears welling up behind the large glasses that swallowed much of her petite face. What a strange day this was turning out to be.

Another woman, Estela de Carlotto, greeted him briefly before receding to a different part of the office. He was led to a room where he sat down with Mariana and two other Abuelas members: Abel Madariaga and Remo Carlotto, Estela's son. Black-and-white photos were pinned to the white walls, and books spilled out of the wooden bookcase. Through the room's tall casement window that looked out at the arches of the Abasto shopping center, the autumn sunlight was softening into dusk. Guillermo took a seat, and the little old woman with the large glasses asked if he'd like to drink anything. He requested a coffee. When she returned, Guillermo could hear the cup clattering wildly against its saucer as her hands shook, splashing the coffee over the sides.

The Abuelas were not accustomed to this sort of situation. Their protocol was to painstakingly gather evidence over the course of months before approaching a suspected grandchild. Even then, they would proceed slowly, tentatively revealing more information and allowing the grandchild to pose questions. With her youthful impulsiveness, Mariana had blown that process apart. Now Guillermo was there in the Abuelas' office on the very same day she had ambushed him. No one quite knew what to do.

Guillermo asked to see what information they had gathered about him. They had recently received two anonymous calls, they explained, suggesting he might be the child of *desaparecidos*. Someone pushed handwritten accounts of the calls across the table.

Guillermo had no idea that military men had stolen children, falsifying their birth certificates and claiming them as their own. He had not been one of the fifty thousand young people to flood into the Plaza de Mayo to take in "Rock por la Identidad," nor had he attended any of the Abuelas' art installations. He had seen *La Historia Oficial*—The Official Story—the movie about a history teacher who begins to doubt the origins of her adopted daughter, but he hadn't thought about it much since.

Reflexively, he reached into his pocket for a pack of cigarettes and pulled one out. The notes about the two anonymous calls were remarkably detailed. The first, dated April 13, 2000, named Teodora Jofré and Francisco Gómez as his "appropriators"—whatever that meant. Some of the notes seemed to have little to do with him: they described a young man who was "blondish" and Germanic-looking, whereas Guillermo had dark hair and eyes. But the call report also included Guillermo's exact home address, phone number, and a description of his workplace down to the uniform he wore there. A long time before, it said, Gómez had admitted to the caller that Guillermo was in fact the son of a medical student who was killed during the dictatorship. It also mentioned that one of Gómez's superiors, known as El Colorado, "had another boy."

The second complaint was transcribed in the same neat cursive that Guillermo had already seen once that day in the letter he opened at Shower. The caller, a woman, wanted to know if the Abuelas had taken any action since she had called the first time. Then she offered new details. Mariana, on the other side of the line, focused on annotating everything the woman said in tidy script: that Gómez had admitted knowledge of "death flights" and he tended to be armed and carry false documentation. The caller also told Mariana that Gómez and another "repressor" had brought Guillermo to her house when he was just a few days old; she had recently given birth to a daughter, she explained, and she had nursed Guillermo.

Guillermo stared at the papers. It was a lot to process. While there were errors, they had so much accurate information about him. He vividly remembered El Colorado from his childhood birthday parties; he had been friends with his son, Ezequiel.

Someone interrupted. To confirm his identity, they told him, he would need to undergo a DNA test.

"Fine," he said briskly. "Take my DNA."

For a moment, no one spoke: not Mariana or the other Abuelas members. Over the past year, the Abuelas had been embroiled in the Evelin Vázquez case. They had grown used to encountering resistance to DNA testing.

After a nervous pause, someone explained that to go through the Banco Nacional de Datos Genéticos, they would need a judge's order. Guillermo replied that he didn't want to wait. He was already there in the office. Now that they had planted the question of whether Mariana might be his sister, he wanted the answer. The group began thinking out loud. *Perhaps they could send his sample to Mary-Claire King in America,* one said. Another agreed that would be faster. Guillermo volunteered—demanded, really—to give his sample that very day.

Mariana and the others gathered were too anxious to extract his blood. Someone brought him a lancet and a small piece of absorbent paper with five small circles traced onto it. Impatient, Guillermo pricked his right thumb and squeezed a drop of blood into each of the circles. As the drops hit the paper, they expanded into red splotches. Those five blots—no bigger than pennies—contained the truth of his past and the fate of his future.

32

Confronting Gómez

May 2000

A week or so after Guillermo's blood sample was carefully packaged and sent by mail to Mary-Claire King, Gómez invited him to dinner at a steakhouse in Morón. The gesture was bizarre—they rarely saw each other, and didn't eat out together except maybe once a year, on Guillermo's birthday. Stranger still was that Gómez had also invited Jofré, with whom he had communicated only sparingly since their divorce. The only explanation Guillermo could think of was that, when he had recently turned twenty-one, Gómez had been released from the obligation of paying monthly child support. Perhaps he was now feeling flush and had no one else with whom to share his newfound gains.

It was also, Guillermo figured, an opportunity. As thick cuts of tenderloin and rib eye sizzled on the black iron grates of the *parrilla*, Gómez got up to wash his hands and Guillermo followed him into the restroom, leaving Jofré behind at the table. As they stood next to each other facing the bathroom mirror, Guillermo told Gómez that a girl had come to visit him where he worked, claiming she was his sister. Guillermo watched as Gómez's normally tan face blanched.

"Take a good look at me, and look at you," he demanded, gesturing toward their reflections. "Are you my father?"

Yes, Gómez insisted in his deep smoker's growl, he was.

Why, then, Guillermo pressed, would this woman claim that he was her brother? What could possibly motivate anyone to lie about that? Gómez maintained that it was all just nasty gossip. Guillermo had always inspired envy among other kids in the neighborhood, he said. His house was large, with not just one but several sun-soaked patios. He had done well in elementary school and at the air force academy. He was a good kid—the only one in the neighborhood with a bright future. This *desaparecidos* story was just to bring him down. And he should not, Gómez added, say anything to his mother.

Guillermo was unconvinced, but a few days later, when Gómez invited him to another meal—this one without Jofré—Guillermo accepted. As waiters milled about, it was Gómez who brought up Mariana. He asked Guillermo to repeat everything that had happened the day she surprised him at work. It seemed he was trying to sketch out just how much Guillermo knew. Guillermo complied, describing Mariana's visit to Shower and the letter she'd written him.

What Guillermo did not share was that he had visited the Abuelas' headquarters, and that he had seen Mariana several times since that day. They had met up at cafés and in parks, searching each other for common traits—how similar their gestures were, and how they both had flat feet. They shared a distaste of Mantecol, a popular Argentine candy made with a peanut butter nougat, and an appreciation for irony. He had learned that the tiny woman with the trembling hands who had served him coffee at the Abuelas' headquarters was Mariana's grandmother, Argentina Rojo. Mariana's other grandmother, whom he had yet to meet, was Rosa Roisinblit, the longtime vice president of the Abuelas.

Guillermo looked at Gómez. He nodded to their hands, resting next to each other on the table—Guillermo's fair, Gómez's bronzed. Again, he asked Gómez if he was his son. Again, Gómez said he was.

They had a third meal, a lunch: Gómez peppered him with the same questions, maintained he was Guillermo's father, and requested to meet again. Finally, as Guillermo got in Gómez's car for the fourth meal, another lunch, and the conversation began to repeat itself, he exploded.

"I have to be at work at four. I don't want to drive somewhere far away just for you to tell me the same thing again," he ranted, his patience frayed. "No, just take me home."

Then Gómez crumbled. He broke into convulsive sobs, tears cascading down his face so heavily that they obscured his vision—Guillermo had to grab the steering wheel from him to avoid flattening a bicyclist crossing the street. Words began to tumble from Gómez's mouth.

Mariana was Guillermo's sister, he admitted. They were the children of two Montoneros, one of whom was a young medical student. Both Guillermo's mother and father had been held at the air force facility where Gómez worked. He promised that while Guillermo's mother was pregnant, no one had hurt her—though he could not say the same for his father, who had been tortured mercilessly.

"You have to understand," Gómez said over and over, between gasps for air. He insisted that he had treated Guillermo's mother kindly, sneaking her extra cartons of milk and hard-boiled eggs when other guards weren't looking. Other days he walked her, blindfolded, around the facility's internal court-yard. Before she was taken away to give birth at the ESMA, Gómez claimed that she had begged him to make a promise: if anything happened to her, she wanted him to take care of her child. "I saved your life," Gómez howled.

Guillermo stared vacantly. Later, he would dream of asking Gómez a million things. What had happened to his parents? Who killed them? When? Where were their remains? But his mind was suddenly blank. Only one response occurred to him: he told Gómez to hire a lawyer.

"You kidnapped the grandson of the vice president of the Abuelas de Plaza de Mayo."

33

Genetics Doesn't Lie

June 2, 2000

As the new millennium dawned, Mary-Claire King's workload had surged. Her lab now handled the most international human rights forensics work in the world and did it all pro bono. She was always on a plane to some far-flung, war-torn place: in addition to Argentina and El Salvador, she had been asked to identify human rights victims in Rwanda, Ethiopia, Cambodia, and Croatia, among other countries. Law enforcement agencies in the United States had begun calling on King for help with their cold murder cases, too. "[The police] got a kick out of [working with] this radical feminist from Berkeley," she would later recall. Since she took on the projects for free, departments thanked her in embroidered ball caps. The unworn police hats heaped in the back of her closet now numbered in the dozens.

In 1994, Myriad Genetics, a private genetic testing company, had won the race to clone the BRCA1 gene. Although King had used the same approach as Myriad, she had far fewer resources, with only one automatic sequencer in her lab. At first, King had been relieved. Now she and other scientists could get on with the real work of understanding how mutations in the gene resulted in breast cancer. But then Myriad obtained patents on BRCA1 and its sister gene, BRCA2, and sent a cease-and-desist letter to King, demanding she stop her research. Instead, King had continued, undeterred, and expanded her work to other genetic mysteries, such as the causes of deafness and schizophrenia. (The US Supreme Court would eventually decide that BRCA1 and BRCA2 are not patentable since they are "products of nature.")

Excited by the groundbreaking advances, Bill Gates and his family had poured tens of millions of dollars into genome sciences at the University of Washington, and in 1995, King had decamped there from Berkeley, setting up her lab in a building near the shores of Portage Bay. Outside the lab's entrance, to warm up the sterile hallway, she displayed a rotating rack full of postcards expressing thanks and encouragement from places like Argentina, Chile, Guatemala, and other countries where King had helped identify human rights victims.

When she wasn't flying around the globe, she could be found pacing the lab and inquiring about the work of her team, a diverse group of about twenty postdoctoral fellows, students, and staff. One reporter likened them to a "multicultural Gap ad." As the team pipetted and centrifuged, scrutinizing vials that might contain breast tumors or the DNA of Haitian villagers whose relatives had been disappeared by their country's military dictatorship, King could be heard offering encouragement ("Wonderful!" "Fabulous!") or issuing challenges—"If this works," she said of one experiment, "I'll buy lattes for a week!" Caffeine was a prized substance in the King Laboratory; its leader was difficult to keep up with, working most evenings and weekends. She had recently taken her first vacation in eighteen years: a boat trip up Alaska's Inside Passage. She thought, moved, and spoke at comet speed. "By comparison," another reporter wrote of King, "one feels trapped in resin."

By then the BNDG had its own mitochondrial DNA team in Argentina. It was a critical development for the Abuelas, as the lab was the sole facility whose results were accepted by Argentine courts to legally change a person's identity. Mitochondrial DNA became the BNDG's first line of inquiry; if samples coincided, the lab ran additional genetic tests to make extra certain of the match. King, though, was still looped into particularly sensitive cases, mainly if the Abuelas needed to compare new samples with the families whose blood she had stored in her deli fridge.

And so, on May 4, 2000, when a small square of filter paper with five splotches of blood arrived at the lab, with the news that it could belong to the grandson of Rosa Roisinblit, King's pulse quickened. That Rosa, the Abuela to whom she felt closest, might have at last located her grandson was almost more than King could have hoped. Rosa—stoic, plucky, devoted Rosa—had waited so long. The geneticist had sometimes joked that, in her work on the Abuelas' project, Estela was her boss and Rosa was her teacher; when King struggled to express complicated genetics concepts in clear Spanish, it was Rosa, the former obstetrician, who served as her patient interpreter. She desperately wanted the results to bear out the Abuelas' suspicions but steeled herself for any outcome. "It doesn't matter how I feel about this," King reminded herself. "All that matters is what it is. . . . Genetics doesn't lie."

Much of the work that had once been done painstakingly by hand—manually pipetting DNA samples into plates of springy gel and applying electric currents to separate the molecules—was now completed by automatic sequencers, but that didn't speed things up much. It would take several weeks of testing and retesting until King felt confident enough to provide a definitive answer.

King's team always jostled to work on a case sent by the Abuelas, and she quickly put them to work. After sterilizing all the equipment with sodium hypochlorite, one of her researchers took a sharp razor, sliced Guillermo's blood blots out of the paper, and soaked them in a small tube filled with Proteinase K solution to release his DNA into the liquid. The resulting mixture was transparent, concealing the complexity and power of the information contained within it. They placed the tube in an incubator where it sat at 55 degrees Celsius for several hours, after which they spun it in a centrifuge until the DNA formed a white tangle of solid strings within the liquid. That DNA was placed in a PCR machine, which copied it millions of times. Finally, it was ready for sequencing in the lab's ABI Sanger sequencing instrument, which resembled a bulky beige printer. The machine clicked and hummed and, after a few hours, finished its work. The result was an image visible on a computer: a series of multicolored peaks and valleys, like a jagged mountain landscape drawn by a toddler. Each color represented the different nucleotides that make up DNA—adenine (A), cytosine (C), guanine (G), and thymine (T).

The team repeated the same process with Rosa's blood sample, which had sat untouched in King's deli fridge for years. Then it was time to compare the sequences. While mitochondrial DNA contains 16,569 nucleotides, most humans differ from the universally accepted reference sequence, which scientists use to compare DNA, in just a handful of spots. King and her team looked at where Rosa's sequence diverged from the reference and compared them to the places where Guillermo's did. The first place coincided: they both had T's. The second place coincided: again, T's. The third and fourth places matched: C and C. Her chest tightening, King examined the fifth and final spot where Rosa's mitochondrial DNA differed from the reference sequence: C. Guillermo's? Also a C.

Guillermo and Rosa were a perfect match.

King furiously repeated and rechecked her work. But there it was: the truth. Late on the evening of June 2, she dialed the headquarters for the Abuelas. Rosa was not available. She was not in Buenos Aires but in Boston, King was told, where she and Estela were due to receive honorary degrees from the University of Massachusetts. King refused to reveal why she was calling before she could talk to Rosa personally.

By the time King and Rosa connected, it was eleven at night on the East Coast. Rosa had just gotten back to the home in Cambridge where she and Estela were staying with Rita Arditti, an Argentine academic who had written extensively about the Abuelas, and her life partner, an artist named Estelle Disch. That night, the University of Massachusetts had hosted a dinner at the John F. Kennedy Library in celebration of Rosa, Estela, and the other honorary degree recipients. Rosa had just changed out of her pale pink dress with lace edging and into a nightgown when she and King finally spoke.

"Rosa," King said through the phone, her voice crackling with joy. "Es tu nieto."

It's your grandson.

Rosa was not one for unbridled displays of emotion. But there, in the middle of her friends' living room, she leapt up and down in her nightgown as Estela and her friends joined in, laughing, crying, and dancing.

That same night, as a cold breeze shook the trees outside in José C. Paz, Guillermo sat at home. The burden of all he had learned felt heavy and he was anxious for an update. He dialed Mariana.

They had continued seeing each other, slowly building trust. Guillermo had not yet revealed what Gómez had confessed to him, and Mariana was intimidated by the strength of Guillermo's conviction that they were siblings. What if she had upended his life for nothing and had to start her search over? Guillermo, meanwhile, was daunted by Mariana's ferocious desire to make up for lost years. During one get-together, he had showed her scars he had from tripping over things as a child, and Mariana had cried for every cut he'd endured without her. They had both grown up lonesome only children wishing for a sibling, but only Mariana had known she was supposed to have one.

Already, living up to her dreams felt impossible. Mariana was hoping for Rodolfo—Rodolfito—and instead had gotten Guillermo—a man with twenty-one years of heavy baggage and a name she couldn't even bring herself to use. Calling him anything other than the name their parents had given him felt, to her, like an affront to their memory. Instead, she used nicknames, like "*nene*" (little one) or "*mocoso*" (brat).

"Any news?" Guillermo asked when Mariana picked up.

His timing was impeccable. Mariana had just heard from Rosa in Boston. His blood had revealed they were brother and sister.

34

Baba

June 2000

Before boarding her flight back to Argentina, Rosa searched for a present to bring Guillermo. When Mariana was younger, Rosa had always brought her dolls dressed in the traditional clothing of whatever place she was visiting. But what to buy for a twenty-one-year-old man she had never met? She selected a white sweatshirt embroidered with a red scorpion and folded it carefully into her suitcase.

Back in Buenos Aires, Rosa arranged to meet Guillermo in the office of one of the Abuelas' lawyers. She was sitting down as he strode in. His height and resemblance to José stunned her to silence. After a pause, she managed to mutter: "Well, I'm your grandmother."

"Ya lo sé, Baba," Guillermo said, using the nickname for her that Mariana had taught him. I already know that, Baba. He bent down and gave her a kiss on the cheek.

A few days later, Rosa and Guillermo went to Mariana's for dinner. The plans had come together quickly: that evening, Mariana, recently interested in theater, had been set to attend the opening of a play she had worked on as part of the Abuelas' Theater for Identity initiative. Titled *On the Subject of Doubt*, the show centered around a young man whose doubts about his identity mounted over the course of the performance. He was as bald as a cue ball, while the man who had raised him had a full mane of hair. But Mariana canceled as soon as her family's reunion had been confirmed.

Mariana was still working on her political science degree at the University of Buenos Aires, but her true love had always been writing. When she was younger, the Abuelas had published some of her poems and letters in a volume titled *Algún Día*, or Some Day. One, from 1986, when Mariana was nine, read: "Dear Brother, when I learned of your existence I was filled with deep happiness, but I also felt sad not to have you next to me."

Now, there he was at her dining table. Rosa pulled out the sweatshirt she had brought from America and gave it to Guillermo. He immediately peeled off the sweater he was wearing and pulled the new one over his head. It was the same color as the kit worn by River Plate, his favorite soccer team, he remarked. And Scorpio was his Zodiac sign. He loved it.

Mariana's twenty-third birthday was coming up, and Guillermo excitedly suggested that Rosa throw her a party. Their parents had been only children, so there were no aunts or uncles to invite, and both of his grandfathers had died. It would be a small affair.

A few weeks later, Guillermo, Mariana, and Argentina gathered in Rosa's apartment, with its honey parquet floors and patterned upholstery, to celebrate Mariana as a family. Rosa had strung pearls around her neck and laid a tablecloth embroidered with turquoise flowers on her dining table for the occasion. Photos of Patricia adorned most surfaces. Guillermo walked over to Rosa's blocky television, where one of the photos was perched, and leaned down to examine it. He nodded at Mariana. "You look like her in this one."

"Like who?" Mariana asked.

"Like Mamá."

As the night came to an end, they lingered over coffee and posed for photos in front of Rosa's elegant hutch. In one, Mariana leaned into Guillermo's shoulder, grinning broadly for the camera. In another, Guillermo stood behind Argentina, resting his large hand on her petite shoulder.

Out on the street below, pedestrians clutched their coats against the winter chill. Yet another economic recession was starting to settle over the country. Inside the small apartment on Riobamba, though, warmth and promise filled the air. Rosa, Mariana, and Guillermo had been robbed of twenty-one years that they could never make up for. But their first days together as a family felt like a start.

The year before she found him, Mariana had written Guillermo a poem about how, one day, when they finally met, she would tell him about his birth in the ESMA. "The story," she titled it.

I'll tell you the story of your arrival to the world, In the depths of fear, on top of a table, it began.

In Spanish, "giving birth" is expressed as *dar a luz*—bring to light. Mariana had worked relentlessly to uncover the details of how Patricia had brought Guillermo to light in the ESMA's airless basement, and everything else about her parents' lives she could possibly find out. Other grandchildren whose siblings had been stolen, like María Lavalle Lemos, had conducted similar familial investigations. Many of them volunteered with the Abuelas and, in 1998, they had begun to wonder what would happen if their grandmothers died before they found their siblings. Who would tell them about their disappeared parents then?

"One must ask what that man or woman recovers when they only learn the names of their parents and the circumstances of their disappearance," Mariana and another Abuelas member wrote. "They recover fragments of their history. But their identity is not restored in the sense that the Abuelas attribute to this word."

These questions inspired the Abuelas to launch a project known as the Archivo Biográfico Familiar—the Biographical Family Archive—along with the University of Buenos Aires. The goal was to collect oral histories about the Abuelas' disappeared sons and daughters so that, when grandchildren were located, they could get to know their parents beyond the grim details recorded in their CONADEP files. Instead of how they died, the focus was on how they lived: who they were friends with, what they liked to eat, whether they had pets, and what pranks they'd played as kids. By transmitting these details, the Abuelas wrote, they could "preserve family memory into the future."

Mariana had worked intensely on the project, hoping to get to know her own parents better in the process. Rosa rarely shrank from telling things like they were, but when it came to Patricia, Mariana felt that her grandmother shared only her daughter's positive characteristics—how beautiful she had been, how smart, and how artistically talented. In adolescence, these one-dimensional descriptions had begun to chafe at Mariana. She wanted to know who her mother and father had *really* been. She began hungrily seeking out friends and relatives of her parents' who might offer a fuller—more complicated—picture of them.

Now, with Guillermo, she shared some of what she'd learned—stories that she herself had pieced together secondhand. Careful not to overwhelm him, she told him slowly about Patricia and José's detention. From her descriptions of the air force facility where the couple was initially held, Guillermo immediately recognized the building where Gómez had brought him as a child. He recalled the place swarming with people—some in starched uniforms, some in plain clothes. There was a large dining area, its walls covered in paintings of planes that had inspired awe in him as a boy. He even knew the base's phone number by heart. They would later learn it was called the Regional de Inteligencia de Buenos Aires, or RIBA.

Eventually, Guillermo heard "the story" Mariana had written about in her poem. How Patricia's contractions had begun early in the morning on November 15. How her eyes had been covered with a mask and she had been led downstairs to the dingy basement infirmary. How she had labored next to torture chambers, and how, when he arrived, she had begged the navy doctor named Magnacco not to cut the umbilical cord connecting them. How his mother's first whispered words to him had been: "Hi, son. It's me." Magnacco, Guillermo learned, told Patricia that she'd been brave during the birth. She'd retorted that she'd been braver the first time she gave birth—in freedom. He found out that his mother had named him Rodolfo Fernando, after two *compañeros* who had been disappeared, and how, a few days after he was born, though no one knew when or where, he had been taken from her.

He began to weave the new story together with another he'd uncovered: about how Gómez and Jofré had tried to have children, but Jofré had suffered several miscarriages, at least one of them precipitated by Gómez's fierce blows. Later, Gómez would fill in more of the blanks. News of the couple's infertility had traveled, and an air force higher-up had offered Gómez a baby—no strings attached—even offering to take care of the paperwork to make things simpler. Gómez would later claim he thought the boy had been abandoned, and that he was doing a noble thing by taking him in. But instead of stating he was adopted, the falsified birth certificate drawn up by the registrar had claimed the boy was the biological son of Francisco Gómez and Teodora Jofré, born on November 24. It was this document that had given him the name Guillermo Francisco Gómez.

35

Thicker Than Water

2001

When Rosa first hugged Guillermo, almost twenty years had passed since democracy was restored to Argentina. But justice for the junta's crimes still seemed unattainable. The Full Stop and Due Obedience Laws remained in force, shielding dictatorship-era military officers from new prosecutions, and many of those accused of torture and murder—and even convicted in the Trial of the Juntas—continued to roam free. After he was detained in the Abuelas' Plan Sistemático case, Videla had been released to house arrest after just thirty-eight days due to his age; Magnacco still worked at the naval hospital despite his firing from Sanatorio Mitre; and Astiz spent many a sunny day clad in boat shoes and blue Bermuda shorts at his yacht club in Mar del Plata, where management considered him a "distinguished member."

In response, frustrated H.I.J.O.S. continued staging *escraches*, and a human rights group known as Centro de Estudios Legales y Sociales (CELS) began organizing "Truth Trials" in Argentina's courts, public hearings in which citizens could testify and share information about abductions and killings—though in most cases judges could not use it to formally prosecute the perpetrators. The impunity had started to attract international attention too. Since Argentine courts could do little to rectify the unthinkable violence perpetrated by the junta, other countries had taken it upon themselves to seek justice. In 1990, a French court had convicted Alfredo Astiz of murdering Alice Domon, the French nun who had been disappeared from the Iglesia de la Santa Cruz at the same time as the Madres Esther Careaga and María Ponce de Bianco, and Léonie Duquet, another French nun associated with the Madres movement who was abducted shortly thereafter. The country had sentenced Astiz in absentia to life in prison for the crimes. More recently, a judge in Spain named Baltasar Garzón had issued arrest warrants for ninety-eight former Argentine military officers for their role in the deaths of six hundred people of Spanish descent. Sweden was preparing to charge Astiz for the murder of Dagmar Hagelin, a Swedish Argentine girl, and Italy planned to do the same for the abductions of Susana Pegoraro, the woman the Abuelas suspected of being Evelin Vázquez's mother; Pegoraro's father, an Italian citizen; and one other Italian Argentine woman.

But Astiz was not extradited, and Argentina's government refused to hand any suspects over to Spain. Next door, Chile's courts had recently stripped parliamentary immunity from the country's former dictator Augusto Pinochet, paving the way to his prosecution, but Argentina seemed in no rush to take similar action. Nor was its government eager to open its books—those that hadn't been destroyed by the military when it left power, anyway. Toward the end of Menem's term in 1999, the Abuelas had urged the then-president to hand over the government's national archives, but he had balked, instead suggesting: "Why don't you ask for the American ones?" Estela and Rosa did just that, flying to Washington, DC, to meet with Hillary Clinton's top advisors to request the US government's secret files related to Operation Condor. Later, Estela also met with Secretary of State Madeleine Albright, who promised that the United States would begin to declassify relevant CIA documents. It was welcome news, but the Abuelas were all too aware that bureaucracy could move at a glacial pace.

Back in Argentina, their persistence was slowly yielding results. By mid-2000, charges in the Plan Sistemático case had ensnared Emilio Massera, the former navy chief; Guillermo Suárez Mason, a general known as the Butcher of Olimpo for his brutality in the Olimpo torture center; and

Héctor Febres, a coast guard officer whom witnesses accused of overseeing pregnant prisoners in the ESMA. In fits and starts, the government had also begun granting reparations to victims of the junta: to the children and spouses of the disappeared, and to those who had been unlawfully detained by the military during the country's state of siege. Before she located Guillermo, Mariana had been awarded bonds amounting to around $334,000 for the disappearances of José and Patricia. She'd been able to cash in enough to pay off debts for Rosa and Argentina and to purchase a charming old home in Colegiales with a patio, where she eventually asked Nilda Noemí "Munú" Actis Goretta, an artist who had been imprisoned with Patricia in the ESMA, to create a vibrant mural on the wall.

Other frustrations lingered as the Abuelas realized that, while fierce custody battles were behind them, reuniting with adult grandchildren dredged up new challenges. In 1999, the Abuelas had located a twenty-one-year-old woman whom they thought might be Claudia Victoria Poblete Hlaczik, a child kidnapped with her mother when she was eight months old; her grandmother, Buscarita Roa, had been searching for her ever since. The young woman, who went by Mercedes Landa, had been raised as a sheltered only child in a wealthy area of Buenos Aires by an army colonel and his wife. She had harbored doubts about her identity as an adolescent, finding it strange that her mother had been in her fifties when she supposedly gave birth, and that there were no photos of her pregnant. Soon thereafter, because of the Abuelas' inquiries, Mercedes was ordered by a judge to submit to genetic testing. In February 2000, the results came back. She was not Mercedes Landa. She was Claudia Victoria Poblete Hlaczik.

Claudia may have given her blood willingly, but she was less quick to embrace the truth. When her real identity was confirmed, she was called to a courthouse, where, unbeknownst to her, Buscarita and other biological relatives were waiting anxiously in another area. Claudia was presented with a thick report whose front pages displayed photos of her biological parents and an image of herself as a baby that she immediately recognized. After she'd had a few minutes to flip through it, the judge asked if she wanted to meet her real family.

"No," she said firmly. "I don't want to."

"They've been waiting a long time," the judge countered.

Grudgingly, Claudia agreed. When she emerged from the courtroom, Buscarita was waiting. "We are your family. Whatever you want, we are here for you," she offered.

"I don't need anything," Claudia spat back.

Her appropriators, Ceferino Landa and Mercedes Beatriz Moreira, were gone by the time she got home. A police car had picked them up while she was in court and taken them to the headquarters of the federal police. "Don't worry about us, we are okay," they wrote in a note they left behind. "We love you a lot." A year later, the judge in Claudia's case ruled that the Full Stop and Due Obedience Laws had violated the constitution—a bold move that allowed not only for the prosecution of her appropriators but also for the reopening of the case against the police officers responsible for her abduction, sending a signal that immunity might not last forever. The rulings were quickly appealed, however, and the case was once again entangled in the courts. In one hearing, Claudia told the judges, "For twenty-two years they were my parents and I love them."

When Guillermo had pricked his thumb in the Abuelas' office, he did so to probe his relationship to Mariana; he had not had time to consider how it might impact Gómez and Jofré. Indeed, King's analysis could not officially confirm that Guillermo was the grandson of Rosa and Argentina in the eyes of the state—only results from the BNDG could do that. But it turned out to be an incriminating piece of evidence. On February 8, 2001, a warm summer Thursday, Francisco Gómez was arrested on charges of kidnapping and the falsification of official documents. The case had been pending for decades—after Rosa had first learned of Guillermo's birth at the ESMA, she had taken the information to the courts; a judge now decided that King's report, which suggested a 99.99999 percent probability of a relationship, and Guillermo's falsified birth certificate were enough evidence to detain Gómez. He was thrown in a coast guard jail behind the city's central train station in Retiro.

Guillermo was livid. He didn't care so much that Gómez was behind bars—until recently, he had hardly seen the man in years—but he dreaded what the arrest presaged: Jofré was surely next. Whether or not they shared the same DNA, he still cared deeply for her. Jofré had raised him. He still lived with her. Ever since he could remember, she had cooked for him and ironed his clothes and hugged him when he was sad. She had been his only source of stability—the one person by whom he felt unconditionally loved. From the beginning, she had denied knowing that he was the child of *desaparecidos*—Gómez had told her that he was the abandoned son of a military man, she explained, and that was what she had believed. Perhaps she knew Gómez was lying, perhaps she didn't. Perhaps, savagely abused by her husband, she hadn't asked too many questions when offered an escape from her misery, a baby of her own to love.

Guillermo found Jofré's tale hard to stomach; she had deceived him about his being adopted for twenty-one years, even when his questions had offered ample opportunities to explain. But he couldn't bear to lose her. It all felt, he would later reflect, like "someone had taken away the ground where you step, and you fall without anything to grab onto."

He lashed out at his grandmothers and especially Mariana, whom he felt had led him to believe that there wouldn't be legal consequences associated with sending his blood to Mary-Claire King. "What good is it to be the son of *desaparecidos*?" he snapped at Mariana. "I don't have even one memory of them, I don't have a gravestone to lay a flower on, I don't know when they died or how they died." He had grown up with parents; she did not know what that was like. He felt a responsibility to Gómez and Jofré that she could not possibly understand. His past life might have been one giant, festering lie. But his new reality was worse.

Ten days after Gómez was arrested, Guillermo gave a scathing interview to *La Nación*, the large and traditionally conservative newspaper, in which he revealed that he had begged for the legal charges against Gómez and Jofré to be dropped, only to be told by his grandmothers that it wasn't possible. The matter was in the hands of the state, which was duty bound to investigate and prosecute the crime that had been committed. To officially change his identity in government registries, the state would require

Guillermo to have his blood drawn by the BNDG. The Abuelas had tried to bribe him to do so, he told the interviewer from *La Nación*, saying that if he gave his DNA to the BNDG, he would receive reparations. He said that "not all the gold in the world" could convince him when it would almost certainly land his "parents" in jail. Adding a personal slight to his slew of grievances about the Abuelas, he described Rosa as "very cold." All *he'd* wanted to know, he insisted, was whether he had a sister; what the Abuelas seemed to want was to hold people—people who might not even know anything—accountable for the deaths of their children. He would not have his blood drawn. He also refused to have his photograph taken. "I want to continue being Guillermo Francisco Gómez," he said. "I want to keep being the son of my parents and not two people that I never met."

Toward the end of their conversation, when the journalist asked Guillermo how he would counsel those with doubts about their identities, Guillermo had a ready answer. First, they should talk to their parents, he replied. If the parents denied wrongdoing, then those with doubts should swallow them. "They should avoid the Abuelas de Plaza de Mayo."

Depression engulfed him. Unable to function, Guillermo quit his job. Then, just as he had feared, Jofré was arrested. (Two months after that, Magnacco, the naval doctor who had delivered him, was detained as well.) Guillermo began to drink heavily—the most he ever had. All alone in the house he normally shared with Jofré, he woke up at odd hours, sobbing. To soothe himself back to sleep, he stared at the gold ring that Jofré had bought him for his twenty-first birthday, which was inscribed with his initials: G.F.G.

When Guillermo was particularly lonely, he would push the tape of his eighteenth birthday party into the VHS player and watch it on repeat. There was cake, friends, food, laughter. He liked seeing Jofré happy. One day, he returned home to find that burglars had torn the place apart. The house looked like someone had scooped it up off its foundation, flipped it over, and shaken everything out. Among the many possessions the thieves had snatched was the treasured tape, which he had stored inside his hand-held camcorder.

Nothing in his life felt secure, and he blamed Mariana and Rosa. He found it slightly less fraught to talk to Argentina. She was not a plaintiff in the legal case for his disappearance—only Rosa was—so it was harder to fault her for the plight of Jofré and Gómez. It also helped that she was like "the perfect granny from films": gentle, affectionate, and a masterful cook. In contrast to Mariana and Rosa, Argentina seemed only to want to know that he was okay. "Are you eating?" she would ask when he picked up the phone. "Do you have clothes?"

In contrast, he felt Mariana and Rosa made no effort to understand his perspective. Mariana still refused to refer to him as Guillermo—sometimes calling him Rodolfo just to rile him, and Rosa bristled when he called Jofré "Mamá." He began to ignore Mariana completely and picked up Rosa's frequent calls only to berate her.

"Why are you calling me?!" he would snarl. "I don't want to see you, I don't want to talk to you." Another time he told her: "Even if you died, I wouldn't want to see you."

Still, Rosa kept calling.

A few months after Jofré was arrested, angry strikes erupted around Argentina. The economy—yet again—had reached a breaking point. Unemployed workers set tires aflame and erected tents in the middle of busy highways, blocking traffic. Argentines rushed to yank their money from the country's banks, stashing the cash under their mattresses or sending it abroad. On one especially frenzied day, $700 million was withdrawn. To prevent a complete banking meltdown, in December 2001, the government prohibited Argentines from taking out more than $250 a week from their accounts—a measure that came to be known as *el corralito*, or little corral. Poor, unemployed Argentines clustered outside supermarkets across the country requesting free food, sometimes busting down the doors to take it themselves. "We don't have any money! We are hungry and we have to eat!" one woman yelled at a television crew filming the looting. In Buenos Aires, citizens poured into the Plaza de Mayo, banging pots and pans to demand jobs. Protesters hurled rocks at police, police fired tear gas and rubber bullets at protesters. Thirty-nine people would end up dying in the chaos.

On December 20, as a fuming crowd jostled outside the windows of the Casa Rosada, President Fernando de la Rúa, who had taken office just two years before, tendered his resignation. De la Rúa had proudly campaigned on the slogan "They say I'm boring," vowing to end the corruption that his predecessor, Carlos Menem, had become known for. (Menem, for all his talk about national unity, had taken to vrooming around Buenos Aires in a red Ferrari and scandalizing Argentina's conservative classes with a rotating cast of busty mistresses.) Afraid of what might happen if he tried to walk out the front door, De la Rúa climbed up to the Casa Rosada's roof, where a helicopter whooshed him away from the furious masses.

Three different interim presidents would try and fail to contain the chaos over the next two weeks. The peso soon lost two-thirds of its value and unemployment exploded. Bedraggled men hauling wood wagons roved the streets of Buenos Aires looking for discarded boxes and cans—anything they could salvage and sell.

Amid the tumult, Jofré returned home. She had been released from prison after complaining of hypertension and other health issues but would need to remain under house arrest while awaiting trial. She sank into a deep, yawning depression that frightened Guillermo even more than his own. Her absence had tormented him, but now that she was back, the rapid reversal of their roles gave him whiplash. Suddenly, he was forced to care for the woman who had always cared for him—only he'd just found out that she might have stolen him. He would later reflect that it was like serving as "the prison guard to [his] own kidnapper."

To afford medicine for Jofré and food for them both, Guillermo urgently needed a new job. As an indication of how much he did not want to be associated with his biological family, he accepted one at a museum operated by the air force.

In his previous life, he might have enjoyed the work—he had always loved planes, and now he spent every day surrounded by them, preparing Gloster Meteor and Pucará fighter planes for exhibition by scuffing out dents, touching up their paint, and dusting their noses. But in his new life, it was not a pleasant environment. Guillermo was the first grandchild the Abuelas had found in the hands of air force operatives; now he worked restoring planes for the same military branch that had used them to throw people like his parents into the Río de la Plata. According to the anonymous caller who had first alerted the Abuelas to Guillermo's whereabouts, Gómez himself had told her about such gruesome flights. Guillermo knew his presence at the museum inspired discomfort. Some colleagues rushed to tell him that the crimes committed during the dictatorship had nothing to do with them. Others simply avoided him, afraid he was a mole who aimed to land them in jail. But he needed the money; he had to stay. His paltry air force salary—400 pesos, or about $120 a month at the time— barely covered the cost of Jofré's hypertension medicine, and jobs were scarce.

A few times a month, Guillermo took the train from José C. Paz into Buenos Aires to visit Gómez. It was a forty-minute ride to Retiro, whose soaring Edwardian station sat between the aluminum-and-brick shacks of Villa 31, one of the city's largest informal settlements, and the grand Parisian apartment buildings of the city's wealthiest neighborhoods. It took Guillermo about an hour of walking—under the Illia highway, past grassy plazas and elegant embassies—to get from the station to the Bosques de Palermo, the city's loveliest park. On the edge of the park, behind the planetarium, was the grubby air force complex where Gómez was being held. Guillermo knew it was strange to devote this kind of effort to the man who had stolen him, but a warped sense of loyalty compelled him. Despite himself, he still strained for Gómez's affection.

The air force facility that held Gómez could hardly be called a prison. Gómez was the only detainee, and he had his own large room, with a big bed, a television, a refrigerator, and a phone. His "guards" were air force colleagues who had served alongside him during the dictatorship, and who had every incentive to ensure that he remained happy—and thus quiet. The air force had largely eluded punishment for the crimes of the dictatorship. While one of its heads was sentenced to four and a half

years in prison during the 1985 Trial of the Juntas, two other top officials were acquitted. No lower-level officers had been convicted since,
and they seemed keen to keep it that way.

Gómez's air force compadres cooked him almost daily *asados*, allowed him
to get roaringly drunk on wine, and invited women over. On weekends, Guillermo sometimes joined them for lunch, eating steak with them at a long
table in between two pavilions. Once, as they sat around after one such meal,
air force officers Guillermo knew by the nicknames Patón (Bigfoot) and El
Oso (The Bear) casually told Guillermo how much he looked like his father
and recalled how stoic José had been in the face of electrical shocks and beatings. *He didn't even complain*, they marveled. That day, neither did Guillermo.
He listened silently as the men defended kidnappings and disappearances.

36

Sea Change

After the anonymous woman twice called the Abuelas' headquarters in April 2000 to denounce Guillermo's kidnapping, the grandmothers had begun to investigate her other assertion: that an air force man she referred to as El Colorado had stolen a child too.

El Colorado's real name was Juan Carlos Vázquez Sarmiento. He had grown up in the Buenos Aires suburbs during the height of Perón's power with a father who worked for Evita's foundation and supported El Líder ardently. After 1955, when Perón was unseated and Peronism was banned, his father had been imprisoned. He was released after a few months, but struggled to find work, forcing young Vázquez Sarmiento to seek employment of his own to avoid starving. At seventeen, he got a job in the air force, and during the dictatorship, he had been an intelligence officer at the same facility where Gómez worked.

In 1977, as the junta's purge entered its brutal second year, Vázquez Sarmiento brought home a baby boy. His wife, Stella Maris Emaldi, who was pregnant at the time with a daughter, would later recall that she'd opened the door to their bedroom to find the infant lying on her bed. When it came time to register the child, the couple did so as though he were their biological son, giving him the name Ezequiel Vázquez Sarmiento. His birth certificate was signed by the same military doctor who had signed Guillermo's falsified document, and the boys sometimes played together when they were young.

Ezequiel was now twenty-four and worked for the air force, just like his childhood friend. The Abuelas had tracked him down in late December 2001, as the country was imploding, but Ezequiel had staunchly refused to have his DNA analyzed by the BNDG. His wedding date was set for the following month, and he had been planning his honeymoon to Disney World in Orlando, where he'd traveled once with his family as a kid. He did not want to do anything that could hurt the people he considered his parents. His case, like the case of Evelin Vázquez, stalled. Ezequiel's, though, had an additional complicating factor: when the judiciary had called on Vázquez Sarmiento to testify in March 2002 about his role in Ezequiel's appropriation, the former intelligence officer had vanished.

Guillermo and Ezequiel had not seen each other in years, and had never discussed the parallels in their stories. But Ezequiel seemed to have heeded the advice Guillermo offered during his 2001 interview in *La Nación*: he stubbornly avoided the Abuelas de Plaza de Mayo.

Guillermo, too, was still resolute in these feelings when, one day at the Retiro station, about to start his regular pilgrimage to see Gómez in Palermo, he recognized a girl with smooth brown hair amid the hubbub of people rushing to catch their trains. Her name was Cintia; Guillermo had first met her when they were both in high school. The house he shared with Jofré sat across from a long, single-story secondary school, which one of his best friends had attended. Sometimes as students arrived, he would perch in his window to see if he could spot this friend and wave at him. That was how he first noticed Cintia, who also studied at the school. She had a round face and serene brown eyes. Guillermo was smitten, and they had started seeing each other in the casual way of high school students—a kiss here and there. But then they had gone their separate ways.

Now Guillermo waved her over and, after remarking on the irony of running into her in Retiro despite living only a few blocks away from one another, asked if he could buy her a drink.

She said no.

A coffee? he asked. A tea? A mate? A soda? She demurred, insisting that she was tired from a long day at the University of Buenos Aires, where she was studying law. Finally, he convinced her to walk with him to nearby Plaza San Martín, where Rosa and Benjamín had enjoyed some of their first dates. Seated on a bench surrounded by lush silk floss, jacaranda, and tipa trees, Cintia suddenly blurted out a confession.

"I dreamed about you," she said.

It was a strange opening, and Guillermo figured she was lying. If he really had appeared in her dreams, it was probably because she had seen the news reports about him—his interview in *La Nación*, the coverage about Rosa finding her grandson at last. Perhaps she was fishing for information, the way people—even kind ones—were apt to do when something dramatic happened to someone they knew.

"Yeah, yeah," he scoffed. "It turns out I'm the son of *desaparecidos*."

To Guillermo's surprise, Cintia looked shocked. Then she burst into tears.

"What?" he asked. "You didn't know?"

"No, I really did dream about you," she said. Guillermo softened. He decided to explain. The past few years had been hard, he said. A lot had happened. As Cintia listened carefully to his story, Guillermo suddenly felt the urge to drop everything just to talk to her. She seemed to see through to his core—beyond the old identity she had known him with, and the new one he was negotiating.

Her quiet acceptance made him feel grounded, and when they started dating officially soon afterward, it was Cintia who gave Guillermo a perspective he hadn't considered. For years, she pointed out, he had been putting Jofré first—and Gómez too. He scrimped to pay for Jofré's medication, which meant that he sometimes ate only one meal a day. When he'd told Gómez of his economic troubles, how he was short on food or couldn't pay taxes, never once had Gómez said, *Stop visiting me here. I'm fine. Take care of yourself.* Nor had Gómez or Jofré ever apologized for the years of deception. Guillermo was making himself miserable, and for people who had brought him extraordinary pain.

Cintia encouraged him to do things for himself, not just for the people who had raised him. Eventually, she planned a trip for them to visit Miramar, a coastal city five hours south of Buenos Aires. They left the dense city streets of Buenos Aires behind and traveled for hours, past flat fields with cows and sheep, before finally arriving at the sand. Together, they watched the waves of the Atlantic crash onto the shore. It was the first time Guillermo had seen the ocean.

Argentina, too, was beginning to more seriously grapple with its past. The country remained a smoldering mess. Not long after De la Rúa zoomed away from the Casa Rosada in a helicopter, the country had defaulted on around $100 billion in debt, becoming the largest sovereign defaulter in world history. More Argentines were living below the poverty line than above it. Nearly a fifth of the country could not find work. Many top politicians strategically sat on the sidelines for the 2003 election, likening a presidential bid to political suicide. One of the candidates, though, had no reputation to tarnish. He was a newcomer to national politics named Néstor Kirchner, who used his lack of public recognition to distance himself from Argentina's disgraced political establishment: "You don't know him that well because he's new. He doesn't belong to the generation of political failure," one of his television ads began.

Not much in Kirchner's history suggested he would one day govern the country. He was born in 1950, around the same time as many of the Abuelas' disappeared children, and grew up far from Argentina's bastions of political power in Río Gallegos, a bleak industrial city on the southern Patagonia coast. It was a flat and empty place, dominated by sheep trading and oil extraction and whipped by fierce winds. (Kirchner's roots in Patagonia would later earn him the nickname El Pingüino—The Penguin—a moniker he wore proudly.) Raised by a postal worker and his wife, Kirchner performed poorly in school. His lazy eye and lisp meant his social life was no brighter than his academic one.

When he got older, he moved north to finish his education, studying law at the University of La Plata, where he joined the Juventud Universitaria Per-

onista (JUP), a leftist youth group who, as its name would suggest, idolized
Juan Perón. It was there that he met Cristina Fernández, whose quick wit,
good looks, and disarming charisma would quickly inspire him to propose
marriage. Fernández, also a law student and a member of the JUP, agreed,
and the couple wed in May 1975, after only six months of dating. In her
autobiography, *Sinceramente*, she would fondly remember those early days
of their relationship, recalling Néstor as having straight hair that stretched
below his ears, square glasses with thick black frames, and an olive-green
jacket that her anti-Peronist father thought made him look like "a guerrilla
coming down from the hills."

Indeed, the JUP was often a feeder to militant groups with armed
branches, and though his electoral rivals would later accuse him of having
been part of the Montoneros, Kirchner and Fernández insisted that they
never accompanied their other university friends into *la lucha armada*—
the armed struggle. Their allegiance was to Perón above all else. When
later asked if his ideology was more informed by the left or right, Kirchner
allegedly responded, "No! I'm a Peronist." According to a college room-
mate, Kirchner even imitated Perón in his sleep, holding a broom in the
dark like a microphone as he sleepwalked.

After university, he served as mayor of his native Río Gallegos, the capital of Santa Cruz province, and later as the province's governor. Fernández, meanwhile, had been elected to Congress and then the Senate, also
representing Santa Cruz. Over the decade in which he served as governor, Kirchner won over many of Santa Cruz's two hundred thousand or
so residents with his redistributive economic policies, funneling money
from the province's vast oil reserves into new highway systems, airports,
and sophisticated hospitals that provided free care for the poor. He also
launched an extensive public housing program, permitting poor families
earning as little as $200 a month to purchase their own homes. But his
forceful approach to governance, which would come to be known as "the K
style," was not for everyone; his opponents accused him of ruling by decree
and doling out high-paying public jobs to assure his electoral success.

According to newspaper reports at the time, Kirchner only entered the

2003 presidential race to boost his profile for a future electoral cycle and never expected to win. Indeed, he attracted only 22 percent of the vote in the first round of elections—but that was enough to propel him into a runoff with political rival and fellow Peronist Carlos Menem, who was seeking office again. When polls showed that Kirchner would trounce Menem, whom many Argentines blamed for the 2001 economic crisis, Menem dropped out of the race and Kirchner became president of the nation by default.

He was viewed by some as a "country bumpkin" who would be devoured by the cutthroat political establishment in Buenos Aires. But once ensconced in the Casa Rosada, Kirchner acted with the bold confidence of someone who had garnered far more than a fifth of the popular vote. He got to work quickly on his vows to "reconstruct a national capitalism" and made a show of playing hardball with Argentina's foreign creditors like the International Monetary Fund (IMF), which many Argentines had long distrusted, if not reviled. He was similarly forceful with Argentina's bondholders, making it clear the country would repay only a fraction of the original value of their defaulted bonds. "If they want to squeeze, let them squeeze," Kirchner told reporters. (Eventually, he would convince the majority to accept new bonds valued at around a third of the originals.)

Perhaps more significantly, Kirchner demonstrated a commitment to justice unprecedented among Argentina's democratic leaders. From his first fiery speech as president, he associated himself with the cause of the Madres and the Abuelas and paid homage to their disappeared children. "I am part of a generation that was decimated and castigated by painful absences," he declared at his inauguration. He quickly purged 80 percent of the corruption-riddled federal police force and moved to clean house in the Supreme Court, which Menem had filled with lackeys. "I haven't come this far to make deals with the past," he had insisted while campaigning. True to his word, once in office, he eliminated the barriers obstructing the prosecution of dictatorship-era crimes. He revoked decrees that protected military officers from extradition—allowing human rights cases related to the dictatorship to recommence abroad—and approved a bill to annul the immunity laws shielding officers from prosecution in Argentina.

Just a few months into his presidency, Kirchner traveled to New York

City and spoke to the General Assembly of the United Nations. Standing before the UN's imposing green marble rostrum, in front of the world's most powerful diplomats, he proclaimed: "We are the children of the Madres and Abuelas of the Plaza de Mayo." With these words, Kirchner signaled a new era for the country.

When Guillermo stepped out of the train station in Retiro to visit Gómez two days before Christmas in 2003, he encountered the perfect summer day—pleasantly warm but not stifling, as Buenos Aires so often becomes around the New Year. In the Bosques de Palermo, shirtless joggers and rollerbladers were making gleeful loops around the glittering lake in the park's center. Sunbathers lazed on benches. It had rained the day before and the air was fragrant with the aromas of roses from the Rosedal, a manicured garden on the lake's south side.

Upon reaching Gómez in the air force compound, Guillermo could immediately tell that the man who had raised him was drunk. He had learned to recognize the signs as a child: the dilated pupils, the swaying movements, the small, pockmarked face pinched with rage. It usually meant that Gómez was about to beat up Jofré. But that day, Gómez's vitriol was directed at Guillermo.

"Look at the mess you got me in by going to see those *viejas*," he spat, referring to the Abuelas. He cursed Guillermo for ruining his chances of reuniting with Jofré, and for his imprisonment. "One day I'll get out of here," he slurred menacingly, "and then I'm going to put a bullet in the foreheads of you, your sister, and your grandmothers."

Guillermo sprang to his feet. *Why wait?* he snarled. *Why not get it over with?*

The prison guards rushed in and peeled the men apart. Still panting, Guillermo spun around to leave. Gómez's outburst terrified him—he had seen Jofré's face bloodied enough times to know what Gómez was capable of. But it also set him free. He would never return to the air force facility in Palermo. For a while, Gómez tried to call him, but Guillermo ignored the calls. He was done yearning for Gómez to behave like a father. His father was José Manuel Pérez Rojo, and he was gone.

37

The Day the Portraits Came Down

2004

Twenty-eight years to the day from when the junta led by Jorge Rafael Videla took power—on March 24, 2004—Néstor Kirchner strode into the Colegio Militar, where the Argentine army educates its officers. Many of the junta's men had passed through the compound's classrooms, including Videla, who had studied there and later led the school. Dressed in a dark suit, Kirchner made his way down a long hallway known as "the gallery." He was flanked by a solemn horde of army officers in camouflage, as well as their current chief, Roberto Bendini.

The president and the military men approached a tan wall where opulent gilt frames held portraits of the college's previous leaders. They paused before the one of Videla. He had been photographed in a navy jacket with gold epaulettes, his eyes staring off to the side as if sizing up an invisible enemy. Bendini climbed a small ladder set up before the portrait and awaited his president's orders.

"Proceed!" Kirchner bellowed. Bendini lifted the portrait off its hook. He handed it to an aide, who promptly shuffled it out of view. Bendini continued, also removing the portrait of Reynaldo Bignone, another former chief of the Colegio Militar who had served as the junta's last president before the return of democracy. The moment would be remembered in Argentina as "el día que Kirchner bajó los cuadros," or the day that Kirchner took the portraits down, and the glaringly empty spots left behind on the wall became a sort of national Rorschach test. Some saw an act of disrespect, erasing all that Videla had done to save the country from anarchy. They accused Kirchner of using human rights for political gain. Others saw a powerful admission and a promising new beginning.

But Kirchner was not done. Earlier that week, he'd arranged a private visit to the ESMA with thirty-two torture survivors, including Miriam Lewin, who had known José and Patricia from the Montoneros and was held in the ESMA for nearly ten months. As the group had entered the property the day of the tour, several drivers speeding down Libertador had shouted "Viva Videla!"—Long Live Videla—as they passed by. Kirchner wound around the vast property for hours, listening to the survivors' stories. Standing in the basement of the Casino de Oficiales, the building where naval officers had held and tortured them during the dictatorship, Kirchner took each survivor aside and, one by one, asked for forgiveness. Then he promised to make the ESMA an emblem of memory and justice, seizing the compound from the navy and converting its grounds into a museum honoring the disappeared.

Five days later, he returned to the former detention site to make good on that vow. A massive crowd awaited him, and as he climbed onstage, people strained to touch him as though he were holy. Fernández stood by his side, dressed in white. Among the thousands before them were Rosa and many other Abuelas and Madres de Plaza de Mayo, their handkerchiefs tied snugly on their heads. It was the first time the public had been allowed on the grounds of the naval school.

Before Kirchner took the microphone, Argentine musicians sang a mournful tune entitled "All Is Recorded in Memory." A pair of activists from H.I.J.O.S. gave a rousing speech. Then came a young man called Juan Cabandié—though he had just decided to start using the name that day. He was the most recent grandchild to have been identified by the Abuelas. Onstage with the president, he described how, a few months before, he had found out that he'd been born in the ESMA while his mother was detained there. After fifteen days, they'd been separated and his mother had never been heard from again. But, he said, "The dictatorship's sinister plan couldn't erase the memory that ran through my veins."

Finally, it was time for Kirchner himself to speak. As blue-and-white Argentine flags flapped in the humid breeze, the president began by addressing the "Abuelas, Madres, [and] Hijos" who "believed and continue believing that the country could change." Then, in an unprecedented move, he again asked for forgiveness, this time for the Argentine government's decades of silence about the dictatorship. The audience roared approvingly.

Dressed in a black tank top with turquoise flowers and a black skirt to beat the heat, Analía Azic was one of the many people clapping in the crowd that day. She had listened to all of the speeches, but the words of Juan Cabandié had sent a chill up her spine. The previous year, the man she'd thought was her father, a former navy prefect named Juan Antonio Azic, had traveled to a desolate port area of Buenos Aires, sat down in front of a statue of the Virgin Mary, put a 9mm pistol in his mouth, and fired. He was rushed to the hospital in critical condition, but alive. As Analía anxiously waited for updates, a breaking news alert had flashed across a hospital television screen in bright red text: Spanish judge Baltasar Garzón had ordered the extradition of forty-six Argentine military officers. Among the names listed was Azic's.

Horrific accusations had emerged in the days that followed. One ESMA survivor, Carlos Lordkipanidse, recognized Azic as one of the men from Task Group 3.3.2, the same torture squad Alfredo Astiz had belonged to. After he was abducted in 1978 and brought to the ESMA with his wife and newborn son, Lordkipanidse recalled having been strapped down to a bed when Azic threatened, "If you don't talk, I will smash your son's head on the floor." He responded that he had nothing to say, prompting Azic to place his twenty-day-old child on his chest. Then Azic shocked Lordkipanidse as his newborn lay atop him.

Analía, who was still making daily hospital visits, was by Azic's bedside when she got a call from a friend. "We need to meet," he said. "It's urgent." In a café around the corner, the friend told her that an investigation by the Abuelas and H.I.J.O.S. had raised suspicions that Azic was not her real father. She might be the daughter of *desaparecidos*.

Analía had always had a rebellious streak. To the chagrin of her buttoned-up parents, she favored short skirts, tight dresses, and high heels; as a law student at the University of Buenos Aires, she had begun volunteering in a *villa* in an industrial suburb of the city, teaching classes at a soup kitchen named after Azucena Villaflor, the disappeared founder of the Madres. In December 2001, when Argentina seemed on the precipice of economic meltdown, Analía had been among the masses who stormed Congress. Her political beliefs diverged sharply from those of her parents, but she had never suspected that she wasn't biologically related to them. Confronted with the possibility, she went home and searched for Azic's revolver, locating it in the back of a kitchen cabinet. She ran a finger over its metal frame before putting it back where she'd found it.

For more than a year, she struggled with what to do next. She wanted to vanish. She had scaled back her activism and swapped her colorful dresses for black ones to draw less attention to herself. Representatives from the Abuelas and H.I.J.O.S. told her that the only way to find out who her real parents were would be through a DNA test, but like so many other grandchildren before her, she was hesitant to take measures that might land those who had raised her in jail.

Now, at the ESMA, with Juan Cabandié's words about memory still echoing in her ears, Analía entered the Casino de Oficiales, which had been opened for visitors to see. She had barely stepped into the building when she broke down. She rarely cried, but now it was as if a levee had broken. She felt like a baby—fragile, defenseless, inconsolable. She was suddenly sure that she had been born there in the ESMA. It was time to find out to whom. "That woman had enough courage to get pregnant, keep fighting for the same society I'm fighting for, and live through torture so that I could be born, and I'm a coward that can't even get blood drawn," she would later recall thinking.

The following day, she called a friend: she was ready to have her DNA tested.

After his last encounter with Gómez, Guillermo had slowly reestablished a relationship with Rosa. But he still resented his grandmother's refusal to accept how difficult it was to abandon the woman who'd raised him. He had no qualms about the man he had thought was his father rotting in prison, and he now recognized that his love for Jofré was unhealthy, like a tree rooted in poisonous soil—but, he tried to explain to Rosa, it was still love, and you can't turn love on and off like a light switch.

Rosa, however, had no patience for lies. "Tell me, Guillermo. That lady you call Mamá—is she my daughter?" she asked him.

Meanwhile, despite Guillermo's best efforts to push her away, Mariana often accompanied him when he was called to court for the ongoing case against Gómez and Jofré. "She put up with all of my mistreatment," he would later say. At first, the case had been handled by a federal judge who happened to be married to a retired air force officer. It had moved at a snail's pace; when the judge did take action, it seemed to Guillermo that she was overly harsh, perhaps to project independence from her husband. Once, a cop car showed up at his house to take him to testify, as though he were a criminal rather than a victim. He was forbidden from leaving the country.

Then, early in Kirchner's term, to Guillermo's relief, the case was passed to a new judge named Jorge Luis Ballestero. Back in the 1990s, Ballestero had handled an appropriations case that had devolved, much like the Juliana Treviño and Ximena Vicario cases, into a media firestorm. He seemed wary to try another. Worried that the judge might return his case to lottery, Guillermo and Mariana went to see him, begging him to stay the course. This had already dragged on for years, they explained, and Guillermo felt he had been mistreated in the process. He promised that he was a low-profile person who had no desire to speak to the press about his situation. Ballestero ultimately agreed to stick with the case.

The following week, Guillermo went to speak with him alone. In Argentina's civil law system, judges take an active role in criminal cases, gathering evidence, spearheading investigations, and keeping victims apprised of their findings. In that first formal meeting, Ballestero urged simply: "Tell me what you need."

It was the first time throughout the case that Guillermo could remember anyone in the judicial system expressing concern for him. Guillermo explained his resistance to having his DNA sequenced by the BNDG, which the previous judge had represented as a necessity to finalize the case. To willingly give his blood felt like a betrayal of Jofré, as it would surely seal her conviction. He did not want to see her suffer. He was also concerned for her security. Someone using a voice distorter had repeatedly called his extension at work, warning it wouldn't be a good idea for the safety of Jofré or Gómez if he underwent the analysis. When Guillermo told Ballestero about the emotional, physical, and financial struggles he faced in caring for Jofré, the judge asked what he did for work. Guillermo mentioned the air force and Ballestero's blue eyes widened. "Does it really seem like *you* should be working *there?*" Guillermo remembers him asking.

Ballestero proposed a work-around to remove the burden from Guillermo. He planned to prove that Jofré had knowingly falsified documents, a crime to which she had already confessed. That way, when Guillermo did give blood at the BNDG, it would merely confirm her guilt, rather than serve as the main piece of evidence that incriminated her. Soon after that conversation, Ballestero contacted Guillermo to offer him a choice between two new jobs: one working for the City of Buenos Aires and the other working for the Ministry of Social Development, which managed Argentina's social assistance programs. Lured by the possibility of traveling around Argentina, which he had never had the opportunity to do, Guillermo chose the latter.

Seemingly overnight, Ballestero had solved all of Guillermo's problems—except one. He and Cintia were growing serious, and they often discussed starting a family. He felt eager to become a father, relishing the chance to create the stable home environment he had lacked. But one thing was holding him back. His name, Guillermo Francisco Gómez, linked him to the man he now thought of not as his father but his kidnapper. A man who had possibly been involved in the deaths of his real parents, and who had recently vowed to kill him too. He could not imagine perpetuating that legacy.

"I didn't have the most elemental thing that a father can offer their child, which is a last name," he would later reflect. "The only thing I had to pass down was [evidence of] the crime that had been committed."

Guillermo liked the idea of adopting Pérez Roisinblit as his new last names, but he and Ballestero sparred over his first name. "You were never supposed to be Guillermo," insisted the judge, urging him to accept his given name of Rodolfo. He countered that he had lived his whole life as Guillermo, and going by anything else was hard to fathom. Rodolfo was an old man's name, Guillermo grumbled, and one he found hideous at that. Perhaps it was true that he was never meant to be Guillermo, he argued. But the years he had lived with the name were still real, and they shouldn't be erased.

Guillermo's new job was scheduled to start on September 21, 2004. But he had to ask permission to show up late to his first day. That morning, Ballestero had called him in. When he arrived at the law office, the judge pushed a stack of papers across the table. Guillermo flipped through them. On the seventh page, near the bottom, capital letters spelled out his new identity: GUILLERMO RODOLFO FERNANDO PÉREZ ROISINBLIT.

"Now you have a name," Ballestero said.

38

Rodolfo Fernando

2005

Nine months later, Argentina's Supreme Court confirmed what Kirchner and Congress had previously decreed: The Full Stop and Due Obedience Laws were unconstitutional. Now it was not just rapes and kidnappings that could be punished—the armed forces could again be pursued for all of the crimes they committed during the dictatorship. Immediately, the decision unleashed a torrent of arrests. The two police officers accused of turning Claudia Poblete Hlaczik over to the Landa family were charged yet again, this time for the disappearance of her parents, making them the first officers to be charged for a disappearance since 1987. Shortly thereafter, three generals and two corporals were arrested for torture and murder. Former interior minister Albano Harguindeguy and thirty-one other retired military officers were apprehended, accused of participating in Operation Condor. For its cover the following day, *Página 12*, the left-leaning newspaper, photoshopped Harguindeguy into striped jail fatigues.

The arrests were celebrated widely—but also decried by some with equal fervor. Former president Eduardo Duhalde, who had helped Kirchner win the election in 2003, accused his onetime ally of ignoring poor Argentines who were still suffering because of the economy—"They are occupying themselves with the human rights of those who are already dead," he spat.

Barely a month later, more news broke: the Argentine Forensic Anthropology Team (EAAF) had made an important discovery in a mass grave in General Lavalle, a sleepy farm village not far from the coastal town of Santa Teresita. There, the team had carefully exhumed seven bodies and extracted mitochondrial DNA from the remains. They had a hypothesis for whom several of the bodies might have belonged to, and after testing the DNA against possible relatives, their suspicions were validated: They had found Esther Careaga, María Ponce de Bianco, and Azucena Villaflor, the three Madres the junta had disappeared in December 1977. From the condition of their bones, the EAAF experts confirmed that the women had been thrown from airplanes. It was the first time since Scilingo's confession about death flights ten years earlier that forensic evidence had proved their existence.

As Azucena's family mulled over how to honor her name—eventually scattering her ashes around the Pirámide de Mayo she had once circled with her fellow Madres—Guillermo was working to embrace his. He had finally given his blood to the BNDG, and the case of his kidnapping had officially implicated Magnacco, who was convicted and sentenced to ten years in prison. Gómez had also been sentenced, to seven and a half years; Jofré had received three and a half, which she had already served over the course of her detention and house arrest. In a rare break with the military's "pact of silence," one air force officer interrogated during the case said he "supposed" that Patricia was "thrown into the sea" after giving birth in the ESMA. It was the only clue Guillermo had to the final resting place of either of his parents.

Guillermo was making sense of what all these things added up to—still struggling to type his new name without staring at his fingers or sign it on official documents without making errors—when he received an invitation to tour the ESMA. Should Guillermo choose to attend the tour, Cristina Fernández de Kirchner would accompany him. Spanish judge Baltasar Garzón would be there as well.

He knew the visit would be gutting. Even those completely unconnected to the horrors that occurred within the ESMA could not help but feel nauseous while taking in the attic where prisoners had been held handcuffed and hooded, or the parking area where they were loaded into trucks to be "transferred," never to be seen again. When construction teams in charge of converting the property to a museum had first entered the buildings, they had found swastikas and messages reading "Here they suppressed and tortured us" on the walls. But as Guillermo wrestled with his new identity, it felt important to see his birthplace, however grotesque. He decided to go. When she caught wind of the decision, Rosa insisted on joining him.

The day of the visit was chilly and gray, one of those Buenos Aires August days when it seems as though the sun will never emerge again. Along with Fernández, Garzón, and several other ESMA survivors and relatives of the disappeared, Guillermo walked tentatively into the Casino de Oficiales. He stuck closest to Cintia, Rosa, and Miriam Lewin, who had again returned to the ESMA to accompany him and share what she knew of Patricia's detention, which had overlapped with her own. Hand in hand with Cintia and his grandmother, Guillermo wove through the immense building's dark rooms. There was the *pañol*, where the ESMA's officers stockpiled the goods they'd pilfered during their raids: mounds of clothing, piles of books, home appliances, furniture. Perhaps it had once held the fur coat that Rosa had lent Patricia, or the furniture that had filled her and José's apartment. There was the *pecera*, or fishbowl, the glassed-in area where prisoners like Miriam who were selected for the *proceso de recuperación* had been forced to clack out propaganda on typewriters. And they stopped in the *capucha*, where most of the ESMA's prisoners had been kept in tiny cubicles that swarmed with what one survivor later described as a "superpopulation" of rats.

Finally, they descended the stairs into the basement. Guillermo felt pressure build in his chest. Maybe his mother's hand had touched the same railing as she was led downstairs to give birth to him. The basement was dim and the air was stale. Guillermo had been told that he was born in an infirmary there, but now, as he looked around, it was hard to envision it. The walls had been knocked out and the furniture removed. As the group milled around, their steps echoing on the hard floor, Guillermo turned to Miriam. "Where was I born?" he asked.

Miriam didn't answer. She stood, silent, her light blue eyes staring at the air vents that provided the basement's only natural light. Guillermo figured that she hadn't heard him, or that the question was too painful. He began to walk away: it was not a place he wanted to dally.

"There, Rodolfo," she said with sudden certainty. He turned around to see her pointing at a spot on the floor beneath one of the vents. "You were born there."

Mixed in with the wave of sorrow and anger that engulfed Guillermo was another feeling: surprise. He had never responded to the name Rodolfo before. Finally, he felt able "to identify with that name, my name. In that place, where it was first spoken by my mother's lips."

Patricia had been a month shy of twenty-six when she gave birth to Guillermo. Guillermo was now twenty-six himself. There, in the exact spot where Patricia had brought him into the world surrounded by torturous strangers, he took Rosa's hand and squeezed tightly, tears streaming down their faces.

A month after Guillermo's visit to the ESMA, Argentina Rojo's heart stopped at the age of eighty-six. Her funeral was held in Villa Crespo, and Guillermo sobbed through the entire service. He felt crushing regret. Still living with Jofré, still unsure of who he was supposed to be, he had spent little time with Argentina. He had not gotten to eat enough of her rich stews or flaky tarts. He had barely gotten to enjoy her hugs, which were so gentle it was as though she thought he was a specter who might evaporate into thin air with too hard a squeeze.

Through his grief, he was still struggling to negotiate his relationships with Rosa and Mariana. Other grandchildren, like Juan Cabandié and Analía Azic, now going by Victoria Analía Donda, seemed to be reconciling with their pasts. After giving her blood at the BNDG, Analía was confirmed to be the daughter of María Hilda Pérez and José María Laureano Donda, and the granddaughter of Leontina Puebla de Pérez, one of the Abuelas' founding members. Victoria had learned that she had indeed been born in the ESMA, as she'd suspected, and discovered something shocking: her biological uncle, Adolfo Donda, had been a leader of Task Group 3.3.2, the same squad as Azic, and he had raised her biological sister after her parents were disappeared and her grandparents could no longer care for her.

But there was no manual for integrating one's old and new lives. As Argentina had grown sick, the tentative bond between Guillermo and Mariana had strained even further. Guillermo sometimes expressed opinions about their grandmother's medical care, and Mariana bristled at his suggestions. Argentina had raised *her*, not Guillermo, who had only appeared in her life recently. She accused Guillermo of not visiting Argentina enough and of neglecting her in her final days. Guillermo countered that she hadn't told him about Argentina's hospitalization for a day or so and, when he did arrive, it was too late.

In the years after Argentina's death, the two bickered over what to do with her ashes. Guillermo eventually suggested sprinkling them into the Río de la Plata so she could be reunited with José. Mariana refused; it had never been confirmed that José and Patricia rested there.

Later, Mariana recorded her thoughts about these fights in writing. Once, she wrote, she had found Argentina's agenda and seen that she had scribbled down Guillermo's phone number with "(grandson)" next to his name, as though she needed reminding as to who he was. "My number," she noted, "wasn't written down anywhere, because she knew it by memory and moreover she saw me every day at [Abuelas], and once a week she came to my house in a taxi to leave me tarts, chard fritters, and rice cakes."

It wasn't just their grandmother that Guillermo and Mariana clashed over. When Guillermo had been unemployed, living off of government subsidies and the charity of neighbors and friends, he had asked his sister to share half the reparations money she'd been awarded for the disappearance of their parents. He was still living with, and trying to support, Jofré, and Mariana was incensed that he would ask her to help fund the thief who had stolen him from her. As Guillermo remembers it, Mariana later invited him to her house only to inform him that she wasn't going to give him a cent. She felt that the state that had disappeared their parents should be the one to pay him his share, not her. They discussed the issue several more times but could never reach an agreement.

Part of the issue was that what "half" of the money meant had changed drastically over the previous years. The 2001 financial crisis had tanked the peso, decimating the value of the bonds Mariana had been awarded. But Guillermo believed the law entitled him to half their original value, not their post-crisis value. "During all of those years, I didn't know what I was supposed to do with those funds. I didn't know if I was supposed to save it for him—he wouldn't speak to me about it—and I had to make decisions amid an enormous financial crisis," Mariana explained later.

Guillermo eventually sought help from the Abuelas, who took his side and caused an even greater rift between the feuding siblings. Mariana was still working for the group, handling investigations and compiling detailed family archives to pass on to the grandchildren they found. When she refused to meet Guillermo's demands, she later recalled, Estela de Carlotto fired her, telling her that her conduct was at odds with the principles of human rights.

As Argentine courts began to issue rulings in the first disappearance and torture cases since the 1980s, Guillermo brought his and Mariana's financial conflict before a judge, who decided to embargo some of Mariana's assets, including her home. Mariana and Guillermo stopped talking—this time, it felt like for good.

39

Complete Memory

2006–2010

One of the first cases to be tried after the annulment of Alfonsín's amnesty laws involved a former police commissioner named Miguel Etchecolatz. During the dictatorship, he had overseen more than twenty clandestine detention centers as the deputy to Ramón Camps, the famously brutal head of the Buenos Aires Provincial Police. Thanks to Menem's pardons, Camps died a free man in 1994. He had previously bragged of having disappeared five thousand Argentines. ("We didn't kill people," Camps once said. "We killed subversives.")

By the time his trial began in June 2006, Etchecolatz was a stooped seventy-seven-year-old with silver hair and a beak-like nose. In 1986, he had been found guilty of ninety-one counts of torture, but was spared from serving his twenty-three-year sentence after the Due Obedience Law was introduced. More recently, in 2004, he had been convicted of stealing a baby—María de las Mercedes Gallo Sanz, grandchild number sixty-two found by the Abuelas—from a woman imprisoned in Buenos Aires Province and gifting her to an ally. Now he was again standing trial for his many other crimes: illegal detention, torture, and murder. (Later, Etchecolatz's own daughter would call her father an "evil narcissist without scruples" and express hope that he would remain in prison for the rest of his days.)

While reticence was the norm among military and police officers involved in the dictatorship, Etchecolatz projected a uniquely strident lack of repentance. "I never had or thought to have, or was haunted by, any sense of blame," he had written in his self-published autobiography. "I was the enforcer of the law made by men. I was the keeper of divine precepts. On both grounds, I would do it again."

If he was counting on his fearsome reputation to keep witnesses quiet, he was mistaken. The terror that had long deterred Argentines from publicly opposing the junta had dissipated, and more than 130 people agreed to testify against Etchecolatz. In the opulent Salón Dorado within La Plata's city hall, under painted ceilings and stained glass windows, person after person recounted horrible episodes, accusing the former commissioner of having led the operation in which Chicha Mariani's daughter-in-law was killed and her granddaughter was stolen, and of masterminding the infamous Night of the Pencils. To the many reporters gathered to cover the trial, Estela de Carlotto praised the detailed nature of such accounts, and celebrated that people had finally "shaken off the fear" they once felt. Through it all, Etchecolatz remained impassive, fidgeting with a rosary on the wooden table before him like a bored child. He insisted that "only God" could judge him.

One of the most moving witnesses was a former construction worker named Jorge Julio López. López had been abducted by the security forces in 1976 and held until mid-1979. Now seventy-six, with a head of white hair and wrinkled face, he took the stand in late June dressed in a red zip-up pullover and, in a cracking voice, described how during his detention, Etchecolatz had once personally ordered his subordinates to increase the charge coursing through his body from wires clamped to his nipples and genitals. "Subí un poco más," López recalled Etchecolatz shouting. Turn it up a little more. Crying, López also remembered how, while detained in one of the centers under Etchecolatz's purview, he watched a mother of young daughters beg for her life only to be shot in the head. "He was a serial killer," López said of Etchecolatz. "He had no compassion."

López had never shared the story of his detention with his two grown sons, who sobbed in court as they listened to his testimony. The day before the trial was set to end, a lazy Sunday in the La Plata neighborhood of Los Hornos, López smoked a few cigarettes with his sons at home before wandering off to catch some soccer on the radio. He wanted to unwind before returning to the soaring columns of city hall for the sentencing the next day. The following morning, when one of the sons prepared to take López to the hearing, he found the clothes his father intended to wear— the same blue cap, red pullover, and shoes he'd worn to each of the court proceedings—neatly laid out in the living room, untouched. His family searched the house and the streets outside. As Etchecolatz was sentenced to life in prison for his crimes, López was nowhere to be found.

Two months later, Cintia gave birth to a baby boy. She and Guillermo had gotten married in early 2006, first in a simple ceremony at the civil registry, where Rosa was among the small crowd of guests that cheered as the happy couple kissed, showing off their new marriage certificate, and then in front of a priest in a Catholic church, with Jofré serving as Guillermo's *madrina*, or marriage sponsor. He had recently moved out of Jofré's house and, with money he had received from the state—compensation for having been born in captivity—he and Cintia purchased a two-story brick house on a quaint corner in Bella Vista, not far from where they had grown up.

The house was just a few blocks from Campo de Mayo, the massive army complex where many Argentines had been detained and tortured during the dictatorship—including, possibly, José, who sometimes had been dragged from the RIBA and tortured elsewhere. This meant that Guillermo and Cintia could often hear the thwap of military helicopters taking off and landing at the property, an odd echo of Guillermo's past. But the house was everything they'd wanted, with a large patio for all the pets they hoped to have and an extensive terrace that Cintia would one day fill with potted plants and twinkling fairy lights.

The day their son was born, Guillermo was afraid to hold him. He seemed so fragile. Soon, though, Guillermo pushed through his jitters and wrapped his baby in an all-encompassing hug—with the same intensity that he wished his father could have embraced him. Staring down at his child's tiny features, which were so similar to Guillermo's own, he could not help but imagine that he was looking at himself as an infant. The thought made the absence of his own parents feel even sharper.

Cintia and Guillermo mulled endlessly over what to name their son, eventually choosing Ignacio. Deciding on a last name was easy: Pérez Roisinblit, just like his father. Guillermo recognized that his son would soon strive to emulate him in other ways as well. For years, he had continued to celebrate the fake birthdate that Gómez and Jofré had picked for him as a baby. He felt immense guilt about celebrating on the actual day, believing that his birth had signed his mother's death sentence. But now, with Ignacio's arrival, he was determined to stop letting his "caprices" govern him, and to set an example for his son. For the first time, Guillermo recognized November 15 as his true birthday.

Rosa took naturally to her new role as great-grandmother, cradling Ignacio and singing him silly songs that she'd made up. Guillermo loved seeing that whimsical side of her—the one he'd missed out on during his childhood. But, despite the joys of new parenthood, anxiety gnawed at him. Even as the country pursued justice with newfound vigor, there were ominous undercurrents. López had not been located after his disappearance during the Etchecolatz trial, and an investigation into his whereabouts had turned up nothing. Meanwhile, resistance to the human rights trials had been mounting, led by vocal sympathizers such as Cecilia Pando, the daughter of a military officer, and Karina Mujica, who had dated Alfredo Astiz and become an enthusiastic cheerleader for the junta. Pando presided over an organization called the Association of Relatives and Friends of Argentine Political Prisoners, which regarded the military officers on trial as "political prisoners"; Mujica ran the Argentine Association for Complete Memory, whose mission was to reclaim the "whole truth" of the dictatorship years. Another group created to resist the trials, known as the Union for Promotions, had recently released a bulletin insisting that "in a context of war, killing your enemy is legal."

The memo had been penned by Victoria Villarruel, a thirty-one-year-old whose father and grandfather had served in the military, and whose uncle, also a military officer, was arrested for dictatorship-era crimes committed at a clandestine detention center but pronounced "incapable" of standing trial. A polished and articulate law graduate, she had been appearing more and more frequently on television and at conferences and schools, weaving a careful counternarrative to those offered by human rights groups like the Abuelas. Her core message was that Argentina had neglected those harmed by leftist violence. The philosophy was informed by her personal experience: In 1973, she alleges her father was taken hostage by the ERP, the leftist group, while recovering from an operation in a military hospital. His hands and feet were bound with wires, and someone pressed a pistol to his skull before ultimately releasing him. In 2006, she founded the Center for Legal Studies on Terrorism and Its Victims, whose mission was to "make visible" those who had been killed not by the junta but by leftist militant organizations like the Montoneros and ERP.

Other groups opposed to the human rights trials took a more threatening tone. In January 2007, Victoria Donda—the grandchild who had previously gone by Analía Azic—returned home to find her front door had been forced open. Donda was preparing to run for Congress at the time and frequently appeared in the media. The intruders had left her a simple but chilling note. "AAA," it read, an apparent allusion to the Argentine Anticommunist Alliance, or Triple A, the right-wing death squad that had killed suspected leftists in the pre-coup era.

Then, in October 2007, before Guillermo and Cintia's son had yet turned one, Gómez was released from prison after completing his sentence for Guillermo's kidnapping. He moved into a humble shack on a dirt road in San Miguel, just a few miles from Guillermo's own home, which turned anxiety to active panic—Gómez could now reach him and Cintia and Ignacio with a quick car ride or easy bus trip. Guillermo recalled how, as a child, Gómez had managed to find him and Jofré no matter where they tried to escape. He scrambled to erase himself from every official registry possible, hoping to make himself disappear before Gómez could. He changed his official address back to Jofré's so he would be harder to find. Cintia signed most official documents on his behalf.

That same month, a new human rights trial began, this one against Héctor Febres, the former ESMA officer who was accused of having overseen the detention of pregnant women like Patricia. Survivors of the ESMA knew Febres as Selva, or Jungle, because he was as savage as "all the animals put together." Sara Osatinsky, one of the women who had helped deliver Guillermo in the basement infirmary, remembered how when she was first dragged into the ESMA and laid on a metal table in one of the school's torture chambers, Febres was the one to slash off her clothing so they didn't have to remove her handcuffs before electrocuting her. Just before pregnant prisoners gave birth, she recalled, Febres would show up with his arms full of luxurious baby items. The tiny clothing he brought was decorated with delicate lace edging and the baby baskets were of the highest quality—the kind only the wealthiest of Argentine families could afford. After the pregnant detainees delivered their babies, Febres would invite the women to write letters to their families that he promised to drop off along with their newborns. Once the ink had dried on the missives, which were never delivered, he was often one of the men to separate the babies from their mothers.

The trial unfolded over several weeks. Survivors described how Febres had held them in cramped wooden stalls and tortured them on metal beds to conduct extra electricity. One identified Febres as the most zealous torturer in the whole compound. "Febres took away the babies," another witness said of the children born in the ESMA. "He knows where they are and could relieve so much pain." Whether compelled by a reflex or genuine agreement, Febres nodded. Despite the monstrous accusations against him, he pled not guilty to the charges of torture, claiming he had never worked in the ESMA at all. Similar to Gómez's situation at the Palermo air force compound, Febres was guarded by his former colleagues and held in a comfortable suite in a coast guard prison up the Río de la Plata in Tigre, a small riverside city seventeen miles north of Buenos Aires.

On December 10, 2007, three days before a verdict was expected in his trial, Febres didn't show up for breakfast. His guards opened the door to his quarters to discover his heavy, lifeless frame sprawled on the floor. An autopsy would later find a large quantity of cyanide in his blood. At first,

Mary-Claire King, Nélida Gómez de Navajas, and Estela de Carlotto admiring DNA in King's lab in Berkeley.

2

(*left to right*) Rosa Roisinblit and Estela de Carlotto.

3

Guillermo's third birthday party, when he was known as Guillermo Francisco Gómez, with Ezequiel Rochistein Tauro pictured on his left.

4

Mary-Claire King.

Jorge Rafael Videla is arrested in June 1998 for his role in the dictatorship's systematic plan to steal babies.

Guillermo, Mariana Pérez, Argentina Rojo, and Rosa Roisinblit celebrate Mariana's birthday shortly after Guillermo is located in 2000.

Néstor Kirchner and Cristina Fernández de Kirchner.

Irma Rojas, Estela de Carlotto, and Rosa Roisinblit celebrate after the Supreme Court ruled that the Full Stop and Due Obedience Laws were unconstitutional in June 2005.

Guillermo and Rosa.

Estela de Carlotto and
her grandson, Ignacio.

President Barack Obama awards Mary-Claire King the National Medal of Science for
"pioneering contributions to genetics, including discovery of the BRCA1 susceptibility gene for
breast cancer; and for development of genetic methods to match 'disappeared' victims of human
rights abuses with their families" in May 2016.

Rosa Roisinblit photographed in her living room with photos of her loved ones visible on her coffee table.

Mariana, Guillermo, and Rosa pose outside of the courthouse after Francisco Gómez, Omar Graffigna, and Luis Trillo were convicted for the disappearance of Patricia Julia Roisinblit and José Manuel Pérez Rojo on September 8, 2016.

Guillermo and Mary-Claire King tour Parque de la Memoria, or Remembrance Park, a memorial to victims of the dictatorship, in September 2023.

Argentine media speculated that Febres's wife and children—who had been detained after accusations they had dined with him the night before his death—had furnished him a pill to commit suicide before his certain conviction. (The family's lawyer denied they had eaten dinner with him, suggesting a friend had instead.) But the judge assigned to the investigation was less sure Febres had willingly ingested the poison. She claimed to have intelligence that, after years of silence, Febres had been planning on revealing information at his sentencing about what had happened to the infants born in the ESMA. "Babies, tell everything," Febres had scribbled in the margins of a court document recovered after his poisoning. The judge deemed his death suspicious.

As the human rights trials restarted, reporters sought out Estela de Carlotto. "Everything that was stalled for nineteen years because the justice system could not act is active again, and that is good," she said. "But they need to hurry. We are elderly women who have waited a long time for justice, and we can't afford to wait much longer."

On June 1, 2008, Licha De la Cuadra died at the age of ninety-two. The first president of the Abuelas had testified just a year earlier at the trial against Christian Von Wernich, a Catholic priest who had served as a police chaplain under Ramón Camps, and was accused of abetting the military in multiple murders, incidents of torture, and kidnappings.

Licha's daughter and son-in-law had crossed paths with the priest while in detention. "Fine, we are subversives," one witness remembered Licha's son-in-law telling Von Wernich in 1977, after his wife—Licha's daughter—had just given birth to a baby girl they'd named Ana Libertad. "But the baby, who is only four days old? What guilt could she possibly have?"

Von Wernich was unmoved.

"The children will pay for the sins of their parents," the witness heard Von Wernich respond. At some point thereafter, Ana Libertad was separated from her parents, who were not seen again.

When Von Wernich was found guilty and sentenced to life in prison—the first Catholic priest to be prosecuted for his role in the dictatorship—a crowd outside the courthouse in La Plata cheered and set off fireworks. Licha, who counted two sons-in-law and two of her five children as disappeared, had also recently been honored by Congress, but she had never found the granddaughter she had sought so tenaciously.

A couple of years earlier, the Madres had called off their annual March of Resistance, announcing that, with Néstor Kirchner in charge, the Casa Rosada no longer housed an enemy; the Abuelas, though, felt more urgency, not less. In August, Rosa celebrated her eighty-ninth birthday. Three months later, Darwinia Gallicchio—Ximena Vicario's grandmother—died. Both had been reunited with their grandchildren, but Estela had not found hers, nor had Chicha, who had created a foundation dedicated to the search for Clara Anahí and other stolen grandchildren after leaving the Abuelas in 1989. "I cannot permit myself to die," Chicha had testified at the trial for Etchecolatz, whom she had hoped would share new information about Clara Anahí's whereabouts. "I have to find my granddaughter."

Fortunately, identifying grandchildren had become slightly easier. For years, the Abuelas had relied on judges to order blood testing of suspected grandchildren, which had sometimes created legal tussles when those possible grandchildren refused to comply. One young woman had responded to a judge's order by going on a hunger strike and threatening to hurl herself under a car. (After detaining her for several days, the judge overseeing her case pronounced her psychologically unfit to continue and released her.) When the case of Evelin Vázquez, which had stalled for years, eventually reached the Supreme Court in 2003, the justices ruled against compulsory blood extraction, arguing that an individual's right to privacy trumped society's collective right to investigate crimes. "My human rights are being violated in the name of human rights," Vázquez had declared to the press. Critics of the Abuelas seized on that same apparent contradiction. "Grandmothers or Vampires?" was the question posed on the cover of a conservative newsmagazine.

But by 2005, Argentine courts had begun accepting results from DNA collected by alternative methods. Drawing blood was no longer necessary; genetic results obtained from testing toothbrushes, hairbrushes, and clothing would also be considered valid. To resolve stubborn cases, judges had begun ordering raids in investigations of potential grandchildren. The first grandchild identified by these means, in 2006, had been Natalia Suárez Nelson, the same woman who had previously promised to starve herself to protest having her blood drawn. One morning, a crew of gendarmerie and doctors arrived at the home she shared with her partner and took her toothbrush and hairbrush, among other items. The DNA drawn from them confirmed she was the daughter of *desaparecidos* María Elena Corvalán and Mario Suárez Nelson. "On one level I wanted to know," she said later. "The raid, in some ways, is the healthiest solution, because the issue needs to be resolved, it can't just stay as it is. Maybe if they had waited for me to do the analysis, I still would not have done it."

Evelin Vázquez, too, was finally identified. In February 2008, a team of police and employees from the BNDG burst into her apartment soon after she had returned from a workout. Vázquez had previously threatened to kill herself rather than give her blood, and as the forensics experts searched her apartment, collecting a pair of tweezers, her underwear, and her toothbrush, police blocked the windows so she wouldn't jump. DNA analysis of the confiscated items confirmed that she was the daughter of Rubén Santiago Bauer and Susana Beatriz Pegoraro—and the grandchild of Abuela Angélica Chimeno de Bauer. Vázquez did not appeal.

In April 2010, cryptic signs began to appear around Buenos Aires. Bold black and red text on a white background spelled out a pointed question: "Can you be 'independent journalists' and serve the owner of a multimedia company that is accused of the appropriation of children of *desaparecidos*?" Below the text were a handful of photos of journalists employed by Clarín, the country's largest media company and the publisher of the eponymous newspaper. Posted anonymously, the signs alluded to a long-simmering scandal: the Abuelas' accusation that the two adoptive children of Ernestina Herrera de Noble, an elegant eighty-four-year-old former flamenco dancer who now ran the media behemoth, were the stolen son and daughter of *desaparecidos*.

The case of Herrera de Noble's two children—Marcela and Felipe Noble Herrera, both adopted in 1976—had long interested the Abuelas, and Chicha Mariani in particular. Back in 1983, Chicha had seen a newspaper photo of Marcela and, recognizing herself in the girl's stockinged legs and her reserved, intelligent manner, thought that she could possibly be Clara Anahí. In 2001, the Abuelas had requested that the children's adoption files be opened, but there was no conclusive information, and a year later, a judge ordered Marcela and Felipe, now adults, to give blood samples to the BNDG. After multiple delays, the judge, impatient, ordered the arrest of Ernestina—a drastic move that scandalized the country and led to the judge's removal from the case. A few weeks later, a freed Ernestina penned an editorial in *Clarín*, claiming that her arrest had been a political maneuver intended to destroy the free press; she insisted that her children would comply with DNA requests when they felt ready. "I've spoken many times with my children about the possibility that they and their parents might have been victims of the illegal repression," she wrote. She did not blame the Abuelas for wanting an answer but insisted she had adopted her children in good faith. "Marcela and Felipe have the right to know who their biological parents were," she wrote. But this knowledge was not to be forced. "It is a right, not an obligation."

The case was soon relegated to the courts—just another ongoing appropriation investigation among many—until a feud between the Kirchners and Clarín reignited the debate over the children's identity. In 2007, news spread that Néstor Kirchner would not be running for reelection. Though his approval rating hovered around 70 percent, a flurry of high-profile corruption cases had rattled his administration. He encouraged his base to vote instead for his wife and political collaborator, Cristina Fernández de Kirchner. Charismatic and a deft communicator, Fernández was, in the popular imagination, like a modern Evita: the daughter of a bus driver in La Plata, she was both glamorous and an advocate of the people. Just as Evita had ordered everyone to speak to her in the familiar *vos* rather than the formal *usted*, Argentines had come to call Fernández by her first name: Cristina. She favored designer clothing and Rolex watches, sometimes toting around a violet crocodile-skin Hermès Birkin bag. "I have painted myself like a door since I was fourteen," she said of her lengthy makeup routine. Even so, her supporters viewed her as a champion for the masses. "Cristina for me signifies love for the humble," one of her supporters would later say. She won the election handily.

But Cristina had proven to be an even more controversial figure than her husband. A week after she took office, *Clarín* published a piece citing allegations that Cristina's recent campaign had been funded with illegal contributions from Venezuelan strongman Hugo Chávez. The Kirchners often cast political opposition as plots against them, and in the aftermath, Cristina became locked in a fierce public battle with the media company. A few months later, she riled Argentina's powerful agricultural interests by increasing export taxes on soybeans in a bid to control domestic food prices and redistribute wealth. Angry farmers across the country staged debilitating strikes—halting exports entirely, which caused financial mayhem—and set up roadblocks that triggered domestic food shortages. The Kirchners, bemoaning *Clarín*'s coverage of these protests as overly sympathetic to the agricultural sector, began to promote the motto "*Clarín miente*"—Clarín lies—and in 2009, tax inspectors were sent to Clarín's offices to conduct a surprise raid. (They found nothing out of the ordinary.) The Kirchners then convinced the national soccer association to yank their broadcasting rights from Clarín and award them instead to the state-run channel. They also introduced a new media law that seemed expressly intended to break Clarín's powerful empire apart.

It was in this context that the case of the Noble Herrera children flared back into view. In November 2009, Congress passed a law formally stating that judges could order compulsory DNA testing, though it specified that the "least intrusive methods" should be used, to protect victims' rights. Victoria Donda, who had by then been elected to Congress, moved many of her colleagues when she took to the floor in support of the law—"None of the nine children of *desaparecidos* who refused to give blood appealed after their raids. Do you know why?" she asked, looking around the chambers. "Because it took a weight off their backs." But some of her fellow lawmakers remained unconvinced. One opposition politician suggested that the law was only being put forward to exert more pressure on the Noble Herrera family.

"That law is not directed at protecting human rights," she complained. "Its specific target is the children of Mrs. Herrera de Noble. This is pure fascism."

A month later, a judge issued a ruling: the Noble Herrera siblings were to give samples of blood and saliva. Marcela and Felipe complied, but there was a problem. The siblings had given the samples at a lab known as the Forensic Medical Corps, not at the BNDG—which, as the Abuelas argued, was the only legal authority for testing in these cases. To rectify this, the judge ordered the confiscation of items from the homes of Marcela and Felipe to be tested at the BNDG, resulting in more legal wrangling.

Soon afterward, the anonymous signs attacking Ernestina Herrera de Noble and her journalists began to appear around Buenos Aires. For many observers, the case's resurgence, and the Abuelas' renewed interest in it after such a long lull, seemed to carry a political charge—an attempt by Kirchner loyalists to put pressure on Clarín and its owners. The Abuelas shot back that they had first started investigating the case long before the Kirchners came to power. And if the Noble Herrera family had nothing to hide, why did they seem so reticent to work with the BNDG?

In May 2010, a new judge summoned Marcela and Felipe to her office. She asked if they would be willing to allow the samples they had previously given to be analyzed by the BNDG, or to give new samples. They refused and climbed into their chauffeured car to return home.

While driving back to Ernestina's marble mansion in Martínez, the siblings' driver noticed that they were being tailed by a green Jeep Cherokee and a motorcycle driven by two men dressed in black. He made a quick turn to test his suspicion; the Jeep and motorcycle followed. By then, someone had affixed a siren to the roof of the Jeep, identifying the car as belonging to the police, but the Noble Herreras' driver did not stop. Instead, he accelerated, swerving through the streets until he reached the iron gates of Ernestina's compound. The police sped in after him and, once inside, ordered Marcela and Felipe to hand over the clothing they were wearing for analysis. Felipe began to sob; Marcela urged someone to call his psychiatrist. Eventually, accompanied by forensics experts wearing gloves, the siblings undressed and handed over their shirts, pants, and socks. Marcela reported that she was then taken to a bathroom, where she was forced to remove her underwear in front of two officers. Within hours, the siblings had gone to the press. "They are trying to break us emotionally," Felipe said in an interview. On a television channel owned by Clarín, Marcela complained that they'd been treated like "criminals."

The scandal crystallized the difficult questions that had long surrounded the Abuelas' work. To whom does identity belong? Is it the sole property of an individual—or does their family and their society also have a right to truth? If someone's identity is falsified—as in the case of the Abuelas' grandchildren—can society force truth on someone who doesn't want to know it? Some argued for identity as a right and not an obligation, as Ernestina had. Julio Strassera, the prosecutor who had successfully convicted Videla and the other junta chiefs in the 1985 Trial of the Juntas, opined: "You cannot try to defend human rights by going against human rights. If an adult person does not want to and refuses to investigate their origins, that must be respected."

For the Abuelas, however, this was unconscionable. As far as they were concerned, the information contained in Felipe and Marcela Noble Herrera's DNA belonged to all of Argentina. Identity was not a choice a person could make. It was a fact. An individual's right to privacy made sense in the abstract, but it could not subsume the collective right to truth—particularly not when a falsified identity was a symptom of a crime as serious as kidnapping. A family had a right to know its members, and a country to know its citizens. Suspected grandchildren could not be expected to pursue their true identities when the decision might punish their appropriators; this was akin to asking an abused spouse to leave their abuser. As Horacio Pietragalla, one recovered grandchild, put it: "The state cannot leave in the hands of a young person, raised by a member of the military, manipulated by guilt, the decision of whether or not to learn his true identity."

———

One month after the Noble Herrera car chase, two police officers parked a car in front of the air force office where Ezequiel Vázquez Sarmiento worked and ordered him to get in.

Having won his legal effort to avoid giving blood, Ezequiel had for years continued evading attempts to have his DNA tested, even with alternative methods. Anticipating a raid, he had once filled a bag with another person's toothbrush and dirty clothes to stall the process. Now, it seemed, his time was up. Police officers dropped him off in the judge's quarters, where the judge's secretary tried, once again, to convince him to give a DNA sample.

"What don't you understand?" Ezequiel snapped. "I don't want to give samples of any kind, and I am an adult person."

After a while, the judge himself entered. They needed the clothes he was wearing.

"Stop messing around, Ezequiel," he remembers the judge admonishing him. "We can do this the easy way, or the hard way." Several strapping police officers walked into the room.

Ezequiel recognized that he was not going to prevail. Even still, he felt compelled to push his resistance to its limit out of love for the woman who had raised him. Turning to the legal secretary, he ordered: "Put it in the report that I'm not voluntarily giving anything, that you're taking it by force." Then, standing in the courtroom, with nowhere to go, Ezequiel stripped naked. (Ezequiel would later recall that, after a while, a court clerk brought him a pair of boxers, which he'd never worn before, to cover up. "The positive side is that from that point on, I discovered boxers. . . . It was a gift from the court.")

Three months after his dramatic court visit, the DNA results came back: Ezequiel was the son of María Graciela Tauro and Jorge Daniel Rochistein, who had been abducted in 1977. He had been delivered at the ESMA in November of that year by the same doctor who would later deliver Guillermo: Jorge Luis Magnacco.

Ezequiel quickly traveled to Mar de Plata to meet his maternal grandmother, Nelly Wuiovich de Tauro, an "angelic" woman who instantly forgave him for the ten years he'd delayed the testing that proved their connection. "All we wanted was to find you," Nelly and his other relatives assured him. Soon after that, Ezequiel invited Nelly to come visit him in the suburbs of Buenos Aires, where he lived with his wife, three young daughters, and Stella Maris Emaldi, the woman who had raised him. Emaldi was terrified of facing Nelly, and almost suffered a nervous breakdown in anticipation of the visit. Sensing her anxiety, Nelly wrapped Emaldi in a warm embrace and comforted her. She asked about Ezequiel's childhood, and thanked Emaldi for raising him so well.

Soon, Ezequiel began going by Ezequiel Rochistein Tauro. He reached out to *Página 12*, the left-leaning newspaper, to give his first public interview, in which he praised the Abuelas and expressed gratitude for the sensitivity they'd shown him. True closure was not yet possible with Ezequiel's appropriator, Juan Carlos Vázquez Sarmiento, still on the run. But Ezequiel felt more peace than he had in a while. "It might seem violent," he said of being forced to strip in the judge's quarters, "but I left the office liberated. They took a backpack off my back."

40

Thank You for Waiting

2010–2012

While his old friend Ezequiel finally embraced his past, Guillermo began studying law, as he had discovered José had done before escalating political violence compelled him to drop out. Guillermo had first felt called to pursue law school during his teenage years, before he found out who his real father was. Maybe his predilection for it was encoded in his genes, Guillermo would later speculate. He relished the intellectual challenge of making arguments, and, at first, his progress was rapid. He managed to pack eight classes into a single year, significantly more than the average course load, but when it came time to take his final exam at the end of his second year, Guillermo melted down. He sat to take the test four times, and each time he froze, unable to speak or write a thing. Professors began suggesting that he abandon law and study something else. Finally, he realized the root cause: José had never finished his second year of law school. The idea of surpassing his father at anything was too much to bear. This understanding, plus intensive therapy, ultimately helped him graduate.

When his second child was born in 2010, a daughter named Catalina, Guillermo continued to feel haunted. Now a parent with two small children, he was in the same position as Patricia and José had been when they were disappeared. As the sleepless days of tending to his newborn passed by in a blur, it was hard not to dwell on how different his family's experience—at home, together—was from that of his mother, who must have shuddered at the sound of every footstep on the ESMA's hard floors. Guillermo had spent just a few days with Patricia before she was led out of the musty basement, cradling him and a bag of his things in her arms.

He was still not on speaking terms with Mariana—another painful absence. She had recently started a new writing project, an irreverent blog she titled *Diario de una princesa montonera*, or Diary of a montonera princess. Her posts recast her experiences through the lens of darkly comic fiction. She would later say that writing a blog, rather than something more formal, had freed her to experiment with language for exploring the dictatorship that didn't feel purple and stale, and she loved the immediate feedback, which gave her the confidence to keep writing.

She was merciless in her depictions of Guillermo, whom she called "Gustavo."

"Once, before we were certain that we were siblings, at the San Miguel station, Gustavo protected me from the rain under his jacket," Mariana wrote in an entry titled "Ten years ago today I found Gustavo." She claimed it was the only act of kindness she could ever remember Guillermo doing for her. In another post, Mariana asks the ghost of Patricia if Guillermo looks like José. "Yes," the ghost of Patricia answers tepidly. "They look alike." Mariana then writes: "I realize that she doesn't see the resemblance because he's too fat."

The siblings had never agreed on what to do with Argentina's ashes and, one day, Guillermo noticed Mariana had uploaded a post titled "Catch me if you can," in which she announced she was taking a night train to Córdoba. "Are you good detectives, readers?" she asked in a note to her audience. Mariana ironically branded her blog as "110% true," and had sometimes written about real events, such as the protest against Magnacco she attended and her tension with Guillermo over Argentina's death. Guillermo interpreted the post as a veiled reference to what Mariana intended to do with Argentina's ashes. He never learned what became of their grandmother's remains after that.

Guillermo's longing for his parents had become crushing. Ignacio, his oldest child, seemed to yearn for them too. *Where were Grandpa José and Grandma Pati?* In heaven, Guillermo told him. *If he went outside, could he see them?* He had just watched *The Lion King,* in which Simba's murdered father watches over him from a cloud. Maybe, Ignacio reasoned, Patricia and José were doing the same. In conversations with Rosa and any of Patricia and José's friends who would speak to him, Guillermo committed each new detail about his parents to memory, as though doing so could somehow bring them back to life. While he continued to see Jofré frequently, and took his children to visit, he stopped calling her Mamá, switching simply to Dora. Jofré accepted the shift stoically, without inquiry. When Ignacio stopped calling her Abuela, however, she could not resist asking why. "Because you're *not* Abuela," Guillermo snapped.

Néstor Kirchner died suddenly of a heart attack, at age sixty, in October 2010; Mariana and Rosa attended his funeral together. As the country mourned, pundits mused about whether Cristina would be able to manage without him. Even Estela de Carlotto expressed concern. "I don't know what will happen with Cristina," she said at the time. "She's all alone now in charge of the country."

As new elections crept closer, Cristina suffered several major public relations setbacks. In June 2011, Marcela and Felipe Noble Herrera finally agreed to give new DNA samples to the BNDG, and the results did not match any of the families they were tested against, fueling critics who saw the whole ordeal as a political stunt. That same month, the Madres—who were closely allied with the Kirchners—also made headlines when the more radical branch of the organization led by Hebe de Bonafini, which the Abuelas had tried to distance themselves from for decades, was accused of misusing funds intended for government-backed housing projects. The Kirchner government had given the group approximately $45 million to complete the buildings for the so-called Shared Dreams project, but opposition politicians complained they were they were only 35 percent done after years. The legal advisor for the Madres was accused of funneling money from the projects into an eighteen-room mansion, a yacht, and a sports car.

If there was good news, it was that testimony in the Plan Sistemático trial had finally begun, after more than a decade of waiting. While the Abuelas' legal maneuvering had resulted in convictions for nineteen individual appropriations, this case would allow them to demonstrate the coordinated nature and scale of baby theft during the dictatorship. Nine defendants—including Videla, Magnacco, and Juan Antonio Azic, the appropriator of Victoria Donda—would be tried for the theft of thirty-five babies.

More than two hundred people testified in the case, including ESMA survivors like Amalia Larralde, Miriam Lewin, and Sara Osatinsky; Ezequiel Rochistein Tauro and other grandchildren located by the Abuelas; and many of the Abuelas themselves. Not everyone was moved by their statements: in one audience, Videla fell asleep and the judge overseeing the proceedings had to order him prodded awake.

Videla's words were just as offensive to the Abuelas as his actions. "All of the pregnant women, whom I respect as mothers, were active militants of the machinery of terrorism," he insisted when called to testify. "Many of them used their embryonic children as human shields in combat."

When her turn came, Rosa told her story with palpable emotion. "In that moment, I didn't understand anything," Rosa said of the time after Patricia's disappearance. "But I never sat around with my arms crossed. I immediately went out to search."

After Gómez and Jofré were first arrested, it had seemed to Guillermo that the Abuelas were simply out for revenge. But now, as a parent himself, he saw their motivations more clearly. They did not just want to find their children's children, they had to. Their drive was instinctual, primal, deeper than fear and stronger than reason. Because what, other than searching for the most precious thing their children had left behind, might momentarily dull the agony of a parent whose child has been stolen? Guillermo felt newly inspired to educate young people about the dictatorship and its ongoing impact in a way he had never been educated. Other grandchildren had poured their energy into politics—Victoria Donda, Juan Cabandié, and Horacio Pietragalla had each held various positions in city and national government.

For his part, Guillermo decided that he would give talks on behalf of the Abuelas, sharing his story at schools across Buenos Aires Province.

In late March 2012, shortly after Magnacco testified in the Plan Sistemático trial, Guillermo made a particularly special visit to Escuela Normal Número 8, where his mother had studied and earned a spot on the honor roll every single quarter, as Rosa liked to remind people. Guillermo relished visiting places he knew his mother had once frequented. As he walked into the school's arched entrance, he drew comfort from the knowledge that her feet had once touched the same tiles as his. Unfortunately, there was a mix-up with the student organizers about his arrival time, and Guillermo found the students he was meant to speak with watching a movie. As soon as he introduced himself to the school's director, she flicked off the film, but by then, he had only ten minutes before the bell rang.

Guillermo apologized for his unintentional tardiness and invited anyone to stay late who wished to. To his surprise, many of the students, who were fourteen and fifteen—usually the age of indifference—enthusiastically took him up on the invitation. They huddled around, peppering him with questions about how he had come to accept his identity, and how he was doing today. At the end, several students wrapped him in tearful hugs.

Late that same night, Guillermo sat down to write the Abuelas an email. The experience at Patricia's old school, he shared, had "filled his soul with affection." He had decided that the following day, he would join the Abuelas and his "siblings"—the other grandchildren the Abuelas had found—in the Plaza de Mayo to commemorate the thirty-sixth anniversary of the coup. It would be his first-ever protest in the plaza where his grandmother had once marched to decry his disappearance. "I believe I let a lot of time pass—perhaps too much—before embracing my own history and the activism that the rest of my family has chosen," he wrote at the end of the lengthy note. "I also believe that it is never too late. . . . Thank you to the Abuelas for waiting for me."

41

Ten World Cups

2013–2016

An unmarked police car rumbled down Florencio Sánchez, a dirt road in the Buenos Aires suburb of San Miguel. The officers stopped the car in front of number 4135, the address they'd been given to surveil, and watched as a man opened an iron gate connected to a humble yellow house and pulled out of the driveway on a motorcycle. The man was wearing sunglasses and a helmet, so they couldn't see his face well enough to tell if he was their guy; when they typed Florencio Sánchez 4135 into their database, the name that popped up did not belong to the person they were searching for. They exited the car and discretely spoke to a few neighbors who informed them that their target in fact lived across the street in 4136, a brick house with an aluminum roof and iron bars over its windows.

As they were talking, a short and wiry man with tan skin and a wide nose approached the door for 4136, and the officers rushed to intercept him. He exactly matched the description they'd been given. The officers identified themselves as police and read the man his rights in front of two witnesses from the neighborhood. He did not resist as they guided him into a car and drove off toward the center of Buenos Aires. After about an hour, they reached the tab of Retiro that houses a cluster of monolithic military headquarters and government buildings. They passed the white Catedral

Castrense Stella Maris, where Madres and Abuelas had long ago begged Monsignor Emilio Grasselli for answers, and arrived at the hulking criminal court building. There, they deposited their charge in a cell within Unidad 29, a courthouse jail that would later become notorious for its decrepit conditions: paint peeling from every surface, collective cells filled with weary men who tried to sleep on the concrete floors.

Since Francisco Gómez was released from prison in 2007, after serving over six years for Guillermo's kidnapping, Guillermo had lived in constant fear he would act on his threat to kill him and his family. Now, at last, on April 16, 2013, Gómez was back behind bars. This time, he was being held for his role in the disappearance of Patricia and José, a crime with the potential to keep him in jail for even longer than the sentence for Guillermo's appropriation that he had already served.

The effects of the Plan Sistemático case were still reverberating around the country. In July 2012, about a year before Gómez was recaptured, the judge overseeing the case had ruled in favor of the Abuelas, confirming that baby theft during the dictatorship had not been the improvised whim of a few depraved actors but a coordinated effort orchestrated by the military's top brass. The lightest sentence doled out to the nine defendants was five years (to Inés Susana Colombo, a woman accused of stealing one of the Abuelas' grandsons). Magnacco, the naval doctor who delivered Guillermo, got another ten-year sentence, while Azic, Victoria Donda's kidnapper, got fourteen. Videla was sentenced to fifty years in jail.

The former dictator would end up serving less than one. On May 17, 2013, a month after Gómez's arrest, Jorge Rafael Videla died in his jail cell at the age of eighty-seven from complications after slipping in the shower. At a press conference the day after his death, Estela de Carlotto made clear that she would never celebrate anyone dying. Instead, she expressed feeling a mix of relief and, at the same time, remorse for "all that Videla did not say."

Guillermo hoped that Gómez would be tried so that his family could avoid the same regrets. Gómez's prosecution would not only offer them a forum to officially record their stories in the collective memory, but also a chance to confront Gómez—to force him to sit, handcuffed, and listen to the seismic impact of his crimes. They wanted those responsible for Patricia and José's disappearance punished. Just as important, though, they wanted them to talk. *Why were José and Patricia taken? By whom? How and when were they killed? And where were their bodies?* The chances of extracting such information were slim, but a trial would be their one opportunity to try. When Gómez was arrested, Rosa was ninety-three. While she was still feisty and lucid, she did not have time to waste.

In June 2014, as the Roisinblit family waited for Gómez to stand trial, the World Cup kicked off in Brazil. On game days, Argentina effectively shut down. Offices closed, and Buenos Aires' normally bustling downtown went eerily quiet; shop windows were redecorated with mannequins in wigs and underwear the colors of the Argentine flag, and vendors set up on every corner, hawking blue-and-white banners and top hats. Every man and child in the country seemed to be walking around in jerseys bearing the number ten, representing Lionel Andrés "Leo" Messi, Argentina's best soccer player and most famous man. A spry forward with phenomenal dribbling skills, Messi had left the country as a youngster to play in the European league. But, every four years, he donned Argentine colors to represent his home country in the World Cup, and Argentines hoped—and prayed, and begged—that this would be the year he would carry them to victory.

For the Abuelas, however, the World Cup resurfaced painful memories from 1978, when the junta had used the games to distract the country from its crimes—"Argentina! Argentina!" the crowds had cheered as the Abuelas searched for their stolen children and grandchildren. Now the Abuelas decided it was their turn to capitalize on the tournament. They reached out to Lionel Messi asking if he'd participate in an ad campaign in support of their cause. Messi, who famously credited his own abuela, Celia Cuccittini, with encouraging his love of soccer, agreed.

The day of filming, Messi and two teammates strolled into a room in a training facility owned by the Argentine Football Association, where a clutch of Abuelas awaited them. The grandmothers seemed to have primped a little extra to meet the dashing athletes, who greeted the women with fond kisses on the cheek. Of the Abuelas assembled, four had found their grandchildren: Buscarita Roa, Claudia Poblete Hlaczik's grandmother; Aída

Kancepolski, whose grandson, Sebastián Rosenfeld Marcuzzo, was found in the 1980s; Berta Schubaroff, who had been married to the poet Juan Gelman and had reunited with their granddaughter Macarena; and Rosa, dressed in a black overcoat with a bold fur collar. Two of the women were still searching: Estela de Carlotto and Delia Giovanola.

As the camera rolled, the Argentine national anthem blared in the background and Messi and his teammates stood with the Abuelas behind a large banner that read: "Resolve Your Identity Now."

"Go see the Abuelas," Ezequiel Lavezzi, one of Messi's teammates, urged. Then the camera cut to Messi himself.

"We have been looking for you for ten World Cups," he said as the Abuelas burst into enthusiastic applause.

Messi and his teammates would end up reaching the World Cup's championship match, only to lose, 1–0, to Germany in overtime. Argentines who had piled into the streets of downtown Buenos Aires expecting to celebrate a win went wild, launching rocks, toppling over streetlights, and breaking into local businesses. A weeks-long gloom settled over the country—except in the Abuelas' headquarters. On July 24, eleven days after the devastating World Cup final, a musician named Ignacio Hurban wandered into the Hospital Durand to give a blood sample to the BNDG. Ignacio had recently been celebrating his birthday with his wife in Olavarría, a small city in Buenos Aires Province near the village where he'd grown up, when he learned a secret from a neighbor: he was not the biological child of the humble farmers he had always believed were his parents. In fact, the neighbor told him, she had it on good authority that he might be the son of *desaparecidos*—or "subversives," as she called them. The couple who raised him had struggled to have children, and when their patron, a wealthy landowner whose property they tended to, offered them a baby, they accepted, acceding to their boss's demand that they keep the whole ordeal a secret. The next night, Ignacio wrote to the Abuelas, expressing doubts about his identity. After several more exchanges, he traveled to the Durand in hopes of finding out who he was.

He gave his blood, pressed his fingerprint on a pad, and posed for a photo to accompany his file. The resulting image showed a thirty-six-year-old man with a long nose that widened at the nostrils and frizzy curls that had already begun to turn gray. Then, he went home to Olavarría to wait.

"If I turn out to be the son of a 'disappeared' couple, I want to be the grandson of the top grandmother, Estela," Ignacio allegedly said while awaiting his results. He had watched Estela give interviews on television and felt moved by the unflagging persistence that had driven her to seek her grandson for so many decades.

On August 5, Ignacio's test results came back: he was Estela's grandson.

Estela announced the news at a jubilant press conference. Rosa, who had accompanied Estela during every twist and turn of her thirty-six-year search, sat next to her old friend, along with several other Abuelas. Behind them stood a handful of grinning grandchildren, excited to welcome Ignacio into their fold. There was Tatiana Britos, one of the first grandchildren located by the Abuelas, Juan Cabandié, and Horacio Pietragalla. And, off to the side, dressed in a blazer and green button-down, Guillermo clapped and cheered.

"Laura, with the anniversary of her murder approaching soon, is smiling from heaven," Estela said of her daughter in a speech that was televised across the country. "She knew before me . . . 'My mother will never forget what they've done to me, and she will pursue them.' . . . Now, she must be saying: 'Mamá, you won. You won a long battle.'" Later in the press conference, she handed the microphone to Rosa, who explained that every time the Abuelas found a grandchild, they had a tradition of toasting with champagne. For years, Rosa had toasted to finding Estela's grandchild next.

"What am I going to do now?" she said with a gleeful laugh.

The news was extolled by Argentina's most famous celebrities and hailed on the covers of all the country's top newspapers. On his Facebook page, boasting nearly sixty-eight million followers, Messi posted a snapshot from the World Cup advertisement he had filmed with the Abuelas accompanied by the message: "Happy and encouraged by the discovery of Estela de Carlotto's grandchild. The fight must continue, there are still many left!" Notwithstanding the Noble Herrera fiasco, even *Clarín* seemed to celebrate the announcement, printing a photo of a giddy Estela on its front page.

Soon after, Ignacio traveled to La Plata to meet Estela and the rest of his biological family. Over beers, a snack board, and little sandwiches, they began to get to know one another. Ignacio immediately called Estela "Abu," the affectionate diminutive for abuela, and their rapport came easily, unburdened by the dynamics that complicated cases like Guillermo's. Ignacio had chosen to seek out his true identity—the people who had raised him were not military officers but humble farmhands with no apparent ties to those who had disappeared his biological parents, and Ignacio fervently believed that they were ignorant of his origins.

"They couldn't have children, and [their boss] gave them the opportunity of bringing them a child born from a woman who didn't want to have it, which was common in those days," he would say later. "They never suspected anything. They believed their boss—he was like God to them: they lived on his land, and he was their only source of income."

Despite the revelation, Ignacio strove to keep his daily existence the same, electing not to change his first name to Guido, as his mother had named him at birth, and continuing to live in Olavarría, where he taught and made music. But aspects of his new life were unavoidably different. A few months after Ignacio was identified, he and Estela met with President Cristina Kirchner, who presented him with a box of documents about his disappeared father. She was not the only world leader to reach out. Ignacio had only ever left Argentina to cross the river to Uruguay, but soon he was on a plane with Estela to the Galápagos, where grandmother and grandson were invited as special guests of Ecuadorian president Rafael Correa. Then the Vatican called. The recently elected pope, an Argentine named Jorge Mario Bergoglio, wanted to meet them. Ignacio initially resisted—he was not religious and resented the church's opposition to gay marriage—but Estela persuaded him by explaining that the main goal of the trip was to convince the pope to open the Vatican's archives, which might contain clues about other stolen grandchildren. In an interview the following year, Ignacio said that people sometimes stopped him to give him hugs, or simply to cry. "Practically all of Argentina has cried on this one," he said, gesturing to his right shoulder.

The news that Ignacio had been found unleashed a flood of calls and visits to the Abuelas. While on a typical day the office received between ten and forty calls, after Ignacio's discovery the number spiked to one hundred. The "Guido Effect," the media called it. Within three weeks, the Abuelas located yet another grandchild. Genetic tests revealed her to be Ana Libertad Baratti De la Cuadra, the granddaughter of Licha De la Cuadra, the Abuelas' late first president. Ana Libertad was living in Europe at the time and had given her blood at an Argentine consulate, which packed the sample in a diplomatic suitcase and sent it to Argentina for testing.

"For me, this means fulfilling my duty to my sister," Licha's daughter, Estela, said, referring to Ana Libertad's mother, Elena De la Cuadra, who was abducted in 1977 at five months pregnant. In yet another celebratory press conference at the Abuelas' headquarters, the group propped up photos of the late Licha and her disappeared daughter and son-in-law on the table as they shared the exciting news with the rest of the country.

"It was in Licha's home where the first meetings of what would later become known as the Abuelas de Plaza de Mayo took place," Estela recalled. "At first, they were just twelve women, but soon we were many more. Licha was the first president of Abuelas, and she looked for her disappeared granddaughter until the day she died."

The following year brought yet another long-awaited victory when, around Easter, a thirty-nine-year-old man with dirty-blond hair and bright blue eyes wandered into the Abuelas' office.

"Hello, I think I'm a child of the disappeared," he said by way of introduction.

His name was Diego Berestycki, and he was an Argentine who had been living in Miami for the past fifteen years, where he ran an electronics export business. His adoptive father, Armando, had never hidden the truth from him: he and his wife at the time were desperate for a baby but struggled to conceive, so Armando had sold his car to pay for Diego when he was a newborn being cared for at a hospital. Given Diego's birth year, 1976, at the peak of the dictatorship, Armando had admitted to his son that he might be the child of *desaparecidos*, but Diego adored Armando, who was playful and affectionate, and never felt comfortable exploring those difficult questions while he was alive. Recently, though, Armando had died of lung cancer, and his stepmother had convinced Diego it was time.

The subsequent genetic results showed that he was the grandson of Delia Giovanola, another of the Abuelas' founding members, and one of its spunkiest—only a few years before, she had gone rappelling at the ripe age of eighty-two. When Delia first connected with her grandson by phone, she shouted into the receiver: "I found you!" On that very same call, he began to call her Abuela. The happy reunion was tinged with sadness, though. In 2011, Delia's granddaughter, Virginia—Diego's sister—had died by suicide, overwhelmed by the pain of fruitlessly searching for her brother for so many years. Now Delia was thrilled to say: "Mission accomplished."

Like Estela's grandson Ignacio, Diego—whom the Abuelas referred to by his given name of Martín Ogando Montesano—had willingly decided to pursue his true identity rather than having it thrust upon him. Perhaps because of this, his reunion with Delia was uncomplicated and joyful. They talked almost every day. In her apartment in the dense Buenos Aires suburban city of Villa Ballester, where photos of Virginia as a blond-haired child adorned an ornate hutch in her living room, Delia cleared out the larger bedroom for her grandson so he could be comfortable when he came to stay with her. She soon went to visit him in Miami, and besides bemoaning the ubiquitousness of air-conditioning and the bananas in Caribbean food, she enjoyed every moment with Diego and his daughters, her great-grandchildren.

Following Estela and Ignacio's visit to the Holy See, Pope Francis ordered in April 2015 that the Vatican's archives from the dictatorship period be opened. There, the truth was finally laid out for all to see: Argentina's bishops had known for certain that the military was disappearing people and chose not to speak out "for fear of weakening [the military government] and for fear of communism." Then, in March 2016, US President Barack Obama visited Argentina to mark the fortieth anniversary of the coup. He placed a wreath on the monument of San Martín, evoking memories of 1977—when Cyrus Vance had honored the Argentine independence hero with the same gesture—and reluctantly performed a tango with a dancer in a slinky gold dress, who dragged him onto the floor during a state dinner. But the most significant aspect of his visit was an announcement: for the first time, Obama declared, the United States would begin releasing previously classified military and intelligence documents from the dictatorship era. "We cannot forget the past," he said. "But when we find the courage to confront it, when we find the courage to change that past, that's when we build a better future."

As the records the junta might have kept about the disappeared were largely destroyed, Argentina had long relied on the archives of other countries to reconstruct the dark period between 1976 and 1983. Cristina Fernández de Kirchner had ordered the remaining archives held by Argentina's armed forces to be pried open in 2010, but that had turned up more bureaucratic logs than bombshells. Over the years, the United States had declassified tranches of memos that its diplomats and intelligence officers had drafted during the dictatorship; one drop, in 2002, included a note that Assistant Secretary of State for Human Rights Elliott Abrams had written in 1982, confirming that he had raised the issue of stolen children with the Argentine military's ambassador in Washington, DC. (The Abuelas pointed to that document in the Plan Sistemático case to show that the highest ranks of the Argentine regime had been fully aware that its men were kidnapping babies.) Now Obama was promising an even more robust release. The United States had never published papers from the military and intelligence services, and Argentine politicians hailed the move.

But the military and its supporters seemed determined to stay as tight-lipped as ever. Monsignor Emilio Grasselli, the naval priest whose poor treatment of the relatives of the disappeared had inspired Azucena Villa-flor to convene the Madres de Plaza de Mayo, had been called as a witness in a trial in 2014, in the hopes that he would talk about the files he had kept on the disappeared and the relatives who were searching for them— some 2,500 names. Before that, he'd been called as a witness six other times, including at a trial for the kidnapping of Ana Libertad, Licha De la Cuadra's granddaughter. He spoke for three hours but gave so little information, claiming not to remember names and revealing so few facts, that one of the plaintiff's lawyers accused him of delivering false testimony.

"There are things he knows and is not telling," the frustrated lawyer told reporters.

42

Something Like Justice

May–September 2016

On May 2, 2016, Rosa walked into a low, unmarked building tagged with graffiti in the Buenos Aires suburb of San Martín. Beside her was Guillermo, his arm wrapped around her shoulders. Inside, they encountered a bare-bones courtroom with fluorescent lighting and benches and chairs for observers. In front of the benches, separated by a wooden banister, several tables had been pushed together to accommodate lawyers for the plaintiffs on one side and the much smaller defense team on the other. In the middle of the lawyers' tables sat a small wood desk that had been outfitted with a microphone.

After three years of legal grappling and delays, the trial for the disappearance of José and Patricia had finally begun. Gómez and two codefendants—Luis Trillo, a former head of the RIBA, and Omar Graffigna, an air force chief during the dictatorship—would, for the first time, face questions about what had happened to the couple. By then, Rosa had turned ninety-six. She had spent nearly four decades waiting for this moment.

Two days after the trial commenced, Rosa was one of the first witnesses to be called. Behind her, among the benches packed with spectators, sat Guillermo and Mariana. To her right hunched Gómez, Trillo, and Graffigna, guarded by penitentiary officers in black bulletproof vests. The men were wrinkled and graying, and, either to ward off the autumn chill or to conceal the shiny metal handcuffs snapped over their wrists, all three wore their overcoats in the courtroom.

Rosa, too, had dressed for the occasion, slicking her lips with pink lipstick and sporting a turtleneck knit with an eye-catching black-and-white design; she was not going to let her emotions make her sloppy—even as she pushed ninety-seven. From a stage facing the witness stand, one of the judges asked Rosa if she swore to be truthful.

"I never stop telling the truth," she retorted. "It's a trait of mine."

"How many kids did you have or currently have, and how many grandchildren?" In other circumstances, it would have been a routine question.

Rosa paused. "I had a daughter, but I don't anymore."

Over the next hour, Rosa detailed everything she knew about Patricia and José's disappearance—from the night of October 6, when the swarm of military men had dropped off Mariana with José's family in Olivos; to her visit to Patricia and José's apartment, where the officers had stolen everything but Mariana's baby crib; to the harrowing months she had spent petitioning the courts, convinced that Patricia was somewhere to be found. "I didn't realize at that time that if I did things like that, I could disappear myself," she said.

She pointed out the cruel irony that Gómez, Trillo, and Graffigna had gotten a trial in which to defend themselves, but Patricia and José had not. "I didn't think I would live to see this moment," she said. "But I did, and here I am, asking once again for justice." For the length of her testimony, she had spoken with the firm confidence of someone who had told her terrible story too many times. Now, suddenly, her voice cracked. "I need the Argentine state to tell me who took them? Why it took them? Who gave them a trial? Who convicted them? Where are they? I want to find the remains of my children," she pleaded, "because then I'd have a place to lay a flower."

Mariana spoke that same day. She had recently moved back to Buenos Aires from Germany, where she'd lived since 2011, pursuing her doctorate in literature. She had gotten married wearing some of Rosa's own wedding finery and, in 2012, her blog, *Diario de una princesa montonera*, had been published in book form.

Mariana's voice trembled with nerves as she began, but she quickly steadied herself. This was the first opportunity she'd had to share her version of events in a judicial forum, and she seemed determined to make the most of it.

Her story, she said, often was flattened: her parents were disappeared, her brother was stolen, she was returned to her family. But to be returned, she first had to be taken—even if it was just for several hours. She too was a victim. "I am not a footnote in this story," she insisted.

Mariana had no concrete memories of the day she was abducted with her mother—she had been just fifteen months old—but she had often imagined it. It was afternoon, so they were probably having a snack. Or maybe she was plopped in front of the television while her mom was studying. Patricia was still eager to finish her medical degree. She was no longer involved in the Montoneros and thought she might be able to safely return to university. Then, the men came. "I don't know if they rang the bell or kicked in the door," Mariana said. "I don't know what I saw, I don't know what I experienced, I don't know what happened to me."

She spoke about the years she had spent searching for her brother, writing him endless letters, giving vial after vial of blood at the Hospital Durand, and working on the Abuelas' investigative team. Once, in hopes of digging up new information, she had even confronted Carlos Orlando Generoso, a former correctional officer who had supposedly arranged her mother's transport to the ESMA to give birth. Generoso denied ever having seen Patricia. But then he cupped Mariana's chin in his hands, closed his eyes, and sighed, as though, Mariana thought, he could envision Patricia in his head. Later, Generoso, who Mariana believed had been with her mother until she was killed, told Mariana that if she came to his house, his wife would make her a Toddy, a drink made from powdered chocolate beloved by Argentine children.

Mariana endured such painful interactions for one purpose. "Finding my brother was my reason for living," she said. But their reunion had not turned out the way she had hoped. She blamed the military for depriving her not just of her parents but of her relationship with Guillermo. Staring at the judges with an even gaze she added, "You are not looking at a happy family."

Twelve days after Mariana's testimony came Guillermo's turn. Dressed in a black-and-gray striped sweater, Guillermo settled into the small wooden desk and positioned the microphone in front of his mouth. Behind him, separated by a banister, Cintia cradled their third child, the three-week-old Helena, in a gauzy swaddle.

"Your full name, please, señor?" the judge began.

"I am Guillermo Rodolfo Fernando Pérez Roisinblit," he answered, later clarifying: "But that was not always my name."

For nearly three hours, Guillermo retold the stories of his two lives: the one he had experienced as Guillermo Francisco Gómez and the one that had unspooled after April 27, 2000, when Mariana had found him. He described how, when he was young, Gómez would take him to the RIBA, treating him to soda in glass bottles. He recounted Gómez's beatings of Jofré, and their attempts to escape him. He recalled the moment when Mariana showed up at Shower and how he'd traveled to the Abuelas that very day, eager to find out if they were siblings. He told the judge how, after several confrontations, Gómez had finally confessed that he was the son of Patricia Julia Roisinblit and José Manuel Pérez Rojo.

Gómez's lawyer asked Guillermo why, after Gómez was arrested in 2001, Guillermo had continued to visit him in prison for two years. "I was confused, because it is not easy to process that this story is my story— that I'm never going to meet my parents and that I was robbed of twenty-one years with my real family," Guillermo responded. He knew that his life with Goméz and Jofré had been built on a lie, and that the love they claimed to feel for him was corrupt.

"Regardless of that," Guillermo said, "my feeling was genuine, not only for her, but also for him."

At the end of his testimony, he honed in on the man he had called Papá for twenty-one years. He was convinced that Gómez had information about his parents' disappearance and the location of their remains. "I hope that he has the compassion to testify," Guillermo said. "I believe that on some level, he owes me that."

Over the following months, around twenty more witnesses were called to the stand. The siblings of Gabriel Pontnau, José's business associate, spoke about the day José and Gabriel were wrestled out of their party supply and toy shop in Martínez, explaining how, after hearing of Gabriel's abduction, their father had rushed to the store and encountered a gang of men loading themselves down with merchandise. The warehouses where José and Gabriel kept overstock were pillaged as well. They had never heard from or of Gabriel again. José and Gabriel's employee, Teresa Izaguirre, took the stand too and described watching her bosses being dragged out of the shop by several strangers, raincoats draped over them. Marcelo Moreyra, José's second cousin, recounted how, after the military men left him a basket with fifteen-month-old Mariana laid inside, his young cousin had offered Mariana bottle of milk, trying to soothe her to sleep. But Mariana kept running frantic circles around the couch, terrified.

Finally, Miriam Lewin and Munú Actis spoke about their conversations with Patricia while she was held in the ESMA, and relayed what she had told them about her detention in the RIBA, where she had been tied to the leg of a desk at eight-months pregnant. Amalia Larralde recounted how when Patricia had given birth to Guillermo, she had wept from a mixture of fear, anguish, and joy. She spoke, too, of watching Patricia as she was led out of the ESMA basement, clutching Guillermo in her arms. It was the last time anyone had seen her. Later, Amalia berated herself for forgetting a few names during her testimony, but Mariana consoled her: "It makes sense you'd forget some things. This trial should have happened forty years ago."

Two months into the proceedings, it was time to hear from the defendants. Gómez's handcuffs were unlocked, and two penitentiary officers led him to the witness desk. Wearing a wine-purple windbreaker over a beige sweater, he sat down in front of the microphone. The guards stood behind him, their hands clasped in front of their bulletproof vests. In a low croak, Gómez delivered a twenty-minute biographical monologue about how he had made it from the fields of Misiones, one of Argentina's poorest provinces, to Buenos Aires, where he met Jofré, who cleaned the home of a man who oversaw the RIBA for a time, Roberto Oscar Sende.

Sende had taken a shining to Gómez and offered him a job at the RIBA. Denying any knowledge of the air force's more sinister operations, Gómez insisted that his roles had always been mundane: tending to the gardens, cleaning offices, and making coffees. When he and Jofré got married, it had been Sende who footed the bill. When they traveled to San Luis to meet Jofré's family, Sende had funded that too. One day, Gómez said, Sende had approached him and said simply: "I have a kid. Do you want it?"

Gómez said he had believed that the baby was abandoned, and since he and Jofré had lost several pregnancies, he agreed to adopt the boy. He claimed that when Jofré and Guillermo had run away from their home in Buenos Aires, he had tracked them down in San Luis not to drag them back to city but to bring them money. He had always made sure Guillermo was dressed like a "little man"—with jackets from America and shoes from the upscale clothing store Grimoldi. Guillermo had the best toys in the neighborhood; he was the only kid for blocks with skates. He had a fan in his room to cool him in the summer and parquet floors that kept his feet warm in the winter. "I raised Guillermo like a true father," he howled. "I loved Guillermo."

The judge cut him off, demanding that he constrain his testimony to the topic of the trial: the disappearance of José and Patricia. "This is not meant to serve as therapy for you," he said. After that, Gómez mostly limited his answers to "No" or "I don't know." Did he ever see guns in the RIBA? "No!" What about detainees? "No! No! No! Never!" He denied knowing Juan Carlos Vázquez Sarmiento, El Colorado, the former air force officer who was still on the run from prosecution in Ezequiel Rochistein Tauro's appropriation case, even though Guillermo vividly remembered him and, during his own testimony, had presented a photo of Ezequiel attending his third birthday party. The answers offered by Trillo and Graffigna were similarly evasive. It seemed that the men would go to their graves without revealing the location of José's and Patricia's.

———————

"I want to make it very clear: we will not permit any demonstration . . . whether it be whistling, or clapping," the judge warned the spectators when it came time to announce the ruling on September 8, four months after Rosa had spoken in the trial's first hearing. Finally, the judge pronounced his verdict. For participating in the disappearance of Patricia Julia Roisinblit and José Manuel Pérez Rojo, he found Gómez, Trillo, and Graffigna guilty. Gómez was sentenced to twelve years in prison, while his superiors were sentenced to twenty-five.

Guillermo and Mariana leaped from the wood bench where they'd taken in the trial and hugged Rosa. Outside the courthouse, speaking to reporters, Rosa pronounced: "I waited thirty-eight years to achieve this." Grandmother and grandchildren squeezed together and posed for the clicking cameras of the press. As they smiled widely, squinting into the sun, their resemblance was uncanny. Had they never confirmed their connection through DNA, Mariana's and Guillermo's similar noses and full lower lips might have seemed proof enough.

Mariana held up two fingers for the pool of reporters—a V for victory. The moment recalled a line from a letter that she had written to Guillermo after they first met.

"When we are together," she wrote, "something very much like justice occurs."

43

A Flower Traveled in My Blood

2022–2023

At the age of 102, Rosa Roisinblit stepped back from her role as the Abuelas' vice president, a position she had held for thirty-three years. She had traveled far and wide championing the group's mission—to Switzerland, France, Cuba, Lithuania, and even North Korea, working to find all the Abuelas' stolen grandchildren long after she had located her own. She had been honored by too many universities, municipalities, and human rights groups to count. Her retirement created a profound absence on the Abuelas' board of directors, and Estela asked Guillermo if he wanted to fill it. "Well," he responded, humbled. "If you think it's a good idea."

Rosa's departure left only a handful of active Abuelas. Soon, their already tight ranks shrank even further. In July 2022, Delia died at the age of ninety-six. "Delia gave everything to this institution," the Abuelas wrote in an homage, but they comforted themselves by pointing out that she had found her grandson. Other grandmothers had not been so lucky. Chicha Mariani, the former president of the Abuelas, passed away in 2018 without ever getting to embrace Clara Anahí. For a few glorious days in late December 2015, Chicha had thought she had found her, a Christmas miracle celebrated by the Abuelas and the country. But additional genetic tests later disproved Chicha's link to the woman she thought might be her granddaughter.

The Abuelas' board was now composed of more grandchildren than the grandmothers who had found them. Among its members was Claudia Poblete Hlaczik, who, after testifying on behalf of her appropriators in court back in 2001, had eventually cultivated a strong bond with her biological family. Now she, Guillermo, and the other grandchildren on the board worked closely with her grandmother, Buscarita, to find their missing peers.

That work seemed to be getting harder. From 2019 to 2022, the Abuelas had not located a single grandchild. The pandemic contributed to the drought: lockdown measures in Argentina had been particularly draconian, with people confined to their apartments for weeks, and the Abuelas' board hadn't been able to meet or investigate in person. But there was a deeper problem. The more than two hundred and fifty grandchildren the Abuelas estimated were still missing were now, like Claudia and Guillermo, in their mid- to late forties. The Abuelas had long sought to inspire possible grandchildren to approach them with a provocative question—*Do you know who you are?*—but this strategy seemed to hold less power now that those grandchildren had reached middle age. Many of them were married, with children of their own. Some had probably absorbed the ideologies of the military officers who raised them and wanted little to do with the Abuelas, even if they did have doubts about their pasts. They felt, perhaps, that they *did* know who they were.

Just before Christmas in 2022, the drought ended. "Nieto 131" was the forty-four-year-old son of Lucía Ángela Nadín and Aldo Hugo Quevedo, a couple from Mendoza who had met at university and participated in the leftist movement. Lucía had been abducted around September 1977 and was held in El Banco, a notorious detention center run out of a building owned by the Buenos Aires Provincial Police, when she was a few months pregnant. Her family had not known she was expecting, complicating the Abuelas' search. In 2004, Lucía's pregnancy was revealed and the next year her family had given blood to the BNDG. The Abuelas eventually located Lucía and Aldo's son in Buenos Aires Province, and when they showed him a photo of his parents, he reportedly stared at it in unblinking disbelief. He had the same jet-black hair, tan skin, and straight nose as his father.

By late July 2023, the number was up to 133—the Abuelas had found one more grandchild shortly after the son of Lucía and Aldo, a forty-seven-year-old man named Juan José Morales, and another long-sought-after grandson, Daniel Santucho Navajas, seven months after that. Soon the Abuelas received more exciting news: the memorial housed at the former site of the ESMA, where around thirty of their grandchildren were born in captivity during the dictatorship, was being named an official UNESCO World Heritage site. The designation was rarely granted to museums commemorating recent history, but UNESCO considered the building to be of "outstanding universal value." The Abuelas were thrilled; the museum was a testament to the preservation of memory, however haunting. Curators had added plaques and art installations to describe how the navy had used the building's various rooms during the dictatorship—to point out where prisoners had been tortured or forced to work. Otherwise, they had largely let the original structure speak for itself. Upstairs, in a cramped, dark room where paint peeled off the walls, large white letters were laid out on the floor: "How was it possible that babies were born in this place?"

Near the main museum, within the ESMA's leafy compound, sat Casa por la Identidad—the House for Identity. A stout white building with brick columns surrounded by rows of tipa trees, the House for Identity held the Abuelas' institutional archive, where hundreds of white plastic boxes contained press clippings, legal filings, and old transcripts of anonymous tips pertaining to their stolen grandchildren. It also housed a warren of echoey rooms hung with photos and posters that told the Abuelas' story from 1977 to the present. In one room, there were images from the Abuelas' early marches, depicting the women gathered in the Plaza de Mayo with white handkerchiefs, clutching photos of their stolen grandchildren. Another room offered a glimpse into the lives of the Abuelas' children before their abductions—walls adorned with photos of pregnant women in flowy dresses and happy couples cutting wedding cakes. A sweeping montage of black-and-white photos of young men and women hung as a tribute to all the parents of the grandchildren sought by the Abuelas since 1977. Among the sea of faces, next to one another, were images of Patricia, smiling, and José, serious.

There was also a room where the timeline of grandchildren located by the Abuelas was traced, from the Britos sisters and Paula Logares to Guillermo and beyond. In the section about recent cases, surrounded by a bold red border, hung an image of Estela de Carlotto grinning widely as she pressed her cheek against Ignacio's face. "This exhibit is dynamic," read a note on one of the posters. "Our grandkids will keep appearing and our search will only end when the last of the children recover their identities."

Occasionally, Guillermo reflected on the anguish he had endured since he pricked his own thumb in the Abuelas' office and watched his blood drip onto the white sheet of filter paper. He thought about how utterly confused and alone he had felt in the years after Gómez and Jofré were arrested. He had lost the people he thought were his parents, only to learn that his true parents were permanently lost. He considered how painful it was to construct a new identity on a foundation of tragedy and trauma. His path had been long and lurching, and, as he helped the Abuelas look for other grandchildren, he understood how difficult it might be for those grandchildren if they were found.

But when asked if he would change his decision to meet with the Abuelas on that day in late April 2000, he did not hesitate. Tears welled up behind the black rectangular frames of his glasses. "I wouldn't change a thing."

If he had made a different choice, then perhaps he would not have Cintia, or their three healthy children, or their home on the corner, where they lived with a menagerie of dogs and cats and fish. He would never have learned that he has the same deep belly laugh as his father, or that his mother had laid him on her chest after giving birth so he could feel her heartbeat. Without accepting the truth himself, he wouldn't have been able to impart a truthful inheritance to his children, or their children after them. And, of course, he never would have met Rosa, whom, despite all their ups and downs, he had come to revere as an icon.

Around the time Guillermo joined the Abuelas' board, Rosa was moved to an assisted care home. After more than one hundred years of fierce independence, she seemed uncomfortable there; when Guillermo visited, he felt she tended to pick fights with him. And yet, Rosa loved him, he had no doubt, and he loved her. Their love wasn't always easy, but it was grounded in truth.

Before Rosa had left her apartment on Riobamba, she had decorated her living room with photos of the most treasured people in her life. They topped every table and lined every shelf. There was the same smiling image of Patricia that Rosa had reprinted hundreds of times during her desperate search, and hundreds more times in her daughter's memory after she had given up hope of finding her alive. There was Benjamín, dapper in a suit and tie, and Rosa's parents, Alte and Salomón. There were frames containing snapshots of Mariana and her children and photos of Rosa with Estela de Carlotto and the other Abuelas. Mixed among them were several images of Guillermo. One depicted Mariana and Guillermo cheek to cheek, smiling—a vestige of their fleeting harmony. Another, tucked into the gold lattice of her large hutch, showed Rosa leaning over to admire her first great-grandchild, Guillermo's son, Ignacio, as he lay in Guillermo's arms.

On the floor, by the sole living room window, Rosa had arranged a tangle of potted plants—a tall leopard lily and a waxy red anthurium, a lacy monstera and a willowy devil's ivy. She relied on a wheelchair to move around, but her hands, whose nails she kept painted Malbec red, were still dexterous. Each day, with the help of her home aide, she used them to tip a stream of water into the pots and remove any dead leaves or branches. She derived particular satisfaction from propagating new plants. Pinching a mature stem between her fingers, she searched for its tiny root nodes. Upon locating them, she snipped the stem. Replanted in fresh soil, the stem would eventually grow its own roots. Then, someday, it would bloom.

Now and Forever

On September 21, 2023, Guillermo found himself at Parque de la Memoria, or Remembrance Park, a memorial to victims of the last dictatorship on the banks of the Río de la Plata. Both its location, separated from the streets of Buenos Aires by a busy highway, and its stark design mean the park is often deserted. Iron gates open to a flat patchwork of concrete tiles and grass. The only shade comes from one measly line of trees and the shadows cast by several giant sculptures. The place feels bleak, exposed, sunburnt. It is not far from Aeroparque, one of the main airports from which the military conducted its death flights. As Guillermo wandered through the front entrance, the rumble of a plane occasionally interrupted the sound of waves splashing against the rocks.

Walking arm in arm with Guillermo that day was Mary-Claire King. She had never seen the memorial before; it was her first trip back to Argentina in three decades. Since the BNDG had become fully self-sufficient in the 1990s, King's work with the Abuelas had been done from afar, in her lab in Seattle. Now, in September 2023, the Abuelas had invited her back to Buenos Aires to reflect on what they'd accomplished together while they still could. Two days before the visit to Parque de la Memoria, King had been awarded an honorary degree by the University of Buenos Aires. There, she had met Guillermo and several other grandchildren for the first time. Her own daughter, Emily, was grown, and King marveled at the interconnected family of grandchildren now standing before her. She had always thought she would have a brood of children, and for years she had wrestled with a mother's guilt over so many long hours in the lab. And yet there before her stood all the sons and daughters her work had helped find. She had studied black-and-white photos of their disappeared parents and the C's, G's, T's, and A's of their mitochondrial DNA sequences. Upon meeting them in person, she realized: she *had* a brood of children after all—133 of them.

During her trip, King had also toured the sleek headquarters of the BNDG, which had moved from the Hospital Durand to an office building operated by the Ministry of Science, Technology, and Innovation in downtown Buenos Aires. The lab was clean and bright and nondescript, save for one clear nod to its mission. On a wall by the entrance hung a large bulletin board called the "Nietera." There, the BNDG's scientists had pinned numbers representing the most recently recovered grandchildren and plastic bags containing corks from the champagne they had sipped upon identifying them. Remembering the Durand's ramshackle hallways, King was thrilled by the lab's modern machinery and sharp director, Mariana Herrera. Like King, Herrera had taught university classes in addition to her lab work, and she was a deft communicator of complex scientific principles. And, to King's amazement, she was related to the Beláustegui Herrera family, the first family to whom King had applied mitochondrial DNA testing back in the 1980s. Three of Herrera's cousins had disappeared during the dictatorship, two of them while expecting children. One, Valeria Beláustegui Herrera, gave birth to a baby boy in December 1977 while detained. In 1988, King conducted mitochondrial DNA analysis of a child the Abuelas suspected might be Valeria's son, but it did not yield a match. Neither he nor the child of Herrera's other cousin, Martín, had been located since, but she had never abandoned hope that one day a BNDG technician might knock gently on her office door and say: "Mariana, we have something to show you. . . ."

Before the end of the lab tour, Herrera surprised King by unveiling a glass plaque etched with her name that she planned to hang on the wall. "In honor of her invaluable contribution to the scientific development for identity, memory, truth, and justice," it read.

Now Herrera joined King, Guillermo, and several others for the visit to Parque de la Memoria. After passing the statues at the entrance, eventually the group reached the park's main exhibit: four long, hulking walls arranged in a zigzag, designed to evoke an open wound. As they approached, they could see that each facade was composed of thousands of rectangular granite plaques stacked on top of one another, towering above visitors' heads. Around 9,000 were inscribed with names and ages; 358 of those bore an additional inscription: *embarazada*. Pregnant. The other 21,000 plaques were blank, representing *desaparecidos* who had not been identified, bringing the total to 30,000—the number of people that human rights groups estimate were disappeared by the state during the dictatorship. The effect was a feeling of both claustrophobia and searing emptiness. Together, King and Guillermo paused before the plaques for Patricia and José—just two stones in the vast walls.

After Gómez was found guilty, the largest trial in Argentine history, known as "the ESMA mega-case," had taken place, investigating the human rights abuses committed against 789 people by 54 defendants. Then, in October 2021, police finally located Juan Carlos Vázquez Sarmiento after almost twenty years on the run. He had recently been convicted of appropriating Ezequiel Rochistein Tauro, and next would be tried for the disappearance of José and Patricia. José's second cousin Marcelo clearly remembered Vázquez Sarmiento as one of the men to drop off baby Mariana in Olivos on the night of October 6, 1978; it was hard to forget a redhead. The trial was another opportunity to learn what might have happened to his parents, but Guillermo wasn't holding out much hope. His own appropriator, Gómez—whom Guillermo called the "personification of his fears"—had died in prison without ever saying another word about his parents. "Do I feel sadness? I don't know," Guillermo wrote at the time. "I do feel impotence because he took with him the truth about what they did to my parents, and also where their bodies are."

The EAAF continued its painstaking work searching for the remains of *desaparecidos*. Just the month before, the team had identified an industrial worker disappeared during the dictatorship after his bones were exhumed from an unmarked grave in the southern suburbs of Buenos Aires. But since the end of the dictatorship, the EAAF had only managed to identify one thousand or so *desaparecidos*. Most of the plaques at Parque de la Memoria represented people whose corpses had never been found. It was precisely this absence that made Guillermo feel so uneasy as he wound around the monuments. The place reminded him of a mausoleum without any bodies. "To accept that you're the child of *desaparecidos* means that you're the child of two people you don't know, and you aren't going to know," he had once said.

The walls of the monument guided Guillermo and King blindly down a gentle slope. When they finally came to an end, Guillermo and King abruptly found themselves at the banks of the Río de la Plata. Before them stretched the area of the river where many victims of death flights were dropped, including, possibly, Patricia. Leaning over the railing that divides the park from the Río de la Plata, Guillermo, King, and the rest of their group tossed red and yellow flowers into the brown water below, chanting: "Ahora y siempre, ahora y siempre!"

Now and forever.

Around the world, in countries attempting to wrestle with histories of violence and trauma, the same questions tend to recur. How should peace be balanced with justice? Is it better, for the health of a society, to pardon or to punish the perpetrators? These quandaries rarely have clear—or static—answers. Almost a century on, they continue to plague Germany, where the Allied forces famously convicted high-ranking Nazis in the Nuremberg trials, but where many of the estimated two hundred thousand perpetrators of Nazi-era crimes were never prosecuted. They played out in South Africa after apartheid and Rwanda after its genocide. In Spain, some have begun to advocate for forgetting their country's Pact of Forgetting, in which both leftist and conservative parties agreed to a blanket amnesty for the crimes of the Franco era. The tension between amnesty and accountability continues to roil Northern Ireland, where sectarian violence known simply as the Troubles gripped the country for thirty years, and where the United Kingdom recently proposed a sweeping immunity law for British soldiers and paramilitary groups involved in the conflict.

Argentina itself has long been viewed as a case study in the classic frictions that afflict such processes of reckoning. From Alfonsín's amnesty laws and Menem's pardons to the Kirchner-era annulment of those initiatives, the country has seesawed between the opposing impulses of reconciliation and justice, between the drive to forget and the obligation to remember. The view of many Argentines is best summarized by the famous saying of Spanish philosopher George Santayana, who witnessed his own country's descent into fascism:

"Those who cannot remember the past are condemned to repeat it." Others embrace the philosophy of Edna Longley, a writer from Northern Ireland, where the Troubles cleaved the country in two. To achieve lasting peace, she advocated "raising a monument to Amnesia, and forgetting where we put it."

But for all the strife since Argentina's military dictatorship ended four decades ago, the country has in many ways been a pioneer in confronting the traumas of its past. Democracy in Argentina had only been restored for three days when Alfonsín vowed to try the junta for its crimes in 1983. The blockbuster Trial of the Juntas that followed represented one of the first major war crimes cases prosecuted since the Nuremberg trials. Argentina's neighbors, who had also lived through dictatorships, eventually launched their own legal processes, but they moved much more slowly than Argentina had: trials of authoritarian regimes in Chile, Guatemala, Peru, and Uruguay did not kick off until the 2000s. CONADEP, which published the explosive report *Nunca Más* the year after the dictatorship ended, is widely credited as the first truth commission to achieve international renown. It inspired similar commissions around the world, including in Chile, El Salvador, and South Africa.

More broadly, groups like the Abuelas have shaped how the country thinks about memory, truth, and justice—the three principles that underpin the Argentine human rights movement. When the impunity laws still reigned, the Abuelas found loopholes that allowed them to prosecute kidnappers and to share their stories through Truth Trials. It is now impossible to walk very far in Buenos Aires without confronting some physical reminder of the dictatorship. Colorful memorial mosaics enliven the sidewalks in front of the buildings where *desaparecidos* were abducted and the schools they attended. In 2011, a law established all former clandestine detention centers as "memory sites." Some were officially converted into museums. Others, like the RIBA, were simply marked with plaques or signs. "Human Rights Crimes were planned and committed here during the period of state terrorism," the sign outside the RIBA's walled compound reads.

The Abuelas' impact, in particular, has extended far beyond Argentina's borders. They were instrumental in persuading the United Nations to introduce the right to identity in its Convention on the Rights of the Child, and are widely viewed as the first group to use genetics to rectify human rights abuses.

Prior to the Abuelas' pioneering work with Mary-Claire King, Víctor Penchaszadeh, the BNDG team, and other scientists, genetic science was more commonly associated with the violation of human rights rather than their defense. Eugenics, the abominable practice by which countries like the United States, Sweden, Hungary, Italy, and Germany enlisted scientists to "perfect" their societies by forcibly sterilizing people from certain racial backgrounds or with intellectual challenges, had given the field a deservedly terrible reputation in the human rights world. With the Index of Grandpaternity, the Abuelas redeemed the image of genetics and inspired similar work across the globe. Since the Abuelas helped found the Banco Nacional de Datos Genéticos in the 1980s, genetic databases dedicated to identifying the disappeared have opened in Colombia and El Salvador. The EAAF, which owes its creation to the Abuelas' tireless lobbying, has helped to identify human rights victims in the Philippines, the Democratic Republic of the Congo, the former Yugoslavia, and more than thirty other countries, including, most recently, Ukraine.

Mary-Claire King herself posits that she and the Abuelas were among the pioneers of genetic genealogy, the combination of traditional genealogical methods like the sketching of family trees with genetic testing to infer family relationships. It is now a large industry populated by companies like Living DNA and Ancestry.com. The Abuelas can also feasibly claim to have spearheaded the use of forensic genetics—the application of genetics to criminal investigations—in a human rights context.

In late 2023, drab-green Ford Falcons like those the military had used to abduct people during the dictatorship began creeping out of garages where they'd been stashed. Since democracy was restored, it had been rare to spot the cars around; they are viewed as provocative symbols of Argentina's darkest days. But suddenly, they were seen cruising about Buenos Aires, their license plates pried off, photos of Videla displayed on the back windshields. A police officer in northern Patagonia posted a video of a Ford Falcon to his social media with the caption: "May the thieves be caught." On a warm, late November day, another Falcon was seen parked outside Argentina's grand Senate building, where inside legislators were preparing for a dramatic presidential transition.

The Falcon owners were seemingly emboldened by the election of Javier Milei, a right-wing populist who had soared to victory in Argentina's elections a few days before. Argentine voters were entertained by his bizarre iconoclasm and, after years of economic mayhem, encouraged by his vow to "destroy" the bloated Argentine government from within. Short and thin with fuzzy sideburns and a mop of unruly hair that looks as though it's never met a comb, Milei allegedly cloned his beloved English mastiff, naming the resulting offspring after his favorite economists: Milton Friedman, Robert Lucas Jr., and Murray Rothbard. Rothbard (the human) originated "anarcho-capitalism," a radical brand of libertarianism proudly championed by Milei that, in its most extreme form, aspires to abolish centralized states.

On the campaign trail, Milei also promised to defend "complete memory," in which the traditional narratives about the dictatorship offered by human rights groups are deconstructed and rewritten. Milei argued that he too was in favor of "memory, truth, and justice" championed by the Abuelas, but he promoted a very different view of what those principles meant. "Let's start with truth: There were not thirty thousand *desaparecidos*," he said in one campaign speech, insisting that the true figure was 8,753—a number even lower than the estimate published in the 1984 *Nunca Más* report. He described what had happened during the 1970s as a "war" in which "excesses" were committed rather than an example of state terrorism and pointed out that "the terrorists in the Montoneros and ERP also killed people, tortured people, planted bombs, and wreaked havoc." He accused human rights groups like the Madres of using their ideology to make money, mentioning the failed Shared Dreams apartment development.

As his vice president, Milei selected the arguable queen of complete memory: Victoria Villarruel, the founder of the Center for Legal Studies on Terrorism and Its Victims, who had vocally pushed back on human rights groups since the early 2000s. While campaigning, Villarruel took direct aim at Estela de Carlotto. "The truth is that Carlotto has been quite a sinister figure for our country," she said. "Because with that kind, grandmotherly face, the reality is that she has justified terrorism." Estela responded by calling Villarruel and Milei "reprehensible" and shrugging that they "shouldn't be given too much importance."

Only now Argentina had voted them into the Casa Rosada, from where they wasted no time in axing several government agencies and initiatives critical to helping the Abuelas in their investigations. Milei cut off subsidies that the Abuelas had received from previous governments. Around the same time, he put an end to the investigative unit of CoNaDI, the governmental body founded by Menem in 1992 to assist in the search for children stolen during the dictatorship. The Abuelas fear that act will significantly slow down their work as they attempt to sift through thousands of outstanding complaints without any state support. Milei's administration disbanded an archive within the Defense Ministry whose team members sometimes unearthed documents relevant to the Abuelas' trials. Recently, they had dug up documentation that helped seal the conviction of Adolfo Donda, the naval officer who was accused of kidnapping Victoria Donda, his own niece, and passing her off to his colleague to raise. Representatives of Milei's party also visited military officers convicted of human rights crimes in prison. Standing under the cross of the jailhouse chapel, they smiled for photos with prisoners including Alfredo Astiz, the naval officer who infiltrated the Madres de Plaza de Mayo, and Juan Carlos Vázquez Sarmiento, El Colorado, his red hair faded to white.

The Abuelas have responded to the provocations as they always have: by taking to the plaza. Their marches are much larger now, and generally safer. Often the Abuelas are joined by workers unions and other human rights groups, and they are usually left alone by police. But the gatherings still retain a flicker of their original revolutionary power, summoning echoes of Azucena Villaflor's vow to march until her legs fell off. The Madres and Abuelas kept Azucena's word: they marched until the junta toppled and never stopped.

At one recent protest on a bluebird winter day, Estela de Carlotto was the only Abuela present to circle the Pirámide de Mayo, which she did once, slowly, with the support of several recovered grandchildren. Exhaustion and sadness darkened her face as the crowd applauded her. Still, she moved her feet, one after the other, across the plaza's tiles.

About This Book

I vividly remember when I first learned about the Abuelas de Plaza de Mayo. It was late 2011 in Buenos Aires. Jacarandas were in bloom, painting the city purple. I had recently graduated from college and had moved to Argentina for what was meant to be a one-year fellowship. I was parked at a charming coffee shop, flipping through a newspaper to get my bearings, when I stumbled on an article that had the opposite effect. It was about the Plan Sistemático case, which was in full swing. While I'd learned about the dictatorship and the Madres de Plaza de Mayo in a college Spanish class, I had no idea that the Argentine military had abducted pregnant women and stolen their babies. Horrified, I immediately did more research—and remember the nausea that spread over me as I learned of suspicions that some mothers were pushed out of planes into the Río de la Plata shortly after giving birth. That nausea soon mingled with awe as I read more about the Abuelas and discovered how they had defied dictators, donned disguises, and pioneered new types of genetic testing in service of finding their stolen grandchildren.

I devoured all the material I could track down about the Abuelas and their grandchildren, but my Spanish was still middling at best, and I found that there was only one book on the subject in English: *Searching for Life*, by the Argentine academic Rita Arditti. It was thorough and compelling, but it had been published in 1999 and was more of a scholarly examination than a narrative history of the type I hoped to read. It did not cross my mind to try to write one myself. While I already nursed ambitions of writing a book someday, I had yet to publish a single article outside of a campus publication.

A few months later, thanks to a generous introduction from Steve Coll—for whom I had recently worked as a fact-checker—I got my first break, publishing a short feature about Argentina's growing drug trade in *Foreign Policy*. The piece caught the eye of Dan Rosenheck, an editor and former Argentina correspondent at the *Economist*. Dan and Mike Reid, the paper's veteran America's editor, gave me the opportunity of a lifetime: to try out as the *Economist*'s Argentina and Uruguay correspondent. Both Dan and Mike were extremely patient as I handed in articles that were double the paper's famously tight word limit and, after a few months on trial, I got the job.

It was a young journalist's dream posting; the news never stopped. Cristina Fernández de Kirchner was president and was locked in fierce fights against her two biggest enemies: Clarín and the economy. She banned Argentines from exchanging their rapidly devaluing pesos for dollars, prompting people to rush to *cuevas*, black-market exchange houses that emerged to buy and sell dollars at a premium. Dogs normally used to detect bombs were trained to sniff out the ink used by the US Mint and deployed to airports to catch Argentines smuggling greenbacks in and out of the country. Not long after that, the Vatican selected Jorge Mario Bergoglio, an Argentine, to lead the Catholic Church as Pope Francis I. I visited the *villas* in Buenos Aires where he'd begun his ecclesiastical career, talking to local priests about his early days and exploring the Argentine Church's complicity in the dictatorship.

Then, in 2013, Jorge Rafael Videla died. The obituary I eventually published in the *Economist* read:

> In what Videla called a "Process of National Reorganisation," Argentines deemed threatening were kidnapped, imprisoned, tortured and killed. Suspects were snatched from their families, subjected to electric shocks, starved, beaten, raped, and held underwater for minutes at a time. Others were pushed out of military aircraft into the River Plate or the Atlantic

to drown. Abducted mothers were separated from their babies, who were sometimes adopted by the military officers responsible for their capture.

(Now, for what it's worth, I would use the word "stolen" instead of "adopted.")

For a foreigner living in Argentina in 2013, the scars from such horrors were often well hidden. Buenos Aires is an enchanting place—pulsing with energy, lush with tall trees, and scented by smoldering charcoal from ubiquitous barbecues of cow parts I didn't even know existed. Perusing the charming antique stores of San Telmo or savoring empanadas at a frozen-in-time *bodegón* in Palermo, it was easy to forget the city had once been host to unthinkable terror.

But some piece of news would inevitably puncture the reverie, reminding me that the wounds from the dictatorship still festered. One day, shortly before Videla died, Argentine media reported that Jorge Luis Magnacco, the gynecologist who had delivered Guillermo and other babies in the ESMA, had violated his house arrest to take his wife shopping at a posh mall where I sometimes got coffee with sources. The next year, in 2014, Abuelas president Estela de Carlotto found her grandson after thirty-six years of relentless searching. Trials—including one over the disappearance of Estela's daughter—were ongoing.

In 2015, I left Argentina, moving to London and then Los Angeles to continue working for the *Economist*. But I never forgot the stolen babies and the tenacious grandmothers who searched for them. When I got pregnant for the first time in 2020, their story suddenly flooded back to me. By then I had left the *Economist* to focus on feature writing and had more bandwidth to pursue longer projects. I began talking to friends, many of whom had studied history in college, as I had, and was surprised by how few were familiar with the Abuelas and their stolen grandchildren. The burst of nervous energy that makes my stomach clench and my hands shake when I stumble on an idea I want to pursue hit me more intensely than ever before. The book I'd wanted to read back in 2011, I now desperately wanted to write.

I officially began this project in February 2021, when I was six months pregnant with my first daughter. COVID was still raging, and vaccines were only just starting to trickle out. Argentina was closed to tourists until November. When it reopened, I was on one of the first flights into the country, with my mercifully cooperative four-month-old strapped to my chest.

During that first trip, I met Rosa in her cozy apartment in Congreso. Her sharp wit made it easy to forget, but she was 102 years old. Estela, whom I thought of as a spring chicken in comparison, was in her nineties. Many other Abuelas had already passed away by the time I began this project. While I managed to connect with almost all of those who were still living, they didn't always recall the details I asked them about. Remembering events from forty years ago is no easy feat for anyone, let alone for someone in their nineties or, in Rosa's case, hundreds.

As my reporting progressed, COVID constraints loosened, but other challenges took their place. In 2022, I got pregnant again—a beautiful and blessed life experience, but not one that particularly facilitates international reporting. I often kicked myself for not having the idea to write this book sooner, back when I lived in Argentina between 2011 and 2015, before I had children or a spouse I dreaded being apart from, and when many more Abuelas were healthy. But it would have been a different book—both because of all that has happened in Argentina over the past ten years, and because my relationship to the story is different now that I'm a parent.

Perhaps the thorniest struggle I faced during this project was deciding where to focus. I heard and read so many incredible—and terrible—stories over my four years reporting this book. There was Victoria Donda, whose navy officer uncle was accused of turning in his own brother—Victoria's father—and who spoke movingly about her enduring love for her appropriator, even after learning that he had tortured and killed. "Love is not like a tap you can turn on and off," she told me in her office in Buenos Aires in December 2022. Or the saga of Manuel Gonçalves Granada (who had previously gone by Claudio Novoa), whose mother saved his life when he was an infant by shoving him in a closet after their house was attacked, and who later discovered that the bassist from the famous band Los Pericos, whom he had grown up idolizing, was in fact his half brother. I was also moved by the experience of Ximena Vicario, who, as an adolescent, had been traumatized by the public firestorm surrounding her case. Years later, she ended up marrying another grandchild located by the Abuelas—perhaps not coincidentally, someone whose story had been equally sensationalized by the media. No less poignant was the story of Tatiana Britos, who, along with her younger sister, was one of the first grandchildren located by the Abuelas. Tatiana grew up to work for the organization as a psychologist, helping recently recovered grandchildren wrestle with their new identities.

All of these stories deserve book-length treatment and, due to the context, omitting anyone's story felt like disappearing them. I sometimes worried that focusing on one family more than the others was incongruent with the collective spirit that had given the Abuelas their power. But I also knew that trying to tell the stories of all of the Abuelas' stolen grandchildren would mean not doing justice to any of them. Repetition can dull the reader's senses and breed jadedness. I felt confident that focusing on one family would be the best way to convey the impact of the Abuelas' story. Along with the need to eat, sleep, and drink, family is one of the only common denominators that unites us all. I felt that the deeper I could delve into one family's story, the more the reader would connect with the grander history of the Abuelas.

After several months of reporting, I decided to pursue the Roisinblit family's story. Rosa had been at the center of the Abuelas movement since its early days, serving as treasurer from 1983 to 1989 and vice president from 1989 to 2022. Not only had she found her grandchild, but she had found him in the hands of a man who was directly implicated in the horrors of the dictatorship.

I knew Guillermo's relationship with his biological family was complicated—a fact that made Guillermo nervous, particularly after he joined the Abuelas' board in 2022. He didn't want his bumpy journey to scare off others with doubts about their identities from coming forward to the Abuelas. He was particularly concerned about how a book might frame his relationship struggles with Mariana. There were many other rosier stories, he pointed out, like Delia Giovanola's. When I visited with Delia, a delightfully impish woman, before her death in 2022, she WhatsApped with her grandson throughout our five-hour meeting, sending him a selfie of us at the café where we had lunch. It was clear that they were in constant contact.

But the complexity of the Roisinblits' story was precisely why I found it so powerful. Guillermo resisted his identity and the Abuelas for many years; now he has joined the organization's board, carrying forward their fight. I wanted to understand how that transformation happened. It struck me as an extreme manifestation of a recurring pattern in many of the Abuelas' cases: even the grandchildren who had most stridently resisted accepting their new identities—like Ezequiel Rochistein Tauro, who had evaded DNA testing for nearly a decade—eventually seemed to embrace the truth. While I dreaded the idea of writing anything that might further inflame tensions between Guillermo and Mariana, their problems, too, seemed emblematic of something larger. Theirs is not a typical family feud. As Mariana herself said in her testimony in the RIBA Trial, the dictatorship "destroyed [her] family, in a destruction that continues to today." Recently, one of her followers on social media suggested that perhaps if the "killers and baby thieves" had not interfered, Mariana and Guillermo might have been best friends. "We'll never know," Mariana responded.

I didn't realize it at the time, but my first meeting with Rosa in November 2021 would be our only one. Before I could travel down for another reporting trip, she'd moved into an assisted living home. When I asked if I could go see her there, Guillermo said she was not in a condition to give interviews, adding: "She's done enough already." As much as I wanted to speak with Rosa again, I didn't feel it would be ethical to push—and I wasn't sure how much doing so would accomplish. Guillermo himself said he'd stopped asking Rosa about his parents and her search for them around 2018. It was too painful for her, and her memories were blurrier than before. To make up for it, I read, watched, and listened to every interview of Rosa's I could find, and spent a full week in La Plata combing through her personal archive at the Comisión Provincial por la Memoria before it was officially opened to the public, poring over old photographs, legal documents, travel notebooks, and correspondence until I had seen every document in all thirty-one boxes.

I also had exclusive access to another particularly special document: Guillermo's Archivo Biográfico Familiar, or Biographical Family Archive. As I have detailed in these pages, since 1998, the Abuelas have gathered extensive oral histories for each of their stolen grandchildren to help them learn about their disappeared parents. Guillermo sent me a digital copy of his archive in June of 2022 after we'd spoken about ten times. A 317-page compilation of interviews with nineteen friends and family members who had known José and Patricia, the archive was packed with vivid anecdotes. Later, Guillermo would express ambivalence about having shared his archive with me. He told me that he had previously thought of the document as something that was his to do as he pleased with. But when he spoke to other members of the Abuelas, they suggested that the archive was meant for his family only, and that the people who had been interviewed for it spoke without necessarily intending for their words to be public. Guillermo never asked me not to use the archive, but I tried to be sensitive to this situation, reaching out to the participants to reinterview them where I could.

Mariana declined to participate in this project, suggesting that she didn't have anything to add to what Guillermo might have told me and that, if I was interested in her side of the story, I should consult *Diario de una princesa montonera*. (Guillermo was not interviewed for Rosa's biography, *Abuela*, which Mariana did participate in.) She asked me not to contact her again after I initially reached out. I respected that wish until the fact-checking stage, when I offered her the opportunity to review the facts related to her story, which I drew mostly from her own writing, court testimony, and interviews she'd granted. She did not respond. Through Comisión Provincial por la Memoria, she did, however, generously grant her permission to use several photos from her grandmother's archive.

I am an incorrigible empath, and when I sometimes grew anxious about telling a painful and intimate family story where not all the family members had spoken to me, I returned to something Rosa had told me as, seated at her dining table, surrounded by photos from her past, I asked her about her hopes for the future.

"I will die, I will die. That's it. I already accomplished everything I could in my life," she said unflinchingly, her manicured hands folded in her lap. "I have always told my story exactly as it is. Nothing more. The truth, before everything."

List of Grandchildren Located by the Abuelas de Plaza de Mayo (as of February 2025)

L isted according to the order in which they were located.

NUMBER	YEAR OF RESTITUTION	FIRST NAME	LAST NAME	NOTES
1	1978	Emiliano Damián	Ginés Scotto	located after his death
2	1979	Anatole Boris	Julien Grisonas	
3	1979	Victoria Eva	Julien Grisonas	
4	1980	Tatiana Mabel	Ruarte Britos	
5	1980	Laura Malena	Jotar Britos	
6	1983	Tamara Ana María	Arze	
7	1983	Martín	Baamonde	
8	1983	Humberto Ernesto	Colautti Fransicetti	
9	1983	Noemí Elena	Ferri Fransicetti	
10	1983	Sebastián	Rosenfeld Marcuzzo	
11	1983	Eduardo	Garbarino Pico	
12	1983		Carpintero - Gatti Casal	died in utero
13	1983	Ana Laura	Hisi	

NUMBER	YEAR OF RESTITUTION	FIRST NAME	LAST NAME	NOTES
14	1984	Bárbara	Lanuscou	
15	1984	Roberto	Lanuscou	
16	1984	Liliana	Bau Delgado	
17	1984	Marina Leonor	Bau Delgado	
18	1984	Juan Pablo	Moyano	
19	1984	Astrid	Patiño Carabelli	
20	1984	Federico Luis	Spoturno	
21	1984	Diego Tomás	Mendizábal Zermoglio	
22	1984	Sebastián Ariel	Santillán Juárez	
23	1984	Paula Eva	Logares	
24	1984	Felipe Martín	Gatica Caracoche	
25	1984	Jorgelina Paula	Molina Planas	
26	1985	Amaral	García Hernández	
27	1985	Carla Graciela	Rutila Artés	
28	1985	María Eugenia	Gatica Caracoche	
29	1985	María Fernanda	Álvarez	
30	1986	Esteban Javier	Badell Acosta	
31	1986	Paula Eliana	Badell Acosta	
32	1986	Ramón Ángel	Pintos	
33	1986	Laura Ernestina	Scaccheri Dorado	
34	1986	Marcos Lino	Moscato	
35	1986	Ximena	Vicario	
36	1986	Paula	Orlando Cancela	
37	1987	Elena	Gallinari Abinet	
38	1987	María José	Lavalle Lemos	
39	1987	Gabriela Alejandra	Gallardo	
40	1988	María Victoria	Moyano Artigas	
41	1988	Hugo Camilo	Ducca	
42	1989		Gayá - Pérez	died in utero

NUMBER	YEAR OF RESTITUTION	FIRST NAME	LAST NAME	NOTES
43	1989	Marcelo Mariano	Ruiz Dameri	
44	1989	Gonzalo Javier	Reggiardo Tolosa	
45	1989	Matías Ángel	Reggiardo Tolosa	
46	1991	Mariana	Zaffaroni Islas	
47	1993		Santilli - Olivier	died in utero
48	1993	José Sabino	Abdala Falabella	
49	1994	María Alejandra	Fuente Alcober	
50	1994	Stella Maris	Fuente Alcober	
51	1994	Raúl Roberto	Fuente Alcober	
52	1994	Carlos	D'Elía Casco	
53	1995	Emiliano Carlos	Castro Tortrino	
54	1995		Franco - Carlevari	died in utero
55	1995		Iwanski - Cabot	died in utero
56	1996	Laura Fernanda	Acosta	
57	1997	Manuel	Gonçalves Granada	
58	1998	Paula	Cortassa Zapata	
59	1998	Javier Gonzalo	Penino Viñas	
60	1999		Bronzel - Pedrini	died in utero
61	1999	Andrea Viviana	Hernández Hobbas	
62	1999	María de las Mercedes	Gallo Sanz	
63	1999	María de las Victorias	Ruiz Dameri	
64	1999	Claudia Victoria	Poblete Hlaczik	
65	2000	Andrés	La Blunda Fontana	
66	2000	Hilda Victoria	Montenegro	
67	2000	Macarena Gelman	García Iruretagoyena	
68	2000	Guillermo Rodolfo Fernando	Pérez Roisinblit	
69	2000	Martín Tomás	Castro Rocchi	

NUMBER	YEAR OF RESTITUTION	FIRST NAME	LAST NAME	NOTES
70	2000	Gabriel Matías	Cevasco	
71	2001	María Eugenia	Sampallo Barragán	
72	2002	Simón Antonio	Gatti Méndez	
73	2003		Castro - Barrios	died in utero
74	2003	Susana	Coloma Larrubia	
75	2003	Horacio	Pietragalla Corti	
76	2003	Gustavo	Godoy Ferreyra	
77	2004	Juan	Cabandié Alfonsín	
78	2004		Libralato - Fonrouge	died in utero
79	2004	Victoria	Donda Pérez	
80	2004	Pedro Luis	Nadal García	
81	2005	Leonardo	Fossati Ortega	
82	2006	Sebastián José	Casado Tasca	
83	2006	Natalia Suárez	Nelson Corvalán	
84	2006	Alejandro Pedro	Sandoval Fontana	
85	2006	Marcos	Suárez Vedoya	
86	2007	Pablo Hernán	Casariego Tato	
87	2007	Silvina Celina Rebeca	Manrique Terrera	
88	2007	Belén Estefanía	Altamiranda Taranto	
89	2008	Evelin	Bauer Pegoraro	
90	2008	Laura Carla	Ruiz Dameri	
91	2008	Milagros	Castelli Trotta	
92	2008	Carlos Alberto	Goya Martínez Aranda	
93	2008	Silvia Alejandra	Cugura Casado	
94	2008	Laura Catalina	De Sanctis Ovando	
95	2008	Federico	Cagnola Pereyra	
96	2008	Sabrina	Valenzuela Negro	
97	2009	Bárbara	García Recchia	

NUMBER	YEAR OF RESTITUTION	FIRST NAME	LAST NAME	NOTES
98	2009	Guillermo	Amarilla Molfino	
99	2009	Mónica Graciela	Santucho	
100	2009	Matías Nicolás	Espinosa Valenzuela	
101	2010	Francisco	Madariaga Quintela	
102	2010	Ezequiel	Rochistein Tauro	
103	2011	María Pía Josefina	Klotzman Barral	
104	2011		Rossetti - Ross	died in utero
105	2011	Florencia Laura	Reinhold Siver	
106	2012	Pablo Javier	Gaona Miranda	
107	2012		Moreno	
108	2012		Malnati - Coutouné	died in utero
109	2013	Pablo Germán	Athanasiu Laschan	
110	2014	Valeria	Gutiérrez Acuña	
111	2014		Vega Ceballos - Romero	died in utero
112	2014		Tion - Tierra	died in utero
113	2014		Ford - De Olaso	died in utero
114	2014	Ignacio	Montoya Carlotto	
115	2014	Ana Libertad	Baratti De La Cuadra	
116	2014	Jorge	Castro Rubel	
117	2015	Claudia	Domínguez Castro	
118	2015	Martín	Ogando Montesano	
119	2015	Mario Daniel	Navarro	
120	2016	José Luis	Maulin Pratto	
121	2016	Maximiliano	Menna Lanzillotto	
122	2017	José	Bustamante García	
123	2017		Amarilla - Benítez	died in utero

NUMBER	YEAR OF RESTITUTION	FIRST NAME	LAST NAME	NOTES
124	2017		Urra Ferrarese - Ossola	died in utero
125	2017	Lucila	Tartaglia	
126	2017	Adriana	Garnier Ortolani	
127	2017	Miriam	Poblete Moyano	
128	2019	Marcos Eduardo	Ramos	
129	2019	Marcela	Solsona Síntora	
130	2019	Javier Matías	Darroux Mijalchuk	
131	2022		Quevedo Nadín	
132	2022	Juan José	Morales	
133	2023	Daniel	Santucho Navajas	
134	2023		Sofía - Vargas	died in utero
135	2023		Scapuzzi - Girardi	died in utero
136	2023		Uncal - Farías	died in utero
137	2023		Rodríguez - Vaccarini	died in utero
138	2024		Villamayor - Portalé	
139	2025		Inama - Macedo	

List of Grandchildren Still Sought by the Abuelas de Plaza de Mayo (as of February 2025)

FIRST NAME	LAST NAME OF BABY	SUSPECTED BIRTHDATE	NOTES
	Agüero - Gómez	March–April 1978	
	Agüero - López	March 1978	
	Agüero - Porcel	January–February 1977	
	Aguirre - Monasterolo	October–November 1976	
	Aguirre - Noce	May 1977	
Mónica Silvia	Alarcón	August 11, 1975	*Disappeared February 26, 1977
Paula Noemí	Albornoz Musacchio	August 1977	*Disappeared January 1978
	Almada - Spotti	November 1977	
	Alonso - Greca	June–July 1977	
	Amono - Bayoni	July–August 1977	
Clara	Anahí Mariani	August 12, 1976	*Disappeared November 24, 1976
	Araldi - Oesterheld	November 1976	
Pablo Daniel Alejandro	Aranda	May 26, 1973	
	Aranda - Duarte	April–May 1978	
	Araoz - Echevarría	September–December 1976	

FIRST NAME	LAST NAME OF BABY	SUSPECTED BIRTHDATE	NOTES
	Arcuschin - Jansenson	April 1977	
	Argüello	July–August 1977	
	Arias - Ormeño	Mid-March 1977	
	Arin - Cuadrelli	March 1977	
	Astorga - Pérez	September 1976	
	Aued - Medici	February–March 1978	
	Ayastuy - Bugnone	March–August 1978	
	Balbuena - Raggio	November 1976	
	Barboza - Ibañez	April–May 1978	
	Basanta - Grillo	April 1977	
	Battistiol - Colayago	November–December 1977	
Cristian Daniel	Becker Barrera	March 13, 1975	*Disappeared June 27, 1975
	Beláustegui Herrera - López Guerra	February–March 1977	
	Benito Choque - Peña	March–April 1977	
	Betelu	August–September 1977	
	Boca	April–July 1976	
	Bocco - Hynes	December 1976–January 1977	
	Buenanueva	June 14, 1976	
	Busemi - Gofín	April 1980	
Claudio Néstor	Caielli Aiub	May 20, 1977	*Disappeared June 19, 1977
	Calabozo - Ferrari	May–June 1977	
	Calleja - Capelli	October–December 1977	
	Cañete - Simerman	November 1977	
	Capella - Arzani	March–April 1977	
	Carballo - Ruiz	February 24, 1976	
	Caro - Assadourian	September–November 1976	
	Carranza - Goeytes	March 1977	
	Carrera - Bonoldi	June–July 1977	

FIRST NAME	LAST NAME OF BABY	SUSPECTED BIRTHDATE	NOTES
	Casanovas - Casello	July–August 1977	
	Castagna - Real Meiners	January 1977	
	Castro - Stritzler	January 1977	
	Cativiela - Prado	June 1977	
	Catnich - Landaburu	October 1977	
	Cena - La Spina	November 1976	
	Chertkoff	February 1976	
	Chirino - Vera	April–May 1978	
	Cian - Soto	December 1976	
	Cisterna	February 1978	
	Clerc - Álvaro	February 1977	
	Cortassa - Zapata	February 1977	
	Corvalán - Delgado	January 1977	
	Courau - Di Cianni	December 1976	
	Cristi Melero - Delard Cabezas	July 1977	
	Cugura - Cayul	June 1978	
	D'Ambra Villares	1976–1977	
	Darroux - Mijalchuk	July 1978	
	De Angeli - Garin	August 1977	
	De Angeli - Godoy	June–July 1978	
	Delgado - Busaniche	February 1978	
	Della Flora	October–November 1977	
	Deria - Vaccaro	January–February 1979	
	Díaz - Alaniz	November 1977	
	Dopazo - Altmann Levy	January 1978	
	Duarte - González	September–October 1977	
	Duclós - Sciutto	September–October 1976	
	Elía - Álvarez	May–June 1978	
	Eroles - Martínez	October–November 1978	

FIRST NAME	LAST NAME OF BABY	SUSPECTED BIRTHDATE	NOTES
	Espín - Torres	September–October 1976	
	Estévez - Funes	February–March 1978	
	Ferreyra	Before July 1977	
	Ferreyra - Luque	August–October 1978	
	Fina - Carlucci	November 1976	
	Fornies - Fariñas	December 1975–February 1976	
	Fortunato - Vacas	November–December 1977	
	Fote - García	December 1977–January 1978	
	Fraga - Grynberg	April 1977	
	Fraga - Paolucci	December 1978–March 1979	
	Fresneda - Argañaraz	October–November 1977	
	Frías - Casado	July–August 1978	
	Galizzi - Baravalle	December 1976–January 1977	
	Galli - Flynn	December 1977–January 1978	
	Garack - Lenain	September–October 1977	
	Garaycochea - Delgado Lizaso	February–March 1977	
	García - Galansky	May–June 1978	
	García - Zelarayan	May 1976	
	García Cano - Quesada	January 1978	
	Garralda - Izurieta	January–February 1977	
	Goldín - Molina	September 1977	
	Gómez	January–February 1977	
	Gómez García - Amarilla	July–August 1977	
	Gomila - Tedesco	January 1978	
	González	January 1977	
	González - Garasa	April 1977	

FIRST NAME	LAST NAME OF BABY	SUSPECTED BIRTHDATE	NOTES
	González - Mazer	December 1976–February 1977	
	Gorga	August–September 1977	
	Grandi - Cournou	November–December 1976	
	Gualdero	June 1976	
	Gudiño - Domínguez	May–June 1977	
	Guede - De Angelis	May–June 1977	
	Guzmán - Frías	May 31, 1976	
Beatriz Lourdes	Hernández Hobbas	February 23, 1961	*Disappeared July 5, 1977
Washington Fernando	Hernández Hobbas	March 24, 1962	*Disappeared July 6, 1977
	Hidalgo - Souto	1976	
	Ibarra - Sosa	May 1977	
	Ignace - Martínez	October 1977	
	Ingegnieros - Pompa	October–November 1977	
	Iturriza - Nusbaum	November–December 1977	
	Iula - Schand	November–December 1978	
	Jakowczyk - Correa Llano	November 1976	
	Jeger - González	September–December 1975	
	Jerez Bordereau - Huarte	November–December 1976	
	Junquera - González	June 1977	
	Jurmussi - Lizarraga	December 1976–January 1977	
	Kofman - Fernández	December 1977–January 1978	
	Lagrutta - Coutada	November–December 1976	
	Laguado Duca - Moreno	March–April 1977	
Matilde	Lanuscou	March 30, 1976	*Disappeared September 4, 1976

FIRST NAME	LAST NAME OF BABY	SUSPECTED BIRTHDATE	NOTES
	Larrieu - Muñoz	July–August 1977	
	Ledesma - Muñoz	December 1978	
	Lescano - Quinteros	November 1976	
	Logares - Grinspon	1978–1979	
	López	June–July 1976	
	López - Feldman	October–November 1977	
	López Mateos - Isabella Valenzi	April 2, 1977	
	López Torres - Capoccetti	December 1977–January 1978	
	Lorusso Lämmle	December 1976	
	Lugones Casinelli - Vásquez Ocampo	January 1977	
	Luzi - Vega	September 1976	
	Machado - González	November–December 1976	
	Maldonado - Molina	November 1979	
	Mancebo	September 1977	
	Mangone - Rapela	October–November 1977	
	Manuele - Ravignani	February 1977	
	Marciano - Mora	November–December 1978	
	Marizcurrena - Caimi	February 1977	
	Marocchi - Valor	March–April 1977	
	Martínez - Pardo	January–February 1977	
	Martínez - Traficante	November–December 1977	
	Martínez - Wlichky	May–June 1977	
	Martinis - Neuhaus	August 1976	
	Medina - Pérez Rey	November–December 1977	
	Mena - Álvarez	April–June 1976	
	Mendoza - Segarra	December 1978–January 1979	
	Mercado	March–April 1976	

FIRST NAME	LAST NAME OF BABY	SUSPECTED BIRTHDATE	NOTES
María	Mercedes Barrera	March 29, 1979	*Disappeared June 27, 1979
	Metz - Romero	April 17, 1977	
	Michelena - De Gouveia	Before March 1978	
Pablo Antonio	Míguez	March 1, 1963	*Disappeared May 12, 1977
	Mirabelli - Nardone	Before August 1979	
	Molina - Falco	October 1978	
	Molina Cuello - Silva	July–August 1976	
	Montes - Dithurbide	April–June 1977	
	Mora - González	April–June 1977	
	Morales - Sans	June–July 1977	
	Morales Von Pieverling - Keim Lledó	May–June 1977	
	Moyano - Navarro	April 1977	
	Moyano - Paulone	January–February 1977	
	Núñez	Mid-1977–Early 1978	
	Ochoa - Blanc	May–June 1977	
	Olmedo - Pujol	March 1977	
	Orona - Leiva	May 1977	
	Orozco - Parodi	June 14, 1976	
	Orzábal - Resnicoff	December 1978–January 1979	
	Orzaocoa - Gómez	May–June 1975	
	Otaño - Manchiola	January–February 1977	
	Ovejero - Castillo Barrios	August–September 1977	
	Palacios - Kazgudenian	June–July 1977	
	Paniagua - Villanueva	May 1979	
	Parada - Cascella	September–October 1978	
	Pastor - Maurer	November–December 1977	
	Patiño - Moavro	March–April 1976	

FIRST NAME	LAST NAME OF BABY	SUSPECTED BIRTHDATE	NOTES
	Patrucco - Bargas	October 1976–February 1977	
	Paz - Chuburu	May–June 1977	
	Pedregosa - Carrizo	September–October 1976	
	Pedregosa - Losada Jimenez	November–December 1977	
	Pellegrini - Luque	November–December 1977	
	Pérez Weiss - Carbonell	January 1977	
	Petrakos - Castellini	April 8–12, 1977	
	Petricca - Lescaray	March–April 1977	
	Placci - Garófalo	May–July 1977	
	Poyastro - Monari	May–June 1977	
	Prieto - Gutiérrez	November 1976	
	Pucheta - Novillo Corvalán	November–December 1976	
	Quevedo - González	June 1975	
	Quintana	April–May 1977	
	Quiroga - Jatib	February–March 1977	
	Ramos - Cerrotta	June–July 1977	
	Rawa Jasinski - Rodríguez	August–September 1977	
	Reale - Baronio	December 1977–January 1978	
	Redel - Viñales	October–November 1976	
	Repetur - Carriquiriborde	December 1976	
	Reynoso - Lescano	January–February 1977	
	Rincón - Maroni	November–December 1977	
	Rivada - Loperena	September–October 1977	
	Robledo - Angerosa	August 1978	
	Robles - Pasatir	1976	
	Rodríguez	August–September 1977	
	Rodríguez - Gerelli	January 1979	

FIRST NAME	LAST NAME OF BABY	SUSPECTED BIRTHDATE	NOTES
	Rodríguez - Santamaría	January 1977	
	Roggerone - Masri	October–November 1977	
	Rojas - Gómez	August–September 1977	
	Roldán - Garaguso	March–April 1977	
	Román	February 1977	
	Romero - Britos	June 1977	
	Rondoletto - Bermejo	March–April 1977	
	Rosemberg - Taboada	Before February 1977	
	Saieg - Roncelli	April 1978	
	Salvatierra	November 1976	
	Sánchez - Ibarra	October 1977	
	Sandoval - Zarza	May 1978	
	Santucho - Delfino	September 1976–April 1977	
	Saun - Farías	July 1976	
	Seindlis - Oesterheld	December 1977–January 1978	
	Serra - Barahona	December 1977–January 1978	
	Sgarbossa - Rojas	June–August 1976	
	Sidaravicius	August 20–21, 1976	
	Silva - Beneyto	October–November 1977	
	Simonetti - Cáceres	September 1977	
	Sobral - Cicero	May–June 1977	
	Soldati - Jiménez	December 1977–January 1978	
	Soler - Moreno	July 1977–February 1978	
	Speranza	April–May 1977	
	Stockdale - Cobo	March–April 1977	
	Suárez - Veiga	February–April 1977	
	Suárez - Villa	February–March 1977	
	Tamburini - Magnet	January–February 1977	

FIRST NAME	LAST NAME OF BABY	SUSPECTED BIRTHDATE	NOTES
	Tapia Contardo - Chelpa	July–August 1977	
	Testi - Morabito	October–November 1977	
	Toranzo - Palacín	September–October 1978	
	Torres	August–October 1976	
	Torres - Segarra	June–July 1978	
	Urtasun - Silveira Gramont	February 1979	
	Uzin - Lijtman	September–October 1977	
	Valenzuela - Negro	Early March 1978	
	Valledor - Castilla	January–February 1978	
	Valledor - Lavalle	May 4, 1977	
	Vargas - Noriega	May–July 1977	
	Vázquez	October–November 1977	
	Velázquez - Carrieri	September 1977	
	Vergara - Ferrer	November 1977–January 1978	
	Villanueva - Valdueza	September–October 1976	
	Vivanco - Abdala	August–September 1975	
	Vivas - De Armas	February–May 1977	
	Waisberg - Beláustegui Herrera	December 1977	
Carlos Osvaldo	Woodley	July 8, 1975	
	Zaffaroni Castilla - Islas Gatti	March–April 1977	
	Zalazar - Peralta	August–November 1976	
	Zeitlin	January–February 1978	

Acknowledgments

As Robert Crassweller so eloquently put it in the opening of his fantastic biography of Perón: books "represent a greater venture in collaboration than the name of a single author would suggest." Many people helped me during the four years it took to report and write this book—both directly and indirectly.

First, I'd like to thank the many Abuelas, grandchildren, scientists, lawyers, historians, judges, and diplomats who spoke to me as I was reporting. I often felt guilty asking Abuelas like Delia Giovanola, Sonia Torres, Elsa Pavón, Estela de Carlotto, and Rosa Roisinblit to relive the darkest moments of their lives. But invariably, they responded with warmth, expressing gratitude that I was sharing their stories with audiences who might not be aware of them. When I ran into reporting challenges or the words just wouldn't come, it was their encouragement that propelled me forward.

Two people in particular stand out for their generosity in the reporting process: Guillermo Roisinblit and Mary-Claire King. Guillermo invited me into his home several times, spent tens of hours talking to me by Zoom, introduced me to his therapist, gamely responded to over three hundred queries during fact-checking, and, as I previously mentioned in "About This Book," generously shared his Biographical Family Archive. Amid her lifesaving work, Dr. King carved out full days to speak with me, inviting me to her lab in Seattle and building time into her busy New York City trips to meet with me in hotel rooms across Manhattan. Our shortest interview lasted three and a half hours. The longest was nine. After that, I learned to prepare for our meetings like a marathon runner might get ready for a race, packing calorie-dense snacks, an external phone charger, and my largest water bottle. (At seventy-eight, she had far more stamina than I did.)

Pablo Wybert was a huge help in connecting me to grandchildren the Abuelas had found. Other Abuelas associates were similarly generous. To weave together this narrative, I relied heavily on legal documents granted to me by the Abuelas' lawyers. I am particularly indebted to Pablo Lachener, who allowed me to download recordings of the RIBA Trial and related documents early in my reporting process. Carolina Villella and Emanuel Lovelli were also helpful, answering my many legal questions and sharing relevant resources, including Carolina's powerful thesis "Apropiación de Niños y Niñas Durante el Terrorismo de Estado en Argentina." Mariana Herrera, the director of the BNDG, was also a pivotal source, touring me around the laboratory and answering many follow-up questions by phone and WhatsApp.

Four archives and their committed archivists were also indispensable in the writing of this book: Marcelo Castillo oriented me at the Archivo Nacional de la Memoria, a state-run archive that contains the CONADEP files and the CLAMOR papers. Carina Carrizo at Memoria Abierta, an alliance of Argentine human rights organizations, sent me dozens of hours of oral testimony from Abuelas, Madres, and torture survivors. Daniela Drucaroff, Paula Erijman, Ana Laura Sucari, Matteo Maiorana, and the rest of the Abuelas archivists were endlessly generous with their time and energy, allowing me to invade their space for weeks as I sifted through dozens of boxes of newspaper clippings, legal filings, and testimony. Finally, Magdalena Lanteri, Virginia Sampietro, Ingrid Jaschek, and Julieta Sahade at the Comisión Provincial por La Memoria in La Plata kindly opened up the Rosa Roisinblit personal archive to me even before they'd officially categorized it.

I must also thank David Millikin, a journalist at the AFP, for tracking down archival newswires and for putting me in contact with former AFP photographer Daniel García, who so generously allowed me to use his epic photo of the Madres and Abuelas in a flooded Plaza de Mayo as the book's cover image. My jaw dropped when the design team showed me their proposal for the first time. García's photo perfectly encapsulates the unwavering commitment of the Madres and Abuelas, and I'm so grateful to him for sharing it. I am also indebted to the Gelman family for allowing me to use "Epitafio," the poem that gives this book its title, and to Ilan Stavans for his beautiful translation.

Mica Duek's research help was invaluable. She efficiently chased down newspaper articles from various archives, helped me wrangle legal documents, and once visited the Abuelas Archive on my behalf. (She was also my designated Argentine slang decoder because, even after four years of residency, the country's *jerga* still eludes me sometimes.) Paola Santos, a talented student journalist at Yale, helped me research how various buildings looked at the time I was writing about them and compiled the list of grandchildren the Abuelas continue to search for. I am also grateful to have had the assistance of Josie Reich, another brilliant Yale journalist, in the prepublication phase. And, in Argentina, I must thank my friend Raul for the long hours helping me dash between interviews in Buenos Aires, the *conurbano*, La Plata, and beyond.

I also want to recognize several people I know primarily through their writing, with Crassweller himself being a good example. I read over 150 books and hundreds more academic articles in the course of writing this one, but certain works were particularly fundamental. Marcela Bublik's *Abuela*, Rosa Roisinblit's biography, was one such book. Marcela wrote a beautiful testament to Rosa that was published in 2013. She also included a great deal of raw testimony, which was extremely helpful for my purposes. Rita Arditti's work was also pivotal. After publishing *Searching for Life*, the only other English-language book about the Abuelas, Rita sadly passed away of cancer. While organizing Rita's drawers, her life partner, Estelle, found the cassette tapes of Rita's interviews with the Abuelas; Estelle generously donated the audio files and over five hundred pages of transcripts to the University of Massachusetts, making them accessible to other researchers. I read every page. These interviews were indispensable, and I only wish

I could thank Rita in person for her thoroughness in conducting them. Juan Martín Ramos Padilla's *Chicha*, Enrique Arrosagaray's *Biografía de Azucena Villaflor*, Ulises Gorini's *Rebelión de las Madres*, Uki Goñi's *El Infiltrado*, and Julio E. Nosiglia's *Botín de Guerra* were hugely important in my understanding of the early days of the Madres and Abuelas. Fabricio Laino's work on the Abuelas is unparalleled in its thoroughness, and he was incredibly generous to me during this process, speaking to me for hours and sending me various documents he'd collected during his own archival research. Enrique Arrosagaray was also very kind, connecting me with various sources, like Azucena Villaflor's daughter, Cecilia, and patiently answering my many questions about the history of the Madres. Ari Gandsman's thesis and academic work were also vital. *Ese Infierno*, a book that compiles conversations between ESMA survivors Munú Actis, Cristina Aldini, Liliana Gardella, Miriam Lewin, and Elisa Tokar, was critical to my understanding of the horrors perpetrated at the ESMA. Joseph Page's *Perón* and Crassweller's *Perón and the Enigmas of Argentina* helped me understand that I will never fully understand Peronism, and anyone who tells you they do is lying.

I am blessed with the best editorial team imaginable. Will Lippincott of Aevitas Creative is a wizard, and his fingerprints are all over this project; I am very grateful to Becky Sweren for introducing us, as well as for her years of patient support. Will is an incisive editor and powerful advocate, as well as a darn good friend. He led me to the perfect editor at the perfect publisher: Julianna Haubner at Avid Reader Press. During the sale process, he told me that picking an editor is like picking a spouse: when you know, you know. I didn't believe him until I met Julianna. Julianna is a whip-smart thinker and elegant stylist: her edits elevated this book immeasurably. Before this book was published, Julianna was given a great opportunity at another publishing house, and after that I was privileged to work with Jofie Ferrari-Adler and Carolyn Kelly to push the book over the finish line. I also want to thank Alexandra Primiani and Eva Kerins for their help in sharing the Abuelas' story with the widest audience possible; Meredith Vilarello, Caroline McGregor, Katya Wiegmann, Wendy Sheanin, Liv Stratman, Toi Crockett, Mary Nubla, Melissa Hurt, Mackenzie Hickey, and Kayla Dee for their marketing magic; Jessica Chin, Alicia Brancato, Allison Green, Cait Lamborne, and Ruth Lee-Mui for their keen attention to detail; Alison Forner, Clay Smith, and Sydney Newman for designing the cover and book of my dreams; Felice Javit and Matt Leish for their careful engagement with the manuscript; Paul J. Pugliese for his beautiful map; and finally, to Janet Byrne for her sharp copyediting and helpful suggestions and Rachael De-Shano for her eagle-eyed proofreading.

Vera Carothers meticulously fact-checked this book, and I am so grateful for her thoroughness, compassion, and committment. Bill Vourvoulias helped with several sections as well and was assiduous and thoughtful. Any errors that somehow snuck in are mine alone. (I ran short chunks of the science-heavy sections by Mary-Claire King herself, after we agreed that she would only offer factual corrections and not editorial suggestions; Mark Stoneking similarly reviewed my descriptions of his work with mitochondrial DNA.) I was also incredibly privileged to work with Gareth Cook, Kate Rodemann, Eli Mennerick, and Chaz Curet at Verto Literary, who were indispensable thought partners and cheerleaders in addition to being the kindest team around.

A year into reporting this book, I was offered my dream job to run the Yale Journalism Initiative, a program dedicated to empowering and equipping Yale students to become journalists. My own experience in the program gave me the confidence to pursue writing as a profession, and I am honored to be back supporting students in the same way I was supported by Mark Oppenheimer when I was an undergraduate. It's a privilege that the professors I long looked up to are now—wildly—my colleagues, and I feel lucky to have had their help during this process. Fred Strebeigh, one of the most generous and incisive writing teachers in the universe, read an early draft of the manuscript in its entirety, offering helpful feedback on pacing, tone, and how to strengthen the core themes. I credit both Fred and Anne Fadiman, another one of the world's most beautiful stylists and giving professors, with sparking my desire to become a writer. Anne, Sarah Stillman, and Sue Dominus offered helpful advice on navigating reporting challenges. Sue released her wonderful book, *The Family Dynamic*, a few months before mine and kindly shared her experiences along the way so the process didn't seem quite so intimidating. Carl Zimmer, an esteemed science writer for *The New York Times* and the author of fifteen books (yes, fifteen!), was kind enough to read through the scientific sections to make sure I wasn't making a buffoon of myself. I am grateful, too, to Steven Brill, Kate Bolick, Graeme Wood, George Levesque, and Jasmina Besirevic-Regan for their support and collegiality. Howard Dean and David Berg have been steadfast mentors since my student days, and I'm grateful for their guidance, which long ago morphed into true friendship. I must also thank the librarians at Sterling Memorial Library, which miraculously had nearly every book I needed for my research—including, to my surprise, Miguel Etchecolatz's self-published autobiography.

Katie Engelhart, Amanda Foreman, Graciela Mochkofsky, Henry Louis Gates Jr., and Patrick Radden Keefe kindly carved time out of their hectic lives to provide me with wise counsel. They are all brilliant writers and intellectuals, and I found great inspiration in their advice, just as I derive it from their incredible work. I am grateful, too, to my closest Argentine friend: Jorgelina do Rosario. Jorgelina is one of the sharpest and most driven reporters I know, and her clear-eyed feedback on the manuscript was indispensable. I am eternally indebted to Steve Coll, Mike Reid, and Dan Rosenheck not only for their thoughts about this project but for my whole career. Working for Steve as a fact-checker on *Private Empire* the summer before I moved to Argentina gave me a firsthand glimpse into the process of crafting excellent narrative nonfiction—and fueled my ambition to write something half as good in my lifetime. If Dan hadn't sent me a Facebook message back in 2012 asking me to try out for the *Economist* job, and Mike hadn't been such a patient teacher, I am not sure where I'd be or what I'd be doing. I am certain, though, that this book would not exist.

And last, but certainly not least, I want to thank my family and friends. My own abuela, Elizabeth, passed away at ninety-nine during the reporting of this project. Well into her eighties, she used to hoover up tomes by the likes of Robert Caro, Walter Isaacson, and Doris Kearns Goodwin. (She had too much to learn about the world, she insisted, to indulge in fiction.)

As I finished this book, I realized she had been the audience I was writing for all along. I'm sad she will never get to read it, but her influence is woven through its pages. Rosa reminded me so much of her. They shared the same endless curiosity, determination, commitment to honesty, love of culture, and thirst for travel. They were both women before their time. My grandma was a multi-hyphenate—an artist, a teacher, a mother of four. She spent many years as a Spanish professor at a small college in Pennsylvania, and she was the first to seed a love of the language in me, even if my pronunciation was never up to her lofty standards. I can still hear her voice as she drilled me in our kitchen. "Not pero, perro! *R-R-R-R-R*! Roll your tongue! Roll it!"

To my siblings, Austin, Lindsay, Jared, I love you. Thank you for tolerating me as I talked your ear off about this book—and in general. And thanks to my adopted family, Alex, Edwina, Isabella, and Tom, too. How lucky I am to have you. To newer friends, who have enriched my life with walks in the woods, winter beach romps, and parental playdates, making home feel like home, and particularly to my oldest ones, who have endured my jabbering about this project for years—thank you for your support. (A special note of gratitude to Soph, for accompanying G and me on my first reporting trip back to Argentina in 2021; to Jess and Ali, for eighteen years of friendship that feels like family; and to Ash for your long-distance sisterhood.)

Candy—thank you for saving us in countless childcare pinches and for your unflagging kindness. Apparently, there is a whole genre of jokes dedicated to mothers-in-law, but I don't get them. You are a dream and I am so grateful for you.

On the topic of childcare, this book would have been impossible without the support of Marta, whose warmth, commitment, and love for my daughters afforded me the mental and physical space to work. Thank you will never be enough. Humongous thanks also to Hilary, Sonia, Leslie, and Sandra.

To those daughters, G.E.G. and C.C.G.: Thank you for revealing new layers of love and for filling my days with gummy grins, blueberry stains, and healthy chaos. Thank you for brightening my reporting trips—G in person three times over, C once in utero—and my life. This story haunted me even before I became a parent, but becoming your mom deepened my visceral understanding of it. I can't say you accelerated my writing process, exactly, but you grounded me in ways I am endlessly grateful for and made sure that, despite the heaviness of my research, I still laughed every day. Books can be all-consuming endeavors—physically and emotionally. Parenting two toddlers while writing ensured that I never got sucked too far into the dark recesses of my head. I poured my heart into this book. But as much as I obsessed over every word, nothing mattered more to me than cuddling with you before bedtime, and that kept me sane.

To Jason: my earliest (and favorite) reader and the foundation upon which everything else in my life rests. Thank you for so carefully reading countless versions of this book—possibly as many as I have—and offering sharp edits and much-needed encouragement. Thank you for making approximately seventy thousand servings of crepes for the girls and coming on multiple reporting trips to Buenos Aires and for picking up the slack as I tried (and often failed) to juggle everything. And thank you, most of all, for building this life with me. It's more than I ever dared to hope for. I love you.

And finally, to my parents, Paula and Richard, whose love and support are gifts beyond measure. I know you would go—and have gone—to the ends of the earth for me (quite literally, when I lived in Argentina!) and for your grandchildren, showing us in countless ways that family is the heart of life. I'll never be able to thank you enough for all you've done for me, but here's a very small start: This book is dedicated to you.

A Note on Sources

This book is the fruit of hundreds of hours of original interviews and my consultation of thousands of hours of court recordings, tens and thousands of archival documents, and hundreds of academic papers and books. Every fact asserted in the book was carefully sourced and the manuscript was subsequently reviewed by professional fact-checkers, to whom I am endlessly grateful. If I mentioned that it rained one day, that is because I looked up historical weather records. Tree descriptions come from interviews, historical photos, or this very handy map of trees in Buenos Aires: https://buenosaires.gob.ar/espaciopublicoehigieneurbana/gestion-comunal/arbopedia/censo-y-mapa-de-arbolado. (Another helpful Buenos Aires map function allowed me to look at aerial photos from 1978 to confirm what buildings and trees were there at the time.) Quotes are derived from original interviews or secondary sources, as cited in the endnotes.

For clarity, I have chosen to refer to the Madres and Abuelas, as well as their grandchildren and disappeared children, by their first names. This is to avoid confusion in instances where members of a family share a last name. In most other scenarios, I refer to people by their last names.

As with any historical research project, I sometimes encountered conflicting accounts during my reporting. In those cases, I have selected the version that my research suggests was most plausible and explained any discrepancies in the endnotes.

There were a few instances in which I could not get my hands on a physical book and had to rely on electronic versions. I have followed *The Chicago Manual of Style*'s protocol for citing those, using chapter numbers instead of exact page numbers, which can differ between users due to text size.

Discerning readers of the endnotes will notice a heavy reliance on US government and journalistic sources in the first half of the book, which focuses on events prior to 1983. During the dictatorship, stringent press censorship meant that foreign outlets provided more accurate reporting on Argentina's internal affairs than local ones.

Readers might also notice something else: despite my best efforts, I did not personally interview any military officers related to this story. This was not for lack of trying. I was rejected by the Federal Penitentiary Service from speaking with Eduardo Acosta, Alfredo Astiz, and Juan Carlos Vázquez Sarmiento, all of whom were imprisoned during the years I reported this book. (In February 2025, as this book went to print, Vázquez Sarmiento passed away at the age of seventy-seven while on trial for the disappearance of Patricia Roisinblit and José Manuel Pérez Rojo.) I sent Jorge Luis Magnacco, the naval doctor who delivered Guillermo, several letters, and I handed his doorman in Buenos Aires a handwritten plea, but I received no response. Many of the other military and police actors mentioned in this book—Francisco Gómez, Jorge Rafael Videla, Miguel Etchecolatz, and Emilio Massera—died before I began reporting.

The manuscript draft I turned over for fact-checking had 3,657 endnotes. To save some trees, in this final version, I have not included endnotes for facts that can be easily found online.

Notes

SOURCE ABBREVIATIONS
AR AIAPM—Abuelas de Plaza de Mayo Institutional Archive
ANM—Archivo Nacional de La Memoria
CPM—Comisión Provincial por la Memoria
Plan Sistemático Trial—1351 – "FRANCO, Rubén O. y otros s/sustracción de menores de diez años"; 1499 – "VIDELA, Jorge Rafael s/supresión del estado civil de un menor de diez años"; 1584 – "AZIC, Juan Antonio s/delito de acción pública"; 1604 – "VAŇEK, Antonio y otros s/sustracción de menores de diez años"; 1730 – "RUFFO, Eduardo Alfredo s/inf. arts. 139, 146 y 293 en función del 292 del C.P."; 1772 – "GALLO, Víctor Alejandro s/inf. arts. 139, 146 y 293 del C.P."
RIBA Trial—Causa N° 3511/16, "GRAFFIGNA Omar Domingo Rubens y otros s/privación ilegal de la libertad (art. 144 bis inc 1° del C.P.)"

PROLOGUE—THE TOY STORE
xxvii *she didn't notice them at first*: RIBA Trial, Causa N° 3511/16, "GRAFFIGNA Omar Domingo Rubens y otros s/privación ilegal de la libertad (art. 144 bis inc 1° del C.P.)," June 13, 2016, Teresa Izaguirre testimony (hereafter cited as the RIBA Trial).
xxvii *preparing for the pre-Christmas throngs*: Legajo CONADEP N° 292, Gabriel Gustavo Pontnau; Mariana Eva Pérez, "Fiestas Que No Fueron," *Decía Mi Abuelo* (blog), September 17, 2008, https://deciamiabuelo.blogspot.com /2008/09/fiestas-que-no-fueron.html.
xxvii *wood-paneled walls hung wreaths*: Mariana Eva Pérez, "Fiestas Que No Fueron," *Decía Mi Abuelo* (blog), September 17, 2008, https://deciamiabuelo.blogspot.com/2008/09 /fiestas-que-no-fueron.html.
xxvii *Superman and Elongated Man comic books*: Archivo Biográfico Familiar Pérez Roisinblit, 66.
xxvii *from the small storefront tucked in a shopping arcade*: RIBA Trial, Fundamentos, October 6, 2016, 111, https://www.mpf.gob.ar/lesa/files/2023/11/12-20161006-RIBA -Fundamentos.pdf.
xxviii *punched José into submission and clamped handcuffs over his wrists*: Legajo CONADEP N° 292, Gabriel Gustavo Pontnau.

xxviii *announced themselves as members of Defraudaciones y Estafas*: Marcela Bublik, *Abuela: La Historia de Rosa Roisinblit, una Abuela de Plaza de Mayo* (Buenos Aires: Marea Editorial, 2013), 77.

xxviii *"Qué hacemos con el rubio?"*: Legajo CONADEP N° 292, Gabriel Gustavo Pontnau.

xxviii *Through the glass walls*: Archivo Biográfico Familiar Pérez Roisinblit, 46.

xxviii *with long beige raincoats*: RIBA Trial, Teresa Izaguirre testimony, June 13, 2016; Elevación vs. RIBA—Causa N° 7273/06, "Scali, Daniel Alfredo y Otros s/ Privación Ilegal de la Libertad Agravada," 216, May 24, 2022.

xxviii *obscuring their faces with women's stockings*: Enrique Arrosagaray, *Biografía de Azucena Villaflor* (Ituzaingó, Provincia de Buenos Aires: Editorial Cienflores, 2014), 102.

xxviii *"Si se los llevan así, es por algo"*: RIBA Trial, Teresa Izaguirre testimony, June 13, 2016; Elevación vs. RIBA—Causa N° 7273/06, "Scali, Daniel Alfredo y Otros s/ Privación Ilegal de la Libertad Agravada," 216, May 24, 2022.

xxviii *The convoy made a brief stop*: Legajo CONADEP N° 292, Gabriel Gustavo Pontnau.

xxix *even boxer puppies*: Juan Martín Ramos Padilla, *Chicha: La Fundadora de Abuelas de Plaza de Mayo* (Buenos Aires: Dunken, 2006), 132.

xxix *the caravan headed south*: RIBA Trial, Fundamentos, October 6, 2016, 111, https://www .mpf.gob.ar/lesa/files/2023/11/12-20161006-RIBA-Fundamentos.pdf; in her most recent testimony for the RIBA II trial, on September 10, 2024, Mariana Pérez said, "We were kidnapped, apparently. Or simultaneously. Or maybe first my dad and his business partner in the store they owned. That day, there were two kidnappings. There were two raids." In every other account I've read, including the one on page 77 of *Abuela* by Marcela Bublik and official court documents in the first RIBA trial, the suggestion is that the same men who abducted José and Gabriel then drove to Palermo to abduct Patricia and Mariana.

xxix *shared six children*: Before 1971, the couple had seven children. That year the couple's third child, Alejandro, who was born with intellectual disabilities, died while living at a facility. Redacción Clarín, "Videla y las Monjas Francesas, un Vínculo Entre la Caridad y la Impiedad," *Clarín*, September 3, 2005, https://www.clarin.com/ediciones-anteriores /videla-monjas-francesas-vinculo-caridad-impiedad_0_HkOl7aDJRFl.html.

xxix *beloved German shepherds*: "Jorge Rafael Videla en Familia," *Para Tí*, February 12, 1979.

xxix *enjoy her delighted expressions*: Archivo Biográfico Familiar Pérez Roisinblit, 273.

xxix *normally thin legs had swollen*: Julio E. Nosiglia, *Botín de Guerra* (Buenos Aires: Abuelas de Plaza de Mayo, 2007), 143.

xxix *"We don't kidnap children"*: Bublik, *Abuela*, 77.

xxix *with their bedroom window facing the street*: Mariana Eva Pérez, "Digresión Lluviosa," *Decía Mi Abuelo* (blog), July 7, 2008, https://deciamiabuelo.blogspot.com/2008/07/dis gresin-lluviosa.html.

xxx *attending to a nephew who had fallen ill*: RIBA Trial, Marcelo Moreyra testimony, May 16, 2016.

xxx *Francisco Beiró 2998*: RIBA Trial, Marcelo Moreyra testimony.

xxx *Eucalyptus trees and Paraná pines*: Interview with Graciela Tobar; Google Maps search and author visit to address.

xxx *gathered at the cottage to celebrate Christmas*: Archivo Biográfico Familiar Pérez Roisinblit, 105; interview with Graciela Tobar.

xxx   *avoided inviting José*: Archivo Biográfico Familiar Pérez Roisinblit, 72.

xxx   *at least twenty of them*: RIBA Trial, Marcelo Moreyra testimony.

xxx   *blocking the doors and windows*: Elevación vs. RIBA—Causa N° 7273/2006, "Scali, Daniel Alfredo y Otros s/ Privación Ilegal de la Libertad," 216.

xxx   *wore starched brown fatigues and carried rifles*: Ibid.; RIBA Trial, Marcelo Moreyra testimony.

xxx   *surveil the cottage from above*: Mariana Eva Pérez, "La Declaración de Marcelo," *Diario de una Princesa Montonera* (blog), February 19, 2018, https://princesamontonera.blogspot.com/2018/02/la-declaracion-de-marcelo.html; Elevación vs. RIBA—causa N° 7273/06, "Scali, Daniel Alfredo y otros s/privación ilegal de la libertad agravada," 216, May 24, 2022.

xxx   *"Open up or we'll knock it down!"*: RIBA Trial, Marcelo Moreyra testimony.

xxx   *getting ready to go out dancing*: Pérez, "La Declaración de Marcelo."

xxx   *cowering under the kitchen table*: RIBA Trial, Marcelo Moreyra testimony.

xxxi   *balanced a basket on the entrance gate*: Ibid.

xxxi   *seemed the most nervous of all*: Mariana Eva Pérez, "Cómo Esconder Un Pelirrojo," elDiarioAR.com, October 10, 2021, https://www.eldiarioar.com/opinion/esconder-pelirrojo_129_8384281.html; RIBA Trial, Marcelo Moreyra testimony.

xxxi   *pushed her back into the car*: RIBA Trial, Marcelo Moreyra testimony.

xxxi   *"Papá, Papá, Papá, Papá, Papá"*: Mariana Eva Pérez, "De doler y de duelar," *Diario de una Princesa Montonera* (blog), June 14, 2016, https://princesamontonera.blogspot.com/2016/06/de-doler-y-de-duelar.html; Archivo Biográfico Familiar Pérez Roisinblit, 274.

CHAPTER 1—THE CASTAWAYS

3   *traumatic miscarriage at five months*: Celeste del Bianco, "Cien Veces Rosa," *Revista Anfibia*, August 15, 2019, https://www.revistaanfibia.com/cien-veces-rosa/.

3   *remain on bed rest for eight months*: Bublik, *Abuela*, 53.

3   *nurses let her admire the sleepy newborns*: Ibid., 54–55.

3   *purses that she made herself*: Ibid., 65.

4   *Saturday classes at the Instituto Bernasconi*: Archivo Biográfico Familiar Pérez Roisinblit, 48.

4   *"Tell your mother not to do your drawings for you"*: Ibid.

4   *"Fine, I'll draw something here"*: Ibid.

4   *helped her with compositions*: Ibid., 47.

4   *plates of Rosa's specialties*: Bublik, *Abuela*, 185.

4   *"My papá taught me"*: Archivo Biográfico Familiar Pérez Roisinblit, 47.

4   *a weekend class at the Peretz*: Bublik, *Abuela*, 64.

4   *"The new Argentina provides us"*: Buenos Aires en el Recuerdo—en 1951 Alumnos de la Escuela "I. L. Peretz" de Villa Lynch, Se Fotografían en el Aula Junto a Su Señorita, la Maestra Felisa Roizman, https://www.facebook.com/buenosairesenelrecuerdo/photos/a.902546853600327/1115151232339887/?type=3.

4   *better off than France and Germany*: Edward L. Glaeser, Rafael Di Tella, and Lucas Llach, "Introduction to Argentine Exceptionalism," *Latin American Economic Review* 27, no. 1 (January 5, 2018): 2, https://doi.org/10.1007s40503-017-0055-4.

5   *soprano's teardrop splash on the stage*: Edward Schumacher, "In Buenos Aires, the Musical Scene Is the Richest in the Third World," *New York Times*, August 30, 1982.

5 *"riche comme un Argentin"*: Glaeser, Di Tella, and Llach, "Introduction to Argentine Exceptionalism," 2.

5 *Customs revenues plummeted*: "Chronology: Argentina's Turbulent History of Economic Crises," Reuters, July 30, 2014, https://www.reuters.com/article/business/chronology -argentinas-turbulent-history-of-economic-crises-idUSKBN0FZ23N/.

5 *wearing their hair too long*: Rodolfo García, "Los Ecos del Pasado," *Página 12*, December 20, 2009, https://www.pagina12.com.ar/diario/elpais/subnotas/137349-44268-2009-12-20 .html.

5 *cutting it before releasing them*: Germán Ferrari, "Entre el Atentado Que No Fue y el Golpe Cordobés," *Caras y Caretas*, February 19, 2024, https://carasycaretas.org.ar/2024/02/19 /entre-el-atentado-que-no-fue-y-el-golpe-cordobes/.

5 *boys were barred from secondary schools*: Valeria Manzano, "'Rock Nacional' and Revolutionary Politics: The Making of a Youth Culture of Contestation in Argentina, 1966–1976," *The Americas* 70, no. 3 (2014): 393–427, https://www.jstor.org/stable/i40124818.

6 *forbidden for being "obscene"*: Valeria Manzano, "Sex, Gender and the Making of the 'Enemy Within' in Cold War Argentina," *Journal of Latin American Studies* 47, no. 1 (July 9, 2014): 1–29, doi:10.1017/S0022216X14000686.

6 *Miloš Forman's* Loves of a Blonde *and Michelangelo Antonioni's* Blow-Up *were banned from theaters*: All details about censorship in the Onganía period in the following paragraph are from "Argentina: Sex & the Strait-Laced Strongman," *Time*, August 18, 1967, https://time .com/archive/6635064/argentina-sex-the-strait-laced-strongman/.

6 *"Today, we had to go to confession"*: Ibid.

6 *"Here you go!"*: Bublik, *Abuela*, 67.

6 *taught mostly patriotic music*: Ibid., 68.

6 *twenty-four-hour café*: Ana Sánchez Trolliet, "'Buenos Aires Beat': A Topography of Rock Culture in Buenos Aires, 1965–1970," *Urban History* 41, no. 3 (October 14, 2013): 525, https://doi.org/10.1017/s0963926813000722.

7 *annoyed by the racket and their frugality*: Ibid.

7 *The single sold 250,000 copies in six months*: Valeria Manzano, *The Age of Youth in Argentina: Culture, Politics, and Sexuality from Perón to Videla* (Chapel Hill: University of North Carolina Press, 2014), 133.

7 *spiraled into barefoot dance parties*: DiFilm, "Happening en el Instituto Di Tella—Martha Minujin 1967," YouTube, December 28, 2013, www.youtube.com/watch?v=q3 _JILTMLlM.

8 *"I'm fed up with a civilization"*: Pipo Lernoud, "Estoy Cansado," *La Nación*, September 21, 2007, https://www.lanacion.com.ar/cultura/estoy-cansado-nid946117/.

8 *"multicolored shirts, tight pants"*: Edgardo Gutiérrez, *Rock del País: Estudios Culturales de Rock en Argentina* (Jujuy: Universidad Nacional de Jujuy, 2010), 250.

8 *a waiter at a café*: "Festival para deliriantes," *Primera Plana*, January 16, 1968.

8 *"Once, I was released"*: Gutiérrez, *Rock del País*, 250.

8 *each time he was jailed*: "El Rock Nacional Tuvo Su Cueva," *Clarín*, January 20, 2014, https://www.clarin.com/ciudades/rock-nacional-cueva_0_S1tV1Ilowmx.html.

8 *honor roll every quarter*: Rosa Roisinblit/Roisinblit, Rosa Tarlovsky de: Entrevista (1/2), interview by Rita Arditti, November 17, 1993, University of Massachusetts–

Boston, Joseph P. Healey Library, https://openarchives.umb.edu/digital/collection/p15774coll10/id/881/rec/35 (hereafter cited as Rosa Roisinblit interview with Rita Arditti).

8 *earned a teaching certificate*: Bublik, *Abuela*, 66.

8 *known as* las avivadas: Ibid., 68.

9 *to change out of an outfit she had stained*: Ibid., 66–68.

9 *"With the legs and ass I have"*: Archivo Biográfico Familiar Pérez Roisinblit, 125. Confirmed by author with Miguel Benasayag.

9 *applied bright red lipstick to her full lips*: Archivo Biográfico Familiar Pérez Roisinblit, 60.

9 *"She made herself up like a doll"*: Bublik, *Abuela*, 69.

9 *"Watching her seduce someone was a party"*: Ibid.

9 *devalued the peso by 50 percent*: Juan Bautista, "El Plan de Krieger Vasena Para Salir de la Crisis Económica en los '60s, el Cordobazo y las Torpezas de Onganía," *Infobae*, July 24, 2022, https://www.infobae.com/sociedad/2022/07/24/el-plan-de-krieger-vasena-para-salir-de-la-crisis-economica-en-los-60-el-cordobazo-y-las-torpezas-de-ongania/.

10 *pushing prices up*: Gustavo Sierra, "Una Protesta Estudiantil, Revueltas y Muerte: Cómo Fue la 'Cocina' del Cordobazo, el Levantamiento Obrero Más Grande de la Argentina," *Infobae*, May 2019, https://www.infobae.com/sociedad/2019/05/01/una-protesta-estudiantil-revueltas-y-muerte-como-fue-la-cocina-del-cordobazo-el-levantamiento-obrero-mas-grande-de-la-argentina/.

10 *steel bars and bolts*: J. P. Brennan and M. B. Gordillo, "Working Class Protest, Popular Revolt, and Urban Insurrection in Argentina: The 1969 Cordobazo," *Journal of Social History* 27, no. 3 (March 1, 1994): 486, https://doi.org/10.1353/jsh/27.3.477.

10 *matches, bottles, and brooms for protection*: Ibid., 487.

10 *describing the mood as "joyous"*: Ibid.

10 *build barricades and bonfires*: Ibid.

10 *Citroën and Xerox stores, the Development Bank, the upscale Jockey Club*: Manzano, *The Age of Youth in Argentina*, 167.

10 *ten million Argentines*: Fernando Ramírez Llorens, "Para Onganía Que Lo Mira por TV: El Rol de la Política Comunicacional y la Expansión de la Televisión en la Cobertura del Cordobazo," *Revista de História*, Departamento de Historia, Facultad de Humanidades, Universidad Nacional del Comahue, Issue 20 (December 26, 2019): 82.

11 *"an excess of freedom"*: "Argentina: Fall of a Corporate Planner," *Time*, June 22, 1970.

11 *"He is very straight, but also very hollow"*: Ibid.

11 *a sanitized curriculum*: Bublik, *Abuela*, 69.

11 *gaining admission without trouble*: Ibid., 66.

11 *"This is the vagina"*: Archivo Biográfico Familiar Pérez Roisinblit, 48.

CHAPTER 2—PERÓN OR DEATH

12 *Aramburu was still in his pajamas*: María O'Donnell, *Aramburu* (Buenos Aires: Planeta, 2020), 42.

12 *a gardener had stumbled on a bomb*: Ibid., 43.

12 *at risk of being killed*: Juan Bautista Tata Yofre, "A 50 Años del Secuestro de Aramburu: El Informe Secreto del Hallazgo del Cuerpo y la Autopsia Que Revela los Detalles del

Fusilamiento," *Infobae*, May 29, 2020, https://www.infobae.com/sociedad/2020/05/29/a-50-anos-del-secuestro-de-aramburu-el-informe-secreto-del-hallazgo-del-cuerpo-y-la-autopsia-que-revela-los-detalles-del-fusilamiento/.

12 *excused herself to go buy meat at the market*: Ibid.

13 *tailored by an amateur*: Eduardo Anguita and Daniel Cecchini, "Así Contaron Los Montoneros El Secuestro Y El Asesinato de Aramburu: 'General, Vamos a Proceder,'" *Infobae*, May 23, 2020, https://www.infobae.com/sociedad/2020/05/23/asi-contaron-los-montoneros-el-secuestro-y-el-asesinato-de-aramburu-general-vamos-a-proceder/.

13 *white Peugeot sedan and sped away*: Norma Arrostito and Mario Firmenich, "Como Murió Aramburu," *La Causa Peronista* 9 (September 3, 1974), https://eltopoblindado.com/wp-content/uploads/2017/01/La-Causa-Peronista-N-9.pdf.

13 *interrupted their programming*: Ibid.

13 *covering him with hay bales*: Ceferino Reato, "A 52 Años, los Secretos del Asesinato de Aramburu," *Perfil*, June 2022, https://www.perfil.com/noticias/sociedad/a-52-anos-los-secretos-del-asesinato-de-aramburu.phtml.

13 *"PERÓN OR DEATH"*: O'Donnell, *Aramburu*, 68.

13 *"gallop for days without finding the end of [their] land"*: "Argentina: New Breed on the Pampas," *Time*, August 21, 1964.

14 *French prostitutes and a year's stash of champagne and foie gras*: Ibid.

14 *kilos of meat, shoes, and toys to adoring crowds*: "Argentina's Evita Was a 'Champion of the Poor': New Exhibit Shows Toys She Gave Out," NBC News, April 26, 2019, https://www.nbcnews.com/news/latino/argentina-s-evita-was-champion-poor-new-exhibit-shows-toys-n998851; "Peronism: Our Sun, Our Air, Our Water," *Time*, November 27, 1972.

14 *button-down shirts*: Nicholas Fraser and Marysa Navarro, *Eva Perón* (New York: W. W. Norton, 1980), 72.

14 *"I once had nothing"*: Alden Whitman, "Peron, After Years as Strongman, Arose from Defeat to Rule Argentina Again," *New York Times*, July 2, 1974.

14 *homeownership shot up*: Isabella Cosse, "Everyday Life in Argentina in the 1960s," *Oxford Research Encyclopedia of Latin American History*, July 27, 2017, https://doi.org/10.1093/acrefore/9780199366439.013.316.

14 *"steak on every plate"*: "Argentina: New Breed on the Pampas."

15 *from a speech that he had delivered*: Lucretia L. Ilsley, "The Argentine Constitutional Revision of 1949," *Journal of Politics* 14, no. 2 (1952): 230, https://doi.org/10.2307/2126520, 230.

15 *shut down forty-five newspapers over their "anti-Argentine coverage"*: "Perón and the Press—Archive, 9 January 1950," *Guardian*, January 9, 2019, https://www.theguardian.com/world/2019/jan/09/peron-and-the-press-archive-1950.

15 Time *magazine was banned in Argentina for over a year*: "The Press: Censored," *Time*, August 8, 1949, https://time.com/archive/6602895/the-press-censored/.

15 *"Shall we burn down the Barrio Norte?"*: Edward Schumacher, "Argentina After the Falklands," *New York Times*, December 26, 1982, https://www.nytimes.com/1982/12/26/magazine/argentina-after-the-falklands.html.

15 *One person might plead for medical treatment*: Fraser and Navarro, *Eva Perón*, 78–79.

15 *the requests would be granted*: Ibid.

15 *"It's the price I have to pay"*: Joseph A. Page, "Evita: The True Life and Strange Cult of the

Long-Running Legend," *Washington Post*, September 20, 1981, https://www.washing
tonpost.com/archive/lifestyle/style/1981/09/20/evita-the-true-life-and-strange-cult-of
-the-long-running-legend/0b98a070-dd65-44e1-846e-35f8c20c918b/.

15   *"An acute bronchitis makes her cough often"*: Ibid.

15   *she lost twenty-two pounds in a single year*: Ibid.

15   *fainted in front of her adoring fans*: "Los Últimos Días de Eva Perón," *Diario Hoy*, July 26,
     2021, https://diariohoy.net/interes-general/los-ultimos-dias-de-eva-peron-170828.

15   *sold 150,000 copies in a single day*: Fraser and Navarro, *Eva Perón*, 150.

15   *one newspaper printed 400,000 copies*: Ibid., 83.

16   *"La vida por Perón!"*: Ibid., 152.

16   *two million people*: "Una Espera Interminable Bajo la Lluvia: Así Fue el Multitudinario
     Velorio Público de Evita," *Clarín*, July 26, 2019, https://www.clarin.com/politica/espera
     -interminable-lluvia-multitudinario-velorio-publico-evita_0_GTcL0Wj9N.html.

16   *some waiting fifteen hours*: "Cien Años de Evita Perón, la Leyenda Religiosa Que Cambió
     Para Siempre Argentina," *El Mundo*, May 7, 2019.

16   *8,340 funeral wreaths*: "Argentina: In Mourning," *Time*, August 11, 1952, https://con
     tent.time.com/time/subscriber/article/0,33009,857294,00.html.

16   *twenty-foot-high piles of flowers*: John Barnes, *Evita, First Lady: A Biography of Eva Perón*
     (New York: Grove Press, 1978), 163.

16   *roses, tulips, and carnations from Chile*: Ibid; Belén Frediani, "El día en que la Argentina se
     quedó sin flores," *Medio Mundo*, August 2, 2020.

16   *wrote to Pope Pius XII to ask that she be canonized*: "Argentina: In Mourning."

16   *brief tenure as a military attaché*: Joseph A. Page, *Perón: A Biography* (New York: Random
     House, 1983), 35–36.

16   *including Rosa Roisinblit*: Memoria Abierta, Testimonio de Rosa Roisinblit, Buenos
     Aires, 2002.

16   *"Eva loves me"*: Mariano Ben Plotkin, *Mañana Es San Perón: A Cultural History of Perón's
     Argentina*, trans. Keith Zahniser (Wilmington, DE: Scholarly Resources Inc., 1961),
     108–9.

16   *lavishing her with gems from Evita's collection*: "The Hemisphere: Daddykins & Nelly,"
     Time, October 10, 1955.

16   *he jailed one curate for "disrespect"*: "Argentina: Back to the Bordello," *Time*, January 10,
     1955, https://time.com/archive/6798534/argentina-back-to-the-bordello/; "The Unex-
     ploded Bomb," *Time*, May 9, 1955.

16   *the Vatican had excommunicated Perón*: "Perón Ban Hinted by Vatican Organ; Excom-
     munication Incurred by Acts," *New York Times*, June 16, 1955, https://www.nytimes
     .com/1955/06/16/archives/peron-ban-hinted-by-vatican-organ-excommunication-in
     curred-by-acts.html.

17   *more than one hundred bombs*: "El Bombardeo de Plaza de Mayo—16 de Junio de 1955,"
     2021, Argentina.gob.ar, June 14, 2021, https://www.argentina.gob.ar/derechoshumanos
     /el-bombardeo-de-plaza-de-mayo-16-de-junio-de-1955.

17   *over three hundred people and maimed more than twelve hundred*: Ibid.

17   *to donate to art students*: "Crackdown Continued," *Time*, December 5, 1955, https://con
     tent.time.com/time/subscriber/article/0,33009,893214,00.html.

17 *Aramburu himself preferred "the monster"*: Antonius C. G. M. Robben, *Political Violence and Trauma in Argentina* (Philadelphia: University of Pennsylvania Press, 2005), 27.

17 *for up to six years*: Felipe Pigna, "Decreto-Ley 4161, del 5 de Marzo de 1956. Prohibición de Elementos de Afirmación Ideológica o de Propaganda Peronista," El Historiador, November 17, 2017, https://elhistoriador.com.ar/decreto-ley-4161-del-5-de-marzo-de -1956-prohibicion-de-elementos-de-afirmacion-ideologica-o-de-propaganda-peronista/.

17 *Valle and twenty-six other military personnel*: Jill Hedges, *Juan Perón: The Life of the People's Colonel* (London: Bloomsbury, 2021), 189–90.

17 *The general supposedly wept*: "Body of Argentina's Kidnapped Ex-President Found," *New York Times*, July 18, 1970.

17 *laying flowers and candles nearby*: Calvin Sims, "Eva Peron's Corpse Continues to Haunt Argentina," *New York Times*, July 30, 1995, https://www.nytimes.com/1995/07/30 /world/eva-peron-s-corpse-continues-to-haunt-argentina.html.

18 *that she was in "Christian hands"*: Fraser and Navarro, *Eva Perón*, 178.

18 *With secret assistance from the Vatican*: Linda Pressly, "The 20-Year Odyssey of Eva Perón's Body," BBC, July 26, 2012, https://www.bbc.com/news/magazine-18616380.

18 *Juan José Valle Command of the Montoneros*: For further reading on the Montoneros, see Richard Gillespie, *Soldiers of Perón* (New York: Oxford University Press, 1982); O'Donnell, *Aramburu*; and María José Moyano, *Argentina's Lost Patrol: Armed Struggle, 1969–1979* (New Haven: Yale University Press, 1995).

18 *twelve young men and women*: Gillespie, *Soldiers of Perón*, 50.

18 *"the liberal oligarchy"*: "Manifesto Político de Montoneros," November 1970, as compiled by Roberto Baschetti, https://www.educ.ar/recursos/128835/manifiesto-politico -de-montoneros.

18 *"intent upon responding to the military violence"*: Gillespie, *Soldiers of Perón*, 87.

18 *"We are peronists"*: "El llanto del enemigo," *Cristianismo y Revolución*, no. 28, April 1971.

18 *a modern Buenos Aires hospital*: Gillespie, *Soldiers of Perón*, 86.

19 *"free, just, and sovereign fatherland"*: O'Donnell, *Aramburu*, 68.

19 *the Montoneros announced*: "Comunicado Nº 3," May 31, 1970, Archivo digitalizado del Centro de Documentación de los Movimientos Armados (CEDEMA), https://cedema .org/digital_items/229.

19 *twice in the head and once in the chest*: O'Donnell, *Aramburu*, 189.

19 *disclosed the whereabouts of Evita Perón's*: Malcolm W. Browne, "Aramburu Case Remains Puzzle," *New York Times*, June 21, 1970.

19 *twenty-two thousand men*: Robben, *Political Violence and Trauma in Argentina*, 112.

19 *lime to dissolve his flesh and bones*: Reato, "A 52 Años, Los Secretos del Asesinato de Aramburu."

CHAPTER 3—PERÓN *AND* DEATH

20 *predicted he had four months to live*: Bublik, *Abuela*, 56–57.

20 *His relatives described him as "a sun"*: Archivo Biográfico Familiar Pérez Roisinblit, 82.

20 *knocking it out to better set the mood*: Bublik, *Abuela*, 48.

20 *or a book he'd picked out for her*: Ibid., 49.

21 *a brown leather album with gilt edging*: Book observed by author, Rosa Tarlovsky de Rois-
    inblit Fondo Personal, Caja 5, Comisión Provincial por la Memoria.

21 *"Rosita, what nice legs you have!"*: Bublik, *Abuela*, 53.

21 *"I sleep in the bed of a king"*: Ibid., 57.

21 *In December 1971, he completed his third book*: Benjamín Roisinblit, *Pampas de Sión: Poe-
    mas Sobre la Fundación de Moisés Ville*, 1971.

21 *he would praise the rock*: Archivo Biográfico Familiar Pérez Roisinblit, 47.

21 *couldn't tolerate the smell of the ink*: Bublik, *Abuela*, 57.

21 *"He wanted to know everything"*: Ibid.

21 *"SHOOTOUT," blared one headline*: "TIROTEO: Atacaron a un Patrullero en Rosa-
    rio: Un Extremista Muerto," *Clarín*, January 13, 1972, https://tapas.clarin.com/tapa
    .html#19720113.

21 *"in Search of Subversive Elements"*: "Gigantesco Operativo Militar en Busca de Elementos
    Subversivos," *Clarín*, January 14, 1972, https://tapas.clarin.com/tapa.html - 19720114.

22 *she had met at the Hebraica*: Bublik, *Abuela*, 69.

22 *where Rosa and Benjamín had also connected*: Ibid., 47.

22 *gathering towels, sheets*: Archivo Biográfico Familiar Pérez Roisinblit, 142.

22 *Benjamín had talked about*: Bublik, *Abuela*, 57.

22 *The whole Roisinblit family adored him*: Archivo Biográfico Familiar Pérez Roisinblit, 60, 142.

22 *"Boys chased after her"*: Bublik, *Abuela*, 69.

22 *"anarchist-hippy"*: Miguel Benasayag et al., "'Rather Than Harbor a Universal Grudge, It
    Is Better to Act': Interview with Miguel Benasayag," trans. Cadenza Academic Trans-
    lations, *Mouvements* 75, no. 3 (2024): 143–56, https://shs.cairn.info/article/E_MOU-
    V_075_0143?lang=en.

22 *"a comfortable middle-class life"*: Bublik, *Abuela*, 71.

22 *"a contagious effervescence in the streets"*: Horacio Baltazar Robles, "Radicalización Política
    y Sectores Populares en la Argentina de los '70s: La Juventud Peronista (JP) y Su Artic-
    ulación con Montoneros en los Barrios Periféricos de la Ciudad de La Plata" (master's
    thesis, Universidad Nacional de La Plata, June 2011), 51.

23 *scrounging for food instead of attending school*: Arthur F. Corwin, "Argentina's War on
    Poverty," *Urban Affairs Quarterly* 5, no. 4 (June 1970): 413, https://doi.org/10.1177/107
    808747000500403, 2.

23 *eighty thousand to eight hundred thousand*: Hugo E. Ratier, *Villeros y Villas Miseria* (La
    Plata: EDULP, 2022), 29.

23 *"Only seldom do we see a car on the villa streets"*: Matilde Mellibovsky, *Circle of Love Over
    Death*, trans. Maria Proser and Matthew Proser (Willimantic, CT: Curbstone Press,
    1997), 104.

23 *weeping as she took in the poverty*: Interview with Miguel Benasayag.

23 *"armed propaganda"*: Gillespie, *Soldiers of Perón*, 110.

24 *"Danger! Dynamited Zone"*: Ibid., 111.

24 *"devoted as much of their energies to proselytizing and legitimate reform as to guerrilla tactics"*:
    Central Intelligence Agency, *The Roots of Violence: The Urban Guerrilla in Argentina*,
    June 9, 1975, https://www.cia.gov/readingroom/document/cia-rdp79t00865a00260013
    0001-0.

24   *"A Maoist would speak to Perón and leave convinced he was a Maoist"*: Whitman, "Peron, After Years as Strongman."

25   *on a chartered Aerolíneas Argentinas jet at three in the afternoon on June 20*: Page, *Perón*, 462–63.

25   *before releasing eighteen thousand doves*: Geoffrey Fox, "Argentina: Putting the 'Perón' Back In," NACLA, September 25, 2007, https://nacla.org/article/argentina-putting -per%C3%B3n-back.

25   *as tall as a ten-story building*: Page, *Perón*, 462.

25   *entertained themselves with broadcasts of faraway boxing matches*: Ibid., 463.

25   *folk music piped from speakers*: Ibid., 463–64.

25   *peel off their overcoats*: Ibid., 464.

26   *banners that stretched 160 feet*: Felipe Pigna, "La Masacre de Ezeiza," El Historiador, November 6, 2017, https://www.elhistoriador.com.ar/la-masacre-de-ezeiza/.

26   *"Look, General, the future runs through us"*: Ibid.

26   *"Perón, Evita, the Peronist Fatherland"*: Page, *Perón*, 464.

26   *a leftist plot to assassinate Perón*: Ibid.

26   *"Perón and Death"*: Ibid., 466.

26   *a "vegetarian lion"*: Whitman, "Peron, After Years as Strongman."

26   *"But it costs a lot"*: Robert D. Crassweller, *Perón and the Enigmas of Argentina* (New York: W. W. Norton, 1988), 288.

27   *"There's only one Evita!"*: Page, *Perón*, 488.

27   *"stupid" and "beardless youths"*: Eduardo Anguita, "'¡Esos Estúpidos Que Gritan!': La Furia de Perón el Día Que Echó a los 'Imberbes' Montoneros de la Plaza," *Infobae*, May 2021, https://www.infobae.com/sociedad/2021/05/01/esos-estupidos-que-gritan-la-furia-de -peron-el-dia-que-echo-a-los-imberbes-montoneros-de-la-plaza/; Page, *Perón*, 490.

27   *poles and stones as they went*: Page, *Perón*, 488–89.

27   *"revolutionary infantilism"*: Ibid., 490.

27   *just as the immune system forms antibodies*: Ibid.

27   *grow stronger by crushing its internal enemies*: Ibid.

27   *"Chau, viejo"—Goodbye, old man*: "Argentina: The Death of El Líder," *Time*, July 15, 1974.

27   *dancer at a Panamanian cabaret called Happyland*: "Argentina: This Is Only a Little Goodbye," *Time*, September 29, 1975.

28   *rhapsodized about the glories of the cow*: Page, *Perón*, 399.

28   *Rasputin of the Pampas*: Martin Andersen, "Argentina Awaits Return of Fugitive Ex-Strongman," *Washington Post*, July 3, 1986, https://www.washingtonpost.com/ar chive/politics/1986/07/04/argentina-awaits-return-of-fugitive-ex-strongman/7b2862 64-c413-4b4b-8f9f-3b1b970c3f06/.

28   *mouthing her words like a wicked ventriloquist*: Page, *Perón*, 497.

28   *"She is a creation of mine"*: Ibid., 492.

28   *Another creation of López Rega's*: Gillespie, *Soldiers of Perón*, 153.

28   *"The AAA makes the leftists look good by comparison"*: Central Intelligence Agency, *The Roots of Violence: The Urban Guerrilla in Argentina*.

28   *"You are hereby informed that you have been sentenced to death"*: Ana Belén Zapata, "Andamios de experiencias: Conflictividad obrera, vigilancia y represión en Argentina. Bahía Blanca, 1966–1976" (Tesis de posgrado, Universidad Nacional de La Plata, Facultad de

Humanidades y Ciencias de la Educación, 2014), 334, https://www.memoria.fahce.unlp .edu.ar/tesis/te.916/te.916.pdf.

28   *two thousand murders in the three years it terrorized Buenos Aires*: Arya Bardo Kazemi, "Political Violence in Argentina During the 1970s" (master's thesis, University of Nevada, Las Vegas, 1997), 31, http://dx.doi.org/10.25669/9vjm-01gt.

29   *detonated 110 bombs*: "The War Against Isabel," *Time*, September 30, 1974.

29   *the most lucrative kidnapping in world history*: Gus Lubin and Shlomo Sprung, "The Biggest Ransoms Ever," Business Insider, September 7, 2012, https://www.business insider.com/the-biggest-ransoms-ever-2012-9#bonus-from-the-pre-modern-era-19; in 2025 terms, the ransom would amount to nearly $400 million.

29   *"It was all very gradual"*: Benasayag et al., "'Rather than Harbor a Universal Grudge, It Is Better to Act.'"

29   *threatened to break up with him*: Archivo Biográfico Familiar Pérez Roisinblit, 128.

29   *arrested soon thereafter anyway*: Interview with Miguel Benasayag.

29   *important pillar of the Triple A*: Alejandro Cánepa, "Triple A, un Debut para el Terror," *Clarín*, November 24, 2023, https://www.clarin.com/revista-n/montoneros-debut-terror _0_ZAGAiOqBH8.html.

29   *torturing or even killing those he arrested*: "A Bomb Kills Chief of Argentine Police," *New York Times*, November 2, 1974.

29   *thirty feet in the sky*: Ibid.

29   *The Montoneros had struck once again*: Ibid.

CHAPTER 4—NOW, NOW, NOW

30   *shooting him between the eyes*: "Argentine Rebels Kill a U.S. Consul," *New York Times*, March 1, 1975, https://www.nytimes.com/1975/03/01/archives/argentine-rebels-kill-a -us-consul-body-of-kidnapped-official-found.html.

30   *Twenty-nine murders*: Page, *Perón*, 498.

30   *Gunfights between police and revolutionary groups were constant*: Federal Bureau of Investigation, *Foreign Political Matters—Argentina*, January 28, 1975, https://www.archives.gov /files/argentina/data/docid-32986507.pdf.

30   *every three hours*: Gillespie, *Soldiers of Perón*, 223.

30   *"to be a smell of death on the streets"*: Kazemi, "Political Violence in Argentina During the 1970s," 34.

30   *"When you see a bomb explode here"*: Bublik, *Abuela*, 71–72.

31   *"one has to commit and push ahead"*: Ibid., 72.

31   *twenty-two-year-old Patricia joined the Montoneros movement*: Archivo Biográfico Familiar Pérez Roisinblit, 267.

31   *tug a carpet over the hole*: Javier Sahade, "La Historia (Jamás Contada) Del Quirófano Subterráneo | Perycia," Perycia, March 24, 2023, https://perycia.com/2023/03/la-histo ria-jamas-contada-del-quirofano-subterraneo/.

31   *identify hypovolemic shock from a gunshot or explosion*: Archivo Biográfico Familiar Pérez Roisinblit, 154.

31   *Patricia worked at a clinic in Quirno*: RIBA Trial, Amalia Larralde testimony, May 30, 2016.

31   *"Everything was now, now, now"*: Bublik, *Abuela*, 74.

31 *"I expect the package with twenty shirts to arrive tomorrow"*: Interview with Miriam Lewin.

32 *lying dead in the street*: Luciana Guglielmo, "Memorias Biográficas de Abuelas de Plaza de Mayo: Dimensión Juvenil y Dimensión Militante en la Construcción de las Representaciones Actuales Sobre sus Hijos 'Desaparecidos' Durante la Última Dictadura Cívico Militar," 2019, 154.

32 *as though he didn't exist*: Ibid.

32 *wore shoes so tattered Rosa was unsure how she could still walk*: Bublik, *Abuela*, 58–59; Archivo Biográfico Familiar Pérez Roisinblit, 207.

32 *just the separate components*: Bublik, *Abuela*, 58.

32 *Rosa decided to downsize*: Ledgers viewed in box 9 of the Rosa Tarlovsky de Roisinblit fondo personal at Comisión por la Memoria suggest that Rosa sold her apartment in Boedo in November 1975.

32 *pass the entire sum on to the Montoneros*: Bublik, *Abuela*, 59.

32 *Patricia handed over her inheritance*: Ibid.

32 *"Mamá, stop insisting"*: Ibid., 58.

33 *toward 1,000 percent*: "Argentina: The Generals Call a Clockwork Coup," *Time*, April 5, 1976, https://content.time.com/time/subscriber/article/0,33009,913982,00.html.

33 *graffiti reading "Chile"*: Kazemi, "Political Violence in Argentina During the 1970s," 34.

33 *"Soldiers, how long must we wait?"*: Juan De Onis, "5 More Policemen Die in Argentina," *New York Times*, October 27, 1975.

33 *six economy ministers, six interior ministers, and four foreign ministers*: "María Estela Martínez de Perón (1974–1976)," Casa Rosada, September 3, 2020, https://www.casa rosada.gob.ar/nuestro-pais/presidentes/93-nuestro-pais/presidentes/47094-maria-estela -martinez-de-peron-1974-1976.

33 *"The coup has been delayed for another day"*: Kazemi, "Political Violence in Argentina During the 1970s," 34.

33 *good enough to perform in one of Argentina's massive soccer stadiums*: Archivo Biográfico Familiar Pérez Roisinblit, 20.

33 *trying to translate the lyrics to Spanish*: Interview with Graciela Tobar; Archivo Biográfico Familiar Pérez Roisinblit, 67.

33 *Paulina, after Paul McCartney*: Archivo Biográfico Familiar Pérez Roisinblit, 28.

33 *a call for attention*: Interview with Graciela Tobar.

34 *led by Mario Bertone*: Mansion Seré IV/RIBA II, Mariana Eva Pérez testimony, September 10, 2024, https://laretaguardia.com.ar/2024/09/juicio-mansion-sere-iv-riba-ii-dia-2 -martes-10-de-septiembre-de-2024-930-horas.html.

34 *built septic tanks, attached roofs to improvised homes, and installed sidewalks*: "Homenaje y Polémica," *Página 12*, July 18, 2016, https://www.pagina12.com.ar/diario /elpais/1-149728-2010-07-18.html; Memoria De Los Pibes De La Union De Estudiantes Secundarios (UES), June 5, 2019, www.facebook.com/secundariosues/posts/los-19-scouts -desaparecidos-durante-la-dictadura-militar-muchos-de-ellos-militan/25340866633 03489/.

34 *sold her sewing machine*: Archivo Biográfico Familiar Pérez Roisinblit, 4.

34 *the Juventud Peronista, Fuerzas Armadas Revolucionarias, and eventually the Montoneros*: Archivo Biográfico Familiar Pérez Roisinblit, 168.

34 *practicing his shooting aim*: Mariana Eva Pérez, "Cosas Que Me Dijeron Sobre Mi Papá,

Ayer, En Caseros," *Diario de Una Princesa Montonera* (blog), 2018, https://princesamon
tonera.blogspot.com/2010/03/cosas-que-me-dijeron-sobre-mi-papa-ayer.html.

34   *"It's not that we want to take over the country"*: Memoria Abierta, Testimonio de Argentina
     Rojo de Pérez, Buenos Aires, 2002.

35   *"fighting like hell against the enemy"*: On October 2, 2022, Mariana Eva Pérez tweeted
     about this letter. I then tracked it down in the October 28, 1977, edition of *La Razón*. The
     title of the article is "El Comando en Jefe del Ejército Dio a Conocer Otro Documento
     Que Fue Secuestrado a la Subversión."

35   *a cache of arms José had hidden*: Interview with Graciela Tobar.

35   *home raids, and detentions*: Gillespie, *Soldiers of Perón*, 244–45.

CHAPTER 5—THE PINK PANTHER

36   *Isabel Perón onto a waiting helicopter*: Paul Hoeffel, "Junta Takes Over in Argentina,"
     Guardian, March 25, 2016, https://www.theguardian.com/world/2016/mar/25/argen
     tina-junta-coup-videla-peron-1976-archive.

36   *"You are under detention"*: "Argentina: The Generals Call a Clockwork Coup."

36   *around three in the morning*: "Día Nacional de la Memoria por la Verdad y la Justicia:
     Cómo Fue el Comunicado Oficial del Golpe de Estado de 1976," *Cronista*, March 23,
     2023, https://www.cronista.com/informacion-gral/dia-nacional-de-la-memoria-por-la
     -verdad-y-la-justicia-como-fue-el-comunicado-oficial-del-golpe-de-estado-de-1976/.

36   *"It is recommended that all inhabitants strictly adhere"*: Comunicado N° 1 de la Junta de
     Comandantes en Jefe de las Fuerzas Armadas, Luego del Golpe de Estado Contra el
     Gobierno Constitucional de María Estela Martínez de Perón el 24 de Marzo de 1976,
     https://backend.educ.ar/refactor_resource/get-attachment/22832.

37   *"a man enduring a pair of boots two sizes too small"*: Martin McReynolds, "Videla May
     Grow More Weary of Chores as Junta's Salesman," *Miami Herald*, August 27, 1977.

37   *"to discuss his job, the infantry, or his children"*: Central Intelligence Agency, "Visiting Hemisphere
     Leaders," September 2, 1977, https://www.cia.gov/readingroom/document/03224637.

37   *"uniformes de civil"*: María Seoane and Vicente Muleiro, *El Dictador: La Historia Secreta
     y Pública de Jorge Rafael Videla* (Buenos Aires: Sudamericana, 2001), 320.

37   *refusing to remove his military jacket*: Ibid., 75.

37   *forbade him from doing so either*: Ricardo Ragendorfer, "La Banalidad del Mal," *Contra-
     editorial*, November 8, 2021, https://contraeditorial.com/la-banalidad-del-mal/.

37   *styled his black hair straight back*: Seoane and Muleiro, *El Dictador*, 126 (hair), 136 (hair
     and sneakers), 142 (handwriting).

37   *he once ratted out a friend*: Ibid., 144.

38   *vowing to return her before dinnertime*: Ragendorfer, "La Banalidad del Mal."

38   *"a stern, self-denying taskmaster"*: Central Intelligence Agency, "Jorge Rafael Videla," Au-
     gust 15, 1978, https://www.archives.gov/files/argentina/data/docid-33065473.pdf

38   *he was "apolitical"*: Felipe Pigna, *Lo Pasado Pensado* (Buenos Aires: Planeta, 2011), "Sec-
     tion: Éramos pocos y llegó Videla," loc. 5700, Kindle.

38   *As Isabel vacationed*: Fernando Agüero, "En Ascochinga, el Retiro de Isabel Aún Genera
     Silencios," *La Voz del Interior*, January 14, 2007, http://archivo.lavoz.com.ar/07/01/14
     /secciones/politica/nota.asp?nota_id=35633.

38   *pressured Isabel into cutting ties with López Rega*: Page, *Perón*, 499.

38   *strong-arming the country's first female president*: Pablo Waisberg and Martín Cortés, "'Fue el Único Golpe de Estado Planificado Hasta el Último Detalle,'" Infojus Noticias, March 23, 2015, http://www.infojusnoticias.gov.ar/entrevistas/fue-el-unico-golpe-de -estado-planificado-hasta-el-ultimo-detalle-121.html.

38   *inevitable step on the path to revolution*: Gillespie, *Soldiers of Perón*, 223.

39   *sometimes wigs*: Arrosagaray, *Biografía de Azucena Villaflor*, 102.

39   *"not only someone who plants bombs"*: Adam Bernstein, "Jorge Rafael Videla, Argentine Junta Leader, Dies at 87," *Washington Post*, May 17, 2013, https://www.washingtonpost .com/world/the_americas/jorge-rafael-videla-argentine-junta-leader-dies-at-87/2013/05 /17/f22ae8d0-2f5c-11e2-a30e-5ca76eeec857_story.html; CELS, *El Mito de la "Guerra Sucia"* (Buenos Aires: CELS, 1984), 24.

39   *wrapped certain books in newspapers*: John Lantigua, "Like Pope, Locals Lived Terror of Dirty War," *Palm Beach Post*, March 26, 2013, https://www.palmbeachpost.com/story /news/2013/03/26/like-pope-locals-lived-terror/7068534007/.

39   *walking against traffic*: Andrew Graham-Yooll, *A State of Fear* (London: Eland, 1986), 39.

39   *scribbling messages behind toilets and mirrors*: Vicente Panetta, "Reporter Remembers Fear in Videla's Argentina," *San Diego Union-Tribune*, May 18, 2013, https:// www.sandiegouniontribune.com/sdut-reporter-remembers-fear-in-videlas-argentina -2013may18-story.html.

39   *Parisiennes and Particulares*: Munú Actis et al., *Ese Infierno* (Buenos Aires: Editorial Altamira, 2006), 66.

39   *buried or burned their copies of* Crisis: Bublik, *Abuela*, 71.

39   *recalled going to see Scorsese's* Taxi Driver: Interview with Miriam Lewin.

40   *in a puddle of blood was a comb belonging to one of her comrades*: Actis et al., *Ese Infierno*, 42.

40   *hidden inside a lipstick tube*: Memoria Abierta, Testimonio de Miriam Lewin, Buenos Aires, 2001.

40   *They spent their days rushing around the city*: Bublik, *Abuela*, 74.

40   *"Against the wall"*: Archivo Biográfico Familiar Pérez Roisinblit, 33.

40   *The whole thing was a ruse*: Ibid.; Memoria Abierta, Testimonio de Argentina Rojo de Pérez, Buenos Aires, 2002.

40   *the apartment was quiet*: Mansión Seré IV/RIBA II Case, Mariana Eva Pérez testimony.

40   *It was raining hard*: Archivo Biográfico Familiar Pérez Roisinblit, 33.

41   *"José, the cops came"*: Ibid., 34.

41   *"I wasn't going to be able to be happy"*: Actis et al., *Ese Infierno*, 60.

41   *"Chicos, let's talk about something else"*: Guglielmo, "Memorias Biográficas de Abuelas de Plaza de Mayo," 158.

41   *"If you want to act that way, do it"*: Bublik, *Abuela*, 60.

41   *Patricia brought happy news*: Ibid.

41   *signing their own death warrants*: Ibid.

42   *had asked Miriam if she'd wait for him*: Interview with Miriam Lewin.

42   *"It was a period where you didn't know"*: Ibid.

42   *"You're wanting to leave the movement"*: Ibid.

42   *on the second floor of a gas station*: Ibid.; Bublik, *Abuela*, 75.

42 *he was also talking about his own*: Interview with Miriam Lewin.

42 *she and José huddled in the tiny maid's quarters*: Bublik, *Abuela*, 60.

42 *after the traumatic raid on their previous home*: Mansión Seré IV/RIBA II Case, Mariana Eva Pérez testimony.

42 *went into labor*: Bublik, *Abuela*, 61.

43 *"It's a girl and she looks just like you!"*: Archivo Biográfico Familiar Pérez Roisinblit, 292.

43 *nine people associated with José's former Scouts group disappeared*: "Festival 'Pasaje de Los Sueños Compartidos,'" *Agencia Paco Urondo*, November 14, 2011, https://www.agencia pacourondo.com.ar/ddhh/festival-pasaje-de-los-suenos-compartidos.

43 *drove him away in an ambulance*: Alejandra Dandan, "Secuestro y Resucitación en el Nosocomio," *Página 12*, August 16, 2013, https://www.pagina12.com.ar/diario/elpais /1-226900-2013-08-16.html.

43 *his family identified his lifeless body*: Acta de acusación de la fiscalía en la Causa nº 761 "ESMA," https://www.legal-tools.org/doc/3e728c/pdf/; "Awaiting Justice in Argentina," *Washington Post*, September 12, 2003, https://www.washingtonpost.com/archive /opinions/2003/09/12/awaiting-justice-in-argentina/5b576e32-3d74-4a2a-8803-f219 c0aa4057/.

43 *lower her eyes from the road*: Bublik, *Abuela*, 61.

43 *She offered to sell her apartment*: Guglielmo, "Memorias Biográficas de Abuelas de Plaza de Mayo," 154.

43 *"Those who leave the country are cowards"*: Ibid.

CHAPTER 6—EL PROCESO

44 *two warring political blocs*: Casa Rosada, Official English Website for the City of Buenos Aires, May 13, 2016, turismo.buenosaires.gob.ar/en/atractivo/casa-rosada; another theory holds that the palace was colored with a mixture of lime and bovine blood, which was rumored to prevent leaks due to the binding properties of the blood. "Curiosidades," Casa Rosada, April 22, 2016, https://www.casarosada.gob.ar/informacion/actividad-oficial /9-noticias/36070-curiosidades#:~:text=%C2%BFPor%20qu%C3%A9%20rosada.

44 *The primary office was regally commanding*: Reynaldo Sietecase, "Las Fotos Favoritas de Víctor Bugge, El Fotógrafo de los Presidentes," Periodismo.com, June 29, 2017, www.pe riodismo.com/2017/06/29/las-fotos-favoritas-de-victor-bugge-el-fotografo-de-los-presi dentes/.

44 *religious art hanging from every wall*: US Department of State, Office of the Historian, "Foreign Relations of the United States, 1977–1980," Volume 24, South America, https://history.state.gov/historicaldocuments/frus1977-80v24/preface; US Department of State, Office of the Historian, "Telegram from the Embassy in Argentina to the Department of State," March 27, 1979, Document 99, Latin America, https://history .state.gov/historicaldocuments/frus1977-80v24/d99.

45 *"Dios nunca me soltó la mano"*: Ceferino Reato, *Disposición Final* (Buenos Aires: Sudamer ican, 2016), ch. 1, Kindle.

45 *"exterminate Marxism"*: "Chile's Strongman," *New York Times*, September 15, 1973, https://www.nytimes.com/1973/09/15/archives/chiles-strongman-augusto-pinochet -ugarte-man-in-the-news-served-in.html.

45 *"who think they are British"*: Calvin Sims, "The World; Formerly Arrogant, Utterly Argentine," *New York Times*, May 24, 1998, https://www.nytimes.com/1998/05/24/weekin review/the-world-formerly-arrogant-utterly-argentine.html.

45 *"A nation traumatized by years of anarchy"*: "Time for a Reckoning in Argentina," *New York Times*, May 13, 1983, https://www.nytimes.com/1983/05/13/opinion/time-for-a -reckoning-in-argentina.html.

46 *two of Videla's own relatives were taken*: Seoane and Muleiro, *El Dictador*, 107; their names were Edgardo Ojea Quintana and Ignacio Pedro Ojea Quintana.

46 *two hundred petitions seeking information*: "Report of an Amnesty International Mission to Argentina: 6–15 November 1976," Amnesty International, 27, https://www.amnesty .org/ar/wp-content/uploads/2021/06/amr130831977eng.pdf.

46 *"more than once or twice"*: "Law: Habeas Corpses," *Time*, April 23, 1979, https://content .time.com/time/subscriber/article/0,33009,920266,00.html.

46 *nearly one hundred lawyers*: Rita Arditti, *Searching for Life: The Grandmothers of the Plaza de Mayo and the Disappeared Children of Argentina* (Berkeley: University of California Press, 1999), 15.

46 *other leftists began using* chupar: Actis et al., *Ese Infierno*—*chupar* is used throughout, including on 134.

46 *"Many of the* desaparecidos *were innocent citizens"*: "Argentina: Hope from a Clockwork Coup," *Time*, April 11, 1977, https://content.time.com/time/subscriber/article /0,33009,918823,00.html.

46 *"ghostly army"*: "Report of an Amnesty International Mission to Argentina: 6–15 November 1976."

46 *"The* desaparecido *is an unknown"*: "Conferencia de Prensa de Videla. Diciembre de 1979," *Lo Pasado Pensado - Archivo Prisma*, 2021, www.archivorta.com.ar/asset/lo-pasa do-pensado-3/.

46 *championing a discounted student bus fare*: Roberto Baschetti, "Falcone, María Claudia," 2017, robertobaschetti.com/falcone-maria-claudia/.

47 *"They tortured us with profound sadism"*: Vladimir Hernandez, "Argentina Marks 'Night of the Pencils,'" BBC, September 14, 2011, https://www.bbc.com/news/world-latin -america-14910859.

47 *or a combination of the three*: Carlos Osorio, Silvia Tandeciarz, and Johanna Weech, "Inside Argentina's Killing Machine: U.S. Intelligence Documents Record Gruesome Human Rights Crimes of 1976–1983," National Security Archive, May 21, 2019, https://nsar chive.gwu.edu/briefing-book/southern-cone/2019-05-30/inside-argentinas-killing -machine-us-intelligence-documents-record-gruesome-human-rights-crimes-1976.

47 *forced to watch*: Charles A. Krause, "Argentine Describes 'Excruciating' Pain of Torture," *Washington Post*, October 29, 1978, https://www.washingtonpost.com/archive/politics /1978/10/29/argentine-describes-excruciating-pain-of-torture/bc19a8c7-ce5e-4362 -a60f-8271ca2c91e4/.

47 *control of their tongues*: Ibid.

48 If your tire pops or goes flat: Interview with Uki Goñi.

48 *machine guns poking out of the windows*: Ibid.

48 *"Cerrar la partida con tres de alfil"*: Legajo CONADEP N° 4816, Graciela Daleo and Andrés Castillo.

48   *fluorescent lights at all hours of the day and night*: Actis et al., *Ese Infierno*, 23.

48   *"El silencio es salud"*: Legajo CONADEP N° 4816, Graciela Daleo and Andrés Castillo.

48   *"Where is the place that"*: Actis et al., *Ese Infierno*, 31.

48   *they put rats in women's vaginas*: Ibid.; the authors of *Ese Infierno* discuss the existence of these rumors in the book, but did not confirm that they were true.

48   *Naval doctors stood by*: Alejandra Dandan, "Los Médicos Que Actuaron en la ESMA," *Página 12*, July 23, 2015, https://www.pagina12.com.ar/diario/elpais/1-277713-2015 -07-23.html; Actis et al., *Ese Infierno*, 251.

49   *not quite muffling*: Abel Gilbert, "Satisfaction en la ESMA," *El Diario*, February 6, 2021, https://www.eldiarioar.com/opinion/satisfaction-esma_129_7198172.html.

49   *were near silent*: The following description of Wednesdays comes from Sara Osatinsky's testimony in the ESMA Trial, June 11, 2010, as provided by the Abuelas' lawyers.

49   *the armed forces loaded groups of prisoners*: Horacio Verbitsky, *El Vuelo* (Barcelona: Seix Barral, 1995), 15.

49   *twenty-two thousand cubic meters of water*: Ismael Piedra-Cueva and Mónica Fossati, "Residual Currents and Corridor of Flow in the Río de La Plata," *Applied Mathematical Modelling* 31, no. 3 (February 16, 2006): 564–77, https://doi.org/10.1016/j.apm.2005.11.033.

49   *"Fish food," the men called them*: Ari Gandsman, "Reclaiming the Past: The Search for the Kidnapped Children of Argentina's Disappeared" (PhD thesis, McGill University, 2008), 6.

CHAPTER 7—WALLS OF GLASS

50   *Ahead of the tournament*: Nicolás Sagaian, "78 World Cup: The Advertising Campaign of Burson-Marsteller," Papelitos, n.d., https://papelitos.com.ar/nota/mundial-78-la-cam pana-publicitaria-de-burson-marsteller?z_language=en.

50   *General Motors and totalitarian countries like Romania*: Robert D. McFadden, "Harold Burson, a Giant in Public Relations, Dies at 98," *New York Times*, January 10, 2020, sec. Business, https:// www.nytimes.com/2020/01/10/business/media/harold-burson-dead.html.

50   *promote a vision of Argentina's true "reality"*: Burson-Marsteller, "Un Programa de Comunicaciones Internacionales para la Argentina," October 22, 1976, 48, https://www .archivosenuso.org/sites/default/files/field_daeci_file/03_1976_oct_programa_com _internacional_bm.pdf.

50   *poured $70 million*: Sagaian, "78 World Cup."

51   *clinic that Patricia had once been a part of disbanded*: Archivo Biográfico Familiar Pérez Roisinblit, 154.

51   *they left behind leaflets*: Department of State, "Montoneros 1977 Material," 1977, 14, https://www.archives.gov/files/argentina/data/docid-32735831.pdf.

51   *began to yearn for peace*: Archivo Biográfico Familiar Pérez Roisinblit, 271.

51   *José was similarly keen*: Interview with Graciela Tobar.

51   *Occasionally, he placed cryptic classified ads*: Archivo Biográfico Familiar Pérez Roisinblit, 270; Mansión Seré IV/RIBA II Case, Mariana Eva Pérez testimony.

51   *she was also the guarantor on the lease*: Plan Sistemático Trial, Causa N° 1351, "FRANCO, Rubén O. y otros s/sustracción de menores de diez años," May 30, 2011, Rosa Roisinblit testimony (hereafter Plan Sistemático Trial).

51   *Patricia and José were thrilled*: Mansión Seré IV/RIBA II Case, Mariana Eva Pérez testimony.

52 *José changed diapers:* Archivo Biográfico Familiar Pérez Roisinblit, 312.

52 *"Ay, Patri!":* Ibid., 272.

CHAPTER 8—SHOW ME THE BODY

53 *a weekly ritual:* Bublik, *Abuela,* 217.

54 *scenes of geishas that Rosa had cross-stitched:* Ibid., 218.

54 *no longer hunting her:* Archivo Biográfico Familiar Pérez Roisinblit, 307.

54 *"Se llevaron a los chicos":* Bublik, *Abuela,* 62.

54 *outlines of the 60:* Ibid.

54 *covered in 170,000 terra-cotta tiles:* "AySA—Palacio," Aysa.com.ar, 2019, https://www
    .aysa.com.ar/lobuenodelagua/gigantes/palacio.

55 *fluttered in the breeze:* Bus route in 1978 and appearance of the Linea 60 buses in that
    period were confirmed by email with Ignacio Gadea, the director of *Revista Colectibondi,*
    an Argentine magazine dedicated to *colectivos.*

55 *Cabildo and Juramento:* Bublik, *Abuela,* 62.

55 *Rosa spotted her in-laws by the swings:* Ibid.

55 *she could muster a few words:* Mariana Eva Pérez, *Diario de una Princesa Montonera: 110%
    Verdad* (Buenos Aires: Capital Intelectual S.A., 2012), 91; Mariana Eva Pérez, "Abuelo
    Universal," *Decía Mi Abuelo* (blog), August 20, 2008, https://deciamiabuelo.blogspot.com
    /2008/08/abuelo-universal.html.

55 *"didn't know anything about anything":* Plan Sistemático Trial, Rosa Roisinblit testimony.

56 *asados, long, leisurely barbecues:* Rosa Roisinblit interview with Rita Arditti, 17, https://
    openarchives.umb.edu/digital/collection/p15774coll10/id/881/rec/35.

56 *who helped her draw up a habeas corpus:* Plan Sistemático Trial, Rosa Roisinblit testimony.

56 *"show me the body":* Different sources offer different translations for "habeas corpus."
    Merriam-Webster offers "you shall have the body." I used the American Civil Liberties
    Union's definition.

56 *later drafted political screeds:* Mariana Eva Pérez, "Mi Abuelo Benjamín," *Decía Mi Abuelo*
    (blog), July 29, 2009, https://deciamiabuelo.blogspot.com/2009/06/mi-abuelo-benja
    min.html.

56 *on October 11:* RIBA Trial, Fundamentos, 159.

56 *ballets and operas with Benjamín:* Bublik, *Abuela,* 46–47.

56 *a line of women like her:* Claudia Bacci, Vera Carnovale, and Alejandra Oberti, *Abogados,
    Derecho y Política* (Buenos Aires: Memoria Abierta, 2010), 42.

57 *"What are they possibly going to do":* Rosa Roisinblit interview with Rita Arditti, 6.

57 *broke the silence in Rosa's apartment:* Rosa Roisinblit letter to Tom Farer, president of the In-
    ter-American Commission on Human Rights (IACHR), undated, Rosa Tarlovsky de Roisin-
    blit Fondo Personal, Caja 12, CPM (hereafter cited as Rosa Roisinblit letter to Tom Farer).

57 *"Mamá, I was mistaken":* Plan Sistemático Trial, Rosa Roisinblit testimony.

57 *the pregnancy was proceeding perfectly:* Nosiglia, *Botín de Guerra,* 143.

57 *"Señora Roisinblit, pay attention":* Ibid.

57 *And she should stay far away:* Rosa Roisinblit letter to Tom Farer; Elevación vs. RIBA, 218.

57 *"The charges against your daughter aren't serious":* Plan Sistemático Trial, Rosa Roisinblit
    testimony.

57   *"But first, you need to prepare yourself"*: Nosiglia, *Botín de Guerra*, 143.

57   *October 17*: Cedula de Notificación, October 17, 1978, Rosa Tarlovsky de Roisinblit Fondo Personal, box 12, CPM.

57   *"You have been notified"*: Ibid.

58   *the shrill ring of her phone*: Rosa Roisinblit letter to Tom Farer.

58   Was Mariana being kept up-to-date: The letter to Tom Farer does not mention vaccines, but in most of her other testimony, including Elevación vs. RIBA, 218, and her testimony in the Plan Sistemático Trial, Rosa mentioned the man on the phone saying that Patricia wanted to ask if Mariana was up-to-date on her vaccines.

58   *Only later would Rosa wonder*: Plan Sistemático Trial, Rosa Roisinblit testimony.

58   *"Behave yourself"*: Nosiglia, *Botín de Guerra*, 144.

CHAPTER 9—WHITE WOOL

59   *Rosa sat as though chained to her telephone*: Rosa Roisinblit interview with Rita Arditti, 6.

59   *paged through each morning*: Bublik, *Abuela*, 222.

59   *Things were heating up*: Robert Barros, "Beagle Channel," NACLA, September 25, 2007, https://nacla.org/article/beagle-channel.

59   *ordered "darkness operations"*: "Se cumplió el operativo de oscurecimiento," *Clarín*, October 25, 1978.

59   *127 percent in less than a year*: Juan de Onis, "Argentina Paralyzed by Inflation," *New York Times*, November 24, 1978.

59   *23 percent in a month*: "Aumentos de precios en octubre último," *La Nación*, November 18, 1978.

59   *Argentines flooded exchange houses*: "Demanda y Suba del Dólar," *Clarín*, November 2, 1978.

59   *fine dresses and children's books*: Bublik, *Abuela*, 101.

60   *"Where is Patricia?"*: Ibid., 102.

60   *she chose white wool*: Nosiglia, *Botín de Guerra*, 143.

60   *forty families, their Torah scrolls*: Bublik, *Abuela*, 20.

60   *amass 600,000 hectares of land*: Silvia Schenkolewski-Kroll, "The Twentieth Century in Iberian and Latin American History," in *Jewish Literatures in Spanish and Portuguese*, ed. Ruth Fine and Susanne Zepp (Berlin: De Gruyter, 2022), 373–416, https://doi.org/10.1515 /9783110563795-013. This number is also mentioned in Ernst Schwarz and Johan C. Te Velde, "Jewish Agricultural Settlement in Argentina: The ICA Experiment," *Hispanic American Historical Review* 19, no. 2 (May 1, 1939): 189, https://doi.org/10.1215/00182168 -19.2.185, though I have also encountered lower estimates in my reading.

60   *150,000*: Diego Armus, "El Once: The Changing Character of an Iconic Jewish Neighborhood," in *The Buenos Aires Reader: History, Culture, Politics*, ed. Diego Armus and Lisa Ubelaker Andrade (Durham, NC: Duke University Press, 2024), https://doi.org /10.1353/book.129068.

60   *an alternative to Palestine*: United Nations, "Origins and Evolution of the Palestine Problem: 1917–1947 (Part I)," Question of Palestine, 2021, https://www.un.org/unispal/his tory2/origins-and-evolution-of-the-palestine-problem/part-i-1917-1947/.

60   *Among the settlers on this particular ship*: Bublik, *Abuela*, 20.

61   *a hamlet near Moisés Ville*: The town was called Las Veinticuatro Casas.

61   *successful ranchers*: Bublik, *Abuela*, 20–21.

61 *four synagogues to choose from*: Alfredo Conti et al., "Moisés Ville: Primer Poblado Judío de Argentina," *Instituto de Investigaciones En Turismo, Universidad Nacional de La Plata*, June 2021, 14.

61 *a series of mysterious murders*: Javier Sinay, *The Murders of Moisés Ville: The Rise and Fall of the Jerusalem of South America* (Brooklyn, New York: Restless Books, 2022).

61 *the mayor was Jewish*: Calvin Sims, "Moises Ville Journal; Sun Has Set on Jewish Gauchos, but Legacy Lives," *New York Times*, May 1, 1996, https://www.nytimes.com/1996/05/01/world/moises-ville-journal-sun-has-set-on-jewish-gauchos-but-legacy-lives.html.

61 *fulfilled his vow*: Bublik, *Abuela*, 21–22.

61 *five girls and two boys*: Ibid., 23.

61 *forced to sell off*: Rosa Roisinblit interview with Rita Arditti, 3.

61 *They read and debated topics*: Bublik, *Abuela*, 23.

62 *knishes and gefilte fish*: Ibid., 24.

62 *scrimped so their children could attend the performance*: Ibid., 40.

62 *horse-drawn cart*: Rosa Roisinblit interview with Rita Arditti, 18.

62 *Spanish school in the morning*: Ibid., 3.

62 *scrambles up trees with her male cousins*: Bublik, *Abuela*, 24.

62 chica del pueblo: Rosa Roisinblit interview with Rita Arditti, 3.

62 "*We planted wheat and grew doctors*": Lawrence D. Bell, "The Jews and Perón: Communal Politics and National Identity in Peronist Argentina, 1946–1955" (PhD diss., Ohio State University, 2002), 41.

62 *concerts and the ballet*: Bublik, *Abuela*, 46.

62 *the local Hebraica*: Ibid., 47.

63 *a long-sleeved gown*: Author Observation of Wedding Photos, Rosa Tarlovsky de Roisinblit Fondo Personal, Caja 5, CPM.

63 *paying the rent*: Plan Sistemático Trial, Rosa Roisinblit testimony.

63 *her youngest sister, Sola*: Bublik, *Abuela*, 99.

63 *nine years younger*: I calculated this age gap using the Archivo Biográfico Familiar. Sola was seventy-five when she was interviewed in July 2003. Rosa was born in August of 1919; the physical description of Sola also comes from the Archivo Biográfico.

63 *Rosa who sang Sola to sleep*: Archivo Biográfico Familiar Pérez Roisinblit, 55.

63 *She had stepped in*: Ibid.

63 *Patricia would sometimes help Sola get ready*: Ibid., 60.

63 *gathering spot for left-leaning youths*: Ibid., 61.

63 "*I am terrified*": Bublik, *Abuela*, 99.

64 *She waited in the car*: Ibid.

64 *balconies that protruded from each floor*: I was able to confirm that the building looked the same in 1978 as it does today via this aerial map from 1978, administered by the city of Buenos Aires: http://www.ssplan.buenosaires.gov.ar/webfiles/mapa_aereas.php.

64 *she called for a locksmith*: Bublik, *Abuela*, 99.

64 *The television and leather chairs*: Ibid.

64 *Mariana's toys had been taken*: Archivo Biográfico Familiar Pérez Roisinblit, 16.

64 *Even the pantry had been ransacked*: RIBA Trial, Rosa Roisinblit testimony, May 4, 2016.

64 *only one item*: Ibid.

65 *a man with a bushy black mustache*: Nosiglia, *Botín de Guerra*, 144.

65 *"Look, señora"*: Plan Sistemático Trial, Rosa Roisinblit testimony.

65 *her modest heels sank into the dirt*: Marta Dillon, "El Relato Sobre el Trabajo y Búsqueda de las Abuelas," Comisión Provincial por la Memoria, n.d., 8.

65 *"This is an open jail"*: Plan Sistemático Trial, Rosa Roisinblit testimony.

CHAPTER 10—NOTHING TO LOSE

66 *"Judío se nace, no se hace"*: RIBA Trial, Rosa Roisinblit testimony.

66 *had grown to 300,000*: Valeria Navarro, "Discriminación y Reconciliación Comunidad Judeo-Argentina y Su Relación con el Régimen Militar Argentino (1976–1989)," *Cuadernos Judaicos* 26 (December 2012), https://doi.org/10.5354/0718-8749.2009.25068.

66 *sold fraudulent Argentine passports*: Tomás Eloy Martínez, "Perón and the Nazi War Criminals," The Wilson Center, 1984; "Wiesenthal Says Nazis Paid $60,000,000 for False Argentine Passports," *Jewish Telegraphic Agency*, March 31, 1967, https://www.jta.org/archive/wiesenthal-says-nazis-paid-60000000-for-false-argentine-passports.

66 *a number of synagogues*: "Memo for George Lister," December 9, 1976, Argentina Declassification Project, https://www.archives.gov/files/argentina/data/docid-32732651.pdf.

67 *looking at their watches impatiently while they talked*: Hernán Dobry, "La DAIA y el Silencio Sobre los Desaparecidos Durante la Dictadura," *Nueva Sion*, September 7, 2014, https://nuevasion.com.ar/archivos/6042.

67 *the organization had used all its political capital*: Ibid.

67 *"Ah, if a Jewish mother comes"*: Bublik, *Abuela*, 105.

67 *"they'll bring me my daughter"*: Ibid., 106.

67 *"Go see our lawyer"*: Ibid.

68 *disappearing at a disproportionate rate*: Uki Goñi, "Jews Targeted in Argentina's Dirty War," *Guardian*, March 24, 1999, https://www.theguardian.com/theguardian/1999/mar/24/guardianweekly.guardianweekly1.

68 *cassettes of Hitler speeches*: Uki Goñi, "Pope Francis and the Missing Marxist," *Guardian*, December 11, 2013, https://www.theguardian.com/world/2013/dec/11/pope-francis-argentina-esther-careaga.

68 *"If he tells me there aren't any"*: Bublik, *Abuela*, 107.

68 *his "supreme duty"*: "The 1970s: Where is Argentina Now?" "'I Have No Right to Be Silent': The Human Rights Legacy of Rabbi Marshall T. Meyer," Duke University Library Exhibits, https://exhibits.library.duke.edu/exhibits/show/ihavenorighttobesilent/whereisargentinanow.

69 *"what wasn't being said in their churches"*: Daniel Goldman and Hernán Dobry, *Ser Judío en los Años Setenta* (Buenos Aires: Siglo Veintiuno Editores, 2014), 166.

69 *imitate Meyer's Hebrew prayers*: Ibid.

69 *constantly rang with death threats*: "How is a Human Being Made to Disappear?" "'I Have No Right to Be Silent': The Human Rights Legacy of Rabbi Marshall T. Meyer," Duke University Library Exhibits, https://exhibits.library.duke.edu/exhibits/show/ihavenorighttobesilent/madetodisappear.

69 *"This Jew is going to walk in"*: Ibid.

69 *"the only thing that distinguishes"*: "I Charge You To Do Something," "'I Have No Right to Be Silent': The Human Rights Legacy of Rabbi Marshall T. Meyer," Duke University Library Exhibits, https://exhibits.library.duke.edu/files/original/e144096a86872fd95cab 174e27fdaf07.jpg.

69 *reached by trudging up a staircase*: RIBA Trial, Rosa Roisinblit testimony.

69 *"tomorrow a bunch of grandmothers"*: Rosa Roisinblit interview with Rita Arditti, 6.

CHAPTER 11—AZUCENA

73 *"I have to tell you something!"*: Arrosagaray, *Biografía de Azucena Villaflor*, 97.

73 *she was proud of his social conscience*: Interview with Cecilia De Vincenti.

73 *build one of the nicest homes*: Ibid.

73 *"Was it really necessary to build such a showy house?"*: Ibid.

74 *"What the hell did you do"*: Daniel Cecchini, "La Incansable Lucha y la Terrible Muerte de Azucena Villaflor, Fundadora de Madres de Plaza de Mayo," *Infobae*, December 20, 2021, https://www.infobae.com/sociedad/2021/12/20/la-incansable-lucha-y-la-terrible-muerte -de-azucena-villaflor-fundadora-de-madres-de-plaza-de-mayo/.

74 *Paco*: Baschetti, "De Vicenti, Néstor"; interview with Cecilia De Vincenti.

74 *a bullet scar on Néstor's leg proved it*: Arrosagaray, *Biografía de Azucena Villaflor*, 96.

74 *the troops lashed Raquel*: Ibid., 97.

74 *Néstor was not being held by the police*: Ibid., 100.

74 *promptly at nine in the evening*: Ibid., 215; specific foods come from an interview with Cecilia De Vincenti.

74 *"made you think of a great fortress"*: Hebe de Bonafini and Matilde Sánchez, "The Madwomen at the Plaza de Mayo," *Argentina Reader*, December 31, 2020, 432, https://doi.org /10.1515/9780822384182-061.

74 *their favorite meals*: "Cecilia De Vincenti: Hija de Azucena Villaflor," *Educación y Memoria*, 2016, www.educacionymemoria.com.ar/cecilia-de-vincenti.

75 *granted only ten visits per day*: Uki Goñi, *El Infiltrado: Astiz, Las Madres, y El Herald* (Biblioteca Uki Goñi, 2018), ch. 4, Kindle.

75 *"help me with this sad situation"*: Arrosagaray, *Biografía de Azucena Villaflor*, 101.

75 *"I'll try to do everything possible"*: Bonafini and Sánchez, "The Madwomen at the Plaza de Mayo," 431.

75 *"maybe he will never reappear"*: Mellibovsky, *Circle of Love Over Death*, 45.

75 *their own* compañeros: Ramos Padilla, *Chicha*, 143–44.

75 *some mothers turned to fortune tellers*: Mellibovsky, *Circle of Love Over Death*, 60.

75 *told Azucena to visit Monseñor Emilio Teodoro Grasselli*: Ricardo Ragendorfer, "Crónica del Secuestro y Asesinato de Azucena Villaflor, Primera Madre de Plaza de Mayo," *Tiempo Argentino*, April 30, 2022, https://www.tiempoar.com.ar/ta_article/los-dos-secuestros-de -azucena-villaflor-primera-madre-de-plaza-de-mayo/; occassionally Grasselli's name is also spelled Graselli. I have chosen the spelling used by human rights organizations Memoria Abierta and CELS, and the Argentine legal news site Infojus Noticias.

76 *Upstairs from the chapel*: Goñi, *El Infiltrado*, 62.

76 *demanded IDs and collected women's purses*: Ramos Padilla, *Chicha*, 120.

76 *take their cigarettes along with them*: Goñi, *El Infiltrado*, 62.

76 *given a number that functioned as a pass*: Comisión Nacional sobre la Desaparición de Personas, *Nunca Más* (Buenos Aires: Editorial Universitaria de Buenos Aires, 1984), 261.

76 *atop which lay a metal coffer*: Ramos Padilla, *Chicha*, 121. There is some ambiguity about whether the coffer was on top of the desk or whether Grasselli had a separate metal filing cabinet he could reach from his desk; Grasselli himself later described the coffer in the Trial of the Juntas. He estimated that he compiled 2,500 cards. Memoria Abierta, Testimonio de Emilio Grasselli, Buenos Aires, 1985.

76 *bore scarlet Ms*: Ibid., 122.

76 *turned these cards over*: "Secuestraron Fichas de Desaparecidos," *La Nación*, May 12, 1999, https://www.lanacion.com.ar/politica/secuestraron-fichas-de-desaparecidos-nid138137/.

76 *under Grasselli's desk*: Alejandra Dandan, "Su Rol Era Desviar Información y Delatar," *Página 12*, September 23, 2015, https://www.pagina12.com.ar/diario/elpais/1-282269 -2015-09-23.html.

77 *"Take a taxi home"*: Ramos Padilla, *Chicha*, 144.

77 *"perhaps he'll come"*: Ana and Virginia Giannoni and Madres de Plaza de Mayo, *Las Viejas: Madres de Plaza de Mayo Línea Fundadora. Cuentan una Historia* (Buenos Aires: Marea Editorial, 2014), 50.

77 *"They're all dead"*: Plan Sistemático Trial, Rosa Roisinblit testimony.

77 *"Christian form of death"*: Verbitsky, *El Vuelo*, 36.

77 *demanded visitors to remove their shoes*: Laureano Barrera, "Hebe: 'Todo Esto Nació Aquel Día en el Que Azucena Villaflor Dijo Basta,'" Infojus Noticias, May 1, 2015, http:// www.archivoinfojus.gob.ar/nacionales/hebe-todo-esto-nacio-aquel-dia-en-el-que-azucena -villaflor-dijo-basta-8378.html.

77 *informed the woman*: Arrosagaray, *Biografía de Azucena Villaflor*, 106.

78 *"All that we're doing"*: Goñi, *El Infiltrado*, 63.

78 *Tapping her leg*: Arrosagaray, *Biografía de Azucena Villaflor*, 105.

78 *"What we have to do"*: Goñi, *El Infiltrado*, 63.

78 *"Let's go to the Plaza de Mayo"*: Ibid.

78 *"But what will we do in the plaza?"*: Arrosagaray, *Biografía de Azucena Villaflor*, 106.

78 *"Nothing special"*: Ibid.

78 *It was decided*: In an interview with scholar Antonius C. G. Robben, Grasselli would later suggest that some people credited him with founding the Madres de Plaza de Mayo because he encouraged women to "walk, ask, walk around streets and squares" (Robben, *Political Violence and Trauma in Argentina*, 286.) But testimony in *Nunca Más* contradicts this version of events; one relative of the disappeared suggested Grasselli told him "not to make much noise" (CONADEP, *Nunca Más*, 261).

CHAPTER 12—THE MOTHERS

80 *"El pueblo quiere saber de que se trata!"*: Jorge Rivas, "El Pueblo Sabe de Qué Se Trata," *Página 12*, May 26, 2011, https://www.pagina12.com.ar/diario/elpais/subnotas/168874 -53848-2011-05-26.html.

80 *having left their pocketbooks behind*: Victoria Ginzberg, "Madres de Plaza de Mayo," Comisión Provincial por la Memoria, n.d., https://www.comisionporlamemoria.org /archivos/educacion/organismos/dossier3.pdf.

80 *"Are you here for the same reason as I am?"*: Ibid.

80 *fourteen women showed up*: Thirteen of the women were related to *desaparecidos*. The fourteenth was a communist activist who did not identify herself by name. Arrosagaray, *Biografía de Azucena Villaflor*, 115–16.

80 *"We were anonymous, distrustful people"*: Bonafini and Sánchez, "The Madwomen at the Plaza de Mayo," 430.

80 *pigeons pecking for scraps in the grass*: Gabriela Naso, "Azucena Villaflor: La Madre Que Dijo 'Vamos a La Plaza,'" AUNO, December 9, 2017, https://auno.org.ar/azucena-villa flor-la-madre-que-dijo-vamos-a-la-pla.

81 *finishing up an official visit to Córdoba*: "Videla Finaliza Hoy Su Visita a Córdoba," *Clarín*, April 30, 1977.

81 *"a disaster"*: Giannoni and Madres de Plaza de Mayo, *Las Viejas*, 54.

81 *"We have to do something!"*: Ginzberg, "Madres de Plaza de Mayo."

81 *"A vos quién te manda?"*: Giannoni and Madres de Plaza de Mayo, *Las Viejas*, 54.

81 *"Together we can do something"*: Ibid.

81 *"Worse luck than we've already had?"*: Ulises Gorini, "La Historia de una Rebeldía," *Página 12*, March 12, 2006, https://www.pagina12.com.ar/diario/sociedad/3-64181-2006-03 -12.html.

81 *They decided to write a letter to Videla*: There is some discrepancy about whom the Abuelas were requesting the meeting with. *Las Viejas*, which is a compendium of first-person testimony from the Madres themselves and *Biografía de Azucena Villaflor* confirm it was Videla. But several other sources, including Gorini, "La Historia de una Rebeldía," suggest it was with Albano Harguindeguy.

81 *He might not know that people were going missing*: Ulises Gorini, *La Rebelión de las Madres: Historia de las Madres de Plaza de Mayo* (La Plata: EDULP, 2017,) 76.

81 *"the mothers who meet every Thursday at three thirty"*: Ibid., 51.

81 *"Your daughter was at the Colegio Nacional"*: Giannoni and Madres de Plaza de Mayo, *Las Viejas*, 38.

81 *"We have to go to the plaza"*: Raquel Radío de Marizcurrena interview with Rita Arditti, November 25, 1993, 6, University of Massachusetts–Boston, Joseph P. Healey Library, https://openarchives.umb.edu/digital/collection/p15774coll10/id/885/rec/26.

82 *"We want a meeting with Videla"*: Giannoni and Madres de Plaza de Mayo, *Las Viejas*, 56.

82 *He was too busy*: Milton Del Moral, "El Día en Que 14 'Locas' Exigieron la Aparición de Sus Hijos: La Primera Ronda de Las Madres de Plaza de Mayo," *Infobae*, April 30, 2023, https://www.infobae.com/historias/2023/04/30/el-dia-en-que-14-locas-exigieron-la -aparicion-de-sus-hijos-la-primera-ronda-de-las-madres-de-plaza-de-mayo/.

82 *Videla isn't interested*: Jean Pierre Bousquet, *Las Locas de La Plaza de Mayo* (Buenos Aires: El Cid Editor, 1983), 51.

82 *agreed to bring them to meet*: There is some ambiguity about whether this meeting was spontaneous or planned in advance. Pages 95 and 96 (chapter 7) of the Kindle edition of *El Infiltrado* by Uki Goñi and pages 121 and 122 of Enrique Arrosagaray's *Biografía de Azucena Villaflor* suggest it was spontaneous. However, Madres scholar Ulises Gorini claims in this news article that more mothers than ever had shown up to the Plaza de Mayo in anticipation of the meeting, implying it was pre-planned: Gorini, "La Historia de una Rebeldía."

82 *dressed in full military regalia*: "El Día en Que las Madres Encararon a Harguindeguy por los Desaparecidos," *Clarín*, July 11, 2007, https://www.clarin.com/ediciones-anteriores /dia-madres-encararon-harguindeguy-desaparecidos_0_SJTWp8e1RKl.html.

82 *"I was happy I wasn't talking to MinInt. Harguindeguy"*: US Department of State, Office of the Historian, "Foreign Relations of the United States, 1977–1980," Volume 24, South America; US Department of State, Office of the Historian, "Telegram from the Embassy in Argentina to the Department of State," March 27, 1979, Document 99, Latin America.

82 *inviting them to sit in armchairs*: "El Día en Que las Madres Encararon a Harguindeguy por los Desaparecidos."

82 *"But, señora, has your daughter still not appeared?"*: Gorini, *La Rebelión de las Madres*, 76.

82 *grabbed a logbook*: "El Día en Que las Madres Encararon a Harguindeguy por los Desaparecidos."

82 *"I have a list of friends"*: Gorini, *La Rebelión de las Madres*, 76.

83 *"My daughter is not a prostitute"*: Memoria Abierta, Testimonio de María del Rosario Cerruti, Buenos Aires, 2006.

83 *charged into the office to see what was happening*: Gorini, *La Rebelión de las Madres*, 77.

83 *"We aren't going to leave the plaza"*: Giannoni and Madres de Plaza de Mayo, *Las Viejas*, 56.

83 *"Franco is a dictator"*: Ibid., 57.

83 *"This meeting"*: Goñi, *El Infiltrado*, 96.

84 *thirty-five reporters had disappeared*: Karen DeYoung, "Associated Press Reporter Missing in Buenos Aires," *Washington Post*, November 11, 1977, https://www.washingtonpost .com/archive/politics/1977/11/11/associated-press-reporter-missing-in-buenos-aires /d8f02788-1deb-4ebd-b21a-90fc6a7ef177/.

84 *Then he swiped her recorder*: Gorini, *La Rebelión de las Madres*, 82. This source spells her name Sally Chari, but the *New York Times* report from the time calls her Sally Chardy: "Argentine Police Arrest 150 Women Protesters," *New York Times*, October 15, 1977.

84 *one woman grabbed his testicles and squeezed*: Gorini, *La Rebelion de las Madres*, 82.

84 *the other police in the plaza made no attempt to arrest the women*: Ibid.

84 *"Plaza Mayo Mothers Protect U.S. Newswoman"*: "Plaza Mayo Mothers Protect U.S. Newswoman," *Buenos Aires Herald*, August 16, 1977.

85 *"It was an honor to scream"*: Goñi, "Pope Francis and the Missing Marxist."

85 *joy was something consigned to her past life*: Gorini, *La Rebelion de las Madres*, 83.

85 *swelled to several hundred*: "Women Arrested after Plaza de Mayo Meeting."

85 *commanding them to disperse*: Gorini, *La Rebelion de las Madres*, 84–85.

85 *"Señoras, tienen que circular"*: Ibid., 84.

85 *"We'll move two by two"*: Ibid., 85.

85 *dragged about fifteen Madres*: "Women Arrested After Plaza de Mayo Meeting," *Buenos Aires Herald*, August 26, 1977.

85 *commandeered five colectivos*: "Argentine Police Arrest 150 Women Protesters."

86 *the buses' floors were blanketed*: Raquel Radio de Marizcurrena interview with Rita Arditti, 5.

86 *"wanted his wife to be at home at all times"*: Arrosagaray, *Biografía de Azucena Villaflor*, 52.

86 *"Basta, Azucena!"*: Cecchini, "La Incansable Lucha y la Terrible Muerte de Azucena Villaflor, Fundadora de Madres de Plaza de Mayo."

86   *"We have to wear something"*: Bonafini and Sánchez, "The Madwomen at the Plaza de Mayo," 435.

87   *"No, we are the Mothers of the Plaza de Mayo"*: Giannoni and Madres de Plaza de Mayo, *Las Viejas*, 76.

87   *held up a sign with black-and-white photos*: Gorini, *La Rebelion de las Madres*, 98.

87   *the priest refused*: Ibid.

87   *they would be impossible to miss*: Gorini, *Rebelión de las Madres*, 85.

88   *burnt with cigarettes, and electrocuted*: John B. Oakes, "Agony in Argentina," *New York Times*, June 29, 1979, https://www.nytimes.com/1979/06/29/archives/agony-in-argentina.html.

88   *After Esther spoke to the* Buenos Aires Herald: Goñi, "Pope Francis and the Missing Marxist."

88   *"I will go on until we find them all"*: "Firman Acuerdo para Desarrollar una Cátedra Sobre Derechos Humanos Abierta a Todo Público," Coordinadora de Derechos Humanos del Paraguay, December 1, 2020, https://www.codehupy.org.py/firman-acuerdo-para-desarrollar-una-catedra-sobre-derechos-humanos-abierta-a-todo-publico/.

88   *wore a white T-shirt that revealed tanned biceps*: Goñi, *El Infiltrado*, 92. There is some debate over when exactly Gustavo Niño appeared. In *Biografía de Azucena Villaflor*, Arrosagaray suggests it might have been in October and that he first introduced himself to Azucena in church on Sunday, October 17, 1977, before attending a march the following Thursday. Uki Goñi's book suggests he infiltrated the Madres earlier, in July.

88   *"You shouldn't be here"*: Goñi, *El Infiltrado*, 92.

88   *he had introduced himself to Azucena*: Arrosagaray, *Biografía de Azucena Villaflor*, 185–86.

88   *handing Azucena a crumpled chit*: Ibid., 130.

88   *Niño gradually won over*: Sam Ferguson, *The Disappeared: Remnants of a Dirty War* (Lincoln: University of Nebraska Press, 2023), 160–61.

88   *"He always looked a little scared"*: Tina Rosenberg, *Children of Cain: Violence and the Violent in Latin America* (New York: Penguin, 1992), 80.

88   *"But—you're crazy!"*: Arrosagaray, *Biografía de Azucena Villaflor*, 187.

CHAPTER 13—THE GRANDMOTHERS

89   *to witness the signing of the Panama Canal treaties*: White House, "President Carter/President Videla Bilateral," Confidential, Memorandum of Conversation, September 9, 1977, President Obama Argentina Declassification Project, https://nsarchive.gwu.edu/document/21950-document-01-white-house-president-carter.

89   *"Because we are free"*: Office of the Historian, US Department of State, "Milestones: 1977–1980"—"Carter and Human Rights," 2019, https://history.state.gov/milestones/1977-1980/human-rights.

89   *"Those who recognized that man"*: White House, "President Carter/President Videla Bilateral."

90   *not only photos of her son and daughter-in-law*: Ramos Padilla, *Chicha*, 129.

90   *had been home in La Plata, knitting*: Nosiglia, *Botín de Guerra*, 21.

90   *four brand-new printing presses*: "Casa Mariani Teruggi Archivo," Asociación Anahí, 2022, https://asociacionanahi.org.ar/casa/.

90   *in the home's smooth white bathtub*: "Juan Carlos Elso—Testigo," Asociación Anahí, YouTube, October 3, 2022, https://www.youtube.com/watch?v=8tbtYYI3fws.

90   *swaddled in a blanket*: Ibid.

90 *signaling for the man to put her there*: Nosiglia, *Botín de Guerra*, 33; "'Chicha' Mariani: 'Para Mí, Marcela Es Mi Nieta Clara Anahí,'" *Página 12*, October 12, 2010, https://www.pagina12.com.ar/diario/ultimas/20-154820-2010-10-12.html.

90 *began steering clear of her*: Francisco Goldman, "Children of the Dirty War," *New Yorker*, March 12, 2012, https://www.newyorker.com/magazine/2012/03/19/children-of-the-dirty-war.

91 *"If you kill me, it doesn't matter"*: Juan Manuel Mannarino, "El Hijo de Chicha Mariani Ya No Será Un NN," Infojus Noticias, March 25, 2015, http://infojusnoticias.gov.ar/nacionales/el-hijo-de-chicha-mariani-ya-no-sera-un-nn-7939.html.

91 *Daniel, too, had been slain*: Eduardo Blaustein, "De La Tierra a La Luna" (Revista Haroldo, August 21, 2018), https://revistaharoldo.com.ar/nota.php?id=318.

91 *"You're very alone, señora"*: Nosiglia, *Botín de Guerra*, 36.

91 *dressed in a pink bathrobe and hair curlers*: Memoria Abierta, Testimonio de María Isabel "Chicha" Chorobik de Mariani, Buenos Aires, 2002.

91 *Licha had been especially battered by tragedy*: In December 1977, after her first meeting with Chicha, Licha would lose another son-in-law to the dictatorship.

91 *On her handkerchief*: Ramos Padilla, *Chicha*, 129.

91 *one hundred other mothers*: "Women Appeal for Vance's Aid," *Atlanta Constitution*, November 22, 1977.

92 *heels were of a sensible height*: These descriptions come from photos of the women published in the following article: "Cumplió intensa actividad Cyurs Vance, que parte hoy," *La Prensa*, November 22, 1977.

92 *turned to pose for the legion of photographers*: "Argentina: Human Rights Statement by Military Government After Visit by U.S. Secretary of State Cyrus Vance (1977)," British Pathé (Reuters, 1977), https://www.britishpathe.com/asset/108233/.

92 *Argentine military officers toting FAL rifles*: Nosiglia, *Botín de Guerra*, 64.

92 *"Vance! Vance! Ayúdenos, ayúdenos!"*: "Women Appeal for Vance's Aid."

92 *He shot his security detail a look*: Nosiglia, *Botín de Guerra*, 64.

93 *"What? You didn't hand yours over?"*: Ibid., 65.

93 *"Help us find our children!"*: "Help Us to Find Our Children; Argentine Mothers Urge Vance," *Miami Herald*, November 22, 1977.

93 *"Those of you who have pregnant daughters-in-law or daughters, step aside!"*: Ramos Padilla, *Chicha*, 134. The Abuelas organization currently celebrates October 22, when Mirta allegedly made this comment, as the date of its foundation. But Chicha long suggested that the true birthday of the Abuelas was the day of the Cyrus Vance march, November 21, 1977.

93 *under the violet blooms of a jacaranda tree*: Ramos Padilla, *Chicha*, 131.

93 *though it didn't stick for long*: The Abuelas officially changed their name to the Abuelas de Plaza de Mayo in 1980: Fabricio Andrés Laino Sanchis, "El Poder y las Armas Contra Biberones y Pañales. La Denuncia por los 'Niños Desaparecidos' y Su Conformación Como Problema Público Durante la Última Dictadura en Argentina (1976–1983)," *Pasado y Memoria*, Issue 26 (January 30, 2023): 433, https://doi.org/10.14198/pasado.22817.

94 *a few months before in La Prensa*: "Solo Pedimos la Verdad," *La Prensa*, October 5, 1977.

94 *aim to publish it on December 10*: Ferguson, *The Disappeared*, 162.

94 *Madre marched to the newspaper's headquarters*: Arrosagaray, *Biografía de Azucena Villaflor*, 199–200.

94 *two mothers stood out front*: Ibid.

95 *the priests had to open a special room to accommodate everyone*: Gorini, *La Rebelión de las Madres*, 138.

95 *Where is Azucena?*: Ibid., 138–39.

95 *Newcomers often mistook him for her son*: Rosenberg, *Children of Cain*, 80.

95 *he kissed Esther Careaga, María Ponce de Bianco, and Sister Alice Domon*: Gorini, *La Rebelión de las Madres*, 139.

95 *five Renault 12s and a Ford Falcon double-parked on the street*: Ibid., 138; Arrosagaray, *Biografía de Azucena Villaflor*, 207.

95 *as she watched her friends hauled away*: Memoria Abierta, Testimonio de María del Rosario Cerruti.

95 *"Why?"*: Gorini, *La Rebelión de las Madres*, 139.

95 *"This is a drug operation"*: Ibid.

96 *"Se las llevaron, se las llevaron!"*: Alejandra Dandan, "La Historia de La Infiltración de Astiz," *Página 12*, November 11, 2010, https://www.pagina12.com.ar/diario/elpais/1-156680-2010-11-11.html.

96 *urged her to try to remember*: The victims who disappeared from the Iglesia de la Santa Cruz are: María Ponce de Bianco, Esther Careaga, Alice Domon, Raquel Bulit, Patricia Oviedo, Ángela Auad, and Gabriel Horacio Horane. The next day, as part of the same operation, Remo Berardo, Horacio Elbert, and José Julio Fondevilla were taken. Gorini, *La Rebelión de las Madres*, 139–40.

96 *"kiss of death"*: In March of 1978, Astiz was dispatched to France to infiltrate a group of Argentine exiles under the alias "Alberto Escudero." He was recognized by one of the exiles who had previously attended meetings at the Iglesia de la Santa Cruz. This is how the Madres learned that the man they thought of as Gustavo Niño had betrayed them. As gathered from: Claudia Feld, "How Do Perpetrators Become Visible? Photographs and Visibility Dispositifs in the Identification of a Perpetrator During the Argentine Dictatorship," *Journal of Perpetrator Research* 6, no. 1 (December 22, 2023): 20–43, https://doi.org/10.21039/jpr.6.1.135.

96 *"I don't want to continue"*: Gorini, *La Rebelión de las Madres*, 140–41.

96 *"Our compañeras were fighting"*: Ibid.

96 *headquarters that afternoon*: There are conflicting accounts of what time the Madres went to the offices of *La Nación*. Page 142 of Ulises Gorini's *La Rebelión de las Madres* suggests that they went in the afternoon. An article in *Página 12* suggests they went at ten in the morning: Dandan, "La Historia de la Infiltración de Astiz."

96 *"If something happens to me, go on without me"*: Naso, "Azucena Villaflor."

96 *unless its content was typed up first*: Gorini, *La Rebelión de las Madres*, 142.

97 *Eventually, the staffer ceded*: Ibid., 143.

97 *"Writing this advertisement is a victory"*: Ibid., 142.

97 *Azucena pressed sheets of paper*: "El Regalo de Azucena a Hebe—Asociación Madres de Plaza de Mayo," 2020, https://madres.org/el-regalo-de-azucena-a-hebe/.

97 *You know you can always*: Ibid. Translation by author.

97 *prepared mate for her husband, Pedro*: Interview with Cecilia De Vincenti.

97   *her regular baker, Aníbal*: Arrosagaray, *Biografía de Azucena Villaflor*, 218.

97   *under an advertisement for a polo store*: "Solo Pedimos la Verdad," *La Nación*, December 10, 1977.

97   *Among the 804 names*: I counted 810 names, but this piece suggests it was 804: Dandan, "La Historia de la Infiltración de Astiz."

98   *just like she did every weekend*: Arrosagaray, *Biografía de Azucena Villaflor*, 65.

98   *"What do you want to eat"*: Ibid., 218.

98   *They shoved her into a Ford Falcon and sped off*: Ibid., 218–19.

98   *Among the detritus*: US Embassy in Argentina, "Report of Nuns [sic] Death," March 1978, 1978BUENOS02346, https://foia.state.gov/documents/argentina/0000A5AF.pdf.

98   *"crashing against hard objects after falling from a great height"*: Cecchini, "La Incansable Lucha y la Terrible Muerte de Azucena Villaflor, Fundadora de Madres de Plaza de Mayo."

98   *ningún nombre, no name*: "Las Cenizas de Azucena Villaflor Fueron Sepultadas en Plaza de Mayo," *Clarín*, December 9, 2005, https://www.clarin.com/ediciones-ante riores/cenizas-azucena-villaflor-sepultadas-plaza-mayo_0_rk8V9LyAKl.html.

CHAPTER 14—A VISIT TO THE TAILOR

99   *dedicated reader of* La Nación: Bublik, *Abuela*, 222.

99   *"I didn't know anything about that"*: Ibid., 111.

100 *pressing their mouths against the floor*: Mellibovsky, *Circle of Love Over Death*, 32.

100 *merely a place to sleep*: Ibid., 34.

100 *"gift to which [they] had no right"*: Ibid.

100 *baked Liliana a cake on her birthday*: Ibid.

100 *proudly defended as her "style"*: Ibid., 38.

100 *fired from point-blank range*: Nosiglia, *Botín de Guerra*, 173.

100 *Later, Rosa would not remember*: In her testimony for the Plan Sistemático case, Rosa recalled meeting Chicha, Licha, and Estela. She said that there was one more Abuela, but that she doesn't recall her identity.

101 *"la tía loca"*: Ramos Padilla, *Chicha*, 134.

101 *more than forty writs of habeas corpus*: Delia Giovanola de Califano interview with Rita Arditti, October 29, 1996, 6, University of Massachusetts–Boston, Joseph P. Healey Library, https://openarchives.umb.edu/digital/collection/p15774coll10/id/863/rec/10.

101 *"waste of time"*: Ibid, 9.

101 *stomp into the offices of military officers*: Ibid.

101 *had charged into the Ministry of the Interior*: Giannoni and Madres de Plaza de Mayo, *Las Viejas*, 103.

101 *arm in arm*: Ibid.

101 *"like a wet little chicken"*: Plan Sistemático Trial, Rosa Roisinblit testimony.

101 *a certain measure of peace*: Rosa Roisinblit interview with Rita Arditti, 7.

101 *"I wanted to fight"*: Plan Sistemático Trial, Rosa Roisinblit testimony.

102 *"to look for our grandchildren without forgetting our children"*: Soledad Iparraguirre, *Delia: Bastion de la Resistencia* (Buenos Aires: Marea, 2022), ch. 4, Kindle.

102 *favoring those with two entrances*: Raquel Radio de Marizcurrena interview with Rita Arditti, 26.

102   *couched their conversation in deceptively cheery code*: Ramos Padilla, *Chicha*, 153.

102   *they laid knitting needles*: Delia Giovanola de Califano interview with Rita Arditti.

102   *empty boxes tied up with ribbon*: Ibid.

102   *during the afternoon siesta*: Ramos Padilla, *Chicha*, 152; Nosiglia, *Botín de Guerra*, 132.

103   *abstained from their cigarettes*: Abuelas de Plaza de Mayo, *La Historia de Abuelas* (Buenos Aires: Abuelas de Plaza de Mayo, 2007), 23, https://escuelaprovincialsdh.mjus.gba.gob .ar/materiales/pdf/abuelas30.pdf.

103   *pooling the money to ensure everyone could eat*: Ramos Padilla, *Chicha*, 163.

103   *on the days the gaggle of grandmothers invaded*: Abuelas de Plaza de Mayo, *La Historia de Abuelas*, 23–24.

103   *Chicha was appointed its executive secretary*: Ramos Padilla, *Chicha*, 164.

103   *a green Royal so old and decrepit*: Ibid., 154.

103   *with just one index finger*: Matilde Herrera and Ernesto Tenembaum, *Identidad Despojo y Restitución* (Buenos Aires: Abuelas de Plaza de Mayo, 2007), 19, https://mail.abuelas .org.ar/resources/identidad_restitucion.pdf.

103   *They sent it by the regular Correo Argentino*: Ibid.

104   *borrowed a small room*: Nosiglia, *Botín de Guerra*, 191.

104   *a twenty-five-minute walk*: The Madres' apartment was on Uruguay 694, on the corner of Uruguay and Viamonte. This address is mentioned in Jean-Pierre Bosquet's *Las Locas de la Plaza de Mayo* and in Fabricio Andrés Laino Sanchis, "Madres-Abuelas. Apuntes Sobre La Formación Histórica de Abuelas de Plaza de Mayo," *Revista del Museo de Antropología*, August 31, 2023, 349, https://doi.org/10.31048/1852.4826.v16.n2.39176.

104   *"I am personally convinced that your children were terrorists"*: Nosiglia, *Botín de Guerra*, 130.

104   *slipping them scraps of paper*: Abuelas de Plaza de Mayo, *La Historia de Abuelas*, 27.

104   *parading around a beautiful baby*: Carolina Villella, "La Genética Forense Como Medio Probatorio de Crímenes Contra la Humanidad: Su Impacto en Causas Judiciales de Apropiación de Niños y Niñas Durante el Último Terrorismo de Estado en la Argentina," *Revista Vía Iuris*, Issue 29 (July 2020): 232, https://doi.org/10.37511/viaiuris.n29a9.

104   *instead they posed as mourners*: Herrera and Tenembaum, *Identidad Despojo y Restitución*, 78.

105   *seven centimeters of bulletproof glass and four locks*: Marcelo Larraquy, "El Misterio de Las Manos de Perón: Una Sierra para Profanar el Cadáver y la Tragedia Que Azotó a los Investigadores," *Infobae*, June 29, 2022, https://www.infobae.com/sociedad/2022/06/29 /el-misterio-de-las-manos-de-peron-una-sierra-para-profanar-el-cadaver-y-la-tragedia -que-azoto-a-los-investigadores/.

105   *a pen hidden among the blooms they carried*: Ramos Padilla, *Chicha*, 183.

105   *"Is there a baby in this house?"*: Abuelas de Plaza de Mayo, *La Historia de Abuelas*, 27.

105   *sought jobs as maids*: Arditti, *Searching for Life*, 67.

105   *Anatole Boris and Victoria Eva Julien Grisonas*: Henceforth I refer to Anatole simply by his first name and Victoria Eva by both her first and middle names to avoid confusion with her mother, who was also named Victoria.

CHAPTER 15—OPERATION CONDOR

106   *previously been in contact*: Caso Familia Julien-Grisonas Argentina N° 13.392, Escrito de Solicitudes, Argumentos y Pruebas, Corte Interamericana de Derechos Humanos,

May 20, 2020, 10, https://www.corteidh.or.cr/docs/casos/julien_grisonas_ar/3_esap .PDF.

106 *she spent several months*: The details of Angélica's search in the following paragraph come from "Renuncié a ellos por amor," *Solidaridad*, June 1982, as viewed in the Abuelas Archive, box 380, AR AIAPM CD 5 380.

106 *"Sometimes I would travel"*: Ibid.

107 *Argentina's armed forces were not alone*: Charis McGowan, "How a Pinochet 'Death Flight' Helicopter Became UK Gamepark Prop," *Guardian*, August 4, 2023, https:// www.theguardian.com/world/2023/aug/04/chile-pinochet-death-flights-helicopter-uk -park; Diego Oré, "Celdas Subterráneas Revelan Pasado Represivo en Bolivia," Reuters, March 6, 2009, https://www.reuters.com/article/world/us/celdas-subterrneas-revelan -pasado-represivo-en-bolivia-idUSSIE525117/.

107 *"leftists, communists, and Marxists"*: Federal Bureau of Investigations, "Operation Condor Cable," September 28, 1976, https://nsarchive2.gwu.edu/NSAEBB/NSAEBB8/docs /doc23.pdf.

107 *known as Operation Condor*: For a more comprehensive exploration of Operation Condor, see: Francesca Lessa, *The Condor Trials: Transnational Repression and Human Rights in South America* (New Haven: Yale University Press, 2022); and John Dinges, *The Condor Years: How Pinochet and His Allies Brought Terrorism to Three Continents* (New York: New Press, 2005).

107 *Ecuador and Peru signed on in 1978*: Francesca Lessa and Lorena Balardini, "No Safe Haven: Operation Condor and Transnational Repression in South America," *International Studies Quarterly* 68, no. 2 (March 14, 2024), https://doi.org/10.1093/isq/sqae035.

107 *urged the US government*: Top Secret Cable from Rio de Janiero, State Department, March 27, 1964, https://nsarchive2.gwu.edu/NSAEBB/NSAEBB118/bz02.pdf.

107 *supported a similar uprising in Bolivia*: Foreign Relations, 1964–1968, Volume 31, South and Central America; Mexico, https://2001-2009.state.gov/r/pa/ho/frus/johnsonlb/xxxi /36271.htm.

107 *in hopes of facilitating a military takeover*: Peter Kornbluh and Savannah Bock, "The CIA and Chile: Anatomy of an Assassination," National Security Archive, October 21, 2020, https://nsarchive.gwu.edu/briefing-book/chile/2020-10-22/cia-chile-anatomy-assassi nation.

108 *"cut out the political science lectures"*: Seymour M. Hersh, "Kissinger Said to Rebuke U.S. Ambassador to Chile," *New York Times*, September 27, 1974, https://www.nytimes.com /1974/09/27/archives/kissinger-said-to-rebuke-us-ambassador-to-chile-kissinger-anger .html.

108 *Most operations took place on Argentine soil*: For a map of Condor operations, see https:// plancondor.org/en/condor-map, compiled by Dr. Francesca Lessa, an associate professor in International Relations of the Americas at University College London (UCL), and her team.

108 *"a hunting ground"*: Sentencia Plan Condor y Automotores Orletti, August 9, 2015, 1225, https://plancondor.org/sites/default/files/2022-09/plan-condor-1era-instancia.pdf; English translation from Lessa, *The Condor Trials*, 220.

108 *"discreetly and through third parties"*: US Embassy Buenos Aires, Cable, Ambassador Rob-

ert Hill to Acting Assistant Secretary for Latin America, "Military Allegedly Wish to Send Representative to Meet with Secretary Kissinger," Secret, EXDIS, February 16, 1976, https://nsarchive.gwu.edu/document/20742-03.

108   *$49 million in military assistance*: Staff Meeting Transcripts, Secretary of State Henry Kissinger, Chairman, Secret, pages 19–23 regarding Argentina, March 26, 1976, National Archives and Records Administration, https://nsarchive.gwu.edu/document /20675-document-02-staff-meeting-transcripts-secretary.

108   *"We want you to succeed"*: Carlos Osorio and Kathleen Costar, "Kissinger to the Argentine Generals in 1976: 'If there are things that have to be done, you should do them quickly,'" National Security Archive, August 27, 2004, https://nsarchive2.gwu.edu//NSAEBB /NSAEBB133/index.htm.

108   *alumni of the School of the Americas*: Galtieri and Viola were both alumni. Richard F. Grimmett and Mark P. Sullivan, "U.S. Army School of the Americas: Background and Congressional Concerns," April 16, 2001, 7, https://sgp.fas.org/crs/intel/RL30532 .pdf.

108   *"fear, payment of bounties"*: Dana Priest, "U.S. Instructed Latins on Executions, Torture," *Washington Post*, September 21, 1996, https://www.washingtonpost.com/archive /politics/1996/09/21/us-instructed-latins-on-executions-torture/f7d86816-5ab3-4ef0 -9df6-f430c209392f/.

108   *intelligence with the FBI, CIA*: Dinges, *The Condor Years*, 123.

109   *the FBI actively investigated*: IACHR, Report No. 273/20, Petition 2253-12, Admissibility, Relatives of Jorge Isaac Fuentes Alarcón, Chile, September 23, 2020, https://www .oas.org/en/iachr/decisions/2020/chad2253-12en.pdf.

109   *secretly owned by the CIA*: "The CIA's 'Minerva' Secret," The National Security Archive, February 11, 2020, https://nsarchive.gwu.edu/briefing-book/chile-cyber-vault-intelli gence-southern-cone/2020-02-11/cias-minerva-secret.

109   *a US military radio network*: Dinges, *The Condor Years*, 122.

109   *used two armored cars to cut off traffic*: Corte Interamericana de Derechos Humanos, *Caso Familia Julien Grisonas vs. Argentina*, Sentencia, September 23, 2021, 26, https://www .corteidh.or.cr/docs/casos/articulos/resumen_437_esp.pdf.

109   *in the bathtub to protect them*: Report No. 56/19, Case 13.392, Admissibility and Merits, Julien-Grisonas Family, Argentina, May 4, 2019, https://summa.cejil.org/en/entity/ds fxwr0tyzh?page=2.

109   *shoving her into the trunk of a police car*: Ibid., 16–17.

109   *Anatole asked to enter the cockpit*: Interview with Anatole Larrabeiti.

109   *the Andes through the windshield*: Lessa, *The Condor Trials*, 3.

109   *a black car with tinted windows*: Ibid., 1.

110   *let them ride its horses around for free*: Interview with Anatole Larrabeiti.

110   *called the Carabineros*: Lessa, *The Condor Trials*, 1.

110   *"If my son and daughter-in-law don't appear"*: "Renuncié a ellos por amor."

110   *including representatives of CLAMOR and UNICEF*: Interview with Anatole Larrabeiti.

110   *"our reason for living"*: Jan Rocha, *CLAMOR: The Search for the Disappeared of the South American Dictatorships* (Warwickshire: Practical Action Publishing and Latin America Bureau, 2023), ch. 8, Kindle.

110   *looked exactly like her mother*: The details in the following paragraph come from "Renuncié a ellos por amor."

110   *was still haunted*: José Luis Baumgartner, *Mamá Julien* (Montevideo: Trilce, 1988), 115–16; interview with Anatole Grisonas; "Renuncié a ellos por amor," *Solidaridad*, June 1982, as viewed in the Abuelas Archive, box 380, AR AIAPM CD 5 380.

110   *ultimately agreed to leave*: "Renuncié a ellos por amor."

110   *"I couldn't make them suffer again"*: Ibid.

111   *Using donations and money*: Ramos Padilla, *Chicha*, 177.

111   *After initially backing Brazil's coup*: Catholic News Agency, "Brazil's Bishops Take Responsibility for Backing Junta," Catholic News Agency, April 5, 2014, https://www.catholic newsagency.com/news/29370/brazils-bishops-take-responsibility-for-backing-junta.

111   *bring back a doll for Clara Anahí*: "Chicha," 2022, Asociación Anahí, 2022, https://asoci acionanahi.org.ar/chicha/. The Asociación Anahí website has photos of many of the dolls Chicha brought home from her trips for Clara Anahí, including one from Brazil in 1979.

111   *wished to be taken to a hotel*: Ramos Padilla, *Chicha*, 178.

112   *hotel staff led them to a room*: Ibid.

112   *"What house are you staying in?"*: Ibid., 179.

113   *Brazilian lawyer Luiz Eduardo Greenhalgh and British journalist Jan Rocha*: Interview with Jan Rocha.

113   *Uruguayan military defectors who shared sensitive information*: Ibid., 16–17.

113   *she proudly underlined for emphasis*: Letter from Rosa Roisinblit to CLAMOR, circa 1980, Colección CLAMOR, Archivo Nacional de La Memoria.

114   *"I haven't heard any news of her"*: Ibid.

114   *a house offered to them by political asylees*: Ramos Padilla, *Chicha*, 180.

114   *Pegoraro gave birth to a baby girl while detained*: Testimony of Lisandro Cubas, Colección CLAMOR, ANM, AR-ANM-CLAMOR.

114   *"barely shadows began to have sexes and birth dates"*: Abuelas de Plaza de Mayo, *La Historia de Abuelas*, 33.

114   *enclosed in shiny wrappers*: Ramos Padilla, *Chicha*, 181.

114   *dirty socks and muddy shoes*: Ibid.

115   *"like a child pulling a prank"*: Ibid.

115   *offered some to the officers*: Memoria Abierta, Testimonio de María Isabel "Chicha" Chorobik de Mariani, Buenos Aires, 2002.

115   *"Who was going to suspect anything"*: Abuelas de Plaza de Mayo, *La Historia de Abuelas*, 33.

CHAPTER 16—THE BRITOS SISTERS

116   *winked at them*: Ramos Padilla, *Chicha*, 182–83.

116   *missives arrived from Costa Rica*: Author observation of correspondence in Abuelas Archive.

116   *who had fled north*: "'Buscamos Alrededor de 300 Nietos Que Tienen 40 y Pico de Años,'" *Mirador Provincial*, April 11, 2023, https://www.miradorprovincial.com/index.php/id _um/361523-buscamos-alrededor-de-300-nietos-que-tienen-40-y-pico-de-anos-tatiana -sfiligoy.html.

116   *the daughters of desaparecidos*: Testimonio de Tatiana Sfiligoy Ruarte Britos, October 18, 2019, Biblioteca Nacional Mariano Moreno, https://www.youtube.com/watch?v=ZO

d9Ryve9ic; interview with Tatiana Sfiligoy Ruarte Britos; interview with Tatiana Sfiligoy Ruarte Britos.

117   *Villarroel 562 in Villa Ballester:* "'Denuncia de Desaparición,'" Tatiana Ruarte Britos, Colección CLAMOR, ANM.

117   *wafted from his windows:* Nosiglia, *Botín de Guerra,* 214.

117   *his head covered by a hood:* "'Denuncia de Desaparición,'" Tatiana Ruarte Britos.

117   *the testimony of the butcher:* Ibid.

117   *someone holding a judicial citation:* Nosiglia, *Botín de Guerra,* 214.

117   *often visited Judge Basso:* Ibid., 215.

118   *"Are these your granddaughters?":* Ibid.

118   *so short it looked almost shaved:* Ibid.

118   *"Those are your granddaughters":* Ibid.

118   *"You think so, Estela?":* Ibid.

118   *visit him three times:* Testimonio de Tatiana Sfiligoy Ruarte Britos, October 18, 2019, Biblioteca Nacional Mariano Moreno.

118   *who else would have sung to them?:* Duolingo, Episode 58: "Los Niños de los Desaparecidos (The Children of the Disappeared)," May 21, 2020.

119   *scared to set foot outside their home:* Tatiana Sfiligoy and Danilo Albín, *En el Nombre de Sus Sueños* (Buenos Aires: Ediciones Fabro, 2013), 140.

119   *"What are the girls' names?":* This and the following dialogue comes from Nosiglia, *Botín de Guerra,* 215.

119   *"living portrait":* Herrera and Tenembaum, *Identidad Despojo y Restitución,* 212.

119   *"Do you recognize me?":* Ibid.; Tatiana herself recalls that all three of her grandmothers were present in the first meeting with the judge, but the Abuelas' official literature suggests there were two separate meetings: one with María Laura and Estela de Carlotto, and another with all three grandmothers.

119   *seemed as though she might faint:* Ibid., 213.

119   *an impassioned speech:* Ibid.

120   *hauled her off:* Testimonio de Tatiana Sfiligoy Ruarte Britos, October 18, 2019, Biblioteca Nacional Mariano Moreno.

120   *"I want you to feel calm":* Mariano Ambrosino et al., "Supresión de Identidad en Niños Apropiados Ilegalmente. Análisis del Material Televisivo 'Televisión por la Identidad,'" Aacademica.org (Facultad de Psicología—Universidad de Buenos Aires, 2024), 39.

CHAPTER 17—THE SURVIVORS

122   *donation from the World Council of Churches:* Ramos Padilla, *Chicha,* 191.

122   *one of the first ever sessions:* "Mandate of the Working Group on Enforced or Involuntary Disappearances," OHCHR, 2020, https://www.ohchr.org/en/special-procedures/wg -disappearances/mandate-working-group-enforced-or-involuntary-disappearances.

122   *one of Argentina's largest private banks:* Daniel Enrique Vaz, "Four Banking Crises: Their Causes and Consequences," Yale School of Management, 1998, https://elischolar.library .yale.edu/ypfs-documents/9629/.

122   *equivalent to 12 percent:* Ibid., 200

123   *blue-and-white sash:* "Argentina: General Roberto Viola Sworn in as New President,"

Reuters Archive Licensing, March 30, 1981, https://reuters.screenocean.com/record /919580.

123   *cavalrymen in feathered top hats*: "Viola Takes His Turn as the President of Argentina," *New York Times*, March 30, 1981.

123   *slowed to a trickle*: According to CONADEP, the vast majority of the 8,960 disappearances recorded took place between 1976 and 1977 (76.6 percent). Emilio Crenzel, "Argentina's National Commission on the Disappearance of Persons: Contributions to Transitional Justice," *The International Journal of Transitional Justice* 2 (2008): 175, doi: 10.1093/ijtj/ijn007; some editions of *Nunca Más* state there were 8,961 disappearances rather than 8,960.

123   *had released scathing reports*: "Testimony on Secret Detention Camps in Argentina," Amnesty International, February 1, 1980, https://www.amnesty.org/en/documents/amr13 /079/1979/en/; "Report on the Situation of Human Rights in Argentina," Organization of American States, 1980, https://www.cidh.org/countryrep/Argentina80eng/toc.htm.

123   *soaring into the triple digits*: Edward Schumacher, "Argentine Regime Severely Strained by Economic Woes," *New York Times*, July 5, 1981, https://www.nytimes.com/1981/07/05 /world/argentine-regime-severely-strained-by-economic-woes.html.

123   *military rule had "run out"*: Edward Schumacher, "Argentina Suffering a Shortage of Political Options," *New York Times*, April 26, 1981, https://www.nytimes.com/1981/04 /26/weekinreview/argentina-suffering-a-shortage-of-political-options.html.

123   *"naughty fat little man"*: Edward Schumacher, "In Argentina, Political Parties Come to Life Again," *New York Times*, October 22, 1981, https://www.nytimes.com/1981/10/22 /world/in-argentina-political-parties-come-to-life-again.html.

123   *Argentines plotted escapes*: "Emigration Becomes a Problem in Argentina," *New York Times*, October 25, 1981, https://www.nytimes.com/1981/10/25/world/emigration-becomes -a-problem-in-argentina.html.

123   *to a "strong presidency"*: "Former Argentine President Jailed for Criticizing Regime," *New York Times*, August 29, 1981, https://www.nytimes.com/1981/08/29/world/former -argentine-president-jailed-for-criticizing-regime.html.

124   *jailed former navy chief*: Edward Schumacher, "Ex-Member of Junta Is Arrested in Argentina," *New York Times*, July 15, 1981, https://www.nytimes.com/1981/07/15/world /ex-member-of-junta-is-arrested-in-argentina.html.

124   *"clinging" to power*: Edward Schumacher, "Though Unpopular, Argentine Armed Forces Cling To Power," *New York Times*, 1981, https://www.nytimes.com/1981/12/13/weekinreview /though-unpopular-argentine-armed-forces-cling-to-power.html?searchResultPosition=778.

124   *chauffeured sedans*: Ibid.

124   *"Baba, I want to go with you!"*: Bublik, *Abuela*, 87; Rosa Roisinblit Travel Notebook as consulted in Rosa Tarlovsky de Roisinblit Fondo Personal, Caja 6, CPM.

124   *Mariana could not pronounce* bobe: Erick Haimovich, "'Aprendí a Amar a Mis Padres, Aún Desde Su Ausencia,'" *Nueva Sion*, December 2014, 13, https://original-ufdc.ufllib .ufl.edu/AA00058024/00842/1j.

124   *"stay a little bit longer with me!"*: Rosa Roisinblit Travel Notebook as consulted in Rosa Tarlovsky de Roisinblit Fondo Personal, Caja 6, CPM.

124   *"how she cried!"*: Ibid.

124   *an intelligence center had been set up*: Eduardo Anguita, "Centro Piloto de París: El

Proyecto Político de Massera, El Misterio de Su Encuentro con Firmenich y el Asesinato Para Silenciar a Elena Holmberg," *Infobae*, October 22, 2019, https://www.infobae.com /sociedad/2019/10/22/centro-piloto-de-paris-el-proyecto-politico-de-massera-el-miste rio-de-su-encuentro-con-firmenich-y-el-asesinato-para-silenciar-a-elena-holmberg/.

124   *las chicas Argentinas*: Travel Notebook, box 380, Abuelas Archive, AR AIAPM CD 5 380.

124   *They met on February 21*: Ibid.

125   *where Rosa and Chicha were staying*: Bublik, *Abuela*, 196.

125   *Rosa was in her room*: Ibid.

125   *Chicha introduced the women to Rosa*: It is possible that Amalia Larralde was also present during this first meeting in Geneva. Rosa mentioned that she was in several pieces of testimony, including when she testified in the Plan Sistemático case. But I only had concrete proof, in the form of a dated letter they sent Rosa, of Sara Osatinsky and Ana María Martí's presence during the 1982 trip. Amalia Larralde later wrote Rosa a similar letter, laying out all she knew about Patricia's detention and experience of giving birth in the ESMA, but that letter was dated from 1983, leading me to believe Rosa did not meet her in Geneva until the year after. When asked if Amalia had been present for the meeting with Rosa in 1982, Ana María Martí said it was possible, as Amalia also lived in Geneva at that time, but she couldn't remember for certain.

125   *Martí and Osatinsky had been tasked*: Interview with Ana María Martí; Plan Sistemático Trial, Sara Osatinsky testimony, October 17, 2011.

125   *live to experience freedom once again*: Interview with Miriam Lewin.

125   *become a Perón-like figure*: Durán Milena, "La Implementación Del Plan Político de Massera a Través de Los Mecanismos Represivos de La Escuela de Mecánica de La Armada," Aacademica.org (Departamento de Historia de la Facultad de Filosofía y Letras. Universidad Nacional de Cuyo, 2013), https://www.aacademica.org/000-010/824.

125   *"la mujer de Matías"*: Letter from Ana María Martí and Sara Osatinsky, February 22, 1982, Rosa Tarlovsky de Roisinblit Fondo Personal, Caja 12, CPM.

125   *Osatinsky had personally witnessed*: Ibid.

CHAPTER 18—A DROP OF LIFE

126   *deep grooves etched into his face like rivers*: Legajo CONADEP N° 03673, Amalia Larralde; and Letter from Amalia Larralde to Rosa Roisinblit, February 26, 1983, Rosa Tarlovsky de Roisinblit Fondo Personal, Caja 12, CPM.

126   *she was blindfolded*: RIBA Trial, Mariana Eva Pérez testimony, May 4, 2016.

126   *returning in even worse shape than before*: Legajo CONADEP N° 03673, Amalia Larralde; and Letter from Amalia Larralde to Rosa Roisinblit, February 26, 1983, Rosa Tarlovsky de Roisinblit Fondo Personal, Caja 12, CPM.

126   *sometimes a guard would lead José upstairs*: RIBA Trial, Amalia Larralde testimony.

126   *a man showed up to take Patricia away*: RIBA Trial, Mariana Eva Pérez testimony.

127   *it was only a few paces long*: Author observation of the room in the ESMA where Patricia Roisinblit was detained.

127   *"a drop of life"*: Ibid., 214.

127   *until the blood-curdling sounds passed*: Actis et al., *Ese Infierno*, 67.

127   *Los Años Locos, El Globo, and Fechoría*: Ibid., 162.

127 *almost always fried calamari*: Ibid., 161.

127 *stalk the hallways at night like a tiger*: Legajo CONADEP N° 4442, Ana María Martí.

127 *"With you, one can talk about movies"*: Actis et al., *Ese Infierno*, 166.

128 *putrid beef sandwiches*: Ibid., 109.

128 *a small room that was painted yellow*: Archivo Biográfico Familiar Pérez Roisinblit, 203.

128 *that were never turned off*: Actis et al., *Ese Infierno*, 23.

128 *a green sheet draped over it*: Alejandra Dandan, "Parir en la ESMA," *Página 12*, November 6, 2011, https://www.pagina12.com.ar/diario/elpais/1-180635-2011-11-06.html.

128 *as Patricia pushed and screamed*: Letter from Amalia Larralde to Rosa Roisinblit, February 26, 1983, Rosa Tarlovsky de Roisinblit Fondo Personal, Caja 12, CPM.

128 *Around noon*: Francisco Gómez, Jorge Luis Magnacco, y Teodora Jofré s/ Sustracción Menor de 10 años, Sentencia Final, April 22, 2005, https://www.saij.gob.ar/jurispruden cia/FA05261086-SU30008610-francisco_sustraccion-federal-2005.htm?1.

128 *pocked by a red rash*: RIBA Trial, Miriam Lewin testimony, May 30, 2016.

128 *sobbing uncontrollably*: Letter from Amalia Larralde to Rosa Roisinblit, February 26, 1983, Rosa Tarlovsky de Roisinblit Fondo Personal, Caja 12, CPM.

128 *"Hola, hijo." Hi, son. "Soy yo"*: *Baldosas X la Memoria II/Barrios X Memoria y Justicia* (Buenos Aires: Instituto Espacio para la Memoria, 2010), 122, https://www.memoria palermo.org.ar/docs/Libro-2-Baldosas-por-la-Memoria.pdf.

129 *"Don't take him away from me"*: Dandan, "Parir en la ESMA."

129 *pull an extra mattress*: RIBA Trial, Amalia Larralde testimony.

129 *shouted desperately from the car*: Letter from Amalia Larralde to Rosa Roisinblit, February 26, 1983, Rosa Tarlovsky de Roisinblit Fondo Personal, Caja 12, CPM.

129 *She'd recognized them immediately*: Ibid.

129 *had hardened and fallen*: Legajo CONADEP N° 03673, Amalia Larralde.

129 *start moving around more*: Letter from Amalia Larralde to Rosa Roisinblit, February 26, 1983, Rosa Tarlovsky de Roisinblit Fondo Personal, Caja 12, CPM.

129 *not theirs to decide*: Ibid.

129 *Patricia was torn*: RIBA Trial, Amalia Larralde testimony.

130 *Forget what you've seen*: Letter from Amalia Larralde to Rosa Roisinblit, February 26, 1983, Rosa Tarlovsky de Roisinblit Fondo Personal, Caja 12, CPM.

130 *cradled in his mother's arms*: Ibid.

CHAPTER 19—LAS MALVINAS

133 *Five days after Rosa returned*: I viewed an entry stamp back to Argentina for March 14, 1982, in one of Rosa Roisinblit's passports held in the Rosa Tarlovsky de Roisinblit Fondo Personal, Caja 1, CPM.

133 *1,700 miles east of Argentina's southernmost tip*: "South Georgia Island," NASA Earth Observatory, September 7, 2002, https://earthobservatory.nasa.gov/images/2764/south-georgia -island.

133 *processing 175,250 whales*: Shafik Meghji, "A World Isolated from Life by 1,400km," BBC, April 2019, https://www.bbc.com/travel/article/20190329-a-world-isolated-from -life-by-1400km.

133 *"pong of bad fish"*: Tim Flannery, "On the Minds of the Whales," *New York Review of*

Books, February 9, 2012, https://www.nybooks.com/articles/2012/02/09/minds-whales
/?lp_txn_id=1542674.

133 *bone saws and harpoons*: "Britain's Abandoned Whale Hunting Stations—in Pictures,"
Guardian, June 10, 2014, https://www.theguardian.com/environment/gallery/2014/jun
/10/britains-whale-hunters-in-pictures.

134 *"The Argies have landed!"*: Margot Hornblower, "Bizarre Salvaging Incident Was Fuse
in Falklands War," *Washington Post*, May 14, 1982, https://www.washingtonpost.com
/archive/politics/1982/05/14/bizarre-salvaging-incident-was-fuse-in-falklands-war
/900d43b6-9dcf-49ab-9e23-6c654449cdba/.

134 *two larger islands and around 220 tiny ones*: "Malvinas," Argentina.gob.ar, May 3, 2018,
https://www.argentina.gob.ar/ejercito/malvinas. This number reflects Argentina's official estimate as well as that in the CIA's World Factbook; other sources, such as the
Falkland Islands Tourist Board, suggest the number of islands is 740.

134 *no arable land*: "Falkland Islands (Islas Malvinas)," Central Intelligence Agency, May 19,
2022, https://www.cia.gov/the-world-factbook/countries/falkland-islands-islas-malvinas/.

134 *4,524 square miles*: "Malvinas," Argentina.gob.ar, May 3, 2018, https://www.argentina
.gob.ar/ejercito/malvinas; CIA World Factbook suggests the area is closer to 4,700
square miles. "Falkland Islands (Islas Malvinas)."

134 *and their 600,000 sheep*: Kieran Mulvaney, "The Improbable Falklands War Still Res-
onates Decades Later," History, April 1, 2022, https://www.nationalgeographic.com
/history/article/falklands-war-history-and-legacy.

134 *"either a prank"*: Margot Hornblower, "Bizarre Salvaging Incident Was Fuse in Falklands
War," *Washington Post*, May 14, 1982, https://www.washingtonpost.com/archive/poli
tics/1982/05/14/bizarre-salvaging-incident-was-fuse-in-falklands-war/900d43b6-9dcf
-49ab-9e23-6c654449cdba/.

134 *"tit for tat, you buggers"*: "'Tit for Tat, You Buggers!': The Falklanders' Response to Argentina's Invasion of South Georgia," Gresham College, July 11, 2022, https://www
.gresham.ac.uk/watch-now/tit-tat-you-buggers-falklanders-response-argentinas-inva
sion-south-georgia.

135 *first such political killing recorded that year*: Edward Schumacher, "Breaking Silence on
Argentina's 'Missing,'" *New York Times*, April 4, 1982, https://www.nytimes.com/1982
/04/04/weekinreview/breaking-silence-on-argentina-s-missing.html.

135 *had cut out a clip about it*: "Argentine: Rivalité de Généreaux Comme Toile de Dond aux
Disparitions," *Tribune de Genève*, February 23, 1982, as viewed in box 380, Abuelas Archive, AR AIAPM CD 5 380.

135 *overwhelming the eighty-four*: "Argentina Seizes Falkland Islands; British Ships Move,"
New York Times, April 3, 1982, https://www.nytimes.com/1982/04/03/world/argentina
-seizes-falkland-islands-british-ships-move.html.

135 *sent a furious stream of telex messages*: "Communications Cut with the Falklands," *New
York Times*, April 3, 1982, https://www.nytimes.com/1982/04/03/world/communica
tions-cut-with-the-falklands.html.

136 *"What are all these rumors?"*: Ibid.

136 *waving blue-and-white flags*: *Clarín*, cover page, April 3, 1982, https://tapas.clarin.com
/tapa.html#19820403.

136 *a pinprick of ground*: "AV-5348 [Cadena Nacional: Discurso de Galtieri en Plaza de Mayo] (Fragmento II)," 1982, https://www.youtube.com/watch?v=QFp5X1KzPGU.

136 *twenty-eight thousand civilians*: "Registros de Voluntarios" (Malvinas Special Commission Fund, 2022), https://www.argentina.gob.ar/sites/default/files/ok_ficha_registro_de_voluntarios.pdf.

136 *total $54 million*: Diego Genoud, "El Enigma Del Fondo Patriótico," *La Nación*, April 1, 2012, https://www.lanacion.com.ar/opinion/el-enigma-del-fondo-patriotico-nid1461096/; Juan Bautista, "La Noche Negra de Cacho Fontana y Pinky: 'Las 24 Horas de las Malvinas,' Donaciones Millonarias y Lingotes de Oro," *Infobae*, July 10, 2022, https://www.infobae.com/sociedad/2022/07/10/la-noche-negra-de-cacho-fontana-y-pinky-las-24-horas-de-las-malvinas-donaciones-millonarias-y-lingotes-de-oro/.

136 *knitting scarves, gloves, hats*: "El Recuerdo de Malvinas Expresado en Tejidos," *La Gaceta*, May 31 2022, https://www.lagaceta.com.ar/nota/945704/sociedad/recuerdo-malvinas-expresado-tejidos.html#google_vignette.

137 *"by the Armed Forces of the dictatorship"*: Eduardo Blaustein and Martín Zubieta, *Decíamos Ayer: La Prensa Argentina Bajo El Proceso* (Buenos Aires: Ediciones Colihue, 2006), 469.

137 *"Massive Euphoria for the Recovery of Las Malvinas!"*: "Euforia Popular por la Recuperacion de Las Malvinas," *Clarín*, April 3, 1982—see Santiago Marani, "Malvinas Argentinas: Las Bochornosas Tapas de Clarín y Otros Medios en Plena Guerra," www.eldestapeweb.com, April 2, 2021, https://www.eldestapeweb.com/politica/malvinas-argentinas/malvinas-las-tapas-de-clarin-y-otros-medios-en-plena-guerra-2021427042.

137 *"We are winning!"*: Ibid.

137 *inventing an entire two-page interview*: Edward Schumacher, "Argentina After the Falklands," *New York Times*, December, 26, 1982, https://www.nytimes.com/1982/12/26/magazine/argentina-after-the-falklands.html.

137 *taken at the ESMA*: Lucía Gardel, "A 40 Años de La Guerra de Malvinas: 5 Desinformaciones Que Circularon Durante La Guerra," Chequeado, April 9, 2024, https://chequeado.com/el-explicador/a-40-anos-de-la-guerra-de-malvinas-5-desinformaciones-que-circularon-durante-la-guerra/.

137 *to stop circulating the* Buenos Aires Herald: Agencias, "Suspendida la Distribución del Único Periódico en Lengua Inglesa," *El País*, April 7, 1982, https://elpais.com/diario/1982/04/08/internacional/387064806_850215.html.

137 *stabbing Argentina in the back with a dagger*: Giannoni and Madres de Plaza de Mayo, *Las Viejas*, 137.

137 *tossed the pamphlets in the air like confetti*: Archivo Prisma, "AV-5402 Madres de Plaza de Mayo, La Historia, Capítulo: La Voz de los Pañuelos (1982–1983)," YouTube, March 3, 2023, https://www.youtube.com/watch?v=R0FTH6gGf8Q.

137 *"They yelled all kinds of insults at us"*: Giannoni and Madres de Plaza de Mayo, *Las Viejas*, 137.

138 *"Las Malvinas Are Argentine"*: SDHArgentina, "Delia Giovanola Sobre el Famoso Cartel 'Las Malvinas Son Argentinas, Los Desaparecidos También,'" YouTube, July 22, 2022, https://www.youtube.com/watch?v=h5Aj0JXxFGE.

138 *sunk to a measly 30 percent*: "Political Monitor—Satisfaction Ratings 1977–1987," Ipsos, 1988, https://www.ipsos.com/en-uk/political-monitor-satisfaction-ratings-1977-1987.

138 *127 warships, helicopters, and submarines*: Imperial War Museums, *A Short History of the Falklands Conflict*, 2024, https://www.iwm.org.uk/history/a-short-history-of-the-falklands-conflict.

138 *gales that reached 100 miles per hour*: "False Start for Operation Paraquet," *Royal Naval Association* (blog), 2021, https://www.royal-naval-association.co.uk/news/21-april-false-start-for-operation-paraquet/; Nicholas Shakespeare, "The Falklands War Revisited," *New Statesman*, January 16, 2019, https://www.newstatesman.com/culture/2019/01/the-falklands-war-revisited.

139 *It was through such photos*: Ferguson, *The Disappeared*, 165.

139 *323 Argentines*: "Crucero ARA 'General Belgrano,'" Argentina.gob.ar, November 9, 2022, https://www.argentina.gob.ar/armada/crucero-ara-general-belgrano.

139 *While the Argentines still outnumbered the Brits*: Imperial War Museums, *A Short History of the Falklands Conflict*.

139 *Chesterfield cigarettes*: Argentinian Ration, Imperial War Museums, 2024, https://www.iwm.org.uk/collections/item/object/30087351.

139 *less than 1,500 calories a day*: Mónica Martin, "Guerra de Malvinas: El Libro Que Figura en Prestigiosas Bibliotecas de EE.UU y Acá Se Ignora," *Perfil*, April 2, 2023, https://www.perfil.com/noticias/sociedad/guerra-de-malvinas-el-libro-que-figura-en-prestigiosas-bibliotecas-de-EEUU-y-aca-se-ignora.phtml.

139 *a huge pile on the side of the road*: Alan Taylor, "30 Years Since the Falklands War," *Atlantic*, March 30, 2012, https://www.theatlantic.com/photo/2012/03/30-years-since-the-falklands-war/100272/.

139 *"The Falkland Islands are once more under the government"*: John Shirley, "War Heroes or Murderers?: A Police Inquiry Must Rule When Death on the Battlefield Is a Crime," *Independent*, August 22, 1992, https://www.the-independent.com/news/uk/war-heroes-or-murderers-a-police-inquiry-must-rule-when-death-on-the-battlefield-is-a-crime-john-shirley-reports-1542024.html.

140 *"not the last link in the national undertaking"*: Edward Schumacher, "Galtieri Bars Peace if Britain Restores Its 'Colonial Rule,'" *New York Times*, June 16, 1982, https://www.nytimes.com/1982/06/16/world/galtieri-bars-peace-if-britain-restores-its-colonial-rule.html.

140 *lit Union Jacks and buses on fire*: PanzerArchivo, "Posible Rendición, Disturbios en Buenos Aires, June 14, 1982," YouTube, February 8, 2024, https://www.youtube.com/watch?v=SAYAj05Y3qM.

140 *Swaying arm in arm*: Richard J. Meislin, "Thousands in Buenos Aires Assail Junta for Surrendering to Britain," *New York Times*, June 16, 1982, https://www.nytimes.com/1982/06/16/world/thousands-in-buenos-aires-assail-junta-for-surrendering-to-britain.html.

140 *in an odd characterization for a dictator, "nice"*: Richard J. Meislin, "Man in the News; A Mild New President for Argentina," *New York Times*, June 23, 1982, https://www.nytimes.com/1982/06/23/world/man-in-the-news-a-mild-new-president-for-argentina.html.

140 *"incompetence among their commanders"*: Katherine J. Roberts, Milt Freudenheim, and Barbara Slavin, "The World in Summary; Argentina Takes Another Plunge," *New York Times*, July 11, 1982, https://www.nytimes.com/1982/07/11/weekinreview/the-world-in-summary-argentina-takes-another-plunge.html.

140　*borrowed $2.2 million from the government*: Juan González Yuste, "El Régimen Militar Argentino Sigue Sin Dar una Explicación Oficial de la Desastrosa Aventura de las Malvinas," *El País*, November 30, 1982, https://elpais.com/diario/1982/12/01/internacional /407545218_850215.html.

140　*plunged 40 percent*: "The World in Summary; Argentina Takes Another Plunge."

141　"*Los desaparecidos . . . que digan dónde están*": Mónica Martin, "La Primera 'Marcha por la Vida,' en 1982, Las Compuertas Argentinas Hacia la Democracia," *Perfil*, October 5, 2022, https://www.perfil.com/noticias/sociedad/la-primera-marcha-por-la -vida-1982-abrio-las-compuertas-argentinas-hacia-la-democracia.phtml.

141　*eighty-eight common graves*: Edward Schumacher, "400 Bodies Are Discovered in Unmarked Graves in Argentina," *New York Times*, October 29, 1982, https://www.nytimes .com/1982/10/29/world/400-bodies-are-discovered-in-unmarked-graves-in-argentina.html.

141　*three hundred bodies in La Plata*: David Rock, *Argentina 1516–1987: From Spanish Colonization to Alfonsín* (Berkeley: University of California Press, 2006), 384.

141　"*beggars and indigents*": Ibid.

141　"*constitutional presence*": Ibid.

141　"*the struggle is not over, nor my role in it*": Ibid., 385.

142　*breathe menacingly into the receiver*: Ramos Padilla, *Chicha*, 199.

142　"*We are going to blow all of you up, old ladies*": Ibid., 200.

142　"*Instead of messing around*": Ibid.

142　*someone had spray-painted*: "Letter from Chicha Mariani to Judge," Ninos Desaparecidos Folder, CLAMOR Papers, Archivo Nacional de La Memoria.

142　"*Madre de Terroristas*": Ibid.

142　*three hundred armed police*: "Around the World; 300 Policemen Block Buenos Aires Protest," *New York Times*, December 10, 1982.

142　*armored cars blocking their path*: "Around the World; Rights Protesters March in Buenos Aires," *New York Times*, December 11, 1982, https://www.nytimes.com/1982/12/11 /world/around-the-world-rights-protesters-march-in-buenos-aires.html.

142　"*La Plaza es de las Madres y no de los cobardes*": Gorini, *La Rebelión de las Madres*, 493.

CHAPTER 20—A BIRD LIVED IN ME

143　"*Can a woman forget her nursing child?*": Isaiah 49:15–17.

143　*she carries her child's genetic material in her veins*: Diana W. Bianchi et al., "Forever Connected: The Lifelong Biological Consequences of Fetomaternal and Maternofetal Microchimerism," *Clinical Chemistry* 67, no. 2 (December 17, 2020): 351–62, https://doi.org /10.1093/clinchem/hvaa304.

143　"*I had to look for my daughter*": David Blaustein, "Botín de Guerra," April 11, 2000, https://www.youtube.com/watch?v=VzLreObkl40, Rosa Roisinblit testimony.

144　*María Eugenia Casinelli*: There is some confusion over whether her name was spelled Casinelli or Cassinelli. The Abuelas website uses both in different places.

144　"*A flower traveled in my blood*": Juan Gelman, *Violín y Otras Cuestiones* (Buenos Aires: Ediciones Gleizer, 1956).

144　"*Wherever he is, I want him to know*": Blaustein, "Botín de Guerra," April 11, 2000, Rosa Roisinblit testimony.

145   *"My mother will never forgive the military"*: "Laura Carlotto: embarazo secreto y parto clandestino de un hijo símbolo," *Cronista*, August 5, 2014, https://www.cronista.com /economia-politica/Laura-Carlotto-embarazo-secreto-y-parto-clandestino-de-un-hijo -simbolo-20140805-0107.html.

145   *"If YOU know something . . . HELP US to find them"*: Edward Shaw, "Afiche de Abuelas de la Plaza de Mayo con Fotos," 1982, https://www.archivosenuso.org/ddhh-archivo/ed ward-shaw?page=6#viewer=/viewer/784%3Fas_overlay%3Dtrue&js=.

145   *with items gathered from their homes*: Rita Arditti interview with Emma Baamonde, September 19, 1993, 6, University of Massachusetts–Boston, Joseph P. Healey Library, https://openarchives.umb.edu/digital/collection/p15774coll10/id/880; Fabricio Andrés Laino Sanchis, "Madres-Abuelas. Apuntes Sobre La Formación Histórica de Abuelas de Plaza de Mayo," *Revista Del Museo de Antropología*, August 31, 2023, 349, https://doi.org /10.31048/1852.4826.v16.n2.39176 suggests they moved from the Madres' apartment to their own rented office in February 1982.

145   *lugged over an armoire*: Bublik, *Abuela*, 113.

145   *inviting their supporters to a party*: Laino Sanchis, "Madres-Abuelas. Apuntes Sobre La Formación Histórica de Abuelas de Plaza de Mayo," 349.

145   *a check for $10,000 had arrived*: Abuelas de Plaza de Mayo, *La Historia de Abuelas*, 35.

146   *distributed to them in cash*: Bublik, *Abuela*, 113–14; and Plan Sistemático Trial, Rosa Roisinblit testimony.

146   *"This envelope belongs to the Abuelas"*: Bublik, *Abuela*, 114.

147   *Carefully tucked into Chicha Mariani's planner*: Plan Sistemático Trial, Chicha Mariani testimony, October 11, 2010. I searched the archives of *El Día* for a copy of the exact article to no avail. The Asociación Anahí archives did not have a copy. Chicha has said several times that she lost the newspaper clipping.

147   *asking her friends who were medical professionals*: Ramos Padilla, *Chicha*, 234.

147   *scratched his face to a pulp*: Guillermo Wulff, *Las Abuelas y la Genética* (Buenos Aires: Abuelas de Plaza de Mayo, 2008), 30, https://www.abuelas.org.ar/resources/Libro Genetica.pdf.

148   *an ashtray to soften the blow*: Ibid.

148   *had been given his name by Isabel Mignone*: Interviews with Eric Stover and Isabel Mignone.

148   *white handkerchiefs over their hair*: In one of our interviews, Stover vividly remembered that they were wearing handkerchiefs when they visited him in Washington, DC, at his office.

148   *he had spent years hitchhiking*: Unless otherwise indicated, information and quotes pertaining to Eric Stover in the following paragraphs are derived from a series of interviews with him between 2023 and 2024.

149   *"To Identify Disappeared Children"*: "Para idenificar los niños desaparecidos," as viewed in the Abuelas Archive, box 380, AR AIAPM CD 5 380.

149   *active in leftist student organizations*: Unless otherwise indicated, information and quotes pertaining to Víctor Penchaszadeh in the following paragraphs are derived from several interviews between 2021 and 2022 and his "Reseña," or long biographical sketch, that he provided me with a copy of.

150   *"Their passion—this mixture of suffering and strength"*: Wulff, *Las Abuelas y la Genética*, 38.

150   *"Who told you that?"*: Interview with Víctor Penchaszadeh.

150   *"there's every reason to be optimistic"*: Wulff, *Las Abuelas y la Genética*, 39.

150   *"You're Argentine and a geneticist"*: Víctor Penchaszadeh's "Reseña."

CHAPTER 21—PAULA

151   *"extinguished"*: Ley 22.924, Ley de Pacificación Nacional, September 22, 1983; The law covered the period from May 25, 1973, to June 17, 1982. It's first article reads: "Criminal actions arising from offenses committed with terrorist or subversive motivation or purpose," from May 25, 1973, to June 17, 1982, are hereby declared extinguished.

151   *a forty-thousand-person march*: Geri Smith, "Chanting 'the Military Dictatorship Will Fall,' 40,000 People Marched," UPI, August 19, 1983, https://www.upi.com/Archives /1983/08/19/Chanting-the-military-dictatorship-will-fall-40000-people-marched /3877430113600/.

151   *thousands of faceless silhouettes*: "Argentina: Self-Amnesty," *Time*, October 3, 1983, https://time.com/archive/6860110/argentina-self-amnesty/.

152   *filing habeas corpus motions for the disappeared*: Jimmy Burns, *The Land That Lost Its Heroes* (London: Bloomsbury, 2002), 120–21.

152   *"With democracy, one does not only vote"*: Sebastián Botticelli, "'Con la Democracia Se Vota, Se Come, Se Cura y Se Educa,'" *Perfil*, December 5, 2023, https://www.perfil.com/noticias /opinion/con-la-democracia-se-vota-se-come-se-cura-y-se-educa.phtml.

152   *misted water onto the crowd*: Martina Jaureguy, "40 Years Later, a Look Back at the Day Argentina Recovered Democracy," *Buenos Aires Herald*, December 9, 2023, https://bue nosairesherald.com/human-rights/40-years-later-a-look-back-at-the-day-argentina -recovered-democracy.

152   *donned their white handkerchiefs*: Ramos Padilla, *Chicha*, 259.

152   *"El pueblo, unido, jamás será vencido"*: Discurso de Alfonsín, December 10, 1983, Facebook, https://www.facebook.com/watch/?v=461838241954623.

152   *"With democracy, we thought that the heavens would open"*: Ramos Padilla, *Chicha*, 259.

152   *others booed and insulted them*: Ibid.

152   *three days after Alfonsín's inauguration*: Testimonio de Elsa Pavón Entrevista Realizada en la Biblioteca Nacional, May 2, 2012, Programa de Derechos Humanos y Departamento de Comunicación, Biblioteca Nacional Mariano Moreno, https://www.bn.gov.ar /uploads/transcripciones/elsa-pavon.pdf; in many interviews Elsa has suggested it was the first working day of democracy.

153   *Paula, who was also hooded, in another*: Ministerio de Ciencia, Tecnología e Innovación Productiva, "Una pregunta. 30 años. Memoria escrita del Banco Nacional de Datos Genéticos," 67, https://www.argentina.gob.ar/sites/default/files/lib_ins_bndg-libro.pdf.

153   *"Just as we could sniff out a policeman"*: Ramos Padilla, *Chicha*, 242.

153   *seemed to say "Paula"*: Irene Barki, *Pour Ces Yeux-Là: La Face Cachée du Drame Argentin les Enfants Disparus* (Paris: Éditions La Découverte, 1988), 252 suggests the photos also included a last name, but, during fact-checking, Elsa Pavón insisted that was not the case.

153   *"You killed this girl's parents"*: Ibid.

153   *"Dios mío!"*: Ibid., 253.

154   *where was her mother?*: Elsa Pavón de Aguilar interview with Rita Arditti, December 19, 1993, University of Massachusetts–Boston, Joseph P. Healey Library, 18, https://open archives.umb.edu/digital/collection/p15774coll10/id/870/rec/6.

154   *hardest areas to investigate*: Ramos Padilla, *Chicha*, 245.

154   *Elsa was careful to change*: Herrera and Tenembaum, *Identidad Despojo y Restitución*, 52; confirmed with Elsa Pavón.

154   *a flash of recognition suddenly struck her*: Interview with Elsa Pavón.

154   *her little legs twisted slightly inward at the ankles*: Barki, *Pour Ces Yeux-Là*, 257; confirmed by Elsa Pavón in fact-checking.

154   *without arousing suspicion*: Herrera and Tenembaum, *Identidad Despojo y Restitución*, 55.

154   *begged the building superintendent*: Ramos Padilla, *Chicha*, 245–46.

155   *Soon they received a tip*: Ibid., 246.

155   *They asked the judge*: "Sinopsis de lo acaecido," n.d., as viewed in the Abuelas Archive, AR AIAPM DEF 1233.

155   *Chicha would rise from her chair*: Testimonio de Elsa Pavón, Programa de Derechos Humanos y Departamento de Comunicación, Biblioteca Nacional Mariano Moreno, May 2, 2012, https://www.bn.gov.ar/uploads/transcripciones/elsa-pavon.pdf.

155   *the responsibility was his*: Alejandra Dandan, "'Ver a la Nena Fue un Shock,'" *Página 12*, May 11, 2011, https://www.pagina12.com.ar/diario/elpais/1-167959-2011-05-11.html.

155   *around one in the afternoon*: Testimonio de Elsa Pavón, Programa de Derechos Humanos y Departamento de Comunicación, Biblioteca Nacional Mariano Moreno, May 2, 2012, https://www.bn.gov.ar/uploads/transcripciones/elsa-pavon.pdf.

155   *might try to escape with Paula*: Elsa Pavón de Aguilar interview with Rita Arditti.

156   *at the bar across the street*: Ibid.

156   *One of the workmen was quite drunk*: Herrera and Tenembaum, *Identidad Despojo y Restitución*, 58; Elsa Pavón de Aguilar interview with Rita Arditti, 24; in fact-checking, Elsa did not remember this detail. But in an interview she gave in 1993, she clearly stated: "So, we were drinking soda, and there were two construction workers—I'll say it again, it was a very hot day—there were two construction workers drinking wine with ice. But I don't know how many times we saw them walking back and forth, and one of them was really drunk, while the other was just getting started. Then, along come two cops, and they say, 'Alright, you two, come over here. I need to do a search, and I need two witnesses.' Look, their drunkenness disappeared in an instant—can you imagine? Just like that! The fright those two men got, you have no idea."

156   *"Alright, you two, come over here"*: Elsa Pavón de Aguilar interview with Rita Arditti, 24.

156   *Elsa had assumed*: Herrera and Tenembaum, *Identidad Despojo y Restitución*, 58.

156   *Elsa and Mirta watched*: Interview with Elsa Pavón.

156   *had given birth*: Ramos Padilla, *Chicha*, 248–49.

156   *nor did her medical records reveal any prenatal visits*: Ramos Padilla, *Chicha*, 248.

157   *Three days after*: "Sinopsis de lo acaecido," n.d., as viewed in the Abuelas Archive, AR AIAPM DEF 1233.

157   *Rosa received a frantic phone call from Chicha*: This anecdote is from Bublik, *Abuela*, 147–48.

157   *a shaggy brown pixie cut*: Descriptions from court sketches as seen on *The MacNeil/ Lehrer NewsHour*; August 14, 1984, https://americanarchive.org/catalog/cpb-aacip-507 -bk16m33s4g; confirmed with Paula Logares.

158   *the one to reach out*: Ministerio de Ciencia, Tecnología e Innovación Productiva, "Una pregunta. 30 años. Memoria escrita del Banco Nacional de Datos Genéticos," 43, https:// www.argentina.gob.ar/sites/default/files/lib_ins_bndg-libro.pdf.

158   *he insisted he could not take on the project*: Ibid.; Víctor Penchaszadeh recalls telling Mary-Claire King about the Abuelas after meeting with them in November 1982. King herself remembers Luca Cavalli-Sforza telling her later, when she was working in his lab.

CHAPTER 22—STORY PROBLEMS

159   *step up to the plate at Wrigley Field*: Unless otherwise indicated, information and quotes pertaining to Mary-Claire King in the following chapter are derived from a series of lengthy interviews between June 2022 and November 2024.

159   *"Ernie Banks is batting .277"*: Ushma S. Neill, "A Conversation with Mary-Claire King," *Journal of Clinical Investigation* 129, no. 1 (January 2, 2019): 1–3, https://doi.org/10.1172 /JCI126050.

161   *some five thousand others*: Greg Whitmore, "Berkeley: A History of Disobedience—in Pictures," *Guardian*, November 15, 2014, https://www.theguardian.com/us-news/gal lery/2014/nov/15/berkeley-a-history-of-disobedience-in-pictures.

161   *every weekday at one in the afternoon*: Mary-Claire King, 2020 William Allan Award address: The American Society of Human Genetics (ASHG) on October 26, 2020. "Genetics As a Way of Thinking—Cultural Inheritance from Our Teachers," DOI: 10.1016/j .ajhg.2021.02.007.

162   *"I couldn't believe people were paid to do this"*: "Autobiography of Mary-Claire King," The Shaw Prize, September 26, 2018, https://www.shawprize.org/autobiography/mary-claire-king/.

162   *"people who were vulnerable"*: Conversations in Genetics, "Mary-Claire King (Human Genetics)," YouTube, March 29, 2016, https://www.youtube.com/watch?v=TiMv8L5sR-Y.

163   *he gamely bailed them out*: Rebecca L. Cann, "Allan Charles Wilson. 18 October 1934–21 July 1991," *Biographical Memoirs of Fellows of the Royal Society* 60 (January 2014): 465, https://doi.org/10.1098/rsbm.2013.0006.

163   *saved his outbursts for racists and creationists*: Ibid.

163   *"If you leave now, you can do good work"*: Interview with Mary-Claire King.

163   *a theory he had explored in his prior work*: A. C. Wilson and V. M. Sarich, "A Molecular Time Scale for Human Evolution," *Proceedings of the National Academy of Sciences* 63, no. 4 (August 1, 1969): 1088–93, https://doi.org/10.1073/pnas.63.4.1088.

165   *"I cannot separate doing science from doing good work"*: Paula Bock, "The Plan of All Plans: Mary-Claire King and Her Team Explore Secrets of DNA," *Seattle Times*, May 31, 1998, https://www.seattletimes.com/pacific-nw-magazine/the-plan-of-all-plans-mary-claire -king-and-her-team-explore-secrets-of-dna/.

165   *breastfed during breaks in her office*: Jane Gitschier, "Evidence Is Evidence: An Interview with Mary-Claire King," *PLoS Genetics* 9, no. 9 (September 26, 2013): e1003828, https:// doi.org/10.1371/journal.pgen.1003828.

165   *splashed across the cover of* Science: Mary-Claire King and A. C. Wilson, "Evolution

at Two Levels in Humans and Chimpanzees," *Science* 188, no. 4184 (April 11, 1975): 107–16, https://doi.org/10.1126/science.1090005.

165 *"I just want you to know you are only here"*: Gitschier, "Evidence Is Evidence."

165 *"I was a young mother, a young scientist and a young wife"*: Natalie Angier, "Scientist at Work: Mary-Claire King; Quest for Genes and Lost Children," *New York Times*, April 27, 1993, https://www.nytimes.com/1993/04/27/science/scientist-at-work-mary-claire-king-quest-for-genes-and-lost-children.html.

165 *"No one's ever reacted like that before"*: "The Moth Presents Dr. Mary-Claire King at the World Science Festival," YouTube, May 29, 2014, www.youtube.com/watch?v=tOP5pUIYhv4.

166 *"I never said that"*: Neill, "A Conversation with Mary-Claire King."

166 *"First Mommy to Walk on Land"*: Alice Park, "Mary-Claire King: The Woman Who Discovered BRCA1," *Time*, June 2, 2014, https://time.com/2802156/lessons-from-the-woman-who-discovered-the-brca-cancer-gene/.

166 *"They are to keep people happy"*: Ibid.

CHAPTER 23—THE INDEX OF GRANDPATERNITY

168 *a year's sabbatical in Cavalli-Sforza's lab*: Correspondence with Pierre Darlu.

169 *approximately eight thousand different types*: Ana Maria Di Lonardo et al., "Human Genetics and Human Rights," *American Journal of Forensic Medicine and Pathology* 5, no. 4 (December 1984): 339–47, https://doi.org/10.1097/00000433-198412000-00011.

170 *"gp" to refer to grandparents, and "c" to mean children*: Ibid.

171 *hurling the mixture of dirt and human remains into the air*: Mellibovsky, *Circle of Love Over Death*, 37.

171 *could not tear himself away from the screen*: Ibid.

172 *to teach the Argentines proper forensic protocols*: Wulff, *Las Abuelas y la Genética*, 43; interview with Eric Stover.

172 *"We want to know who the murderers are"*: Alison Brysk, "The Politics of Measurement: The Contested Count of the Disappeared in Argentina," *Human Rights Quarterly* 16, no. 4 (November 1994): 688, https://doi.org/10.2307/762564; ultimately, in 1986, the Madres split into two separate organizations: La Asociación de Madres de Plaza de Mayo, led by Hebe de Bonafini, and Las Madres de Plaza de Mayo – Línea Fundadora. The group of Madres led by Hebe de Bonafini refused to recognize that their disappeared children were dead.

172 *in February 1984*: Christopher Joyce and Eric Stover, *Witnesses from the Grave* (New York: Ballantine, 1992), 221.

172 *"diagnostician of death"*: Douglas Martin, "Leslie Lukash, Medical Examiner, 86, Dies," *New York Times*, August 25, 2007, https://www.nytimes.com/2007/08/25/nyregion/25lukash.html.

172 *leather cowboy boots and a jaunty felt fedora*: "Remembering Clyde Snow," Physicians for Human Rights, n.d., https://phr.org/our-work/resources/remembering-clyde-snow/.

172 *drooped out of his mouth*: Interview with Lowell Levine.

172 *fated to plunge to the earth*: Jody Bales Foote, "Profiles in Science for Science Librarians: Clyde Snow: Forensic Anthropologist, Social Justice Advocate, and Super Sleuth,"

Science & Technology Libraries 33, no. 3 (July 3, 2014): 216–17, https://doi.org/10.1080 /0194262x.2014.944297; Joyce and Stover, *Witnesses from the Grave*, 24.

172   the *"Sherlock Holmes of Bones"*: "Clyde Snow—Obituary," *Telegraph*, May 19, 2014, https://www.telegraph.co.uk/news/obituaries/10841938/Clyde-Snow-obituary.html.

174   *some of which were American-owned*: "Anaconda Reaches Accord with Chile," *New York Times*, July 25, 1974.

174   *attempted to mount a coup*: US State Department, Office of the Historian, "The Allende Years and the Pinochet Coup, 1969–1973," 2019, https://history.state.gov/milestones /1969-1976/allende.

174   *he was shot dead*: "Gunmen Murder Aide to Allende," *New York Times*, July 28, 1973, https://www.nytimes.com/1973/07/28/archives/gunmen-murder-aide-to-allende-navy -captain-is-shot-down-on-balcony.html.

175   *jittery soldiers would fire*: "Chile: The Bloody End of a Marxist Dream," *Time*, September 24, 1973, https://time.com/archive/6841772/chile-the-bloody-end-of-a-marxist-dream/.

175   *Colwell recalled that the TV screen went blank*: Interview with Robert Colwell.

176   *had been killed during the brutal days after the coup*: Marvine Howe, "2 Americans Slain in Chile: The Unanswered Questions," *New York Times*, November 19, 1973, https:// www.nytimes.com/1973/11/19/archives/2-americans-slain-in-chile-the-unanswered -questions-accident-widely.html.

176   *around eight thousand*: "Chile: The Generals Consolidate Their Coup," *Time*, October 1, 1973, https://time.com/archive/6875791/chile-the-generals-consolidate-their-coup/.

176   *massive makeshift torture camp*: Ibid.; This source suggests that the stadium could seat 100,000. But most other sources suggest its capacity was between 45,000 and 60,000.

176   *"place of blood"*: "Empty Seats in Chile's Estadio Nacional Tell a Haunting Story," WBUR, June 20, 2015, https://www.wbur.org/onlyagame/2015/06/20/empty-seats -estadio-nacional-chile.

176   *told to shut up or die*: David Waldstein, "In Chile's National Stadium, Dark Past Shad-ows Copa América Matches," *New York Times*, June 17, 2015, https://www.nytimes.com /2015/06/19/sports/soccer/in-chiles-national-stadium-dark-past-shadows-copa-america -matches.html.

176   *"fractured, fractured French"*: Conversations in Genetics, "Mary-Claire King (Human Ge-netics)," YouTube, March 29, 2016, https://www.youtube.com/watch?v=TiMv8L5sR-Y.

177   *"We would like to invite"*: Robert Colwell, Memoir in Progress, Shared with author in December 2024.

177   *concealed cash in film canisters*: Interview with Robert Colwell.

CHAPTER 24—MADAME DEFARGE

178   *"Seminar on the Forensic Sciences and the Disappeared . . . All welcome"*: Joyce and Stover, *Witnesses from the Grave*, 218.

178   *Abuelas, government officials, and relatives of the disappeared*: Interview with Morris Tidball-Binz.

178   *"absolute precision"*: "Los niños desaparecidos," *Diario Popular*, June 24, 1984.

178   *She began to bumble*: Joyce and Stover, *Witnesses from the Grave*, 218.

178   *burst into tears*: Ibid.

179   *several marches with the Abuelas*: Interview with Morris Tidball-Binz.

179   *"Tell me, Doctor"*: Mary-Claire King, "My Mother Will Never Forgive Them," *Grand Street* (1992): 35, https://doi.org/10.2307/25007525.

179   *all wrapped in a green blanket*: Joyce and Stover, *Witnesses from the Grave*, 220; detail about teddy bear is derived from Amelia Herrera de Miranda interview with Rita Arditti, November 1, 1993, University of Massachusetts–Boston, Joseph P. Healey Library, 5, https://openarchives.umb.edu/digital/collection/p15774coll10/id/854/rec/27.

179   *"Then Matilde is still alive"*: King, "My Mother Will Never Forgive Them."

180   *It was Rosa Roisinblit who opened the door*: Unless otherwise indicated, all information and quotes pertaining to Mary-Claire King's story in the following chapter are derived from a series of lengthy interviews between June 2022 and November 2024.

182   *rusted bright orange*: Descriptions of the Durand in the 1980s are derived from NOVA, *The Search for the Disappeared*, 1986.

182   *"an oasis in the middle of a desert"*: Ibid.

182   *their work was completed her way*: Interview with Marisa Mena, former employee of the immunology section of the Hospital Durand.

183   *all their calculations by hand*: "Genética. Avances científicos sobre las leyes de la herencia," *Tiempo Argentino* (Suplemento La Salud), June 27, 1984, 1–2.

183   *99.82 percent*: Fabricio Laino Sanchis, "La Creación del Banco Nacional de Datos Genéticos. Acción Colectiva y Políticas Públicas por los 'Niños Desaparecidos' Durante la Posdictadura en Argentina (1984–1989)," *Folia Histórica del Nordeste*, no. 46 (April 3, 2023): 69, https://doi.org/10.30972/fhn.4606492.

CHAPTER 25—NUNCA MÁS

184   *stopped insisting Paula was his daughter*: Lucia Iañez, "Proyecto de Declaración: De Beneplácito por el 35° Aniversario de la Fundación Banco Nacional de Datos Genéticos (BNDG)," March 23, 2022, https://intranet.hcdiputados-ba.gov.ar/proyectos/22-23D1113012022-03-1813-51-53.pdf.

184   *would be too traumatic*: King, "My Mother Will Never Forgive Them."

184   *Lavallen at the Brigada de San Justo*: Abuelas press release, October 22, 1984, as viewed in the Abuelas Archive, AR AIAPM DEF 1233.

184   *"Paula Eva Logares: kidnapped by a repressor and prisoner of the justice system"*: Televisión Pública, "Paula Logares- Nietos, historias de identidad," YouTube, November 23, 2012, https://www.youtube.com/watch?v=aX0PMxDAhLg.

185   *"Paula cannot continue as 'war booty'"*: Abuelas press release, October 22, 1984, AR AIAPM DEF 1233.

185   *initial print run of forty thousand copies*: Luciana Bertoia, "Los 'Conadepianos': Los Que Hicieron el Informe Nunca Más," *Página 12*, September 20, 2023, https://www.pagina12.com.ar/589790-los-conadepianos-los-que-hicieron-el-informe-nunca-mas.

185   *"Many of the episodes recounted here will be hard to believe"*: CONADEP, *Nunca Más*, 15.

185   *to pull sheets over their heads*: Ibid., 24.

185   *340 clandestine torture facilities*: Ibid., 54.

185   *"services rendered"*: Ibid., 155.

185   *involved some sort of torture*: Ibid., 26.

186 *8,960*: I have sometimes seen the number cited as 8,961. But my copy of *Nunca Más* says 8,960.

186 *all records related to disappearances be destroyed*: "Murió Reynaldo Bignone, El Último Dictador de la Junta Militar," *La Nación*, March 7, 2018, https://www.lanacion.com.ar /politica/murio-reynaldo-bignone-el-ultimo-dictador-de-la-junta-militar-nid2114804/; Alberto Amato, "Reynaldo Bignone, El Dictador Que Ordenó Destruir Toda la Documentación Sobre los Desaparecidos," *Clarín*, March 7, 2018, https://www.clarin.com /politica/reynaldo-bignone-ultimo-dictador-ordeno-destruir-toda-documentacion-desa parecidos_0_HJGZItp_f.html.

186 *twenty-two thousand people had been disappeared in Argentina by July 1978*: Carlos Osario, Marcos Novaro, and John Dinges, "On 30th Anniversary of Argentine Coup: New Declassified Details on Repression and U.S. Support for Military Dictatorship," National Security Archive, March 26, 2006, https://nsarchive2.gwu.edu/NSAEBB/NS AEBB185/index.htm#19780715.

186 *wanted to "adopt"*: CONADEP, *Nunca Más*, 303.

186 *"When a child is torn from their legitimate family"*: Ibid., 326.

187 *"Where is my teddy bear?"*: Abuelas de Plaza de Mayo page dedicated to the case of Paula Logares, https://www.abuelas.org.ar/nietas-y-nietos/243; King, "My Mother Will Never Forgive Them."

CHAPTER 26—A MOTHER'S MARK

188 *"But why? Why?"*: Andrés Jaroslavsky, *El Futuro de la Memoria* (London: Latin America Bureau, 2004), 206.

188 *observe the images in silence*: Mariana Eva Pérez, "Las Fotos del Aparador," *Decía Mi Abuelo* (blog), November 16, 2007, https://deciamiabuelo.blogspot.com/2007/11/las -fotos-del-aparador.html; Archivo Biogfáfico Familiar Pérez Roisinblit, 282.

189 *"I wish you could go with your mother, too"*: RIBA Trial, Mariana Eva Pérez testimony.

189 *it would just be like a "mosquito bite"*: Jaroslavsky, *El Futuro de la Memoria*, 206.

189 *eleven other grandchildren*: Ariel Reira, "Los Hijos y Nietos Recuperados a lo Largo del Tiempo," Chequeado, August 31, 2015, https://chequeado.com/el-explicador /%E2%80%A8los-hijos-y-nietos-recuperados-a-lo-largo-del-tiempo/.

189 *Mariana became convinced*: Memoria Abierta, Testimonio de Mariana Eva Pérez, Buenos Aires, 2002.

189 *watching every one of his broadcast speeches*: Jaroslavsky, *El Futuro de la Memoria*, 206.

189 *an unlikely friendship with the repair technician*: Mariana Eva Pérez, "Una Relación Rara," *Decía Mi Abuelo* (blog), February 3, 2008, https://deciamiabuelo.blogspot.com/2007/09 /burrone.html.

189 *"Argentinos! The dictatorship is over"*: Discurso de Raúl Alfonsín en el cierre de la campaña electoral Buenos Aires, Plaza de la República 27 de octubre de 1983, https://www.alfon sin.org/wp-content/uploads/2018/12/Discurso_de_cierre_de_campana_en_el_Obe lisco-1-1.pdf.

189 Señorita Maestra *or* Burbujas: Mariana Eva Pérez, "Mi Alfonsín particular," *Decía Mi Abuelo* (blog), April 1, 2009, https://deciamiabuelo.blogspot.com/2009/04/mi-alfon sin-particular.html; it appears the official title of *Burbujas* was *Odisea Burbujas*, but I have hewed to Mariana's language in this section.

190 *"I am disappointed with Alfonsín"*: Guglielmo, "Memorias Biográficas de Abuelas de Plaza de Mayo," 162.

190 *She imagined leading him to school*: Josefina Giglio, "La Joven que Pudo Encontrar a su Hermano Desaparecido," *La Nación*, February 18, 2001, https://www.lanacion.com.ar /politica/la-joven-que-pudo-encontrar-a-su-hermano-desaparecido-nid52825/.

190 *"Sometimes I think, when we find one another"*: Jaroslavsky, *El Futuro de la Memoria*, 207.

190 *"terrorist subversion" during the dictatorship were "unimpeachable"*: Manuel Tarricone, "¿Qué Fue El Juicio a Las Juntas?," *Chequeado*, September 29, 2022, https://chequeado .com/hilando-fino/que-fue-el-juicio-a-las-juntas/.

190 *"the greatest genocide"*: "Fragmento de la acusación del fiscal Strassera," *El Historiador*, https://elhistoriador.com.ar/22-de-abril-de-1985-se-inicia-el-juicio-a-las-juntas-mili tares/.

190 *"The guerrillas kidnapped, tortured, and murdered"*: William D. Montalbano, "9 Argentine Junta Leaders Face Their Accusers in Courtroom," *Los Angeles Times*, September 12, 1985.

190 *One particularly gut-turning session*: Personas Desaparecidas BA, "Adriana Calvo de Laborde en el Juicio a las Juntas Militares—Año 1985," YouTube, 1985, www.youtube .com/watch?v=ouRn9hnBxy8.

191 *"That day I made a promise"*: Ibid.

191 *"I still love Videla"*: Juan Manuel Trenado, "'Argentina, 1985': El Giro de la Madre de Moreno Ocampo, Su Cariño por Videla y el Impacto de una Nota de *La Nación*," *La Nación*, October 5, 2022, https://www.lanacion.com.ar/politica/argentina-1985-el -giro-de-la-madre-de-moreno-ocampo-su-carino-por-videla-y-el-impacto-de-una-nota -de-nid05102022/.

191 *"I want to use a phrase that doesn't belong to me"*: IP Noticias, "Argentina, 1985: 'Señores Jueces, Nunca Más,'" YouTube, April 22, 2024, www.youtube.com/watch?v=f13UMZR_sMA.

191 *paging through a Bible*: Natalia Benavídez, "Juicio a Las Juntas: La Trastienda Periodística y Fotográfica," *La Vanguardia*, December 10, 2022, https://lavanguardiadigital.com .ar/index.php/2022/12/10/juicio-a-las-juntas-la-trastienda-periodistica-y-fotografica/; Agencias, "Videla: De Los Derechos Humanos al Homicidio," *El País*, December 9, 1985, https://elpais.com/diario/1985/12/10/internacional/503017213_850215.html.

191 *93 episodes of torture, 306 cases of illegal privation of liberty, and 26 robberies*: "Sentencia Causa 84/13," December 9, 1985, 296, https://www.comisionporlamemoria.org/archi vos/comunicacion/causa_13_sentencia.pdf.

191 *It was the first time in Latin American history*: "Leaders Facing Justice: 1945–2021," Council on Foreign Relations, https://www.cfr.org/timeline/leaders-facing-justice#:~: text=The%20Argentine%20government%20initiates%20trials,2013%20while%20serv ing%20his%20sentence.

192 *alone in the presidential residence*: Patricio Zunini, "La Historia Secreta de la Quinta de Olivos: Del Tigre de Perón a la Noche en Que la Policía Abandonó a de la Rúa," *Infobae*, July 15, 2017, https://www.infobae.com/grandes-libros/2017/07/15/la-historia-secreta-de-la-quinta-de olivos-del-tigre-de-peron-a-la-noche-en-que-la-policia-abandono-a-de-la-rua/.

192 *lawsuits lodged against military officers skyrocketed*: Juan Pablo Csipka, "Semana Santa del 87: El Desafío Militar Que Llevó a la Obediencia Debida," *Página 12*, April 16, 2022,

https://www.pagina12.com.ar/415383-semana-santa-del-87-el-desafio-militar-que-llevo -a-la-obedie.

192   *Rosa was among the massive crowd*: Bublik, *Abuela*, 164–65.

193   *"I only hope that you think"*: Jaroslavsky, *El Futuro de la Memoria*, 208.

193   *in her fifties at the time she gave birth*: Ramos Padilla, *Chicha*, 305; confirmed with María José Lavalle Lemos.

193   *Paula Logares's appropriator had also worked*: "Ficha Perteneciente a LOGARES GRINGSPÓN, Paula Eva," Niñas y niños víctimas de secuestro, desaparición, apropiación y restitución de identidad por responsabilidad y/o aquiescencia del Estado, Equipo de Investigación Histórica, November 21, 2012.

193   *stripped off her own shirt*: Ramos Padilla, *Chicha*, 306; confirmed with María José Lavalle Lemos.

193   *so the infant would smell her scent*: Correspondence with María José Lavalle Lemos.

193   *same gait as María Lavalle Lemos*: Ramos Padilla, *Chicha*, 307.

193   *his heart weakened by grief*: Haydée Vallino de Lemos, interview with Rita Arditti November 5, 1993, University of Massachusetts–Boston, Joseph P. Healey Library, https:// openarchives.umb.edu/digital/collection/p15774coll10/id/842/rec/22.

193   *their son had also been disappeared*: Ibid.

194   *she all but gasped*: Interview with Mary-Claire King.

194   *"Mirá, Mariquita"*: Jaroslavsky, *El Futuro de la Memoria*, 41.

195   *the first "biobank" of its kind in the world*: Sebastián A. Vishnopolska et al., "Genetics and Genomic Medicine in Argentina," *Molecular Genetics & Genomic Medicine* 6, no. 4 (July 2018): 481–91, https://doi.org/10.1002/mgg3.455.

195   *More than three hundred*: The Abuelas have long estimated that 500 of their grandchildren were stolen, but the count of official cases on their website is 392. They theorize that many other people might not have known that their daughters and daughters-in-law were pregnant at the time of their disappearances.

195   *"Go back to Berkeley, dear"*: King, "My Mother Will Never Forgive Them"; interview with Mary-Claire King.

195   *an electron microscope at chick embryos*: Dorothy R. Haskett, "Mitochondrial DNA (MtDNA)," *The Embryo Project Encyclopedia*, December 19, 2014, https://embryo.asu .edu/pages/mitochondrial-dna-mtdna.

196   *The idea had come from Cristián Orrego*: Interview with Mary-Claire King.

196   *recently begun working at UC Berkeley*: Jorge A. Santiago-Blay, Ashlee J. Loewy, and Michael Goldman, "Juan Cristián Orrego-Benavente (January 31, 1944, Santiago, Chile– December 12, 2018, San Salvador, El Salvador," *Life: The Excitement of Biology* 6, no. 2 (February 25, 2019): 57–70, https://blaypublishers.com/wp-content/uploads/2019/02 /santiago-blay-et-al.-leb-62-25-january-2019.pdf.

196   *blast rock and roll*: Rebecca L. Cann, "Allan Charles Wilson. 18 October 1934—21 July 1991," *Biographical Memoirs of Fellows of the Royal Society* 60 (January 2014): 466, https:// doi.org/10.1098/rsbm.2013.0006.

196   *Bon Jovi or Aerosmith*: Mark Stoneking could not specifically remember what music played in the lab, but recalled that they listened to the radio rather than cassettes or CDs. These were two of the most popular artists of the time period.

196 *yank the stereo's plug out of the outlet and start talking*: Cann, "Allan Charles Wilson. 18 October 1934–21 July 1991," 467.

197 *"Grey Eminence"*: Ibid., 464.

197 *"belly-dancer enthusiasts"*: Ibid., 465.

197 *quipped that his lab had all the women*: Jane Gitschier, "All about Mitochondrial Eve: An Interview with Rebecca Cann," *PLoS Genetics* 6, no. 5 (May 27, 2010): e1000959, https://doi.org/10.1371/journal.pgen.1000959.

197 *personally carried her placenta*: Interview with Mary-Claire King.

197 *attend Lamaze classes to source placentas*: Alasdair Wilkins, "The Scientists Behind Mitochondrial Eve Tell Us about the 'Lucky Mother' Who Changed Human Evolution Forever," Gizmodo, January 27, 2012, https://gizmodo.com/the-scientists-behind-mitochondrial-eve-tell-us-about-t-5879991. Confirmed with Mark Stoneking.

197 *twenty-six from Indigenous New Guineans*: Rebecca L. Cann, Mark Stoneking, and Allan C. Wilson, "Mitochondrial DNA and Human Evolution," *Nature* 325, no. 6099 (January 1987): 31–36, https://doi.org/10.1038/325031a0.

197 *an entire frozen alligator*: Cann, "Allan Charles Wilson. 18 October 1934—21 July 1991," 467.

197 *sterile Waring kitchen blender*: This and the following details about the process of extracting and analyzing mitochondrial DNA come from an email exchange with Mark Stoneking, a geneticist who coauthored "Mitochondrial DNA and Human Evolution," with Rebecca Cann and Allan Wilson.

197 *high-speed centrifuges*: John Tierney, Lynda Wright, and Karen Springen, "The Search for Adam and Eve: Scientists Claim to Have Found Our Common Ancestor—a Woman Who Lived 200,000 Years Ago and Left Resilient Genes That Are Carried by All of Mankind," *Newsweek*, January 11, 1988.

198 *published their work in* Nature *in January 1987*: Cann, Stoneking, and Wilson, "Mitochondrial DNA and Human Evolution."

198 *"Lucky Mother"*: Wilkins, "The Scientists Behind Mitochondrial Eve."

198 *"This will work"*: Interview with Mary-Claire King.

199 *she never had more faith that God was a woman*: Ibid.

CHAPTER 27—DAUGHTERS OF THE STATE

200 *strode into the immunology lab of the Hospital Durand*: Ramos Padilla, *Chicha*, 315; "La Historia Secreta de la Nieta Que No Fue," *Mendoza Post*, December 26, 2015, https://www.mendozapost.com/nota/25613-la-historia-secreta-de-la-nieta-que-no-fue/. Treviño and Rivarola had begun trying to find out Juliana's true identity in 1983 but, according to José Treviño's testimony as printed in "Estamos firmemente convencidos," *Página 12*, August 25, 1988, the case was delayed for years.

200 *in the throes of moving to a larger space*: The Abuelas moved to Corrientes 3284 in February 1988, according to *Historia de Abuelas*, 194.

200 *a genetic condition*: Ramos Padilla, *Chicha*, 316.

200 *"Did my parents abandon me because they didn't love me?"*: Ibid., 315.

200 *watching the film* La Historia Oficial: Gabriel Levinas and Sergio Serrichio, "Ramos Padilla: Los Conocidos de Siempre," *Clarín*, March 18, 2019, https://www.clarin.com/politica/ramos-padilla-conocidos-siempre_0_F2FZFGLuV.html.

201   *a boy born in January 1978*: "La Historia Secreta de La Nieta Que No Fue," *Mendoza Post*, December 26, 2015, https://www.mendozapost.com/nota/25613-la-historia-secreta-de -la-nieta-que-no-fue/.

201   *pregnant again*: "La Historia Secreta de La Nieta Que No Fue."

201   *there was a 98.91 percent*: Ramos Padilla, *Chicha*, 321.

201   *"She needs separation from her adoptive family"*: Horacio Verbitsky, "Juliana de Vuelta al Hogar con 2 Hermanos y 32 Primos," *Página 12*, August 3, 1988.

202   *flitted in and out*: Ibid.

202   *drew pictures of mountains and birds*: Ibid.

202   *tawny thing named Coli*: Ramos Padilla, *Chicha*, 325; Jorge Llistosella, "Los Métodos Que Buscan La Verdad," *Página 12*, May 27, 1990.

202   *José Treviño declared*: "Declaración de José Benigno Treviño, Padre Adoptive de Juliana Sandoval como Imputado no Procesado, el 29 de Junio de 1988," as reprinted as "Estamos Firmemente Convencidos," *Página 12*, August 25, 1988.

202   *which the magazine published*: Ramos Padilla, *Chicha*, 324.

203   *"The identity of Juliana"*: Horacio Verbitsky, "Cambio de Domicilio," *Página 12*, August 31, 1988; "Será Justicia?" *Página 12*, cover, August 28, 1988.

203   *"Juliana should have been home with us"*: Horacio Palma, "Caso Juliana Treviño (Tiempo Nuevo)," YouTube, October 27, 2009, www.youtube.com/watch?v=cwAgaK LsHJU.

203   *Rivarola brought up the inconsistency*: Gandsman, "Reclaiming the Past," 206.

203   *"It doesn't matter"*: "Declaración de José Benigno Treviño, Padre Adoptive de Juliana Sandoval como Imputado no Procesado, el 29 de JHunio de 1988," as reprinted as "Estamos Firmemente Convencidos," *Página 12*, August 25, 1988.

203   *biologically related to Fontana-Sandovals*: Ramos Padilla, *Chicha*, 335.

203   *Mamá de Juliana*: Claudia Acuña, "La lógica de la Corte Suprema," *Página 12*, August 28, 1988; "Será Justicia?" *Página 12*, cover, August 28, 1988.

203   *"Have heart"*: A.R., "Al Juez Solo le Piden Que Aplique Ética y Corazón," *Página 12*, August 28, 1988.

203   *curled up in the fetal position*: Andrea Rodríguez, "Las Últimas Horas en el Juzgado," *Página 12*, August 31, 1988.

204   *"Hasta mañana"*: "El Día Despues," *Página 12*, August 31, 1988.

204   *"they've stolen my granddaughter"*: Matt Prichard, "Child's Fate Reopens Argentina's War Wounds," *Roanoke Times & World News*, October 9, 1988.

204   *"is part of a campaign"*: Ibid.

204   *the anniversary drew 150,000 people*: "Hubo 150,000 Jóvenes en el Festival de Rock," *Clarín*, December 28, 1988.

204   *five years of waiting*: Some official documents such as lawsuit Darwinia Rosa Mónaco de Gallicchio v. Argentina, Comunicación No. 400/1990, U.N. Doc. CCPR/C/53/D/400/1990 (1995), suggest that Ximena was located in 1984. In an interview, Ximena herself recalled that it was earlier, in 1983. That is corroborated by sources like Amnesty International's September 1990 report on missing children, visible at: https://www.amnesty.org/en /wp-content/uploads/2024/04/AMR130051990ENGLISH.pdf; and Marianela Scocco, "La Historia de Una Búsqueda. Darwinia Gallicchio, Madre Y Abuela de Plaza 25 de

Mayo de Rosario.," Aacademica.org (Departamento de Historia de la Facultad de Humanidades, Universidad Nacional de Catamarca, 2011), 8, https://www.aacademica.org /000-071/342.

204 *to pick up the infant's passport*: Abuelas de Plaza de Mayo, *La Historia de Abuelas*, 78, suggests that Stella Maris was picking up passports for the whole family; in an interview, Ximena Vicario herself maintained that her passport was the only one being processed in Buenos Aires that day.

204 *Pedro de Elizalde, a children's hospital*: "Restituirán a Su Familia a una Niña Que Fue Localizada," *Clarín*, April 16, 1986.

204 *Ximena did not fit the profile*: Interview with Ximena Vicario.

205 *"Daughter of guerrillas"*: Ramos Padilla, *Chicha*, 354; this detail has been widely reported in other sources. Ximena herself suggests that her parents were not involved in the leftist movement. But the Abuelas website and the official database of victims of the Parque de la Memoria both list Stella Maris Gallicchio and Juan Carlos Vicario as having been members of the PRT-ERP.

205 *one of the hospital's hematologists*: Susana Siciliano is often referred to as a nurse. In an interview, Ximena Vicario suggested she was actually a doctor.

205 *tried to convince her young granddaughter*: Jaroslavsky, *El Futuro de la Memoria*, 103.

205 *late 1985*: "Restituirán a Su Familia a una Niña Que Fue Localizada."

205 *the judge sent a technician to her house*: Jaroslavsky, *El Futuro de la Memoria*, 101.

205 *99.82 percent*: Laura Oren, "Righting Child Custody Wrongs: The Children of the 'Disappeared' in Argentina," *Harvard Human Rights Journal* 14 (March 3, 1997): 167, https:// journals.law.harvard.edu/hrj/wp-content/uploads/sites/83/2020/06/14HHRJ123 -Oren.pdf.

205 *"cut off my hands"*: Horacio Vargas, "La Familia Espera En Rosario," *Página 12*, January 4, 1989.

205 *kept in a locked box*: A.R., "Desde Ayer, Ximena Vicario Reside con Su Verdadera Abuela," *Página 12*, January 4, 1989.

206 *dispatched security forces*: Ibid.

206 *multiple men with rifles in her room*: Interview with Ximena Vicario.

206 *Ximena's fuzzy cocker spaniel, Pamela*: George De Lama, "'Dirty War' Still Tears at Families in Argentina," *Chicago Tribune*, January 17, 1989.

206 *a tank top and white hoop earrings*: A.R., "Desde Ayer, Ximena Vicario Reside con Su Verdadera Abuela."

206 *"I'm not going with that old lady!"*: Ibid.

206 *"Let me stay with my mommy please!"*: "Young Victim of 'Dirty War' Is Taken from Adoptive Mom," *Deseret News*, January 4, 1989, https://www.deseret.com/1989/1/4 /18790117/young-victim-of-dirty-war-is-taken-from-adoptive-mom/.

206 *vowing to commit suicide*: "The Lost Generation," *Newsweek*, February 8, 1993, https:// www.newsweek.com/lost-generation-195078.

206 *Ximena continued crying*: A.R., "Desde Ayer, Ximena Vicario Reside con Su Verdadera Abuela."

206 *"Ximena's case kept me up for nights"*: "The Lost Generation," *Newsweek*, February 8, 1993, https://www.newsweek.com/lost-generation-195078.

CHAPTER 28—FALLOUT

207 *"XIMENA VICARIO IS WITH HER GRANDMOTHER"*: "Ximena Vicario Está Con Su Abuela," *Página 12*, January 4, 1989.

207 *"A daughter of desaparecidos resisted"*: "Una Hija de Desaparecidos Se Resistió a Dejar a Su Madre Adoptive," *Clarín*, January 4, 1989.

207 *"why don't they respect what the girl wants?"*: Sergio Ciancaglini, "El Torpedo," *Página 12*, January 5, 1989.

207 *"How can they separate the girl from the people who raised her?"*: Ibid.

207 *"from a human point of view"*: De Lama, "'Dirty War' Still Tears at Families in Argentina."

208 *had left twelve of them to grow up*: Eduardo Videla, "Ximena, después de la tormenta," *Página 12*, January 5, 1989.

208 *named Siciliano one of its people of the year*: Gandsman, "Reclaiming the Past," 227.

208 *appear on Tiempo Nuevo*: Ramos Padilla, *Chicha*, 355–56.

208 *he accused the Abuelas of "kidnapping"*: Ibid.

208 *"You won't be with us anymore"*: ISHIR, "Homenaje a Darwinia Mónaco de Gallicchio," YouTube, March 29, 2023, www.youtube.com/watch?v=WfuAxFgryIM.

208 *the only place she allowed herself was to cry was the Plaza de Mayo*: Nélida Gómez de Navajas interview with Rita Arditti, November 8, 1993, University of Massachusetts–Boston, Joseph P. Healey Library, 25, https://openarchives.umb.edu/digital/collection/p15774coll 10/id/886/rec/28.

209 *detail-oriented and demanding*: Ramos Padilla, *Chicha*, 346. Estela has never publicly spoken about her rift with Chicha. What follows is from Chicha's biographies. I sent Estela a fact-checking memo to allow her to respond to Chicha's narrative and share her thoughts about the rift, but she did not respond.

209 *Estela was more inclined to wade into partisan politics*: Ibid., 365.

209 *relishing media attention*: Ibid., 345.

209 *Estela was supportive*: Laureano Barrera, *La Casa de la Calle 30* (Buenos Aires: Tusquets Editores S.A., 2022), ch. 12, Kindle.

209 *under a jacaranda tree after Cyrus Vance's visit*: This origin story is told in Ramos Padilla, *Chicha*, 131, and also in Chicha Mariani's testimony to the Biblioteca Nacional, https://www.bn.gov.ar/uploads/transcripciones/chicha-chorobik-de-mariani.pdf.

209 *coincide with her birthday*: Estela Barnes de Carlotto interview with Rita Arditti, December 22, 1994, University of Massachusetts–Boston, Joseph P. Healey Library, https://openarchives.umb.edu/digital/collection/p15774coll10/id/882/rec/12.

209 *"I have tolerated insolence from Estela"*: Barrera, *La Casa de la Calle 30*, 211.

209 *Chicha Mariani left the Abuelas*: Ibid., 221.

209 *Abuela Vilma Gutiérrez later remembered*: Ramos Padilla, *Chicha*, 364.

210 *"had been broken"*: Barrera, *La Casa de la Calle 30*, 221.

210 *let their personal animus affect their mission*: Ramos Padilla, *Chicha*, 363–64.

210 *invited in 1990 to receive a prize*: Ibid., 352.

210 *she used two advanced technologies*: "Los Métodos Que Buscan la Verdad," *Página 12*, May 27, 1990.

210 *not shared by any of her supposed grandparents*: Sergio A. Lozano, "La Huella Incierta," *Página 12*, June 9, 1990.

210 *would blame Di Lonardo and the BNDG*: "Dios, el Metodo y las Abuelas," *Página 12*, April 25, 1992.

211 *"had no reason to doubt"*: Ibid.

211 *"How curious"*: "La Genetista de Los Derechos Humanos," *La Nación*, October 20, 1996, https://www.lanacion.com.ar/lifestyle/la-genetista-de-los-derechos-humanos-nid211334/.

211 *No other judicial decision*: Gandsman, "Reclaiming the Past," 216.

211 *did not have photocopiers*: Jorge Llistosella, "Otro Banco en la Picota," *Página 12*, July 22, 1990.

211 *Di Lonardo had to drive her personal Citroën*: Ibid.

211 *waiting impatiently for him in the arrivals area*: Interview with Eric Stover.

211 *"And these chemicals, where do they come from?"*: Ministerio de Ciencia, Tecnología e Innovación Productiva, "Una pregunta," 32.

212 *it would have essentially ceased functioning*: Jorge Llistosella, "Otro Banco en la Picota," *Página 12*, July 22, 1990.

212 *the "hysterical decision"*: Ramos Padilla, *Chicha*, 353.

212 *"allows one to question similar cases"*: Gandsman, "Reclaiming the Past," 215.

212 *spiked to the triple digits*: Juan Pablo Csipka, "Hiperinflación: A 35 Años del Inicio de una Experiencia Traumática | El 6 de Febrero de 1989, El Dólar Saltó de 17 a 24 Australes y Comenzó la Crisis Que Liquidó al Gobierno de Alfonsín," *Página 12*, February 6, 2024, https://www.pagina12.com.ar/710712-hiperinflacion-a-35-anos-del-inicio-de-una-experiencia-traum.

212 *exasperated housewives blocked roads in protest*: "El Vendaval," *Página 12*, May 30, 1989.

212 *At least fourteen people died*: "Alfonsin Steps Aside," *Los Angeles Times*, June 15, 1989, https://www.latimes.com/archives/la-xpm-1989-06-15-me-2207-story.html.

213 *Videla denied the request*: "Menem 1976–1981: El Mismo Preso, Otra Historia," *Clarín*, June 7, 2001, https://www.clarin.com/politica/menem-1976-1981-mismo-preso-historia_0_H1rgxOgAKg.html.

213 *"The final stop for murderers is jail"*: "El Punto Final para los Asesinos es la Cárcel," *La Rázon*, December 9, 1986.

213 *"power more than anything, including his family"*: Clifford Krauss, "Argentina's Former President Still at Center Stage," *New York Times*, January 3, 2000, https://www.nytimes.com/2000/01/03/world/argentina-s-former-president-still-at-center-stage.html.

213 *"I know there will be those who are unhappy"*: "200 Military Officers Are Pardoned in Argentina," *New York Times*, October 8, 1989.

213 *just able to make out the birdlike face and rangy gait*: "Officers Go Free in Argentina," UPI, December 29, 1990, https://www.upi.com/Archives/1990/12/29/Officers-go-free-in-Argentina/9009662446800/.

CHAPTER 29—THE DELI FRIDGE

214 *head of the Human Genome Project*: Angier, "Scientist at Work."

214 *approached to lead the National Institutes of Health*: Ibid.

215 *The officers demanded to see the books*: Jorge Llistosella, "Singular Allanamiento al Banco de Datos Genéticos," *Página 12*, March 28, 1991; and "Allanan un banco de datos genéticos," *Clarín*, March 28, 1991.

215 *HLA data scribbled in red ink*: Banco Nacional de Datos Genéticos, *Ciencia X la Identidad: Historia Viva del Banco Nacional de Datos Genéticos*, March 2022, 97.

215 *"You all studied the grandparents of the girl"*: Llistosella, "Singular Allanamiento al Banco de Datos Genéticos."

215 *"Dear Mary"*: Fax from Estela de Carlotto to Mary-Claire King, August 27, 1991, box 170, AR AIAPM CD 1170.

216 *in at least one dozen labs*: Mary-Claire King, "'The Race' to Clone BRCA1," *Science* 343, no. 6178 (2014): 1462–65, https://doi.org/10.2307/24743524.

216 *her twenty-person team*: Angier, "Scientist at Work."

216 *called the contest to clone BRCA1 just as intense*: Neill, "A Conversation with Mary-Claire King."

216 *"if not 24/7, at least 14/6"*: King, "'The Race' to Clone BRCA1."

216 *she would do the work at no cost*: Fax from Mary-Claire King, August 23, 1991, box 170, AR AIAPM CD 1170.

216 *"It's not infectious"*: Mary-Claire King interview with the Archivo Institucional de Abuelas de Plaza de Mayo, September 18, 2023, Casa por la Identidad, Ciudad Autónoma de Buenos Aires.

217 *"specifically for the Abuelas"*: "Dios, El Metodo y las Abuelas," (Special Insert) *Página 12*, April 25, 1992.

217 *"rather correct"*: Ibid.

217 *"essentially infallible"*: Ibid.

217 *600 millionths of an ounce*: Matt Crenson, "New DNA Test Matches Mother to Child Through Genetic Pattern," *Anchorage Daily News*, October 9, 1992.

217 *even the most degraded remains*: Interview with Mary-Claire King.

217 *quickly matched two bodies*: Andrew A. Skolnick, "Mitochondrial DNA Studies Help Identify Lost Victims of Human Rights Abuses," *Journal of the American Medical Association* 269, no. 15 (April 21, 1993): 1911, https://doi.org/10.1001/jama.1993.03500 150015004.

217 *stamps from faraway places*: Interview with Mary-Claire King.

218 *She helped analyze the remains of the Romanovs*: Interview with Mary-Claire King. In that particular case, she worked with bones, not teeth, to extract mitochondrial DNA.

218 *"bring the missing children back to life"*: Mary-Claire King interview with the Archivo Institucional de Abuelas de Plaza de Mayo, September 18, 2023, Casa por la Identidad, Ciudad Autónoma de Buenos Aires.

218 *189 people representing ninety families*: Abuelas application to Fundación Pro Victimas in 1992, as viewed in the Abuelas Archive, AR AIAPM CD 4 440. (The organization is based in Geneva and, in French, its name is Fondation Pro Victimis.)

218 *"Very merry Christmas"*: Fax from Mary-Claire King to the Abuelas, December 23, 1993, as viewed in the Abuelas Archive, AR AIAPM CD 4 440.

CHAPTER 30—A SYSTEMATIC PLAN

219 *in 1994*: Michael J. Farrell, "New Light on Argentina's Dirty War Brings Spotlight Back to Pio Laghi," *National Catholic Reporter*, September 20, 1996.

219 *a former Montonero*: "Horacio Verbitsky, Sobre Su Época en Montoneros: 'Tuve la Su-

erte de No Matar a Nadie,'" *Noticias,* May 19, 2018, https://noticias.perfil.com/noticias/politica/2018-05-19-horacio-verbitsky-sobre-su-epoca-en-montoneros-tuve-la-suerte-de-no-matar-a-nadie.phtml.

219 *"I was at the ESMA":* Verbitsky, *El Vuelo,* 11.

219 *"We did worse things than the Nazis":* Ibid., 14.

220 *long rumored to be true:* In March 1978, an ESMA prisoner named Horacio Domingo Maggio escaped and confirmed the existence of death flights. He was later recaptured and killed. For more, see: Archivo Nacional de la Memoria, "Los 'Vuelos de La Muerte' En Campo de Mayo," November 13, 2023, https://www.argentina.gob.ar/sites/default/files/2023-11-13-icm6-los-vuelos-de-la-muerte_compressed.pdf.

220 *"rubbing salt in old wounds":* Semana, "Por Fin la Verdad," Semana.com Últimas Noticias de Colombia y el Mundo (Revista Semana, May 29, 1995), https://www.semana.com/por-fin-la-verdad/25635-3/.

220 *without men throwing punches at him:* Calvin Sims, "Retired Torturer Now Lives a Tortured Existence," *New York Times,* August 12, 1997, https://www.nytimes.com/1997/08/12/world/retired-torturer-now-lives-a-tortured-existence.html.

220 *"I could have smashed a glass over his head":* Francisco Peregil, "'I Started the "Escraches" When I Came Across the Man Who Tortured My Dad,'" *El País,* April 17, 2013, https://english.elpais.com/elpais/2013/04/17/inenglish/1366207043_710769.html.

221 *"I was following orders":* "Los Nietos Marchan por la Memoria," AUNO, March 21, 2018, https://auno.org.ar/los-nietos-nacidos-en-cautiverio-marchan-por-la-me.

221 *"Magnacco: Torturer and Thief of Lives":* "H.I.J.O.S.: Primer Escrache," Canal Encuentro, YouTube, April 13, 2020, www.youtube.com/watch?v=CHoZVrglDvE.

221 *forced to resign from Sanatorio Mitre:* "¡Cuidado! El Partero de la ESMA Anda Suelto," *La Tinta,* March 5, 2018, https://latinta.com.ar/2018/03/05/cuidado-partero-esma-suelto/.

221 *neighbors had asked him to move:* Natalia Chientaroli, "El Escrache, de Argentina al Mundo," *El Diario,* March 6, 2013, https://www.eldiario.es/sociedad/escrache-escrachar-argentina-hijos-represion_1_5601866.html.

221 *holding an enlarged photo of Patricia:* Maribel Rams Albuisech, "Fotografía, Narración y Posmemoria en España y Argentina. Cristina Fallarás y Mariana Eva Perez," *Pasavento Revista de Estudios Hispánicos* 12, no. 1 (May 2024): 17, https://doi.org/10.37536/preh.2024.12.1.2207.

221 *a no-nonsense outlook on life that Mariana identified with:* Archivo Biográfico Familiar Pérez Roisinblit, 295.

221 *"starring in a suspense movie":* Pérez, *Diario de una Princesa Montonera,* 41.

222 *rape and the kidnapping of minors were still prosecutable offenses:* "Argentina: Amnesty Laws Struck Down," Human Rights Watch, June 14, 2005, https://www.hrw.org/news/2005/06/14/argentina-amnesty-laws-struck-down.

222 *eight kidnapping cases:* Carolina Villella, "Apropiación de Niños y Niñas Durante el Terrorismo de Estado en Argentina: Respuesta Judicial Entre los Años 1975–2015," 2023, https://bibliotecavirtual.unl.edu.ar:8443/handle/11185/7757.

222 *"received verbal and written orders":* Seoane and Muleiro, *El Dictador,* 512. The doctor's name was Jorge Caserotto, and he was the chief of gynecology at the Hospital de Campo de Mayo.

222 *knotting his tie around his gangly neck*: "Detienen a Videla en un Caso por Robo de Bebés," *Clarín*, June 10, 1998, https://www.clarin.com/politica/detienen-videla-caso-robo-bebes _0_By7GwsJJ8nx.html.

223 *red Peugeot 405 he kept downstairs in the garage*: Romina Calderaro, "No Se Prive de Nada," *Página 12*, June 10, 1998, https://www.pagina12.com.ar/1998/98-06/98-06 -10/pag03.htm.

223 *"We have an order to detain you"*: "Detienen a Videla en un Caso por Robo de Bebés."

223 *black winter coats and black peaked caps*: Di Chiara DiFilm archive, "Detienen a Jorge Rafael Videla–Fotos—DiFilm (1998)," YouTube, October 5, 2017, www.youtube.com /watch?v=DckZLVzHwDg.

223 *One of them held a piece of paper*: "Detienen a Videla En Un Caso Por Robo de Bebés."

223 *"facilitating and promoting"*: Seoane and Muleiro, *El Dictador*, 15.

223 *he strained to cover his face*: Horacio Verbitsky, "Videla Es Mundial," *Página 12*, June 10, 1998, https://www.pagina12.com.ar/1998/98-06/98-06-10/pag03.htm.

223 *duck into the back of a white sedan*: Ibid.

223 *hardly even blinking*: Seoane and Muliero, *El Dictador*, 16.

223 *"Asesino! Hijo de puta!"*: Ibid.

224 *a wide grin spread across her face*: "La Sonrisa de Estela Carlotto: 'No Se Me Borra,'" *Página 12*, July 4, 1998, https://www.pagina12.com.ar/1998/98-07/98-07-04/pag 03.htm.

224 *"What news do you have of your grandson?"*: ArchivoDiChiara, *Estela de Carlotto Pablo Diaz Adriana Calvo Pedro Aznar con Mirtha Legrand 1998 DiFilm*, April 10, 2018, www .youtube.com/watch?v=_Z-k3-hdQpQ.

224 *"I am a grandmother"*: Ibid.

224 *Estela was declared one of the "People of the Year"*: *Gente*, December 17, 1998.

224 *"For decades we have been looking for our grandchildren"*: Interview with Mary-Claire King.

CHAPTER 31—GUILLERMO

227 *maybe he could take a Sunday off*: Unless otherwise indicated, all information pertaining to Guillermo's story in the following chapter is derived from a series of over a dozen interviews with him between March 2021 and November 2024.

234 *"Finally, Gelman found his granddaughter"*: "Al Fin Gelman Encontró a Su Nieta," *Clarín*, April 1, 2000.

234 *"I have been looking"*: Jorge Elías, "Gelman Halló a su Nieta, Desaparecida," *La Nación*, April 1, 2000, https://www.lanacion.com.ar/el-mundo/gelman-hallo-a-su-nieta-desapa recida-nid11329/.

234 *his eyes visibly red*: Redacción Clarín, "El Poeta Gelman Encontró a su Nieta Desaparecida en Uruguay," *Clarín*, March 31, 2000, https://www.clarin.com/politica/poeta-gel man-encontro-nieta-desaparecida-uruguay_0_BJlehSjgCYe.html.

234 *"El Gordo José"*: Gabriel Tuñez, "Victoria Montenegro, Nieta Recuperada y Abuela: 'No Imagino a Mi Nieto en Otros Brazos Que No Fueran Los Míos,'" *El Diario*, March 24, 2023, https://www.eldiarioar.com/politica/victoria-montenegro-nieta-recuperada-abuela -no-imagino-nieto-brazos-no-fueran_1_10061933.html.

234 *reunited with her brother*: "María de las Victorias Ruiz Dameri," DNA: January 4, 2000, Abuelas.org.ar, 2017, https://www.abuelas.org.ar/nietas-y-nietos/280.

235 *Evelin Vázquez*: In many sources, Evelin's name is spelled Evelyn. But on her own social media profiles and on the Abuelas website, Evelin's name is spelled with an "i."

235 *"divine mandate"*: Raúl Kollman, "Sucursal de la ESMA en Mar del Plata," *Página 12*, August 1, 2001, https://www.pagina12.com.ar/2000/00-01/00-01-08/pag03.htm.

235 *"God put the baby in my hands"*: Ibid.

235 *But a week later, she reneged*: Ari Gandsman, "'A Prick of a Needle Can Do No Harm': Compulsory Extraction of Blood in the Search for the Children of Argentina's Disappeared," *Journal of Latin American and Caribbean Anthropology* 14, no. 1 (April 2009): 166, https://doi.org/10.1111/j.1935-4940.2009.01043.x.

235 *"If for twenty-two years, he has been my father"*: María Elena Polack, "Acepta el ADN, Pero No Acusar a Su Padre," *La Nación*, August 20, 2000, https://www.lanacion.com.ar/politica/acepta-el-adn-pero-no-acusar-a-su-padre-nid29641/.

235 *still hundreds of stolen grandchildren*: As of January 2025, the Abuelas listed 392 cases on their website. But they have long estimated that as many as 500 grandchildren were stolen. They explain some women disappeared before their families knew they were pregnant.

235 *"Vos sabés quién sos?"*: María Luisa Diz, "Los Spots Para Televisión de Abuelas de Plaza de Mayo: Entre El Nombre, la Sangre y el Testimonio," *Comunicación y Sociedad* 31 (January 1, 2018): 73–94, https://doi.org/10.32870/cys.v0i31.6861.

235 *held massive rock concerts*: Abuelas de Plaza de Mayo, *La Historia de Abuelas*, 127.

235 *five o'clock showing of* Botín de Guerra: Movie Section of *Página 12* on April 27, 2000.

235 *The director had spliced together*: Blaustein, "Botín de Guerra."

236 *going by Claudio Novoa*: This was the name with which he was raised, which he had not yet changed. Today he goes by Manuel Gonçalves Granada.

236 *María Carolina Guallane*: This was the name with which she was raised, which she had not yet changed. The name given to her by her biological family is Paula Cortassa Zapata.

236 *"I hope he knows that he has two Abuelas"*: Blaustein, "Botín de Guerra."

236 *"It must be terrible for these young people"*: Ibid.

236 *crackly voice of a smoker*: Mariana Eva Pérez, "Chau Pucho," *Decía Mi Abuelo* (blog), August 19, 2008, https://deciamiabuelo.blogspot.com/2008/08/chau-pucho.html.

237 *fifty thousand young people*: Abuelas de Plaza de Mayo, *La Historia de Abuelas*, 127.

237 *The notes about the two anonymous calls*: I personally viewed copies of this and the second denuncia in the Rosa Tarlovsky de Roisinblit Fondo Personal, Caja 12, CPM.

238 *Gómez had admitted knowledge of "death flights"*: Ibid.

238 *They had grown used*: Adriana Meyer, "Análisis Genético a Evelyn," *Página 12*, April 15, 1999.

239 *five small circles*: Guillermo does not explicitly remember if they were circles or rectangles, but every photo I've seen of such absorbent cards used to collect blood samples depict circles.

CHAPTER 32—CONFRONTING GÓMEZ

240 *dinner at a steakhouse in Morón*: Unless otherwise indicated, all information pertaining to Guillermo's story in the following chapter is derived from a series of over one dozen interviews with him between March 2021 and November 2024.

240   *The only explanation Guillermo could think of*: RIBA Trial, Guillermo Pérez Roisinblit testimony, May 16, 2016.

240   *"Take a good look at me"*: Daniel Enzetti, "Como puede estar tranquilo, con sangre de las secuestradas en su conciencia?" *Tiempo Argentino*, February 11, 2013.

242   *"I have to be at work at four"*: RIBA Trial, Guillermo Pérez Roisinblit testimony.

242   *to avoid flattening a bicyclist crossing the street*: Daniel Enzetti, "Cómo Puede Estar Tranquilo, con Sangre de las Secuestradas en Su Conciencia," *Tiempo Argentino*, February 11, 2013.

242   *"You have to understand"*: Guillermo Pérez Roisinblit, Tweet from March 10, 2018, X (formerly Twitter), accessed November 25, 2024, https://x.com/Guillogo_/status /972611660337819648.

242   *"I saved your life"*: Ibid.

242   *"You kidnapped the grandson"*: Daniel Enzetti, "Cómo Puede Estar Tranquilo, con Sangre de las Secuestradas en Su Conciencia," *Tiempo Argentino*, February 11, 2013.

CHAPTER 33—GENETICS DOESN'T LIE

243   *the most international human rights forensics work*: Bock, "The Plan of All Plans."

243   *"[The police] got a kick out of"*: Unless otherwise indicated, all quotes and information pertaining to Mary-Claire King in the following chapter are derived from a series of lengthy interviews with her between June 2022 and November 2024.

244   *tens of millions of dollars*: Randy Trick, "Gates Gives $70 Million to UW," *The Daily of the University of Washington*, April 25, 2003, https://www.dailyuw.com/news/gates-gives -70-million-to-uw/article_c615af4d-645f-54fa-955c-f5304647319c.html.

244   *"multicultural Gap ad"*: Bock, "The Plan of All Plans."

244   *"I'll buy lattes for a week!"*: Ibid.

244   *"one feels trapped in resin"*: Angier, "Scientist at Work."

245   *on May 4, 2000*: Mary-Claire King and Kelly Owens, "Nucleotide Sequence Analysis of Mitochondrial and Nuclear DNA of Guillermo Gomez, Rosa Rosenblitt [sic], Mariana Eva Perez and Argentina Rojo," University of Washington School of Medicine, August 30, 2000, as consulted in Rosa Tarlovsky de Roisinblit Fondo Personal, Caja 12, CPM.

246   *hosted a dinner at the John F. Kennedy Library*: Estela Barnes de Carlotto and Rosa Tarlovsky de Roisinblit from Las Abuelas de Plaza de Mayo at UMass Boston Honorary Degree Dinner, June 2, 2000, https://openarchives.umb.edu/digital/collection /p15774coll10/id/821/rec/19.

246   *into a nightgown*: Interview with Estelle Disch.

247   *laughing, crying, and dancing*: Ibid.

247   *Mariana was intimidated*: RIBA Trial, Mariana Eva Pérez testimony, May 4, 2016.

247   *Mariana had cried for every cut*: Victoria Ginzberg, "A los 22 Años la Historia Verdadera," *Página 12*, February 9, 2002, https://www.pagina12.com.ar/2001/01-02 /01-02-09/pag15.htm.

247   *"nene" (little one) or "mocoso" (brat)*: Ibid.

CHAPTER 34—BABA

248   *a white sweatshirt embroidered with a red scorpion*: Plan Sistemático Trial, Rosa Roisinblit testimony.

248 *"Well, I'm your grandmother"*: Ibid.

248 *"Ya lo sé, Baba"*: Ibid.

248 *gave her a kiss on the cheek*: Ibid.

248 *A few days later*: In this article, Mariana mentions she missed the opening of the play *A Propósito de la Duda* due to the dinner: Hinde Pomeraniec, "Mariana Eva Pérez: 'La Militancia Armada Sigue Siendo el Elefante en el Cuarto,'" *Infobae*, April 17, 2022, https://www.infobae.com/leamos/2022/04/17/mariana-eva-perez-la-militancia-armada-sigue-siendo-el-elefante-en-el-cuarto/. This journal article suggests the opening was on June 5, 2000: Federica De Filippi, "A Propósito de la Duda, de Patricia Zangaro: Dramaturgia e Identidad," *Boletín GEC*, no. 29 (June 30, 2022): 179–91, https://doi.org/10.48162/rev.43.021.

248 *had been set to attend the opening*: Pomeraniec, "Mariana Eva Pérez."

249 *"Dear Brother, when I learned of your existence"*: Mariana Eva Pérez and Yamila Grandi, *Algún Día* (Buenos Aires: Abuelas de Plaza de Mayo, 1990).

249 *suggested that Rosa throw her a party*: Plan Sistemático Trial, Rosa Roisinblit testimony, May 30, 2011.

249 *embroidered with turquoise flowers on her dining table for the occasion*: Photo provided to author by Guillermo Pérez Roisinblit.

249 *"You look like her in this one"*: Rosa Roisinblit interview with Rita Arditti on January 26, 2006, https://openarchives.umb.edu/digital/collection/p15774coll10/id/877/rec/36.

249 *resting his large hand on her petite shoulder*: Photos provided to author by Guillermo Pérez Roisinblit.

250 *I'll tell you the story*: Actis et al., *Ese Infierno*, 246.

250 *"One must ask what that man or woman recovers"*: Milena Durán, "Los 20 Años del Archivo Biográfico Familiar de Abuelas de Plaza de Mayo," *Historia, Voces y Memoria* 12 (December 10, 2018): 33, https://doi.org/10.34096/hvm.n12.6239.

251 *"preserve family memory into the future"*: Ibid.

251 *one-dimensional descriptions had begun to chafe at Mariana*: Archivo Biográfico Familiar Pérez Roisinblit, 283–95.

251 *Guillermo immediately recognized the building*: RIBA Trial, Guillermo Pérez Roisinblit testimony.

251 *He even knew the base's phone number by heart*: Ibid.

251 *early in the morning*: In her testimony about Guillermo's birth, Sara Osatinsky said that the contractions started at dawn. Francisco Gomez, Jorge Luis Magnacco, y Teodora Jofre s/ Sustracción Menor de 10 años, Sentencia, April 22, 2005, http://www.saij.gob.ar/jurisprudencia/FA05261086-SU30008610-francisco_sustraccion-federal-2005.htm?1.

251 *covered with a mask*: Miriam Lewin Testimony, Juicio a las Juntas, 1985.

251 *"Hi, son. It's me"*: Baldosas X la Memoria II/Barrios X Memoria y Justicia, 122.

251 *after two* compañeros *who had been disappeared*: Archivo Biográfico Familiar Pérez Roisinblit, 3.

252 *at least one of them precipitated by Gómez's fierce blows*: RIBA Trial, Guillermo Pérez Roisinblit testimony.

252 *that he was doing a noble thing by taking him in*: Gómez, Magnacco, y Jofré s/ Sustracción Menor de 10 años, Sentencia Final, April 22, 2005.

CHAPTER 35—THICKER THAN WATER

253 *after just thirty-eight days*: Lucía Cholakian Herrera, "Jorge Rafael Videla: The Dictator Who Died in Jail," *Página 12*, May 17, 2023, https://Buenosairesherald.com/Human-Rights/Jorge-Rafael-Videla-The-Dictator-Who-Died-In-Jail.

253 *still worked at the naval hospital*: "¡Cuidado! El Partero de la ESMA Anda Suelto."

253 *"distinguished member"*: Luis Bruschtein, "El Insólito Yacht Club," *Página 12*, November 2, 2003, https://www.pagina12.com.ar/diario/elpais/1-27615-2003-11-02.html.

254 *sentenced Astiz in absentia to life in prison*: "Extradite Astiz, Argentine Government Urged," Human Rights Watch, July 28, 2001, https://www.hrw.org/news/2001/07/27/extradite-astiz-argentine-government-urged.

254 *ninety-eight former Argentine military officers for their role in the deaths of six hundred people*: Joshua Hammer, "In Argentina, Justice Delayed," *Newsweek*, September 25, 2000, https://www.newsweek.com/argentina-justice-delayed-159303.

254 *one other Italian Argentine woman*: Astiz was also sought for the disappearance of Angela María Aieta.

254 *"Why don't you ask for the American ones?"*: Luciana Bertoia and María Eugenia Ludueña, "Archivos: Desclasificar el Silencio," Revista Anfibia, March 24, 2016, https://www.revistaanfibia.com/archivos-desclasificar-silencio/.

254 *Hillary Clinton's top advisors*: Victoria Ginzberg, "Las Abuelas Viajan para Desclasificar Archivos," *Página 12*, September 21, 1999, https://www.pagina12.com.ar/1999/99-09/99-09-21/pag12.htm.

254 *Estela also met with Secretary of State Madeleine Albright*: Werner Pertot, "Nuevos Secretos Pueden Salir a la Luz," *Página 12*, March 18, 2016, https://www.pagina12.com.ar/diario/elpais/1-294874-2016-03-18.html.

255 *overseeing pregnant prisoners in the ESMA*: Plan Sistemático, Fallo, September 17, 2012, 653.

255 *to the children and spouses of the disappeared*: Pablo De Greiff, *The Handbook of Reparations* (New York: Oxford University Press, 2006), 26.

255 *amounting to around $334,000*: Thread from Mariana Eva Pérez, August 16, 2024, https://x.com/princesamonto/status/1824564998351491354; Confirmed figure with Guillermo Pérez Roisinblit; Nora Lloveras and Sebastián Monjo, "Las Indemnizaciones a Cargo del Estado Nacional en los Casos de Desaparición Forzada de Personas," *Jurisprudencia Argentina* 7 (2013), https://rdu.unc.edu.ar/bitstream/handle/11086/551702/Las%20indemnizaciones%20a%20cargo%20del%20Estado%20Nacional%20en%20los%20casos%20de%20desaparici%C3%B3n%20forzada%20de%20personas.pdf?sequence=3&isAllowed=y.

255 *She'd been able to cash in enough*: Thread from Mariana Eva Pérez, August 16, 2024.

255 *to create a vibrant mural*: Pérez, *Diario de una Princesa Montonera*, 85.

255 *there were no photos of her pregnant*: Interview with Claudia Poblete Hlaczik.

255 *In February 2000, the results came back*: Federico Bianchini, *Tu Nombre No Es Tu Nombre: Historia de una Identidad Robada en la Dictadura Argentina* (Madrid: Libros del K.O., 2023), 9.

255 *"I don't want to"*: Ibid.

256 *taken them to the headquarters of the federal police*: Ibid., 8.

256 *"Don't worry about us"*: Ibid., 9.

256 *"For twenty-two years"*: "Desaparecidos: Poblete Reafirmó su Identidad," *La Nación*,

June 23, 2001, https://www.lanacion.com.ar/politica/desaparecidos-poblete-reafirmo-su-identidad-nid314780/.

256 *arrested on charges of kidnapping and the falsification of official documents*: RIBA Trial, Guillermo Pérez Roisinblit testimony.

256 *a 99.99999 percent probability of a relationship*: King and Owens, "Nucleotide Sequence Analysis of Mitochondrial and Nuclear DNA of Guillermo Gomez, Rosa Rosenblitt [sic], Mariana Eva Perez and Argentina Rojo."

256 *behind the city's central train station in Retiro*: RIBA Trial, Guillermo Pérez Roisinblit testimony.

256 *Guillermo was livid*: Unless otherwise indicated, all information and quotes pertaining to Guillermo's story in the following chapter are derived from a series of over one dozen interviews with him between March 2021 and November 2024.

257 *"the ground where you step"*: "Guillermo Rodolfo Pérez Roisinblit," Educación y Memoria, 2016, https://www.educacionymemoria.com.ar/guillermo-rodolfo-perez-roisinblit.

257 *gave a scathing interview to* La Nación: "'Quiero Ser Hijo de Mis Padres, No de Gente Que No Conocí,'" *La Nación*, February 18, 2001, https://www.lanacion.com.ar/politica/quiero-ser-hijo-de-mis-padres-no-de-gente-que-no-conoci-nid52827/.

258 *"I want to keep being the son of my parents"*: Ibid.

258 *"They should avoid the Abuelas de Plaza de Mayo"*: Ibid.

258 *was detained as well*: "¡Cuidado! El Partero de la ESMA Anda Suelto."

259 *"the perfect granny from films"*: Matthew Bremner, "The Secret Police Killed His Parents. Then One of Them Adopted Him," *1843*, December 4, 2023.

259 *"Why are you calling me?!"*: Plan Sistemático Trial, Rosa Roisinblit testimony.

259 *$700 million was withdrawn*: Clifford Krauss, "Argentine Economy: Postponing the Inevitable," *New York Times*, December 4, 2001, https://www.nytimes.com/2001/12/04/world/argentine-economy-postponing-the-inevitable.html.

259 *$250 a week*: Joaquin G. Gutierrez and Fernando Montes-Negret, "Argentina's Banking System: Restoring Financial Viability," World Bank Office for Argentina, Chile, Paraguay, and Uruguay, January 2004.

259 *"We don't have any money!"*: Alex Bellos, "Argentina Besieged by Looting Spree," *Guardian*, December 20, 2001, https://www.theguardian.com/world/2001/dec/20/argentina.alexbellos.

260 *"They say I'm boring"*: "Dicen Que Soy Aburrido. Spot de La Rua." YouTube, March 22, 2021, www.youtube.com/watch?v=CXF6vcXn7_4.

260 *vrooming around Buenos Aires in a red Ferrari*: Uki Goñi, "Argentina Collapses into Chaos," *Guardian*, December 21, 2001, https://www.theguardian.com/world/2001/dec/21/argentina.ukigoni.

260 *rotating cast of busty mistresses*: John Simpson, "Menem's Miracle," *The Spectator*, March 21, 1992, https://archive.spectator.co.uk/article/21st-march-1992/13/menems-miracle.

261 *throw people like his parents into the Río de la Plata*: Juan Ignacio Irigaray, "Destapan Que La Fuerza Aérea Argentina También Ejecutó 'Vuelos de La Muerte,'" *El Mundo*, June 24, 2010, https://www.elmundo.es/america/2010/06/24/argentina/1277392343.html.

261 *told her about such gruesome flights*: Denuncia, April 24, 2000, Rosa Tarlovsky de Roisinblit Fondo Personal, Caja 12, CPM.

262 *No lower-level officers had been convicted since*: "Lesa Humanidad: La Lista de Todos los Procesados," Centro de Información Judicial, 2018, https://www.cij.gov.ar/nota-972-Lesa -humanidad--la-lista-de-todos-los-procesados.html. According to this list, the first air force officer convicted of human rights crimes was in 2004.

CHAPTER 36—SEA CHANGE

263 *supported El Líder ardently*: Interiew with Ezequiel Rochistein Tauro.

263 *forcing young Vázquez Sarmiento to seek employment*: Ibid.

263 *to find the infant lying on her bed*: Constanza Hola Chamy, "'Cómo Cambió Mi Vida Saber Que Soy un Nieto Recuperado,'" BBC, August 7, 2014, https://www.bbc.com/mundo /noticias/2014/08/140806_nietos_recuperados_testimonios_como_cambia_vidach.

264 *who had signed Guillermo's falsified document*: "Vázquez Sarmiento y Otros s/ Supresión del Estado Civil y Otros," Procesamiento, November 15, 2021. The doctor's name was Pedro Alejandro Canela.

264 *where he'd traveled once with his family as a kid*: Interview with Ezequiel Rochistein Tauro.

265 *apologized for the years of deception*: RIBA Trial, Guillermo Pérez Roisinblit testimony.

266 *around $100 billion in debt*: Rafael Di Tella and Fernanda Miguel, "Breaking Bad (the Rules): Argentina Defaults, Inflates (and Grows), 1997–2015," Harvard Business School Case 714-036, December 2013 (Revised March 2024).

266 *becoming the largest sovereign defaulter in world history*: Rafael M. Di Tella and Ingrid Vogel, "The 2001 Crisis in Argentina: An IMF-Sponsored Default?," Harvard Business School Case 704-004, October 2003.

266 *More Argentines were living below the poverty line than above it*: "Report No. 26127-AR: Argentina, Crisis and Poverty," *World Bank*, July 24, 2003.

266 *Nearly a fifth of the country could not find work*: Ibid.

266 *"You don't know him that well"*: Ariel Pirogovsky, "2003—Spot Campaña Nestor Kirchner," YouTube, September 30, 2014, www.youtube.com/watch?v=zaquZ95zFWo.

266 *a moniker he wore proudly*: Gastón Garriga, "El Pingüino Bonaerense," *Página 12*, October 27, 2022, https://www.pagina12.com.ar/492847-el-pinguino-bonaerense-un-caso -muy-particular.

266 *his social life was no brighter than his academic one*: Jorge Lanata, "The Mysterious Mr. K," *NACLA*, March 13, 2008, https://nacla.org/news/mysterious-mr-k.

266 *Juventud Universitaria Peronista (JUP)*: First Néstor joined the Federación Universitaria de la Revolución (FURN) and Cristina was more active in the Federación de Agrupaciones Eva Perón (FAEP). Then they both joined the JUP; Aldo Duzdevich, "Violencia Política: Cristina, No, 'Alguna', Sí," *Perfil*, December 18, 2022, https://www.perfil.com/noticias/elobservador/violencia-politica-cristina-no-alguna -si.phtml.

267 *quickly inspire him to propose marriage*: Uki Goñi, "Cristina Fernández de Kirchner: Is the Fairytale Ending for Argentina's New Evita?," *Guardian*, February 21, 2015, https:// www.theguardian.com/world/2015/feb/20/cristina-fernandez-de-kirchner-argentina -president-political-turmoil.

267 *"a guerrilla coming down from the hills"*: Cristina Fernández de Kirchner, *Sinceramente* (Buenos Aires: Sudamericana, 2019), 61.

267 *part of the Montoneros*: "Kirchner aclaró que nunca fue montonero," *Clarín*, May 5, 2003, https://www.clarin.com/ultimo-momento/kirchner-aclaro-montonero_0_Byp -I9WeCte.html.

267 *"No! I'm a Peronist"*: Julie McCarthy, "Argentina's Unusual Approach Leads to Big Gains," NPR, May 30, 2007, https://www.npr.org/2007/05/30/10554006/argentinas-unusual -approach-leads-to-big-gains.

267 *Kirchner even imitated Perón in his sleep*: Lanata, "The Mysterious Mr. K."

267 *earning as little as $200 a month*: Larry Rohter, "Argentine Contender Dogged by Questions," *New York Times*, May 12, 2003, https://www.nytimes.com/2003/05/12/world /argentine-contender-dogged-by-questions.html.

267 *known as "the K style"*: Larry Rohter, "Cautiously, Argentines Warm to the 'K Style,'" *New York Times*, June 29, 2003, https://www.nytimes.com/2003/06/29/world/cau tiously-argentines-warm-to-the-k-style.html.

268 *never expected to win*: Larry Rohter, "Man in the News—Néstor Carlos Kirchner; Argentina's Backwoods Leader-To-Be," *New York Times*, May 16, 2003, https://www.nytimes .com/2003/05/16/world/man-in-the-news-nestor-carlos-kirchner-argentina-s-backwoods -leader-to-be.html.

268 *"country bumpkin"*: Ibid.

268 *"reconstruct a national capitalism"*: "Discurso del Señor Presidente de la Nación, Doctor Néstor Kirchner, Ante la Honorable Asamblea Legislativa," May 25, 2003, https://www .casarosada.gob.ar/informacion/archivo/24414-blank-18980869.

268 *"If they want to squeeze, let them squeeze"*: Juan Forero, "Ex-President Helped Solve Argentina's Financial Crisis," *Washington Post*, October 28, 2010, https://www.washingtonpost .com/archive/local/2010/10/28/ex-president-helped-solve-argentinas-financial-crisis /e58c05a6-e223-11df-a21e-de205020554d/.

268 *"I am part of a generation that was decimated"*: "Discurso del Señor Presidente de la Nación, Doctor Néstor Kirchner, Ante la Honorable Asamblea Legislativa."

268 *He quickly purged 80 percent*: Larry Rohter, "Cautiously, Argentines Warm to the 'K Style,'" *New York Times*, June 29, 2003, https://www.nytimes.com/2003/06/29/world /cautiously-argentines-warm-to-the-k-style.html?searchResultPosition=34.

268 *"deals with the past"*: Rohter, "Man in the News—Néstor Carlos Kirchner; Argentina's Backwoods Leader-To-Be."

269 *"We are the children of the Madres and Abuelas of the Plaza de Mayo"*: "Discurso de Néstor Kirchner en la ONU," September 25, 2003.

269 *two days before Christmas in 2003*: RIBA Trial, Guillermo Pérez Roisinblit testimony.

269 *Why wait? he snarled*: Bremner, "The Secret Police Killed His Parents. Then One of Them Adopted Him"; confirmed with Guillermo Pérez Roisinblit.

CHAPTER 37—THE DAY THE PORTRAITS CAME DOWN

270 *known as "the gallery"*: Televisión Pública, "Informe: El Día Que Kirchner Hizo Bajar los Cuadros—40 Años de Democracia," YouTube, August 9, 2023, www.youtube.com /watch?v=xTG-pihZ_WQ.

271 *"Viva Videla!"*: Ailín Bullentini, "'Ahí Donde Nos Habían Torturado, Kirchner Nos Pidió Perdón y Prometió Que la ESMA Iba a Ser Emblema de No Olvido,'" *Página 12*, March 18, 2024, https://www.pagina12.com.ar/721732-ahi-donde-nos-habian-torturado-kirchner-nos-pidio-perdon-y-p.

271 *strained to touch him as though he were holy*: "Discurso Completo de Néstor Kirchner en la Ex ESMA/24 de Marzo de 2004," YouTube, March 20, 2015, www.youtube.com/watch?v=lQORpg3Yb6A.

271 *using the name that day*: Email exchange with Juan Cabandié.

272 *"The dictatorship's sinister plan"*: "Discurso Completo de Néstor Kirchner en la Ex ESMA/24 de Marzo de 2004," YouTube, March 20, 2015, www.youtube.com/watch?v=lQORpg3Yb6A.

272 *"Abuelas, Madres, [and] Hijos"*: Ibid.

272 *Dressed in a black tank top with turquoise flowers*: Victoria Donda, *Mi Nombre Es Victoria* (Buenos Aires: Sudamericana, 2009), 21.

272 *put a 9mm pistol in his mouth*: "Azic, el Prefecto Que Torturó a Bebés y Quiso Matarse de Cara a la Virgen," *Clarín*, July 26, 2003, https://www.clarin.com/politica/azic-prefecto-torturo-bebes-quiso-matarse-cara-virgen_0_ByYfOhxlRKx.html.

272 *a breaking news alert had flashed*: Mei-Ling Hopgood, "I Learned at 26 That I Had Been Kidnapped at Birth and My Identity Changed," *Marie Claire*, June 20, 2011, https://www.marieclaire.com/culture/news/a6233/victoria-donda-parents/.

272 *"If you don't talk"*: "Azic, el Prefecto Que Torturó a Bebés y Quiso Matarse de Cara a la Virgen."

272 *"It's urgent"*: Hopgood, "I Learned at 26 That I Had Been Kidnapped at Birth and My Identity Changed."

273 *short skirts, tight dresses, and high heels*: Ibid.

273 *among the masses who stormed Congress*: Ceferino Reato, *Doce Noches* (Buenos Aires: Sudamericana, 2015), ch. 1, Kindle.

273 *She ran a finger over its metal frame*: Donda, *Mi Nombre es Victoria*, 17–18.

273 *swapped her colorful dresses for black ones*: Ibid.

273 *She felt like a baby*: Ibid., 23.

273 *"That woman had enough courage to get pregnant"*: Victoria Ginzberg, "'Me Di Cuenta Que Había Nacido Ahí en la ESMA,'" *Página 12*, March 21, 2005, https://www.pagina12.com.ar/diario/elpais/1-48768-2005-03-21.html.

273 *he still resented*: Unless otherwise indicated, all information and quotes pertaining to Guillermo's story in the following chapter are derived from a series of over one dozen interviews with him between March 2021 and November 2024.

274 *"Tell me, Guillermo"*: *Al Jazeera Español* video, August 30, 2020, https://x.com/ajpluses panol/status/1300116075003015168.

275 *"I didn't have the most elemental thing"*: Juan Manuel Ciucci, "Derecho a la Identidad: 'Pasás a Ser Libre, Pasás a Ser Vos y Eso No Tiene Precio,'" *Broquel*, October 12, 2022, https://broquel.ptn.gob.ar/2022/10/12/derecho-a-la-identidad/.

276 *On the seventh page*: As viewed in the Rosa Tarlovsky de Roisinblit Fondo Personal, Caja 12, CPM.

276 *GUILLERMO RODOLFO FERNANDO PÉREZ ROISINBLIT*: Ibid. The document does not contain any accents even though Pérez is normally spelled with one.

CHAPTER 38—RODOLFO FERNANDO

277 *the first officers to be charged for a disappearance since 1987*: Goldman, "Children of the Dirty War."

277 *photoshopped Harguindeguy into striped jail fatigues*: *Página 12*, July 13, 2004.

277 *"They are occupying themselves with the human rights of those who are already dead"*: "Ahora Duhalde Contra Kirchner: 'Se Están Ocupando de Los Derechos Humanos de los Que Ya Han Muerto,'" *Ámbito*, June 11, 2004, https://www.ambito.com/portada-principal /ahora-duhalde-contra-kirchner-se-estan-ocupando-los-derechos-humanos-los-que-ya -han-muerto-n3277192.

278 *extracted mitochondrial DNA from the remains*: Victoria Ginzberg, "'No Se Puede Hacer Desaparecer Lo Evidente,'" *Página 12*, July 9, 2005, https://www.pagina12.com.ar/diario /elpais/1-53475-2005-07-09.html.

278 *confirmed that the women had been thrown from airplanes*: Victoria Ginzberg, "'La Buro-cracia Siempre Deja Huellas,'" *Página 12*, July 17, 2005, https://www.pagina12.com.ar /diario/elpais/1-53809-2005-07-17.html.

278 *Guillermo was working to embrace his*: Unless otherwise indicated, all information and quotes pertaining to Guillermo's story in the following chapter are derived from a series of over one dozen interviews with him between March 2021 and November 2024.

278 *Jofré had received three and a half*: Gómez, Magnacco, y Jofré s/ Sustracción Menor de 10 años, Sentencia Final, April 22, 2005.

278 *"thrown into the sea"*: Ibid.

279 *"Here they suppressed and tortured us"*: Author observation at the ex-ESMA museum.

279 *Rosa insisted on joining him*: Rosa Roisinblit interview with Rita Arditti on January 26, 2006.

279 *"superpopulation" of rats*: Actis et al., *Ese Infierno*, 24.

279 *Guillermo felt pressure build in his chest*: Victoria Ginzberg et al., "La Memoria y la Ver-dad Como Hijas de la Lucha Colectiva," *Página 12*, October 22, 2018, https://www .pagina12.com.ar/150377-la-memoria-y-la-verdad-como-hijas-de-la-lucha-colectiva.

279 *"Where was I born?"*: Ibid.

280 *"There, Rodolfo"*: Ibid.; confirmed with Miriam Lewin.

280 *"to identify with that name, my name"*: Ibid.

280 *tears streaming down their faces*: Rosa Roisinblit interview with Rita Arditti on January 26, 2006.

280 *Her funeral was held in Villa Crespo*: "Adiós a una Luchadora," *Página 12*, September 5, 2005, https://www.pagina12.com.ar/diario/elpais/1-56070-2005-09-05.html.

281 *Mariana bristled at his suggestions*: Pérez, *Diario de una Princesa Montonera*, 52; confirmed with Guillermo Pérez Roisinblit.

281 *it had never been confirmed that José and Patricia rested there*: Ibid., 56.

281 *"wasn't written down anywhere"*: Ibid., 57.

281 *Mariana was incensed*: Twitter thread from Mariana Eva Pérez, August 16, 2024, https://x.com/princesamonto/status/1824564998351491354.

282 *"During all of those years, I didn't know what I was supposed to do"*: RIBA Trial, Mariana Eva Pérez testimony.

282 *handling investigations and compiling detailed family archives*: "Mariana Eva Perez," n.d, Uni-versität Heidelberg, https://www.uni-heidelberg.de/rose/erc/personen/mperez.html.

282   *her conduct was at odds with the principles of human rights*: Twitter thread from Mariana
      Eva Pérez, August 19, 2024, https://x.com/princesamonto/status/1825519525137461753.

CHAPTER 39—COMPLETE MEMORY

283   *more than twenty clandestine detention centers*: "Argentina Dirty War: Killer Etcheco-
      latz Gets House Arrest," BBC News, December 28, 2017, https://www.bbc.com/news
      /world-latin-america-42502240.

283   *died a free man in 1994*: Daniel Cecchini, "'Cumplí Con Mi Deber': El Día Que Ramón
      Camps Fue Condenado Por Sus Atroces Crímenes Durante La Dictadura," *Infobae*, De-
      cember 2, 2021, https://www.infobae.com/sociedad/2021/12/02/cumpli-con-mi-deber
      -el-dia-que-ramon-camps-fue-condenado-por-sus-atroces-crimenes-durante-la-dictadura/.

283   *having disappeared five thousand Argentines*: Ibid.

283   *"We didn't kill people"*: José Pablo Feinmann, "Amenazas," *Página 12*, March 20, 2006,
      https://www.pagina12.com.ar/diario/contratapa/13-64507-2006-03-20.html.

283   *ninety-one counts of torture*: "Sentencia contra Etchecolatz por crímenes contra la humani-
      dad," September 19, 2006.

283   *he had been convicted*: Victoria Ginzberg, "Etchecolatz y Bergés van a juicio por la ap-
      ropriación de una niña," *Pagina 12*, February 21, 2004, https://www.pagina12.com.ar
      /diario/elpais/1-31757-2004-02-21.html.

283   *"evil narcissist without scruples"*: "Argentina Dirty War: Killer Etchecolatz Gets House Arrest."

283   *remain in prison for the rest of his days*: Juan Manuel Mannarino, "Marché Contra Mi
      Padre Genocida," *Revista Anfibia*, May 12, 2017, https://www.revistaanfibia.com/mar
      che-contra-mi-padre-genocida/.

284   *"I never had or thought to have"*: Miguel Osvaldo Etchecolatz, *La Otra Campana Del
      Nunca Más*, 1988, 124.

284   *"shaken off the fear"*: Larry Rohter, "Argentina's Dictatorship Stands Trial," *New York
      Times*, August 20, 2006, https://www.nytimes.com/2006/08/20/world/americas/ar
      gentinas-dictatorship-stands-trial.html.

284   *"only God" could judge him*: Brian Murphy, "Miguel Etchecolatz, Enforcer of Argenti-
      na's 'Dirty War,' Dies at 93," *Washington Post*, July 5, 2022, https://www.washingtonpost
      .com/obituaries/2022/07/05/etchecolatz-argentina-dirty-war-dies/.

284   *"Subí un poco más"*: Comisión por la Memoria, "TESTIMONIO JORGE JULIO
      LÓPEZ," YouTube, September 15, 2021, www.youtube.com/watch?v=MnSUcmqBK1s.

284   *"He was a serial killer"*: Ibid.

284   *who sobbed in court as they listened to his testimony*: Luciana Rosende, "Un Tal Jorge Julio
      López," *Política Argentina*, September 17, 2016, https://www.politicargentina.com/notas
      /201609/16658-un-tal-jorge-julio-lopez.html.

285   *catch some soccer on the radio*: Daniel Cecchini, "Los Últimos Pasos de Julio López Antes
      de Su Desaparición y los Secretos Que Etchecolatz Se Llevó a la Tumba," *Infobae*, Septem-
      ber 17, 2023, https://www.infobae.com/sociedad/2023/09/18/los-ultimos-pasos-de-julio
      -lopez-antes-de-su-desaparicion-y-los-secretos-que-etchecolatz-se-llevo-a-la-tumba/.

285   *neatly laid out in the living room, untouched*: "Desaparecer Esperando la Condena, la His-
      toria de Jorge Julio López," *Clarín*, September 18, 2013, https://www.clarin.com/politica
      /anos-desaparecer-jorge-julio-lopez_0_HyVPYWVjDmx.html.

285 *López was nowhere to be found*: As this book went to print in early 2025, Jorge Julio López had still not been found.

285 *Cintia gave birth to a baby boy*: Unless otherwise indicated, all information and quotes pertaining to Guillermo's story in the following chapter are derived from a series of over one dozen interviews with him between March 2021 and November 2024.

285 *where Rosa was among the small crowd of guests*: Plan Sistemático Trial, Rosa Roisinblit testimony.

285 *dragged from the RIBA and tortured elsewhere*: RIBA Trial, Amalia Larralde testimony, May 30, 2016.

285 *often hear the thwap of military helicopters*: Author observation from two visits to Guillermo's home.

285 *with the same intensity that he wished his father could have embraced him*: "Nietos, Historias Con Identidad—Guillermo Pérez Roisinblit (1 de 2)," YouTube, August 15, 2012, www.youtube.com/watch?v=lt8VcoKEX0Q.

286 *singing him silly songs that she'd made up*: Canal Encuentro, "Conurbano: Guillermo Roisinblit (Capítulo Completo)—Canal Encuentro," YouTube, July 7, 2017, www.youtube.com/watch?v=b-FpJaTlYPQ.

286 *"in a context of war, killing your enemy is legal"*: Victoria Villarruel, "Lesa humanidad, el delito que no es," Anexo al Boletín N° 4 de la Unión de Promociones, April 2006. Thanks to Cristian Palmisciano at Universidad Nacional de Mar del Plata for generously sharing this document, which is no longer available on the internet.

286 *The memo had been penned by Victoria Villarruel*: Ibid.

287 *"incapable" of standing trial*: "Primer Cuerpo de Ejército: El Juez Rafecas Elevó a Juicio Oral una Causa por Crímenes de Lesa Humanidad en 'El Vesubio,'" Centro de Información Judicial.

287 *her father was taken hostage*: Maia Jastreblansky, "Victoria Villarruel," *La Nación*, September 5, 2023, https://www.lanacion.com.ar/politica/victoria-villarruel-que-piensa-del-indulto-como-explica-sus-visitas-a-videla-y-las-historias-nid05092023/#/.

287 *her front door had been forced open*: Martín Piqué, "Una Joven Que Nació en la ESMA Denunció Que Recibió Amenazas," *Página 12*, January 25, 2007, https://www.pagina12.com.ar/diario/elpais/1-79541-2007-01-25.html.

287 *Cintia signed most official documents on his behalf*: Bremner, "The Secret Police Killed His Parents. Then One of Them Adopted Him."

288 *"all the animals put together"*: "Comenzó el Primer Juicio Oral y Público Contra un Represor de la ESMA," *Página 12*, October 18, 2007, https://www.pagina12.com.ar/diario/ultimas/20-93169-2007-10-18.html.

288 *Febres was the one to slash off her clothing*: ESMA I Trial, Sara Osatinksy testimony, June 14, 2007.

288 *the kind only the wealthiest of Argentine families could afford*: Plan Sistemático Trial, Sara Osatinsky testimony, October 17, 2011.

288 *he was often one of the men to separate the babies from their mothers*: "El Juicio Mutilado: Muerte Dudosa y el Último Gesto de Febres," *La Vaca*, December 12, 2007, https://lavaca.org/notas/el-juicio-mutilado-muerte-dudosa-y-el-ultimo-gesto-de-febres/.

288 *the most zealous torturer in the whole compound*: Hernán Cappiello, "Los Sobrevivientes de La ESMA Acusan al Prefecto Febres," *La Nación*, October 24, 2007, https://www .lanacion.com.ar/politica/los-sobrevivientes-de-la-esma-acusan-al-prefecto-febres-nid 956029/.

288 *"Febres took away the babies"*: "El Juicio Mutilado: Muerte Dudosa y el Último Gesto de Febres," *La Vaca*, December 12, 2007, https://lavaca.org/notas/el-juicio-mutilado -muerte-dudosa-y-el-ultimo-gesto-de-febres/.

288 *claiming he had never worked in the ESMA at all*: "Juicio Oral: El Represor Febres Negó Haber Estado en la ESMA," *Clarín*, October 19, 2007, https://www.clarin.com/edi ciones-anteriores/juicio-oral-represor-febres-nego-esma_0_ry6g_NyyAKg.html.

288 *held in a comfortable suite*: "Argentine Torture Defendant May Have Been Silenced," Reuters, January 7, 2008, https://www.reuters.com/article/economy/argentine-torture -defendant-may-have-been-silenced-idUSN07332719/.

288 *lifeless frame sprawled on the floor*: Adriana Meyer, "Antes de las Últimas Palabras," *Página 12*, December 11, 2007, https://www.pagina12.com.ar/diario/elpais/1-96023-2007-12 -11.html.

289 *dined with him the night before*: "Indagaron a los Familiares de Héctor Febres," *La Nación*, December 16, 2007, https://www.lanacion.com.ar/politica/indagaron-a-los-famil iares-de-hector-febres-nid971400/.

289 *The family's lawyer denied*: "La Familia Niega Haber Cenado Con Febres," *La Nación*, December 16, 2007, https://www.lanacion.com.ar/politica/la-familia-niega-haber-cenado -con-febres-nid971694/.

289 *planning on revealing information*: "Presume Jueza Que Intentaron Callar a Febres," *Ámbito*, January 7, 2008, https://www.ambito.com/judiciales/presume-jueza-que-inten taron-callar-febres-n3479567.

289 *"Babies, tell everything"*: Raúl Kollmann, "'Quizás el gordo le metió el veneno,'" *Página 12*, January 5, 2008.

289 *The judge deemed his death suspicious*: Reuters Staff, "Argentine Torture Defendant May Have Been Silenced," Reuters, January 7, 2008, https://www.reuters.com/article/econ omy/argentine-torture-defendant-may-have-been-silenced-idUSN07332719/.

289 *"Everything that was stalled for nineteen years"*: Rohter, "Argentina's Dictatorship Stands Trial."

289 *"Fine, we are subversives"*: "El Rol Que Tuvo von Wernich en el Secuestro y Apropiación de la Nieta 115," *Diario Uno*, August 23, 2014, https://www.diariouno.com.ar/pais /el-rol-que-tuvo-von-wernich-en-el-secuestro-y-apropiacion-de-la-nieta-115-08232014 _SJbRYIBMBQ.

289 *cheered and set off fireworks*: Pablo Morosi, "Condenaron a Reclusión Perpetua a von Wernich," *La Nación*, October 10, 2007, https://www.lanacion.com.ar/politica/conden aron-a-reclusion-perpetua-a-von-wernich-nid951794/.

290 *the Casa Rosada no longer housed an enemy*: "37—Última Marcha de la Resistencia— Asociación Madres de Plaza de Mayo," Madres.org, https://madres.org/37-ultima-mar cha-de-la-resistencia/.

290 *"I cannot permit myself to die"*: "Chicha Mariani: 'No Me Puedo Permitir Morirme, Tengo Que Encontrar a Mi Nieta,'" Comisión Provincial por la Memoria, July 5, 2006, https://

www.comisionporlamemoria.org/chicha-mariani-no-me-puedo-permitir-morirme-tengo
-que-encontrar-a-mi-nieta/.

290   *pronounced her psychologically unfit to continue and released her*: Gandsman, "A Prick of a
      Needle Can Do No Harm," 170.

290   *"My human rights are being violated"*: Ibid., 172.

290   *"Grandmothers or Vampires?"*: Ibid.

290   *But by 2005*: Interview with Mariana Herrera, head of the BNDG.

291   *"On one level I wanted to know"*: Wulff, *Las Abuelas y la Genética*, 121.

291   *a pair of tweezers, her underwear, and her toothbrush*: Diego Martínez, "Cuando Una Ver-
      dad Demora Treinta Años," *Página 12*, April 23, 2008, https://www.pagina12.com.ar
      /diario/elpais/1-102925-2008-04-23.html.

291   *police blocked the windows so she wouldn't jump*: Goldman, "Children of the Dirty War."

291   *did not appeal*: "Una Certeza Que No Se Discute," *Página 12*, April 24, 2008, https://
      www.pagina12.com.ar/diario/elpais/1-102998-2008-04-24.html.

291   *"Can you be 'independent journalists'"*: "La Pelea con *Clarín*: ¿Ahora van Contra los Pe-
      riodistas?," *La Política*, April 16, 2010, https://www.lapoliticaonline.com/nota/nota
      -64909/.

292   *thought that she could possibly be Clara Anahí*: Goldman, "Children of the Dirty War."

292   *"I've spoken many times with my children about the possibility"*: "'Hay un Sector Político
      Que Quiere Ir Limpiando el Terreno Para Adueñarse de Todo el Poder,'" *Clarín*, Jan-
      uary 12, 2003, https://www.clarin.com/politica/sector-politico-quiere-ir-limpiando-ter
      reno-aduenarse-poder_0_r1AraGgRtl.html.

292   *Rolex watches*: "Cristina Se Presentó en Tribunales con un Rolex de 35 Mil Dólares,"
      Realpolitik, July 18, 2021, https://realpolitik.com.ar/nota/44559/cristina-se-presento
      -en-tribunales-con-un-rolex-de-35-mil-dolares/.

293   *Hermès Birkin bag*: Belén Papa Orfano, "Cristina vs. Juliana: Dos Colecciones de Car-
      teras Que Valen Lo Mismo Que un Departamento," *Cronista*, February 1, 2019, https://
      www.cronista.com/economia-politica/Cristina-vs-Juliana-dos-colecciones-de-carteras
      -que-valen-lo-mismo-que-un-departamento-20190201-0034.html.

293   *"I have painted myself like a door since I was fourteen"*: Uki Goñi, "As Argentina's Queen Cristina
      Says Farewell, Her Enemies Wait in the Wings," *Guardian*, November 22, 2015, https://www
      .theguardian.com/world/2015/nov/22/argentina-heads-right-after-cristina-reign.

293   *"Cristina for me signifies love for the humble"*: Goñi, "Cristina Fernández de Kirchner: Is
      the Fairytale Ending for Argentina's New Evita?"

293   *illegal contributions from Venezuelan strongman Hugo Chavez*: Graciela Mochkofsky,
      Pecado Original: Clarín, Los Kirchner y la Lucha por el Poder (Espejo de la Argentina
      /Planeta, 2011), 314.

293   *tax inspectors were sent to Clarín's offices to conduct a surprise raid*: Silvio Waisbord, "All-
      out Media War," *Columbia Journalism Review*, September 30, 2010, https://www.cjr.org
      /reports/allout_media_war.php.

293   *"None of the nine children of desaparecidos"*: "Aprobaron la Extracción de ADN," *La
      Política*, November 5, 2009, https://www.lapoliticaonline.com/nota/nota-61252/.

294   *"That law is not directed at protecting human rights"*: "Repudio a Carrió por Expresiones en
      Contra del Examen Obligatorio de ADN," *La Capital*, October 17, 2009, https://www

.lacapital.com.ar/politica/repudio-carrioacute-expresiones-contra-del-examen-obligato
rio-adn-n310658.html/amp.

294 *Forensic Medical Corps*: Goldman, "Children of the Dirty War."

294 *tailed by a green Jeep Cherokee and a motorcycle driven by two men dressed in black*: Mochkofsky, *Pecado Original*, 361.

295 *Marcela urged someone to call his psychiatrist*: Ibid., 362.

295 *forced to remove her underwear in front of two officers*: Marcelo Veneranda, "'Buscan Mostrar
Abuso de Autoridad y Quebrarnos,'" *La Nación*, May 29, 2010, https://www.lanacion.com
.ar/politica/buscan-mostrar-abuso-de-autoridad-y-quebrarnos-nid1269790/.

295 *"They are trying to break us emotionally"*: Ibid.

295 *complained that they'd been treated like "criminals"*: Mochkofsky, *Pecado Original*, 363.

295 *"You cannot try to defend human rights by going against human rights"*: Martín Piqué, "El
ADN y las Caras de la Política," *Página 12*, November 23, 2009, https://www.pagina12
.com.ar/diario/elpais/1-135783-2009-11-23.html.

295 *"The state cannot leave in the hands of a young person"*: "Argentina Forces DNA Tests in
'Dirty War' Cases," Associated Press, November 20, 2009, https://www.nbcnews.com
/id/wbna34071255.

296 *ordered him to get in*: Unless otherwise indicated, all information and quotes pertaining
to Ezequiel Rochistein Tauro's story in the following chapter are derived from a series of
interviews between 2022 and 2023.

297 *"All we wanted was to find you"*: Victoria Ginzberg, "'Cerré una Etapa y Abrí Otra,'" *Página 12*, April 10, 2011, https://www.pagina12.com.ar/diario/elpais/1-165964-2011
-04-10.html.

297 *expressed gratitude for the sensitivity they'd shown him*: Ibid.

CHAPTER 40—THANK YOU FOR WAITING

298 *political violence compelled him to drop out*: Archivo Biográfico Familiar Pérez Roisinblit, 268.

298 *Guillermo would later speculate*: Unless otherwise indicated, all information and quotes
pertaining to Guillermo's story in the following chapter are derived from a series of over
one dozen interviews with him between March 2021 and November 2024.

299 *freed her to experiment with language*: "Ficciones de una Princesa Montonera," *Clarín*,
April 29, 2012, https://www.clarin.com/literatura/mariana-eva-perez-diario-princesa
-montonera_0_HkvjsNhvme.html.

299 *"Once, before we were certain that we were siblings"*: Pérez, *Diario de una Princesa Montonera*,
106. Many of the posts mentioned here have been deleted from Mariana's blog but are included in the book version of *Diario de una Princesa Montonera*, which is what I cite here.

299 *"I realize that she doesn't see the resemblance"*: Ibid., 112.

299 *"Are you good detectives, readers?"*: Ibid., 58.

300 If he went outside, could he see them?: Enzetti, "Cómo Puede Estar Tranquilo, Con Sangre de Las Secuestradas En Su Conciencia."

300 *Mariana and Rosa attended his funeral together*: Pérez, *Diario de una Princesa Montonera*,
190.

300 *"She's all alone now in charge of the country"*: D.R., "Back to a Vacuum," *Economist*, October 27, 2010, https://www.economist.com/americas-view/2010/10/27/back-to-a-vacuum.

300   *$45 million to complete the buildings*: Brian Murphy, "Hebe de Bonafini, Strident Voice for Argentine 'Dirty War' Victims, Dies at 93," *Washington Post*, November 22, 2022, https://www.washingtonpost.com/obituaries/2022/11/22/hebe-bonafini-mothers-argentina-dies/.

300   *opposition politicians complained*: Annie Kelly, "Scandal Hits Argentina's Mothers of the Disappeared," *Guardian*, June 12, 2011, https://www.theguardian.com/world/2011/jun/12/scandal-argentina-mothers-funds.

300   *an eighteen-room mansion, a yacht, and a sports car*: Ibid. As of 2024, the case against Schoklender had still not concluded.

301   *Videla fell asleep*: "Videla Se Quedó Dormido y Fue Apercibido por el Tribunal," *El Día*, March 26, 2012, https://www.eldia.com/nota/2012-3-26-videla-se-quedo-dormido-y-fue-apercibido-por-el-tribunal.

301   *"All of the pregnant women"*: "Videla: 'Muchas Parturientas Usaron a Sus Hijos Embrionarios Como Escudos Humanos al Momento de Ser Combatientes,'" *Página 12*, June 26, 2012, https://www.pagina12.com.ar/diario/ultimas/20-197273-2012-06-26.html.

301   *"In that moment, I didn't understand anything"*: Plan Sistemático Trial, Rosa Roisinblit testimony.

302   *only ten minutes before the bell rang*: Email from Guillermo to the Abuelas and Nietos, March 24, 2012, Rosa Tarlovsky de Roisinblit Fondo Personal, Caja 23, CPM.

302   *"filled his soul with affection"*: Ibid.

302   *"I believe I let a lot of time pass"*: Ibid.

CHAPTER 41—TEN WORLD CUPS

303   *rumbled down Florencio Sánchez*: Unless otherwise indicated, information about Francisco Gómez's 2013 capture comes from the following document: "Diligencia Judicial—Captura," April 16, 2013; court document provided to the author by Dr. Daniel Rafecas, the judge in the case.

304   *notorious for its decrepit conditions*: "Penosas Condiciones de Detención en la Unidad 29," Procuración Penitenciaria de la Nación, July 11, 2019, https://www.ppn.gov.ar/index.php/institucional/noticias/2274-penosas-condiciones-de-detencion-en-la-unidad-29.

304   *slipping in the shower*: "Ex-Arg. Dictator Videla Died After Shower Fall," Associated Press, May 20, 2013, https://apnews.com/general-news-57bd13c48f62463c84f26ef1c49d8c55.

304   *"all that Videla did not say"*: Ailín Bullentini, "'Se Fue un Hombre Deshumanizado,'" *Página 12*, May 18, 2013, https://www.pagina12.com.ar/diario/elpais/1-220288-2013-05-18.html.

305   *hawking blue-and-white banners and top hats*: Author observation from her time living in Argentina during this period and photos taken during that time.

305   *who famously credited his own abuela*: Arthur Parashar, "Messi Spoke to His Late Grandmother Before Montiel's Winning Penalty," *Daily Mail*, January 17, 2023, https://www.dailymail.co.uk/sport/football/article-11644787/Lionel-Messi-looked-said-to-day-grandma-Argentinas-winning-penalty.html.

305   *strolled into a room in a training facility*: CTA Provincia de Buenos Aires, "Spot la Selección Hincha por las Abuelas," YouTube, June 12, 2014, www.youtube.com/watch?v=EVexvlYm4zA.

305 *Aída Kancepolski:* The Abuelas website spells her name Aída Kancepolski on their web-site, but other sources suggest her last name ended in "y."

306 *launching rocks, toppling over streetlights, and breaking into local businesses:* Adam With-nall, "World Cup 2014: 60 Arrested in Buenos Aires Riots as Argentina Takes Final Loss Badly," *Independent,* July 14, 2014, https://www.independent.co.uk/news/world/americas/world-cup-2014-60-arrested-in-buenos-aires-riots-as-argentina-takes-final-loss-badly-9603924.html.

306 *On July 24:* "El Final Feliz de Estela e Ignacio: '¡Encontré a Mi Nieto!'" Cosecha Roja, Au-gust 6, 2016, https://www.cosecharoja.org/la-historia-del-encuentro-entre-estela-e-ig nacio-encontre-mi-nieto/.

306 *might be the son of* desaparecidos: Ibid.

306 *posed for a photo to accompany his file:* Ibid.

307 *"If I turn out to be the son of a 'disappeared' couple":* Uki Goñi, "A Grandmother's 36-Year Hunt for the Child Stolen by the Argentinian Junta," *Guardian,* June 7, 2015, https://www.theguardian.com/world/2015/jun/07/grandmothers-of-plaza-de-mayo-36-year-hunt-for-stolen-child.

307 *Guillermo clapped and cheered:* "C5N—Sociedad: Nieto 114, Habla Estela de Carlotto," YouTube, August 5, 2014, www.youtube.com/watch?v=dq3j02o3RT0.

307 *"Laura, with the anniversary of her murder":* Ibid.

307 *"Happy and encouraged by the discovery":* "Messi También Se Emocionó con la Aparición del Nieto de Carlotto," *Infobae,* November 25, 2017, https://www.infobae.com/2014/08/06/1585703-messi-tambien-se-emociono-la-aparicion-del-nieto-carlotto/.

307 *giddy Estela on its front page:* "Carlotto consiguió recuperar a su nieto," *Clarín,* August 6, 2014.

307 *beers, a snack board, and little sandwiches:* Marina Abiuso, "Ignacio Guido Montoya Car-lotto: La Sorprendente Historia del Nieto Ideal," *Noticias,* August 17, 2014, https://noticias.perfil.com/noticias/informacion-general/2014-08-17-guido-montoya-carlotto-la-sorprendente-historia-del-nieto-114.phtml.

308 *"They couldn't have children":* Goñi, "A Grandmother's 36-Year Hunt for the Child Stolen by the Argentinian Junta."

308 *who presented him with a box of documents about his disappeared father:* Casa Rosada, "23 de Oct. Audiencia de Cristina Fernández con Estela y Guido Carlotto," YouTube, October 23, 2014, www.youtube.com/watch?v=bBSnp-BdyLQ.

308 *soon he was on a plane with Estela to the Galápagos:* "Los Secretos del Reencuentro Entre Estela Carlotto e Ignacio 'Guido,'" *Infobae,* November 29, 2017, https://www.infobae.com/2015/06/13/1734692-los-secretos-del-reencuentro-estela-carlotto-e-ignacio-guido/.

308 *convince the pope to open the Vatican's archives:* Ibid.

308 *"Practically all of Argentina has cried on this one":* Goñi, "A Grandmother's 36-Year Hunt for the Child Stolen by the Argentinian Junta."

309 *spiked to one hundred:* Ignacio de los Reyes, "El 'Efecto Guido' en las Abuelas de Plaza de Mayo Que Aún Esperan en Argentina," BBC, August 7, 2014, https://www.bbc.com/mundo/noticias/2014/08/140806_abuelas_plaza_mayo_nieto_guido_carlotto_irm.

309 *"For me, this means fulfilling my duty to my sister":* "'Ana Libertad Está Feliz, Se Ríe Todo

el Tiempo,'" *Página 12*, August 25, 2014, https://www.pagina12.com.ar/diario/ultimas /20-253780-2014-08-25.html.

309 *"It was in Licha's home where the first meetings"*: "Visión 7—Abuelas de Plaza de Mayo Hallaron a Ana Libertad y Suman 115 Nietos Recuperado," YouTube, August 22, 2014, www.youtube.com/watch?v=I9sF226YT0k.

309 *"Hello, I think I'm a child of the disappeared"*: Bridget Huber, "The Living Disappeared," *California Sunday Magazine*, March 30, 2017, https://story.californiasunday.com/the-living-disappeared/.

309 *sold his car to pay for Diego*: Ibid.

310 *rappelling at the ripe age of eighty-two*: Ibid.

310 *"I found you!"*: Fernando Soriano, "A los 96 Años, Murió Delia Giovanola, Una de las Fundadoras de Abuelas de Plaza de Mayo," *Infobae*, July 18, 2022, https://www.infobae .com/sociedad/2022/07/18/a-los-96-anos-murio-delia-giovanola-una-de-las-fundado ras-de-abuelas-de-plaza-de-mayo/.

310 *"Mission accomplished"*: Ibid.

310 *adorned an ornate hutch in her living room*: Author observation from visit on November 15, 2021.

310 *Delia cleared out the larger bedroom*: Lucía Cholakian Herrera, "Decades after Argentina's Dictatorship, the Abuelas Continue Reuniting Families," *NACLA*, March 24, 2020, https://nacla.org/news/2020/03/24/argentina-dictatorship-abuelas.

310 *bemoaning the ubiquitousness of air-conditioning and the bananas in Caribbean food*: Huber, "The Living Disappeared."

310 *Vatican's archives from the dictatorship period be opened*: Uki Goñi, "Pope Francis Orders Vatican to Open Files on Argentina Dictatorship," *Guardian*, April 29, 2015, https://www.theguardian.com/world/2015/apr/29/pope-francis-argentina-orders-vati can-open-files-dictatorship.

310 *"for fear of weakening [the military government]"*: Gerard O'Connell, "New Research Reveals Argentine Bishops Knew the Military Junta Was 'Disappearing' People and Chose Not to Speak out Publicly," *America Magazine*, June 23, 2023, https://www.americamagazine.org /faith/2023/06/23/argentina-dirty-war-pope-francis-bishops-disappeared-245548.

310 *reluctantly performed a tango with a dancer in a slinky gold dress*: "Dancer Who Tangoed with President Obama Was Initially Forbidden from Doing So," *ABC News*, April 2016, https://abcnews.go.com/Politics/dancer-tangoed-president-obama-initially-forbidden /story?id=38081748.

311 *"But when we find the courage to confront it"*: Barack Obama, "Remarks by President Obama and President Macri of Argentina at Parque de la Memoria," March 24, 2016, https://obamawhitehouse.archives.gov/the-press-office/2016/03/24/remarks-presi dent-obama-and-president-macri-argentina-parque-de-la.

311 *pried open in 2010*: "Desclasifican Más Documentos Militares Sobre la Represión," *Clarín*, January 7, 2010, https://www.clarin.com/ediciones-anteriores/desclasifican-doc umentos-militares-represion_0_HyuX49wA6Kg.html.

311 *included a note that Assistant Secretary of State for Human Rights Elliott Abrams had written in 1982*: Department of State, Memorandum of Conversation, December 3, 1982, https://nsarchive.gwu.edu/document/23927-department-state-memorandum-conver

sation-december-3-1982-redacted-version; "STOLEN BABIES: Argentina Convicts Two Military Dictators," National Security Archive, July 5, 2012, https://nsarchive2.gwu .edu/NSAEBB/NSAEBB383/.

311   *The Abuelas pointed to that document*: The original document was heavily redacted. With support from the National Security Archive, an archival institution operated by George Washington University, the Abuelas requested that the entire memo be released, which the US agreed to in December 2011 while the Plan Sistemático trial was ongoing. "STOLEN BABIES: Argentina Convicts Two Military Dictators," *National Security Archive*, July 5, 2012.

311   *he'd been called as a witness six other times*: Alejandra Dandan, "La Lista de Grasselli," *Página 12*, September 21, 2014, https://www.pagina12.com.ar/diario/elpais/1 -255768-2014-09-21.html.

311   *"There are things he knows and is not telling"*: Alejandra Dandan, "El Cura de Las Fichas de Desaparecidos," *Página 12*, August 29, 2014, https://www.pagina12.com.ar/diario /elpais/1-254050-2014-08-29.html.

CHAPTER 42—SOMETHING LIKE JUSTICE

312   *On May 2, 2016*: Noelia Pirsic, "'Mi Nombre No Siempre Fue Así,'" *ANCCOM*, May 18, 2016, https://anccom.sociales.uba.ar/2016/05/18/mi-nombre-no-siempre-fue-asi/.

312   *his arm wrapped around her shoulders*: Ibid.

312   *fluorescent lighting and benches and chairs for observers*: Author observation from watching court recordings.

313   *turtleneck knit with an eye-catching black-and-white design*: RIBA Trial, Rosa Roisinblit testimony, May 4, 2016.

313   *"I never stop telling the truth"*: Ibid.

313   *Rosa's own wedding finery*: Bublik, *Abuela*, 94.

314   *"I am not a footnote in this story"*: RIBA Trial, Mariana Eva Pérez testimony, May 4, 2016.

315   *"Your full name, please, señor?"*: RIBA Trial, Guillermo Pérez Roisinblit testimony, May 16, 2016.

316   *kept running frantic circles*: RIBA Trial, Edith Clutet testimony, June 13, 2016.

316   *tied to the leg of a desk at eight-months pregnant*: RIBA Trial, Miriam Lewin testimony, May 30, 2016; RIBA Trial, Sara Osatinsky testimony, May 30, 2016.

316   *clutching Guillermo in her arms*: RIBA Trial, Amalia Larralde testimony, May 30, 2016.

316   *"It makes sense you'd forget some things"*: Noelia Pirsic, "'Esa Nenita Que Fue Robada Hoy Es una Señora Que Exige Justicia,'" *ANCCOM*, June 1, 2016, http://anccom.sociales.uba.ar /2016/06/01/esa-nenita-que-fue-robada-hoy-es-una-senora-que-exige-justicia/.

316   *he sat down in front of the microphone*: RIBA Trial, Francisco Gómez testimony, July 13, 2016. The following account of Gómez's testimony all comes from court recordings granted to the author by the Abuelas' lawyers.

318   *"I want to make it very clear"*: RIBA Trial, Sentencia, September 8, 2016. Unless otherwise indicated, the following account of the RIBA sentencing all comes from court recordings granted to the author by the Abuelas' lawyers.

318   *"I waited thirty-eight years to achieve this"*: "Ex-Head of Argentina Air Force Sentenced," *Guardian*, September 8, 2016, https://www.theguardian.com/world/2016/sep/08/ar gentina-air-force-head-sentenced-abduction-prison-omar-graffigna.

318 *a V for victory*: "Treinta y Ocho Años Esperando Justicia," *Clarín*, September 8, 2016, https://hd.clarin.com/post/150129692054/sentencia-juicio-riba-condena-a-25-a%C3%B1os-para-el.

318 *"When we are together"*: Gandsman, "Reclaiming the Past," 321.

CHAPTER 43—A FLOWER TRAVELED IN MY BLOOD

319 *"If you think it's a good idea"*: Interview with Guillermo Pérez Roisinblit.

319 *"Delia gave everything to this institution"*: Fernando, "A los 96 Años, Murió Delia Giovanola," *Infobae*, July 18, 2022.

320 *even if they did have doubts about their pasts*: Interview with Juan Pablo Moyano, the eighteenth grandchild located by the Abuelas.

320 *Her family had not known she was expecting*: Alejandra Dandan, "La Historia del Nieto 131: Cuando una Foto Vuelve a Dar Vida," *Página 12*, December 23, 2022, https://www.pagina12.com.ar/510512-el-poder-de-una-foto-que-despierta-la-vida.

320 *stared at it in unblinking disbelief*: Ibid.

321 *where around thirty*: "Nacer en la Esma," Museo Sitio de Memoria Esma, 2021, http://www.museositioesma.gob.ar/item/nacer-en-la-esma/.

321 *"outstanding universal value"*: "ESMA Museum and Site of Memory—Former Clandestine Center of Detention, Torture and Extermination," UNESCO World Heritage Centre, 2023, https://whc.unesco.org/en/list/1681.

321 *"How was it possible that babies were born in this place?"*: "ESMA Museum and Site of Memory—Former Clandestine Centre of Detention, Torture and Extermination," UNESCO, 2018, https://whc.unesco.org/en/list/1681/gallery/.

321 *A stout white building with brick columns*: The following account is from author observation, photos, and videos of the Casa por la Identidad.

322 *Guillermo reflected on the anguish*: Unless otherwise indicated, all information and quotes pertaining to Guillermo's story in the following chapter are derived from a series of over one dozen interviews with him between March 2021 and November 2024.

323 *photos of the most treasured people in her life*: Unless otherwise indicated, the following paragraphs are derived from author observation and transcripts of an interview with Rosa Roisinblit on November 19, 2021.

EPILOGUE—NOW AND FOREVER

325 *Guillermo found himself at Parque de la Memoria*: "Celebramos la Visita de Mary-Claire King," Argentina.gob.ar, September 22, 2023, https://www.argentina.gob.ar/noticias/celebramos-la-visita-de-mary-claire-king.

325 *one of the main airports*: "Los 'Vuelos de la Muerte' en Campo de Mayo."

326 *a large bulletin board called the "Nietera"*: Author observation from visit to the BNDG laboratory on July 15, 2022.

326 *"Mariana, we have something to show you"*: Interview with Mariana Herrera.

326 *"In honor of her invaluable contribution"*: Instagram post from the Banco Nacional de Datos Genéticos, January 4, 2024, https://www.instagram.com/p/C1rb4f6uhfw/.

327 *designed to evoke an open wound*: "Argentina: Parque de la Memoria," April 2, 2021, https://archis.org/projects/article/argentina-parque-de-la-memoria/.

327 *358 of those bore an additional inscription*: Base de Datos, Parque de la Memoria, http://

basededatos.parquedelamemoria.org.ar/buscador/?nombre_o_apellido=&anio_en_mon
umento=&estudio=&militancia=&trabajo=&centro_clandestino=&sexo=&embaraz
o=True&lugar=.

327 *the largest trial in Argentine history:* "ESMA MEGA-CASE," CELS, https://www.cels
.org.ar/especiales/megacausaesma/en/#cierre-en-palabras-de-vera-jarach.

327 *tried for the disappearance of José and Patricia:* As this book was finalized, Juan Carlos
Vázquez Sarmiento was still on trial for the disappearance of Patricia Julia Roisinblit and
José Manuel Pérez Rojo. In one audience in 2024, which was conducted by videoconference,
he stood from his bench and urinated in a bucket, exposing himself to the camera. Ezequiel
Rochistein Tauro, who grew up believing Vázquez Sarmiento was his father, explained:
"His legal strategy is to say he is not psychologically fit to stand trial." In February 2025,
Vázquez Sarmiento died at the age of seventy-seven.

327 *Marcelo clearly remembered Vázquez Sarmiento:* RIBA Trial, Marcelo Moreyra testimony.

327 *"personification of his fears":* Guillermo Pérez Roisinblit on X, April 26, 2020, https://
x.com/Guillogo_/status/1254524238922428416.

327 *"Do I feel sadness? I don't know":* Tweet by Guillermo (@guillogo_), April 26, 2020,
https://x.com/Guillogo_/status/1254524238922428416.

327 *one thousand or so* desaparecidos: Lorenzo Tondo and Uki Goñi, "Argentina Sends out
DNA Kits in Drive to Identify Thousands 'Disappeared' Under Dictatorship," *Guardian*,
May 28, 2021, https://www.theguardian.com/global-development/2021/may/28/argen
tina-sends-dna-test-kits-embassies-find-juntas-disappeared-victims.

328 *"To accept that you're the child of* desaparecidos": *Al Jazeera Español* video, August 30, 2020.

328 *"Ahora y siempre, ahora y siempre!":* Parque de la Memoria Instagram, October 2, 2023,
https://www.instagram.com/p/Cx6V3OcPfQP/?next=%2Fronbar21%2F&hl=af.

328 *a sweeping immunity law:* Rafa de Miguel, "The UK's Controversial Amnesty for Atrocities Committed During Northern Ireland's Troubles," *El País English*, September 13,
2023, https://english.elpais.com/international/2023-09-13/the-uks-controversial-am
nesty-for-atrocities-committed-during-northern-irelands-troubles.html.

329 *"Those who cannot remember the past are condemned to repeat it":* George Santayana, *The
Life of Reason: Reason in Common Sense* (New York: Charles Scribner's Sons, 1905), 284.

329 *"raising a monument to Amnesia, and forgetting where we put it":* David Rieff, *In Praise of
Forgetting: Historical Memory and Its Ironies* (New Haven: Yale University Press, 2016), 28.

329 *clandestine detention centers as "memory sites":* "Sitios de Memoria," Argentina.gob.ar,
August 30, 2017, https://www.argentina.gob.ar/derechoshumanos/sitiosdememoria
/centrosclandestinos.

329 *"Human Rights Crimes were planned and committed here":* Author observation and photo
on December 9, 2022.

329 *Convention on the Rights of the Child:* Ana Laura Sucari, "Entre el Derecho a la Identidad y la Impunidad," *Avances del Cesor* 17, no. 23 (December 5, 2020), https://doi.org
/10.35305/ac.v17i23.1293.

330 *the pioneers of genetic genealogy:* Interview with Mary-Claire King.

330 *feasibly claim to have spearheaded:* Lindsay Smith, "'Genetics Is a Study in Faith': Forensic
DNA, Kinship Analysis, and the Ethics of Care in Post-Conflict Latin America," *The
Scholar and Feminist Online* 11, no. 3 (2013).

330 *photos of Videla displayed on the back windshields*: Valen Iricibar, "Dictatorship-Era Threat: Green Ford Falcon Parked Outside Senate," *Buenos Aires Herald*, November 26, 2023.

330 *"May the thieves be caught"*: "'Que Se Agarren Los Chorros': El Repudiable Video del Falcon Verde Que Posteó un Comisario," *Clarín*, November 21, 2023, https://www.clarin .com/policiales/agarren-chorros-repudiable-video-falcon-verde-posteo-comisario_0_dgzj D8X5Kf.html.

330 *parked outside Argentina's grand Senate building*: Iricibar, "Dictatorship-Era Threat: Green Ford Falcon Parked Outside Senate."

331 *proudly championed by Milei*: Newsroom Infobae, "Milei: 'Estoy Orgulloso de Ser Anarcocapitalista,'" *Infobae*, February 20, 2024, https://www.infobae.com/america/agencias /2024/02/20/milei-estoy-orgulloso-de-ser-anarcocapitalista/.

331 *"Let's start with truth: There were not thirty thousand desaparecidos"*: La Nación, "Milei: 'No Son 30,000 los Desaparecidos, Son 8,753,'" YouTube, October 1, 2023, www.you tube.com/watch?v=rLvNQY99yXU.

331 *"the terrorists in the Montoneros and ERP"*: Ibid.

331 *"The truth is that Carlotto"*: Ayelen Segovia, "Villarruel, Sobre Carlotto: 'Con Ese Cariz de Abuelita Buena, Justificó el Terrorismo,'" *Perfil*, September 5, 2023, https://www.perfil .com/noticias/politica/victoria-villarruel-sobre-estela-de-carlotto-es-un-personaje-bas tante-siniestro.phtml.

332 *"shouldn't be given too much importance"*: Ibid.

332 *Milei cut off subsidies*: "El Gobierno Afirmó Que Rescindirá un Fondo Destinado a Abuelas de Plaza de Mayo," *El Diario*, September 30, 2024, https://www.eldiarioar.com/politica /gobierno-afirmo-rescindira-fondo-destinado-abuelas-plaza-mayo_1_11695445.html.

332 *he put an end to the investigative unit of CoNaDI*: Iván Pérez Sarmenti, "Milei Cierra un Organismo Oficial Que Buscaba a los Niños Apropiados Ilegalmente Durante la Última Dictadura en Argentina," CNN, August 23, 2024, https://cnnespanol.cnn.com/2024 /08/23/milei-cierra-organismo-ninos-apropiados-dictadura-argentina-orix/.

332 *sift through thousands of outstanding complaints*: Ibid.

332 *disbanded an archive within the Defense Ministry*: Martina Jaureguy, "This Archive Team Brought Dozens of Dictatorship Criminals to Trial. Now It's Gone," *Buenos Aires Herald*, September 1, 2024, https://buenosairesherald.com/human-rights/this-archive -team-brought-dozens-of-dictatorship-criminals-to-trial-now-its-gone.

332 *smiled for photos with prisoners*: "Argentine Dictatorship Criminal Visited by Lawmakers Stands Trial for Kidnapping," *Buenos Aires Herald*, August 27, 2024, https:// buenosairesherald.com/human-rights/argentine-dictatorship-criminal-visited-by-law makers-stands-trial-for-kidnapping.

332 *with the support of several recovered grandchildren*: Author observation from July 4, 2024, march in the Plaza de Mayo.

ABOUT THIS BOOK

338 *"destroyed [her] family"*: RIBA Trial, Mariana Eva Pérez testimony, May 4, 2016.

338 *"We'll never know"*: Mariana Pérez on X, August 16, 2024, https://x.com/ezeferrero /status/1824625207031505179.

Further Reading

Abalos, Ezequiel. *Rock de Acá 2*. Buenos Aires: Ezequiel Abalos Ediciones, 2011.

Abuelas de Plaza de Mayo. *La Historia de Abuelas*. Buenos Aires: Abuelas de Plaza de Mayo, 2007.

Actis, Munú, Cristina Aldini, Liliana Gardella, Miriam Lewin, and Elisa Tokar. *Ese Infierno*. Buenos Aires: Editorial Sudamericana, 2001.

Alcoba, Laura. *La Casa de Los Conejos*. Buenos Aires: Edhasa, 2018.

Alexander, Robert J. *Juan Domingo Peron*. Boulder: Westview Press, 1979.

Altamirano, Claudio. *Identity: A Pedagogy on Collective Memory*. Ushuaia: Universidad Nacional de Tierra del Fuego, Antártida e Islas del Atlántico Sur, 2006.

Andersen, Martin Edwin. *Dossier Secreto*. Boulder and Oxford: Westview Press, 1993.

Arditti, Rita. *Searching for Life: The Grandmothers of the Plaza de Mayo and the Disappeared Children of Argentina*. Berkeley: University of California Press, 1999.

Argento, Analía. *De Vuelta a Casa*. Buenos Aires: Marea Editorial, 2008.

Arrosagaray, Enrique. *Biografía de Azucena Villaflor*. Ituzaingó, Provincia de Buenos Aires: Editorial Cienflores, 2021.

——. *Los Villaflor de Avellaneda*. Buenos Aires: Ediciones de La Flor, 1993.

Bacci, Claudia, Vera Carnovale, and Alejandra Oberti. *Abogados, Derecho y Política*. Buenos Aires: Memoria Abierta, 2010.

Barki, Irene. *Pour Ces Yeux-Là: La Face Cachée Du Drame Argentin Les Enfants Disparus*. Paris: Éditions La Découverte, 1988.

Barnes, John. *Evita, First Lady: A Biography of Eva Perón*. New York: Grove Press, 1996.

Barrera, Laureano. *La Casa de La Calle 30*. Buenos Aires: Tusquets Editores S.A., 2022.

BARRIOS X MEMORIA Y JUSTICIA. *Baldosas X La Memoria II*. BARRIOS X MEMORIA Y JUSTICIA, 2010. https://www.memoriapalermo.org.ar/docs/Libro-2-Baldosas-por-la-Memoria.pdf.

Bascomb, Neal, and Mazal Holocaust Collection. *Hunting Eichmann: How a Band of Survivors and a Young Spy Agency Chased down the World's Most Notorious Nazi*. Boston: Houghton Mifflin Harcourt, 2009.

Basconi, Andrea. *Elena Holmberg. La Mujer Que Sabía Demasiado.* Buenos Aires: Sudamericana, 2012.

Bass, Thomas A. *Reinventing the Future: Conversations with the World's Leading Scientists.* Reading, MA: Addison-Wesley, 1994.

Baumgartner, José Luis. *Mamá Julien.* Montevideo: Trilce, 1988.

Bianchini, Federico. *Tu Nombre No Es Tu Nombre: Historia de Una Identidad Robada En La Dictadura.* Madrid: Libros del K.O., 2023.

Blaustein, Eduardo, and Martín Zubieta. *Decíamos Ayer: La Prensa Argentina Bajo El Proceso.* Buenos Aires: Ediciones Colihue, 2006.

Borges, Jorge Luis. *On Argentina.* New York: Penguin Books, 2010.

Bousquet, Jean Pierre. *Las Locas de La Plaza de Mayo.* Buenos Aires: El Cid Editor, 1983.

Bouvard, Marguerite Guzman. *Revolutionizing Motherhood the Mothers of the Plaza de Mayo.* Wilmington, DE: Sr Books, 1995.

Brennan, James P. *Argentina's Missing Bones: Revisiting the History of the Dirty War.* Oakland: University of California Press, 2018.

———. *Peronism and Argentina.* Wilmington, DE: Sr Books, 1998.

Brodersen, Juan. "Qué Fue 'La Noche de las Corbatas', Otro Oscuro Episodio de la Dictadura Militar Del 76." *Clarín,* August 15, 2016. https://www.clarin.com/sociedad/corbatas -oscuro-episodio-dictadura-militar_0_SJ0cH5wK.html.

Brum, Pablo. *The Robin Hood Guerrillas: The Epic Journey of Uruguay's Tupamaros.* Charleston, SC: Createspace, 2014.

Bublik, Marcela, and Rosa Roisinblit. *Abuela: La Historia de Rosa Roisinblit, Una Abuela de Plaza de Mayo.* Ciudad De Buenos Aires: Marea Editorial, 2013.

Burns, Jimmy. *The Land That Lost Its Heroes.* London: Bloomsbury, 2002.

Cociovitch, Noé. *Génesis de Moisés Ville.* Buenos Aires: Editorial Milá, 1987.

Cohen Salama, Mauricio. *Tumbas Anónimas.* Catologos Editora, 1992.

Comisión Nacional sobre la Desaparición de Personas. *Nunca Más.* Buenos Aires: Editorial Universitaria de Buenos Aires, 1984.

Confino, Hernán. *La Contraofensiva: El Final de Montoneros.* Buenos Aires: Fondo de Cultura Económica Argentina, 2022.

Cox, David. *Dirty Secrets, Dirty War: Buenos Aires, Argentina, 1976–1983: The Exile of Editor Robert J. Cox.* Charleston, SC: Evening Post Pub. Co. With Joggling Board Press, 2008.

Crassweller, Robert D. *Perón and the Enigmas of Argentina.* New York: Norton, 1988.

De Greiff, Pablo. *The Handbook of Reparations.* New York: Oxford University Press, 2006.

Dinges, John. *The Condor Years: How Pinochet and His Allies Brought Terrorism to Three Continents.* New York: New Press, 2005.

Donda, Victoria. *Mi Nombre Es Victoria.* Buenos Aires: Sudamerica, 2009.

Erlich, Henry A. and Eric Stover. *Silent Witness: Forensic DNA Evidence in Criminal Investigations and Humanitarian Disasters.* New York: Oxford University Press, 2020.

Etchecolatz, Miguel Osvaldo. *La Otra Campana Del Nunca Más,* 1988.

Feitlowitz, Marguerite. *A Lexicon of Terror.* New York: Oxford University Press, 2011.

Ferguson, Sam. *The Disappeared.* Lincoln: University of Nebraska Press, 2023.

Fernández de Kirchner, Cristina. *Sinceramente.* Buenos Aires: Sudamericana, 2019.

Finchelstein, Federico. *The Ideological Origins of the Dirty War: Fascism, Populism, and Dictatorship in Twentieth Century Argentina*. New York: Oxford University Press, 2017.

Fisher, Jo. *Mothers of the Disappeared*. London: Zed Books, 1995.

Folco, Javier. *Estela: La Biografía de Estela de Carlotto*. Buenos Aires: Editorial Marea, 2015.

Foss, Clive. *Juan and Eva Perón*. Gloucestershire: Sutton, 2006.

Fraser, Nicholas, and Marysa Navarro. *Eva Perón*. New York: W. W. Norton, 1980.

Gasparini, Juan. *Mujeres de Dictadores*. Barcelona: Ediciones Península, 2002.

Gelman, Juan. *Violín Y Otras Cuestiones*. Buenos Aires: Ediciones Gleizer, 1956.

Giannoni, Virginia, and Madres De Plaza De Mayo (Association). *Las Viejas: Madres de Plaza de Mayo Línea Fundadora Cuentan Una Historia*. Ciudad Autónoma De Buenos Aires: Marea Editorial, 2014.

Gillespie, Richard. *Soldiers of Perón*. New York: Oxford University Press, 1982.

Giussani, Pablo. *Montoneros, La Soberbia Armada (Edición Definitiva)*. Buenos Aires: Sudamericana, 2011.

Goldman, Daniel, and Hernán Dobry. *Ser Judío En Los Años Setenta*. Buenos Aires: Siglo Veintiuno Editores, 2019.

Goñi, Uki. *El Infiltrado: Astiz, Las Madres, y El Herald*. Biblioteca Uki Goñi, 2018. Kindle Edition.

———. *The Real Odessa*. London: Granta Books (UK), 2002.

Gorini, Ulises. *La Rebelion de Las Madres: Historia de Las Madres de Plaza de Mayo*. La Plata: EDULP, 2017.

Graham-Yooll, Andrew. *A State of Fear*. London: Eland, 1986.

Guerriero, Leila. *La Llamada*. Barcelona: Anagrama, 2024.

Guest, Iain. *Behind the Disappearances: Argentina's Dirty War against Human Rights and the United Nations*. Philadelphia: University of Pennsylvania Press, 1999.

Gutiérrez, Edgardo. *Rock Del País*. Jujuy: Universidad Nacional de Jujuy, 2010.

Hayner, Priscilla B. *Unspeakable Truths: Transitional Justice and the Challenge of Truth Commissions*. London: Routledge, 2011.

Healey, Mark A. *The Ruins of the New Argentina: Peronism and the Remaking of San Juan after the 1944 Earthquake*. Durham, NC: Duke University Press, 2011.

Hedges, Jill. *Juan Perón*. London: Bloomsbury, 2021.

Herrera, Matilde, and Ernesto Tenembaum. *Identidad Despojo y Restitución*. Buenos Aires: Abuelas de Plaza de Mayo, 2001.

Hodges, Donald C. *Argentina's "Dirty War."* Austin: University of Texas Press, 2014.

Hora, Roy. *The Landowners of the Argentine Pampas*. Oxford: Clarendon Press, 2001.

Iparraguirre, Soledad. *Delia*. Buenos Aires: Marea Editorial, 2022.

Jaroslavsky, Andrés. *El Futuro de La Memoria*. London: Latin America Bureau, 2004.

Joyce, Christopher, and Eric Stover. *Witnesses from the Grave*. New York: Ballantine, 1992.

Lacunza, Sebastián. *El Testigo Inglés*. Buenos Aires: Paidós, 2021.

Larraquy, Marcelo. *Fuimos Soldados*. Buenos Aires: Sudamericana, 2021.

Lede, Ariel, and Lucas Bilbao. *Profeta Del Genocidio*. Buenos Aires: Sudamericana, 2013.

Lessa, Francesca. *The Condor Trials: Transnational Repression and Human Rights in South America*. New Haven: Yale University Press, 2022.

Lewin, Miriam, and Olga Wornat. *Putas y Guerrilleras*. Buenos Aires: Planeta, 2013.

Lewis, Paul H. *Guerrillas and Generals*. Westport, CT: Praeger, 2002.

Lewis, Paul H., and Carolina. *The Crisis of Argentine Capitalism*. Chapel Hill: The University of North Carolina Press, Cop, 1992.

Lipis, Guillermo. *Nueva Sión, Periodismo Crítico*. Buenos Aires: Milá, 2004.

Llonto, Pablo. *El Juicio Que No Se Vio*. Buenos Aires: Ediciones Continente, 2015.

Ludueña, María Eugenia. *Laura*. Buenos Aires: Planeta, 2015.

Luna, Félix. *A Short History of the Argentinians*. Buenos Aires: Planeta, 2000.

Manfroni, Carlos, and Victoria E. Villarruel. *Los Otros Muertos*. Buenos Aires: Sudamericana, 2014.

Manzano, Valeria. *The Age of Youth in Argentina: Culture, Politics, and Sexuality from Perón to Videla*. Chapel Hill: The University of North Carolina Press, 2014.

Marchak, Patricia, and Queen's University (Montreal). *Reigns of Terror*. Montreal: McGill-Queen's University, 2003.

Martínez, Juan Carlos. *La Abuela de Hierro*. Lumbre, 2012.

Meijide, Graciela Fernández. *La Historia Íntima de Los Derechos Humanos En La Argentina (Reedición Actualizada)*. Buenos Aires: Sudamericana, 2020.

Mellibovsky, Matilde. *Circle of Love Over Death*. Willimantic, CT: Curbstone Press, 1997.

Meyer, Marshall T. *You Are My Witness*. New York: St. Martin's Press, 2014.

Michael, William. *The Fate of Freedom Elsewhere: Human Rights and U.S. Cold War Policy toward Argentina*. Ithaca, NY: Cornell University Press, 2013.

Mignone, Emilio Fermín. *Iglesia y Dictadura*. Buenos Aires: Ediciones Colihue SRL, 2006.

Mochkofsky, Graciela. *Pecado Original*. Espejo de La Argentina: Planeta, 2011.

Moyano, María José. *Argentina's Lost Patrol: Armed Struggle, 1969–1979*. New Haven: Yale University Press, 1995.

Mukherjee, Siddhartha. *The Gene: An Intimate History*. New York: Scribner, 2016.

Neilson, James. *El Fin de La Quimera*. Buenos Aires: Emecé Editores, 1991.

Norman, Theodore. *An Outstretched Arm: A History of the Jewish Colonization Association*. London: Routledge & Kegan Paul Books, 1985.

Nosiglia, Julio E. *Botín de Guerra*. Buenos Aires: Abuelas de Plaza de Mayo, 1985.

Nuguer, Jaime. *Un Hábeas Corpus En Dictadura: Las Acciones Judiciales Por Inés Ollero Que Culminaron Con El Encarcelamiento Del Jefe de La ESMA*. Carapachay, Buenos Aires: Lenguaje Claro, 2014.

Ocampo, Luis Moreno. *Cuando El Poder Perdió El Juicio*. Buenos Aires: Capital Intelectual, 2022.

O'Donnell, María. *Aramburu*. Buenos Aires: Planeta, 2020.

———. *BORN*. Buenos Aires: Sudamericana, 2015.

O'Donnell, Pacho. *La Nueva Vejez*. Buenos Aires: Sudamericana, 2023.

Page, Joseph A. *Perón*. New York: Random House, 1983.

Pérez, Mariana Eva. *Diario de Una Princesa Montonera: 110% Verdad*. Buenos Aires: Capital Intelectual S.A., 2012.

Pérez, Mariana Eva, and Yamila Grandi. *Algún Día*. Buenos Aires: Abuelas de Plaza De Mayo, 1990.

Pigna, Felipe. *Evita. Jirones de Su Vida*. Buenos Aires: Planeta, 2012.

———. *Lo Pasado Pensado*. Buenos Aires: Planeta, 2011.

Plotkin, Mariano Ben. *Mañana Es San Perón: A Cultural History of Perón's Argentina*. Wilmington, DE: Scholarly Resources Inc., 1961.

Quesada, María Sáenz. *La Primera Presidente*. Buenos Aires: Sudamericana, 2016.

Ramos Padilla, Juan Martín. *Chicha*. Buenos Aires: Dunken, 2006.

Ramus, Susana Jorgelina. *Sueños Sobrevivientes de Una Montonera*. Buenos Aires: Ediciones Colihue SRL, 2000.

Ratier, Hugo E. *Villeros y Villas Miseria*. La Plata: EDULP, 2022.

Reato, Ceferino. *Disposición Final*. Buenos Aires: Buenos Aires: Sudamericana, 2016.

———. *Doce Noches*. Buenos Aires: Buenos Aires: Sudamericana, 2015.

———. *Los 70, La Década Que Siempre Vuelve*. Buenos Aires: Sudamericana, 2020.

Rieff, David. *In Praise of Forgetting: Historical Memory and Its Ironies*. New Haven: Yale University Press, 2016.

Robben, Antonius. *Political Violence and Trauma in Argentina*. Philadelphia: University of Pennsylvania Press, 2007.

Robledo, Pablo. *Montoneros Y Palestina*. Buenos Aires: Planeta, 2018.

Rocha, Jan. *Clamor: The Search for the Disappeared of the South American Dictatorships*. Warwickshire: Practical Action Publishing and Latin America Bureau, 2023.

Rock, David. *Argentina 1516–1987: From Spanish Colonization to Alfonsín*. Berkeley: University of California Press, 2006.

Rodríguez, Laura Graciela. *Universidad, Peronismo y Dictadura*. Buenos Aires: Prometeo Libros, 2015.

Roisinblit, Benjamín. *Pampas de Sion: Poemas Sobre La Fundación de Moisés Ville*, 1971.

Romero, José Luis. *Breve Historia Contemporánea de La Argentina 1916–2010*. Buenos Aires: Fondo de Cultura Económica, 2012.

Romero, Luis Alberto. *La Larga Crisis Argentina*. Buenos Aires: Siglo XXI Ediciones, 2013.

Rosenberg, Tina. *Children of Cain: Violence and the Violent in Latin America*. New York: Penguin, 1992.

Ruiz Moreno, Isidoro J. *Comandos En Acción*. Buenos Aires: Claridad, 2011.

Rutherford, Adam. *A Brief History of Everyone Who Ever Lived: The Stories in Our Genes*. London: Weidenfeld & Nicolson, 2017.

Seoane, María, and Roberto Caballero. *El Nieto*. Buenos Aires: Sudamericana, 2015.

Seoane, María, and Vicente Muleiro. *El Dictador*. Buenos Aires: Sudamericana, 2001.

Sfiligoy, Tatiana, and Danilo Albín. *En El Nombre de Sus Sueños*. Buenos Aires: Ediciones Fabro, 2013.

Sheinin, David M. K. *Consent of the Damned*. Gainsville: University Press of Florida, 2012.

Sheinin, David M.K., and Ranaan Rein. *Armed Jews in the Americas*. Boston: Brill, 2021.

Shumway, Nicolas. *The Invention of Argentina*. Berkeley: University of California Press, 2003.

Simpson, John, and Jana Bennett. *The Disappeared*. London: Sphere, 1986.

Sinay, Javier. *The Murders of Moisés Ville: The Rise and Fall of the Jerusalem of South America*. Brooklyn, NY: Restless Books, 2022.

Solomon, Andrew. *Far from the Tree*. New York: Simon & Schuster Books for Young Readers, 2017.

Stark, Lizzie. *Pandora's DNA: Tracing the Breast Cancer Genes through History, Science, and One Family Tree*. Chicago: Chicago Review Press, 2014.

Taylor, Diana. *Disappearing Acts: Spectacles of Gender and Nationalism in Argentina's "Dirty War."* Durham, NC: Duke University Press, 1997.

Timerman, Jacobo. *Prisoner without a Name, Cell without a Number.* Madison: University of Wisconsin Press, 2002.

Torres, Sergio, and Cecilia Brizzio. *ESMA.* Buenos Aires: EUDEBA, 2021.

Vallejos, Soledad M. *Olivos.* Buenos Aires: AGUILAR, 2017.

Verbitsky, Horacio. *El Vuelo.* Barcelona: Seix Barral, 1995.

Walsh, Rodolfo. *Operación Masacre.* Buenos Aires: Planeta, 1998.

Watson, James D. *DNA: The Story of the Genetic Revolution.* London: Arrow Books, 2017.

Wulff, Guillermo. *Las Abuelas y la Genética.* Buenos Aires: Abuelas de Plaza de Mayo, 2008.

Yofre, Juan B. *Fuimos Todos.* Buenos Aires: Sudamericana, 2011.

———. *Nadie Fue (Edición Definitiva).* Buenos Aires: Sudamericana, 2011.

Yount, Lisa. *Disease Detectives.* San Diego, CA: Lucent Books, 2001.

Zimmer, Carl. *She Has Her Mother's Laugh: The Powers, Perversions, and Potential of Heredity.* New York: Dutton, 2019.

Zunino, Marcos. *Justice Framed: A Genealogy of Transitional Justice.* Cambridge: Cambridge University Press, 2019.

ARCHIVES CONSULTED

Abuelas de Plaza de Mayo Archivo Institucional

Archivo Nacional de La Memoria

Argentina Declassification Project

Biblioteca del Congreso de la Nación - Hemeroteca and Hemeroteca Revistas

Biblioteca Nacional Mariano Moreno - Hemeroteca

Disappeared Children in Argentina: Rita Arditti's Interviews with the Grandmothers of Plaza de Mayo, Joseph P. Healey Library, University of Massachusetts, Boston

Memoria Abierta

Patricia M. Derian papers, David M. Rubenstein Rare Book & Manuscript Library, Duke University

Robert J. Cox papers, David M. Rubenstein Rare Book & Manuscript Library, Duke University

Rosa Tarlovsky de Roinsinblit Fondo Personal, Comisión Provincial por la Memoria

Image Credits

INSERT 2

1. Abuelas de Plaza de Mayo Institutional Archive—13-16-001
2. Rosa Tarlovsky de Roisinblit Fondo Personal, Comisión Provincial por La Memoria
3. Courtesy of Guillermo Pérez Roisinblit
4. Photo by Cindy Charles, Abuelas de Plaza de Mayo Institutional Archive
5. AFP/Getty Images
6. Courtesy of Guillermo Pérez Roisinblit
7. Juan Mabromata/AFP/Getty Images
8. AFP/Getty Images
9. Rosa Tarlovsky de Roisinblit Fondo Personal, Comisión Provincial por La Memoria
10. Leo La Valle/Getty Images
11. Drew Angerer/Getty Images News
12. Juan Mabromata/AFP/Getty Images
13. Juan Mabromata/AFP/Getty Images
14. Photo by Santiago Tarelli, Abuelas de Plaza de Mayo Institutional Archive

Index

About the Author

HALEY COHEN GILLILAND is a journalist and the director of the Yale Journalism Initiative. She previously worked at *The Economist* for seven years, four of which were spent in Buenos Aires as the paper's Argentina correspondent. Following her time at *The Economist*, she has focused on narrative nonfiction—bringing history and current events to life through fact-based storytelling. She has published long form feature articles in *The New York Times*, *National Geographic*, *Bloomberg Businessweek*, and *Vanity Fair*, among other publications. She lives in New York State with her husband, two children, and dogs.

Avid Reader Press, an imprint of Simon & Schuster, is built on the idea that the most rewarding publishing has three common denominators: great books, published with intense focus, in true partnership. Thank you to the Avid Reader Press colleagues who collaborated on *A Flower Traveled in My Blood*, as well as to the hundreds of professionals in the Simon & Schuster advertising, audio, communications, design, ebook, finance, human resources, legal, marketing, operations, production, sales, supply chain, subsidiary rights, and warehouse departments whose invaluable support and expertise benefit every one of our titles.

Editorial
Jofie Ferrari-Adler, *VP and Co-Publisher*
Carolyn Kelly, *Editor*

Jacket Design
Alison Forner, *Senior Art Director*
Clay Smith, *Senior Designer*
Sydney Newman, *Art Associate*

Marketing
Meredith Vilarello, *VP and Associate Publisher*
Caroline McGregor, *Senior Marketing Manager*
Kayla Dee, *Associate Marketing Manager*
Katya Wiegmann, *Marketing and Publishing Assistant*

Production
Allison Green, *Managing Editor*
Hana Handzija, *Managing Editorial Assistant*
Jessica Chin, *Senior Manager of Copyediting*
Ruth Lee-Mui, *Interior Text Designer*
Alicia Brancato, *Production Manager*
Cait Lamborne, *Ebook Developer*

Publicity
Alexandra Primiani, *Publicity Director*
Eva Kerins, *Publicity Assistant*

Subsidiary Rights
Paul O'Halloran, *VP and Director of Subsidiary Rights*
Fiona Sharp, *Subsidiary Rights Coordinator*